**Books are to be returned or renewed
before the last date below**

**South Leicestershire College Library.
To renew, telephone:**
0116 264 3527

Edward Carpenter

Edward Carpenter:
A Life of Liberty and Love

SHEILA ROWBOTHAM

VERSO
London • New York

First published by Verso 2008

1 3 5 7 9 10 8 6 4 2

Verso
UK: 6 Meard Street, London W1F 0EG
USA: 20 Jay Street, Brooklyn, NY 11201
www.versobooks.com

Verso is the imprint of New Left Books

ISBN-13: 978-1-84467-295-0

British Library Cataloguing in Publication Data
A catalogue record for this book is available from the British Library

Library of Congress Cataloging-in-Publication Data
A catalog record for this book is available from the Library of Congress

Typeset by Hewer Text UK Ltd, Edinburgh
Printed by Scandbook AB, Sweden

Contents

List of Illustrations

Introduction

Edward Carpenter possessed a knack which helped to prod the modern world into being. Rejecting his upper-middle-class upbringing, he adopted outlooks and ways of life before they crystallised into an alternative culture. In 1874, a decade ahead of the liberal middle-class 'discovery' of the slums, he left his comfortable clerical fellowship at Trinity Hall, Cambridge, and went to commune with 'the people' through teaching in an adult education movement, University Extension. Then, in the early 1880s, he settled at Millthorpe in the countryside outside Sheffield, where he proceeded to advocate growing your own produce and the 'simple life' several years before the intelligentsia took to country cottages. He was sitting at the feet of a holy man in Sri Lanka (then Ceylon) in the early 1890s – well in advance of the early twentieth-century bohemians who embraced Eastern mysticism. Some of his perceptions were strangely prescient; nearly a hundred years before the advent of Gay Liberation, Carpenter contemplated an organisation of men who were attracted to members of their own sex.

In so far as he is known nowadays it is as a pioneer sex reformer who wrote on homosexuality, the emancipation of women and mutuality in loving. He was, however, associated with a wide swathe of other movements and causes. During the early 1880s, when the first socialist and anarchist groupings emerged in Britain, Carpenter was among the first to challenge capitalism as a social and economic system, linking external transformation with new forms of relating and desiring. Attuned to this utopian moment in radical politics, partly by the distress he had experienced in being forced to conceal his own sexual feelings towards men, Carpenter devised a flexible version of socialism with anarchist stripes which put the emphasis on changing everyday living and behaviour. Stretching socialism towards environmental and humanitarian causes, he campaigned for clean air, prison reform and animal rights. He came to symbolise the possibility of a new lifestyle without the trappings of Victorian bourgeois respectability by propounding the merits of recycling woolly coats, wearing sandals and bathing nude. Resolutely resisting the fear and guilt surrounding sexuality, he found inspiration by looking backwards as well as forwards, holding forth on the most diverse topics from pagan sun worship to Plato's *Phaedrus*. Carpenter's critique of the values of his own society was strengthened by an interest in Eastern spirituality which led him to repudiate not simply Western imperialism, but more fundamentally Western 'civilisation'.

His friend the Cambridge classicist, Goldsworthy Lowes Dickinson, observed that 'Carpenter was a mystic . . . but his feet were pretty firm on the ground . . . I remember asking him once how he related this with this Socialism. He replied that he liked to hang out his red flag from the ground floor and then go up above to see how it looked.'[1] Though Carpenter was drawn to mysticism, he eschewed asceticism. He had learned from his exuberant mentor the American poet Walt Whitman to celebrate the body electric and he struggled all his life to combine matter and spirit, body and soul. As he put it in 1910: 'The spiritual must have the material to give it body; the material has no meaning without the spiritual';[2] this insight enabled him to reinvent himself in the early twentieth century as a modern sage proclaiming self-expression, energy and flux.

Carpenter defied the hierarchies of class deference endemic in the society of his day. His life was marked by close, long, sometimes intimate relationships with working-class men and a host of more peripheral attachments. While the impulse was partly sexual, his commitment to personal comradeship was not just about sex. He was incontestably kind, generous not only with his money but with his time, and his ever-expanding friendship network embraced the great and the good from social and literary movements along with an assortment of waifs and strays. He drew people from all walks of life towards him.

Carpenter exerted a remarkable influence during his lifetime. In the early twentieth century his books and his personal contacts extended not only into Europe but to India, Sri Lanka (or Ceylon as it was then known), Japan, Australia and North America. Though Carpenter's reputation began to fade after his death in 1929, many of the people in his enormous network of friends and acquaintances have remained well-known figures. They include writers: Olive Schreiner, E.M. Forster, George Bernard Shaw, the Webbs, Siegfried Sassoon, Rabindranath Tagore; along with politicians, Ramsay MacDonald and Keir Hardie; the trade union leader Tom Mann; the anarchist Emma Goldman and the feminists Charlotte Despard, Lady Constance Lytton and Isabella Ford. He collaborated closely with the pioneering sex psychologist Havelock Ellis and was supportive to the British birth control campaigner Marie Stopes and her American counterpart, Margaret Sanger. Admirers of his work included Tolstoy, Jack London and Romain Rolland. The list could go on and on.

Edward Carpenter has been lurking around in my life a very long time indeed. I first came across him in 1959 in a biography of Havelock Ellis by Arthur Calder-Marshall,[3] a present I had requested for my sixteenth birthday. It was my introduction to a circle of dissidents who invented their own ways of living, but at the time I did not register Carpenter, instead I was captivated by Ellis and his love the South African 'new woman' novelist, Olive Schreiner. Ellis' interest in reconciling religion and materialism intrigued me, as did the search for an inner morality guided by spirit rather than external rules. In 1964, when I began a PhD thesis on University Extension, Carpenter was among a little cluster of oddball lecturers who went into the adult education movement. Several became his friends: Goldsworthy Lowes Dickinson; the arts and crafts designer and architect, Charles Ashbee; and the art critic Roger Fry. Carpenter's networks were beginning to expand. They grew even wider when the social historian E.P. Thompson, who I had met while I was an undergraduate, sent me off to read the Carpenter papers in Sheffield. His description of Carpenter as one of the middle-class socialists who had raised ideas of sexuality which had been partly, but not completely, accepted by the labour movement, made me prick up my ears. Too shy to admit I could not quite understand what he meant, I tried to piece together an answer from the manuscripts in the Carpenter Collection and the books in the Thompsons' home, gathered in the course of writing *William Morris: Romantic to Revolutionary* (1955).[4] I learned about a socialist Leeds which contrasted with my own Tory background in the city; about Carpenter's close friends, the feminist Isabella Ford, the handsome photographer and poet, Tom Maguire, and the engineer and trade union organiser, Alf Mattison. Then in the Brotherton Library in Leeds I uncovered more about them all in the manuscripts kept by the historically minded Mattison.

During the 1960s the skeins of memory were close enough for some personal contacts. Dorothy and Edward Thompson had known Mattison's wife, Florence, who was active in women's labour circles and was, they said, very open-minded on sexual issues apart from homosexuality, a remark which gave me another puzzle to ponder on. In Manchester, I was introduced to a friend of a man called Charles Sixsmith, a member of the Whitmanite circle in Bolton who had been close to Carpenter. He was still chuckling in the mid 1960s about 'Charlie's' eccentric reputation, and I made my first stab at reading the collection of material Sixsmith collected on Carpenter in the John Rylands Library in Deansgate. Around this time a chance encounter with E.M. Forster in the quad at King's College, Cambridge, was my first direct link with someone who had known Carpenter. The second, oddly, was familial; in the 1970s I met a distant relative who happened to have delivered milk as a boy to Carpenter and his working-class lover, George Merrill, at Millthorpe. He recollected Carpenter, the gentleman, rebuking Merrill for swearing in front of a child. The socialist Fenner Brockway later told me of another Carpenter, the writer on sex who had helped him as a young man to question conventional morality.

In 1974, a talk I gave to the newly formed Gay Culture Society at the London School of Economics was to send me back up the hill to the Sheffield library where the Carpenter Collection was then stored. The emergence of the Women's Liberation and Gay Liberation movements, intent on breaking with existing conditions and resolutely utopian in their aspirations, made Carpenter seem suddenly relevant for a new politics. The hopes of transforming human relationships and culture, which socialists had put on one side, were resurfacing. Inequality was being questioned, not simply in terms of the ownership of things, but in how the subordinated were defined. During the 1970s, Carpenter's efforts to connect the personal and the political absorbed me, as did the insights his papers revealed about the interior world of the Sheffield socialists and anarchists. These were the themes I emphasised when Jeffrey Weeks and I collaborated on Carpenter and Ellis in *Socialism and the New Life* (1977) and in two subsequent articles in the seventies and eighties.[5]

The ramifications of Carpenter's life and work are a treasure trove for historians, and since I wrote on him in *Socialism and the New Life* there have been a range of studies which have examined aspects of his activities and thought in depth. These have tended to 'do' him in bits, putting the emphasis on his links to the labour movement, his writings on criminology or on his thinking about sex or Eastern religion. He also appears as a character in the wings in biographies of other figures who became prominent through politics or literature. I have been able to draw on this work, most of which was not available when I initially wrote about him, and have also used many smaller collections of documents to complement the material in Sheffield, Manchester and Leeds. This time around I have sought to bring out the remarkable range of *interconnections* evident in his life, through his networks, his mix of causes, his interests and his thinking.

Carpenter was not unique in making links which in retrospect appear surprising. Many of his friends and acquaintances shared his utopian faith in the possibility of transforming the economy and politics along with daily life and human relationships. However few of them accepted quite as many connections *between* causes as Carpenter, or were so adept at uniting apparently opposing polarities. While a preoccupation with various forms of spirituality was not particularly strange among late nineteenth-century socialists, over the years most people tended to opt for one or the other. Similarly, those who experimented in their personal lives during the 1880s and 1890s were inclined to grow more conventional as they got older. Not so Carpenter, whose alternative lifestyle lasted into old age, blowing the stereotype of the stuffy Victorians.

Carpenter was courageously frank in his published work and was careful to leave a private correspondence which revealed much more. Thanks to Carpenter, it is possible to trace not only how new theories around homosexuality emerge, but see these interacting with personal encounters which were uncertain, tentative and experimental. Expecting to figure in history, he kept a careful record for posterity and his friends added yet more. He did live his political beliefs in his personal relationships and he wanted us to know what many people would conceal because he believed a future would come in which his desires, and those of his friends, would not be regarded with contempt. Close friends wondered at his ability to evade not only censorship but ostracism and the law. He was a careful strategist. In 1894 when he was producing a series of pamphlets on sex he remarked to Roger Fry that the 'manner' in which the topic was treated was as important as the 'matter', and the radical lawyer E.S.P. Haynes recollected Carpenter advising him to permit the enemy a bridge for retreat on matters of controversy.[6] Even though Carpenter was uncompromising in his convictions, he was an accomplished propagandist who pronounced with a deceptive urbanity.

Reading the vast collection of writings and letters is rather like sauntering through a department store. Initially you imagine that you wander as you list, then the realisation dawns that the manner in which the goods are displayed has been carefully planned even though the traces of design are well covered. Carpenter's project of making his own life demonstrate his politics disguises as well as reveals, making the personal man actually more elusive, for when aspects of private intimacy migrate into the public sphere a new realm of secrecy is inclined to tuck itself away. The exceptional record he has left is also a reminder that the charting of intimacy is far more complex than what is said, that only stray aspects of sexual experience are ever chronicled, that sexual feelings, being transient, are inclined to burst like bubbles when you try and catch them. As I grew more and more immersed in his life through writing this biography, the tracker-dog element in my historian's nosiness sniffed furiously over tiny hints.

I quickly realised that writing his life involved writing his circles and his times, an engrossing and frustrating endeavour that left me metaphorically puffing and panting in an effort to keep up with him. It was rewarding nonetheless, for looking at Carpenter in the round provides myriad clues to links which have been retrospectively buried. Along with the insights into a broad, humanitarian socialism and the emergence of an alternative culture of the everyday and new sexual values, his life opens up a series of intellectual trails. Profoundly influenced by both Romanticism and German idealism, Carpenter sought the union with Nature which inspired F.W.J. von Schelling, William Wordsworth and Percy Bysshe Shelley while folding Arthur Schopenhauer's pessimism about Western progress into his left perspective. Interested in hidden traditions of knowledge, he looked back to Pythagoras, Plotinus and the Gnostics, to Emanuel Swedenborg and William Blake. Though he carefully kept his distance from esoteric groupings interested in the occult which were popular in the late nineteenth and early twentieth centuries, he was associated with people who were part of these movements. Similarly Carpenter knew several scientists who were engaged in psychical research and was himself preoccupied with connecting contemporary findings in science to a metaphysical search for spiritual transcendence.

Carpenter's refusal to acknowledge any boundaries between areas of knowledge makes following his intellectual trajectory daunting indeed, for he zoomed from industrial democracy to theories of consciousness, from the evils of vivisection to reorganising domestic labour. He studied anthropology, psychology, physiology, neurology or the history of religion and esoteric thought as the need arose, solving mathematical theorems and acquiring an intense understanding of Beethoven's music in between times. He also sought to connect how he lived to what he believed. When Carpenter's autobiography, *My Days and Dreams*, was published in 1916, he defied the destruction and disillusionment of war with his unabashed utopianism; insisting that he wanted a 'revolution in human life' which would involve international harmony between peoples, non-governmental societies based on 'the Communalization of Land and Capital', sexual equality and freedom, closeness to Nature, direct relations between human beings, 'by plain living, friendship with the Animals, open-air habits, fruitarian food and such degree of Nudity as we can reasonably attain to'.[7]

Theorising is, of course, always rather easier than putting ideas into practice and Carpenter ruefully realised that gaining a reputation for living one's politics did bring certain disadvantages. His home at Millthorpe near

Sheffield became a place of pilgrimage for the politically correct of his day who flocked to observe the simple life in action and recruit him to their causes; 'sometimes I had almost to barricade myself against them'.[8] The libertarian in Carpenter disliked telling people what to do and he always refuted any suggestion that his behaviour was ideological. In response to a congratulatory letter that was presented to him on his seventieth birthday in 1914, he declared that his political agitation, market gardening and sandal making had all been done simply 'because of the joy I had in doing it, and to please myself'.[9]

The truth was rather more complicated. Carpenter was undoubtedly led by a desire to divest himself of the accoutrements of a 'Victorian' middle-class lifestyle, however his 'simple life' was also posited on a puritanism rooted in a very 'Victorian' rectitude. The twentieth century was being invented in the nineteenth and Carpenter bridges the complex shifts in attitudes and behaviour as one century gave way to the other. That he was at once a 'Victorian' and a 'modern' reveals how structures of feeling overlapped. At the same time his trajectory reveals just how difficult it was to foster new ways of being in the world. While Carpenter burned his dress clothes as the outer symbols of class privilege, the inner signs, which his humanitarian socialist friend, Henry Salt, described as 'the tattoo-marks of gentility', remained, and Carpenter, despite himself, was never able to discard them. Salt recalled meeting Carpenter one day near Millthorpe 'walking and talking with a very ragged tramp whom he had overtaken on the high road. The tramp accosted me, as if wishing to explain matters: "This gentleman" – he began indicating Mr. Carpenter. "I'm *not* a gentleman", sharply interjected the philosopher.'[10] Carpenter's libertarianism contained a vein of autocracy, while the spontaneity and directness he so admired in his mentor, the poet Walt Whitman, would be qualities he could never emulate himself. Carpenter remained self-conscious, gentlemanly and restrained.

Nor was the simple life so simple. Carpenter might don sandals, a Walt Whitman broad-brimmed hat, silk cummerbunds and tweedy plus fours, but his outfits were noticeably well tailored. Indeed, Salt remembered Carpenter dressing 'rather nattily . . . in a velvet coat'; this was simplification with style.[11] The vegetarian diet, the market gardening and the lack of furnishings at Millthorpe were buttressed by a large inheritance, and Carpenter always kept his escape routes open. He would take off to London, Italy, France, even Ceylon, in pursuit of sun, sex and spiritual stimulation.

Carpenter's contradictions are delightfully revealing, but they exasperated some of his contemporaries. George Bernard Shaw, who darted about on the outskirts of Carpenter's circle, snorted scornfully about 'Carpenterings and illusions',[12] branding him as 'that ultra-civilized impostor and ex-clergyman of Millthorpe'.[13] Shaw, with his sharp nose for role-playing, scented the effort to assume another persona, but the brittle wit did not allow for any magnanimity about the tension between Carpenter's genuine democratic intent and the ingrained habits of superiority lingering from his upbringing. A host of working-class and lower-middle-class socialists – especially in the North of England – were less picky than Shaw about the chafing diffidence and prepared to acknowledge effort and purpose. They respected the commitment that led Carpenter to tour the country addressing meetings in shabby halls, and loyally came to listen to him holding forth on small-holdings, allotments, pollution, anti-vaccination, the conditions of work, non-governmental society, sex, science, and Eastern religion. Razor-grinders, labourers, engineers, quarry-men, garden-ers, clerks and schoolteachers tucked his books into their pockets and walked out into the countryside to dream of better days.

The dilemma Carpenter lived so strenuously, how to imagine an alter-native without becoming trapped in a prescriptive construct, is as relevant for rebels now as it was then. In order to go beyond protest it is necessary, in E.P. Thompson's words, to conceive a new 'vocabulary of desire'.[14] But there are many discomfiting historical instances of how these can ossify into repressive dystopias. Instead of casting ideals in stone, Carpenter kept utopia in his mind's eye in the immediate changes he proposed. As Terry Eagleton has said, such a way of thinking implies that alternatives are always 'in some sense immanent in the present'.[15] This was the spirit in which many of Carpenter's admirers took his writings into their hearts.

The influence he exerted came partly from the sponge-like manner in which he was able to assimilate and synthesise concepts, attitudes and aspirations while they were still in flux. Carpenter was such an absorbent thinker and kept a finger in so many ephemeral fractions, groupings, circles and movements, that his political and intellectual trajectory runs like a roller-coaster ride through the highways and byways of late nineteenth-century and early twentieth-century thought and activism, signalling currents of opinion and patterns of assumption which have dissolved from view. The story of Carpenter and his interwoven friendship networks is packed with suggestive knots as reminders of routes covered over and routes not taken, and his biographical allure lies in his refusal of confinement.

PART I

'At home I never felt really at home'

When Carpenter began his autobiography, *My Days and Dreams*, in 1890, he already had his life mapped out like a play with four acts. 'My life . . . divides into four pretty distinct periods', he announced, with the clarity of one accustomed to giving lectures. The first part, up to the age of twenty, is presented as predominantly a bad dream in which he describes himself as 'embedded in a would-be fashionable world which I hated'.[1] *My Days and Dreams* is the main source for our knowledge of Carpenter's youth, and he uses broad brushstrokes in order to demonstrate contrasts with his later life. Vivid and playful, *My Days and Dreams* is an adroit piece of propaganda for the alternative values and lifestyle he had adopted; the account of childhood he has left us is accordingly slanted to fit the rest of the script.

Carpenter was endowed with a strong sense of drama and there are two villains in the story: his hometown of Brighton and the Carpenter family house at 45 Brunswick Square. Carpenter's niece Ida Hyett, who inclined towards the bohemian and literary circles in which he moved, knew about his childhood from her aunts and from her mother Ellen. In an essay on her uncle which appeared in 1931, Hyett confirmed that when he was growing up in the 1850s and '60s Brighton was indeed, 'associated . . . with the type of vulgarity denoted by the word "smart"', adding, 'In Brighton in the reign of Victoria one had to be smart or die socially.'[2] The town had become fashionable in the eighteenth century, and the apogee of style during the Regency era. By the early 1840s, when the Carpenter family moved to Brighton, a booming holiday resort was developing out of the former fishing village. From 1841 the London to Brighton railway brought upper-class visitors into the bracing sea air for a mini-season in February and March and enabled a pot pourri of less elegant summer pleasure-seekers to reach the seaside. Brighton's architecture reflected the social gradations of its tourists and, during the bustling Victorian era, proceeded to burst out in ostentatious flourishes. The Grand Hotel, described by a contemporary commentator as a 'cyclopean pile'[3] was going up in 1864, just as Carpenter was escaping from the town. The even showier Norfolk Hotel was to follow the year after. This was the Brighton Carpenter reviled; he never mentions the other Brighton, the damp, lichen-coated walls of the houses of the poor, or the warm pubs and brothels in which working-class men took refuge. But then topography was not his concern; Brighton, for Carpenter, was not so much a place as a metaphor. Ida Hyett believed that his perception of the town in this early part of his life lay at the root of his revulsion against 'Victorianism'. 'He saw the England of his youth as a magnified Brighton.'[4]

The house that Carpenter disliked so much at 45 Brunswick Square belonged to the Regency days of Brighton's glory and still stands, grand and lofty, on the western side of Brighton with a blue municipal plaque in his memory. The Square had been started as part of a Regency speculative building project which had spread over a former brickyard. With its Corinthian columns and cornices on Ionic columns, it was designed to look prestigious, proclaiming wealth and privilege, while retaining the austerity and restraint of the eighteenth century. The Carpenters were able to live in style in this fashionable square thanks to a large legacy from Edward's paternal grandfather, Admiral James Carpenter, who died in 1845. Grandfather James Carpenter had fought against revolutionary France, suppressing the rebellious peoples of St Vincent, Grenada and Dominica, before accumulating his wealth through investments. Carpenter's father Charles had also served in the Navy, becoming a lieutenant in 1818, but did not take to the life, entering the legal profession instead. Nonetheless, he was proud of the family's military pedigree, which could be traced back to the thirteenth century. The Carpenters were endowed with a sense of heraldic destiny and service to King and country.

Seafarers were part of Carpenter's ancestry on both sides. In 1833 Charles married Sophia Wilson, the daughter of a Scottish naval officer turned shipbuilder. The early years of their married life were somewhat unsettled. Sophia's father, a widower, had made it a condition of their marriage that the young couple live with him in Walthamstow, then a village outside London. Divided from Hackney by the marshes and the River Lea, Walthamstow was cut off from London and the difficulties of travelling to and fro contributed to Charles Carpenter abandoning his career at the Bar. He had also started to display an anxiety and restlessness which calmed over time, but never entirely left him. The young couple's relationship was thus emotionally troubled, though fecund. Between 1835

Carpenter in 1857, aged thirteen

and 1841 Sophia bore six children in rapid succession; Sophy, Charles, Eliza, Emily, Ellen and George. Edward was the seventh child, born on August 29, 1844; another brother, Alfred, and two younger sisters, Alice and Dora, were to follow. The large house in Brunswick Square must have been a relief to Sophia with this growing brood.

Even though the Admiral's legacy enabled her to keep six or seven servants, she had been reared by a strict Scottish mother from whom she had ingested principles of work, duty and Sunday observance. Carpenter remembered his mother as relentlessly sacrificing herself to the needs of her husband and family. The result was an externally well-regulated domain in which daily routines were invariable and conventions unquestioned. Unlike his younger brother Alfred who was always getting into scrapes, Carpenter tried to please his mother by being good, a ploy he found hard to shed. Yet, to the small, bewildered boy the house was replete with hidden 'mustn'ts' and ineffable rules governed by the mysterious 'dread of appearances', which seemed to permeate Brighton society and hover ominously over number 45. It was also packed with siblings, especially sisters, and he cherished the rare and precious moments of intimacy, when his mother smoothed his pillow at night, the 'gazelle-like eyes'[5] looked down and he could see the moonlight through his bedroom window.

The older sisters bossed, patronised and petted little 'Teddie', who was so unlike the heroic and manly older brother Charles. Already at ten he was disrupting assumed gender roles by trying to play the piano. They would exercise female authority by hustling him off the piano stool; whereas they had to acquire music as an accomplishment, it was regarded as inappropriate for a boy. He describes in *My Days and Dreams* how eventually his mother took pity on him and taught him some notes. He would stumble through Beethoven sonatas in the evenings when the sisters were not practising. A love of music, and of Beethoven in particular stayed with him all his life.

Sophia Carpenter was kindly and protective towards her sensitive son, who adored her. Nonetheless, he found it difficult to draw close to his mother. In *My Days and Dreams*, he explained that she had been brought up to regard 'all expression of tender feeling as little short of a sin; and this reserve, inculcated in youth, became in later days involuntary and inevitable'.[6] Moreover, as the hub of the family, Sophia was scrupulously fair and had many other claims on her time and attention, including the younger children. Her warmth and affection was expressed mainly through a non-verbal love of animals, especially dogs and horses, and in the delight she took in being outdoors looking after them and gardening. As Carpenter grew older he became aware of her powerful inner spirit, but her dutiful rigidity made it impossible for him to reach her. He remarked in his auto-biography, 'My mother had very gracious manners, of gently-smiling dignity, yet her inflexible sense of truth and justice – inflexible especially as regards her own life and conduct – was easily apparent beneath the gentle exterior.'[7]

Ironically his description of his mother resembles the identity he was to acquire over the years. Regardless of his rejection of externally imposed conventions in the very different life he had chosen, he too was led by principles, and evinced the same sense of obligation that drove Sophia. He observed in 1892 that she had been the main influence on his character, adding, 'She was one of the Spartan mothers, of whom there seem so few now; who urge their children to sacrifice much or all for the public good, when need is.'[8] He worked very hard to perfect the outer composure and inner resolve demonstrated by his mother. She bequeathed him her sense of duty. Yet he also yearned for free spontaneous expression. The result was to be a profoundly controlled naturalness which concealed a nervous vulnerability. Despite all Carpenter's efforts to eradicate self-consciousness the very effort belied the endeavour and some deep dissatisfaction left him restless and questing. The knot of need and distance was to remain with him long after the death of his mother.

While Sophia exercised an external control over the household and an inner control over herself, Carpenter's father dwelt in a transcendent zone of abstract thought. He did not have a study at 45 Brunswick Square, and instead he would sit in the dining room, immersed in the German mystic, Johannes Eckhart, or in the Idealist Philosophers, Immanuel Kant or George Wilhelm Friedrich Hegel, while the large household buzzed and clattered around him. On occasion he would pace around reading abstruse passages out loud, until interrupted by protests from Sophia and the girls. Carpenter was imbibing fragments of Romanticism and Idealism from his father, long before he could distinguish aesthetic and philosophical currents. Charles Carpenter, too, affected the cast of his son's thinking, even though his influence was less discernible than Sophia's iron will. As he grew older Carpenter could acknowledge his intellectual debt to his father, but he was not an easy man for a child to connect to. In a poem 'Out of the House of Childhood', which appears in the fourth part of his *Towards Democracy* published in 1902, Carpenter refers to his father as the man he 'used to meet so often on the stairs'.[9] Charles Carpenter seemed to be at once there and yet not there.

Carpenter later described his father as a conservative philosophically and a Liberal in politics; a verdict which underestimated Charles Carpenter's inclinations to radical heterodoxies.[10] Charles went from being a sceptical Anglican to non-attendance at Church, a real act of defiance in this era, and he moved in quite unconventional circles. He had met the Romantic poet Samuel Taylor Coleridge, and his friends included the controversial revolutionary Brighton clergyman, Frederick W. Robertson, the unorthodox Christian Socialist, F.D. Maurice, and Brighton's radical MP, the blind Cambridge political economist, Henry Fawcett, who believed in extending the franchise to workers and to women. Fawcett married the advocate of women's rights, Millicent Garrett, in 1867. In her autobiography, *What I Remember*, Millicent Fawcett describes how she gave her first suffrage speech of any length in Brighton in 1870, encouraged by Mr Carpenter, 'a delightful old gentleman with a charming family of musical sons and daughters'.[11]

The Carpenter family circle also included survivors from the Regency era. Many years later, writing to the radical lawyer E.S.P. Haynes, Carpenter related how when visiting Haynes' great aunt, 'Gussie' Nicolas, she had presented him with a rosebud, a gesture so startling and unfamiliar that, as a stiff, repressed ten-year-old, he had refused it. Haynes recalls how his great aunt's alarming Regency pronouncements on sex used to ruffle dinner parties; nonetheless she was completely acceptable to the Carpenters.[12] Though Carpenter insisted he was bullied and suppressed by his family, they did not really fit the Victorian stereotype he put them into. There was more dissidence and more leeway in his background than he acknowledged.

Reflecting on his childhood, Carpenter remarked, 'at home I never felt really at home'.[13] This inner dislocation was a powerful force in driving him to make a new 'home', both in his own lifestyle and in society at large. Utopia was to be everything that his family home and Brighton were not. Despite this reaction, the house still exercised a hold over him; it was, after all, part of his autobiography. Years later, when his parents had died and the house was about to be sold, he wrote to the man he loved, the Sheffield razor-grinder, George Hukin, 'Someday perhaps we will come down and look at the outside of the old house.'[14] Number 45 and the memories it evoked, however painful, were necessary in explaining himself.

Carpenter's recollections of childhood were by no means exclusively unhappy. The reflective small boy spent hours gazing out at the grey-blue sea with the water washing in at his feet. He found great joy in the music his sisters played. Eliza (known as Lizzie) was his favourite sister and he would turn over the pages of Beethoven's sonatas for her hour after hour, entranced by her piano playing. Ida Hyett depicts Lizzie as Tennysonian. 'She was one of those invalids, like Elizabeth Barrett, in whom her generation specialised, and the life of the house centred round her sofa.'[15] The tender and sympathetic Lizzie could empathise with the intense, interior world of the little boy who was making melodies in his head long before he became aware of poetry. Many years later Carpenter could still recall the sounds of his sisters playing or singing in the evenings, the wind in the chimney, the distant thud of the sea outside, the tattoo of his father's fingers on the table as he read some striking passage and the creak of his boots as he paced reciting to himself. The evenings when the whole family would sit reading round the fire are remembered as times of contemplative peace amidst the bustle.

The family, apart from Lizzie, were athletic as well as musical. When Edward Carpenter's older sisters looked back on their childhood, they recalled a rumbustious felicity of family games, walks on the Downs, swimming in the sea, gardening and much loved pets. Carpenter shared these memories. As a young boy he enjoyed the noisy, romping games, the perils of hide and seek in the dark or chasing one another up and down the front and back stairs. The communal garden in the square was overrun by neighbouring children amidst whom the young Carpenters defended their athletic prowess with staunch family pride. Carpenter's sister

Ellen was a great walker and took him with her as he grew older on long treks across the Downs, which, along with the sea, became the place his thoughts could stretch and wander. Other favourite pastimes were experiments with his brother Charles' discarded chemistry set and playing with the pets in the back garden, 'pigeons, seagulls with clipped wings, rabbits, tortoises, guinea-pigs and smaller fry'.[16] Though he abandoned the chemistry, music, walking and a strong connection to animals were childhood heritages he took with him into later life. Ida Hyett comments on how the contact between her eccentric 'Uncle Ted' and her mother Ellen was maintained on the basis of their mutual 'passion for the open air, for animals and for growing things'. Ellen passed this outdoor energy on to her own family who took to the new bicycles with enthusiasm, though otherwise 'Uncle Ted' was regarded as 'an amiable crank with impossible theories and still more impossible friends'.[17]

How surprised his sisters would have been to learn that they themselves had contributed to his unique disposition in the family to question how things were ordained. It was not only that combat over the piano stool; as a boy of nine or ten under the table playing with his marbles, he used to listen to his sisters and their friends 'talking freely and unconsciously with each other about some ball of the night before, and their partners in the dances'.[18] This eavesdropping on women's talk about men percolated into his consciousness, part of the intimated meanings which for the imaginative child lurked half-hidden in the spaces and tones of the large busy house.

Yet, amidst this most comfortable of worlds, he experienced a persistent feeling of discomfort:

> At the age of eight or nine, and long before distinct sexual feelings declared themselves, I felt a friendly attraction toward my own sex, and this developed after the age of puberty into a passionate sense of love, which, however, never found any expression for itself till I was fully 20 years of age . . . My own sexual nature was a mystery to me. I found myself cut off from the understanding of others, felt myself an outcast and with a highly loving and clinging temperament was intensely miserable.[19]

In 1854 Carpenter went to Brighton College. His father had been closely involved with the school since its foundation in 1845 and all four Carpenter boys were to be pupils. Set in spacious grounds in Kemp Town, the other side of Brighton from Brunswick Square, it resembled an Oxbridge College. The Gothic-style entrances and the dining hall with its church-like roof must have instilled awe in a new boy of ten. But awe recedes quickly once a place becomes familiar and Carpenter, as a day boarder, was to escape the fate of many sensitive Victorian schoolboys exposed to the rigour of more elite public schools. Moreover, he records that his older brother Charles, who had been among the first intake of pupils in 1847, was a hero at Brighton College. Sociable, athletic and first in everything, Charles paved the way for his younger brother who inherited the family nickname 'Chips', which followed him through life, along with his sisters' 'Teddie' and the slightly less familiar 'Ed'. Though several of the masters who inclined to heretics remembered him with affection, the school never really knew what to make of the younger Carpenter brother. In the College records it is Charles who is the star. Carpenter was not a notable pupil and the form his later celebrity took made him a potential embarrassment. After he began his simple life and embraced socialism, the 1886 College Register chronicled him tersely as a 'Farmer and Fruit-grower' and listed some of his writings without evident enthusiasm.[20] Subsequently, his description in My Days and Dreams of the head, Dr Griffith, as muddle-headed and a little touched in the head, provoked outraged protest from Brighton College.

Between 1856 and 1857 the family moved to Paris for a year giving Carpenter no choice but to become fluent in French. He and his brother Alfred attended the classically symmetrical Lycée Hoche, where the boys were marched with military discipline from lesson to lesson. Carpenter proved outstanding in arithmetic and did well in classics and French language; the first glimmer of the range of his intellectual abilities had emerged, though back at Brighton College, perhaps overshadowed by his brother's reputation, he did not appear particularly scholarly. Nor was he as athletic as Charles, though he enjoyed football and hockey. He concentrated on being an average kind of schoolboy, holding his own despite an inward timidity. Years later he was ashamed by acts of meanness; he had teased the French master, bullied an 'idiot boy', felt remorse, bullied again.[21] On the other hand there were also countervailing moments of kindness, acts of generosity, and the defence of more vulnerable pupils. There were no signs yet of the great circles of friends, though one friendship with a slightly younger boy, Henry B. Cotterill, who wrote an account of the 'African Slave Trade' in 1877, survived into adulthood.

Behind the screen of ordinariness the Brighton College schoolboy was experiencing the most disturbing sensations about his classmates and teachers. These were more intense than the customary hero-worship of school crushes, impossible for him to define or articulate at the time. Desire, held at arm's length, indefatigably wiggled its way down the most contorted paths of fantasy:

I dreamed about them at night, absorbed them with my eyes during the day, watched them at cricket, loved to press against them unnoticed in a football melly [sic], or even to get accidentally hurt by one of them at hockey, was glad if they just spoke to me or smiled; but never got a word farther with it all.[22]

When a master was kind, Carpenter repaid him with unworded devotion – but to his disappointment the teacher made no further move.

Many years later when his friend Havelock Ellis was embarking on his study of the psychology of 'sexual inversion' with the writer on Greek culture, John Addington Symonds, Carpenter confided to them that his forbidden desires had left him with a terrible self-loathing which made him feel a monstrosity. Most difficult was the prurient hush surrounding the body and desire. Nobody spoke to him about sex, either at school or at home. Amidst this silence, men who desired men inhabited a zone of stealth and fear, even though homoerotic relationships were pervasive in all-male institutions from the public schools onwards into the Universities, the Church, and the Armed Forces. Nonetheless Victorian moral attitudes were less clear-cut than they appeared and, among sections of the governing classes, the real crime was to let the side down by being found out. Among the privileged, a strong protective code of discretion operated. Symonds, surrounded by the same daunting silence as Carpenter, recoiled from the brutality of sex at Harrow, but the Greek classics presented him with an alternative ideal: he thrilled to Homer's description of Hermes going to meet Priam, 'Like a young prince with the first down upon his lip, the time when youth is most charming.'[23]

When Carpenter and Symonds were growing up homosexual desire was not only lonely, it could be extremely dangerous. Until 1861 the death penalty was still technically in force for what the law called 'sodomy', but because attitudes had changed, mid-century juries had become reluctant to convict. Instead the 1861 Offences Against the Persons Act substituted life sentences with penal servitude for sodomy, along with between two to ten years for a vaguer category of offences, termed indecent assault. Though upper-middle-class schoolboys were not likely to fall foul of the Offences Against the Persons Act, which anyway was not strenuously enforced, the harsh legal framework contributed to the psychological apprehension and shame that surrounded homosexual desire. In response, as they became young men, Symonds and Carpenter retreated behind a protective barrier of reserve which transmuted into an internalised prohibition. Both were to find dissolving their inner defences as difficult as negotiating the outward constraints upon them. The painful psychological struggle which ensued would propel them in differing ways to become passionate proponents of change.

As Carpenter entered adolescence inner confusion accentuated his feelings of alienation from his family. He took to escaping at night by clambouring along the stony beach, defying the wind and gazing out at the wild, white breakers and distant vessels. His other refuge was the Downs where he would walk for hours, his mind free-floating, or, like the nature writer Richard Jefferies, whose work he later came to admire, he would lie in a hollow, brooding and watching the clouds go by. The silence and isolation of the Downs acted as an antidote to Brighton; the distant bark of a dog, the rumble of a train far away and the occasional shepherd huddling against a gorse-bush the only intrusions. In the sparse beauty of the curving chalklands covered in blue-green turf, splashed with red clover, pink centaury, madder, dwarf-broom and yellow lotus, he marvelled at the natural world which he came to love and depend upon more and more as he grew older. He first acquired the observant eye for tiny flowers and fauna on the Sussex Downs, which he retained throughout his life. Long afterwards, the now well-travelled walker would notice the same yellow lotus in the Alps and again in the Himalayas.

When he returned to Brunswick Square, daily life there came to seem vacuous and unbearable. In *My Days and Dreams* he describes his sisters dabbling in painting and music and wandering aimlessly from room to room to see if anything was going on. Any break in the monotony was nearly as bad, for he would then be subjected to the rituals of fashionable life, which he excoriated in an early poem: 'the first introductions, the curtseys, the bows, the tentative remarks, the bombast, the grimaces, the grotesque baffling masks . . . the peacock display'.[24]

In a 'Little Women' style portrayal, in which each of the sisters are apportioned distinctive characteristics, Ida Hyett depicted Emily as spiritual and thoughtful and Eliza (Lizzie), as musical and poetic. Ellen (Ida Hyett's mother) was the walker and gardener; Dora was summed up as 'brilliant', while poor Alice was 'odd and weak-minded'. The oldest sister, Sophy, was the forceful, controlling one in the family and it was she who embraced fashionable society, causing her younger sisters to whisper, 'Sophy has no soul.' Ida Hyett mused, 'I suspect that the alien atmosphere in which the young Edward grew up was partly of her creation.'[25] The frissons of horror against smart sets, department stores and managing women that shudder through his writings over the years emanate partly from this formidable older sister.

As the children grew older, the divided destinies of male and female became ever more apparent. Charles entered the Indian Civil Service in 1857. Four years later, Alfred joined the Navy at fourteen, continuing the family tradition, while George (who Carpenter rarely mentions) went into the Army. In contrast his sisters were compelled to negotiate the immediate world of Brighton society, for the wider vistas of their brothers' lives were closed to them. Despite Charles Carpenter's liberalism and his interest in education, he did not pay much attention to the education of his daughters. And neither parent possessed the worldly know-how which could steer a daughter through the rungs of the upper-middle-class to a 'good' marriage. The sisters were left to drift, despite Sophy's efforts to gain some hold in the swirling currents of 'society'. At a time when a minority of middle-class women were striving for higher education, they were to fall between two stools, being neither learned and 'advanced' nor entirely comfortable in the conventional mode. In the sixth form and aware that he too was soon to escape, the youthful, introspective Carpenter experienced a greater degree of discomfort about the demarcations of gender than was common among men of his class and era. He flailed against the shallowness and futility of the lives mapped out for his sisters, his thoughtful nature-loving cousin Janet McNair and their young women friends, believing that they were capable of so much more than the custom-ary rituals of balls, dinner parties, theatres and concerts, the round of shopping or loafing up and down the parade gossiping.[26]

Outwardly the adolescent 'Teddie' had grown into a rather severe and priggish young man; the more turbulent his internal feelings became, the more devout he appeared on the surface. By the time he left school he was ostensibly more conformist than his radical and enquiring father and, after sighting a handsome young curate, had started to consider going into the Church. The whole family, for differing reasons, appear to have lined up with their mother against Charles Carpenter's heterodoxies. Even Lizzie, who believed fervently in the fearless pursuit of ideas, groaned when her father descended on her and a young woman acquaintance, dropped a few heresies and commenced to read aloud from the French Enlightenment freethinker, Comte de Volney.[27] Charles Carpenter seemed incapable of knowing what constituted appropriate behaviour in the company of Brighton young ladyhood.

Periodically, nervous depression would strike Charles and anxiety about his investments would penetrate the clouds of Idealism. The mathematical Edward would then be summoned to study railway company reports, maps, gazetteers, newspaper cuttings into the early hours of the morning, acquiring a knowledge of the social basis of market forces that would foster his later questioning of abstract economic laws. Despite his dreaminess and spasms of anxiety, Charles proved a competent investor and the family fortune grew.

The Carpenters present in cameo a wider economic and social phenomenon. By the 1850s and '60s more and more families were living off
unearned capital, buoyed up by the accumulated inheritances of parents
and grandparents. This rentier group were instrumental in British capitalism's
transition into a second phase of industrialisation in which finance played
a defining role. Wealth flowed into the country from their investments in
many distant lands, padding the aura of earnestness and culture that the
Carpenters and other upper-middle-class Victorians exuded. The return on
their capital appeared only as figures on a balance sheet, nonetheless, the
immigrant poor of America, who laid the tracks for the railway that linked
the East and West coasts, had unknowingly contributed to the splendour
of 45 Brunswick Square. In later years, this dependence on the toil of others
came to seem an immoral parasitism to Carpenter. Nevertheless, it made
the cultivation of his intellect as a young man possible.

In the summer of 1863 Charles Carpenter could afford to send his prim
and scholarly son off on a walking holiday along the zigzagging paths of
the pine-covered Swiss mountains near Vevey, and then on to Heidelberg,
the following year, to learn German. Edward was to stay five months in
Germany; this, his first long journey away from home, signalled that his
route as a young man had clearly diverted from that of his sisters. The
introspective youth spent a rather solitary time at Heidelberg, wandering
through the nearby woods and hills, and eating sausages with the sceptical
professor with whom he lodged. Despite his new freedom, he still tussled
to fulfil both parents' contradictory expectations; letters home to his mother
assure her that he is going to church and not getting into any duels.[28]
The professor and his wife teased him because he still wore his tall hat
to the English church on Sundays; though outwardly conformist, he could
not be content with his mother's unquestioning religious faith. He was
beginning to explore the ideas of unorthodox religious thinkers who had
valued mystical illumination and defied the Church. An early, undated
notebook, written in German and French, contains references to Blaise
Pascal, François Fénelon and Emmanuel Swedenborg.[29]
    When Carpenter went to Germany the generation who followed Kant
in philosophy were intent on examining their inner selves as a source for
understanding universal truths about human destiny. Carpenter had already
acquired an orientation towards Romanticism and Idealism from his father,
absorbing a respect for intuition, a belief in the power of consciousness
and a conviction that a transcendent spirituality resided in every individual.
German Idealism would influence him profoundly and result in a search
for an ever-expanding consciousness, while conversely yearning for some

lost union with nature. At nineteen, however, he wanted to learn about the new scientific work of Gustav Robert Kirchoff and Robert Wilhelm Bunsen in physics and chemistry and took himself off to their lectures. This fascination with science would persist as a love-hate relationship. Like the German Idealists, he, too, would try to reconcile philosophy and the natural sciences, while circumventing materialism and positivism.

The atmosphere of the beautiful old German university town was affecting Carpenter, almost despite himself, by exposing him to a new outlook about what mattered. In Heidelberg, Brighton 'smart' did not rule supreme, and he could not resist a dig at sister Sophy in a letter to his father; 'the students here go about in all manner of costumes so I don't think I have excited much attention by my bag like appearance'.[30] Father and son could share the life of the mind and unite safely against petty trivialities of dress. Charles Carpenter no doubt congratulated himself on enabling his son to acquire German and breathe the atmosphere of European thought as a counter to English parochialism.

This period abroad away from his family and Brighton fostered a new tone of confidence; Heidelberg was an important staging post before he went on to university in Britain. Carpenter's interest in mathematics had made Cambridge an obvious choice and he was resolved that Trinity Hall should be his college. When his father began to dither in favour of St John's the steely determination which would later startle friends used to his customary gentle demeanour came flashing out: 'I thought we had quite decided that Trinity should be my college.'[31] When he later argued that Trinity Hall was a gentlemanly college, Charles Carpenter laughed at his son; Brighton had left its mark after all. Though he kept it up his sleeve, Carpenter had a further, boyish reason for selecting Trinity – it was 'Head of the River' and he admired good oarsmen. Like many young people he had made a momentous decision for incongruous reasons. Notwithstanding, Charles Carpenter backed down and Trinity Hall it would be.

2

The Cambridge Radical

An intriguing painting by Robert Farren, 'Senate House Hill: Degree Morning' (1863), still hangs in Trinity Hall. It captures the intense all-male world of self-regarding power and strong, if suppressed, emotion, that Carpenter was about to enter. A section depicts the Master of Trinity Hall, Thomas Charles Geldart, shaking the hand of a rather glazed-looking Robert Romer who had just been classed as senior wrangler and was also a renowned oarsman. A sardonic Henry Latham, who would teach Carpenter mathematics and eventually became Master himself, holds a small wooden spoon which was customarily given to the student who came bottom in the Mathematical Tripos. At the back of the academic cluster stands the blind Henry Fawcett, the vigorous radical whose efforts to democratise Cambridge would greatly influence Carpenter. He stands leaning on a stick with an air of detachment, as if he is waiting for change to come.[1]

And, indeed, the years Carpenter spent at Cambridge between 1864 and 1874 did see major political and educational reforms in society and to a lesser extent in the University. Campaigns for women's education were under way and the first women's college, Girton, started with five students in a rented house in 1869; Newnham followed in 1871. In the same year the religious tests which had excluded non-conformists were abolished. Religious scepticism had hit Cambridge during the 1860s and some of the more liberally minded dons wanted to break the ties between the University and the Anglican establishment by ending the tradition of appointing men to clerical fellowships and scrapping the celibacy requirements on fellows. Nevertheless, Cambridge was, after all, Cambridge, and old ways died hard. Tradition was personified by the elderly Master of Trinity Hall, Thomas Charles Geldart, who was renowned not for his learning, but for his love of fishing and his appreciation of good wine. His wife was the proverbial power behind the throne and represented a

Detail of 'Senate House Hill: Degree Morning 1863',
by Robert Farren

redoubtable force for conservatism. The suffrage campaigner, Millicent Fawcett, maintained in *What I Remember* (1924) that Mrs Geldart was so orthodox in religion she controverted the credentials of several bishops, while her loyalty to the Royal Family belonged to the time of le Roi Soleil.[2]

In *My Days and Dreams*, Carpenter dismissed Cambridge as his 'intellectual'[3] period, but in fact, while he was there, he encountered active reforming lobbies which affected his political outlook. The successful agitation for the Reform Act had encouraged hope for women's suffrage along with the extension of higher education to women and to the working class. The Fawcetts were key campaigning figures, along with the modernising moral philosopher, Henry Sidgwick. Sidgwick, a staunch supporter of efforts to bring women students to Cambridge, was equally committed to taking university education beyond the walls, proudly telling his sister in November 1867 that an association of 'school mistresses and other enlightened people' had been formed in the North of England to encourage the higher education of women.[4]

The cause of reform was invigorated by the arrival in 1867 of a radical Scot, James Stuart. Stuart was unusual in being linked to the world of manufacturing which Cambridge so disdained, and his interest in working-class education had begun when he started an evening school for apprentices at his father's factory in Scotland. Stuart was appalled by the gulf between classes at Cambridge and critical of the contempt in which applied science and technology were held. He became a supporter of the Ladies' National Association's campaign against the Contagious Diseases Acts which allowed the police in military towns to arrest women suspected of being prostitutes. The women, who were forcibly examined, would be detained if they had a sexually transmitted disease in order to protect the troops. Defying the taboos against discussing sexuality, middle-class women reformers were able to mobilise both non-conformists and radicals in protest against the violation of working-class women's rights. The movement was led by Josephine Butler, who was also promoting women's higher education in the North of England, and Stuart drew on these links when a few years later with the support of Sidgwick, he launched a new venture into adult education, University Extension, which would take Carpenter away from Cambridge.

Along with the spirit of hopeful activism, Carpenter also encountered cultural aspirations for change. Henry Sidgwick would later remark that during the 1860s, he and his generation had been searching for 'a complete revision of human relations, political, moral, and economic'.[5] Sidgwick's own writing articulated the enthusiasms and angsts of an era in which intellectuals wrestled not only with democracy, but with the fallout from Charles Darwin's *Origin of Species* (1859). Sidgwick and other agnostic dons agonised over whether they should dissemble about their religious doubts in order not to destroy the faith of others. This clash between individual conscience and social duty triggered Sidgwick's theoretical attempts to elaborate a rational basis for ethics and impinged on his life; in 1869 he felt compelled to resign from a clerical fellowship. While Carpenter does not refer to Sidgwick in his autobiography, a Sidgwickian concern to balance individual happiness and social responsibility would be his life's endeavour, though he gave it a quite different rendition. In later years they would take contrary paths, for Sidgwick, a friend of J.A. Symonds, urged cautious casuistry about homosexuality.

Carpenter's autobiography does mention the other great figure he encountered at Cambridge, his father's friend, the heterodox F.D. Maurice, who had been the inspiration for the Working Men's College in London in 1854. Maurice became Professor of Moral Philosophy at Cambridge in 1866, and though a devout Anglican and a conservative, was regarded as both theologically and politically heretical by the establishment. He rejected the doctrine of eternal damnation and did not ground morality in the Bible or religious doctrine, but in personal, loving relationships which he saw stretching outwards from the family into society. Maurice's belief in a transcendent inner divinity derived from Wordsworth and the Romantics and he deplored the utilitarian focus on external change which influenced Sidgwick. Nevertheless, both men saw their role not simply as formal educators; they wanted to infuse their students with a moral and social mission of tolerance and empathy. And, in this spirit, Sidgwick welcomed Maurice into the coterie of intellectual reformers who were intent on transforming the ethos of the University.

Maurice's effect was almost despite himself, for his message was often unintelligible and always vague and convoluted. In *My Days and Dreams* Carpenter chuckles over Maurice lecturing on moral philosophy, 'tapping his forehead with his fingers, shutting his eyes, and still only framing broken sentences'.[6] Yet somehow the spirit of the man fired many undergraduates and University teachers. Stuart took Maurice's emphasis on personal empathy as a foundation for social action, first into a series of lectures for Northern workers and then into University Extension. Carpenter also absorbed Maurice's approach much more than he admits. In the long term Maurice's cultural influence would be far more pervasive than Sidgwick's, reverberating in attitudes to politics, culture and personal relations for many years.

★   ★   ★

Cambridge was waking up not only to social reform, but to a new enthusiasm for athleticism. Carpenter's boisterous upbringing stood him in good stead and he soon became part of a large friendship network of enthusiastic rowing men. Despite spending time rowing, a sport made popular by muscular products of the reformed public schools, Carpenter came top in his first term college examinations which qualified him to study under the imposing Henry Latham for the honours degree in mathematics, called the Tripos. While impressing Latham in mathematics, Carpenter soon demonstrated the wide-ranging interests that would mark his subsequent intellectual trajectory. In 1866 Carpenter won a Trinity Hall prize for an essay, 'On the Continuance of Modern Civilisation', pressing for equal educational opportunities and less extreme class divisions. Beautifully written in flowing copy-plate handwriting, the essay was an imposing piece of work from a twenty-two-year-old. Carpenter begins with a proposition that uncannily heralds his future intellectual path. Instead of simply examining 'the nature and character of man as an individual', he posits the need to 'map out his destinies as part of the great whole of humanity and to foretell the workings of his energies in forwarding the progress of Civilisation'. This grand project is no sooner laid out when he gulps and adds, 'our courage may well fail us. Life is all too short for such a task.'[7] His cousin, Janet McNair, who seems to have had a special affection for him, wrote saying that she liked it 'extremely'. She added, 'I hope you mean to go on writing things, and let us have the benefits of them, it is a duty you owe to society and me in particular, for I like just the kind of things you explain.'[8] Though Carpenter was later to interrogate 'civilisation' more harshly than he does in this early essay, his interest in examining the individual in relation to human society was already being sketched out. The organic evolutionary image of the seed of the future lying dormant, which recurred in his later writing, also makes its first appearance in this early essay.

His record as an undergraduate was so outstanding that when Leslie Stephen decided his conscience would not allow him to continue as a clerical fellow in 1867, Carpenter was sounded out about the position by Henry Latham, even though he had not yet taken his degree. When he gained a first-class degree and the honour of being placed tenth wrangler in the demanding Mathematics Tripos in 1868, the fellowship was confirmed. He wrote with understandable pride to tell his father of the good offer while expressing doubts about an academic career.

> I have always thought that the life of a don is a rather stagnant sort of life and I do not think I could make up my mind to settle down altogether as such. At the same time I do not know that I ought to

refuse such a good openings [sic], because even if I do not remain here altogether, it will be very likely to lead to something else, and a few years spent here would not have been time wasted.[9]

Clearly uneasy about admitting to his sceptical father that he was about to take a clerical fellowship, he tries to be placatory: 'Besides, the satisfaction of being able to turn to account all the money you have spent on my education is a great inducement to me to close with the offer at once.'[10] The conscientious son was still trying to do the impossible and please both parents. Though Sophia's delight at having a clergyman in the family might have been tempered had she heard Carpenter explaining to the Bishop of Ely, who was to ordain him in June 1870, that Abraham's offering of Isaac as a sacrifice was undoubtedly a remnant of Moloch-worship.[11] The Bishop himself was troubled, but the Anglican Church contained such a mixture of evangelicals, 'high' churchmen who flirted with Rome, 'broad' church advocates of salvation through good works, along with quietly epicurean agnostics, that oddness in theology could be accommodated.

The Bishop may well have noted some unruly sentiments in Carpenter's essay on 'The Religious Influence of Art' which was awarded the Burney Prize in 1869. Published in 1870, this argued that art was 'more cognate' to religion in an inner spiritual sense than to any external code of morality. Carpenter believed that music, architecture and Nature could intimate a spiritual presence. Like the Romantics, he presents the artist as endowed with transcendent perceptions, and, following Wordsworth, stresses the wordless understanding that comes from contact with Nature. His interest in science is evident in references to debates about continuity and variation in the classification of species, as well as to atoms and crystals. Taking a sideways swipe at the overemphasis in women's education on imitation and sensibility, he sees in Nature a balance; every little plant and animal fulfils 'a happy individuality', while being linked by 'sympathetic dependence to every other part of creation'.[12]

Art, nature, science, women's emancipation, the balancing of individuality and connection, body and soul, would be long-term preoccupations. Praising the Stoics, he says the Greeks valued the development of personality, but is equally drawn to a 'Brahmanism' which seeks mystic union. He had been reading the Neo-Platonists, the late Hellenic grouping which gathered around Plotinus (203–70 AD), whose thinking carries echoes of Buddhism and Hinduism as well as the influence of Plato. While expressing unease at the reduction of Nature to a passive principle in the Neo-Platonic tradition, Carpenter nonetheless found turning away from asceticism a struggle. Later in the essay he criticises a 'false excitement' of art, yet insists he does not want to inveigh against the indulgence of sensual enjoyment, adding that this shows 'How difficult or impossible it is to draw any marked dividing line between our higher nature and our more animal instincts.' Convinced that he had 'seen the light', the prize-winning young essayist was resolved to go forth with his face 'beaming like that of Moses, to give light to others to shine in the darkness, though the darkness comprehend it not'.[13]

Duly ordained and hence a college fellow, Carpenter was expected to deliver sermons in the college chapel. Being assiduous, and deciding he was in need of practice, he began acting as a curate to F.D. Maurice at St Edward's church which was connected to Trinity Hall. The appointment of Maurice had been strenuously opposed by Mrs Geldart, who attended St Edward's and abhorred both his politics and his theological views. In the ensuing fracas of college politics poor Geldart had tumbled completely out of his depth. When asked at Trinity Hall's high table about the source of his objections to Maurice's views, he could hardly say they came from his wife. As Geldart resorted to muttering vaguely about other people, the radical Henry Fawcett had guffawed over his chop and the table erupted in hilarity. Eventually a way out had been found by means of a letter from the Bishop of Carlisle endorsing Maurice as the incumbent.[14] With such a pile of eggshells, a curacy at St Edward's was not exactly low profile.

Fawcett's guffaw resounded far beyond Trinity Hall's high table. When Carpenter started working with Maurice, religion was implicated at once in politics, the class structure and an existential sense of self. Intense anxieties were provoked by religious deviation and agnosticism alike, partly because they appeared to undermine the social fabric of the status quo into which the Anglican Church was inextricably woven. Conservatives feared that without religion to calm the lower orders, society might tumble down like a pack of cards. Moreover disbelief shattered the Broad Church compromise between faith and reason; it cast individuals adrift. Even liberal thinkers were troubled by the prospect of living without any accepted framework, with all assumed reference points dissolved. Doubt opened a void from which a swarm of questions arose. How could an alternative basis for altruism be established? How could humanity flourish in a purely materialist world? Was it legitimate to conceal one's own disbelief in order to protect others from the pain of living without God?

By accepting the gratifying clerical fellowship and then agreeing to stand up and pronounce in St Edward's, Carpenter had blundered into the ethical minefield Sidgwick was struggling to theorise. Meanwhile the spate of reforms in Britain, the agitation of the left-wing First International, a small but articulate Republican movement, and the revolutionary eruption of the Commune in Paris, were polarising Cambridge opinion. Carpenter's sermon notes from the early 1870s have survived and record him using the pulpit to expunge his own religious doubts through radical social exhortation. They are packed with calls for the rich to give up their wealth and adopt a life of social service. On one occasion he took as his text, 'For whosoever shall do the will of my Father which is in heaven, the same is my brother and sister and mother.' Admonishing the congregation to eschew materialism, Carpenter reminded them that the rich lived on the labour of the poor. He asked rhetorically, 'If we have really hoodwinked this thing, this huge human creature and made it our beast of burden – what if it one day come [sic] to know this, and shrug up its back and shake us into the dust.'[15]

In case anyone was still feeling complacent, he warned that 'the people' had been kept ignorant and their passions were running high. He then referred the congregation to Professor Fawcett's friendly criticisms of the First International's programme, explaining that this kind of dialogue was the best way to avert revolution. Carpenter urged St Edward's, 'Let us above all beware of ascribing to these men, though we may differ from them, evil motives, there is enough ill feeling already between class and class in England.'[16] If Mrs Geldart was in the congregation, this was a remark likely to conjure up horrifying spectres of marauding First International desperadoes advancing on the cherished Geldart wine cellars, while a bunch of advanced liberals – Carpenter, Fawcett and their ilk – adjured the dons, fellows and undergraduates who were meant to be her first line of defence to 'Be polite! Be polite!'

Carpenter's sermon notes mark a shift away from the confident hopes in political and educational reform expressed in his prize-winning essay of 1866. Racked with uncertainty about capitalism as a social and economic system, they echo John Ruskin's Cassandra-like declarations of imminent doom and calls for a moral economy in which the selfish rich rectify their covetousness and 'occult theft' of the labour of others.[17] However, Ruskin's eccentric authoritarian Toryism was hard to square with the democratic radicalism Carpenter had assimilated at Cambridge. Instead, Carpenter evoked the Italian republican and insurrectionary, Giuseppe Mazzini, who fused the duty of social cohesion with the rights of citizens: 'Class feeling, class exclusiveness is one of the great curses of England, the drag on progress, the foe of that ideal state of society for which we look. We have talked for centuries about our rights, let us go and fulfil the duties which we have not spoken of.'[18]

The idealistic young Cambridge curate was not alone in his admiration for Mazzini. The latter's essays on association, liberty, civic consciousness and the ideal state had been published in English as the *Duties of Man* in 1860. Mazzini spent long periods as a political exile in Britain where his enthusiasm for working-class education and his emphasis upon social harmony based on a combination of duties with rights caused him to be lionised by the liberal intelligentsia. His republicanism was harder to swallow. However, in the late 1860s and early 1870s, Queen Victoria's popularity was at a low ebb; after the death of Prince Albert, she had gone into retreat from public life, there were rumours about her relationship with her Scottish servant John Brown, and the mounting cost of her large family resulted in complaints about the monarchy. This mood of dissatisfaction occurred at a time when working-class agitation on a mass scale had died down, but it did result in the formation of several Republican groupings including one among Cambridge intellectuals, instigated by Henry Fawcett.

After delivering his sermons on Sunday evenings, Carpenter would rush off to read Mazzini's *Duties of Man* with members of the Cambridge Republican Club at King's College. Well fuelled by claret and tobacco, the little band would sit subverting society, Christianity and the monarchy late into the night. Its secretary was the brilliant young mathematician, William Kingdom Clifford, who combined these heresies with his interest in Georg Friedrich Bernhard Riemann's ideas about a non-Euclidian geometry. Clifford described this geometry, which would have practical consequences for navigation, as a 'bending of space'.[19] Speculations about curved space and manifold dimensions continued to unfurl around Carpenter in later life, but in the early 1870s, it was the Socratic, paradoxical Clifford with his 'Satyr-like face . . . and blasphemous treatment of the existing gods',[20] who constituted an exciting challenge. Carpenter found the Club a good deal more interesting than St Edward's. However, the French Commune in 1871 swiftly hardened the public mood, a panic about revolution broke out in the press and the Cambridge Republican Club was signalled out for censure.[21] Carpenter, who was never actually a member of the Club, backed off, to the relief of his sister Lizzie who had decided that 'Mr Fawcett' was going mad.[22]

Between 1870 and 1872 Carpenter was oscillating between sharply contrasting polarities. Around the time he was attending the Republican Club, he was being considered as a possible tutor for two of the royal princes, Albert Victor and George of Wales, who he had seen at Osborne House on the Isle of Wight and found 'natural and pleasant'.[23] Amidst these political and religious disjunctures, he became tortured by doubt as to whether he had taken the right step in accepting the clerical fellowship.

Writing his sermon notes was an agony because he did not know how to speak with sincerity. He made an attempt at Sidgwickian strategic caution and seemed to be thinking out loud in one sermon: 'If a belief is not a living faith in us the least we can do is to keep it in suspense as it were, till we feel it distinctly our duty to discard it or adopt it.'[24] It was hardly a rousing call to fill the pews and it left him feeling unhappy. Most of his friends counselled hypocrisy. Among them was the thoughtful and devoted John Dalton, who actually took the royal post. Dalton urged Carpenter not to give up on the fellowship. What would he be succumbing to if he flinched, but 'the forces you most despise, Mrs Geldart, and Kings-Parade-tradesmen – Philistinism'?[25] F.D. Maurice, for his part, could not understand why his earnest curate could not reconcile himself to holding a historical-philosophical view of the Bible and Anglican doctrine. Carpenter explains in *My Days and Dreams* that though he had been initiated into this Broad Church attitude by his father, his problem was in presenting Christian belief to congregations who he knew accepted the Bible as fundamentalist truth.[26] On the other hand he quailed at secularism.

His letters home must have expressed the strain. Sophia Carpenter, who knew that her dearest Teddie was inclined to nervous ailments, worried that he was in such an overworked state he would break down altogether. She was contemplating intervening herself with a plea to F.D. Maurice for time off.[27] Impossible to tell his mother that it was the inner conscience she herself had bequeathed which made him feel such a wretched dissembler speaking from a Christian pulpit. There was, moreover, something else disturbing his fragile equanimity – something he could never explain to his mother or Maurice or even Lizzie. He was falling in love.

Something approximating love had already occurred. A sexual experience when he was twenty is mentioned in the self-analysis Carpenter wrote for Havelock Ellis, and he has left other clues in scraps of notes and poetry. In 1865 he described feelings of physical attraction to an unnamed man. Declaring 'I dare not think the thoughts I might entertain about him', he then proceeded to articulate them:

> He and I are human beings, and the thought will suggest itself to me; why cannot my fate be linked with him. I cannot, cannot keep away this thought . . . the more I try the more it overwhelms me. I think if I could know he loved me, nothing can be wanting to make me feel entirely blest. Why should this feeling, this conviction be presenting itself to me when I know that its realization is utterly impossible?[28]

Poetry became his outlet for these impossible desires. A verse dated May 1868 describes a love in secret for a man with sweet brown hair. This time his feelings are overtly physical; he is entranced by the hair, the eyes, the smile, the sensuality that the voice arouses. But this love too is unrealised and he is left with only his own dreams and woes as companions through the night.[29] Hopeless longings and insomnia became a pattern which it would take many years for him to cast off.

The most serious of these early loves was a slightly younger man from a modest Norfolk background, called Edward Anthony Beck. They first grew close when Beck was a bright classics student who shared Carpenter's penchant for poetry. After Beck became a Fellow, they had adjoining rooms and spent the evenings together talking and reading each other's writings; then during the vacations they visited one another's homes. College life at Cambridge was conducive to intense friendships between young men, but this particular close friendship was edged with sexual feeling. In their letters they invoke the homoerotic icons of male love, with Beck cast as Jonathan to Carpenter's David. After a magical day viewing Turner's paintings together at the National Gallery in the Spring of 1871, a dazzled Beck wrote, 'I remember a great blurring of barriers, my Ganymede, and all the Turners encauticized [sic] into one great burning line of sunset sea, all set in a halo of Carpenter.'[30] Carpenter, already acquiring the charisma which subsequently became more pronounced, did what he would do on many occasions later in his life – take a man who attracted him on a journey in Europe. During the summer vacation he and Beck travelled through Switzerland, Italy and Germany.

They parted in Paris, where evidence of the recent fighting during the Commune was everywhere visible. The sublime holiday concluded in a burlesque incident when Carpenter was arrested by Prussian soldiers who suspected him of being a French spy. His English passport was in luggage which had been sent on and things were looking bad until his guard, writing a description of his captive's physiognomy, summed up his nose with the German word 'stumpf'. The literal meaning of 'stumpf' is 'turned up', but metaphorically it denotes intellectual arrogance! Carpenter was not familiar with the word but the sound made him burst out laughing in delight at the expressiveness of the German language. The ice broke, the soldier joined in the mirth and let him go. Carpenter always regarded his large nose with its slightly bulbous tip, as one of his weak points, but this time he had been saved by the 'stumpf'.[31]

On September 1, 1871, back home at Castle Rising, Norfolk, Beck composed a long, laboured letter to Carpenter. His memories of their time together were assuming a 'Turneresque glow' again, but he was coming down to earth and realising he was having difficulty relating the welter of impressions to the humdrum actuality of life at home. The letter assumes a determinedly chatty style as Beck tries to hold emotions at a distance, exercising the irony that made him so popular at Trinity Hall. Carpenter is quintessentially poetical; in contrast Beck presents himself as the realist: 'You have no idea how practical I am. Everybody acknowledges it.' He announces how he is drinking beer, smoking his pipe and making vacant conversation; 'I have utterly abjured all poetry, both for reading and writing. I look at the rising moon unmoved. I wad my ears against all manner of sentiment: will not allow myself to cry or ache inwardly at any sorrow or injustice. I systematically train myself into a consistent brutality. I am utterly changed – it is all the reaction from you.' Momentarily Beck drops his guard and becomes simply a frank young man remembering something extraordinary he cannot deal with but is unable to dismiss. 'Of all places I am so glad we stayed at Munich – and that not because of the beer and notwithstanding the diarrhoea.' Yet this letter signalled emotional withdrawal, striking an ominous note with 'Be as jolly as you can.'[32]

On September 5th Carpenter revealed his feelings for Beck in a letter to a mutual friend, Charles Oates. Oates, who had left Cambridge the previous year, was in London preparing to be a barrister. Taciturn, retiring and never given to extreme enthusiasms, Oates too was a homosexual and, like Carpenter, inclined to fancy sexually ambivalent young men. Despite the differences in their characters, this secret bond ensured that Oates remained Carpenter's close confidant from the late 1860s until his death in 1901. Without mentioning the beer, Carpenter recounts how he and Beck had gone 'up to heaven in an incense-cloud of art at Munich'. Yet he knew Beck's responses differed from his own, intimating that some barriers could not be blurred, 'it is the half-inarticulate dread, it is the scarcely-confessed nightmare dream of divided love; nay! of hopeless, impossible love'.[33] While some part of him foresees estrangement, half-knowing that their separation was inevitable did not make it any easier to bear. The failed relationship with Beck would be the first real crisis of passion in Carpenter's life.

Beck also was aware that something momentous had occurred. This was no ordinary friendship, nor was it to be easily shaken off. A year later in September 1872 Beck, indefatigably amiable, told 'My dear polemic' that he was 'the most difficult person in the world to write to because one has so much to say to you that one knows not what to choose; trifles so light as not to be worth writing; and confidences too intimate to be congealed on paper.' On the whole Beck felt on safer ground with trifles rather than intimacy but he could not be quite content with them; 'To say I enjoyed your company would be too commonplace – I do not like to use the same word for you as of walnuts and cucumber.'[34]

Carpenter's sole recourse was his poetry: 'Yet I behold but thee in all', he wrote obsessively around 1873. The memory of Beck stayed with him over the years, a dull stab of buried pain. An allusion to 'Love in absence' in a poem is later changed to 'distant'; then 'the old intense joy' is crossed out, and becomes 'unfulfilled joy'.[35] He was still fiddling about with these verses in 1915. The following year, in *My Days and Dreams*, Carpenter affirmed that there had been a touch of romance in their friendship – a surprising admission given contemporary attitudes. His explanation for the severing of the relationship was that Beck's 'vein of poetic feeling and romance, possibly too soon ripe, ran itself out. . . . His mind . . . took on a slightly cynical cast.'[36] The two men's lives forked in contrasting directions. Beck, who after all had a living to earn, became a respectable Cambridge don and eventually Master of Trinity Hall. He died in 1916 and Carpenter, the socialist and sex reformer, carefully folded away and kept the obituary of his first great love which appeared in the *Cambridge Chronicle* on April 19th that year.[37]

Looking back in his autobiography, with an awareness of his sexual desires he had not possessed in the 1870s, Carpenter observed that his relationship to Beck was one of several strong attachments he had formed while at Cambridge. He regretted how he had been paralysed by an education that repressed self-expression, by the prejudices of public opinion and his own reserve. Carpenter's upbringing as an upper-middle-class young man had taught him to intellectualise rather than to confront emotion, while the need to conceal forbidden sexual desires had made him adept at maintaining a conventional front of humorous irony, gossiping lightly in his letters to friends about Cambridge characters. In contrast, his friendship with Oates was particularly precious because they could talk without restraint; not simply about personal relationships but about Carpenter's love of nature, Beethoven, Tennyson or Shelley. Yet even with Oates he remained inhibited, aware that when he tried to say simply how he valued their conversations it came out in 'a medley of Kant, Comte and Christianity'.[38] He would struggle with his reserve and his cerebral approach to relationships throughout his life.

In retrospect he concluded, 'By concealing myself I was unfair to my friends, and at the same time suffered torments which I need not have suffered.'[39] However, this was hindsight; an opinion formed after Carpenter had become an initiator of the conscious attempt to bring sexual desires of all kinds out into the open. In the 1870s things were very different. The ambiguity of strong friendships in the 1870s blurred any explicit expression of sexual passion. It was possible to at once know and not know that feelings were sexually charged, leaving space for exploratory emotions but making actual physical moves difficult. The equivocal attitudes to homosexual desire in Cambridge in the late 1860s and '70s created a perplexing kind of freedom which had to be intimated within bounds which could never be explicitly marked out.

In this opaque and shifting terrain, Carpenter, like other Victorian homosexual intellectuals, found in ancient Greek culture mirrors which could be the source of coded signals. In December 1870 he told Oates:

> you have two sides to your existence (everyone has I suppose in a way) – the one you live in Duke Street and digest law and perform the usual functions of life (breathing excepted); the other you spend in an ideal world . '. . I have just been reading a translation of Plato's Phaedrus – that is the essence of what you dream of – do read it.[40]

Plato's *Phaedrus*, translated by the Cambridge classicist, W.H. Thompson in 1868, was subversive stuff. Plato's convoluted dialogic text presents ideal love as a sensual and erotic communion of such intense mutuality that it transcends sexual penetration. Despite the lofty ethics, the style is playful and teasing; Plato writes about arousal graphically – 'it throbs and aches and tickles' like 'cutting teeth' or 'the soul of a man who is beginning to sprout wings'. He describes the pain of unrealised desire, 'remembering the boy with his beauty', the lover is both 'strong all over' and in a state of rejoicing; caught between agony and ecstasy, he is unable to sleep at night or keep still by day.[41]

It was not just the vivid language which expressed so precisely the edginess of the passions men like Carpenter and Oates were forced to conceal. Plato's assumption that a love between an older and a younger man could be the most noble of all human relationships was electrifying and revelatory; it shook contemporary presumptions to the core. Upper-middle-class homosexual men like Carpenter, whose own culture silenced any overt discussion of same sex love, felt that their own hidden longings were sanctioned when they read Plato at school or university. Plato touched the recesses of the imagination and turned received values upside down; paradoxically they seemed to belong with the Greek philosopher-lovers rather than to their own times.

However, the cultural affirmation that the Greeks provided did present a difficulty for a man, like Carpenter, with a radical disposition, for it remained undeniably aristocratic and elitist. An alternative democratic ideal of male comradeship came from across the Atlantic as the American poet, Walt Whitman, started to gather British adherents. In 1868 the Pre-Raphaelite writer and critic, William Michael Rossetti, edited a British version of Walt Whitman's poems. The story of this edition is a curious one. Thomas Dixon, a cork cutter in Sunderland, had come across a volume of Whitman's poems by chance. Dixon, to whom John Ruskin had addressed his letters to workers, *Time and Tide, by Weare and Tyne*, knew the Pre-Raphaelite art teacher and painter, William Bell Scott, and it was via Scott that the poems found their way to Rossetti. Though Whitman's break with conventional poetic metre was disturbing to a Victorian ear, the critic was enthusiastic and made contact with Whitman who authorised this British edition.

When a Trinity Hall friend handed him the blue-covered Rossetti edition of Whitman shortly after it was published, asking 'What do you think of this?', Carpenter relates in *My Days and Dreams* how he lay on the floor with the book, poring over it in wonder. Whitman's style was startling to anyone accustomed to literary English. Unlike other American poets he did not emulate the British; instead he translated the language he heard around him into poetry. For the first time the British were receiving the English tongue in the literature of another, quite different, culture, learning anew the language that they had assumed only they possessed. Carpenter recalled that initially the idiom of the poems seemed so unfamiliar, 'I could not make the book out.' Despite the shock of the unfamiliar form, 'What made me cling to the little blue book from the beginning was largely the poems which celebrate comradeship.' The straightforward open physicality about the body in Whitman's writing was an exciting introduction to another mode of experiencing the world. Whitman had evoked what Carpenter called 'a current of sympathy' so powerful that it would eventually take him away from Cambridge.[42]

Yet Rossetti's selection had excluded the more overtly sexual works. Most of the 'Children of Adam', 'Calamus' and even 'Song of Myself' were omitted. Carpenter was not to read an unexpurgated 'Leaves of Grass' until a few years later. Even so, he became one of a small group of British Whitmanite enthusiasts who delighted in the bracing style of the American poet. For J.A. Symonds Whitman's 'Calamus' conveyed 'strong democratic enthusiasm, a sense of the dignity and beauty of simple healthy men'.[43] Whitman always insisted that his relations with men were not sexual and, when Symonds later tried to pin him down on the homosexual implications of 'Calamus', Whitman emphatically rejected the category. Then, charac-teristically, he added, 'I maybe do not know all my meanings.'[44]

Whitman's advocacy of an 'adhesive' democratic manly comradeship was attractive to Carpenter because it provided a new homoerotic possibility, and at the same time touched a political nerve. Whitman's essay 'Democratic Vistas' (1871), presented adhesiveness as the complement to individualism, a brotherhood in which all races fused as comrades. The extension of the franchise by the Tory, Benjamin Disraeli, in 1867, had produced a dual response among intellectuals in Britain. From the right, Thomas Carlyle, in his article 'Shooting Niagara and After', thundered that culture itself would be threatened in Britain and America by 'swarming' workers and blacks. In contrast, British radicals wanted democracy to spread more extensively into daily life through the diffusion of education and personal contact between classes. In the very different context of the United States, Whitman, who had begun his 'Democratic Vistas' as a passionate refutation of Carlyle, was becoming increasingly aware of the dangers of democracy in terms of corruption and manipulation, and after the Civil War oscillated in his attitudes to race.[45]

These American nuances were lost on Whitman's British supporters like Carpenter, who started to urge his relations and friends to read Whitman.

Walt Whitman, c. 1876

Among those he was able to persuade was an unconventional woman, Jane Olivia Daubeny, who Carpenter writes about as 'Francesca' in his *Sketches of Life in Town and Country* (1908) and as 'Olivia' in *My Days and Dreams*. She was fifty and still beautiful when they came into contact through his sister Emily's marriage into the Daubeny family. Jane Olivia Daubeny, who had doubly defied propriety by separating from her husband and remaining friends with him, had spent many years in Italy, was knowledgeable about art and literature and open to new ideas. When Carpenter met her, she was living with a young woman, who, he says equivocally, was engaged as a companion, but became something more than a companion.[46] Jane Olivia Daubeny entered his life at a crisis point when he was confused and vulnerable, and he states that she was the only woman, apart from his mother, who acted upon him 'as a strong motive-force or inspiration or as a help or a guide in doubt or difficulty'.[47] Perhaps for her there was something more; she told him: 'I thought of you a long, long time in the night . . . To me it seems our affections are given us for torture . . . I am afraid you will think my morals bad.'[48] Instead she confirmed his rejection of external moral codes. The antithesis of Sophia Carpenter, who embodied sacrifice, Jane Olivia Daubeny believed in Romantic self-realisation and she exhorted Carpenter to break the pattern of his life.

In the Spring of 1873, with her encouragement, Carpenter set off on a long trip to Rome, Naples and Florence. While he was away he read about art and studied the mystical pantheism of Johannes Eckhart, the medieval German heretic liked by his father. He also became interested in the German philosopher, Arthur Schopenhauer, and mentions Eastern philosophy in a letter from Rome to Oates that April.[49] Schopenhauer opened several very important pathways for Carpenter. Hinduism and Buddhism had led Schopenhauer to a concept of spirituality apart from any religious institution, based on the human mind in relation to nature. Moreover, Schopenhauer accentuated the irrational creative force of the will over a purely intellectual apprehension. Similar concepts would be incorporated into Carpenter's later writings, however, this journey to Italy was not primarily about ideas but about being; Carpenter was intent on self-discovery and regeneration. The trail was already well marked. In this period the Mediterranean South represented a place of sensuous emotion and exotic adventure to Romantic English visitors escaping from grey skies and puritanical values. Italy was the place where the English could discard their inhibiting Englishness, and was particularly cherished by homosexuals as a land of love without fear. In a country where hidden aspects of feeling could be uncovered and unknown selves revealed, the

Greek statues, exiled so long ago, fused with Whitman's poetry, to awaken a deep germinating awareness within Carpenter. Something else could be. Amidst the sculpture and the sun, he wrote to Geldart resigning his clerical fellowship.[50]

When he returned to Cambridge that June he went to see Geldart. He was hoping for a lay fellowship and spent the rest of 1873 waiting in limbo. A volume of his verse, *Narcissus and Other Poems*, dedicated to his favourite sister Lizzie, was published in the autumn. It contained references not only to the mythical youth gazing haplessly at his own image but to 'sad echoes of sweet voices'.[51] By December it was evident to the aspiring poet that he was not going to be the poetic sensation of the season, nor was an embarrassed Trinity Hall intending to grant him a lay fellowship. The realisation that he would have to leave not only the Church but Cambridge, led him to seek out James Stuart early in 1874 and enquire about the adult education courses just being established through Stuart and Sedgwick's networking with workers and women in the North of England. Their experimental project of taking higher education to those excluded from the Universities would result in the establishment of the Cambridge University Extension Movement in 1875. The new movement was suffused with Maurice's vision of social harmony through personal contact, along with Matthew Arnold's concern that the working class should be saved from the 'Philistine' attitudes of those in trade.

It was agreed that Carpenter could start a circuit of peripatetic lecturing in the following autumn of 1874. He was pleased with the prospect of going North; it promised possibilities not only of personal release but of that spiritual merging to which, in their distinct ways, both F.D. Maurice and Walt Whitman had alluded. An added bonus was that University Extension would enable him to be close to Charles Oates, who had given up his legal ambitions to live with his ailing mother and administer the family's large estate at Meanwoodside near Leeds. The two young men were finding more and more to discuss. It was Oates who found Whitman's poem, 'Passage to India', first, and Oates who sent Arthur Hugh Clough's 'Amours de Voyage' in March 1873.[52] Perhaps he thought Clough's clever and intricate account of a heterosexual affair between two travellers in Italy that never quite took off might cheer up his lovesick friend. Or perhaps it was a more general empathy with Clough's complicated radicalism and alienated loneliness as a young man which made him think of Carpenter.

In February 1874, Carpenter was enthusing to Oates about the light and sound and colour in Edmund Gosse's *On Viol and Flute*. Gosse had been influenced by Whitman's eye for the body and the senses, but dedicated his volume to the Pre-Raphaelite, William Bell Scott. Though Carpenter expresses some unease about what he calls 'the somewhat narrow pathway of Preraphaelitism [sic]',[53] he is generous in his praise of Gosse, for the bitter truth was that Gosse's work had received far more attention than his own 'Narcissus'.

Despite the setbacks Carpenter experienced during 1873, he did not abandon his hopes of being a writer. Early in 1874 he was at work in Brighton on a drama in blank verse about Moses. Moses, the prophetic leader working from within, struggles to overcome the apathy of the people in order to lead them to the Promised Land – just the hero for an admirer of Mazzini about to set off as a University Extension lecturer.

In May 1874, the first letter came from Ponnambalam Arunachalam, a student from Sri Lanka (then Ceylon) who had just left Cambridge and was reading for the Bar in London. It was the beginning of a long correspondence between the two men whose friendship had started with Cambridge walks and boat trips. The photograph Arunachalam enclosed in his first letter shows a forthright young man with dreamy eyes, a large forehead and broad features. He has a slight beard and his hair, a little longer than was customary at the time, is parted in the middle. He wears a Western jacket with broad lapels. An extraordinary future lay ahead of him. From a wealthy Tamil family that had settled in Ceylon, Arunachalam was the first Sri Lankan to pass the examination for the Civil Service. He went on to become Police Magistrate and a District Judge and then, after his retirement, devoted himself to social reform, labour rights and the cause of self-rule. As a student Arunachalam was enthusiastic about the West and modernity, though he challenged the Archbishop of Canterbury over insulting remarks about Eastern religions. As he grew older he took a more critical stance towards Western civilisation. Carpenter recounts in My Days and Dreams how he learned a great deal about India and Ceylon from Arunachalam on their early Cambridge rambles. As the years went by he would keep on learning.[54]

Carpenter luxuriated in his last summer vacation in Cambridge, reading, canoeing on the river, bathing, playing fives or rackets and walking with friends along country lanes, resting and talking on turfy banks. This was the idyllic Cambridge he found hard to leave. Yet those exasperating Geldart coils contrived to entangle him still, for that July, a tiresome Geldart daughter had invited his sister Sophy, of all people, to stay. Sophy, anxious as ever about matters of etiquette and worried about her wardrobe, wrote to enquire, 'Do the ladies wear evening dress at the Hall dinner'?[55] This was not at all the kind of question he wanted to be thinking about.

After Sophy and a friend had been visiting for a fortnight, Carpenter grizzled to Oates that they made a fellow tear his hair in desperation: 'Women have not the faintest conception of what work means. And they placidly absorb you for hours and hours without the faintest suspicion of the struggle you go through to make both ends meet while they are absent.'[56]

In the same letter he confided to an act of supreme daring: 'What do you think? I wrote to Walt Whitman the other day – a long letter at 4 a.m.'[57] This extraordinary letter to Whitman from Trinity Hall, written on July 12th, during one of Carpenter's insomniac nights, reveals how seductive he could be. Carpenter's capacity to charm, which can be glimpsed obliquely in the passionate responses he evoked throughout his life from other people, on this occasion is there on the page, in lyrical prose.

> My dear friend – it is just dawn but there is light enough to write by, and the birds in their old sweet fashion are chirping in the little College garden outside. My first knowledge of you is all entangled with that little garden. But that was six years ago; so you must not mind me writing to you now because you understand, as I understand, that I am not drunk with new wine.[58]

The ostensible reason for Carpenter's letter is to reassure Whitman that he was read by people in England. Thinking no doubt of the enthusiasts he had recruited personally, like Jane Olivia Daubeny, Carpenter tells the poet how he was particularly popular among women. Whitman, himself, frequently invoked women along with workers as the agents who would redeem society and Carpenter expresses the same idea in this letter. The 1860s dream of the adolescent boy, to release his sisters from Brighton frippery instead of the proverbial tower, has transposed itself into an insight that women did not have to be regarded as victims. It was not just a chimera; while Carpenter was at Cambridge an alliance was being forged between middle-class advanced women and radical working-class men in the campaign against the Contagious Diseases Acts. After the 1870 Education Act these connections were taken into electoral work around the School Boards in many parts of the country. Carpenter sought to convey his sense of the flickering utopia their association could bring to Whitman in Hegelian terms: 'the new, open life which is to come; the spirit moving backwards and forwards beneath the old forms – strengthening and reshaping the foundations before it alters the superstructure'.[59]

Most of all though, Carpenter has a personal perception to impart to Whitman: 'Yesterday there came (to mend my door) a young workman with the old divine light in his eyes – even *I* call it old though I am not thirty – and perhaps, more than all, he made me write to you.' Whitman's poems about working-class masculinity had awakened in him a new way of looking at other men:

> Because you have, as it were, given me a ground for the love of men
> I thank you continually in my heart. (– And others thank you though
> they do not say so). For you have made men to be not ashamed of
> the noblest instinct of their nature. Women are beautiful; but to some,
> there is that which passes the love of women.[60]

Carpenter tells Whitman there is nothing vital in Cambridge and that he is leaving the university to lecture to working men and women in the North who want 'to lay hold of something with a real grasp'.[61] Carpenter has transmuted the rejection by Trinity Hall into his own repudiation of a stuffy, over-intellectual hot-house world and cast himself as a Whitmanite pioneer, heading to an unknown frontier. He would stick with this story all his life. Though not entirely true, it was considerably more dramatic than being turned down for a fellowship and spotting an alternative.

He closes by saying,

> Farewell; wherever the most common desires and dreams of daily life
> are – wherever the beloved opposition is, of hand to hand, of soul to
> soul – I sometimes think to meet you.
>   I have finished this at night. All is silent again; and as at first I am
> yours.[62]

Whitman, the poet, loved this first letter; 'It is beautiful, like a confession', he observed to his amanuensis Horace Traubel in 1888. 'I seem to get very near to his heart and he to mine in that letter: it has a place in our personal history – an important place. Carpenter was never more thoroughly Carpenter than just there, in that tender mood of self-examination.'[63] The two men met for the first time in 1877 and then again in 1884 when Carpenter travelled to America, and the correspondence continued until Whitman's death.

The letter is redolent of the future Carpenter. In a photograph taken around this time a dapper handsome young man with a moustache, but no beard, looks out with a shy charm. He is wearing a floppy tie and a three-piece tweed suit and is evidently still in the 'tender mood'. Having resolved to throw in his 'lot with the mass-people and the manual workers',[64] this is the man who went North to meet them.

3

Discovering the North

The North was a shock; Carpenter felt as if he had arrived in another country. While anticipating that he might not be immediately appreciated in his role as redeemer, he had not bargained for Leeds, the black, grimy town at the centre of his University Extension lecture circuit. It was not just the dirt, or the absence of beauty, or even the lack of culture in the place. The attitudes and mores of the people he met negated all his Cambridge-bred assumptions in a most disorientating manner. Carpenter was alarmed by the directness, the rough, bluff heartiness of manner. In Leeds the greatest virtue in a man was his hard-headedness; the capacity to make money was openly respected. People made no bones about knowing their own mind. Instead of the tentative, many-sidedness of Broad Church Anglicanism, the certainties of Dissent prevailed. All this jarred on Carpenter, yet in a vain effort to fit into this new world, he shaved off his Cambridge beard hoping he would look more respectable, leading a little nephew to shout out in the Christmas vacation, 'O doesn't he look like the shop man.'[1]

When Carpenter discovered Leeds, the woollen trade which was the basis of the town's prosperity had diversified into clothing, flax-spinning, printing and engineering. The variety of trades in Leeds had helped to prevent the severe hardship of the smaller towns which focused on one industry, and its fortunes had been augmented by its mercantile wealth. Leeds had not, however, attained the municipal grandeur of Manchester, nor could it match the larger city's culture. Leeds' Liberal Dissenting establishment tended towards science and technology as opposed to the arts and humanities associated with gentlemanly Oxbridge. By the early 1870s the old intellectual core of Leeds' business and professional classes, the Philosophical and Literary Society, had gone into decline. The University Extension Movement attracted a newly emerging group, the wives and daughters of Leeds' provincial elite who were active in the

Leeds Ladies' Educational Association, some of whom were connecting their bid for better educational opportunities to women's rights. This lobby, combined with the movement's emphasis on the higher education of artisans, gave University Extension a hint of daring, for reaching out to workers implied a new inclusive brand of liberalism.

University Extension's meaning for the established universities was less radical. After the extension of the franchise, criticism of the elitism of Oxford and Cambridge had raised the spectre of disendowment and dismemberment. James Stuart's Extension plan enabled them to appear progressive without drastic internal reform or loss of their considerable resources. The University Extension Movement was a characteristically English compromise, for it was evidently preferable to extend rather than to be dismembered, especially when the main costs of Extension were borne by the local branches of the movement, not by the universities. The economic structure of Extension would thus ensure that the middle class rather than the working class comprised the bedrock of the movement.

The pioneer lecturers from Cambridge endowed University Extension with a variety of social meanings. They entered the movement with a troubled mixture of hope in the new 'democracy' and fear that civilisation's sweetness and light were about to be swamped in philistinism. Carpenter was unusual in his desire to merge; lecturers were more likely to see themselves as leading working-class students towards the high-minded spiritual values they believed were an integral part of education. The more materialist-minded sought to persuade workers that political economy, which had fallen into disrepute as a science, was not necessarily just a gloss on the status quo. Amidst all the confusion of differing assumptions, one thing was certain: worker students were in a minority.

Carpenter went hurtling around on his Extension circuit which covered Leeds, Halifax and Skipton, lecturing on astronomy, mainly to the aspiring middle classes. To his undoubted disappointment, handsome young carpenters with divine lights in their eyes were not conspicuous among his Extension students, though he did do a lecture for Leeds Co-operators on 'Materialism' in November 1874, in which he urged them not to worship matter. Carpenter told the co-operators to challenge the all-knowingness of science and learn 'to see through the sights and sounds of this outer world', referring them to Eastern culture.[2] In a letter to John Dalton, urging him to encourage the Prince Consort, Albert Victor's artistic interests, Carpenter did admit that it would not be easy to integrate working-class students into his Extension classes.[3] But, like his fellow Extension lecturer, the economist Herbert Somerton Foxwell, the

The dapper young Carpenter, c. 1875

Northern manufacturing towns convinced Carpenter that the sciences were partly shaped by human action and values.[4]

Carpenter and Foxwell were transplanted by University Extension from the familiar all-male world of Cambridge into a predominantly female sphere of authority where their destinies were decided by the Leeds Ladies' Educational Association. Whereas in Cambridge Carpenter could idolise women as redeemers from afar, the Leeds Ladies' Educational Association controlled his bread and butter. It was a disquieting gender reversal. Most formidable was the Extension secretary, Lucy Wilson, who was resolutely committed to demonstrating to the hard-headed men of Leeds that higher education for women through University Extension could pay. She had already acquired an organisational track record in the campaign against the forced search of women under the Contagious Diseases Acts, and later joined the Vigilance Association for the Defence of Personal Rights which campaigned on social purity issues such as prostitution. Having tried unsuccessfully to be elected to the newly formed Leeds School Board in

1870, University Extension provided Lucy Wilson with an alternative sphere of activity and she took her responsibility as Local Secretary seriously, exercising iron discipline. Carpenter remembered her somewhat ruefully as 'extremely good looking and capable, and a good organiser', but 'very doctrinaire'.[5] Wilson's militant advocacy of women's rights assumed the superiority of women and differed from the more polite versions Carpenter had come across in Cambridge. She belonged to a new political species, which would shortly acquire a name in English – 'feminists'. According to Carpenter, Lucy Wilson hated men.

In such circumstances knowledge was power, and when the Cambridge men met for dinner in their lodgings, they compared notes and joked about the scandals and rivalries that pervaded the Leeds Ladies' Educational Association. They soon discovered that among Lucy Wilson's rivals for the post of secretary was another advanced young woman, Theodosia Marshall. The Marshalls were a leading manufacturing family in Leeds; having made their money from flax spinning, they played a prominent philanthropic role. Though Carpenter made fun of Theodosia, he found her more amiable than Lucy Wilson. 'Theo Marshall' was still in his address book of 1890.[6]

The Marshalls were close friends of the tolerant and enlightened Quaker Ford family. In meeting the Fords, Carpenter became acquainted with a bevy of congenial advanced women. Hannah Ford, one of the founders of the Leeds Ladies' Educational Association, had also been involved in the Campaign Against the Contagious Diseases Acts. Her three younger daughters, Emily, Bessie and Isabella, were all members and shared their mother's belief in women's and workers' rights. The sisters had taught mill-girls in a school started by a shoemaker in east Leeds, learning from their pupils about the class divide. Carpenter first became friendly with Emily Ford, who went off to study at the newly opened Slade School of Art in the late 1870s and lived in her own flat in London. But his closest, long-lasting friend would be Isabella, who was only twenty when they met in 1875.[7] Like many other people in her generation who were searching for a more inclusive liberalism, she ended up becoming a socialist. Carpenter acted as a lodestar in Isabella's life.

The Fords were immediately recognisable, for they belonged to the political and intellectual network he knew from Cambridge; James Stuart, the Fawcetts, Henry Sidgwick. Yet they were also radical Northerners and could introduce him to the broader dimensions of Dissent in Leeds, including the probing Unitarians from the famous Mill Hill Chapel, Joseph Estlin Carpenter and William Henry Channing. In Carpenter's first year in Leeds, his namesake, a scholar in the history of religion, was a welcome companion whom he greatly regretted losing.[8] However the American, Channing, who replaced him, proved even more interesting. Channing, who was linked to the high-minded Romanticism of the Transcendentalist writers, introduced Carpenter to the ideal of the simple life; elegance rather than luxury, refinement rather than fashion, and living 'content with small means'.[9] It was an appropriate lifestyle for a University Extension lecturer on a slender salary.

The Fords lived at Adel, well outside the grime of Leeds, and their commodious Gothic-style house, Adel Grange, provided Carpenter with a welcome refuge. Adel Grange, with its landscaped seven acres of gardens, carefully contrived rustic walks and lake, was an aesthetic and intellectual oasis which helped him to overcome his alienation from the North. Now an old people's home, in the late nineteenth century the house throbbed with political argument and ideas. Conveniently, Adel is not far from Meanwoodside, where Carpenter's college friend Oates was living with his mother, and Carpenter introduced him to the Fords.

In *My Days and Dreams*, Carpenter relates that his friendship with Oates deepened into 'intimacy' while he was working in the Leeds area.[10] 'Intimacy' is used ambiguously by Carpenter, so we cannot assume any physical connection, but he certainly needed Oates emotionally in those early years in the North. They shared all those Cambridge memories and, most importantly, Carpenter was able to be frank about his sexual feelings. Oates could understand Carpenter's response in December 1874, when Edward Anthony Beck was married, surrounded by everyone from the inner circle at Trinity Hall. Carpenter had sat through the ceremony unseen in a pew, telling his friend, 'I have just come back – a sadder and wiser man. Indeed I feel older than fate itself.'[11] Beck's wedding brought home to him the break with his life in Cambridge; indeed many years later, in a letter to Dalton, Beck expressed the view that the 'net' could not hold Carpenter within Trinity Hall.[12] Carpenter buried his humiliation at the twofold rejection, but Cambridge continued to haunt him. He kept reliving precious but painful recollections. On a visit in August 1875, he wrote to Oates describing the little back garden in Trinity Hall. The rain was 'pattering upon the mulberry trees and the marigolds and fennel' and the garden was 'so full of reminiscences and associations, from Walt Whitman to the W.C.'[13] Like Cambridge as a whole, he could not decide whether the college garden was dreadful or sacred to him.

The undemonstrative Oates was, however, inclined to go to ground. An exasperated Carpenter complained in August 1876, 'WHY do you preserve this abysmal secrecy about your own doings? WHAT are you doing?' He added 'Alas! let me burst! – I am going mad.'[14] This pattern of easy familiarity, broken by occasional outbursts from Carpenter when his friend failed to respond to an emotional crisis persisted throughout their long relationship.

Drifting between northern landladies during term time and Brighton in his vacations, Carpenter was desperate for someone to whom he could express the welter of perceptions and emotions his new life was provoking. Walt Whitman, far away across the Atlantic, seemed to be the only person who could comprehend the inchoate intimations he found so hard to communicate. Early in January 1876, still wrestling with the metaphor of redemption, he wrote to Whitman from Brunswick Square.

> A few weeks ago I sent you a book of mine – Moses: a drama. It is an effort to represent the character of one who, being far beyond his time, has conceived a new idea, a new development for mankind, and by the very force with which he has conceived it wills it to shape out, and shapes out, the way of its realisation – standing himself all the while alone, solitary, upon earth.[15]

'Moses' as the deliverer embodied an ideal of visionary leadership which echoes Shelley's Romantic concept of the poet as saviour. Carpenter, who had long admired Shelley, now cast Whitman in the role of Redeemer. 'Dear friend you have so infused yourself that it is daily more and more possible for men to walk hand in hand . . .'. Whitman had 'planted the seed of a spiritual union and identity above all space and time' in the midst of a 'material and mechanical' age. From Whitman came a sense of personal destiny; 'I feel that my work is to carry on what you have begun. You have opened the way: my own desire is to go onward with it.'[16] Carpenter had found in Whitman an intimation of spiritual revelation arising from direct human experience which he would continue to explore all his life. Whitman was later to muse to Traubel, busily taking notes of the old poet's every word and gesture, that Carpenter 'was never nobler than then, in that period of interrogating enthusiasm.'[17]

During the mid 1870s a conjunction of circumstances brought Carpenter and Whitman together. If the younger man needed acknowledgement, the older poet wanted adulation. Though much published and reviewed, it was becoming evident that Whitman's dream of being the national poet of America was not to be fulfilled, partly because of the content of his verse and partly because of his innovative style of writing. In disappointment, he had begun to construct a narrative which exaggerated his rejection in his own land and presented himself as indigent and

neglected. On January 3, 1876 Carpenter wrote in distress to Whitman
having heard rumours that no American publisher would take on his
works. Carpenter said he considered it outrageous that anyone treated
Whitman's poems as immoral, for he saw only purity and health in
them. It must be the distortions imposed by modern civilisation which
shocked people when they read them and, Carpenter hoped, 'After ages
perhaps man will return *consciously* to the innocent joyous delight in his
own natural powers and instincts which characterized the earlier
civilizations.' In Carpenter's opinion, it was only because present-day
society was so narrow and one-sided that Whitman was being misunderstood; 'People's minds are dwarfed: one portion of their nature grows
up in the dark (and ceases to be healthy).'[18] Views about the corrupting,
distorting effect of civilisation and an earlier golden age of naked
innocence were implicit within the Romanticism and Idealism which
had helped shape Carpenter's thought. Whitman confirmed them and
provided an evangelical twist.

Carpenter and Whitman's mix of Romanticism and Puritanism arose
from quite different sources, but merged in this translation of sexuality
into healthy, innocent wholesome improvement. The device of presenting
an unorthodox outlook as a moral tonic was to enable Carpenter to steer
through some dangerous shoals in the years to come, and it was partly
acquired from Whitman. However, Carpenter the upper-middle-class
Victorian was rather more squeamish about physicality than the farmer-
craftsman turned poet. Wriggling uncomfortably, he had to admit to his
mentor that 'there are things in your writings which make it difficult,
sometimes impossible to commend them to some who might otherwise
profit by them, yet I feel it is best that they should be there'.[19] Even if
they hindered Whitman's message in the present, Carpenter declared he
was convinced that they would be accepted. Carpenter's response amused
the American, whose attitudes to sexuality had been formed by the rough
and tumble of life among the country people and workers of New Jersey
and Brooklyn and amidst New York's mid-century gangs and bohemia.
Even as an old man intent on respectability, he could chuckle to Traubel,
'Carpenter seems to have been just a bit dubious about the Children of
Adam poems then: just a trifle, staggers, reels, wonders, just a little; comes
back at once of course: recovers – stands up.'[20]

An anonymous article appeared in the *West Jersey Press* on January 26,
1876 announcing that Walt Whitman's poems were being treated with
'determined denial, disgust and scorn' by American authors, publishers
and editors.[21] These narrow-minded gatekeepers of the nation's culture,
it appeared, had caused the poet's works to be still-born and had left him

in poverty. The author of the article was none other than Walt Whitman, whose days as a jobbing journalist had taught him how to spin. Moreover, the crafty infuser made quite sure that copies reached his English admirers. Accordingly they upbraided Americans for ignoring the great poet and angry ripostes flew back across the Atlantic. All this fuss raised Whitman's visibility wonderfully; the poet basked in the adulation of his growing circle of British admirers and happily opened the large drafts of cash sent by Carpenter, the Fords and others.

Early in 1876, encouraged by his friendship with W.H. Channing, Carpenter was toying with the idea of going to visit Whitman himself, when his older brother Charles died suddenly in India after a fall from his horse.[22] A bland obituary in the Allahabad *Pioneer* recorded Charles Carpenter's rise in the Civil Service, his skill in cricket and tennis, summing him up as 'a typical English gentleman'.[23] Carpenter sent a comforting letter to his mother,[24] while confiding to Oates that his brother was a comparative stranger to him, having left home when he was still young.[25] Carpenter did not return immediately to Brunswick Square because he had to finish his course of lectures and then fell ill, reporting on April 5th to his dearest Mother that he was still too weak and unfit to travel.[26]

Meanwhile the sisters were coping at Brunswick Square; Lizzie, who was longing for her 'dearest Boy' to arrive, nonetheless sought to put his mind at rest, assuring him, 'Mamma will not break down anymore now I think, with her the first <u>shock</u> did its work: it went straight home, and has taken away from her the brightness of her remaining years.'[27] The death of her eldest son had finally pierced the patina of control Sophia Carpenter had formed around herself, and her sensitive younger son was incapable of staunching his mother's grief.

The family's financial affairs provided Carpenter with the opportunity of finally meeting Whitman. In March 1873 Charles Carpenter had written to his son about problems with his American shares; it was still just a nibble of doubt. Indeed, in the same letter he was equally troubled about whether intelligent life could be found in plants and insects.[28] The arch-materialist, Thomas Huxley, had recently raised this bothersome matter in a lecture to the Metaphysical Society, entitled 'Has a Frog a Soul and if so, of what Nature is that Soul?' Quite a furore had ensued in which John Ruskin had entered the lists.[29] The souls and intellects of frogs still seemed more absorbing than the tiny storm clouds of a depression. Life had been prosperous for so long, serious economic dislocation appeared inconceivable, and a few months later Charles Carpenter was reassuring

his son that all was well with their American shares.[30] All was not entirely
well however. In 1873 a crash had occurred in the German and American
railways. Deflation, a decline in profits and a fall in the rate of interest
would follow. The British economy was not to recover until the mid
1890s. The term 'Great Depression', used to describe this period, is somewhat misleading, for the depression oscillated over time and varied by
trade and region, while falling prices made these golden years for consumers.
If the Great Depression was somewhat contradictory in material terms,
its psychological and cultural effects were serious, for it sowed doubts in
the system and made the British uncomfortably aware of their competitors
in Germany and the United States. Thanks to the Great Depression,
Carpenter was despatched in the Spring of 1877 to the United States to
report on the American economy and sound out the possibilities for
investments. He informed his father that the financial system seemed somewhat rackety and slip-shod and concluded that bonds would be safer than
shares. It was evident that fortunes might be easily made and just as easily
lost in this brash, vibrant economy making its way up in the world willy-
nilly. The display of luxury and modernity he encountered on the East
Coast amazed the young English visitor. When he travelled by steamer
from Boston to New York, he told Charles Carpenter that the ship not
only had 'four decks', but was equipped with 'thick piled carpets, gorgeous
armchairs, gilt and frescoes and mirrors, gas laid on in chandeliers'.[31]

Carpenter found an utterly different America when, on his way down
the Hudson, he arrived at the home in Esopus of Walt Whitman's friend,
John Burroughs; they walked through the woods together talking of
bird-lore. Already a popular writer on nature, Burroughs would become
a great advocate of the simple outdoor life, espousing conservation values
which acted as a counter to the rush for profits.[32] Urged by his father to
make contact with the Transcendentalists and with a letter of introduction
from W.H. Channing, Carpenter also paid a visit to the influential writer,
Ralph Waldo Emerson, who had woven together American Puritanism,
Romanticism and Eastern religion into a critique of his country's thrusting
commercial culture. 'Civilization crowed too soon . . . what we bragged
as triumphs were treachery', warned Emerson.[33] Influenced by the early
nineteenth-century Indian reformer, Rammohan Roy, who had moved
in British Unitarian anti-slavery circles, Emerson possessed an erudite
knowledge of Indian history and religion, proudly showing Carpenter his
translation of the Hindu sacred work, the *Upanishads*. Carpenter was
already familiar with Emerson's idea of a transcendental deity and would
incorporate Emerson's 'Oversoul' or 'Divine Mind' into his own spiritual

beliefs. Though drawn to Emerson's critique of 'civilisation', the personal encounter was somewhat stilted, particularly when Emerson expressed distaste for Whitman's vulgarity.[34]

For it was, of course, Whitman that Carpenter had really come to see. He arrived in Camden, New Jersey, early in May and Whitman came down to meet him, leaning heavily on the banisters. His long beard was almost white and made him look old, but the florid face and grey-blue eyes were youthful. Carpenter related in a letter to a friend in Leeds, called Benjamin: 'He held my hand for a long time, looking with clear blue eyes into mine.' Whitman seemed to possess an 'intense perceptive power'.[35] Carpenter was fascinated by the American custom of sitting out on the doorstep and thought Whitman looked 'like some old god' in the middle of the group.[36]

The 'old god' was sixty, though ragged and battered by life and shaken by a recent stroke. By 1877 he had buried his earlier self, the rumbustious Brooklyner who had hung out with tough, street-wise New York 'b'hoys', recasting himself as the sagacious 'good grey poet' and democratic patriarch. In this persona he was accustomed to receiving acolytes. A Canadian admirer, Dr Richard Maurice Bucke, who arrived a few months after Carpenter, also felt that he was meeting a god or some 'preter-human' being, graphically recording the poet's 'big fleshy ears, the thin wrinkles and red complexion, the ample snow-white beard, and the heavy lidded eyes above which arched the high eyebrows'.[37]

Carpenter made notes on the visit which he would write up for the *Progressive Review* in 1897 and then publish in a book, *Days with Walt Whitman*, in 1906. He describes how Whitman, like Emerson, talked about Hindu culture and was particularly intrigued by the poet's water-baths and sun-baths at a nearby creek. When he returned to Britain, Carpenter adopted these himself, regardless of the unpropitious climate in the North of England. Whitman's relationship to nature and to the body convinced Carpenter that 'Leaves of Grass' had been written from personal experience. Meeting Whitman revealed:

> The same deliberate suggestiveness about his actions and manners that you find in his writings – only, of course, with the added force of bodily presence; and far down too there were clearly enough visible the same strong and contrary moods, the same strange omnivorous egotism, controlled and restrained by that wonderful genius of his for human affection and love. 'Who has the most enamoured body?' were words which somehow his presence often suggested.[38]

Gavin Arthur, a young man who visited Carpenter many years later in the early 1920s, recorded he had told him that Whitman 'thought that people should "know" each other on the physical and emotional plane as well as in the mental. And that the best part of comrade love was that there was no limit to the number of comrades one could have – whereas the very fact of engendering children made the man-woman relationship more singular.'[39] According to Arthur, Carpenter also claimed to have himself 'slept' with Whitman. There is no way of knowing whether this second-hand account written in the 1960s, long after Arthur met Carpenter, is accurate. However there certainly were homoerotic frissons during Carpenter's stay which were impossible to convey in his published notes. In an undated letter Carpenter expressed distress at what felt like Whitman's rejection:

> I have loved you (I don't know why I should not confess it) with a deep personal love for many years, and all I have seen of you since I have been here has just tended to make that feeling deeper. . . . For a long time I have cherished the thought that if I came to know you and be known by you, I might be the beginning, or at least one of a small band of followers who by the force of personal intercourse and attachment might have the strength (which it is so hard to have alone) to move the world, or rather to form the nucleus – you being at the heart of it – for all that great vitalized organization of human love and fellowship which must be – without which modern civilization will be merely nothing. That thought has seemed to justify my love to you – for I myself believe that love is only right and pure and true when it becomes the inspiring energy of some work which has to be done.[40]

He assured Whitman that nothing would deflect him from carrying on the work the poet had begun, for he would never marry.

Whatever the nature of his relationship with Whitman, Carpenter brought intense emotional expectations of his own destiny to the encounter with the poet. Carpenter was also greatly taken with Whitman's friend, the nineteen-year-old Harry Stafford who came from a local farm. Carpenter enquired about the young man from Whitman after he left the United States, asking for his photograph. Stafford was even more affected by his meeting with Carpenter, cherishing their friendship all his life.[41]

Carpenter was impressed by Whitman's rapport with working-class men on the ferry and trams to Philadelphia, and aspired to emulate what seemed to him to be personal acts of democratic comradeship. Yet this ease of manner was not all that it seemed. Whitman had grappled with his feelings for Peter Doyle, a young tramway conductor with whom he had fallen in love in 1865. Whitman believed that the key to the body electric was balance between what he saw as the amative and the adhesive aspects of love; if either were to become overactive psychological break-down could ensue. What troubled Whitman about Doyle was that the young man evoked obsessive emotions in him rather than amative male comradeship.[42] The prophet of paths untrodden and the ocean of life, who opened up such vistas of transformatory possibility, was, in his own way, as preoccupied as Sophia Carpenter with self-control.

Nevertheless Carpenter's meeting with Whitman reinforced the tentative insights accumulating since he decided to give up his clerical fellowship. In *My Days and Dreams* he described Whitman's influence as enabling him to see that a purely intellectual perspective was not as important as he had believed.[43] Not only did Whitman allow him to appreciate that wonder of being and body he had glimpsed in Italy, he observed during the time he spent with Whitman how the poet possessed 'a knack of making ordinary life enjoyable, redeeming it from commonplaceness'. Instead of 'the Present' seeming like a 'squalid necessity to be got over as best may be, in view of something always in the future, he gave you that good sense of nowness'.[44] This was later to be a capacity many friends associated with Carpenter. Meeting Whitman clarified new ways of seeing, feeling and being for Carpenter, giving him a different means of denoting significance. It was the start of an alternative outlook on the world.

Whitman was 'magnificent', Carpenter enthused to Oates when he returned from the U.S., 'I stayed in the house with him for a week.'[45] He could not conceal the pride with which he described how he and Whitman had become great friends. He and Oates must meet so they could talk things over, it was impossible to convey everything that had happened by letter. The self-conscious Englishman particularly admired Whitman's ability to draw men and women to him as the central figure in a circle – a characteristic he soon attained himself. Whitman, though accustomed to visitors and often notoriously gruff with them, also took a liking to Carpenter, and would later concur with Traubel's assertion that he was 'the handsomest' of all his friends.[46]

Carpenter might be handsome but he was not happy. His life in the North was not fulfilling his early hopes. When he had written to Whitman in January 1876, he had still been enthusiastic about the 'working artisans' he had met. 'There is undoubtedly an entirely new (social) state of affairs coming about through their rise, and I hail it with delight.'[47] A note of doubt had, however, crept in. The new future was not as close at hand as he had thought in 1874; when one went out into the world, it became evident that change was likely to take a very long time indeed. These misgivings were to grow, and the visit to Whitman only served to accentuate them.

During 1876 and 1877 Carpenter's lecturing beat shifted to Nottingham, York and Hull; he left Leeds, lodging first at Nottingham and then at Hull. His initial enthusiasm waned as it became evident how few working-class students he was reaching. This experience was widespread. The working-class students who had greeted James Stuart's pilot lectures quickly fell away; as the Secretary of the Cambridge Extension Movement, Robert D. Roberts, another idealistic Whitmanite, sadly admitted, 'some of the seed had fallen in stony places'.[48] This was partly because of the high cost of the courses but it was also a question of ethos. Worker-students complained that some of the University lecturers spoke in a removed, abstract manner, while the grand philanthropic families who formed the backbone of University Extension in the large cities were perceived as patronising. Indeed, by 1879 James Stuart had changed tack; in a speech to the Co-operative Congress he envisaged a 'floating, yet permanent Co-operative University . . . accepted by the ancient Universities as a younger sister'.[49] But this scheme was never to be realised.

Carpenter continued to circulate, consuming his Northern landladies' chops and rice puddings, worrying about his mainly young lady students and the fierce local feuding among the organisers. The travelling was exhausting and when he arrived he had to set up the halls for the experiments that accompanied his lectures, making his own oxygen gas for the lantern. 'I have been in a whirlpool of people and apparatus', he told Oates in 1879.[50] Never a natural speaker, in these early years he would be so nervous that sometimes he stumbled as he sought desperately for the right words. Afterwards, because University Extension lectures were big events in provincial cities, he would be whisked off to dine with some local manufacturer who might be subsidising the course, and compelled to socialise into the small hours, only to get up next morning and move on. Agitated by the strain of lecturing and finding himself amidst the northern equivalent of the Brighton circles from which he had fled, Carpenter became increasingly frustrated with his way of life. He started to suffer from a painful eye condition which he felt sure was stress-related.

In the vacation when his round of lecturing came to an end, he would return to Brunswick Square, where he was once again surrounded by sisters, whom he considered to be 'wearing out their lives and their affectional capacities with nothing to do and nothing to care for'.[51] Emily and Ellen had married during the 1860s; Emily's husband being a young army officer, Edward Daubeny, and Ellen's a college friend of Carpenter's,

Francis Adams Hyett. In 1878 Lizzie agreed to a marriage of convenience to an older man who was a relative of Emily's husband, Lieutenant General Sir Henry Charles Barnston Daubeny, thus becoming Lady Daubeny. Her letters to her beloved brother took on a conspiratorial tone as she assured him he could write anything, because her husband never asked to see her correspondence.[52] Her marriage did, however, curtail her close connection with her brother. The other three sisters, Sophy, Alice and Dora, remained unmarried, causing Carpenter to deplore the unnecessary suffering caused by the Victorian refusal to recognise women's sexual needs.

His own sexuality was also a cause of unhappiness. He was in his early thirties, and compelled to be utterly secretive about his desires. It was many years before he could write of this long period of sexual suppression. In his privately published pamphlet 'Homogenic Love' in 1894, Carpenter reflected:

> It is difficult for outsiders not personally experienced in the matter to realise the great strain and tension of nerves under which those persons grow up from boyhood to manhood – or from girl to womanhood – who find their deepest and strongest instincts under the ban of the society around them, who before they clearly understand the drift of their own natures discover that they are somehow cut off from the sympathy and understanding of those nearest to them, and who know that they can never give expression to their tenderest yearnings of affection without exposing themselves to the possible charge of actions stigmatised as odious crimes.[53]

The orotund prose muffles the frustration and despair he had experienced as a young man, but the pangs continued to stab away.

Men of Carpenter's class and background were necessarily affected by the guilt which pervaded sexual desire and the body. Unable to synchronise lust with ideals, both homosexual and heterosexual men turned to the lower classes for forbidden sex, partly because the codes of correct behaviour did not hold with outsiders. Casual cross-class sexual encounters were part of the underground culture of the nineteenth century. Many of these would be overtly commercial transactions and they always carried complex nuances of power. The illegality of homosexual acts gave these contacts a particularly furtive quality, edged with the danger of blackmail or exposure. Though this transgressive loving might stimulate excitement about working-class men who could be, in fantasy, the forbidden 'other', for sensitive and self-conscious intellectuals with democratic aspirations, these commercial outlets for male sexuality were problematic. J.A. Symonds, who like Carpenter had been profoundly affected by reading Whitman, held the animal desire which he called 'the wolf' at bay, until 1877 when he met a 'strapping young soldier with . . . frank eyes and pleasant smile' in a male brothel in London. When they talked, Symonds was intrigued that the young man felt no guilt and had come away convinced that 'the physical appetite of one male for another may be made the foundation of a solid friendship'.[54]

Carpenter, too, tried going to Paris to seek out male prostitutes, only to return from this attempt to dip into the demi-monde feeling exhausted and hopeless.[55] Unlike Symonds, he was not able to translate his encounters with prostitutes into a human relationship; his redemptive ideals conflicted too starkly with the predatory role of the client paying a working-class youth. While the romance of sex between men of divergent classes attracted him, pleasure was not enough, he wanted a democratic fusion. When Carpenter groped across the class divide, he was yearning for love to be a means of deliverance. For Whitman had given him a way of reimagining love which contained a millenarian impulse. 'Will it ever be that human love – strong to meet with adventurous joy all chance and change – will cease to be a mere name? that men will "understand" – eat of the tree of knowledge of good and evil, and so be immortal?'[56]

For Carpenter it followed that if sex were to change, society must too. From Whitman he had acquired new eyes for the everyday; looking at the desolation of the industrial towns around him, he imagined the wretched present transcended: 'I see it everywhere – in face after face in the streets . . . – clear, unmistakable, as if just about to be disclosed, the divine "everywhere – equal" life';[57] the faces began to enter the poetry he was still jotting down on scraps of paper and in notebooks. Now he was no longer just searching for meaning beneath the surface of his own desires but turning outwards, questing for union.

In 1877, back from America, and excited by his contact with Whitman, Carpenter announced to Oates, 'I believe I shall live at Sheffield.'[58] He was attracted by the hills and the beautiful, craggy countryside that surrounded the town. Unfortunately, on the autumn day he arrived in Sheffield, it was pouring with rain: 'And for three days thereafter it rained soot and blacks incessantly . . . I was lecturing on Astronomy; but it was not much use, because no one could tell whether I was speaking the truth or not – since the stars were seldom or hardly visible.'[59] Carpenter had already lived in West Yorkshire smoke, but Sheffield's blast furnaces and coke ovens made its air far worse. In deciding to settle in Sheffield, Carpenter had landed in the midst of an environmental disaster; the industrial expansion of the previous decades had devoured an endless supply of raw materials without regard for the consequences. The better off people evaded the smog by building their homes up on one of the town's hills, but in the low-lying parts of the centre not only was the sun frequently blocked by pollution, terrible smells rose from untreated sewage and from rubbish in the streets. As well as the smoke, acid dust took its toll, causing high rates of pulmonary and bronchial illness – including silicosis which was known as 'grinders' disease'. In 1871 Ruskin had bemoaned the poisonous smoke and the 'dry black veil . . . partly diffused in mist' which hovered over nearby Matlock.[60] The inhabitants of the industrial regions were apt to regard the veil surrounding them as simply a fact of life; not so Carpenter, and during the 1880s when 'Smoke Abatement' became a cause for public concern, he was among the first eager anti-pollution converts.

Though temporarily daunted, Carpenter did take lodgings in Sheffield, drawn by a geniality and warmth about the people there. In a letter urging John Dalton to persuade the Queen to admit his nautical younger brother, Alfred, into the Royal Yacht Club, he told his old friend that while the town was 'filthy beyond words', his students took up his lectures in the 'most spirited way'.[61] He discovered that long walks in the surrounding countryside helped him to survive the Sheffield air and relax from his teaching, and he attempted to winkle Oates out of Meanwoodside to join him. He had more success when Arunachalam came to stay in 1879; the two men renewed their Cambridge friendship, ambling from Midhurst to Haslemere along blackberry-lined paths, amidst buttercups and honey-suckles, happily talking about Whitman and Mazzini.

Carpenter's visit to Whitman had awakened in him a desire for contact with nature. It also made him more bold sexually; he embarked on exploratory encounters with working-class men, 'railway-men, porters, clerks, signalmen, ironworkers, coach-builders, Sheffield cutters', discovering he could 'knit up alliances more satisfactory to me than any I had before known'. These new relationships resulted in a powerful sense of well-being: 'I felt I had come into, or at least in sight of, the world to which I belonged, and to my natural *habitat*.'[62]

Carpenter's life was changed that year by one of those coincidences which appear insignificant at the time, yet in retrospect can be seen to have altered the whole course of things. Despite his political radicalism, he was inclined to be conservative about the daily arrangements of his existence, evincing a peculiar passivity throughout long periods of unhappiness before making a break. This pattern, already evident in Cambridge, was being repeated painfully in University Extension, when one of his Sheffield students, a scythe-maker called Albert Fearnehough, invited Carpenter to visit himself and a fellow student, a farmer called Charles Fox. They lived in the small Derbyshire hamlet of Bradway. Carpenter began to go regularly and enjoyed their company as well as helping with the farm work.

Through this meeting he was introduced to manual labour and a rural way of life, both of which he loved. In the spring of 1880 he told Walt Whitman how he intended never to abandon working outdoors,[63] describing Fearnehough in a letter of July that year as 'the best friend I ever had'.[64] In *My Days and Dreams*, Fearnehough is depicted as muscular and powerful, and there are hints in *Towards Democracy* of a sensuous connection to the scythe-maker.[65] Fearnehough was a man of few words, and despite his long connection to Carpenter left few visible traces about his own feelings and opinions, apart from a few early letters to 'Chips' which show a deep affection and warmth of character.[66] Though Carpenter continued to respect Fearnehough's uncommercial spirit and his unassuming 'transparent sincerity',[67] the slow, ponderous Fearnehough eventually became rather a bore, yet Carpenter retained a strong sense of debt towards the one time 'best friend' who had enabled him to escape bourgeois life.

When Carpenter first met Fearnehough, he was living in a small cottage on Charles Fox's farm, with his wife, Mary Ann, who helped him in his trade of scythe-making. Their daughter Annie still lived at home and their son George, who was apprenticed to a carpenter in Sheffield, returned at weekends. Fox's cows would peep over the low wall between cottage and farm and there was an orchard of cherry, apple and pear trees.[68] Fox was one of the small independent proprietors who had stubbornly survived; many of the farms were being rented from large landowners. When Fearnehough first described his friend, Charles Fox, to Carpenter, he had respectfully stressed how Fox was 'well up in book learning'.[69] Carpenter has left a deft account of Fox in *Sketches from Life in Town and Country* (1908) under the pseudonym 'Martin Turner', showing how false the stereotypes of conservative, conforming country dwellers can be. Outwardly Fox might look like a clodhopping farmer with the florid face of the outdoors man that betrayed little emotion. But Fox was a great reader, had a lively mathematical brain and a sceptical outlook. Poker-faced, he would torture the local Methodist preacher who saw the Bible as literal truth. Were light and the darkness mingled together before God divided them?, the Socratic Fox would enquire. Was it like a mist dotted black and white or in layers – darkness, light, darkness; like streaky bacon perhaps? And how was it if God created Adam and Eve in his own likeness that he was customarily seen as having a long, white beard? Slapping his knee, Fox proposed that God might well be like a beautiful woman.[70]

Such talk earned him a reputation as 'daft' in the neighbourhood. After Fox's mother died, his sister, who had had an illegitimate son, came to keep house for him, confirming the household's reputation for oddness. But Fox did not bother himself about the opinion of other people. At Bradway, in Derbyshire dialect, Carpenter heard the philosophic scepticism of a countryman: 'People go about fussing to get on . . . toiling away, and taking no rest at nights – but it comes to nowt. . . . Best take it quietly and make the most of the days as they come. They'll never come back again.'[71]

Fox's words must have resonated with Carpenter, treading water in University Extension. In the summer of 1879, when Carpenter's Sheffield circuit of lectures ended, Fox wrote to say he was sorry, qualifying this with a characteristically sardonic observation that he did not think great pleasure could be derived from 'lecturing to a lot of ignorant people having corns'.[72] Though the contact with Fearnehough and Fox had thrown his ritualised University Extension existence into question, Carpenter dithered before following his feelings. Another year passed before he migrated to the countryside. There was not enough room for him to live and write in the Fearnehoughs' small home, so he and the family all transplanted that summer to Woodland Villas in nearby Totley within sight of the moors, returning to Bradway the following year when a larger cottage turned up.

Flights to nature were not unprecedented; there had been Britain's Lakeside Romantics, then European artists had gone in search of the inner soul of peasants and fishermen and started to don their stripy Breton jumpers. Through the 1870s Ruskin too had been energetically propounding the value of manual labour on the land, and, by chance, happened to have a special interest in Totley. However these enthusiasms were somewhat specialised, and Carpenter's move was deemed highly eccentric by many of his associates. He had some difficulty explaining the attraction of cottage life at Totley and Bradway to Oates, who was not given to romantic enthusiasms. Carpenter feared that 'the roughness of our accommodation might be <u>too</u> much for you. Imagine yourself going to stay with one of your old pensioners in the tumble downdest [sic] of old cottages on a fare of potatoes and gruel – if your heart does not quail at the prospect then come!'[73] In contrast, Arunachalam supported the move, telling Carpenter that life in the cottage with the Fearnehoughs and the gardening sounded very attractive, indeed, he had thought of it himself but his garden was not big enough.[74]

Arunachalam was wondering whether it had been the right decision for him to enter the Civil Service, but having succeeded felt he could not desert his post. He was struggling between Western and Eastern culture; his upbringing and education meant he was connected to both worlds. However, on returning to Ceylon the implications of imperialism had started to trouble him more. He explained to Carpenter that Westernised Indians and Ceylonese were 'abandoning everything that is valuable in their civilisation in their eagerness to adopt indiscriminately every detail of European life'.[75] Moreover the Raj was fostering a travesty of European civilisation.

Arunachalam wrote with mischievous delight of the arrival of a group of Westerners, the Theosophists, who had embraced Eastern religion and philosophy and rejected distinctions of race and caste. Their presence demonstrated to the Ceylonese people that all 'white Masters were not necessarily Christian', and the Theosophists had been most helpful in defending local Buddhists.[76] Arunachalam was enjoying their effect on the British authorities who suspected subversion.

He wanted Carpenter to visit India and Ceylon, sending threats that he would come to Britain and kidnap him. Letter after letter flowed from his pen with alluring accounts of mangoes and mountain streams. As these made their long meandering journeys to the North of England, Arunachalam sat on his veranda after work, surveying the shadows of the trees in the moonlight and composing yet another letter to his friend far away. Carpenter, meanwhile, was eating his potatoes and gruel with the Fearnehoughs and sallying forth on his University Extension circuit to expound on the evolutionary theories of Charles Darwin and Jean Lamarck. The correspondence between the two men initiated an offensive against the vaunting superiority of Western civilisation which would preoccupy them all their lives.

Carpenter had followed his emotions in his flight from his own 'civilisation'; Fearnehough and Fox enabled him to feel happy, healthy and relaxed. His response was, however, also tinged with Romantic and Whitmanite ideals; the two country men represented for him 'a life close to Nature and actual materials, shrewd, strong, manly, independent, not the least polite or proper, thoroughly human and friendly'.[77] Moreover Carpenter brought with him an intellectual's construct of rural existence. Being in imagination everything that the city is not, the countryside appeared as a blank which could then have 'Innocence', 'Simplicity' and 'Escape' projected upon it.[78] Like many urban migrants, Carpenter soon discovered that the countryside, far from being simple, was full of the unexpected, and that Charles Fox was not the only dissident to be found around Bradway and Totley.

4

Becoming a Socialist

The region around Sheffield which Carpenter had chosen as his 'natural habitat' was scattered with small workshops run by 'little mesters'. Craftsmen grinders used their own stones drawn from the local quarries to make tools and cutlery, while down the scale were a host of low-paid workers, some of whom worked at home. This system of production had arisen in the days of water power, when the combination of sandstone, which was so good for grinding and the fast-running rivers and streams of the area, had created a landscape in which the division between industry and rural life was not hard and fast. In the early 1870s the villages and hamlets were still as likely to include men who made tools, or worked in the quarries as agricultural workers. Moreover differing ways of making a living would be combined; if times were hard, metal workers turned to gardening and, if they stayed bad, men went on the tramp for work. Despite the rise of large iron and steel works in Sheffield, in the light metal trades craft skills remained the crucial factor in production. A pre-industrial rhythm of work continued to prevail, with workers often taking Mondays and even Tuesdays off, then labouring all hours to finish before Sunday.

So in the place where the casings for international capital were being cast, customs and attitudes persisted tenaciously. The Sheffield locality was marked by an enclosed, behind the times ethos which belied the modern technology of large-scale steel production, and the adaptive flexibility of the small-scale cutlery business. Change nonetheless was afoot, for, from the early 1870s, international competition was putting pressure on the light metal trades and, as unemployment mounted, the men who had lost their jobs set up their own small workshops, squeezing their profits still further. Either they found themselves scamping on craft pride in an effort to keep costs down or they adopted Fearnehough's bull-headed stance. Accordingly a ferocious independence characterised both masters and journeymen who resented any form of regulation, while trades unionists maintained a dogged resistance to mechanisation. Politically this was expressed in Sheffield's radical Liberalism which had its roots partly in religious non-conformity and partly in the Owenite and Chartist movements, though from the late 1870s a populist Toryism began to gain votes in the Town Council elections.

The Owenite Hall of Science in Rockingham Street provided a centre for a plebeian underground of rebels and utopians, embracing men and women affected by the radicalism of the first half of the century, along with Secularists, Unitarians and Quakers. In the early 1870s, one such cluster gathered in the Hall of Science to talk about mutual improvement and ended up debating 'communism'. Among them were several future Sheffield Socialists including Joseph Sharpe, who would be an inspirational figure for Carpenter. A veteran of Chartism, Sharpe was a harpist playing at the village feasts and floral well-dressings which invoked good harvests and fertility. Argumentative and obstinate, he was a great reader and debater, wrote poetry and watched the stars. Sharpe and his companions at the Hall of Science decided that in order to live as communists they should establish a communal farm, though they lacked any experience of farming. They did not have much capital to buy land so they gave what they could from their savings and subscribed a penny a week. The realisation that this penny communism would take a long time indeed was dawning, when John Ruskin offered to lend them £2,025 to buy land to the south of Sheffield in Dore and Totley. Ruskin had started an organisation called the Guild of St George, a moral brotherhood which would enable a supposed peasantry to cultivate the land and benefit from the honest labour he regarded as so uplifting. Needless to say, the stroppy, rebellious communists did not fit this paternalistic idyll at all and were wary of the autocratic rules of the Guild. Nonetheless they accepted the offer, believing they could pay back the loan.

Things did not go according to plan. By the time Carpenter came to live nearby it was evident that the failure to recruit farmers, as opposed to boot makers, ironworkers, opticians and harpists, constituted a fatal flaw. Moreover the schismatic communists became locked in dogmatic disputes with each other causing Ruskin to lose patience and bring in his own manager, John Harrison Riley. Riley, who had joined the Guild in 1878, was a more cosmopolitan figure than the Totley communists and would impart to Carpenter the political and social radicalism that flowed from the break-up of the Chartist movement. From the republican left and a follower of the Chartist Bronterre O'Brien, he had met not only Karl Marx in the First International but Walt Whitman while working as a commercial traveller in America. Throughout the 1870s Riley propagated political reform along with producers' co-operatives and the nationalisation of the land and public services. When his grand plans did not gain support he tried smaller projects; in 1875 he and his wife started a temperance cultural centre, open to both sexes, the Social Improvement Institute at 6 Brunswick Square, Bristol. Arriving in Sheffield in 1877, he began to edit a paper called *The Socialist*, in which he expounded his version of Christian Socialism.

Riley used to take his papers and pamphlets up to Charles Fox at Bradway, where Carpenter first came across him in 1879. When they met, Riley was agitating for a 'Mutual Producers' Co-operative Land Emigration and Colonisation Company' to set up communities in the United States, and prodding Ruskin to create model co-operative villages in Britain. A harassed Ruskin advised him not to be in a hurry, adding that he did not believe such a project was possible with their existing resources.[1] Ruskin had already extended himself too far; the Guild was turning into a financial and administrative burden and in 1878 the mental illnesses which were to plague his later years had begun.[2] Riley seems to have enthused Carpenter however, for an excited Arunachalam wrote to enquire of his friend, 'What is the scheme of co-operation you are working at? What does Ruskin propose to do with the farm now? Have you met him, he must be a charming man.'[3] Unfortunately Ruskin at this particular juncture was more disgruntled than charming. He and Riley soon fell out too, and Ruskin resorted to bringing in an old family retainer to evict everyone with a pitchfork.[4] In the spring of 1880 Carpenter tried to intervene in Riley's defence by writing to Ruskin. Ruskin was, however, implacable, declaring his former manager liked smoking better than digging.[5] Ruskin expressed some curiosity about Carpenter's position in life, remarking, 'I see you to be a gentleman'[6] – those tattoo-marks of gentility were inscribed in his correspondence, as well as voice and bearing.

The communists' farm at Totley was a kind of volcanic mole-hill which left fragments in all directions. Riley emigrated to the United States where he tried unsuccessfully to join various utopian communities, eking out a living as a journalist and devising hopeless plans to call Ruskin and the Guild to account. Joseph Sharpe was economically ruined by Totley, though his indomitable spirit rallied to the utopianism of 1880s socialism. Another member of the Totley project, M.A. Maloy, who, like Sharpe, also joined the Sheffield Socialists, was still erupting in rage over Ruskin's behaviour in William Morris' paper *Commonweal* in 1888.[7]

The name 'St George's Farm' survived, however, and Carpenter helped to retrieve something of the communitarian spirit by negotiating for George Pearson, a radical who knew about farming, to rent it. In *My Days and*

Dreams Carpenter recounts how Pearson and his friend John Furniss, who helped farm Totley, were men of stern stuff. They would think nothing of walking five or six miles over the moors to speak for radical causes at the Pump or the Monolith in Sheffield and then striding home again in the middle of the night. Furniss had worked on a farm as a child, before leaving home to be a quarryman. After becoming disillusioned with Methodism, he had adopted his own independent-minded brand of Christian Socialism and set up a utopian community, Moorhay Farm, a long, grey stone building, with an outhouse attached, situated in remote countryside on the edge of Linacre Wood not far from some old quarries. Radicalised by his hatred of large landlords, John Furniss' name was to be first on the list when the Sheffield Socialist Society was formed in 1885. Carpenter described him as 'wiry in mind and body', and even the disenchanted Riley conceded that the new Totley tenant was a remarkable and noble man.[8] Between them, Joseph Sharpe, George Pearson, John Furniss and John Harrison Riley introduced Carpenter to divergent strands of a left which linked Chartism to the socialism that emerged in the 1880s.

Riley had scattered subversion with such profligacy he was hard pressed to see himself what it all amounted to. His letters from America assumed the tone of a man disappointed by history, which seemed to have made a detour around him. Nonetheless, all that agitation left ripples which continued even when he was far away. Two members of Riley's Bristol Social Improvement Institute, the brothers John and Robert Sharland, helped found the local socialist movement in 1884, bringing to it the musical talents which Riley had encouraged. Carpenter's connection with the Sharlands through Riley contributed to his long association with the Bristol socialists, who remained heterodox in spirit and enthusiastic singers. In Sheffield, two grocer brothers who Riley had recruited to socialism, John and Robert Bingham, joined the Sheffield Socialist Society. Though never within Carpenter's personal circle, their fiery activism in first the socialist and then the anarchist movement made the Binghams figures to be reckoned with. In their youth they were always on the look-out for an insurrectionary opportunity, before settling down as established doyens of the Sheffield labour movement. By a strange coincidence Riley also introduced an Eton schoolmaster who became a friend of Carpenter's, Henry Salt, to socialist ideas. They met through Ruskin, while Salt was on holiday in the Lake District during the winter of 1878–9. At the time Salt could hardly decide which was most shocking, Riley's political views or Ruskin's attack on Tennyson's poem 'Maud'.[9]

It was unfortunate for Riley that his energetic agitation occurred at a time when left causes were in the doldrums; the Russian revolutionary

Prince Peter Kropotkin, who arrived in London in 1881, was equally discouraged. Britain might offer him refuge but politically it was such a bore that he departed for the continent, despite being hounded by the police forces of Europe. Yet, as Kropotkin, with his astute eye for grassroots consciousness, subsequently remarked, social movements had 'periods of slumber and – periods of sudden progress'.[10] Totley and Riley together provide a glimpse of how tiny networks formed in the slumbering years can be of surprising consequence. The late 1870s and early 1880s proved to be the lull before the storm.

In January 1881 Sophia Carpenter died. With a daughter's dread of mirroring her mother, Emily Carpenter wrote sadly to her brother reflecting, 'Her life was so unfulfilled in many ways.'[11] With Sophia's death the kernel of the household disintegrated. Ellen, now Mrs Hyett, reported, 'Poor Father has seemed not to understand it all, he hardly realised she was seriously ill and now can only say, "It was my fault", but he seems to feel little grief.'[12] Charles Carpenter was suffering from senile dementia.

When his friend Havelock Ellis' mother died in 1888, Carpenter would write 'a Mother's death must after all alter all one's life, as it changes too the whole household. Perhaps you will still however feel her very near you.'[13] He was drawing on his own experience. Carpenter relates in *My Days and Dreams* how his mother's death brought to the surface the invisible tie which had exerted such a powerful hold over his life. Once she was no longer there in the flesh, this was transmuted into an inward sense of her being. 'For months, even years, after her death, I seemed to feel her, even see her, close to me – always figuring as a semi-luminous presence.' Yet his mother's death also signalled a release. He describes himself as 'exhaling the great mass of feelings, intuitions, conceptions, and views of life which had formed within me, into another sphere'.[14] In Latin 'exhalare' means to expire, as well as to breathe out; an ending can be a beginning, and, with the external devout monitor gone, Carpenter's internalised, ethereal mother could be freely transposed. Henceforth doing the right thing could acquire the gloss Carpenter determined for himself. Thus freed, he could assume control.

Suddenly he was making decisions. In March 1881 a cottage became vacant on Fox's land and the handy farmer merged this with the Fearnehough's former home to make enough room for Carpenter. Once again they could all be together at Bradway. This was undoubtedly welcomed by Fearnehough who had been forced by poverty to go on the tramp in search of work. Carpenter too was happy at Fox's farm, with its combination of sociability and outdoor life, telling Whitman, 'It is possible that Albert and I might take a small farm, but we shall see. I feel that I must write at present – I can't keep my fingers off it – but still that takes only a small fraction of the week and leaves plenty of time for other work.'[15] If Carpenter was not sure about the farm, he knew it was time to break with University Extension. He had been growing increasingly restive, telling the students in his last course, on 'The History and Science of Music', that 'the culmination of all expression is Simplicity (not Sandford and Merton simplicity) to say what you want, neither more nor less; "singleness", "directness", "ease", "naturalness"'.[16] With this early intimation of 'the simple life' came a practical resolve. He had savings from his Cambridge days which yielded between fifty and sixty pounds a year; he calculated that he could just live on this income at Bradway.

Around this time Carpenter was reading a copy of the *Bhagavad-Gita* sent by Arunachalam. Translated into English in 1785, it had been one of the first Hindu Sanskrit works to be translated and had inspired both the Romantics in Europe and the Transcendentalists in North America. Since the 1860s Western Orientalist scholars had tended to focus more on the earlier Vedic texts, however the Gita was being reclaimed in India when Arunachalam sent the book to Carpenter. For Arunachalam spiritual revival and moral renewal were integral to self-rule, and aptly the mature statesman-like Krishna in the *Bhagavad-Gita* enjoins the warrior Arjuna to action based on social and religious duty. The book resonated equally with Carpenter. Through the *Bhagavad-Gita* the former Anglican curate could find in another spiritual idiom an endorsement of the selfless endeavour to serve others which he, like so many of his contemporaries, still valued after discarding the Christian faith. Through the Gita he could conceive another kind of redemption.

In *My Days and Dreams* Carpenter tells how, in a mood of exaltation he knocked up a kind of wooden sentinel-box in the garden at Bradway and began to write. Thus cocooned he could achieve the singleness and directness which had eluded him in the years of lecturing. He began to work through all the scraps of poetry he had accumulated and go over the impressions and reflections he had not been able to articulate during the pent-up years at Cambridge and in University Extension. His afternoons were spent hoeing, singling turnips or picking potatoes with Fearnehough and Fox; manual labour was turning out to be the antidote for the nervous tension that had troubled him on his rounds of lectures. Now he was seeing beauty everywhere, and, when he paused in the lanes or the fields, he could sense a possibility of an unbounded freedom and gladness. 'I was haunted by an image, a vision within me, of something like the bulb and bud, with short green blades, of a huge hyacinth just appearing above the ground. I knew that it represented vigour and abounding life.'[17] After a long, slow beginning his life was at last taking creative root.

The huge hyacinth turned into a prose poem, *Towards Democracy*. Originally about a hundred pages long when it was published in 1883, it kept growing over the years, with new parts appearing in 1885, 1892 and 1902. Its epic ambitions mark a decisive shift from his earlier collection *Narcissus*. The 1883 version contains his observations of the poverty he saw in the streets of the northern cities, the crushing, destructive working conditions, and the lack of human contact between people of differing classes. These are mixed together with Ruskinian diatribes against commercialism and the decline of craft and a Romantic, Whitmanite embracing of all humanity, however despised or outcast.

He was still writing in April 1882 when he was called back to Brighton by the death of his father. Charles Carpenter left a substantial fortune of £20,744, much of which came from overseas railway investments, including 926 shares in the Pennsylvania Railroad. Carpenter had to go through these, selling and negotiating in order to divide up the legacy. He spent the whole summer at Brunswick Square, chafing and fretting as he dutifully sorted out the family's finances. It was especially onerous after the freedom of his Bradway sentinel box, and the irritation creeps into *Towards Democracy*, which went to Brighton with him. 'I hate those nearest me, and am closed, captious and intolerant. I sweep a great space round me and sulk in the middle of it.'[18] No doubt the Carpenter sisters gave 'Teddie' a wide berth in such moods.

Towards Democracy is also permeated by the organic images of Carpenter's new life at Bradway – bulbs, buds, chrysalises breaking open. Growth is accompanied by decay and renewal, for within the husks the unknown, the about-to-be, rests immanent. He was later to borrow a word from Whitman to sum up this vision of transformation which continued to play itself out in his thinking: 'exfoliation'. Never comfortable with a Darwinian emphasis on external explanations for change, Carpenter devised a Romantic adaptation of Lamarck's theories of inner need. Human desire is the force which causes the chrysalis of convention to crack in *Towards Democracy*, opening the way out of the grim and vacuous circumstances of the everyday. Though the poem celebrates the real in the beauty of the natural world and exalts the body and human love, it expresses a suspicion of outer forms which persisted in all Carpenter's writing. German Idealism, Hindu spirituality and his reading of Plato converge; inwardness is more real than appearances. The 'democracy' he sought was neither political nor economic, but a new way of being human, a new manner of encountering others.

I look upon him who makes all things.
I sit at his feet in silence as he lights his pipe, and feel the careless
resting of his fingers upon my neck.
I see the fire leaping in the grate; I see the nodding of grasses and
blackberry sprays in the hedges; I hear the long surge and hush of the
wind; I hear his voice speaking to me.[19]

His democracy is personal and momentary – a flash of loving recognition,
a closeness to nature and the loving comradeship of men.

In *My Days and Dreams* Carpenter designated *Towards Democracy* as the
'start-point and kernel of all my later work, the centre from which the other
books have radiated'.[20] This was, however, in retrospect. At the time he
was more low-key, writing to Whitman from Bradway in March 1882:

I have about finished what I am writing at present. It is in paragraphs,
some short (half a line or so), some long in the ordinary prose form
tho poetical in character . . . I have thought for some time of calling
it Towards Democracy and I do not see any reason for altering the
title – though the word Democracy does not often occur in it.[21]

When *Towards Democracy* appeared in print its similarity in style and
content to Whitman was noted. In a perceptive review the radical journalist
Edward Aveling declared, 'He is an English Walt Whitman.' Though
critical of a certain poesy in the style, Aveling detailed Carpenter's strengths,
a keen eye and skill in juxtaposing images which created their effect 'by
the collision of the incongruous'.[22] In contrast, Havelock Ellis, then a
young medical student with literary ambitions, initially dismissed it as
'Whitman and water',[23] though he was later to change his opinion. Carpenter himself felt the need to disavow any suggestion that he had merely
copied Whitman, insisting that his use of a Whitmanite style arose because
he wanted to find a means of direct communication.[24] Writing in 1894,
he explained the similarities in terms of his closeness in outlook and
temperament to Whitman, saying that *Leaves of Grass* had 'filtered and
fibred' his blood. Whitman was not complaining. Indeed, back in 1852,
his 'Song of Myself' in *Leaves of Grass* had exhorted his readers to look
and listen to the world and filter their own impressions.[25] He presumably
regarded Carpenter's emulatory efforts as a kind of tribute, just like the letters
he kept over the years. On Carpenter's poems, the diplomatic Whitman
remarked enigmatically, 'Edward is young: his time is yet to come.'[26]

Carpenter thought that *Towards Democracy* differed in tone from Whitman's
poetry. In contrast to the craggy American, whose words were hewn out

of the rock of his being, Carpenter saw his own work as 'Tender and meditative, less resolute and altogether less massive', adding that 'it has the quality of the fluid and yielding air rather than of the solid and uncompromising earth'.[27] There were, however, other contrasts in both style and stance. Carpenter lacked Whitman's capacity to weave emotions and thoughts so tightly together that the boundaries are barely visible. *Towards Democracy* contains some graphic observations – Carpenter was at his best in describing individuals – but the overall flaccidity of the writing turns the work into a monotone.

In his letter to Whitman in 1882 Carpenter explained that *Towards Democracy* was 'a good deal made up of previous writings of the last five or six years *squeezed out* – a drop or two here and there.'[28] In some instances the original drops read rather better than the revised manuscript. For instance his manuscript notes contain the passage:

> When the surface test is final;
> And society slowly disintegrating under it.
> A trick of clothing or speech, metallic clink in the pocket.
> White skin, soft hands;
> Everywhere the thrust of alienation,
> The bond of redemption nowhere.[29]

The printed version became: 'When the surface test is final – the rainbow-colored scum – and society rolling down beneath it; a trick of clothing or speech, metallic chink in the pocket, white skin, soft hands, fawning and lying looks – everywhere the thrust of rejection, the bond of redemption nowhere.'[30] He has padded out and over-written until the intensity of the original has been muffled.

It is not simply that Whitman is a better poet. The assertion of personal democracy in Carpenter's work is less convincing than in Whitman's poems of the 1850s and '60s, because Whitman was writing about a young nation in which – superficially at least, and between whites – there was a direct, egalitarian way of relating. Whitman could elaborate on a theme which was recognisably part of the culture, and credibly position himself with the deckhand canal-boys, opium-eaters and prostitutes. Carpenter, writing in the highly stratified England of the 1880s, is looking at the poor and outcast and *willing* himself among them – the self-conscious effort veils the directness of expression he wanted to achieve. Whereas Whitman's poems are suffused by a sensuousness which overflows, Carpenter's anxiety is communicated even as he finds release for emotion. A shyness and long habits of concealment make his treatment of physicality abstract rather than immediate. His equivalent to J.A. Symonds' imagined wolf, the transgressive and forbidden, lurks in fantasy – the 'goat-legged God' of the Greeks or the 'black and horned Ethiopian'[31] – the white man's projected dangerous other self.

Carpenter might have wanted to embrace all and sundry; publishers were more wary. Eventually 500 copies were published at the author's own expense. After two years 400 of these had been sold – many distributed by Carpenter as gifts. The feminist Millicent Fawcett's lips were still metaphorically pursed when she recalled in her autobiography how Edward Carpenter 'sent me his little book *Towards Democracy*: my copy was characteristically bound into its cover upside down'.[32] Yet Aveling was right to spot in *Towards Democracy* a presentiment: 'He has caught before, as I think, any other singer the first inarticulate notes of the sighing of the people for the land.'[33] *Towards Democracy* brought them a promise of fulfilment rather than Christian denial – 'Sweet are the uses of life'[34] – along with an existential millennium, 'a time when men and women all over the earth shall ascend and enter into relation with their bodies – shall attain freedom and joy'.[35] Over the next few decades Carpenter's poem slowly gathered an enthusiastic following among socialists, sexual rebels and spiritual searchers. As the years went by, it became no longer quite so alarming to read, 'Sex still goes first, and hands eyes mouth brain follow; from the midst of belly and thighs radiate the knowledge of self, religion, and immortality.'[36] In the 1880s the words leapt transgressively off the page.

Carpenter wrote into *Towards Democracy* all the vigour and energy he was experiencing by working on the land at Bradway, and the directness and ease of his friendship with Fearnehough and Fox. In the poem he roams metaphorically, while in real life he would go into Sheffield looking for adventures during the evenings after work. He describes these euphemistically in *My Days and Dreams* as nocturnal expeditions 'with new companions among new modes of life'.[37] Not only was the sociability pleasurable, these encounters have a sexual edge. He confided to Havelock Ellis: 'Gradually . . . I came to find there were others like myself. I made a few special friends and at last it came to me occasionally to sleep with them and to satisfy my imperious need by mutual embraces and emissions.'[38] He appears also to have sought adventures in London, mentioning to Oates in January 1882 that he had met 'a young fellow . . . of doubtful character but to me interesting'.[39] Caution prevailed on this occasion. In Sheffield, however, there was a wonderfully legitimate setting in which he could look at naked men – the local foot-races. In the early 1880s male nakedness in bathing or sport was not explicitly sexualised any more than the hugs of contemporary footballers would be today. The young working-class men ran naked or wore only a strip of cloth between their legs. Carpenter took to watching. 'I used to stroll down by myself on many a summer afternoon and witness these contests.' The races went one better than the Greek statues for here were actual, beautiful men who moved; 'What held my attention was the sight of the fine free figures and of their proud movements.' Though a little prim about what he regarded as the vulgar aspects of the race, such as betting, he was riveted by the sight of so many 'men and youths of fine figure and development'.[40] Carpenter made a new companion among the runners, a young marine engineer called Joe Potter. Carpenter was finally discovering what he wanted sexually, 'a powerful strongly built man, of my own age or rather younger – preferably of the "working class"'.[41]

When Carpenter returned to Bradway from Brighton in September 1882, he walked into his sentinel box no longer a man with £60 a year, but one with an inheritance of around £6,000 – a very considerable sum. This opened up possibilities of simplification on an altogether grander scale. In *My Days and Dreams* he says that he made up his 'mind to buy a piece of land and work on it as a market-gardener' and then persuaded Fearnehough to join him.[42] Walt Whitman remembers the move rather differently: 'C. had been "much attached" to a young man whose great ambition had been to get a farm of his own to work, to live upon. Edward encouraged him. When he came into money Edward invested in land.'[43] Whitman's interpretation was presumably based on Carpenter's account of his fondness for Fearnehough along with his hesitancy about getting a farm while at Bradway, and he may well have over-emphasised Fearnehough's part because of an intuitive recognition of the closeness between the two men. Whatever the reason, Carpenter's decision to buy three fields at Millthorpe, a tiny, remote settlement nestling in the Cordwell Valley near the village of Holmesfield, and embark on the arduous labour of market-gardening, was indeed an extraordinary step for a Cambridge mathematician and would-be poet.

During the spring and summer of 1883 Carpenter had a grey stone, two storey house with a grey slate roof built, at some speed, a few yards from the road on Cordwell Lane. It was in the style of the local farms, consisting of a sitting room, kitchen, scullery, coach house and stable in a long, thin row without any hall or corridor. Simple and serviceable, Millthorpe Cottage, as it was known, was the antithesis of Brunswick Square's lofty grandeur. Albert Fearnehough, with his wife Mary Ann and two children, George and Annie, along with a spaniel dog, Bruno (named after the heretical philosopher Giordano Bruno), moved in.

Carpenter dutifully set to, helping Albert Fearnehough in digging drains, loading manure, grooming and bedding down the horse. When he drove in to sell their produce at the local market, the sight of a Cambridge MA costermongering caused quite a stir. Breaking taboos was all very well, but he does admit in *My Days and Dreams* that he soon began to doubt the wisdom of his decision. For though he loved the beauty of his surroundings and the close proximity of the moors, the nearest railway station was at Totley about four miles away; it was consequently less easy to get into Sheffield. He tried visiting his neighbours in the tumble-down farmhouses, entering dim, dingy, slightly fusty rooms with low ceilings and scanty furniture which contained redoubtable matriarchs, strapping young men and fierce cats that terrorised poor Bruno. However, the possibility of conversation locally was limited. He had buried himself, 'amidst a perfectly illiterate unprogressive country population (much more so than at Bradway)'. The devoted Fearnehough, without Fox's wit, lacked sparkle: 'my friend and his family . . . though good and true people were also quite limited to material interests'.[44] When he read Thoreau's book about the ideal, simple life in 'Walden', his unease was intensified. For instead of the transcendental peace Thoreau described, he had landed himself with a market-gardening business and a household of Fearnehoughs.

While writing *Towards Democracy* Carpenter had been preoccupied with an exploration of his own mind's eye; this inward-looking restorative spell allowed him to return afresh to the ethical dilemmas that had troubled him from his Cambridge days about how individuals should act in a society where human beings' destinies were so unequal. The question was given an added urgency by his own recently acquired wealth. In March 1883, just before going to live at Millthorpe, Carpenter gave a lecture on 'Co-operative Production' in the Hall of Science. He was going against the grain. The British Co-operative Movement had largely shifted to consumer co-operation, though from 1882 the Co-operative Productive Federation helped the surviving producer co-ops to market their goods and obtain capital. Carpenter keenly promoted the theories of the French producer co-operator E.J. Leclaire, who advocated profit-sharing and workers' participation. There was some interest in these ideas among thoughtful liberals who wished to avoid labour disputes, while a shadowy vision of co-operation as an alternative system to competitive capitalism still lurked within working-class co-operative circles.

In his lecture Carpenter insisted that the maintenance of grand people by masses of others, many of whom were half-taught boys and girls toiling in dirt and polluted air, was manifestly wrong. Regardless of the sophisms of political economy, there could be no justification for so much human degradation simply to satisfy the rage for cheap commodities. Carpenter's critique of current economic theory, and the connection he makes between pollution, consumption and production, are Ruskinian. So is his resolve to make 'the common occupations, honourable and enviable'.[45] However he is far more bothered about inequality than either Ruskin or the liberal enthusiasts for profit-sharing. Having observed in practice how little it was possible to live upon, he was convinced that he, and members of his class, had become accustomed to the most wasteful luxury. He decided that co-operative production was the way out. 'We will show in ourselves that the simplest life is as good as any, that we are not ashamed of it – and we will so adorn it that the rich and idle shall enviously leave their sofas and gilded saloons and come and join hands with us in it.'[46] Carpenter's approach to social change was imbued with the idea of personal action.

Shortly after giving his lecture in the Hall of Science, Carpenter discovered a book called *England for All* (1881) by the pioneer of British socialism, Henry Hyndman, which dramatically altered the essentially moral stance he had taken towards social and economic questions. Hyndman's starting point was in accord with his own: 'It is impossible to survey our modern society without at once seeing that there is something seriously amiss in the conditions of our everyday life.'[47] However the book contained a way of looking at capitalism which seemed to grip hold of its inner workings and make sense of the alienating financial transactions with which Carpenter had become familiar through handling his father's investments. In his autobiography Carpenter states that the instant he read the chapter on surplus value 'the mass of floating impressions, sentiments, ideals, etc., in my mind fell into shape – and I had a clear line of social reconstruction before me'.[48] Like many British socialists Carpenter had alighted upon Marx via Hyndman and, for a while, Marx's ideas provided a satisfying synthesis for Carpenter the mathematician and Carpenter the Idealist philosopher. Though by the time he read a French edition of Marx's *Capital* he was shuffling off the coils, writing in the margin: 'Labour value implies man himself and is therefore not analysable.'[49]

The author of *England for All* was a surprising recruit to Marxism. After studying at Eton and Trinity Hall, Cambridge, Hyndman had gone into business and as a result understood, unlike most socialists, how the City operated. He had been so enthusiastic after reading Marx's *Capital* in 1880 that he had haunted the Marx household, delivering bombastic perorations in the midst of family charades. Marx had tolerated him as a self-satisfied chatterbox until he had opened *England for All* to find his own work plagiarised and unacknowledged. Hyndman's justification that the English would never take their ideas from a foreigner was an argument that did not go down well among a family of internationalist political refugees.

Carpenter observes in *My Days and Dreams* how Hyndman was always

filled with fervent revolutionary anticipation. The early 1880s just happened
to be Hyndman's moment. In the dead-as-a-doornail year of 1881, he
had solemnly called a Socialist Congress which, according to Kropotkin,
was so small Mrs Hyndman received most of the delegates in her home.
Hyndman, who was not prone to doubt, went on to organise the Democratic Federation and later the Social Democratic Federation (S.D.F.)
regardless. As fortune would have it, the dogged Hyndman had managed
to knit together his little band of radical workers and dissident intellectuals
just before socialism emerged as a movement.

Dressed in his habitual stockbroker's black frock coat, Hyndman met
Carpenter one evening in 1883, and took him along to the basement of
a shop in Westminster Bridge Road where the committee of the newly
formed Social Democratic Federation were holding a conspiratorial meeting. Carpenter encountered two very different men there, both of whom
would have a significant bearing on his life. One was a striking, gaunt-
faced young man with red curls down his neck, James Leigh Joynes,
known to friends as 'Jim'. Joynes had been a schoolteacher at Eton, before
enthusiasm for the ideas of the American land nationaliser, Henry George,
had ended his career. Through Joynes, Carpenter would meet his sister
Kate and her husband Henry Salt – the same Henry Salt who had come
across Riley and Ruskin a few years before. The other more celebrated
figure Carpenter saw sitting at the table was the artist and poet William
Morris. In 1883, Morris was nearly fifty and his lion-like mane of hair
was speckled with grey; aesthetic and moral outrage against the human
and environmental devastation of capitalism had brought him into the
S.D.F. In marked contrast to Hyndman, Morris had adopted a plain blue
linen sailor shirt; a refusal of airs and graces that added to his charismatic
power in the early socialist movement.

Carpenter donated £300 to *Justice*, the paper Hyndman started early
in 1884. To Hyndman this constituted a membership fee to the S.D.F.,
though it is not clear whether Carpenter viewed it quite so literally. The
mission statement of Britain's first Marxist paper contrived to be dismissive
of the parliamentary system while at the same time calling for universal
suffrage, annual parliaments, payment of members, equal electoral districts
and proportional representation. It was an early hint of a schizophrenia
which always haunted Britain's first and longest surviving Marxist organisation. Some of the problems of the S.D.F. were common to those of all
revolutionary sects intent on rejecting capitalism in its entirety while being
forced to work within it for change, but others derived from Hyndman's
personal intransigence and insensitivity. As Carpenter recalled in *My Days
and Dreams*: 'We used to chaff him because at every crisis in the industrial

situation he was confident that the Millennium was at hand.' Then the
S.D.F. would be ready and waiting with Hyndman at the helm 'to guide
the ship of the State into the calm haven of Socialism!'[50] Hyndman, who
took himself very seriously, was easy to tease.

During 1883 and the early months of 1884, however, contradictions,
difficulties and personalities did not matter. Tom Mann, an engineer active
in both the Co-operative movement and the Malthusian movement for
population control, regarded the formation of the S.D.F. as a catalyst:
'*Justice* had been started and those who were able to sense the situation
recognised that something was buzzing.'[51] The buzzing of a new social
movement emanated partly from the rumblings of doubt and pessimism
which surrounded the years of the Great Depression. After being seen as
the unquestioned source of prosperity and progress, capitalism was looking
like a charlatan, powerless to overcome the falling rate of profit and the
consequent unemployment. Political thinking was shifting too, as the
radical wing of the Liberal Party became disillusioned with Gladstone,
and the Party split over Irish nationalism.

As the tiny tributaries of dissent swelled, Hyndman's new organisation
provided them with a ready-made channel, enabling land nationalisers,
Co-operators, Malthusians and self-educated trade unionists, to join with
Secularists and Christian Socialists. Among the first few hundred recruits
to socialism were insurrectionaries, utopians and hard-headed municipal
reformers. Some put the emphasis on direct action, others on the creation
of communal alternatives, yet others on parliamentary representation. In
each town and city, as these little networks of heresy coalesced to become
the cores of the new movement, the emphasis would differ slightly,
depending on the particular composition of the new branches and the
remembered traditions of the locality. The connections between Chartism
and Christian Socialism, embodied by Sharpe and Riley, were complemented by an historical memory of radical resistance handed down through
families to the next generation. One of the founders of *Justice*, Jonathan
Taylor, came from a Sheffield Chartist family, and had himself been
campaigning since the 1860s around education and housing. As a local
radical, who Carpenter calls 'lean, logical and conclusive', he knew the
ornery Totley farmers, John Furniss and George Pearson.[52]

The S.D.F. also acted as a magnet for rebels from the metropolitan
intelligentsia, a growing strata which ranged from the privileged on large
private incomes, to the low-paid literary hacks, and down-at-heel new
professionals, earning a living in elementary school teaching or on the
bottom rungs of the civil service. Their feelings of alienation contributed
disproportionately to the buzzing utopianism of the early 1880s, for they

were a loquacious lot, forming countless small discussion groups and short-lived journals to air their opinions. Several early SDFers, Hyndman, Joynes, Eleanor Marx and Edward Aveling, were familiar with this precarious gossipy world, in which *The Doll's House* by the Norwegian playwright, Henrik Ibsen, figured as prominently as the works of the American advocate of land nationalisation, Henry George or Eleanor's father Karl.[53]

Radicalised sections of the intelligentsia had not only come to the conclusion that the capitalist economy was running down; like Ibsen's rebellious heroine, Dora, they were prepared to break personally with past conventions. As an emergent social *couche*, they were inclined to regard attitudes and opinions as infinitely fictile. Busily remaking themselves culturally, they assumed they could shape new ways of seeing and being that would be accepted by the whole of society. Priding themselves on being so close to the pulse of the present, they believed they were on the fast-track to the future, inscribing their journals with names like 'Modern Thought', 'Papers for the Times', 'Progress'. While not all of these marginalised metropolitans identified as socialists, they were being dubbed as 'progressive' – a term which carried a fashionable French tinge. From this milieu came the early enthusiasts of Carpenter's *Towards Democracy*, which they hailed as thoroughly modern in its unusual subject matter and its call for new values.

Carpenter had foreseen the buzz of consciousness in *Towards Democracy*, proclaiming, 'When a new desire has declared itself within the human heart, when a fresh plexus is forming among the nerves – then the revolutions of nations are already decided, and histories unwritten are written.'[54] He could not, however, have envisaged the whirlpool of meetings and manifestoes which were to pull him away from his Millthorpe market-garden. As Whitman put it in his jumbly, but apposite way, 'Edward was not always there, yet mainly.'[55] Carpenter might wax romantic about his rural base, in reality he was that rare oxymoron, a rooted cosmopolitan. He was no sooner settled than he started to wander. Though he had grumbled about all the travelling on trains in his Extension days, he reproduced this peripatetic behaviour in his talks for the socialist movement and radical causes for the rest of his life. And a delight in far-flung journeys, stimulated when he was young by his father's encouragement of broad vistas, never subsided.

In the summer of 1884, Carpenter travelled once more across the Atlantic. Uncomfortable among the first-class passengers, he was moved by the drama of the migrant poor from Ireland, Germany, Hungary, Poland, Holland, Norway, Lapland, Sweden and Russia. So many lives and so much hope crowded together on the deck, heading towards the unknown, with their battered boxes and scratched brown suitcases. Carpenter reached out to them in his imagination, recording his impressions in a poem, 'On an Atlantic Steamship', which was to appear in the second part of *Towards Democracy*. His eye settled on an old grey-bearded Russian Jew, praying, hour after hour, mainly from memory, eating only dry bread, 'sitting alone with his thoughts among strangers'.[56] He was a tailor, going to join his son-in-law and an unimaginable future in Texas. Carpenter turned the sounds of the ship into words: the old man's chanted prayers, love-making, bible-reading, jingles of music, hymns, comic-songs, dances. On the way home he was to desert his class and travel steerage himself; another taboo had been broken.

During his second North American trip, Carpenter paid a visit to John Harrison Riley in Massachusetts, adding a stone to Thoreau's cairn at Walden and renewing his friendship with Whitman. This time Carpenter was no longer such a reverential devotee and could appraise the American poet in a more distanced way. The Whitman he now saw was a compound of cussedness and absorbent fluidity; of self-regarding egotism and all-embracing love. The gulf between their outlooks had widened as Carpenter's views had set. Both covered over their differences; Carpenter emphasising his old mentor's affinities with the common people and Whitman treating Carpenter's socialism as an eccentric English quirk.

Whitman gave Carpenter a letter of introduction to his fan, Dr Richard Maurice Bucke and he set off, across the vast Lake Erie, to meet the Canadian Whitmanite, who was in charge of an insane asylum in the town of London. Whitman had been sending him Bucke's writings on spirituality, psychology and physiology, stimulating Carpenter's interest in the Canadian doctor's views on the close connection between humans and animals and his theories of an emotional consciousness distinct from the brain, associated with the 'Great Sympathetic' nerve. Bucke's paper on the Great Sympathetic had led Carpenter to puzzle away to Whitman over its relationship to the soul.[57] The 1884 meeting with Bucke went well, setting in train an ongoing collaboration. Carpenter adopted the theory of the Sympathetic as an alternative source for consciousness and Bucke visited Britain, meeting up with Carpenter and other Whitman enthusiasts.

Back in Millthorpe that August, Carpenter was keen to import congenial company, a persistent impulse which would turn the isolated spot into a hive of hospitality. A young man who had attended Carpenter's Chesterfield University Extension course during 1880 and 1881, Raymond Unwin, happened to be staying in Chesterfield that summer with his wealthy cousins, the Parkers. Unwin, who was training as an apprentice engineering draughts-man/fitter, had been brought up by his idealistic and unworldly father to despise money-making. Uncle Parker disapproved of both his nephew's indigence and his politics, especially when his daughter Ethel and young Raymond fell in love. Unwin related to her his delight on sighting Millthorpe as he walked from Chesterfield through moorland and down the hill:

> The house he has built is a long one only one room deep, as all the rooms face South, and look over to a beautiful ford. One field is laid out in oats for the horse and wheat for fowl use, the other is in grass with a few young apple trees in it, the centre one in front of the house is planted with fruit, vegetables and flowers – lots of young rose trees – there is a stream running at the bottom where primroses grow.[58]

He spent many weekends at Millthorpe, talking with Carpenter late into the night. When Unwin left Chesterfield in October, Carpenter gave him *Towards Democracy*; it opened a new world, releasing him from 'an intol-erable sheath of unreality and social superstition'.[59] Carpenter exerted a profound and continuing influence, and, when Unwin worked with Ethel's brother, Barry Parker, in designing garden cities and early council housing in the early twentieth century, Millthorpe stayed with him as an ideal.

By the time Carpenter returned from North America to Britain the utopian desire within the human heart he had envisaged was not playing out too well; instead of stepping in democratic harmony towards the Socialist Commonwealth, the Social Democratic Federation was riven by animosities. An anti-Hyndman revolt was brewing on the Committee in London; it included Eleanor Marx, who had inherited the family vendetta against Hyndman; Edward Aveling, now Eleanor's lover; and William Morris. Carpenter commiserated with both camps, trying to remain neutral and going to see Morris when he came up to Chesterfield to talk about the schism in December. Morris, weary of the in-fighting, told Georgiana Burne-Jones, 'I listened with a longing heart to his account of his patch of ground, seven acres: he says that he and his fellow can almost live on it: they grow their own wheat, and send flowers and fruit to Chesterfield and Sheffield markets.'[60] It sounded so agreeable to Morris, especially after all those fractious meetings, and his encounter with Carpenter led him to reflect 'that the real way to enjoy life is to accept all its necessary ordinary details and turn them into pleasures by taking interest in them'. He toyed momentarily with the dream 'of a decent community as a refuge from our mean squabbles and corrupt society; but I am too old now, even if it were not dastardly to desert'.[61]

In January 1885 Carpenter went down to London where he contacted Hyndman as well as Morris. However the time for peace-making had passed. The Morris cabal had conquered on the committee on December 27th, but knowing that they could not win over the local branches of the S.D.F., they left to form the Socialist League, taking with them the blessing of Frederick Engels and little else. In response to consternation among the Bristol socialists, Carpenter told Robert Sharland that Morris, deceived by certain schemers, had led his little band out into the wilderness.[62] The schemers were Eleanor Marx and the dubious Edward Aveling, whose financial honesty had been challenged by Hyndman. At this point Carpenter believed that the S.D.F. had kept the best people and, despite Hyndman's failings, respected his sacrifices for the cause.

However, while he thought the S.D.F. was worth defending as an organisation, Carpenter felt no animosity towards Morris, sending off a copy of *Walden* as an offering and asking Morris to come and speak in Sheffield. Morris, who had thrown himself into building the new Socialist League, was carefully measured on Thoreau. He thought 'It would be an immense gain to get rid of hypocrisy and other artificialities.'[63] On the other hand he was sceptical about a Thoreau-style detachment, politically and personally. Morris, though resolutely private about his own sexual emotions, had lived through much unhappiness. His wife Jane had been involved with the Pre-Raphaelite artist Dante Gabriel Rossetti and had recently embarked on an affair with the free-thinking, philandering Wilfred Scawen Blunt. Morris himself was secretly and hopelessly in love with Georgiana Burne-Jones, married to his best friend, and he knew that the heart could be contrary. 'The passions have to be reckoned with by almost everyone, and thence come all kinds of entanglements, which we could not wholly get rid of in any state of society.' Morris added, 'I know from experience what a comfortable life one might lead if one could be careful not to concern oneself with <u>persons</u> but with things, or persons in the light of things.'[64]

This statement was in direct accord with Carpenter's socialism. Both men's politics arose from a longing for free and equal human relations and both imagined these as enabling individuals to realise aspects of themselves denied under capitalism. Morris and Carpenter were utopians in the sense that they regarded politics as the means to an end; the end being a new way of living. Their conception of socialism was broad in sweep, carrying perceptions, relationships, daily life, the environment and art along with it. Yet despite this concurrence, significant differences existed. Morris hid his subjective feelings about his friendships and loves; his eroticism was veiled in romances of pining swan maidens. Detailing a requirement for 'a powerful strongly built man', even in confidence, was inconceivable to Morris.[65] Carpenter's thrashing around with his yearnings in *Towards Democracy* was as alien to Morris as the Whitmanite declamatory style. Morris was a bon viveur who loved wine, beautiful objects, rich textures, and old books, spent money freely and supported his family in style. Carpenter's attempt to live out ideals of simplification was not for him; according to Henry Salt, Morris described Carpenter as 'a dreary cove' after one of his stays at Millthorpe.[66] Renunciation did not figure in Morris' socialism unless it was forced on him by the exigencies of struggle. Nor was Morris interested in spiritual redemption like Carpenter, he saw himself fighting alongside workers or sharing craft skills with them, not as a deliverer or a seer. These personal and psychological dissimilarities meant the two men were never close, despite the confluence in their politics.

In the first half of 1885 they were skirting around one another. Morris was wooing Carpenter politically by carefully cultivating the core of recognition between them. It was not all ideals; Morris had a business streak in him and Carpenter was a rich man, intent on divesting himself of his wealth. *Commonweal*, the new journal of the Socialist League, like *Justice* gobbled up funds. Morris, an adept recruiter with a sure psychological touch, had bedazzled young Raymond Unwin into the Socialist League in Manchester.[67] He subdued Carpenter's doubts with the same intellectual charm. That September a happy Morris wrote to Millthorpe, 'I am very glad that you will join the League.'[68] He had hooked his man. Nonetheless, Carpenter continued to diversify his investments in the socialist millennium. In the month that he joined the Socialist League, he made a donation to a Social Democratic Federation Library started by Robert Sharland in Bristol. His £5 helped a young Scot, Ramsay MacDonald, to become the librarian.

While Morris was busy creating the League, Carpenter was part of an attempt by the Working Man's Radical Association in Sheffield to put up an independent labour candidate. John Furniss, the treasurer of this Association, staunchly defended their break with the Liberal establishment at a meeting in November 1885. He saw electing a labour candidate as the key to a world without either aristocracy or 'moneyocracy', where all would dwell on the earth 'which we ought to possess in common'.[69] Though the independent candidate was defeated, several future Sheffield Socialists were associated with the campaign, including Jonathan Taylor and the sister of the two Bingham brothers, Louisa Usher. By February 1886, when Morris finally managed to set time aside to visit Sheffield, the political atmosphere had become highly charged. Mounting unemployment had resulted in angry demonstrations in Trafalgar Square and the police, edgy about the infiltration of foreign 'agitators', had attacked a march led by the S.D.F., wielding their batons. The escalating violence in the capital had made Morris all the more convinced of the need to organise, and his talk, 'Socialism in Relation to the London Riots', in the Hall of Science could not have been more topical. However Sheffield was not London, and the subsequent smaller meeting to set up a branch of the Socialist League did not go as he had hoped. Instead of signing up for the Socialist League, the Sheffield socialists decided to form their own Socialist Society. Morris concluded that they hung back because in a provincial town 'people are so much more known and as it were ticketed than in London'.[70] He underestimated the independent spirit of the Northerners. It was more likely to have been the doubts expressed at the meeting about religion and the League's rejection of parliament. John Furniss, who joined the Sheffield Socialist Society, had become a Christian Socialist after moving away from Methodism. Moreover Furniss, along with Louisa Usher and Jonathan Taylor, who also joined the new group, had campaigned for labour representation and municipal reforms. What seemed like inconsequential palliatives to Morris mattered to them.

The Sheffield Socialists: Carpenter seated first on right

Among the first forty-four Sheffield Socialists were the names of two men who played central roles in Carpenter's life: George Hukin and George Adams. Hukin, the man with whom Carpenter soon fell irrevocably in love, was a razor–grinder and trades unionist of Dutch descent. Adams, an orphan from the age of thirteen, had worked as a gardener for a phil-anthropic family, who encouraged his interest in art. He was earning his living as an insurance collector when he joined the Socialist Society and would later move to Millthorpe with his family, where he gardened, painted and made sandals. The initial list also included the grocer inspired by Riley's propaganda, Robert Bingham; his brother John became involved later, as did Joseph Sharpe and 'Mrs Maloy', the only other woman besides Louisa Usher. Over the next few years, Carpenter would be in regular contact with this little band of activists.

Carpenter helped draft the statement of the new society, trying to include everyone's views. Describing themselves as an 'Association', a word that evoked not just the Working Man's Radical Association, but the utopian socialism of the 1830s and '40s, their aim was 'a regenerate society in which everyone who can shall work', and in which those incapable of working would be provided for by the community. They directed their fire at both the big landlords and the capitalists, calling for an end to monopolies in land and capital, demanding a 'cumulative income tax',[71] the gradual nationalisation of large industries and services, including the railways, and the municipal ownership of gas, water and trams. Their programme also pressed for labour representation in parliament, in local government, on the School Boards and on the Boards of Guardians who administered Poor Relief. It was a political project which harked back to the traditions of working–class radicalism, while anticipating the policies of the Fabians and the Independent Labour Party.

That July, Carpenter addressed a meeting of the new Socialist Society at a radical haunt, the Wentworth Café in Holly Street. He spoke of his personal experience on the land, asserting that the land should be in the hands of the 'nation'. A sympathetic report in the *Sheffield Weekly Echo: An Anti-Whig Journal*, recorded an audience of about a dozen people, described as 'of the hardworking sort into whose lives not much of the joy of existence had entered'.[72] They were a tiny little huddle, without any discernible influence or power, but they were Carpenter's new world, and their lives and dreams would entwine with his.

5

Widening Circles

Carpenter's unusual circumstances as a Millthorpe market gardener endowed him with a certain mystique amidst the newly radicalised intelligentsia earnestly debating poverty, class inequality, sexual relations, new ethical codes and alternative spiritualities. Between 1883 and 1886 he was becoming known not simply as the author of *Towards Democracy*, but through his lectures and articles in the new socialist periodicals, including *To-day*, edited jointly by Hyndman and Joynes, and *Justice*, the paper of the Social Democratic Federation. Carpenter put his mathematical skills to work for socialism, just as he had for his father. 'The Cause of Poverty' in *Justice*, February 1885, carefully computed the proportion of the profits distributed to shareholders and workers. Adopting a time-saving device of recycling that he would employ all his life, he adapted the article into a pamphlet, 'A Letter to the Employees of the Midland and other Railway Companies', and used it as the basis for thirteen lectures during 1886–7.[1]

Other lectures given in the mid 1880s, 'Justice Before Charity' and 'Private Property', called for the redistribution of wealth and nationalisation of the land along with a national system of co-operative production. In these he accepted state ownership, but stressed that nationalisation had to be part of broader changes. He wanted to democratise relations between state and society, rather than utilising the state as it was, an unease about the state that positioned him on the libertarian wing of the socialist movement.[2] He also envisaged a combination of small co-operative ventures alongside state intervention. While putting his materialist foot forward in these early writings and talks, the topics that really animated him were more diffuse ethical questions about how to live the good life and how the individual should behave. He stressed, as he had done in *Towards Democracy*, that the moral elements in historical movements were the key to change because they caused men and women to desire an alternative. Questions of conscience relating to wealth, poverty and interest run through all the lectures or articles from *To-Day* or *Progress* produced between 1883 and 1887 and published together in *England's Ideal, and Other Papers on Social Subjects* (1887). Carpenter focused on 'the sorrows of the well-to-do',[3] insisting that they, too, had an incentive to leave the 'frantic dividend-dance'[4] for the deeper satisfactions of egalitarian co-operative production. He proposed that the rich should consume less. 'It has for some time been one of the serious problems of Political Economy to know how much labor [*sic*] is really required to furnish a man with ordinary necessaries.' Though Carpenter maintained that 'the ordinary wages of manual labor represent very much less than the value already created',[5] he cited Thoreau rather than Marx as the theorist of appropriate needs; Thoreau had demonstrated that it was possible to support yourself and have leisure to spare.

Ideas about self-sufficiency and appropriate consumption spoke to an unease about the superfluity of things entering middle-class homes amidst the poverty of sections of the working classes. Carpenter's comments on work touched yet another neuralgic spot. The mid-nineteenth-century emphasis on virtue as embedded in work had been overtaken by the actuality of the 1880s in which a substantial chunk of the upper middle class were living off inherited wealth. Carpenter's worried readers knew their Ruskin and their Morris, so when asked whether they were able to make a piano or build a house and admonished on the superiority of craft-based learning to their books and talk, they were ready to concede their inadequacy. This was a generation reared in the shadow of evangelical Christianity and susceptible to guilt. In rejecting the Christian faith, ethical imperatives remained strong, and though bereft of religious certainties many radicals and socialists continued, like Carpenter, to pursue spiritual insights alongside the movements for social change.

Carpenter was acquiring a reputation not simply as a thinker but as the practitioner of an alternative style of living. Millthorpe might have been geographically remote from the intense metropolitan coteries edging around one another in the British Museum Reading Room, packing themselves into the tiny offices of 'progressive' publishers and editors, or debating Ibsen and the meaning of life in one of the proliferating discussion groups, but Millthorpe, as an ideal, struck deep chords. Carpenter and his cottage merged into a model of how to make changes in the here and now, landing him with a dilemma that would dog his life. His penchant for the prophetic stance and 'can-do' style was offset by an abhorrence of prescription. He hated the idea of a new set of inhibiting moral rules substituting for existing ones, warning in *England's Ideal* against regarding any one change in life and surroundings as the secret of happiness.[6] He was equally chary about outlining the future utopia for which the new converts to socialism longed. While he believed that it would see new relations of honesty, he was otherwise disinclined 'to foreshadow' the 'new Ideal of Humanity'.[7] For Carpenter, 'There is a millennium, but it does not belong to any system of society that can be named, nor to any doctrine, belief, circumstance or surrounding of everyday life.'[8] Yet regardless of his protestations, he and Millthorpe kept being cited as exemplars.

Among the many debating groups that studded London during the first half of the 1880s was the Fellowship of the New Life, an association explicitly committed to combining the personal with the political. It was started on October 24, 1883, when around fifteen people crammed into the Regent's Park lodgings of the Ford sisters' cousin, Edward Pease, who was studying carpentry in order to acquire a manual skill. Isabella Ford was there, along with Jim Joynes whose vegetarianism inclined him to the 'New Life'. Also present were two idealistic members of yet another grouping, the Islington Green 'Progressive Association', Percival Chubb, a government clerk, and the medical student Havelock Ellis, whose studies were being interrupted by his predilection for meetings. Carpenter did not attend the early meetings of the Fellowship of the New Life and indeed had rather discouraged Chubb's utopian hopes in March 1884: 'I have not founded any community, nor have any intention of founding one.'[9] However it would not be long before he was drawn into the orbit of the Fellowship.

Chubb was a great admirer of the inspirational initiator of the group, Thomas Davidson, and it was he who had brought Havelock Ellis along to hear Davidson address the first meeting on 'The New Life' and propose the creation of a fellowship dedicated to simple living and elevated thinking. Davidson had come across the Transcendentalists on his travels in the United States, and combined an enthusiasm for utopian communities with a powerful conviction in the capacity of individuals to do whatever they desired. However, the Fellowship could not decide precisely what it was that they should do. The minutes of the first meeting record a resolve to found a 'communistic society' while seeking a 'higher life'.[10] Vague plans for a community were mooted, though it was not clear whether it was to be in the U.S., Brazil or the British countryside. Ellis did not hit it off with Davidson, who soon departed to Italy, and it was left to Chubb and Ellis to define the aim of the Fellowship that December as 'the cultivation of a perfect character for each and all'.[11] Whereupon, in January 1884, sceptics like George Bernard Shaw, who believed personal perfection would take far too long, departed to set up the pragmatic Fabian Society. Among those who migrated was Pease, who soon became secretary of the Fabians.

Shaw presented the split between the Fellowship and the Fabians as a clear-cut division between those who were exclusively preoccupied with inner contemplation and the practically minded ones who wanted external change – 'one to sit among the dandelions, the other to organise the docks'.[12] In reality the distinction between the two groupings was never so definitive. The Fellowship of the New Life was concerned about social as well as individual transformation, and its members could also be in the Fabian Society. Chubb was in both groupings, as was Sidney Webb's friend in the Colonial Office, Sydney Olivier. Carpenter himself maintained an association with both the Fellowship of the New Life and the Fabians.

It was true, though, that while the Fabians addressed the intelligentsia as potential leaders with practical expertise, the Fellowship of the New Life appealed to them as spiritual pathfinders. The Fellowship also provided greater scope for a hankering after mystical routes to understanding the self; Ellis might reject Davidson, but he had been profoundly influenced by the meandering manuscripts of James Hinton, a surgeon and philosopher who had been involved in the Metaphysical Society with John Ruskin. Hinton, the author of several acclaimed books questioning absolute moral laws, had died in 1875 of inflammation of the brain, leaving voluminous notes which Ellis tried to sort out. In these Hinton propagated the interrelatedness of good and evil, a concept he had mined from the seventeenth-century vision-ary, Jakob Boehme, along with another seventeenth-century heresy that resurfaced in the early nineteenth century – redemption by women. 'A woman-age is coming', Hinton had declared, 'that is an age of postponing self to others'.[13] When it transpired that Hinton not only saw women as the symbols of love, but had been physically involved with a circle of admirers, Ellis was somewhat embarrassed. However, from Hinton, Ellis acquired ideas about complementary differences between the sexes and a powerful psychological portent – 'the terrors that have haunted us, the evils we have shunned, were but dark shadows from the blackness in ourselves'.[14] Travelling along the back corridors of nineteenth-century thought, Hinton and Davidson's ideas exercised a remarkably pervasive influence. From Davidson came the assertion of individual action and from Hinton the rejection of conventional notions of sin. The two men acted as bridges to modernity and their ideas melded into the tacit assumptions of late nine-teenth- and early twentieth-century cultural dissent. Carpenter drew on both Davidson and Hinton more than he chose to admit.

While the exact date of Carpenter and Ellis' first meeting is not clear, Ellis recalled his first impression vividly. He was sitting at a Fellowship meeting with his back to the door, listening to the speaker, a Russian exile. On hearing the door quietly open, he turned around and found himself looking into 'two bright brown eyes in friendly twinkle';[15] Carpenter had already acquired a charisma. Before they met, Ellis had initiated what was to be a long correspondence with a letter telling Carpenter how much he liked *Towards Democracy*. When the poem had first come out Ellis had been dismissive, but by the time he contacted Carpenter in 1885 he was in love with the South African writer, Olive Schreiner, whose novel of adolescent awakening *Story of an African Farm* (1883) had made her a London celebrity, and it may have been her enthusiasm about the copy of *Towards Democracy* Ellis had given her in May 1884 which led him to reassess Carpenter's work. Schreiner saw the poem as expressive of the spirit of the times, articulating 'what is in our hearts; ours of today'.[16] Ellis confided to Schreiner in September 1885 how he longed for a friendship with Carpenter, though he suspected Carpenter imitated Whitman in many ways.[17] The following month he had shifted again, assuring Carpenter that he did not think *Towards Democracy* was an imitation; he found the poem 'in no bad sense <u>feminine</u>', while Whitman was 'so strenuously masculine'.[18] In October 1885, Ellis wrote saying that 'Miss Schreiner' would be glad to see Carpenter when he came to London.[19] But by the end of the year a shadow had fallen between the two lovers. Schreiner was attracted to the exacting and logical statistician Karl Pearson. Pearson, who ran yet another little discussion group, the Men and Women's Club, approved of forthright New Women in theory, though the real life Olive appears to have disturbed him.

Olive Schreiner's passionate directness troubled and fascinated many men while she was in Britain. A photograph of her from this period shows an attractive strong-featured face. The pronounced curves of her body are clad in a demure dark dress with a lace collar and she is holding a book. The energy and movement are evident even in this formal study. Her body is straining against the Victorian dress; it is as if her very being utterly refused confinement. She was in a vulnerable and exposed position as a visiting female celebrity. Adulation put her in a goldfish bowl; every move she made was public and she was apt to crash through the unspoken taboos which prevailed even in the heterodox circles in which she moved. Schreiner, like her close friend Eleanor Marx, was among a little band of Ibsenite women pushing at the boundaries of behaviour.

When Carpenter read *Story of an African Farm* he joined the crowds of Schreiner admirers, recalling in *My Days and Dreams* how, in the 1880s, Schreiner's very deportment marked her out:

> When 'ladies' took the greatest care to bridle in their chins and speak in mincing accents, a young and pretty woman of apparently lady-like origin who did not wear a veil and seldom wore gloves, and who talked and laughed even in the streets quite naturally and unaffectedly,

Olive Schreiner at the time she met Havelock Ellis, c. 1885

was an unclassifiable phenomenon and laid herself open to the gravest suspicions.[20]

Though Schreiner might appear natural and unbridled, she was constrained by the harsh evangelical tenets of her upbringing. The tensions erupted into illnesses and in 1887, troubled and wounded, Schreiner fled to Switzerland and Italy. She discovered in Carpenter someone in whom she could confide, scrawling letter after letter in haste in an effort to comprehend: 'The question of sex is so very <u>complex</u> and you cannot treat it adequately at all unless you show its <u>complexity</u>.' She observed that Ellis had a lethargic reserved spirit, assuring Carpenter: 'The tragedy of his life is that the outer man gives no expression to the wonderful, beautiful soul in him.'[21] Ellis, despite being so hurt, could never stop himself from intellectualising his friends and lovers as case studies. In December 1887 he commented to Carpenter on Schreiner's inner contra-dictions, '(as Schopenhauer says), even when we take the course of action that is most suited to us, those faculties which would have been exercised on an opposite course, are still within us, crying out for satisfaction'.[22]

Carpenter, troubled by his own sexual angsts, found in Ellis and Schreiner two friends who were, like him, intent on examining sexual responses and attitudes. All three were searching after a new ethic of honesty and frankness which could dispense with external moral codes and conventional judgements. Each took a different tack. Ellis distanced himself from his subject, drawing on his medical training; Schreiner, the novelist, generalised through intuition and observation, while Carpenter hovered somewhere between the two, proposing to Ellis in December 1885 that an oscillation between mystical insight and 'intellectual science' should be the desired approach.[23] Carpenter grew particularly close to Schreiner in the late 1880s, when both he and she were unhappy in love and their connection would continue to be more emotional than his relationship with Ellis. Nevertheless Carpenter greatly respected Ellis as an intellectual critic throughout his life. In *My Days and Dreams* a note of exasperation appears about Ellis, the tireless categoriser, with his very English 'love of order . . . and command of particulars'.[24] But he was aware that Ellis possessed other aspects; a fine aesthetic sense and a fascination for everything forbidden, and so he relented and portrayed his bearded friend with the Dionysian head and figure of Pan. Ellis was rather pleased about being compared to Pan and the satyrs.

The initial rapport between the two men was based on Ellis' familiarity with London's progressive intellectual circles. Though Ellis was much younger, he was better connected than Carpenter in this metropolitan milieu and took it upon himself to steer Carpenter through the concealed shoals of

progressive London. Despite his Millthorpe retreat, Carpenter clearly wanted
to make his mark among the intelligentsia, invoking his friendship with the
Fords in a letter to their cousin Edward Pease in December 1885 when
offering to speak for the Fabians. Noting the Fabians' full programme,
Carpenter assured Pease with disarming modesty that he would understand
if they could not fit him in.[25] Carpenter did indeed address the Fabians on
'Private Property' on January 1, 1886. London radical audiences, however,
were far more sophisticated and sceptical about speakers than Carpenter's
Northern Extension students or working-class co-operators, and the irreverent
Shaw took merciless and hilarious notes. In attendance was a wealthy woman
from Hampstead, Charlotte Wilson, soon to head off towards the anarchists,
and the children's author Edith Nesbit, married to the Fabian, Hubert Bland.
Shaw recorded: 'Awfully dull meeting. Wilson yawned like anything – No
wonder! Infernal draught from the window . . . something making frightful
noise like the winding of a rusty clock. Mrs Bland suspected of doing it
with the handle of her fan. Wish she wouldn't. Two or three meetings like
this could finish up any society.'[26] Fortunately the same lecture went down
much better when Carpenter repeated it for William Morris' Hammersmith
branch of the Socialist League on January 3rd.

In December 1885 Carpenter had proposed to Ellis that he should
lecture for the Fellowship of the New Life on 'Some Economies of Daily
Life',[27] and predictably the New Lifers were appreciative when he tested
out his ideas on simplification at their meeting in the Williams Library,
Gower Street in January 1886. Carpenter urged them to change their
décor, clothing and diets. Drawing on his own experience in the Northern
countryside, Carpenter pronounced stone floors to be the best solution
for downstairs because thick boots were likely to be in and out all day.
Upstairs Carpenter recommended varnished wood with rugs or bits of
carpet. Such simplified interiors, he pointed out, were easier to clean than
fitted carpets which were apt to smell, thus the make-over he proposed
had the added benefit of reducing housework.

Clothing was to be similarly pared down. Carpenter had demolished
his dress clothes when he went to live at Millthorpe. Now, in order to
simplify without appearing too odd, he advocated a good woollen coat.
No lining was necessary, it could be worn with a woollen shirt and pants.
The great advantage of wool was that it could be reprocessed; cut up,
the coat could become a hearth rug and this in turn could eventually find
its way into the dog kennel en-route to the manure heap. At Millthorpe
the benefactor of this particular aspect of simplification was likely to be
Bruno, the spaniel who appears in a photograph with Albert Fearnehough
in *My Days and Dreams*. Carpenter, who was shortly to discover sandals,

considered liberating the feet to be of the utmost importance. By going barefoot one could feel 'the pleasure of grasping the ground – the bare earth'.[28] Carpenter combined his evangelical call for a new lifestyle with an alternative moral economy. This recycled, self-sufficient praxis involved growing your own vegetables, keeping hens and using local not imported grain – American produce was forcing down British farmers' prices. The detail involved was to be his undoing; henceforth, like it or not, 'simplification' became Carpenter's logo regardless of his protestations that really he did not wish to decree how others should live.

Carpenter's talk went down so well that the chairman at the Fellowship meeting even proposed they should go home and do some little thing themselves to simplify.[29] Ellis attended the meeting, sending favourable comments on January 13th, though he protested against Carpenter's advocacy of vegetarianism on the grounds that meat was a 'stimulant'. Ellis wanted to know why meat? Why not potatoes? Was not all food a stimulant? Ellis also considered Carpenter's creed too austere and ascetic; he had neglected 'The aesthetic side of things . . . simplicity is really allied with beauty.'[30] Solicitous about his friend's London reputation, Ellis warned Carpenter that his work was being criticised as unpractical. He then softened the blow by saying that while others might be branding Carpenter as a crank, he himself had not found the talk at all faddish; moreover Olive Schreiner and various other women were enthusiastic about Carpenter's writing. Already at twenty-seven, Ellis was adopting the tone of an eminence grise. Carpenter was grateful for Ellis' 'hints' and agreed that he should tone down his observations on vegetarianism. 'People of course will take the paper as a statement of an ideal way of living, instead of (as I rather intend it) as a dry suggestion of how to get thro' life with less work or bother than at present.'[31] His prediction proved all too accurate. Carpenter's punctilious and protective Pan was unable to shield him from an ironic Shaw watching in the wings, who soon had a nickname for Carpenter, 'The Noble Savage'.[32]

Carpenter might have exasperated practical, rigorous, scientific or aesthetic socialists with his back-to-nature enthusiasms, but he also gained staunch adherents. In extolling the simple life, Carpenter not only touched a puritan nerve of guilt, he was flowing with a current, evident since Rousseau and the Romantics, which equated nature with integrity, truth and renewal. In an article in To-day in October 1886, entitled 'Does It Pay?', Carpenter suggested that it might be possible to 'Keep at least one spot of earth clean; actually to try and produce clean and unadulterated food, to encourage honest work, to cultivate decent and healthful conditions for the workers and useful products for the public.'[33] Simplification and a clean spot of earth possessed a practical as well as a romantic appeal for the growing strata of middle-class intellectuals. Escalating standards of consumption were making it harder for them to establish conventionally acceptable households and those on private incomes felt the pinch of the Great Depression. Rebels dissatisfied with bourgeois respectability detected the possibility of an alternative lifestyle on limited means which relieved them of the guilt of parasitism and the responsibility of servants. Carpenter's proposals were attractive because they cut the knots in their purse strings as well as in their consciences. Ideas of nature, the new life and simplification folded into a new ethic.

Henry Salt was one of the first who tried to live out Carpenter's ideas about the simple life. Inspired by Carpenter's account of Millthorpe, he left his job at Eton and went with his wife Kate to live in the Surrey village of Tilford, near Farnham. Salt would later explain that two social movements had attracted those like himself who were breaking away from bourgeois backgrounds in the 1880s. 'Socialism, the more equitable distribution of wealth, and simplification, the saner method of living.'[34] Carpenter, who spanned both, supported the humanitarian causes that became Salt's life's work, though it was Jim Joynes' sister, Kate Salt, who became a

Kate and Henry Salt

closer friend. He describes her in *My Days and Dreams* as raven-haired and large eyed with a 'sensitive, somewhat sad, Dante-like profile'.[35]

Salt came, like Carpenter, from an upper-middle-class background. He had studied at Cambridge, where Jim Joynes had encouraged him to rebel against the inner sinews of class privilege. Salt, like Joynes, decided that it was wrong to live off the labour of others and to eat animals. Accordingly, in 1884 he went to the headmaster, Dr Edmond Warre, to hand in his resignation from Eton, declaring he was a vegetarian, had lost his faith in the public school system and had become a socialist. Horrified by this roll call of apostasies, Warre exploded, 'Then blow us up, blow us up! There's nothing left for it but that.'[36] It is unlikely that Dr Warre subscribed to *Justice*. If he had, over the course of 1885 he would have read Salt attacking the Eton schoolboy's mission in Hackney Wick and, even more sacrilegiously, the Eton–Harrow cricket match at Lords. But vegetarianism proved to be contentious on the left as well as at Eton, and Salt was soon in conflict with the Socialist League newspaper, *Commonweal*, which declared vegetarianism was an employers' plot to force workers to accept a lower standard of living. Salt blasted back from the pages of the S.D.F.'s *To-day*. 'Food Reform' was not just about saving money, but a matter of 'Justice and humanity towards animals and a more healthy alternative than the overeating common among the upper classes'.[37]

Henry and Kate Salt's move, accompanied by books and piano, to a labourer's cottage at Tilford hardly seems remarkable today, but it caused a minor media stir in 1884, after Hyndman announced at a public meeting that Salt had left Eton. Resolutely Salt cut his academic gown into strips for fastening creepers to walls and used his top hat for shading a young vegetable marrow. But it was hard work at Tilford and both he and Kate missed their old life. They began to reconstruct it in a rural setting and, just like Millthorpe, their supposed retreat was soon attracting visitors. Edward Carpenter came and played Beethoven with Kate; not to be outdone, George Bernard Shaw pounded out Wagner while Kate sang. Shaw penned parts of *Plays Pleasant* in the heather outside, and dutifully did his share of the washing-up because he liked 'Sunday husbanding', as he called it, and Kate Salt in particular.[38] Hyndman meanwhile was not at all happy about this outbreak of noble savagery in the ranks. He, too, came down to Tilford to tell the Salts: 'I don't want the movement to be a depository of odd cranks; humanitarians, vegetarians, anti-vivisectionists, arty-crafties and all the rest of them. We are scientific socialists and have no room for sentimentalists, they confuse the issue.'[39]

The issue, however, continued to be confused by socialist intellectuals who insisted on communing with nature. The Salts stayed at Tilford until

1891, inspiring less extreme country cottagers, Jim Joynes, the Fabian Sydney Olivier and his new wife Margaret, who rode tricycles about the village. Even Sidney Webb and Beatrice Potter (later Webb), with hair streaming, appeared at the local pub on bicycles. Another recruit to the simple life, Harold Cox, was living next door to the Salts in the mid 1880s. During 1884 Cox had paid several visits to Millthorpe while working as a University Extension lecturer and had been inspired by Carpenter to start a farm 'colony'. Carpenter gave Cox money to start his community at Craig Farm in Tilford, and Cox imported an agricultural labourer from Kent, called Gibbs, and his family to help. The idea was that Cox would experience manual labour in the raw and corroborate Carpenter's faith, based on Totley, Moorhay and Millthorpe, that small-scale co-operative projects could be pursued as well as the wider scheme of land nationalisation. Cox, who was a member of the Social Democratic Federation with connections to the Fabians through his brother-in-law and former school friend at Tonbridge, Sydney Olivier, shared Carpenter's political convictions, but he lacked his ability to acquire practical knowledge. Cox soon alienated Gibbs and his experiment was not an agricultural success. However through Cox, Carpenter became friendly with three young Cambridge men: Goldsworthy (Goldy) Lowes Dickinson, Charles Ashbee and Roger Fry – a connection which was as important for him as it was for them.

Goldsworthy Lowes Dickinson arrived to help at Craig Farm one evening in April 1885, struggling through bracken and heather from Farnham station in the dusk. He approached the farm 'colony' in a highly theoretical manner; Cox's project was meant to help him resolve intellectual polarities. 'The social question' was ingrained in Lowes Dickinson, whose artist father had links to F.D. Maurice and the Christian Socialists; and, when he took the train to Farnham, his head was full of the ideas of the land nationaliser, Henry George. Yet at Cambridge he had come under the influence of the Theosophists, then targeting British elite circles in an effort to give the group respectability. Lowes Dickinson had been impressed by the leading Theosophist A.P. Sinnett's book *Esoteric Buddhism* (1883) and completely overawed when the brilliant young Indian convert to Theosophy, Mohini Chatterjee, spoke in Cambridge. Chatterjee advised him to read Plato; Lowes Dickinson did, and went on to study the contemplative and ascetic Plotinus. Plotinus provided a route between Plato and Hindu mysticism by asserting an inner human divinity in union with nature while accepting a consciousness beyond reason, but he was not too hot on class struggle and the land question. Consequently Lowes Dickinson was in a terrible muddle and meanwhile had to prepare his University Extension lectures on Carlyle, Emerson and Robert Browning for the following autumn. Pulled in all directions, he came to Craig Farm in the hope of finding himself amidst nature and farm work.

Instead he discovered that the farm was not quite as he had imagined. For a start manual labour proved more tricky than he had expected; his back aching from hoeing, Lowes Dickinson wrote plaintively to his friend Charles Ashbee, who was still at King's, 'I can not milk a cow'.[40] Ashbee might think it looked easy but you had to manipulate the teat in a particular way that Lowes Dickinson was not able to fathom. Then relations at the farm turned out to be far from utopian. Lowes Dickinson told Ashbee that the agricultural worker from Kent, Mr Gibbs, grumbled about Harold Cox, that it was impossible to converse with Mrs Gibbs as she was so deaf, and a shocked Lowes Dickinson had seen the pretty Gibbs daughter, Annie, sitting on Cox's knees drinking cocoa, after the parents had retired to bed. As for their intellectual neighbours, Lowes Dickinson considered Salt 'rather petulant and something of a fool',[41] though he enjoyed playing duets with Kate, was amused by Shaw, and exceedingly pleased when he eventually met Carpenter.

'Crankie Farm', as Lowes Dickinson named it, was to fail soon after he left in June. Harold Cox gave up rural simplicity and land colonisation in England and went off to teach mathematics at the Muhammadan Anglo-Oriental College, in Aligarh, India, where a Cambridge friend, Theodore Beck was Principal. Cox had no sooner arrived when he was writing to Carpenter bemoaning the unpopularity of the English and the lack of women.[42] With no Annies at Aligarh, Cox's only physical outlet was cricket. Though Beck stayed, Cox was back in England within two years and became a successful journalist, turning into an uncompromising opponent of state intervention and socialism later in life.

Cox's *Dictionary of National Biography* entry in 1949 refers rather grandly to Carpenter influencing Cox in his efforts 'to gain an insight into the life of English labourers'[43] through Craig Farm. Clearly neither Mr Gibbs, nor local villagers who sneered at Craig Farm's spindly radishes, were consulted. Indirectly, though, Cox's farm 'colony' did produce several off-shoots. Cox introduced Carpenter to sandals by sending him a pair from 'Cashmere', whereupon Carpenter began to make his own for friends.[44] Eventually the Millthorpe sandals turned into a little rural business, creating a prototype for innumerable copies which entered the wardrobe of bohemians in the years to come. Moreover, because of Cox, Carpenter made contact with Beck and the college at Aligarh while travelling through India in 1891, a journey which had profound effects on his subsequent thinking. Even Neo-Platonism was of consequence. Carpenter might tease Lowes Dickinson about 'Plotinion muzziness',[45] but he too turned to Plotinus when he started to ponder the links between Western and Eastern thought, and the second-century Egyptian was soon to inspire the symbolist artists and Henri Bergson. More immediately, Plotinus secured Lowes Dickinson a fellowship at Cambridge and a close relationship with Roger Fry, with whom he fell in love. Craig Farm brought Carpenter and Lowes Dickinson together too, and this contact, made during the mid 1880s, sent a whole series of intellectual and personal ripples flowing out into the twentieth century. So, in unexpected ways, Cox's venture did result in rather more than radishes.

Lowes Dickinson began his University Extension lectures in the autumn of 1885, still hopelessly wrapped up in Plotinus. In the first term a supportive Carpenter went to hear his lecture on Carlyle in Chesterfield. It was pouring with rain that night and Carpenter took him back to Millthorpe in a cab. Lowes Dickinson was struck by Carpenter's simple, friendly manner when he spoke to the cab driver and by the way the older man put him at his ease. 'There was a bright fire in the little kitchen, and I soon felt at home – what we talked about was not Socialism but mysticism. Carpenter lent me the *Bhagavad-Gita*, of which I had never heard.'[46] Otherwise things did not go too well in the North. University Extension exhausted Lowes Dickinson, who did not impress his students. He mumbled his lectures, turned his back on the audience, and no one could read his writing. His courses were disastrous, reaching a crunch in the second term with a complaint from the Chester class about a verse he read out from Emerson which they regarded as shockingly sexy. Still, Lowes Dickinson's friendship with Carpenter was established and, through Lowes Dickinson, Carpenter acquired another devotee.

In December 1885 Charles Ashbee travelled North to visit the struggling Extension lecturer. A little younger than Lowes Dickinson, Ashbee was more susceptible to the socialism wafting through Kings in the mid 1880s. Lowes Dickinson described his effusive friend at this time as 'a long youth, enthusiastic, opinionated, Schwärmerisch'.[47] The 'long youth' had already met Carpenter briefly in May 1885 when they had discussed land nationalisation, but the visit he paid to Millthorpe that December established a bond which transformed Ashbee's life. He was introduced to the Fearnehoughs, Carpenter showed him pictures and letters from Walt Whitman, and an elated Ashbee decided Carpenter was 'nearer to one's ideal of The Man than anyone I have ever met'.[48] The trip to Millthorpe inspired Ashbee and Lowes Dickinson to read Plato's *Phaedrus* together, debating in a Lincoln pub whether physical desire was indeed a distraction from the soul, no doubt to the wonderment of the locals.

Carpenter's defiance of class barriers and old-style social conventions endowed him with a pioneering, prophetic status to the idealistic young Cambridge men. The combination of powerful inspirational qualities with a disarming Peter Pan-like demeanour which dissolved age differences allowed Carpenter to be both the wise and the winsome one simultaneously. Carpenter was equally taken with his enthusiastic disciples, for he invited 'Goldy' and Ashbee to the lecture he was about to give in January 1886 to the Hammersmith Socialist League on 'Private Property', and, already networking, suggested they might like to meet the people in the Fellowship of the New Life. The Socialist League meeting was a dramatic occasion for the two young Cambridge men. In his memoirs, Ashbee, in contrast to Shaw, designated Carpenter's 'Private Property' lecture as 'beautiful' and described his excitement when William Morris invited them to supper. He related how Morris banged his hand upon the table and asked, '"If we had our Revolution tomorrow what should we Socialists do the day after"? "Yes . . . what" we all cried. And that he could not answer. "We should all be hanged, because we are promising the people more than we can ever give them."' Despite this gloomy prognosis, an exhilarated band, Ashbee, Lowes Dickinson, Carpenter, two Miss Carpenters – undoubtedly Dora and Alice – and Bernard Shaw left the meeting, heading in the direction of Tottenham Court Road talking of 'the coming Revolution and the collapse of the Capitalistic System'.[49]

During 1886, an uncertain Lowes Dickinson continued to be troubled by how to reconcile his practical and reflective life, exclaiming in distress to Ashbee, 'Really with Political Economy on the one hand and mysticism on the other what is a poor fellow to do.'[50] The unemployed were clashing with the police in Trafalgar Square, causing his middle-class Extension students to denounce 'Hyndman and Co.' Lowes Dickinson was troubled by the turmoil: 'The unemployed shriek to one "Are you not a man and a brother?" and all one's soul cries out "yes" and has to leave its philosophic contemplation to do so.'[51] Ashbee did not share Lowes Dickinson's introspective dilemmas. He thought Carpenter's approach to socialism as a religion ought to resolve his friend's vacillation between the spiritual life and social action.[52]

Ashbee was preoccupied with economics, work and technology, rather than either Plato or Plotinus, when he returned to stay with Carpenter that Spring. The Ruskinian in Ashbee was shocked by the grimy, grinding monotony of work which the conventional political economy he had learned from Henry Fawcett at Cambridge had failed to mention. Yet he also responded in Whitmanite fashion to the aesthetics of modern steel production, when Carpenter took him to John Brown and Company's Atlas Steel and Ironworks. 'Vast engines, plying armour plates. Great brawny men wheeling . . . molten nuggets of steel . . . the blast furnace shooting its white blaze of light and sparks into the sky.' He decided 'it is to this our art must turn'.[53] Ashbee was to spend his life trying to develop a radical aesthetic, pulled between rejection and awe in the face of technology and modern industry.

Ashbee, who seems to have been rather fitter than Lowes Dickinson, helped Carpenter with the hoeing and replanting of raspberries, chatting about socialism, democracy and Wagner as they worked. He was delighted to meet 'several of the labourers – Carpenter's friends' and longed to get nearer to them. 'If one could only shake off this "churlish gentility."'[54] His own background was in fact only ostensibly genteel; his father Henry Spencer Ashbee was a successful exporter whose hobby was collecting and listing erotic books.

That April Ashbee left Millthorpe for his friend Roger Fry's reserved Quaker home still infectiously enthusing about Whitman.[55] In July 1886 Carpenter went to see Ashbee at Kings and met Fry. It was a triumphant return for Carpenter in his new role as socialist sage, and Virginia Woolf records in her biography of Fry that the visit created a great impression on the Kings' students. Carpenter 'made them read Walt Whitman and turned Roger Fry's thoughts to democracy and the future of England'.[56] Gently insinuating sex along with Whitman and Ruskin, Carpenter also introduced the Cambridge young men to the metaphysical surgeon James Hinton's hetero- dox ideas about love. Ashbee was particularly delighted when Carpenter took him for a 'walk through the green cornfields in the afterglow', unfolding 'a wonderful idea of his of a new free masonry, a comradeship in the life of man which might be based on our little Cambridge circle of friendships. Are we to be the nucleus out of which the new Society is to be organised?'[57] It was wonderful to be thus chosen and most flattering to be declared harbingers of the future. Ashbee sensed a frisson, something about Carpenter he could not define. 'We are knit together by a presence I don't understand. I only feel the influence.'[58] These were pre-Freudian days and he decided it must be because they had a hero among them.

This is the first account of Carpenter's proselytising for the band of male comrades. His scheme had been germinating ever since the initial visit to Walt Whitman and may have been encouraged by the Fellowship of the New Life's vision of an enlightened elect, but it had acquired a new urgency because of changes to the law. The 1885 Criminal Law Amendment Act had made explicit the illegality of acts of 'gross indecency', not only in public places but in private. This was not, in fact, completely innovatory, for sodomy cases in private homes had surfaced earlier, though most prosecutions tended to be for soliciting in public places. Nonetheless, it seemed to contemporaries to constitute an extension of the law into the private sphere and the Act was regarded by those hoping for a relaxation in the law on sodomy as a blow. The amendment had been introduced when a radical M.P., Henry Labouchere, added it to a Bill aimed at stopping child prostitution. The new measure was backed by social purity campaigners, a lobby which included radicals, liberals and non-conformists. Their efforts to protect the vulnerable contributed to a focus on personal behaviour which had unforeseen consequences for sexual relations between men. The insistence that private morality should be reflected in the public sphere opened up a terrain of conflict about who should determine morality and how new boundaries between personal behaviour and the public sphere were to be configured. Alignments were complicated by the fact that the protagonists tended to be in the reform camp yet were putting forward contrary moral agendas on sex. Though the Criminal Law Amendment Act targeted brothel keepers rather than upper-class men wandering in Cambridge cornfields, during the 1880s homosexual acts became more visible and attitudes towards them began to crystallise. This was the context which caused Carpenter to conceive of some kind of conscious defence.

The beauty of Cambridge in the summer evoked many memories for Carpenter; the contrast with Sheffield's workplaces was all too evident. He wrote to 'Dear Charlie' about the divide between the North's 'practicality, deadly dull, worn out and grimy' and Cambridge's 'lawn-tennis and literature' – 'and four men to support each of you: what is to be done?' He prodded Ashbee's class guilt, a little meanly, asking, 'How to reconcile that freedom and culture of life with self-supporting labour?'[59] Ashbee was worrying away over the same question listening to William Morris on how the machine should be 'auxiliary to the man',[60] and starting voluntary work at the Oxford University Settlement in East London, Toynbee Hall. Named after the idealistic Arnold Toynbee, who had died young after going to live in Whitechapel in an effort to bring about class reconciliation, the Settlement was booming amidst the social conflicts of the mid 1880s. Ashbee found it bristling 'with social reformers in a hurry'[61] who aimed to investigate and reform conditions through personal contact with workers.

Carpenter, who planned with precision, wrote in July inviting Ashbee to stay again at the end of August and early September. On this trip to Millthorpe, Ashbee was impressed by John Furniss and the nine other men and three women living at Moorhay. They had taken the remote farm on a twenty-one year lease, convinced that all land would be nationalised by then. While Carpenter helped the men load hay, Furniss showed Ashbee and Lowes Dickinson the fields and the three quarries they worked communally, sharing the profits. Sitting with Lowes Dickinson in the kitchen with its huge brown grate and beams, and looking at the enthusiastic faces of the Moorhay 'communists', Ashbee felt as if he had entered 'a community of early Christians pure and simple'.[62] Roger Fry, in contrast, was beginning to fret under the pressure of 'this enthusiasm of Humanity business',[63] announcing to Ashbee early in September that he was more preoccupied with enthusiasm for himself. Ashbee was worried; the nucleus of the new society could not be allowed to flake so soon. Deciding that Fry was just being 'gloomy and pippy' he tried to cheer him up by saying Carpenter had asked for his photograph. Ashbee himself was facing the future with some trepidation. He had resisted his father's desire that he should enter the family firm. Instead he was about to join an architect's office where the world of top hats, dress coats and dinner parties awaited him. Ashbee told Fry he admired how Carpenter had 'burnt his boats (i.e. his dress suit etc.)', but for the time being there was nothing for it but to conform. Nonetheless he urged Fry on: 'we must help each other fight the many headed, many tailed . . . monster social convention'.[64] The young architect did his bit by marching defiantly into the City in a soft felt hat.[65]

Every evening Ashbee left his office and headed East to lecture on Ruskin in radical workers' clubs, writing with pride in his diary on November 22, 1886, 'the "B.W.M." is no longer a terror to me'.[66] Fry teased Ashbee about his worker students, who he called 'Toynbeests'. In contrast he did not think art had a social purpose.[67] Class conflict troubled Fry for a quite subjective reason; it forced him to make his mind up about what position to take. Carpenter, who could accept that there were many roads to truth, especially where charming young men were concerned, sent him a pair of sandals nonetheless.[68] The consequences of these friendships were far-reaching for all of them. Meeting 'Goldy' Lowes Dickinson, Ashbee and Fry enabled Carpenter to reconnect with Cambridge and inspired him to fuse F.D. Maurice's vision of personal relationships with Whitman's democratic comradeship and ideas of the 'new life' into his 'free masonry'. Carpenter's glimpse of an alternative collectivity was transposed by Ashbee into the Guild and School of Handicraft he formed out of his East London classes in 1888. Drawing on his experience at Toynbee Hall and his admiration for Morris' ideas of linking art and craft skills, Ashbee's Guild embodied Whitmanite ideas of comradeship, tinged with homoeroticism. The Guild and School of Handicraft would carry Ashbee's convictions about changing the conditions and relations of work, along with how things were designed, into the emerging arts and crafts movement. Lowes Dickinson, too, was deeply affected by Carpenter's faith in comradeship, though he inclined to an Hellenic trope rather than the rumbustious Whitman.

These close connections made among the London intelligentsia and the earnest young men from Cambridge would be lifelong. Carpenter was already displaying the extraordinary talent for friendship which would draw so many people towards him. This gift for relating can be attributed partly to the intensity of his focus in one-to-one encounters and his responsiveness towards the people he met, but it was also associated with that capacity to make the mundane incandescent which he had noted in Whitman. The wider implications of these personal links were characteristic of the times. Carpenter's emergence as a visible figure coincided with a unique period of utopian flux when the communicative power he possessed could take on a wider cultural and political significance. In the initial upsurge of the new socialist movement the division between personal liberation and social transformation seemed to blur. Carpenter internalised and articulated the whirling spirals of longing for new forms of communality and fellowship and a closer relation to nature which intertwined with a search for personal equality, sexual freedom and deeper understanding of the psyche.

He connected diverse aspirations for change and he linked people with overlapping interests, for he moved so easily between differing groupings. Already in the inchoate years from 1883 to 1886, he had emerged as the consummate communicator and networker. His networking was not primarily instrumental but an aspect of his receptivity, and the same absorbent quality was evident in his ability to assimilate and synthesise ideas which earned him a reputation for foresight. He was able to keep a metaphorical ear to the ground and sniff what was in the air. And so he picked up shifts which were less explicit than concepts, called them desires, and somehow cleared space for them to come into being. Havelock Ellis observed this already in 1886; writing on the extended version of *Towards Democracy*, he said Carpenter had 'loosened' the 'bounds of personality'.[69]

The loosening of the personality, along with simplification, country cottages, the Fellowship of the New Life and sexual honesty, were all somewhat ahead of their time. The utopian energy which carried Carpenter and his friends along in the early 1880s overflowed into subsequent decades, inspiring ventures in communal living and working, progressive educational experiments, alternative diets, fashion and décor. It also fostered ideas about ethical consumption and a conviction that theorising social change involved living some part of the future in the here and now. Carpenter threw himself into the rush of meetings and causes, pausing from time to time for his own little moments of 'Plotinion muzziness'.

6

Love and Loss

Carpenter was a man living several lives: in July 1886, the same month in which he was inspiring the Sheffield Socialists in the Wentworth Café and dazzling Ashbee and Fry at Kings, he was entering a passionate relationship with the man who would be the love of his life. The razor-grinder, George Hukin, was twenty-six when they first became lovers. In a poem called 'In the Stone-floored Workshop', Carpenter evoked Hukin's large, dove-grey eyes and the light curls escaping from under his cap, dusty from the grinding stones.[1] The dust took its toll on the grinders' lungs and Hukin suffered from asthma and eczema aggravated by his trade. Despite working in unhealthy conditions, Hukin was a skilled craftsman able to earn around 30 to 40 shillings a week, sometimes employing a few other less skilled workers when he had a good run of work. Nevertheless conscience and a strong sense of justice made him try to unionise other grinders and join the Sheffield Socialist Society – a step that transformed his life. He quickly became the lynchpin of the group because of his considerable organisational skills and steadiness of judgement. Thoughtful and discerning, Hukin always saw through blather. He also displayed a redoubtable tenacity in putting proposals into practice and the calm diplomacy of the backroom committee man. Tolerance was part of his Dutch family heritage, but with Hukin it went deeper. The man who ineradicably marked Carpenter's life was blessed with a rare comprehension of the complexity of human behaviour. Hukin saw much more than he said, his openness and sensitivity veiled behind stoical humour. Carpenter responded intuitively to this tacit philosopher; the two men complemented each other, one full of words, the other implicit in his expression.

There were times however when this difference led to difficulties between them. Throughout their long correspondence the working-class scholar laboured over letter writing, apologising frequently for not being able to communicate his feelings and for not sending longer, more frequent

The young George Hukin

letters. The very first letter to Carpenter, dated July 8, 1886, was clearly among the most difficult. The words, in careful copybook handwriting, are painfully ground out, expressive in their starts and stops of Hukin's inner perplexity of feeling. Facing the unknown, Hukin backs off and yet inclines towards the unfamiliar upper-class man who has singled him out by presenting him with Olive Schreiner's *Story of an African Farm*:

> I think you are right. I would rather withdraw from, than approach any nearer to you. I feel so mean and little beside you! altogether unworthy of your friendship. It is not your fault that I feel so, I know you have always tried to put me at my ease, to make me feel at home with you. How I should like! – Yet I feel I can't.
>
> Excuse the fewness of these lines, but I really can't say (– I don't know how I mean) what I feel just now.
>
> Forgive me for calling you Mr. I know I've offended you often by doing so. I won't do so again.[2]

This is reminiscent of Beck's withdrawal. Perhaps Carpenter still courted too hard, rushing Hukin as he had Beck, with an excess of concentrated devotion. But there were reasons for Hukin's awkward awe that were beyond Carpenter's control. At forty-two, Carpenter was physically imposing, his natural good looks having been enhanced by his outdoor life – 'tall, spare with browned bearded face', according to the *Sheffield Weekly Echo*.[3] Not only was he a well-known figure, he was erudite and confident about ideas and a literary culture, to which the thoughtful Hukin aspired. While the socialist movement had brought them together, the immensity of the class divide in the mid 1880s still made close cross-class friendships unusual.

Yet Hukin, unlike Beck, was not decisively moving away. He might be alarmed and uneasy in Carpenter's presence, nonetheless he felt his life was illuminated by him. The stubborn streak of defiance, which, despite his mildness, had made him an organiser and a socialist, also enabled him to put aside convention and follow strong feeling. 'I have been thinking of you all week',[4] he wrote on July 23rd. It is not clear whether Hukin initially knew he was being wooed, but over the course of the summer and autumn of 1886 the two men relaxed into an intimate friendship. When they were separated in October, because Carpenter went to Brighton to sort out the contents of 45 Brunswick Square, Hukin wrote, 'It is so good of you to love me so. I don't think I ever felt so happy in my life as I have felt.' He added, however, 'And I am sure I love you more than any friend I have in the world.'[5]

Did Hukin see Carpenter as friend or lover? There is no indication that he had ever known a sexual relationship with a man or that he had any terms of reference for conceiving of another man as a lover. Hukin's working-class world was heterosexual, he had married in 1883 when he was twenty-three, but his young wife had died the following year. Nevertheless Hukin came from a culture in which a degree of physical contact between men was common. Men and women inhabited distinct worlds and all-male company was the norm, not only at work but also outside it. Young men would swim naked, like the runners Carpenter had enjoyed watching, while at the village feasts Carpenter had attended with the harpist Joseph Sharpe and his son, men danced together because few women were there. It was not at all unusual for working-class men to share a bed because of lack of space. This unselfconscious physical contact fostered a tacit acceptance of occasional sexual encounters between men in private; these co-existed, like incest, alongside and in addition to the social conventions of sex within marriage and the pride of fatherhood.

Whatever happened between Hukin and Carpenter quickly moved beyond any passing arousal Hukin might have known from his boyhood and youth. Emotions were spilling over and sweeping both men along. Their divergent union flowed without format or ritual. Carpenter, who knew rather more than Hukin about what was happening between them, nonetheless played this relationship by ear, telling the stalwart Oates, 'My friend George has turned out too good almost to be true.' Inclined to self-censor even letters to his close friend, he promised, 'I will tell you about it sometime.'[6] Hukin made Carpenter so happy he could even feel amiable towards sister Sophy, remarking sympathetically to Oates, 'Life is awfully hard on an unprotected female on the shady side of 40.'[7]

In the summer of 1886, back in Brighton, Hukin was constantly in Carpenter's thoughts. Suffused with passion, he sat on the beach, just below Brunswick Square, letting the sea lap at his feet, just as he had done so many times as a boy. He watched the glow of the sunset and a crescent moon appearing among the clouds. Then, as darkness fell, he returned to his room and wrote it all down in a letter to Hukin. He had tried to persuade Hukin to accompany him to Brighton wanting, lover-like, to show the working-class man the childhood he had fled. Hukin had been unable to leave work and sober reflection convinced Carpenter that it was for the best. 'I shld. [sic] have been all in a muddle.'[8] The muddle would not have been simply subjective; in Brighton the taboos of class and sex would have made it impossible for them to love as equals.

Miraculously, in Sheffield crevices could be contrived. Regardless of the illegality of homosexual acts, convictions were rare and the ambiguity of close male friendship still provided protective cover. In December 1886 Carpenter confided to Oates that Hukin was as good as ever and said they were great 'chums'. 'Chums' has acquired a risible ring of *Boys' Own Paper* heartiness, but to Carpenter it denoted warmth and intimacy. He found Hukin did him good because he was 'very easy going and comic, yet deep feeling underneath';[9] Carpenter, ever the redeemer, trusted that he helped Hukin too. He had come across Plutarch's account in *Pelopidas* of the Theban band of lovers, and, intrigued and fascinated, recommended the book to Oates. He had discovered a fitting image for Hukin and himself as socialist warrior-lovers.

A no doubt envious Oates was informed how Hukin was staying with him on Saturday nights, either at Millthorpe or sleeping over 'at my quarters in Shffd [*sic*]'.[10] With Hukin's help, Carpenter had rented premises for the Sheffield Socialists in the old debtor's jail in Scotland Street. On the ground floor they established their very own coffee-house to rival the Wentworth radical café. Upstairs was a meeting hall, and above that an attic Carpenter used as his pied-à-terre. These 'quarters' in Scotland Street were hardly sybaritic. Carpenter told Ellis he was 'in the midst of the slums in an air laden with smoke and the sound of clogs'.[11] In *My Days and Dreams* he recalled how he was '*almost* high enough to escape the smells of the street below, but exposed to showers of blacks which fell from the innumerable chimneys around'.[12] The smells, noise and pollution did not matter; Scotland Street was special because of Hukin, who he called his 'Pippin'.

Quite what happened there between the two men remains concealed. The ingrained habit of discretion made Carpenter Delphic about details, and he was a dab hand at sounding frank while carefully qualifying. The anonymous statement sent to Havelock Ellis in the early 1890s when he began collecting material for his study of 'Sexual Inversion' leaves us guessing. In this Carpenter told Ellis that he had 'never had to do with actual pederasty, so called'. He is referring to anal intercourse rather than attraction to boys, for he adds that pederasty, 'either active or passive', would only seem appropriate if he loved someone very devotedly and the other person reciprocated his feelings.[13] Well, Hukin certainly reciprocated; when Carpenter went off to speak on socialism in Bristol in January 1887, Hukin assured him that his 'Dearest Pippin'[14] was longing for him. On the other hand Carpenter also explained to Ellis: 'My chief desire in love is bodily nearness or contact, as to sleep naked with a naked friend; the specially sexual, though urgent enough, seems a secondary matter.'[15] The old debtors' prison, demolished now, has kept the lovers' secrets.

The relationship between Carpenter and Hukin was interwoven with the exhilaration of being part of a new movement. In these early years socialism generated an evangelical energy along with a startling clarity and confidence. It appeared that the world was indeed about to be turned upside down; new human beings, new ways of relating, seemed just visible. In such extraordinary circumstances Hukin was able to follow emotions he did not fully understand and Carpenter found the courage to love unreservedly once again.

Carpenter and Hukin experienced the heady joy of working together filled with hope in a cause that seemed indubitable. Through the summer and autumn of 1886 mounting unemployment and the acute distress it brought with it were gaining an audience for the socialists' street meetings which were regularly reported in the Socialist League paper *Commonweal*. Carpenter fulminated against landlords and railway shareholders (like himself) who collected millions for doing nothing. He was joined by John Furniss, Jonathan Taylor and Mrs Maloy, who had recently become the second woman member of the Socialist Society, and they began to attract crowds of around two to three hundred people, competing with the Salvation Army and barrel organ men at the corner of Fargate and Surrey Street. When the police tried to close them down, the excitement which ensued only added to their audience. Jonathan Taylor, wily in local politics, began an outraged letter-writing campaign presenting himself as a member of the public, upset at the curtailing of free speech. By September their listeners were reaching four to five hundred.

Having your own premises signalled that you had arrived on the local political scene. In February 1887 when the new premises in Scotland Street formally opened as the 'Commonwealth Café', the sympathetic *Sheffield Weekly Echo* reported that the Sheffield Socialists, who, 'Some little time back . . . might have been counted on the fingers', now not only had their own hall, but could fill it to overflowing, while the *Sheffield and Rotherham Independent* noted that there were even a few ladies in the audience, though it derided their shrill 'hear hears'.[16] John Furniss was in his element quoting the Bible and Ruskin and explaining that the 'common' in 'Commonwealth' meant 'the common people', by which he did not mean one class, but that they were all 'of one common flesh and blood'.[17] The ethos of the Commonwealth Café was open and eclectic. The unemployed were welcome along with speakers of varying political hues: William Morris, Annie Besant and Havelock Ellis from the London socialist milieu, Peter Kropotkin and Charlotte Wilson from the anarchists. Kropotkin filled the largest hall in Sheffield in March 1887 and his Hampstead-based companion, Charlotte Wilson, who had recently left the Fabians, was delighted with the 'smart and tempting coffee house'[18] in Scotland Street. She appears to have overlooked any smoke or smells.

The emerging socialist movement acted as a vibrant popular university for reflective workers such as Hukin. Not only did the barriers to knowledge seem to be melting away as they listened to speakers, a process of mutual education stemmed from discussions with others coming into the movement. Carpenter's political connections and personal contacts brought ideas and stimulation from around the country to Sheffield. During 1886 and 1887 links were being made between the Sheffield Socialists and other similar groupings in Leeds, Glasgow, Manchester and Bristol. Tom Maguire, a young Irish socialist and trades unionist from Leeds, was in the audience at the opening of the Commonwealth Café. Bob Muirhead, a mathematics teacher from the Glasgow Socialist League, with whom Carpenter had stayed on a Scottish speaking tour in 1886, helped out with the open-air propaganda; Raymond Unwin came over from Manchester. The excitement was not just intellectual. The early socialist movement was packed with would-be musicians, artists and poets, all inspired by William Morris' combination of creativity and agitation, and each little group was sprouting a culture of clubs, cafés, halls and institutes where, amidst all the talk, there would be social gatherings with recitations, songs and music. These generated a need for material, and, in collaboration with the Bristol Sharland brothers, Carpenter began to compile a songbook, *Chants of Labour*. It appeared in 1888 and included work by Morris, Whitman, Ellis and Carpenter himself. The artist Walter Crane designed its cover.

The aspiration Carpenter voiced at the opening of the Commonwealth Café early in 1887 expressed a broad current of feeling. Socialism was not merely a movement for industrial emancipation, it 'meant the entire regeneration of society in art, in science, in religion and in literature and the building up of a new life in which industrial socialism was the foundation'.[19] William Morris too conceived socialism as a new culture, worrying away over how the discontent of the unemployed could transmute into the birth of a new society, though Carpenter put greater stress on creating a new way of living and stimulating new desires. Nevertheless, having observed Totley and heard accounts of American utopian communities, Carpenter remained sceptical about attempts to live completely apart from capitalism, observing in *Commonweal* that he would not like to be part of a community of less than a million because of the danger of being watched, though he conceded that each venture broke new ground and helped the 'cause'.[20] The Manchester Socialist Leaguer, Raymond Unwin, similarly argued that no small society could be socialistic when surrounded by capitalist competition, proposing instead that alternative co-operative values could be fostered by a range of 'social experiments' and by what he called 'living in spite of conditions'.[21]

Unwin could not have known how his phrase carried a particular meaning for Carpenter whose sexual desire for George Hukin made living against the grain a necessity as well as a choice.

In April 1887 Carpenter was so wrapped up in his love affair with Hukin that he was even loathe to join Oates on a holiday they had planned in Italy. Hukin came to stay with him at Millthorpe and they went walking in the Derbyshire hills. Carpenter described his lover to Oates as 'so disinterested and tender I hardly dare think it true'.[22] Just before Carpenter left to join Oates in Acqui, that flicker of doubt materialised into a dreadful certainty. As they lay in bed together Hukin told him that he was in love with a woman called Fannie and that they were to marry. Ever since the first time they had slept together Hukin had been trying to explain about Fannie. 'You don't know how miserable I have felt all along, just because I wanted to tell you, and yet somehow I was afraid to but I shall not be afraid to tell you anything in future if you would only let me Ted.'[23] Hukin had felt a tremendous relief that he and Carpenter had talked about it finally. However when Hukin said goodbye to Carpenter he had sensed that all was not well. Somewhat bluntly he told Carpenter how he had felt depressed until he and Fannie had gone for a walk and cheered each other up.[24]

Hukin was right; Carpenter was, indeed, concealing his distress. He confided to Whitman in a letter from the Commonwealth Café on April 20th that he had spent the night wondering whether there was any sense in the world.

I have had a baddish time the last few days and feel tired out and sick. A very dear friend of mine – we have been companions day and night for many months now – has taken to girl [sic] whom I can't say I much care for. She is right enough – and they both have behaved awfully well to me: but just now I feel as if I had lost him and am rather dumpy – tho' I don't know that it will be altogether bad in the end.[25]

Behind the stiff upper lip and contrived vernacular, Carpenter's desolation is evident.

An oblivious Hukin was pleased when Carpenter's first letter from Acqui arrived, writing back on May 15th to say he hoped that none of them would feel 'so weighed down again'.[26] Was Fannie weighed down by Carpenter leaving or because Hukin was so profoundly affected by his strange friend's departure? The latter is more likely. Hukin was prone to meld Fannie's feelings into his own.

Those months with Carpenter had nurtured ideals of non-possessive co-operative-style loving which rebounded in the letter Hukin wrote to Carpenter on May 21st:

> Don't think we have forgotten you dear Ted! for if we didn't both of us love you so much, I don't think we should love each other as much as we do, I'm sure we both love you more than ever, Ted, and you really must come and live with us when we do marry. You will won't you Ted? We shall all be so happy then and you will always have someone near you who loves you and whom you can love.[27]

Divided hopelessly between Carpenter and Fannie, Hukin was evidently missing his male lover physically. He did not find it so nice sleeping alone as he used to.

On the face of it Carpenter was in idyllic circumstances. He loved Italy, which, like many other nineteenth-century homosexuals, he invested with the promise of sensuous freedom. Oates' villa, Nuove Tèrme, was near Acqui, a beautiful old Roman hill town with narrow, winding streets, the balconies on either side festooned with oleanders, pinks and grape vines. In a letter dated May 22nd, to the working-class paper *The Yorkshire Free Press*, Carpenter contrasted the Italian town with the harsh ugliness of the North of England's urban landscape.[28] Ostensibly his letter purported to portray how towns need not all be like Sheffield or Leeds, though he may well have been sending a coded indication to Hukin of what he was missing.

Charles Oates and his young Italian friend, Guido, cosseted Carpenter in the villa. But neither their kindness nor Acqui's loveliness could salve his misery. A six-day gap between Hukin's letters caused him to panic and give vent to the desperation he had been holding within him in a letter to Sheffield which has not survived. It is not clear whether Hukin destroyed it at the time or whether it was lost or removed later as being too raw and exposed. Hukin's reply on May 24th makes it apparent that Carpenter had been unable to contain his emotions of despair and grief. Carpenter's unfamiliar vulnerability and loss of control left Hukin utterly distraught. The letter had made both Fannie and himself 'feel very bad' – so bad indeed that Hukin's syntax went all awry: 'Surely Ted, if you knew how we both love you, you would not be so unhappy, and cause us to be so miserable. We would do anything to make you happy and we can't be happy ourselves without you are, I'm sure. So if you still love us you must be happy, Ted, for our sakes.'[29] It was the nearest he ever got to a reproach.

Wretched because all he could do was make the two people he loved unhappy, Hukin said it would be better if he were to die. 'Then your wound might heal the sooner – and Fannie might forget all about me then.'[30] Carpenter acted quickly, sending a reassuring telegram from the post office in Acqui. As he walked back over the fields to Nuove Tèrme in the twilight he felt acutely aware of Hukin's presence surrounding him.[31] On Whit Monday, Carpenter wrote promising never to doubt Hukin and Fannie's love again and apologising for all the pain he had caused them.[32] Hukin had written to Acqui on Sunday, after Carpenter's telegram arrived, apologising too.[33] More apologies followed, along with two letters from Fannie, which expressed concern about Hukin's health. These have not survived but Carpenter refers to them in his replies to Hukin. Both men were turning themselves inside-out in altruistic empathy for the other's distress.

Early in June Carpenter was putting on a brave face, announcing to Hukin how he felt his 'sexual nature returning'[34] and was getting on pretty well with an Italian youth, Francesco. If the wounded lover sought to stir jealousy, he was keen also to communicate that Hukin was not being replaced. He and Francesco had walked a long way in silence; the young Italian was thinking of his Clotilde; Carpenter refrained from mentioning who his thoughts had been with – but Hukin would have read between the lines.

On the train going over the Alps towards France Carpenter could not sleep; instead he gazed at the mountains and fantasised about two Italian men in his compartment. Then, in Paris, where he had arranged to meet up with Olive Schreiner, everything fell apart. Schreiner, pining with unrequited love for Karl Pearson, was too dismal herself to relate to his woes. In his misery the world turned sour, and the Parisians' faces seemed to leer at him with 'satyr lust' in contrast to the loving openness he associated with Italy. He and Schreiner sought to divert themselves with a visit to a salon, which proved a mistake. Carpenter related his disgust to Oates at the pictures they saw 'of naked women in the most obscenely distorted attitudes'.[35] Male nudity he found aesthetic and delightful; female nudity disturbed him and provoked a curate-primness. Oates, he knew, would empathise with his recoil.

As he and Olive Schreiner came 'steaming mournfully into Dover'[36] on a foggy chilly day, Carpenter fingered the remnants of the rosebud Oates' Italian friend Guido had given him. It was still in his pocket, a reminder of how the young Italian and Oates had assuaged the worst of this crisis. He put off returning to Sheffield, dawdling in London where yet another letter from Fannie awaited him. He asked Hukin not to tell anyone when he was returning, for he needed a little time. Solicitous about Hukin's exhaustion, he promised to take up the work of the Socialist Society again; just a little rest and he would be ready. It had become a chore now, and they were two yoke-fellows bound by duty. Carpenter politely hoped he and Fannie were well. But of course it was Hukin with whom he wanted to be. The most painful loss was not physical, but, as he had told Whitman, the denial of intimacy. On June 3rd he wrote to Hukin, 'I rather dread coming back because I wd [sic] almost rather not see people that I love than see them just for a few moments and then get interrupted – and that is always what it comes to.'[37]

Carpenter's fears about his homecoming were well-founded. At Millthorpe, Albert Fearnehough was disgruntled by the presence of unwelcome guests, particularly the aesthetic New Life Fabian, Percival Chubb, to whom his daughter Annie had taken a liking. Personal strife had broken out in the Sheffield Socialist Society, the numbers attending meetings were falling off and the Commonwealth Café was turning into a relief station doling out bread and coffee to the unemployed. It was losing about £100 a year.

George Hukin and Fannie were married on July 26th and Carpenter nobly acted as their witness. However he found spending time with them acutely painful, his nervous tension and insomnia returned and he decided that to protect himself he had to withdraw from Hukin. In an incoherent letter to Oates on July 27th, part of which is missing, he announced, 'I must try and stand alone a little, because the nearer I get to them the more miserable I seem when I am away.' Carpenter beseeched Oates to come away with him for a few days; 'The whole affair is very complicated, too long to ask you to write about.'[38] Carpenter was desperately dependent on Oates, who, in contrast, was in an unusually elated frame of mind, having just met a young clerk, Arthur Coles. Coles was married, which disposed Oates to dispense worldly-wise advice about the advantages of falling in love with married men as this made it easier to develop a philosophical attitude towards their wives.[39] The loyal, trustworthy Oates tried to express affection but it came out as ponderous platitudes about 'the kindly hand of Time' and in pompous counsel 'not to ignore the philosophical and moral beauties which are blossoming around you'.[40] After pronouncing on birds in the bush and gathering rosebuds while you could, Oates gave up on responding to Carpenter's continuing distress over the ensuing months. Never very forthcoming, Oates went into retreat, until Carpenter grew impatient with his guarded friend, exploding,

'One feels like the suitor in the Sleeping Beauty who left their bones in the hedge in the vain effort to get through.'[41] Whereupon a period of estrangement followed between the two old friends.

Uncharacteristically, Carpenter, in lonely desperation, confided in Olive Schreiner. Two more dissimilar confidants than Oates and Schreiner can hardly be imagined. At the other end of the emotional Richter scale from the buttoned-up Oates, Schreiner tingled with such intense sensibilities that she caught other peoples' emotions too easily for comfort and as a result could not be relied upon as a buffer for grief: 'Just now I am not good for you. You are suffering much more than you know. . . . You must not write to me about the subject on which you talked to me unless it is restful to you, but my mind will always be wandering after you.'[42] It was several months before she fully comprehended Carpenter's feelings for Hukin: 'I didn't know that you and he ever came quite close to each other still; I thought your life was all quite empty.'[43]

Schreiner, who struggled to regulate her own emotions with stringent inner codes of behaviour, was one of the few friends who decreed to Carpenter what he was feeling. It was a role he usually took upon himself in relation to others. The problem was that butterfly-like she jumped from one solution to another. He should rest, he should work, he should go to America to see Walt Whitman, he should stay in Millthorpe, he should be alone. He clung to one comment in her letters: he must 'harden'.[44] Carpenter's uncustomary defencelessness disturbed the assumed pattern of their relationship. Initially it had been Schreiner who confided in him about Ellis and Pearson. Carpenter had been the helping one, the mother; now he was suddenly being transposed into being her brother, her beautiful boy, her son to mother. Yet Schreiner was flooded with so many disturbing feelings of her own and always desperate to write. Accordingly when he suggested seeing her, she urged that he needed to be alone.

Carpenter did refrain from his usual sociability that summer. Raymond Unwin, having given up his attempt to organise the Manchester Socialist League, was in the neighbourhood again from May 1887 when he found a job as a draughtsman at the Staveley Coal and Iron Company at Barrow Hill near Chesterfield. Unwin was lonely in his digs, pouring over Kant, Ruskin and James Hinton and faithfully keeping a diary in the form of letters to his love 'Ettie' (Ethel Parker). At the weekends he would walk for miles, seeking companionship with George Hukin or with John Furniss at Moorhay. Carpenter's elusiveness puzzled Unwin, who began to worry that they had somehow become estranged. Though when he did finally meet Carpenter at Chesterfield in July he was reassured, deciding that 'Edward . . . Only wants to quieten his brain a bit.'[45]

That summer, isolated and agitated, Carpenter shifted his affections to Hukin's friend George Adams, who he described in *My Days and Dreams* as slight and thin with a forward stoop, a shock of black hair and an impetuous artistic temperament. Adams' 'temperament' would cause trouble in the future, but in the late 1880s he responded happily to Carpenter's attention. Adams was miserable working as an insurance agent, he had glimpsed another way of life when he had worked as a gardener for the kindly family who had enabled him to attend art classes, and he knew he wanted to paint.[46] Carpenter must have appeared as his way out. Early in August they set off to Whitby together. 'George A and I are on our way', Carpenter wrote to Oates while still on the train heading for the moors and sea. On reflection he had decided that it was probably right that Oates had not come after all and announced that he was 'healing and hardening nicely and beginning to think of other people, other possibilities – which is a good sign'. He was glad to have put some distance between himself and the Hukins, for seeing them was agonising. Carpenter related to Oates how, when he had called to say goodbye, George Hukin was ill and under stress in bed, and had kissed him with such a loving look in his eyes, it had been unbearable. Moreover encountering Fannie evoked terrible spasms of jealousy, leading Carpenter to confess to Oates the overpowering fierce longing he felt for a mate and his resentment of 'the mockery of woman always thrust in the way'.[47] Aching with thwarted desire, he felt bitterly aware that women, and Fannie in particular, could vaunt the legitimacy of their feelings while it seemed that love between men would be always pushed aside. Despite desperately struggling to subdue his emotions, they kept bursting through.

It was Schreiner who perceived how Fannie might be feeling. After visiting Carpenter and Adams in Whitby, she remonstrated, 'you must be gentle to her because its [sic] hard for her too; and she hasn't got the large things to fall back on that you have'.[48] Carpenter did not keep Fannie's early letters to him, so her feelings remain blanked out of the record and we can only infer how she reacted to being part of a love triangle. Though she was thirty-seven when she married George Hukin, and not a young girl without any experience of life, she can hardly have expected to share her husband with an upper-class socialist man. If Fannie's assumptions about marriage received a jolt, to Carpenter that September Schreiner's 'the large things' must have seemed like the booby prize. Fannie had his beloved George Hukin. Carpenter was too bitter to make the imaginative translation and display empathy towards her. Eventually he pushed down his jealousy, though he continued to skirt around her. Relating to Fannie was an effort he made because of George

Hukin; apart from Hukin loving them both, they had little else in common.

Lucy Adams, George Adams' wife, assumes even less of a voice than Fannie Hukin in the surviving record. A local socialist journalist, Harold Armitage, remembered 'a blue-eyed golden-haired girl with pink and white complexion', apart from that he could think of little else to say about Lucy, except that she was constantly cleaning.[49] There are hints of dissonance though in her relationship with her husband, who was a more convoluted angry character than the open-hearted Hukin. In an undated letter to Carpenter, Adams remarked that Isabella Ford might be right in her opinion that men were more selfish than women, but he blamed women for making them so. 'They never think, only of getting a husband and then expect to be treated as though they were China and we pot. I always feel so mad with their sly ways, and their treatment of one another.'[50] So perhaps Lucy possessed hidden depths beneath the golden hair. In contrast, Adams admired and respected the upper-middle-class Ford sisters and was attracted to Schreiner, to whom he would send his love via Carpenter. She reciprocated by sending hers back to him. Adams wanted to enter Carpenter's world much more than Hukin ever did, moreover his intellectual and creative interests made him particularly acceptable to Carpenter's middle-class circle. Ellis was flattered that Carpenter and Adams liked the volume of Heine's work he edited,[51] while Schreiner impulsively suggested that Carpenter and Adams might come out to South Africa.[52] As he and Lucy already had one child and were expecting another, this was not a practical proposition. For a few months though it appeared as if Adams might fill Hukin's place. Thanking Carpenter for a present of a tie, and looking anxiously forward to seeing him, Adams stressed, 'You needn't have sent it to make me think of you.'[53] Yet Carpenter's inner feelings were ambivalent. He was searching for other 'possibilities', putting out homoerotic feelers, rather than ready for another love.

Just after Carpenter and Adams returned from Whitby, Unwin came across to Sheffield to lecture on 'Socialism and Happiness', recording in his diary for 'Ettie': 'Edw came after it was over and I slept with him and we were all right again and talked a good bit he asked about you and I told him how things stood he was very kind and oh Ettie he said he had just been knocked back by something of the kind but he was getting over it a bit.'[54] Unwin was too tactful to enquire further, but grieved for Carpenter and for all men, including himself, deprived of love. To Unwin the encounter was one of intimacy and comradeship, not sex, though it was sensuous too, in some ambiguous way he could not quite comprehend. He related to Ettie how he was surprised to find, as he and

Carpenter lay with their arms around one another, that he could not 'help longing for the time when I might be able to have your arms around me at night'.[55] Afterwards Carpenter – who would, no doubt, have experienced their night differently – told Unwin that they trusted one another. Unwin took this at face value without recognising any complicit pact of secrecy.

The scope for frustrating misunderstanding was considerable; on the other hand the vague affinities of spiritual comradeship also put up a protective screen around which meanings and interpretations folded imperceptibly. During the autumn and winter of 1887 Carpenter renewed his friendship with his Cambridge 'freemasons' who were replete with their own ambiguities. Lowes Dickinson wrote in October confiding, 'it is always well with me when I have Fry and without him damnable'.[56] The two young men revelled in one another's company; however Lowes Dickinson was realising that his feelings towards Fry were sexual and, even more troubling, masochistic. He decided they could never be consummated physically; 'I believed it would lower our love.'[57] It was not just a Plotinus-like denial of the body; he knew Fry loved him without desiring him, a problem that would recur in Lowes Dickinson's later life. While Fry and Lowes Dickinson were spending their nights at Byron's Pool in Cambridge, Ashbee was consumed by his idea of a Guild of Handicraft in the East End of London which he thought might be a prototype for a community of the future, uniting men of differing skills and differing classes. Carpenter wrote encouragingly in October, 'I think you might do something with your Guild ideas and I believe you have a real love for the rougher types of youths among the "people" . . . without which indeed one could do little.'[58] It was a somewhat vague endorsement, but Carpenter was preoccupied with his emotional troubles.

On November 13th this long phase of concentrated subjective absorption was shattered. A series of demonstrations by the unemployed and protests against the Tory–Liberal Unionist government's coercion in Ireland culminated in a massive demonstration of Radicals, Irish Nationalists and Socialists in Trafalgar Square. Carpenter was there with Bob Muirhead from the Glasgow Socialist League; the two men stood aghast as the police attacked marchers before they reached the Square and then charged on horseback into those who had already assembled. A regiment of Guardsmen with drawn bayonets followed the mounted police into Trafalgar Square to clear any stragglers. When Muirhead and Carpenter did not move away fast enough, a policeman seized Muirhead by the collar; Carpenter remonstrated, only to be batoned in his face. The gentlemanly voice had gone unheard and Carpenter had glimpsed an aspect of the British state rarely revealed to Englishmen of his class. He was hailed by Hukin and Adams as a local hero; their only regret was that Carpenter had not been able to give the 'peeler' a 'smack' in return.[59]

Behind the brave talk, 'Bloody Sunday', as November 13th came to be known, sent a shudder of apprehension through the socialist movement. The draconian response of the authorities left three men dead and countless others wounded. It showed all too clearly how a disciplined armed force could deal with a large crowd. It was a watershed, marking a shift in the mood of hopeful anticipation which had characterised the early years of the new socialist movement. Three broad responses emerged. Those around the Fabian group resolved to eschew confrontation, while a minority of militants in the Socialist League concluded they must fight the state more overtly. A troubled and confused majority, including Carpenter, started to rethink their assumptions and look around for alternative strategies.

Carpenter was down in London again on December 14th, visiting the East London settlement Toynbee Hall. The settlement worker and journalist, Henry W. Nevinson, was charmed by a brief meeting there with the author of *Towards Democracy*, noting 'the mild brown eyes . . . fine irregular face' and the brown hair and short beard that was just beginning to grow grey.[60] Carpenter was inspired by his trip to London, and probably by conversations with Ashbee about his Guild, declaring to Oates:

> We are going to form by degrees a body of friends, who will be tied together by the strongest general bond, and also by personal attachments − and that we shall help each other immensely by the mutual support we shall be able to give to each other. The knowledge that there are many others in the same position as oneself will remove that sense of loneliness which one feels so keenly at times − especially when plumped in the society of the Philistines − and which is really almost unbearable.[61]

Knowing Oates was not an enthusiastic joiner, he tried to lure his friend into the shadowy Theban band with a young man he had just met in London, called Frank Deas, as bait. Oates failed to respond, but Deas remained in Carpenter's circle and both he and Ashbee adhered to the idea of 'the body of friends'.

In November Carpenter presented the Hukins with a bed; a symbolic and decisive gesture of his acceptance of their union. But Hukin still hankered after his dream of loving them both. When he wrote sending his thanks, he told Carpenter that the bed was much softer and wider than the one he and Fannie had before and sank in the middle 'which

somehow throws us together, whether or no'. The wideness of the bed
set Hukin thinking:

> I do wish you could sleep with us sometimes Ted, but I don't know
> whether Fannie would quite like it yet and I don't feel I could press
> it on her anyway. Still I often think how nice it would be if we three
> could love each other so that we might sleep together sometimes without
> feeling that there was anything at all wrong in doing so.[62]

By December Carpenter had contained his pain in a 'hidden chamber',
though it reawakened whenever he saw Fannie. He observed to Oates
that Fannie 'seemed to draw off a little – or perhaps it is my own reflection
in her that I see – but he is very affectionate as much as ever – the
position is a little difficult for me'.[63] The attraction between Carpenter
and Hukin proved resilient. In January 1888 they went walking and slept
together again at the village of Baslow. Carpenter was confused but pleased,
confiding to Oates, 'It is a funny business – but I think I am getting used
to it.'[64] In February the two men spent the night together again. The
following day Carpenter stayed with Hukin and Fannie and felt that 'we
seemed as a trio, to get on better than at any time hitherto. I cannot say
that I love him so passionately as once, but my love is very sincere – and
jealousy troubles our mutual relations less.'[65]

There were no known patterns for their criss-crossing emotions. Yet
somehow, without any maps to guide them, they had contained the pain
and prevented it from breaking out in ugliness and anger. This must have
required a tremendous effort of will on the part of all three of them. In
the long term it would hold – but in the meantime desire died hard.
When Hukin was at work he allowed himself to dream of Carpenter –
perhaps in this male terrain it did not infringe on the love that belonged
to Fannie. That Whitsuntide, a year after the telegrams, letters, pain and
panic, Hukin carefully planned his and Fannie's visit to Millthorpe. He
took the precaution of saying he hoped there would not be a lot of other
people around.[66] Carpenter's predilection for Theban bands combined
with his networking meant that the narrow stream of visitors which had
broken the monotony when Carpenter first lived there had swollen into
a steady flow. Yet, despite the hurly-burly, Hukin would always be a
special guest at Millthorpe, and Fannie and Carpenter – well – they found
a way of adjusting to being together.

Olive Schreiner, still wrestling with her feelings for Pearson, told
Carpenter, 'The true love is that which you fight against, struggle against
year after year, and which is always there.'[67] Carpenter would not have put

it quite so dramatically, though his love for Hukin was indeed indestructible. Nearly twenty years after they met he wrote a poem, 'Philolaus to Diocles', reflecting on the laughter and thoughts which entwined them. 'Years bring no shadow between us.' Not being together had suspended their love in time; the separation that had seemed so unbearable in 1887 protected them from the familiarity, 'Of too much nearness, and love dying so / Down to mere slackness.'[68]

7

Political Dilemmas

'Everybody seems out of sorts and depressed; there seems to be an evil wave travelling over us',[1] wrote a gloomy Carpenter to Olive Schreiner's friend, the children's novelist Edith Nesbit, who had sent a contribution to his socialist songbook, *Chants of Labour* (1888). This was not just solipsism. The millennial optimism of the early socialist days was beginning to dissipate in a malaise of doubt and uncertainty about what to do. All over the country socialist groups were splitting and going into decline. In Sheffield the mutterings and back-biting seethed away in the Commonwealth Café. In February 1888 Carpenter admitted to Oates that he was thoroughly sick of the coffee shop; it had brought him nothing but trouble.[2] That Spring, while Carpenter was again seeking the sun, this time in the South of France, a hard-headed Hukin insisted that the Scotland Street premises had to go. The town was overrun with coffee shops; there was no point in them joining the long list of struggling shopkeepers. The indefatigable Hukin had his eye on the Temperance Hotel in St James' Street and by April he was fixing up a meeting room there, helped by Jonathan Taylor, Louisa Usher and a friendly neighbour, Thomas Gascoigne. Before long though, even Hukin was beginning to wonder if it was worth holding lectures, for the numbers attending became embarrassingly low.[3]

Carpenter's initial response was to hurl himself into propagandising with even greater zeal. 'England Arise! The long, long night is over' proclaimed his contribution to *Chants of Labour*; it was as if he hoped that socialism could be sung into being. *Chants of Labour* received a sympathetic review from Oscar Wilde, who praised the socialists for using art to build their 'eternal city', but could not resist tweaking their earnestness. Thebes, he reminded them, had been constructed to music, yet it turned out to be an exceedingly dull place. Nonchalantly, Wilde threw out one of his far-sighted epigrams about the socialist project: 'For to make men Socialists is nothing, but to make Socialism human a great thing.'[4]

Carpenter, who knew from personal experience that making socialists was far more arduous than Wilde could imagine, was equally determined that socialism should be human and not dull, though his notion of dullness was not exactly Wilde's. Fun for Carpenter was heading off to speak in Chesterfield market, in the company of one of the new members of the Socialist Society, Jim Shortland, 'with a bicycle between us'.[5] Shortland, 'handsome fiery and athletic', belonged to the new breed of workers employed in the big Vickers' steelworks making armour plating for the Admiralty. He was tough and pugnacious and hence a reliable 'chucker out' for the socialists if there was any trouble.[6] Happier in male company than in his marriage, Shortland was drawn towards the growing circle of young men Carpenter was gathering around him at Millthorpe.

The new-fangled bicycle did not replace Carpenter's love of walking. He persuaded another handsome socialist, the dark-haired, pale-skinned Tom Maguire, who had attended the opening of the Commonwealth Café, to accompany him on propaganda trips to local beauty spots. Maguire came from the Leeds Irish Catholic community. He became a socialist at 18 in 1883 after reading a copy of *The Christian Socialist* edited by Jim Joynes and H.H. Champion, joining first the S.D.F. and then the Leeds Socialist League, which he helped to form. As a result Maguire had been ostracised by the Leeds Irish Catholics for whom socialism was akin to godlessness. A poet, singer and photographer, Maguire combined creativity with considerable organisational, strategic and oratorical skills. Unfortunately, Carpenter's penchant for scenic routes led him to apathetic audiences; in picturesque Hathersage the villagers stayed carefully just out of earshot while Maguire bellowed away from his pitch before giving up in disgust.

Given the chance, however, Maguire could be persuasive and among those he recruited at his open-air meetings at Vicar's Croft, Leeds, was a young engineer called Alf Mattison, who was soon joining the propaganda rambles. Mattison became one of Carpenter's closest friends. They met for the first time at the Socialist League Club in the Clarendon Buildings, Victoria Road, late in 1889. Young Mattison regarded Carpenter, who was speaking at the meeting, with reverence. When he shook Mattison's hand, the twenty-year-old 'thrilled at the touch'.[7] The whole event stayed vividly in Mattison's memory.

We mustered in full force and, with a few unattached sympathisers made up an audience of about fifty, the largest indoor meeting of our four years' existence. And what a motley crew we were to be sure, made up of English, Irish and Scotch; Polish Russian and German Jews, a Frenchman and two Germans – one . . . had been expelled from his native land for his work in the Old International.[8]

This Leeds gathering was utterly unlike a socialist meeting in Sheffield; the migrants and refugees brought memories and understanding from many lands, not simply of class but of national and ethnic struggles. They were brimming over with stories, and, after Carpenter finished speaking, gathered round the fire talking and singing songs from their homelands.

Outside the fog that night was too dense for Carpenter to reach the Fords' house at Adel, so instead he went to working-class Hunslet to stay with Mattison and his mother. Mattison guided Carpenter through the dark streets and as they walked together Carpenter put his arm in his. The gentlemanly visitor received a warm welcome from Mrs Mattison. The house was cramped so Carpenter shared Mattison's bed, and while his guest slept the working-class man 'lay awake thinking of all the circumstances of this sudden and unexpected happening'.[9]

Carpenter followed up their initial encounter by sending Mattison a copy of Towards Democracy and inviting him to visit Millthorpe. Having seen the highly respectable Mattison household, he knew that the young skilled worker would feel compelled to dress up in clothes he could not afford to damage and thoughtfully warned, 'we are quite rough in our ways out in the country and the lanes are muddy so don't put on anything that will get spoiled'.[10] Carpenter's matter-of-factness helped to allay some of the hero-worship and draw Mattison towards him as a friend. Scholarly and intelligent, regretful of his lack of schooling, having worked half-time in a mill since he was eleven, Mattison was hungry for an intellectual mentor, and Carpenter was charmed by the beauty, sensitivity and thoughtfulness of 'little Alf'.

Despite the downturn in socialist morale, Carpenter's friendship circle was expanding. Early in 1889 he announced to Walt Whitman, 'I am brown and hardy – and tho' I live mostly alone I have more friends almost than a man ought to have.'[11] His speaking and writing kept adding to the network. The Sharland brothers frequently invited him to Bristol where he took to a gentle working-class Christian Socialist, Robert Weare, and was adopted by two unconventional 'new women' members, Helena Born and Miriam Daniell, who had left the Women's Liberal Association for the Bristol socialists. Active in organising women workers, they had left Bristol's middle-class suburbs for a house at 9 Louisa Street in the slums, which they turned into a model of simplification. They tinted the walls, waxed the uncarpeted floors and improvised aesthetic furniture, a Carpenter-style makeover which was intended to indicate alternative possibilities of décor to their working-class neighbours, whose opinions, perhaps fortunately, go unrecorded. Like Mattison, Born and Daniell regarded Carpenter with awe. When he was expected early in 1890 Helena Born had 9 Louisa Street shining with beeswax and elbow grease in his honour.[12] The socialist movement might be democratic and free-spirited, nonetheless it cleaved to its personages, and by 1890 Carpenter was firmly established as one of these more visible comrades. They were not leaders exactly, but they wielded influence and their inspirational role became more important as the movement became increasingly embattled and disorientated.

As well as propagandising and networking Carpenter concentrated on the 'one little spot' approach he had floated in 'Does it Pay?' in 1886.[13] Over the course of 1887 he had been talking with Raymond Unwin about focusing on specific projects while agitating for wider change. Doubt about the immanent revolution had already set in, and Unwin explained Carpenter's approach to Ettie by saying that the small things might do some good while they lasted, in case the 'large change' were to fail.[14] Carpenter's first local cause was one close to his heart – bathing. In a 'yours disgusted' letter to the *Sheffield Independent* in June 1888, he complained because young men were being kept shivering in Endcliffe Wood until nine at night waiting for a policeman to blow his whistle before they were allowed to clamber into the water in the bathing drawers issued to them by an anxious Town Council. Carpenter fulminated against this prurient restriction on their desire for cleanliness and healthy recreation. Immorality in his opinion was in the eye of the beholder. At Eton and Harrow sports days or on the river at Cambridge, mothers, sisters, cousins did not blanch at the sight of a naked male arm or leg. The inference was that *real* ladies, accustomed to casting their eyes over Greek statues, would not be offended if the young men in Endcliffe Wood were permitted to bathe in the warmth of the day. Carpenter suggested that any excessively 'decent' ladies along with others liable to be shocked by anything not clad in a tall hat and frock coat might forego the pleasure of Endcliffe Wood for the sake of those in need of a bath.[15]

This is Carpenter in full spate against the Mrs Grundyism of his era, throwing health and cleanliness in for good measure to unsettle his social purity opponents. He saw the ban on bathing as akin to putting muslin on the legs of pianos and expurgating Shakespeare, and his protest coincided with an aesthetic celebration of the 'natural'. Just when municipal authorities and social purity reformers were becoming nervous about youths bathing naked, painters Henry Scott Tuke and William Stott, along with photographers Peter Henry and Frank Meadow Sutcliffe, were portraying them as playful innocents. These images, framed and exhibited, contrived to rearrange what had been unremarkable. Boys without clothes were being viewed consciously when Carpenter protested about bathing in Endcliffe Wood, and this generated unease. The male body, and the young male working-class body in particular, hovered on the edge of ambiguity, aesthetically acceptable, yet indicating a certain destabilising frisson. There was, indeed, a sub-text. The 'ladies', of whom Carpenter made so much in his letter, were decoys. It was, of course, unmentionable that the young men might stir arousal in other *men*. Meanwhile the male body was being variously sexualised through the social purity campaigners' legislation and well-publicised scandals, as well as by the camera. For the camera made possible, not only the water babies and waifs of art photography, but an expanding trade in overtly pornographic images. A confluence of undercurrents flowed into Endcliffe Woods. Carpenter and the young men in their bathing drawers were in deeper water than might appear at first sight.

Carpenter's other supposedly small local causes were similarly inclined to ramify. His next foray, directed against the Duke of Rutland who owned the land around Holmesfield, broadened into a challenge to the considerable economic and social power wielded by the aristocracy in the countryside. 'Our Parish and Our Duke' originated as a lecture given in Chesterfield in December 1888. Carpenter repeated it in Bristol in January 1889 and then in Sheffield's Hall of Science in February, and it appeared as a pamphlet later in the year. How absurd, declared Carpenter, that the five hundred hard-working farmers, farm labourers, miners and tradesmen of Holmesfield handed over £2,200 in rents every year. He estimated that from an average family income of £50, £20 went to the Duke. Carpenter did his history as well as his sums; by studying the Parish Awards Book he traced how common land had been enclosed in 1820 and demanded that it be returned by Act of Parliament. Moreover, he declared that instead of enriching the Duke, the £2,200 should be paid into a common fund and used for roads, care of the old and higher wages for parish workers. The locals remained silent but his protest against the Duke was printed in the London newspaper the *Star* and the pamphlet sold around twenty thousand copies.[16]

Carpenter was adding his voice to a wider critique of aristocratic landholders as the best guardian of rural interests. Bad harvests and the importation of American corn had resulted in a crisis in agriculture during the 1880s; farms and cottages had been emptied as their occupants left for the cities and parts of the countryside were desolate and neglected. Land still occupied a crucial place in the radical agenda and the agitation for land nationalisation in the 1870s and early 1880s had led to a discussion about alternative forms of ownership and relationships in the countryside. By the time Carpenter wrote 'Our Parish and Our Duke', disputes had arisen on the left as to the merits of centralisation versus decentralisation. Instead of the state farms mooted by some socialists, Carpenter inclined towards the Russian anarchist Kropotkin's enthusiasm for establishing small-scale production in industrial villages and combining industry with farming. When Kropotkin had seen the small cutlery workshops in Sheffield he felt as if he were in one of the Russian cutlery villages, and was fascinated by the survival of older forms of production amidst the big factory system. He thought there was a vitality and flexibility worth saving despite the bad conditions. Carpenter provided him with information about the 'putting out' system, which Kropotkin used in an article in the *Nineteenth Century* in October 1888, called 'The Industrial Village of the Future', and subsequently elaborated into a call for participatory democracy and small-scale co-operative ventures in *Fields, Factories and Workshops* (1898).[17] For Carpenter too, transforming the rural economy would be a long-term preoccupation; 'Our Parish and Our Duke' marked the beginning of his assault on the immense power of rural vested interests.

Carpenter's next campaign was to be equally long-lasting. Sheffield turned him into a pioneer environmentalist. He was not entirely alone; awareness of pollution from blast furnaces, coke ovens and boilers had been mounting during the 1870s and 1880s, leading to royal commissions and legislation. Though the Public Health Act of 1875 gave local authorities powers to combat industrial smoke, in practice they did little. Domestic fires were partly to blame, but it was the unfettered development of manufacturing that escalated the hazards.

Over the course of the summer Carpenter studied the history of anti-pollution legislation from medieval times, ploughed through reports and learned papers and acquired an impressive knowledge of recent technologies designed to reduce smoke emissions. Not content with second-hand information, he took himself off to view gas-furnaces and the new kind of boilers which were fitted with mechanical stokers in Lancashire, Yorkshire and London. Excited by this state of the art technology, he packed his newly acquired erudition into a series of lectures that autumn in Sheffield, Bradford, Hull, York and Manchester. Carpenter was enthusiastic about mechanisation because it obviated the practice of banking up the fires when the hand-stokers were sent to do other jobs, and thus resulted in less smoke. When his advocacy of the mechanical stokers was criticised by a boiler inspector who argued that they would put men out of work, Carpenter's response was pragmatic. While it was true that emissions might be similarly reduced if workers were given more space and time to hand-fire, employers were less likely to improve labour conditions and take on more men than to put in new technologies. He could not resist showing off to the inspector his newly acquired understanding of the specifics of draughts, the rates of evaporation depending on load, and the effects of differing types of coal.[18] One step forward was made in 1890, when, with Hukin's help, all the candidates for the City Council promised that they would 'go straight for the smoke fiend'.[19] Putting promises into effect was another matter, and Carpenter's evangelising against the 'smoke nuisance' would prove another long haul. From 1900 electricity slowly spread through the industry but even in the early 1950s around forty to fifty thousand hand-fired boilers were still belching away in Sheffield.[20]

Carpenter's last local project of the 1880s, a 'new school', was insti-gated by an eccentric schoolteacher he had met through the Fellowship of the New Life, Cecil Reddie. After working with the scientist and urban planner Patrick Geddes in Edinburgh, where he formed a secret society called the Gild of the Laurel to encourage sex education, Reddie had become a teacher at the boy's public school Clifton College in Bristol in 1887. On a visit to Bristol that year, Carpenter went on an exciting ramble with Reddie over the downs, talking about setting up a 'new school' which they decided would create a new man. Carpenter was sufficiently enthused to write to Reddie in December offering him the grounds at Millthorpe for his project and suggesting that he should run the school with the Scottish Socialist Leaguer, Bob Muirhead, who was out of a job. Carpenter offered to teach boxing at the school, adding, 'I don't advise you to undertake it unless you like organisation (I hate it).'[21]

In April 1888 Reddie arrived, staying until October. He was at Millthorpe so long he had to be steered into a neighbouring cottage – Carpenter was learning how to manoeuvre adhesive guests. Reddie with his military bearing, grey tweed Norfolk jacket and purple ties proved a somewhat irascible visitor. That August Fannie Hukin relayed to Carpenter news of 'such an argument'[22] between Reddie and Raymond Unwin. It should have been a warning, but nevertheless the 'new school' project went ahead. Reddie was the driving force; dismissing the classics, arguing for the study of modern societies, envisaging inter-disciplinary links between history and geography. A Ruskinian, he was a firm believer in craft education and manual work; not only would the boys study carpentry, instructed by a member of Ashbee's Guild, Reddie wanted cooking and butter-making to be part of the curriculum. Carpenter's partiality for market-gardening added yet more manual labour in the form of potato picking to the school's regimen.

Early in 1889 the dream took shape when Carpenter produced a financial backer, the Scottish businessman William Cassels, who invested £2,000. Ashbee and Lowes Dickinson were brought in as supporters and Bob Muirhead joined the teaching staff. In July the first issue of the Fellowship of the New Life's magazine *The Sower* (later *Seed-Time*) announced that the new school in Derbyshire, 'Abbotsholme', aimed to develop all the faculties, manual as well as intellectual, so that the boys would understand 'the conditions of labour and handicraft'.[23]

Carpenter had backed out by the time the article appeared, pleading too much work. He did have his book to do and his many lectures, but sustained contact with the autocratic and intransigent Reddie had probably made it evident that one small educational venture could absorb an inordinate amount of energy. Before the first term was out Cassels and Muirhead were at loggerheads with the headmaster, whose interpretation of new life fellowship was strictly Reddie-led. Muirhead complained to his Scottish Socialist League friend, John Bruce Glasier, that Reddie's 'sneering' manner had turned the whole project sour for him.[24] An equally disgruntled Cassels was paid off by December and the publisher Charles Kegan Paul replaced him as the backer; Muirhead was contracted to work for another term, after which he resigned with relief.

Reddie remained on genial terms with Carpenter, whom he continued to admire. However he was a difficult man to work with and Muirhead and Cassels were not the last colleagues to conflict with Reddie; Abbotsholme had a high turnover in its early years. Reddie moved quickly away from his Ruskinian and socialist ideas of education towards more abrasive Germanic theories of turning out a hardy elite. Germanic schooling methods fell out of favour in the First World War, and he grew increasingly isolated and paranoid. He was eventually persuaded to sell Abbotsholme, which survived under less astringent rule. Nonetheless Reddie's 'new school' did have an impact on British education because the breakaways developed differing aspects of Reddie's vision, from progressive Bedales to robust Gordonstoun.

For Carpenter, an immediate and propitious spin-off from the new school scheme was the chance to spend more time with Muirhead, whose athletic good looks reminded him sometimes of Greek statues and sometimes of Jim Shortland. Muirhead stayed at Millthorpe in April 1889, bicycling off with Carpenter and Shortland on their propaganda trips. It was a novel experience for Carpenter to be with an attractive, like-minded man with whom he could puzzle over mathematical theorems. Muirhead had what Carpenter described as 'a romance of affection' with a tailor and aspiring poet from the Scottish Socialist League, James Brown.[25] It is conceivable that Brown may not have felt too happy to hear from Carpenter how 'Bob' and 'Jim' had 'chummed a little', or been exactly reassured by Carpenter's remark, 'I keep hugging Bob for you.'[26]

By June it was evident that Brown was seriously ill with Bright's disease, but Muirhead was young, drifting, open to encounters and reluctant to accept responsibilities, attracting both men and women.[27] Towards the end of July Schreiner was dilating on the 'beautiful' day she had spent with Muirhead on the river.[28] Messages followed for 'Bob' in her letters through 1889 and 1890. A beady-eyed George Adams, who was also the recipient of Schreiner's messages of love in letters to Carpenter, gossiped to Alf Mattison about his suspicion that Bob Muirhead had 'designs' on 'Olive'.[29]

In the autumn of 1889, James Brown, who had become too ill to work, found refuge at Millthorpe. He and Carpenter took sunbaths and gazed at the stars. The two men read together and Carpenter played Beethoven sonatas for him on the piano. Carpenter's capacity for intense one-to-one engagement made every day vibrant. Bowled over, Brown wrote to his and Muirhead's friend from Glasgow, John Bruce Glasier, 'I never weary with Carpenter.'[30]

Then, after Brown returned to Scotland, rumours began to reach him about Muirhead and Schreiner. Carpenter wrote in January to allay his anxiety by assuring him 'Bob's' feelings for 'Olive' were 'quite apart from sexual'. Even if he were to marry it would not alter his relationship with Brown for marriage could not provide 'that precious something which is only found in comradeship'. This letter may not have entirely cheered Brown, for it also related how he and Muirhead, alone for the first time at Millthorpe, had bathed in the brook and run through the garden naked. 'His figure is splendid and his face too.'[31] Many years later Carpenter would muse on how 'wonderfully handsome and athletic'[32] the young Muirhead had been. He must have been hardy too, accompanying Carpenter on his rigorous regime of naked bathing in January!

Whatever Brown thought, Carpenter himself divined trouble ahead.

He confided to Oates that he had been 'wonderfully happy and contented lately – too much so almost, for I am afraid it forebodes doom'. But the attraction was too strong for him to heed warnings of emotional danger and he added that he was going with the flow, 'sailing along enjoying just what Destiny has saved up'.[33] Early that March 'Destiny' exploded. 'You will be surprised to hear that I slept with Bob at Derby', wrote Carpenter to Brown. 'I hope you won't be jealous; but I don't think you are. It was good to have him. . . . He was very loving and good and we did not forget you.'[34] Brown's feelings go unrecorded. His friendship with Carpenter and with Muirhead survived, but he was ill and poor, and fast becoming dependent. It is hard to accept that he felt no pain.

Many years later in 1925, Muirhead, married with a respectable academic career behind him, sent a bundle of James Brown's letters to Carpenter and reflected on the fancies that had wafted around him in his youth: 'You and he idealised me a good deal. I am really a very ordinary person, inspite [sic] of my mathematical prowess and philosophic abilities and I daresay I have often been very disappointing to the idealists.'[35] Just as Carpenter's small changes turned out to be larger than he imagined, the vision of non-possessive loving comradeship proved far more muddled in practice than any theory could envisage.

While these intricate micro-coils of love and comradeship were playing themselves out, a new working-class movement was coming into being. A crucial breakthrough occurred in August 1889 when the London gas-workers, led by Will Thorne, won the eight-hour day. Thorne's Gaswork-ers' and General Labourers' Union possessed a unique bargaining tool; the gas-stokers and firemen could bring the country's economy to a halt. Next came the London dockers' strike; a rebellion of casualised, humiliated men that transformed the mood of East London. Olive Schreiner, who was staying in the East End, wrote to Carpenter in great excitement on September 4th: 'Isn't the strike splendid.'[36] She empathised with the spirit of silent, confident elation she felt around her. Carpenter, however, remained on the sidelines of new unionism, even though several of his friends were key organisers.

Unlike the old craft unions, new unionism's reach was inclusive. In the autumn of 1889, Maguire, Mattison and Isabella Ford combined in support of the low-paid Leeds tailoresses without success, but by March 1890 the Socialist League had managed to unionise bricklayers and gas-workers. When Carpenter wrote to inform Mattison of a new book by Havelock Ellis on Whitman, Tolstoy, Ibsen and Heine, called *The New*

Spirit, Mattison did not have much time for reading – he was rushing between the gas-workers, the Socialist League and Leeds Jewish Workers' Society. A vague, benign, uncomprehending Carpenter mused, 'Everything seems to be rushing on faster and faster! Where are we going? Niagara, or the Islands of the Blest.'[37]

A new spirit certainly was abroad, though not quite as Ellis had conceived it.

In June the Gas Sub-Committee of the Liberal-dominated municipal council in Leeds brought in scabs to break the militant gas-workers. Whereupon, supported by other workers and by women, the militants attacked not only the interlopers, but the heavily protected city worthies. Leeds was in turmoil for several days with Hussars, swords drawn, confronting the workers. The new power of the gas-workers prevailed; the untrained scabs could not do their work and the city depended on gas. Amidst jubilation in the streets, the authorities backed down, after which everyone wanted to join a union and Maguire and Mattison were even busier.

The working-class 'new spirit' had hit Bristol the previous autumn when gas-workers and women cotton-workers took strike action. Carpenter's admirers, Helena Born and Miriam Daniell, helped to build the Bristol branch of the Gasworkers' Union by organising the women cotton-workers. Daniell wrote a pamphlet on why equality between the sexes must be the hallmark of the new unionism, with the secretary of the strike committee, a worker called Robert Allan Nicol, who was soon being invited to Millthorpe. In Bristol, militancy was matched with moral persuasion. Robert Weare accompanied the cotton-workers every Sunday on a tour of the churches, to tug at the consciences of the middle classes. When they walked in their white aprons to the altar rail at Clifton's fashionable All Saints Church in silent protest, a Cambridge graduate teaching at Redland High School, Katharine St John Conway, felt the shame of privilege. She duly presented herself at the Bristol socialists' smoky coffee-house in the Old Rope Walk, only to be viewed with suspicion, until the kindly Christian Socialist Robert Weare shrewdly handed her Carpenter's *England's Ideal*. Its impact was life-changing; she felt as if a 'window had been flung wide open and the vision of a new world had been shown me'.[38]

Some workers proved beyond the reach of even new unionism's enthusiastic evangelical zeal; Born and Daniell's subsequent effort to organise women seamstresses who worked at home failed, and, forced to concede defeat, they sailed across the Atlantic to make a new life among Boston's anarchists and Whitmanites. However, the Bristol left's traditions of women's emancipation were maintained when another communicant from the All Saints Church and university graduate, Enid Stacy, took over from Daniell as Secretary of the Association for the Promotion of Trade Unionism Amongst Women and, along with St John Conway, joined the Bristol Fabians.

Sheffield's new unionist activists inclined to the anarchism which was gaining adherents within the local Socialist Society as well as in the Socialist League nationally. In December 1889 Hukin reported to Carpenter that twenty-eight men were on strike at John Brown and Company's works.[39] They received zealous support from Robert Bingham and a young anarchist from Walsall, known as Fred 'Charles' (his real name was Slaughter), who was working as a clerk in the Bingham brothers' shop. Bingham's bluster about killing scabs being no murder led to his arrest on a charge of incitement to murder. The jury at Leeds Assizes found him not guilty, but he was convicted of using language which could have inflammatory consequences. Bingham's trial exacerbated the tensions between socialists and anarchists in the Sheffield Socialist Society, and the energy that went into his defence was taxing.

The new unions proved difficult to sustain institutionally, a weakness exacerbated in Sheffield by the anarchists' resolve to form exclusively revolutionary unions. Not only the anarchists' purism, but local labour conditions resulted in new unionism being rather a damp squib. In the late 1880s the labour movement in Sheffield still consisted of the grinders, forgers, hardeners and cutters of the metal trades, along with bricklayers, masons, tailors and printers. The small craft societies that represented them responded to threats of mechanisation not by creating a new trades unionism but by amalgamating. Hukin's razor-grinders joined with the forgers and filers in 1890. It was not until the 1890s that the trades union movement established a permanent base in the large steelworks then developing as arms producers.

Though Carpenter remained outside the practical side of new unionism he recognised that its implications were profound, arguing that the demand for the eight-hour day claimed back time from the relentless pressure for increased productivity. The overt class confrontation within new unionism was not his style, instead he spotted the seeds of an alternative vision of industry which centred on the health and welfare of the workers as human beings, rather than upon profits. Moreover, when he went as a delegate from the Sheffield Socialists to the International Socialist Congress in Paris during July 1889, it became evident that the resolve to regulate capital was being articulated more widely by an emergent European movement. Despite the discord at the Congress, it revealed to him how 'a new era in the Labour Movement had begun'[40] in many other countries as well as Britain. This new term, 'the labour movement', now lodged itself in his political vocabulary and enabled him to outline a larger scope for trades unions which included creating a new consciousness. Early in 1890, speaking on 'The Breakdown of our Industrial System', Carpenter told audiences in Bristol and Nottingham that the unions had an important role in winning higher wages and securing the eight-hour legislation, but that their most vital contribution lay in developing 'solidarity' among workers.[41]

The new political trades unionism and agitation for the eight-hour day coincided with pressure from several divergent groups for state regulation of what was being called 'sweated work' or 'the sweating system'. Never precisely defined, these terms broadly covered low-paid, labour-intensive labour which involved sub-contracting. In 1888 a House of Lords Sweating Committee under the chairmanship of Lord Dunraven was set up to investigate. Eight bemused lords sat boggle-eyed as the secretary of the Sheffield Trades Council, Stuart Uttley, sought to explain the intricacies of merchants, little masters and outworkers. 'It is rather complicated I am aware for persons that are not accustomed to it',[42] he propitiated. When it was George Hukin's turn to give evidence in such an unfamiliar setting, his replies to their lordships were initially gruff and terse as he struggled to explain he was a workman not a little master. He acknowledged low pay was a problem for the less skilled men, but insisted overwork affected everyone in his trade. Questioned on the causes of 'sweating', he thought it was a 'phase of economic development' in which merchants, little masters and workers were all caught because of the drive for cheap goods.[43] The remedy, he believed, was the eight-hour day, regardless of the piece-work system. When challenged he agreed that prices would have to rise.

Hukin's economic analysis of 'sweating' was confirmed as the committee accumulated more and more evidence. However an alternative account of sweating was being loudly trumpeted by the right-wing, anti-immigration lobby to which Lord Dunraven belonged. A sensationalist writer, Arnold White, was blaming foreigners for causing both unemployment and sweating, explicitly signalling out the Chinese, still a tiny minority of seamen and laundry workers, and Polish Jews who came to Britain after being expelled by Bismarck from Prussia in 1886. As more and more Jewish immigrants followed, fleeing persecution from the Russian Tsar Alexander III, economic fears quickly assumed a racialised dimension not only on the right, but among some liberals, trades unionists and socialists.

Sheffield had its own advocate of trade protection and immigration control, the Liberal M.P. for Sheffield Central, Sir Howard Vincent, and many craftsmen fearful of foreign competition were impressed by his arguments. Carpenter tackled the topic in a speech at the Hall of Science in March 1890 on 'Socialism and the Foreigner'. His commitment to simplification made him an opponent of the international division of labour; what could be more absurd than sending 'Razors to Germany to be ground',[44] he asked, knowing this would strike home with a Sheffield audience. But then Carpenter went on to the movement of labour, opposing the free entry of Polish Jews and Chinese immigrants. The reason he gave, that immigrants made it harder to achieve the eight-hour day, was a real dilemma for the labour movement, but his proposal that they should not be let in until shorter hours had been won was not the only option he could have presented to his audience. In Leeds, Tom Maguire, Alf Mattison and Isabella Ford took an internationalist stand. Maguire's 'Song of the Sweater's Victim' affirmed solidarity with workers of every land and was sung, in broken English, by the organised Jewish workers who themselves backed the eight-hour day.[45] The anarchists in East London were similarly closely allied with immigrant workers. Instead Carpenter, who had previously opposed the chauvinist strand in the S.D.F., played on the anti-immigration sentiments whipped up by men like White and Vincent. His attitudes aroused criticism. When Carpenter was eighty in 1924, a Russian tailor called John A. Dyche, who had been in the Leeds Socialist League in the 1880s, wrote thanking Carpenter for the help he had given him in migrating to America all those years ago, while censuring his anti-Jewish prejudices as unworthy.[46]

Carpenter subsided quickly on the immigration issue. Over time he developed a respect for Chinese culture and tried to counter the racism of the 'Yellow Peril' scares which swept through Britain and America in the late nineteenth and early twentieth centuries. A personal connection with a Jewish immigrant worker from the Leeds Socialist League made him understand the desperation that led Jewish immigrants to pay agents to smuggle them across borders. From the early 1890s, Max Flint (originally Flynke) became a semi-permanent resident at Millthorpe. After fleeing from Slobodka, near Kovno in Poland, to evade conscription into the Tsar's Russian army, Flint had ended up, like many others seeking asylum, in a Leeds clothing sweatshop. Radicalised by his experiences, he had broken with religion and moved towards socialism, whereupon, like Maguire, he had been rejected by his own community. People pelted him with mud and stones in the street and the woman he was to marry renounced him. When Carpenter encountered Flint at a Socialist League meeting in Leeds, he was already suffering from consumption. Whisked off to Millthorpe to recuperate, Flint made several attempts to get back to work in Manchester, where he had an aunt. But gradually his illness overtook him and he stayed at Millthorpe for several years, where Carpenter supported him, nursed him and eventually paid for a convalescent home in Bournemouth.

Carpenter's close involvement with Flint did not, however, eradicate his anti-Semitism. Not only did Carpenter continue to fulminate against Jewish financiers, he decided there were differing types of Jews, contrasting those who were slender-nosed and delicate like Flint to others with 'the Jewish proboscis'.[47] Perhaps Carpenter's discomfort about his own 'stumpf' contributed to this absurd preoccupation with noses.

Carpenter's support for the eight-hour day, the regulation of labour conditions and indeed his opposition to immigration all involved legislation, yet theoretically he was inclined to be in opposition to the state. He was not the only one tangled up in this contradictory knot; when he attended the International Socialist Congress in Paris in the summer of 1889 the state was at the nub of contention. Not only did it divide the reformists, who met at a separate Congress, it was wrenching apart the revolutionaries too. While some socialists believed in calling for legislative change, the anarchists were fiercely opposed to using the state, which they saw as inherently oppressive. These divisions had a direct bearing on action. Hukin, who saw union organisation and legislation as complementary, was exasperated by the way Robert Bingham veered from supporting the demand for an eight-hour day to denouncing it as a 'palliative' and insisting that only the nationalisation of all capital would do.[48] The militant grocer was soon endorsing the anarchists' refusal to have any truck with the state at all.

A little group of anarchists within the Socialist League were not merely criticising the state, but intent on provoking it. Having convinced themselves that capitalism was on its last legs, and keen to expose it in its true repressive colours, they were prepared to give law and order an extra shove. In a fluster of melodrama and high-flown heroics they were set to court martyrdom if need be. Robert Bingham's inflammatory attack on the scabs at John Brown's was swiftly followed by a violent speech at the Jubilee Monument in December 1889 by the London anarchist Charles Mowbray. The speech, hailed in *Commonweal* and denounced in the local press for profanity and blasphemy, divided the Sheffield Socialists.[49]

Carpenter's response was to try to ride out the mounting dissension.

In January 1890 the Socialists, now a 'Club' rather than a 'Society', moved to new premises at Lady's Bridge Buildings, 63 Blonk Street, not far from the Binghams' shop in the Wicker, and Carpenter helped them to cobble together a new Manifesto.

He explained to Bob Muirhead's friend James Brown, who was inclining towards the anarchists: 'We are getting into rooms at Sheffield and bringing out a Manifesto. I have had great trouble to reconcile the opposing parties over the Manifesto, but I think it is done with, and you shall see it soon.'[50] Of course it was not 'done with' for the little gang of passionate anarchists were convinced they were absolutely right.

The Sheffield Socialist Club's 1890 Manifesto echoed not just the divergent views of those who believed, like Bingham and Charles, in anarchism and those, like Hukin and Jonathan Taylor, who favoured trades unionism and municipal politics, it reveals Carpenter's own ambiguities about the role of the state and trades unions. While endorsing the 1886 assertion that land and capital should not be in private hands, the Blonk Street Manifesto specified that industry should be under the people's control. It aimed at an active democracy as part of a transformatory process rather than simply stressing a change in ownership. This 1890 Manifesto dismissed trades union action unless it was consciously seeking the creation of a co-operative 'free society' producing for use, not profit. But then it lurched towards Hukin and other trades union minded members by adding: 'We hold ourselves ready to help in the general labour movement that is going on – in the direction of a shorter Working Day, suppression of the contract and sweating systems, spread of Trade Unions etc.' A rapid renunciation of reformism followed: 'But while glad to assist in securing a temporary improvement in wages or other conditions, we look upon all these measures as of little use unless they ultimately establish the power of workers to take over the various industries into their own hands.'[51]

Only a hairbreadth's difference separated the anarchists' policies from those held by the Socialist League in the mid 1880s. The stress on popular control, freedom, consciousness, and indeed the purism, had all been there. Yet, pushed to the nether edge of confrontation, these were beginning to assume new meanings. An exasperated Tom Maguire wrote to Carpenter saying that while he believed in the use of physical force as a last resort, it was 'midsummer madness' on the part of the anarchists 'to advocate it on the public platform'.[52] Maguire wanted to hide in a corner and write poetry to overcome his bitterness as the Socialist League fragmented around him. Instead, he struggled on, organising the Labour Electoral Union, a reassertion of John Furniss' dream of labour representation. Victimised for his political activism, Maguire was plunged into poverty, made worse by his increasingly heavy drinking.

In Sheffield Carpenter's friends were divided. Practically minded members of the Society were inclined to withdraw into union work or municipal campaigns. Hukin, as uncomfortable in the company of the wild-talking anarchists as he had been at the House of Lords, lingered on out of loyalty to Carpenter. Carpenter meanwhile was personally drawn towards the irreverent, fun-loving Fred Charles who was becoming friendly with Jim Shortland as well as James Brown. His liking for Charles and his sympathy with some of the anarchists' ideals was nevertheless tempered by a vein of realism. In May 1890 Carpenter agreed with Bruce Glasier, who was similarly torn, that one did get 'rather sick waiting for the S.R. at times. I sometimes think it will never come in this country – only an S.E.'[53]

Social evolution rather than revolution might be disappointing; but Carpenter's greatest fear was that the vision of a transformed way of living which had been glimpsed in the mid 1880s was fading. His efforts to will it back into being resonated; a vast crowd came out to hear him speak on 'The Future Society' in February 1890 in the Albert Hall, Glasgow. Instead of the fear that ruled present-day Britain, Carpenter urged them to imagine a society in which everyone would be entitled to the necessities of food, clothing and housing, where everyone would work without compulsion and 'the variety of tasks and energies wd meet – the variety of social need'. He explained to his audience that he saw this 'ideal' as Anarchist-Communism; while Collectivist Socialism constituted the 'Transition'.[54] With the revolution deferred, Carpenter's strategy of transition suggested what could be done in the meantime. The lecture was repeated in London, Nottingham, Chesterfield, Liverpool, Manchester and Sheffield over the course of 1890, and Carpenter would return to the idea of transition again and again over the coming decade.

Carpenter set out to construct a broad highway between the gradualist statism of the Fabians and the 'midsummer madness' of the anarchists and, over the years, he would rework his transitional perspective. However he was not able to answer the question as to quite how the metamorphosis was to occur. If foreigners, for example, were to be held at bay during the transition, why would they be greeted with affection come Anarchist-Communism? And how could a strong state melt itself sweetly down into free association and mutuality? Nonetheless, he had located the problem both socialists and anarchists confronted – the widening gap between present circumstances and their aspirations for utopia. Unfortunately the

Carpenter with Oates and Mrs Oates

space for open enquiry was closing up; political discord had become too acrimonious for calm strategic discussions.

Early in 1890, weary from the toils of Manifesto-making, Carpenter returned to Cambridge. He reflected to Oates how romance still hung about the place. But it had become impalpable and no longer disturbed him. 'I dined with Beck however, and played games with his <u>five</u> children (ye Gods!).'[55] One ghost at least had been settled. Nevertheless he was careful to avoid Trinity, staying instead at Kings with Goldsworthy Lowes Dickinson, Roger Fry and their Hegelian philosopher friend, James McTaggart. An admiring Lowes Dickinson decided that Carpenter was the only young man over forty he had ever encountered and attributed Carpenter's perpetual youthfulness to his capacity to be always positive about possibilities rather than dwelling on failures.[56] Yet visiting Cambridge had made Carpenter aware of time irrevocably passing. It was sobering to realise that seven generations of undergraduates had gone through since he and Oates had been students.[57]

While he was in London that July, Carpenter took to sitting in St Pancras' Churchyard, where Percy Bysshe Shelley and Mary Godwin used to meet by Mary Wollstonecraft's grave. In this oasis of peace, surrounded by traffic, trains and industry, he started to jot down the autobiographical notes which eventually transmuted into *My Days and Dreams*.[58] He was nearly forty-six and aware that he needed to pause. The external political momentum that had carried him through the 1880s had wound itself down and he could see that the fourth phase in his life story had ended. Like all breaks, it had been preceded by a new modality. Throughout 1888 and 1889, amidst all the politicking and personal entanglements, he had been plumbing new sources of creativity; the rethinking went into his next book, *Civilisation: Its Cause and Cure*, which appeared at the end of 1889. Even more than *England's Ideal*, it steered his conception of socialism on a course which brought him devoted adherents and peptic opponents.

8

Challenging Civilisation

Carpenter floated an extract from his new book on January 4, 1889, at a gathering of Social Democratic Federation and Fabian heavyweights that included Hyndman, Shaw and Edith Nesbit's husband, Hubert Bland. He had no sooner delivered his paper on 'Civilisation: Its Cause and Cure' when the firing began. Carpenter was arraigned for glorifying 'the condition of savagery' (Hyndman), distorting Hegel's theory of history (Hyndman and Shaw) and, most serious of all, misleading 'the ignorant Philistines as to what socialists were aiming at' (Bland). Shaw was particularly scathing; had Carpenter attended the recent course of Fabian Society lectures he would not be presenting this shaky interpretation of Hegel. His approach could only 'bring contempt on the Socialist Cause when delivered to outsiders'. The report in *To-day* referred in muffled fashion to a 'chorus of adverse criticism',[1] but it was sufficiently heated for Shaw to repent in his diary: 'Attacked Carpenter rather strongly over his lecture – perhaps too strongly. I believe my nerves are getting too high strung.'[2] According to *To-day*, a 'nettled' Mr Carpenter responded by expressing 'his surprise at finding that the Fabian Society was unable to follow an argument' and defending 'himself with considerable smartness'.[3] The searing memory of this meeting stayed with Carpenter all his life.

Carpenter's discomposure indicates that he had not realised just how many sensitive trigger-points his paper would activate. And, not being a political animal, he did not see that he personally represented a threat to the leaders of the S.D.F. and the Fabians through the charismatic influence he wielded on audiences who were outside their own enclosed circles. Regardless of disagreements among themselves, both Hyndman and the Fabian leadership were convinced they should be the ones who put the official stamp on socialist theories before they were delivered to the 'masses'. Carpenter's wandering emanations steeped in German Idealism and Transcendentalism deliquesced their carefully deliberated certainties. In response they sought to marginalise him as the simplifying 'Noble Savage' who wanted everyone to live out of doors and wear fewer clothes.

The disputed 'Civilisation: Its Cause and Cure' gave its name to the collection of papers on modern society, custom, evolution, ethics, criminality and science published towards the end of 1889. The book would be one of Carpenter's long-lasting successes, reaching many more 'ignorant Philistines' than his opponents could have imagined. It went into eighteen editions in English between 1889 and 1938 and was also translated into French (1896), Dutch (1899), German (1903), Russian (1906), Bulgarian (1908), Danish (1913), while extracts appeared in Japanese.

Carpenter sought to bring together two parallel rebellions against the competitive society he equated with 'civilisation': the struggle for 'a social-istic and communal life' and the Romantic quest for 'Nature and Savagery'. He argued that this 'nature-movement', which had its origins in 'literature and art', was manifesting itself in an opposition to machinery and excessive consumption and was creating new ways of living, inspired by what he jokingly branded 'a gospel of salvation by sandals and sunbaths'.[4] His case was carefully qualified; technology, science and elaborate modern products were not to be 'refused' but prevented from dominating human beings:

> Our locomotives, machinery, telegraphic and postal systems; our houses, furniture, clothes, books; our fearful and wonderful cookery, strong drinks, teas, tobaccos; our medical and surgical appliances; high faluting sciences and philosophies, and all other engines hitherto of human bewilderment, have simply to be reduced to abject subjection to the real man. All these appliances, and a thousand others such as we hardly dream of, will come in to perfect his power and increase his freedom; but they will not be the objects of a mere fetish-worship as now. Man will use them, instead of their using him.[5]

Carpenter did not oppose invention; he was simply sceptical about his era's faith in automatic progress as a result of external changes in science, technology, productivity and material prosperity. In dissenting from the prevailing view he was in a minority but not entirely alone, for the nine-teenth century was not of one mind, harbouring forthright critics, on both right and left, of Panglossian 'Victorian' complacency.

Carpenter's concept of historical stages evolving through a transcendent synthesis was, as Hyndman and Bland recognised, Hegelian. He had also been reading the evolutionary anthropology of Lewis Morgan and Frederick Engels, whose work was still in German, along with his old school friend Cotterill's observations of the Africans he had met around Lake Nyasa in the 1870s and Charles Oates' brother Frank's diary of travelling in Matabele Land. Positive accounts of the health and vigour of contemporary 'primitive' people led Carpenter to see an early stage of society as containing features which needed to be preserved rather than overcome and discarded. For Carpenter, as for the Romantics, change from one historical era to another involved both loss and gain. 'Man must first fall; in order to know, he must lose.'[6] He believed that there had been an early stage of communal unself-conscious solidarity, a unity decimated by competition and alienation. The ensuing stage of isolation had generated a self-consciousness, nurturing a movement 'both in the individual and society'. Carpenter envisaged that this inner and outer rebellion could enable the impact of man to mount 'deliberately and consciously back again towards the unity which he has lost'.[7] This was a philosophic gamble, infused with the Christian redemption which had featured in *Towards Democracy*. Carpenter was chary however of prescribing the redeemed future, apart from the assurance that it would involve a return to nature and community. The image of the 'chrysalis' returns. 'Man has to undo the wrappings and mummydom of centuries' and be resurrected in 'the light of the sun'.[8] Even Hyndman would have to shed his black frock coat in this socialism of sandals and sun.

The tardiness of the revolution had made Carpenter uneasily aware that humanity could display a curious attachment to the wrappings and shells he regarded as so unnecessary. *Civilisation: Its Cause and Cure* sought to address the hold of custom and common-sense assumptions and suggest how new values could be intimated. 'How can we, gulfed as we are in the present whirlpool, conceive rightly the glory which awaits us?'[9] asked Carpenter, proposing that a break in apprehension could be effected through an historical realisation that capitalism had not always existed and by the desire of human beings for new ways of living. For Carpenter, civilisation's cure rested in a form of consciousness which united thought, understanding, yearning and revelation.

In searching for alternative ways of knowing he drew on a mystical tradition that asserted inner energy against external restrictions; Boehme, Swedenborg and Blake were intriguing him more and more. Mixing mathematical speculations with his mysticism, he was also toying with 'a fourth-dimensional consciousness to whose gaze the interiors of solid bodies are exposed like mere surfaces – a consciousness to whose perception some usual antitheses like cause and effect, matter and spirit, past and future, simply do not exist'.[10] Uncomfortable with Darwinian evolution which he called the 'mechanism-theory of the survival of the fittest',[11] Carpenter transmuted Lamarck's concept of an inner necessity into a desire. In Carpenter's Whitmanite theory of 'exfoliation', 'Desire, or inward change, comes first, action follows, and organisation or outward structure is the result.'¹² Though Carpenter accepted that forms and structures may affect desire, he granted the human spirit the determining role in their shaping. He continued to adhere to this vitalist approach in which the immaterial is the transcendent force all his life.

Carpenter's commitment to inner desire over external form and his urge to reconnect human existence with the natural world led him to imagine an organic architecture for communal use, 'to front the sky and the sea and the sun, to spring out of the earth, companionable with the trees and the rocks, not alien in spirit from the sunlit globe itself or the depth of the starry night'.¹³ The organic integration with nature would prove rather more popular as a basis for architectural design than the association with communality.

An awkwardness left hanging in *Civilisation: Its Cause and Cure*, and indeed in Carpenter's thinking in general, was the relation between the communal union sought by his socialism and those aspects of the 'nature-movement' in art which focused on individual self-expression. While arguing that human realisation was always in relation to others, he was recasting Thomas Carlyle's heroes as catalytic outsiders who tore through Hegel's construct of morality embodied in the state. Society needed anarchical law-breakers, Carpenter had declared in 'Defence of Criminals: A Criticism of Morality', which had been initially published in the February and March 1889 issues of *To-day*.

This was his first sally into criminology and prison reform, topics which would be of lifelong interest to him. Carpenter was able to draw on recent work by the Italian pioneer of criminology, Cesare Lombroso. Lombroso sought to understand instead of simply condemning criminals morally, but his elaborate typologies of criminal brains wired into evil were too deterministic for Carpenter, whose emphasis on criminality as created by society was more akin to Kropotkin's approach. He went a step further; by presenting the 'criminal' as a cultural catalyst, Carpenter was moving towards a celebration of social deviancy. Remarking how Roger Bacon, the thirteenth-century mathematician, philosopher and alchemist, along with the early Christians, and the 'Jew money-lender' in the Middle Ages, were all treated with contempt before becoming respected and powerful, Carpenter proclaimed memorably, 'The Outcast of one age is the Hero of another.'¹⁴

His own sense of sexual alienation contributed to this sympathy with outcasts and made him prepared to question established moral assumptions. Carpenter reminded his readers that in *Phaedrus* Plato presented a white horse and a black horse as images of 'heavenward and earthward' yearnings, without ever suggesting that the black horse be destroyed. Echoing James

Hinton, Carpenter deduced that the fierce, earthy passions were 'half the driving force of the soul', while 'sensuality . . . underlies all art and the high emotions'.[15] He wanted to validate physical desires denigrated by Christianity, and homosexuality peeps gingerly out from the pages of *Civilisation: Its Cause and Cure*, smuggled in under cover of the classics.

The book not only touched on sexual taboos and upset shibboleths of progress, modernisation, law and ethics, it also undermined assumptions about science and indeed the very processes of knowing. Carpenter contested the negative view of health in Western medicine. Instead of a narrow definition of health as the absence of disease, he invoked old words which embraced body, mind and spirit; 'heal, hallow, hale, holy, whole, wholesome', adding the Sanskrit 'atman, breath or soul' for good measure.[16] Making it clear that he was not out to restore 'rib-story' Christianity, Carpenter challenged science's claims to be value-free.[17] He was as interested in mathematics and the physical sciences as he had been when he was young, it was the overweening authority of science he disliked. Carpenter argued that scientific work was framed by the assumptions of particular cultures and epochs and the scientist did not stand outside the object of study in either the physical or the social sciences. Consequently 'science' did not in itself offer proof, and the findings of scientists were always open to question. Insisting that science was not as exact as it appeared, he contested the separation of pure intellect and subjective attitudes as illusory. '"Facts" are at least half feelings.'[18] The purported objectivity concealed implicit values.

Writing at a time when the scientific objectivity of economic laws was being fiercely debated, Carpenter had lunged into the fray with an article entitled 'The Value of the Value Theory' in *To-day* in June 1889. Taking revenge for his January drubbing, Carpenter accused Shaw and Hyndman alike of wielding economic theory like 'blunderbusses'. He asserted:

A theory is necessary to think by – we must have generalisation for daily use; sometimes it is convenient to generalise the facts of exchange on a basis of labour, sometimes on the basis of utility (final or other) sometimes on a basis of custom, and so on. These different aspects of the problem vary in relative importance at different times and places, and according to the facts envisaged; and one theory may involve fewer untenable positions than another, but it is certain that none is, or can be, impregnable.[19]

For Carpenter the process of theorising was dynamic and always approximate, an approach he reiterated in *Civilisation: Its Cause and Cure* and would take into his later work.

In *Civilisation: Its Cause and Cure* Carpenter was, moreover, groping towards a critique of purely intellectual apprehension. He felt the key was the physiological theory he had picked up via Whitman through Dr Bucke; 'Behind the brain and determining its action stands the great sympathetic nerve – the organ of the emotions. In fact here the brain appears as distinctly transitional. It stands between the nerves of sense on the one hand and the great sympathetic.'[20] After reading Havelock Ellis' *The New Spirit* in 1890 he decided it corroborated Bucke's theory about the great sympathetic.[21] Carpenter remained attached to Bucke's view of the sympathetic nerve, in defiance of contemporary physiology, because he saw it as the source of a different kind of perception. In *Civilisation: Its Cause and Cure* he postulates that a kind of knowledge or consciousness constituted the axiomatic ground on which thought structures were built and that this grew even as the brain slept. Open to the idea of there being differing kinds of 'knowing', Carpenter saw consciousness as sensuous and emotional as well as rational. In a reference to Schopenhauer on music, Carpenter remarked that a Beethoven symphony could not be understood by examining the notes alone 'but by *experience* of their relation to deepest feelings'.[22] *Civilisation: Its Cause and Cure* took Carpenter along lines of enquiry with outcomes he could not envisage.

Carpenter's friends divided sharply on the book. John Bruce Glasier, like most socialists, saw external, environmental factors as determining human destiny and believed that the raison d'être for political, social and economic change rested on this perspective. Carpenter countered Glasier's criticisms by asking why creatures responded differently to the same environment. He was convinced that variation was determined 'by something in the creature itself and not mainly in the environment'.[23] Olive Schreiner's objections were more difficult for Carpenter to refute. He, the 'over taught' one, could not imagine the 'joy and peace' that she acquired from being able to exercise her intellect. In Schreiner's view, it was not the intellect and nature that were at war, but the 'personal and impersonal'.[24] Conversely, the Bristol new woman, Helena Born, picked up on the critique of material progress, and was inspired by Carpenter's belief in what she described as 'the Great Spirit of love which animates the universe'.[25] A less reverent Whitman claimed Carpenter's 'Defence of Criminals' was taken from his own philosophy of life.[26]

James Brown, who had been staying at Millthorpe in autumn 1889 when the book was being finished, identified both with Carpenter's recognition of a direct, emotional way of knowing and with the outcast as hero. Teasing Bruce Glasier about his dismissal of Theosophy and his lingering attachment to respectability, Brown told his friend that the new book was the best work Carpenter had ever written.[27] The romantic tailor believed that in the 'New Society' a feeling of Brotherhood would 'overcome all wrong-doing by love'.[28] Brown's personal revolt against convention, along with his friendship with Fred Charles, was leading him towards the anarchists in the Socialist League. This strand of anarchism was pushing Carpenter's questioning of objective reasoning and his praise of outcasts further than Carpenter himself intended and would soon throw Carpenter's own position as a committed intellectual into question. If reality would not stay still and if subjectivity was ever part of what was observed, how could a convincing case be made against the status quo? The anarchists stressed instead the kind of consciousness in motion which arose through action. The next few years were to reveal, often painfully, that this too had its limits.

Arunachalam had not given up his wish to bring Carpenter to Ceylon. By the late 1880s he was in the process of rediscovering the Hinduism his Western education had caused him to reject as a young man. He found a teacher in Ramaswamy, the disciple of a famous guru from a wealthy family, Tilleinathan Swami, who in the 1850s had left a life of privilege to seek enlightenment in the forest, symbolically carrying a despised pariah dog around his neck.[29] Ramaswamy, who had been an adviser to the Maharajah of Tanjore and a scholar of Tamil language and philosophy before becoming an adept, helped Arunachalam to calm the warring 'Western' and 'Eastern' identities within his being. In the outer world Arunachalam acted as a distinguished reforming magistrate, District Judge and administrator, keeping up with Western ideas and politics while adhering to Hindu traditions in his personal life. Indeed on questions of marriage and the position of women he was conservative.[30]

Influenced by the movement for 'authenticity' which was rejecting the rituals which had accrued within Hinduism, and filled with confidence by Ramaswamy, in November 1888 Arunachalam had urged Carpenter to visit Ceylon and 'seek the truth' insisting, 'You of all my friends are most ripe.'[31] Just over a year later, after reading *Towards Democracy*, *Chants of Labour* and *Civilisation: Its Cause and Cure*, Arunachalam again encouraged his friend, carefully expounding the Tamil saiva-siddhanta beliefs of Ramaswamy and stressing the importance of self-understanding.[32] Arunachalam needed his friend from the West to complement his own efforts at holding disparate ways of seeing in tandem and he struggled to explain his religious views to Carpenter at considerable length. Though Carpenter showed little interest in the distinctions between Ramaswamy's Saivite Hinduism and other varieties, more generally Arunachalam acted as an important impetus for Carpenter's interest in Hindu philosophy and his questioning of Western 'civilisation'. He would later acknowledge the great debt he owed to Arunachalam.[33]

The receptiveness Arunachalam sensed in Carpenter had been formed partly by their early friendship, as well as by Carpenter's interest in Neo-Platonism, Schopenhauer and the Transcendentalists. Moreover during the 1880s other Westerners were turning towards the relativism of the Orientalists' religious scholarship or seeking a union of religious enlightenment in Theosophy. In *My Days and Dreams* Carpenter comments, 'I too felt a great desire to see for myself one of these representatives of the ancient wisdom.'[34]

Despite the efforts of A.P. Sinnett to elevate their profile, the Theosophists retained many of the features of a sect, sporadically blighted by bitter internal feuds over who held the truth and embarrassing sexual scandals. The charismatic Mohini Chatterjee, who had so impressed Lowes Dickinson at Cambridge, had to be shipped hastily back to India for 'Don Juanic crimes'.[35] Nonetheless they exerted considerable influence in the West, presenting Eastern religion as an alternative source of spirituality to Christianity. Though Carpenter adopted an arch attitude towards the Theosophists and carefully distanced himself from them in *My Days and Dreams*,[36] he was more affected by them than he would admit and did not disdain to contribute a poem, enigmatically entitled 'Underneath and After All' to their monthly journal *Lucifer*, in May 1890. In this he announced, 'I am the space within the soul, of which space without is but the simultude [*sic*] and mental image.'[37]

The East was in vogue aesthetically as well as philosophically in the late 1880s and early '90s. The Millthorpe sandals, modelled on the pair Cox had sent from Kashmir, were being considered in 1890 as entries in the next Arts and Crafts exhibition. An amused Henry Salt wrote to tell Carpenter that Shaw had shown a sandal catalogue to Lady Colin Campbell, who liked them. He predicted Carpenter would start a new fashion: 'New Bond Street full of sandaled Respectables! You had better take out a patent in time.'[38]

Carpenter's friendship with Harold Cox was another factor which inclined him to look Eastwards. Through Cox he had learned of the modern Muslim identity emerging in India at the Muhammadan Anglo-Oriental College at Aligarh. The college represented a unique synthesis; its founder Sayyid Ahmad Khan sought to draft Western science on to a modernised Islamic theological culture, while its principal Theodore Beck transported Cambridge in the image of F.D. Maurice to India. Carpenter was impressed by what was then a subversive warning in Beck's *Essays on Indian Topics* (1888): the

Empire would collapse unless Indians could meet the British on equal terms in civil society.[39] More personally, a story Cox had told him about two pupils at Aligarh haunted Carpenter; they loved one another so deeply that, when they were parted, one drowned himself and the other flung himself in front of a train. Carpenter had noted down this cameo of tragic love and it continued to play on his imagination.[40]

The English winter of 1890, along with the muddles in his personal life and a sense of political impasse, combined to produce a feeling of restlessness. In a letter to Oates written from the greenhouse at Cox's large family home in Tonbridge, Carpenter announced that he wanted 'to renovate my faith and unfold the frozen buds wh. [sic] civilisation and fog have nipped!'[41] The habit of roaming and a hankering after sun, with him since his youth, were stirring. By the summer he had decided to go to India. He knew he had made a momentous decision. 'What a leap into space!' he exclaimed to James Brown, telling him the idea had been lurking for some time but 'now Arunachalam says I must come'.[42] Of course Arunachalam had been saying this for several years, but in 1890 Carpenter had reached a plateau. He needed the space for inner reflection that India and Ceylon seemed to offer in his imagination.

By coincidence that summer he met a socialist friend of the Fords' at Adel, called Harrison, who Carpenter nicknamed 'Ajax'. He was planning a trip to Ceylon and the two men decided to travel together. Although it was a big step, Carpenter was already a seasoned traveller and, having brothers in the Indian civil service, army and navy, came from a family accustomed to venturing off.[43] The Empire had familiarised the Victorians with travel to far-flung parts, but Carpenter had no intention of going as a member of the British Raj. Early in October he informed Oates that he was looking forward to taking part in 'native life' with the help of Arunachalam.[44] He was heading towards democracy, regardless of Empire, person to person. It was to be his longest journey.

Carpenter sailed off to Colombo, Ceylon in October 1890. He spent his time on the long crossing learning Tamil and befriending a lascar crew member, Kaludesaya (Kalua). Kalua was about twenty-eight and from a Sinhalese peasant family. He had led a varied life, having been a temple devil dancer as a child and later performed for Europeans as well as travelling as a seaman. When he went on deck Carpenter wrapped himself up in the warm shawl Kate Salt had knitted for him. They had recently grown very close. She revered and adored him and was uncritically receptive to his interest in spirituality while he lolled playfully in her admiration, adopting a fond, teasing, brotherly tone in his early letters to her. Carpenter's sister Alice would later notice a striking physical resemblance between Kate Salt and Lizzie.[45] Carpenter had drifted apart from his favourite sister after her marriage to Lord Daubeny and Kate substituted for a time. While he was in Ceylon and India he sent her long accounts of his trip.

He was still wearing his shawl when he reached Arunachalam's home at Kurunegala, a small town fifty miles from Colombo. Arunachalam had been politely exiled there as District Judge after advocating self-government reforms, but to Carpenter the remote spot was delightful. He took walks through the lush green foliage and sunbaths in the woods, telling Oates that after nearly a month with Arunachalam and his 'sweet native wife and three children' he was 'becoming quite native in my ways and habits'.[46] He was greatly impressed by the gentleness Arunachalam and his wife, Svarnam, displayed to the 'little creatures' which surrounded them; lizards, beetles, spiders, centipedes and scorpions were all left to their own devices.[47] He found Arunachalam somewhat stouter but much the same in temperament as in their college days; together the two men pored nostalgically over a faded picture of Oates in an old photograph album. Knowing that Oates would be interested in Kalua, he compared him to Guido in Italy and described him as 'a good looking chap of the peasant class'.[48]

Encouraged by Kate Salt, Carpenter complemented the graphic letters to friends by writing up his journey in *From Adam's Peak to Elephanta*. Produced after his return in 1892, Carpenter's book provided an alternative travel guide to a Raj few visitors from Britain saw. In it Carpenter tells how he visited Kalua's little cabin outside the ancient city of Kandy and describes their travels around Ceylon together. The friendliness of Kalua and his brother reminded him of the Transcendentalist, Herman Melville's account of the peoples of the Marquesas Islands in *Typee* (1846).[49] Carpenter says that Kalua was 'remarkably well-made and active and powerful', adding a little shyly that he looked 'quite handsome'.[50] A photograph in *From Adam's Peak to Elephanta* reveals this to be an understatement; Kalua, who has the bearing of a dancer, holds himself with athletic pride. Indeed, when he and Carpenter climbed up the precipitous 7,341 foot mountain, 'Adam's Peak', which was reputed to bear the footprint of Buddha, the Englishman had to admit himself outdone by Kalua's agility and stamina. Far down below, mist wrapped the lower lying hills, while a white rolling sea stretched out as far as the eye could see and at night it was so cold that even the hardy Carpenter stayed awake shivering, though Kalua slept soundly.[51]

It was hot during the day, and, on hearing that Carpenter had sunbathed on Adam's Peak, an envious Henry Salt sent a humorous verse:

TO EDWARD CARPENTER IN CEYLON

O'er Ceylon's Isle the spicy breezes
Blow soft, while torpid Britain freezes.
Say, Bard of Brotherhood, is't fair?
We shivering here, you basking there?
Is this your 'Towards Democracy'?
Are we your freeborn comrades – we,
Left wandering thus like spirits lost.
In purgatorial fog and frost,
While you sit calm, 'neath summer skies,
On Adam's Peak in Adam's guise.[52]

While marvelling at Kalua's 'savage strength and *insouciance*', as they floated in a boat lazily down the River Kalu Ganga, Carpenter could recognise that Ceylon had its less idyllic aspects – the tough-looking priests who collected a toll from pilgrims on Adam's Peak and the Tamil immigrant workers labouring in grim conditions on a tea plantation.[53] Nonetheless, he contrasted the people's closeness to the 'sun and air' with the enervated Europeans, ridiculous in their inappropriate clothes.[54]

He was particularly fascinated by a Hindu festival at Taypusam on the first full moon of January 1891, where he witnessed a procession of 'hundreds of men and boys, bare-bodied, barehead and barefoot, but with white loin-cloths all in a state of great excitement'. With trumpets and horns blasting, it was not like any religious ceremony he knew from Christianity, being more of a spectacle and carrying the anticipation he associated with 'the commencement of a theatrical performance'.[55] Carpenter realised he was observing a form of communal celebration which was quite new and strange to him. Like many Westerners intrigued by the East, he saw an absence of piety and guilt about the body; sexual energy seemed to charge spiritual ecstasy. When they arrived in the temple, Carpenter noticed a relief of the god Siva at a shrine – 'the perpetual dance of creation'. In the distance he could just see the sacred lingam surrounded by lamps. He had come across phallic shaped versions of the lingam in the outer courts of temples, but he knew the lingam in the inner sanctum would be an egg-shaped, blue-veined white stone.

Thus the worship of sex is found to lie at the root of the present Hinduism, as it does at the root of nearly all the primitive religions of the world. Yet it would be a mistake to conclude that such worship is a mere deification of material functions. Whenever it may have been

Kalua

that the Vedic prophets descending from Northern lands into India first discovered within themselves that capacity of spiritual ecstasy which has made them even down till to-day one of the great religious forces in the world, it is certain that they found (as indeed many of the mediaeval Christian seers at a later time also found) that their ecstasy had a certain similarity to the sexual rapture.[56]

Carpenter was careful not to reduce the religious meaning of the lingam to sex, instead he conceptualises it as comparable to sex. His speculation was that the Vedic prophets gave the rude phallic worship of primitive times a new meaning, through which sex became not simply earthly joy but was brought into 'relation to the one supreme and heavenly fact, that of the soul's union with God'.[57] The lingam signified the dilemma of how to reconcile sex and spirit which troubled him all his life.

While staying with Arunachalam he spent many hours with Ramaswamy, who Carpenter calls the Gnani, because he practised a contemplative 'jnana' yoga. The imposing seventy-year-old, dressed in 'a white muslin wrapper wound loosely round his lithe . . . active dark brown form', expounded prophetically on how to attain 'consciousness without thought', while they walked with Arunachalam along the country roads or up on Elephant Hill above the town.[58] Carpenter sat at Ramaswamy's feet in a little bungalow where snakes and rats hissed and scuttled in the ceiling.[59] Though he had learned some Tamil, he needed Arunachalam to translate the teacher's sayings, but the 'expression of *illumination*' communicated something beyond words; Ramaswamy seemed suffused by a mystic joy.[60] While Carpenter had read about Hinduism, contact with the Gnani brought a direct connection with an oral tradition of ancient knowledge and another dimension of understanding.

In a letter to Walt Whitman from Kurunegala in December 1890, Carpenter related how he had met Arunachalam's 'Guru or Teacher' and discovered that those who attained union with 'the universal consciousness' cast off external hierarchies, 'so that one finds here behind the outer religion of the people a hidden few who are perfectly democratic and whose watchwords are Freedom, Equality and Joy'.[61] In *From Adam's Peak to Elephanta*, Carpenter suggests a correspondence between Eastern and Western religions. At several points in the book he alludes to a tradition from the Eastern sages to Pythagoras, Plato, Paul, the Gnostics and the medieval alchemists and German mystics. Similarities do exist; the Gnostics were indeed preoccupied with withdrawal and the inner soul and there was a persistent interaction between cultures; however the details of historical transmission remain hazy. While Carpenter concedes that ideas may have arisen spontaneously, this idea of a hidden tradition crossing over from the East, clearly interests him. Occult quests for an underground knowledge of the inner mysteries of being flourished in the late nineteenth century. He was unusual however in wanting this lineage of a consciousness beyond thought to be democratic rather than remaining esoteric in an elitist way. He conceived it as a 'kind of tacit understanding and free masonry' a counter-knowledge held by a few but potentially there for everyone.[62]

The significance of his sessions with the Gnani was not simply spiritual but psychological. In the letter to Walt Whitman from Arunachalam's home, Carpenter compared the process of meditation to 'the suppression of Thought' in Leaves of Grass and remarked how it made it possible to attain mastery to use thought, or not, as you wished.[63] He had come to realise that reason alone was not sufficient in quietening emotions, yet his background had drilled into him the merits of self-possession. He came away from Gnani Ramaswamy with a most powerful insight which related to the crisis he had undergone over Hukin in the summer of 1887, when it had seemed as if he was about to lose his psychological balance. In From Adam's Peak to Elephanta, he reflected on how in the West people were dominating nature through technology and science while neglecting mastery over their inner thoughts and feelings. As a consequence Carpenter could see how 'moderns' like himself were apt to be 'prey to the bat-winged phantoms' that 'flit through the corridors' of their own brains.[64] Aware of hypnosis and ideas of 'a secondary consciousness' which were currently being discussed by early psychologists,[65] Carpenter was also familiar with Schopenhauer's theory that conscious thoughts merely skimmed along the surface of the mind. The Gnani indicated a method of entering another consciousness and securing peace.

After meeting Arunachalam's religious teacher, Carpenter would feel able to pronounce on the suppression of thought and the space within the soul as one who had been there. And, despite his desire for a democratic hidden tradition, he displayed a hint of that competitiveness over authenticity common among seekers after enlightenment. The Theosophists were doing good work, he remarked to Kate Salt in November 1890, 'although their teaching was of a somewhat second hand character'.[66] On the other hand, regardless of his admiration for the culture of Ceylon and for the Gnani's teaching, Carpenter could not swallow it all uncritically. In From Adam's Peak to Elephanta he observed how the absorption with the inner self left no place for an outgoing love of one's fellows.[67] The gentle submission of the people also troubled him; he wrote to Kate Salt: 'one feels that a dash of the Western materialism will be good for them'.[68] As an intellectual, too, he could see the evident disadvantage of knowledge handed down by tradition; it denied the importance of scepticism. While Arunachalam struggled with his 'Eastern' and 'Western' selves, Carpenter the Westerner, who wanted so much to be open to the 'East' of his imagining, left Ceylon puzzling how to tuck sex, love, inner will and reason into the 'space within'.

Leaving Colombo at the end of January, Carpenter took the steamer to India. He had read the learned James Fergusson on the history of Indian architecture and followed his guide around temples in South India.[69] He also dropped by to visit the Theosophists at their base in Adyar and had to admire their villa with its 'roomy lecture-hall and library',[70] set in woods by a river about half a mile from the sea. Annie Besant, already moving towards Theosophy, would settle in India in 1893 and often spoke in this imposing lecture-hall. Theosophists like Besant were going over similar ground to Carpenter in their efforts to draw on spiritual insights from Eastern religion, while espousing movements of resistance. Nevertheless, though Besant praised his work, Carpenter remained guarded about the group.

As Carpenter traversed the vastness of India, to Calcutta, then Allahabad where he met Indian Civil Service friends of his brother Charles, followed by Delhi, Aligarh, Agra and Bombay (Mumbai) he became aware that India was not the homogenous entity he had imagined from tiny Britain far away. Writing to Kate Salt from Agra on February 22, 1891, he exclaimed, 'Nations races languages creeds customs and manners are whirling in my brain. I just realise what an immense place India is.'[71]

Carpenter made a special detour to see Theodore Beck at the Anglo-Oriental College at Aligarh, noting how the equality in personal relations Beck had initiated contrasted with the customary aloofness of the colonisers. Acknowledging the courage and scholarship of Sir Sayyid Ahmed, Carpenter was uneasy with what he felt was his contempt for the Hindus.[72] Nonetheless, the college included Hindus as well as Muslims, and Carpenter made friends with one of the Hindu teachers, Bhagavan Das, a social reformer who respected folk culture and expressed interest in *England's Ideal* and *Civilisation: Its Cause and Cure*.[73] At Agra University College too, he met an impressive group of intellectuals, among them the Professor of Mathematics, A.C. Bose, who had been reading W.K. Clifford's *The Common-Sense of the Exact Sciences* and wanted to talk about crumpled space and the fourth dimension. They all wanted to send their sons to study in England and were anxious about what kind of reception they would have. An embarrassed Carpenter said they must not think ill of the English because of the unfortunate gulf between the races in India.[74]

Uncomfortable in the colonial India of tidy villas and imperial architecture, he sought out post office clerks and railway workers, hung around with tumblers, tightrope walkers and opium sellers, as well as canvassing factory workers' views. He had to admit to Alf Mattison that it was difficult to imagine socialism making headway.[75] Still, looking at the items of Sheffield cutlery and shoddy Lancashire cotton goods scattered around by international trade, he dreamed of a direct person-to-person workers' internationalism through which his British working-class friends, toiling amidst the dust and the cold, could come out 'to enjoy the glorious sunshine and fraternise with . . . the despised darkie!'[76] In fact a trades union movement was soon to begin in both India and Ceylon, which would result in a more formal kind of workers' internationalism.

Carpenter learned from the educated professionals he met how offensive the British Raj was to them. He sympathised politically with the Nationalists, agreeing that the Raj would have to concede more political power or withdraw, otherwise violence would ensue, even though it was still hard to conceive of India without the British. Carpenter particularly abhorred the grotesque personal alienation of imperialism.[77] In Ceylon a solicitor called Monerasingha related how the English behaved normally when they first arrived, but after a few months imbibed the values of the Raj and refused to acknowledge educated men like himself.[78]

A contradiction which troubled Carpenter was one shared by Nationalists and social reformers. Modernisation and industrialisation seemed the only way out of the subjection and poverty of the mass of the people, yet these very processes would destroy the spirituality and communality he valued. The dilemma was compounded because, despite his friendship with Arunachalam, Carpenter brought to Ceylon and India his own yearnings for the savage and the natural as opposed to the distorting complexities of civilisation. Part of him had frozen the sub-continent into the Hegelian dream-state, which supposedly preceded the awakening of reason and self-conscious subjectivity, and therefore he had great difficulty in assimilating the contrary evidence he encountered on his travels. He kept sidelining signs of capitalist graft and dismissed the interest Indian intellectuals evinced in the moderniser, John Stuart Mill. Moreover, holding on to his fixed ideal, and dazed by the beauty of so many brown male bodies, he could not subjectively comprehend Arunachalam's painful sense of division or Kalua's discontent with his cabin after glimpsing Europe. Carpenter's myth of the East remained unitary, even though the Ceylon and India he delineated in From Adam's Peak to Elephanta were differentiated and contradictory societies. Theoretically he was prepared to argue that the British Raj had sown the seeds of its own destruction in the idea of 'modern democracy'. But he could not follow the implications through in his own personal apprehension.

Carpenter winced at the behaviour of his own class and wrote ironically of the lower-class 'Tommy Atkins' sitting lordly in a two-wheeled gig being pulled along by 'the toiling "nigger"'.[79] He uses the pejorative 'nigger' in inverted commas, as a term used by the British, but he himself refers to 'darkies'. Arunachalam, well aware of the blind spots in even the enlightened Western gaze, 'chaffed' him for referring to everyone in Ceylon as 'natives' without recognising that they were Tamils, Muhammadan or Cingalese. Arunachalam remarked that it was 'as if we were so many *oysters*'. Carpenter resented this amiable correction, reverting to blustery public school humour with 'Ajax' – 'There was nothing for it after that but to call them all oysters.'[80] Yet something registered, for he recorded this awkward jolt in their friendship in *From Adam's Peak to Elephanta*.

Carpenter exoticised Kalua in his book. He is not quite a person but a type who possesses the 'soft giraffe-like eyes of the Cingalese, and the gentle somewhat diffident manner which they affect'.[81] Kalua is represented as 'masculine' in his strength, 'feminine' in his softness. Overtly ascribing 'femininity' to a man was for Carpenter not derogatory; indeed in an early manuscript draft of *My Days and Dreams* he wondered, 'Was I really a woman born in some inner unknown region of my nature?'[82] However, implicitly, his relationship to femininity was ambiguous, because it was culturally enmeshed in subordination. Interestingly the 'feminine' characteristics allotted to Kalua resemble those ascribed to Max Flint, the Jew. In both cases Carpenter takes for granted his power to be their definer.

In *From Adam's Peak to Elephanta*, Carpenter chronicled some unsavoury physical traits among the lower castes, but the people he most despised were those busy making money or rising socially. In Ceylon he deplored the 'chetties' with 'Avarice in their faces', and in India, the Brahmins, who he characterised as having 'sharp eyes, rather close together, and a thin aquiline nose'.[83] Carpenter's assumption that physiognomy denotes character was common in this period, but odd from one so opposed to determinism. In fact the snobbery of the upper-class Cambridge man folds into his racial categories, and he never queried his own tacit presumption that the lower classes and subordinated races were to be defended when vulnerable and abject, but trounced with contempt when they sought individual advancement.

Carpenter's particular mix of left politics, anti-Western philosophy and sexual empathy did take him to an unusual cultural place. He did reject many conventional assumptions that prevailed in the British Raj, and he did break out of accepted forms of behaving and take quite startling new turnings. But casting off Western superiority had many more levels than he envisaged, and suddenly his perceptions would clog. Carpenter wanted to become 'a native', without conceding the power to decree what a suitable 'native' should be like.

Carpenter's journey had begun at Adam's Peak, an apt symbol of the juxtaposition of faiths. Buddha's footprint on the mountain could be Adam's to the Muslims, Jesus' to the Christians and that of the creator-destroyer, Siva, to the Hindus. Carpenter met Siva again in a temple carved from the rock of Elephanta Island off the coast of Bombay. Elephanta was the metaphorical end piece in his quest for the 'real' India. Yet he recoiled from the dualistic Siva with male genitals and female breasts. The statue appeared to him as a 'monstrosity'. He could accept androgyny as a psychological concept, but was revolted by the physical representation of this hybrid God, 'with its left side projecting into a huge breast and hip'.[84] The extraordinary ambivalence of gender in the statue did not intrigue him at all. Instead his response was akin to the disgust he had felt at seeing the female nudes in the French exhibition in 1887. Acceptable femininity consisted of lithe young men and supportive, tom-boyish sister figures.

Back in Sheffield Carpenter lectured on the 'Social Movement in India' at the Hall of Science in October 1891. He commented on caste in relation to trade guilds and praised the strength of family and communal loyalties, before considering the impact of Western education, scientific ideas, materialism and commercialism. He explained to his Sheffield audience how the Nationalist Congress Movement had been consolidating since 1885, mentioning their attempts to gain representation on municipal councils, which he knew would strike a chord among his working-class listeners.[85] Carpenter made no reference to the Theosophists or to the movement for women's emancipation in India. He also maintained a discreet silence on the Gnani and Siva, though he did discuss his spiritual experiences with working-class friends, for George Hukin and James Brown were arguing fiercely about Mahatmas in October 1891, while a circumspect Fannie simply thanked Carpenter for his present of tea.[86]

In *From Adam's Peak to Elephanta*, however, he was more daring, and its publication in 1892 ruffled the Empire's press. Bhagavan Das, to whom Carpenter had sent the Fellowship of the New Life's journal, *Seed-Time*, posted him the review from the *Pioneer* early in 1893.[87] The influential Anglo-Indian paper, which had ejected the Theosophist Sinnett from its editorship for unsound views, was particularly rattled about the 'Cingalese solicitor' who criticised the British for being unfriendly. Poor Monerasingha was warned sternly that he would be far worse off under the brutal Russians. As for the socialist Carpenter, he should understand that the

English had not come to India to 'Orientalise' or study philosophy, 'but to rule the country on sound and civilised principles'.[88] The *Times of India* labelled Carpenter 'An Original Globe-Trotter' and adopted a tone of condescending humour, before dismissing his lack of knowledge.[89]

Carpenter had collected a strange piece of information after he returned, when a District Sessions Judge, C.E. Crawford, who had read *England's Ideal* and *Civilisation: Its Cause and Cure*, wrote from Thana, Bombay, to tell him about the 'Fellowship of the Naked Trust', a group of Britishers who believed nudity was good for the health, opposing 'false shame' and the 'morbid curiosity' it aroused about the body. Crawford was careful to explain that at these nude social gatherings they were careful to avoid any discussion of politics.[90] The image of the Raj with no clothes appealed to Carpenter's sense of mischief. His revelation of this secret nudist colony among the British disturbed *The Athenaeum*, which spluttered that the reader could judge the value of the kind of author who would disclose such a thing as a guide 'through the Eastern labyrinth'.[91] In contrast the *Tribune* in New York, no doubt remembering the Americans' own revolution against colonisation, enthused about *From Adam's Peak to Elephanta*.[92]

The reviewer in *Lucifer*, the Theosophists' journal, commended Carpenter's 'friendly intercourse with all classes of the native population'. However his encroachment into the zone of Eastern spirituality, which the Theosophists considered they had exclusively staked out, brought the gloves off. Readers were informed that Carpenter's account of the spiritual teaching of the Gnani contained nothing that would be new to Theosophists and warned that *From Adam's Peak to Elephanta* was marred by crucial mistakes about the stages of enlightenment.[93] This was the Theosophist equivalent of being accused by the S.D.F. and the Fabians of misleading 'the ignorant Philistines'.

Carpenter was recovering from a political tornado by the time these reviews appeared in 1893. For, while he had been contemplating the oneness of being and scouting around for the 'real India', Siva had decided to drop into Sheffield. Creation–destruction arrived in the person of a small fiery Irish anarchist called John Creaghe; from the moment he materialised, the Sheffield Socialists were destined to go up in smoke.

9

Utopian Mutations

John Creaghe appeared in Sheffield in the autumn of 1890, just after Carpenter had left for Ceylon. Creaghe, a 'sixpenny doctor' who practised among the poor, was inspired by the Italian anarchist Errico Malatesta, whose faith in direct action made Kropotkin look like a determinist. Creaghe interpreted Malatesta's ideas bluntly; he believed that deeds spoke louder than words and thrived on action and controversy. He was resolved to shake Sheffield up.

On November 15th William Morris broke with the anarchists, reflecting sadly in *Commonweal*: 'Men absorbed in a movement are apt to surround themselves with a kind of artificial atmosphere which distorts the proportions of things outside, and prevents them from seeing what is really going on.'[1] It was in part self-criticism, but Morris was also fingering the militant anarchism of men like Creaghe. Predictably, the confrontational Creaghe was not bashful in responding. He claimed to have read Morris' words 'with a shiver', accusing him, calumny of calumnies, of 'Fabian' tendencies.[2]

Through the winter of 1890–91 a disconsolate George Hukin penned gloomy accounts of the anarchists in Sheffield to the travelling, abstracted Carpenter. 'I have not been down to the club much lately, don't feel I can get on with the set one finds there now.' There was too much talk of 'blood and vengeance' for the realistic Hukin, who was convinced it could only lead to trouble.[3] In January 1891 he wrote to Carpenter in India, worried because James Brown, who had moved down to the area, was staying over at Fred Charles' far too often and not sleeping until 3 or 4 in the morning. His health was deteriorating as a result of this roistering. Hukin also remarked how, despite himself, Charles had a way of putting everyone in the Socialist Club at loggerheads.[4] By the end of January the anarchists had split from the Club; Hukin heard they had a new banner with the motto 'No God, No Master', and were going to hold separate meetings at the Monolith.[5] Not content with propaganda and banner-making, that March, Creaghe started a 'No Rent strike' – all on his own – at the dispensary where he treated the poor. The local newspapers bristled with the story of how he had assaulted a bailiff and a police constable with a poker. Hukin carefully cut the reports out for Carpenter and posted them off to India.

When Carpenter returned to Sheffield in April, James Brown proudly showed him Creaghe's leaflet advising criminals not to abandon their present mode of life for that of the wretched wage slave. Bruce Glasier, already angry about Creaghe's attack on his mentor Morris, had been appalled by it, telling Brown he was considering a rival addressed to 'Baby Farmers, Brothel Keepers and Wife Beaters'.[6] A smug Brown was able to inform Bruce Glasier that Carpenter had agreed with the Manifesto addressed to Sheffield's criminals.[7] Indeed how could the author of the 'Defence of Criminals' do otherwise? In appealing to the outcast and in emphasising inner volition the anarchists were in consonance with Carpenter. He also shared their rebellion against the 'respectables' and their distrust of the state. However, whereas Carpenter sought a broad consensus and was accomplished in the mild-sounding presentation of startling opinions, Creaghe was the opposite. Nuance was equivalent to apostasy; for Creaghe, everything was clear-cut.

The small band of anarchists hurtled through that summer and autumn in a flurry of defiance. In June, when the idolised explorer Henry Morton Stanley came to speak in Sheffield, Creaghe and John Bingham took gallery seats and sold a pamphlet by the anarchist editor of *Commonweal*, David Nicoll, documenting the Africans Stanley had killed in the course of his explorations. *Commonweal* frankly announced how *Stanley's Exploits, or, Civilising Africa* had 'sold like hot cakes' because the audience, not seeing the irony in the title, had believed it to be praising the explorer. But when Creaghe and Bingham tried hissing the hero of the hour, the crowd howled them down.[8] Undaunted, the anarchists busied themselves with 'No Rent' meetings, boldly telling their audiences that they should refuse to pay rent and learn the noble art of self-defence – 'that is the use of bombs'.[9] *Commonweal* faithfully chronicled this inflammatory propaganda.

The propaganda efforts became increasingly turbulent. Early in September *Commonweal* indignantly reported that 'A lot of counter-jumpers [clerks] police spies and boys encouraged by middle-class cowards', had attacked Cyril Bell, a London medical student in the anarchist ranks. The hostile crowd had sung such 'bosh' as 'Hi-tiddly-hi-ti' and 'The Bogy Man'. Whereupon the 'Bogy Men' had defended themselves by hurling copies of *Commonweal* and *Freedom* at their audience. With a certain inconsistency, given the anarchists' theory of the state, *Commonweal* was outraged that the police had laughed and egged on their opponents. Eventually Creaghe had come to the rescue with a 'detachment' of the 'boys'.[10]

Outdoor propaganda was complemented by the publication of the *Sheffield Anarchist* by Creaghe, Charles, Bell and a French man, Auguste Coulon, who had gained respect in anarchist circles for his work at the school run by Louise Michel, the refugee survivor of the Paris commune of 1871. The *Sheffield Anarchist* revelled in all forms of direct action, including poaching on the Duke of Devonshire's estate. It was defiantly anti-respectable, calling on unmarried mothers and prostitutes to join the movement and enthusiastically endorsing free love.[11] The anarchists took the emphasis on consciousness and human agency common on the libertarian left to extremes; according to Cyril Bell the revolution was subjective: 'We do not look forward to a revolt in the future but from the moment we become anarchists.'[12] Consciousness, however, could only take you so far. By November the anarchists could no longer pay for the *Sheffield Anarchist* to be printed and Creaghe decided to relocate to Liverpool.

Creaghe's parting shot was a blistering letter in *Commonweal* on November 28th, accusing Carpenter of being half-hearted in support of the anarchists' propaganda and hobnobbing with Fabians and trades unionists. 'For my part, I do not understand such people, and to the devil pitch them be they ever so literary and artistic.'[13] This open declaration of war aroused the spirit of grandfather, Admiral Carpenter, and on November 29th, Carpenter, who was on a speaking tour, informed Alf Mattison that he was going to give it to Creaghe in next week's *Commonweal*.[14] The result was designed to infuriate Creaghe.

> Certainly comrade Creaghe, I stick up for Fabians and Trade Unions just as much as I do for the Anarchists. I have never disavowed the Anarchists. What can be more obvious? We are all travelling along the same road. Why should we be snarling at each other's heads? . . . I take it we all have our work to do in our time. For goodness sake let us do it without so much jaw.[15]

Creaghe loathed Carpenter's confident English upper-middle-class tone with its easy assumption of the high ground. 'With what an air of the superior person he dismisses my jaw', he spluttered in reply, incensed against 'this man', in his 'comfortable retirement', who had undermined the efforts of the 'comrades in Sheffield, Sunday after Sunday struggling with the apathy of their hearers'.[16] Creaghe was not simply making Carpenter the scapegoat for the anarchists' failure, the Irishman wanted to destroy Carpenter's credibility with anarchist supporters who remained friendly with him – James Brown, Jim Shortland, and the Leicester hosiery workers' leader Tom Barclay, who leapt to Carpenter and Morris' defence in *Commonweal*.[17]

Political differences as well as personal animosity were behind the conflict. As socialists and anarchists polarised over the difficult question of the state during the early 1890s, Carpenter was trying to keep open a middle ground for people who could accept some role for the state while viewing centralisation askance. Creaghe sneered at this ambiguity, declaring that Carpenter and his socialist cronies wanted to build the state on 'wider and firmer' foundations making 'freedom . . . impossible', rather than recognising, like the anarchists, that the aim had to be the destruction of the state.[18] Moreover, having convinced themselves that revolution was just around the corner, the anarchists in Sheffield saw themselves as igniting the conflagration simply by being individuals of greater will than their fellows. As Creaghe put it, he was acting of his own volition, not for the sake of working men who did not desire the 'Revolution nearly as much as men like himself'.[19] Creaghe, the extreme proponent of democracy, had turned full circle; the professional revolutionary, being desire incarnate, knew best and thus need not waste time considering the view of others.

Even as they were arguing, the state, in the shape of a stout, moustachioed police inspector called William Melville, was prowling around Walsall railway station checking on the comings and goings of anarchists. Melville, who spoke French and Italian, specialised in anarchists and was well versed in European police tactics. He had Auguste Coulon in his pay and when Fred Charles returned to Walsall, Coulon had drawn him, along with several members of the Walsall Socialist Club – including its secretary, Joe Deakin, a French stoker, Victor Cailes and an Italian shoemaker, Jean Battola – into a 'plot' to make bombs, supposedly to defend revolutionaries in Russia. Before the police picked them up early in January, Coulon melted mysteriously away. The police produced a sketch of a bomb and a statement found at Fred Charles' lodgings in Cailes' handwriting recommending attacks on various public and religious buildings in Britain. According to the editor of *Commonweal*, David Nicoll, Cailes had copied it for discussion at a meeting.[20] If this was the case it was insouciance indeed, for the anarchists knew that they were being followed. There was, however, no evidence against the other men, until the police tricked Deakin into a confession.[21]

Carpenter was dismayed by the fiasco of the foiled bomb plot, observing in a letter to Bruce Glasier that if the manifesto really was by Cailes he must be crazy. He suspected that the police may have had a hand in it, but fell back on a general indictment of capitalism. 'After all the point is that "society" by its damnabilities drives people to such extremities – makes the scourge for its own back – its crimes begetting the hatred wh. avenges them.'[22] Carpenter told Bruce Glasier he was going down to visit Charles and find out what his plans were for a defence. The London anarchists around *Commonweal* started a defence fund organised by David Nicoll. It was agreed in Sheffield that Robert Bingham and Carpenter would collect money, and their efforts were publicised through the anarchist-communist paper, *Freedom*, edited by Kropotkin and Charlotte Wilson. However Nicoll, contemptuous of the *Freedom* group, refused to merge the two funds, causing confusion among the frail network of supporters. Glasier wrote anxiously to Carpenter as the remnants of the Glasgow Socialist League, one of the last branches to hold together, wrangled about which fund should receive the money they had collected. Carpenter responded by sending a summary of his Defence Fund's accounts.[23]

Some S.D.F. branches, members of the Sheffield Socialists and friends of Carpenter's such as Henry Salt contributed to the defence fund, but the accused men were dangerously isolated, for even those who personally sympathised with their predicament deplored bomb-making. Bruce Glasier thought the anarchists had lost 'all perception of the actual living wall of millions of hostile people that surrounds them', telling James Brown, 'Recent events have destroyed my hope in Revolutionary action in this country.'[24] Carpenter too had had private doubts about the 'Revolution'; nonetheless, when he testified on behalf of Fred Charles' good character, he stated in court that he was himself an anarchist. The defence hastily persuaded him to submit a written statement explaining that he did not agree with violence or believe that it was integral to anarchism. But in the atmosphere of panic such niceties hardly mattered.

Conflict dogged the trial. Carpenter appointed a solicitor friend from the Bristol socialist group, Hugh Holmes Gore, whom Nicoll regarded as far too conciliatory. Gore did not agree with the radical barrister W.M. Thompson's attempts to reveal in court that Coulon was in police pay. The arrest of the Walsall anarchists coincided with harsh repression towards anarchist violence in France and Spain and the British state was in no mood for liberality. The judge at the Stafford Assizes, whose nickname was 'Hangman' Hawkins, sentenced Charles, Cailes and Battola to ten years' penal servitude and Deakin, who had provided information to the police, to five years.

The severity of these sentences transmitted the message of fear that the authorities intended. 'Anarchists' became in the public imagination murderous foreign bombers slipping from country to country to spread havoc and destruction, and the anti-immigration lobby were able to conflate anarchists with foreign refugees. *The Times* declared that anarchists endangered not only all governments but society itself. *The Saturday Review* smeared Carpenter, the 'Theoretical Anarchist', as the harbinger of the bomb plot.[25] It was not the most comfortable time to declare yourself an anarchist. Yet Carpenter not only lined up with the anarchists during the trial, he supported the imprisoned men by raising money and campaigning for their release. He kept in touch with Fred Charles over the years and made sure that the two foreign prisoners were not forgotten. But his relationship with the *Commonweal* support group, and especially with David Nicoll, was never easy. One painful repercussion of the 'Bomb Plot' was the hostility of James Brown. In March 1892, Brown told Bruce Glasier that a complete estrangement between Carpenter and himself was inevitable because Carpenter had refused to offer bail for Fred Charles, and had sidelined Robert Bingham by taking over the Sheffield defence fund with Gore. Brown was confused; bail had already been put forward for Charles, so Carpenter had paid up for the despised Deakin.[26] Carpenter ran his fund with mathematical precision and he no doubt considered it better that Robert Bingham, who now had a police record, should stay in the background when he made appeals outside anarchist circles.

After the men had been convicted, disagreement erupted over the basis on which an appeal might be made. Nicoll continued to blame the defence for not revealing police provocation sufficiently. Carpenter tried to explain himself in November 1892 in *Freedom*, asserting that while the sentences were barbarous and the real criminal was society, a viable appeal could not be made on the grounds that none of the accused had ever contemplated violence. There was just too much evidence to the contrary – police plots or no police plots.[27]

Walsall marked the beginning of the end for the *Commonweal* phase of insurrectionary anarchism in Britain. The police, prodded by their European counterparts, and encouraged by the anarchists' growing isolation, harried them throughout the 1890s. Several other arrests followed the Walsall trial and the anarchists, caught in a web of paranoia, began to vilify one another. Carpenter ignored the animosity and concentrated on the predicament of the imprisoned men, who were carefully equable in their thanks to all wings of their support network. In 1895 the radical newspaper *Reynolds News* printed the memoir of an ex-Detective Sergeant McIntyre who claimed he had been forced out of the police because he was regarded as too soft on the anarchists. After this appeared, hopes revived that the

Walsall verdict might be reconsidered. Carpenter, along with Morris, was part of an attempt to build a broad coalition which drew in socialists of various persuasions and reached out towards liberals. In Sheffield Carpenter managed to cobble together an alliance that included the radical Sheffield M.P., H.J. Wilson, and the volatile David Nicoll, who had moved up north. However, in 1895 the Tory Unionists had replaced the Liberals in power, and in 1896 the Home Secretary rejected the appeal. When Carpenter visited a depressed Fred Charles in November that year the prison authorities were making it difficult for him to get books. 'Starvation of the mind', Carpenter told the socialist Fred Henderson, adding that Charles had resorted to studying Greek grammar.[28]

Charles, Cailes and Battola were not released until 1899. By this time an insurgent anarchism had turned into a distant memory, yet Carpenter was still badgering friends for money to help the freed prisoners. Isabella Ford, beset by numerous appeals protested, 'Forgive this grumble, but it is a little inconvenient all this continued impunity.'[29] She paid up nonetheless to his fund, as he knew she surely would. Carpenter's bonds of friendship were confirmed by the support he received from Isabella Ford, the Salts, Oates, Unwin and Muirhead. They gave money because of comradeship, not because of ideological agreement.

The irrepressible Creaghe transported the Sheffield anarchists' ideas across the ocean to Argentina, where they sprouted on more fertile ground. He helped to found the militant Argentinean Federation of Workers (FORA), which grew into a mass union. Creaghe's hostility towards Carpenter mellowed over time. A Spanish *Defensa de los Criminales* by Edward Carpenter was published in Buenos Aires in 1901. A copy was sent to Carpenter in 1903, addressed 'to the distinguished author and companero' (replaced with the word 'comrade') 'by his old acquaintance and admirer John Creaghe and present Editor of "La Protesta Humana".'[30]

The personal comradeship Carpenter valued above all else did hold fast regardless of the acrimony arising from the thwarted bomb plot. He was reconciled with the ailing Brown who had not long to live, for Bright's disease was taking its toll on his kidneys and heart. In Brown's last days, during the spring of 1893, Carpenter, George Hukin and George Adams took turns by his bedside, along with Jim Shortland, who had become his closest friend. As Brown lay dying, Bruce Glasier warned Carpenter that he might find hostile references in Brown's papers as a result of 'the counsel of some of our more impetuous friends.'[31] Carpenter reassured Bruce Glasier that he would not be offended, for Brown had described being 'possessed' by his illness.[32] After Brown died in April 1893 Carpenter produced a little book of the Scottish tailor's verses mentioning his socialism

Carpenter in his 'very anarchist overcoat'.
Portrait by Roger Fry, 1894

and anarchism along with his interest in secularism and Theosophy.[33] Both Bruce Glasier and Carpenter knew that Brown's death signalled a closure. The Scottish poet's romantic plebeian radicalism had flowed through the Socialist League into anarchism, but then the politics of infinite possibility had run into the unyielding ground of reality. Those who were left stranded had no choice but to search for alternative paths.

Roger Fry painted a portrait of Carpenter in 1894 in an urban aesthetic setting. It now hangs in the National Portrait Gallery and shows a hand-some, bearded man standing in a bare room in which one low chair is reflected in a large mirror. His town shoes are highly polished and his clothes beautifully cut. Fry told his mother with delight that he had painted Carpenter with 'a very anarchist overcoat on'.[34] The overcoat is long, black and elegant; its upturned collar that of an upper-crust bohemian, not a down-and-out conspirator. Overlapping theoretical affinities and personal empathy attracted Carpenter towards anarchism, yet eggs in one basket were never his style and the negative repercussions of Walsall made him acutely aware of the dangers of isolation. The early 1890s saw him propelled in apparently contrary directions.

Carpenter now had an established lecturing circuit, speaking not only in Sheffield, Rotherham and Chesterfield, but extending outwards to West Yorkshire and Lancashire, along with Nottingham and Derby. He was also frequently in Bristol and London and did tours of Scotland. Completely eclectic in accepting invitations, in 1893, he addressed the Social Demo-cratic Federation in London, as well as the Fabians and the Liberal club in Sheffield. Not only did he range widely, he could gather huge crowds of around a thousand people to some of these meetings. Carpenter continued his University Extension habit of having a basic stash of lectures which he recycled in differing places. In the first half of the 1890s these were: 'The Future Society'; 'Parties in the Labor Movement'; 'The Way Out'; 'The Changed Ideal of Society'; 'The Future of Labor'. Insisting that the 'ideal' of an anarchist spontaneous free society was also the aim of 'nearly all Socts. [sic]', he invoked Dr Bucke and Melville's *Typee* as suggestions of what this might be. Carpenter really grappled in these lectures with how to *reach* the utopian future, searching for an alternative to both the state and the self-defeating defiance of the anarchists who, he noted 'Tear their hair at one'.[35] Along with a proposal of a transitional period of collective socialism, en route to spontaneous freedom, Carpenter focused on the process of change, arguing for a combination of methods, including the formation of links between working-class institutions such as trades unions and co-operative societies. Like the new unionist leader, Tom

Mann, Carpenter was thinking in terms of a *labour movement* comprising diverse kinds of working-class organisations and socialist groupings. It was a dynamic perception which kept the way open for differing political outlooks and approaches.

After the collapse of the Socialist League, some working-class northern socialists, including Tom Maguire, had turned towards the Fabians and provincial groups began to spring up. Carpenter toyed with the same idea, announcing to Mattison in July 1892 that along with Hukin and Unwin, he intended to 'hunt up' the Sheffield Fabians.[36] However a completely new national party demanding 'labour' representation was in the making. Over the course of 1892 and the early months of 1893 new groups were sprouting ad hoc, indeed Carpenter's efforts helped to bring some of these into being. Yet the mood remained undecided; when Carpenter spoke in Chesterfield in October 1892, he had encouraged those at the meeting to link up with the Independent Labour Party, but instead they decided to call themselves a 'Labour Association'.[37] While with hindsight these diffuse local initiatives appear as part of the historic formation of the I.L.P., to contemporaries everything seemed more confused.

The core of the new Party was indubitably in West Yorkshire. Maguire wrote to Carpenter in November, a little bashful about his association with reformism, but nevertheless daring once again to hope for a new beginning. The new Independent Labour Party had, he believed, 'caught the people as I imagine the Chartist movement did'.[38] He urged Carpenter to come and see for himself. Early that December Carpenter recounted to the Bolton socialist who shared his enthusiasm for Whitman, James William Wallace, how the 'labor movement' in Halifax and Bradford was 'going on gorgeously'.[39] The I.L.P. emerged amidst an impulse towards a wider-reaching socialism. Shortly after its founding conference in 1893, Carpenter observed that in coming late the I.L.P. had the advantage of drawing on a variety of ideas and urged it to 'keep broad'.[40] It was always the *movement* rather than the Party itself that he cherished. All those years of fissile sects with their inviolable certainties had bred in Carpenter, and in many other socialists, a yearning for a broad labour movement connected by a shared mentality rather than by strict doctrine.

Far away in Ceylon, Arunachalam was following the fortunes of the new 'Labour Party'.[41] Several of Carpenter's friends and acquaintances gravitated towards the I.L.P. Isabella Ford, impressed by the West Yorkshire I.L.P.'s commitment to women's emancipation, joined after a tea party in the Colne Valley where the *men* 'poured out the tea, cut the bread and butter, and washed everything up'.[42] She, along with Alf Mattison and the Bolton Whitmanite, Wallace, became stalwart supporters, while Enid Stacy and Katharine St John Conway from Bristol emerged as star I.L.P. speakers. A disillusioned Bruce Glasier discarded his bohemian anarchist dreams of revolution and morphed into an I.L.P. national figure. Tom Mann, having left the S.D.F., became the national secretary of the I.L.P., while the Bristol librarian who had been involved in the Fellowship of the New Life and the Fabians, Ramsay Macdonald, eventually rose to be leader of the Party. From the start the I.L.P. displayed an extraordinary range of radical political strands and a marked degree of regional variegation. The ethos of spiritual aspiration and personal fellowship in which Carpenter felt at home in West Yorkshire or Bolton contrasted with the real politick at the centre of the organisation. Alongside the ex-Socialist League dreamers, the I.L.P. attracted clumps of experienced trades unionists, accustomed to jockeying for position and prepared to negotiate with the Liberals. In Sheffield, the hard-headed trades unionists led by the file-cutter, Stuart Uttley, who had given evidence alongside Hukin on sweating, were preponderant. Accordingly Carpenter's relationship with his local I.L.P. was quite different from his engagement with the Socialist Society. He remained a semi-detached sympathiser who spoke at meetings and graced social occasions such as I.L.P. dances.

Carpenter was more comfortable amidst the non-aligned organisations that appeared alongside or flourished on the periphery of the I.L.P. One of the most successful meetings on Carpenter's Scottish tour of 1892 had been hosted by the 'Labour Army', a campaigning body created by a former member of the Salvation Army, Frank Smith.[43] Carpenter also spoke frequently under the auspices of the Labour Church, an organisation formed in 1891 by John Trevor in Manchester. Dissatisfied with the rational liberalism of Unitarian Christianity, Trevor was attracted to the enthusiasm of evangelical Christianity while opposed to its narrowness. He was searching for a Christianity in which a working-class ethos could prevail, when he met an anarchist-inclined Socialist Leaguer called William Bailie in Upper Brook Street, who persuaded him that a socialist equivalent to the Salvation Army was needed.[44] By 1892 Trevor was editing the Labour Church's journal, *The Labour Prophet*, which propagated an ideological melange of Ruskin, Whitman, Carpenter and Mazzini. It bore a quote from Mazzini on its masthead, 'Let Labour be the Basis of Civil Society', a slogan Carpenter could happily endorse.[45] *The Labour Prophet*'s broad take on socialism could embrace municipal elections, William Morris, Walt Whitman and Fred Charles. Despite being closely bound up with the I.L.P., it also worked alongside the S.D.F., the Fabians and the lively new socialist paper, the *Clarion*, edited by the Manchester journalist, Robert Blatchford. Both papers provided Carpenter with welcome non-aligned outlets in the early 1890s.

Propelled outwards by the schisms and feuds, Carpenter took up the cause of the railway workers, claiming that their long hours of work contributed to accidents.[46] He also supported the Derbyshire and South Yorkshire miners, including his friends at Barlow, who, kept on short time with reduced wages and then locked out, rose in rebellion against the colliery owners' autocracy. Miners, declared Carpenter, should regulate their own hours and prices, and, when Monkwood Colliery was closed in 1893, his name was on the relief fund appeal.[47] Eschewing sectarian purity, Carpenter supported diverse wings of the movement. On March 7, 1892, he was speaking with the dockers' leader Ben Tillett and Isabella Ford to an audience a thousand strong in Rawdon in West Yorkshire. He greeted the victory of the radical Progressive municipal alliance which saw the election of the Fabian, Sidney Webb, and Fred Charles' friend Fred Henderson to the London County Council, exclaiming in excitement to Hukin, 'Oh my! is the British lion really awakening?'[48] Lecturing on 'The Way Out', in Sheffield, Chesterfield, Leeds, Healey, Bradford, Rochdale and Derby during 1893 and 1894, Carpenter referred to the days when the Social Democrats, Hyndman, Morris, Joynes and the rest had been 'Voices Crying in the Wilderness' at street corners. The 'mustard seed' they had planted had made it possible to look ahead to the practical recasting of socialism.[49]

Nonetheless he did not want to abandon the transformatory vision of the emancipation of body and spirit which had inspired *Towards Democracy*. Writing in *The Labour Prophet* in 1894 on how he had created his long prose poem, Carpenter stated that he had '*felt* that this region of Self existing in me existed equally (though not always equally *consciously*) in others. In regard to it the mere diversities of temperament which ordinarily distinguish and divide people dropped away and became indifferent, and a field was opened in which all might meet, in which all were truly Equal.'[50] Carpenter's adherence to socialism and anarchism alike sprang from this inward perception; it was always more real to him than external political definitions, sustaining him through all the squabbles. When Alf Mattison was upset about the movement in Leeds in January 1893, Carpenter wrote saying, 'Public life and all its lies and slanders is very odious – I always dread it myself.'[51] He was not alone. During the early 1890s the egalitarian mysticism which had been the impulse behind *Towards Democracy* struck a profound chord among the growing numbers joining the labour movement. The I.L.P., *Clarion* and the Labour Church movement were attracting a new generation of upper-working-class and lower-middle-class spiritual searchers. In moving away from the established Christian churches, they still articulated their socialism in quasi-religious terms. Moreover they wanted not only economic changes but new kinds of human relationships in society and personal life. These aspirations made them receptive to some of the dreams of the 1880s, and, consequently a transformative politics was grafted onto their struggles for everyday reforms. Utopia had mutated, albeit with a less grandiose sweep than in the previous decade. If a sense of loss accompanied the demise of the Socialist League, the early 1890s was a period of encouraging expansion too.

Dreaming democracy was one thing, practising it proved more tricky. Carpenter made a sudden dive into the mechanics of inter-party democracy in an article in the *Clarion* in 1894. Among the I.L.P.'s successful municipal candidates was the upper-class socialist from Halifax, John Lister, a friend of the Fords and Alf Mattison. When Lister was accused of working too closely with the Liberals, a row broke out over the degree to which socialist organisations should exert control over elected representatives. The Fabian Webbs had come out in opposition to the strict mandatory policy of some trades unions towards their delegates on the grounds of inefficiency. Carpenter disagreed with what he called the 'dancing doll' theory of democracy for a different reason; he thought it denied the individual any rights of conscience. Characteristically he also believed the personal character of the delegate was the key to democracy rather than strict monitoring.[52] The editor of *Clarion*, Robert Blatchford, took an opposing position, defending the delegate system in terms of the democratic rights of the rank and file.

These disputes occurred in the context of a wide-ranging debate about forms of democracy on the left. *Clarion* was mounting a strong critique of the Fabians' advocacy of representative democracy, posing direct democratic participation through the referendum as a preferable alternative to the election of political parties to Parliament. Characteristically, Carpenter equivocated, 'I do not say that the *Referendum* is not a good idea.' He was reluctant however to give up on the existing representative democratic framework and convinced that while elective bodies existed, 'our men must take their heads with them and not be decapitated before they go'.[53]

Carpenter pronounced on the need for tolerance to Blatchford and the readers of the *Clarion*; they must cultivate 'larger hearts' and recognise they were all working on the same building, even if they busied themselves on different parts. 'Don't go and kick the hodman's ladder down because you individually are not going to use the bricks which he is bringing up.'[54] John Lister took up the cudgels on January 5th, in defence of individual conscience, but Carpenter, who preferred to present himself as the benign mediator floating above sectarianism, backed off from the scrum.[55]

The London County Council victory and the success of socialists in local elections raised hopes about the democratic potential of local government. Accordingly, when the Local Government Act established parish councils in 1894, Carpenter and George Adams, who had moved to Millthorpe, put themselves forward as candidates in Holmesfield. This caused a flurry of controversy in the neighbourhood and they were accused of working on the Sabbath, advocating the burning of the Bible, as well as proposing to raise the rates. The two socialist candidates were not successful, though Carpenter would later be elected. From 1894 Carpenter enthusiastically advocated participation in 'parish councils' in his lectures. He had high hopes they would enable divergent views and interests in the countryside to be expressed, not just those of the Anglican Church and the landlord, but the chapels, the secularists, farmers, agricultural labourers and industrial workers like the miners. He had not forgotten his strictures against big landlords, such as the Duke of Rutland, and imagined that the parish councils might be a means of appealing against their rents and that they might be able to restore common rights to land and contribute towards a self-sufficient social economy in rural areas by hiring out allotments for growing food.[56]

Sidney Webb also considered the establishment of parish councils significant, and in 1893 the Fabians published a tract 'Parish and District Councils' full of brass tacks about 'What they are and what they can do', which Carpenter made use of in his lectures.[57] During the summer and autumn of 1894 the Webbs decamped to Borough Farm, near Godalming in Surrey, to investigate attitudes in the countryside. While Sidney dispensed advice to village radicals on election tactics, a more cynical Beatrice opined that rural democracy was a dead duck.[58] Carpenter regarded rural life more favourably and was inclined to idealise the parish council as a kind of Russian village 'mir' of communal democracy, but he came down with a bump when he actually served on the Council in Holmesfield. The farmers were terrified of their landlords, while the parson, 'bound by golden chains to the Lord of the Manor', snoozed through the interminable meetings, which deliberated ponderously on how to avoid spending any money whatsoever. Carpenter's one achievement was saving the Award Book which recorded the enclosure of the common lands of Holmesfield. It took him a year to persuade the parish council to have a chest made to secure it. In *My Days and Dreams*, he wondered whether he should 'have fought things out a little more, but wrangling is an occupation which I detest, and to fight questions to a practical finish always means the expenditure of much time – time I could ill afford'.[59] Duty might lead him towards taking a practical role but he was in essence an ideas man. This contact with local government convinced him, yet again, that outer institutional forms mattered less than culture and consciousness.

Carpenter was always happier with issue-based politics and there were no end of issues to be agitated around in the 1890s. His friend Henry Salt provided him with a new umbrella organisation for them in the shape of the Humanitarian League in 1891. The remit of this new grouping was ethical and 'progressive' rather than overtly political. It ranged from arms control and international arbitration to the establishment of public hospitals; from animal rights to the humanising of the Poor Law and the Criminal Justice system. Its focus was on humane values and rights in civil society rather than on state power or industrial conflict, and it could reach out to involve 'New Lifers' and the dissident spiritual groupings of the Theosophists and Esoteric Christians around Edward Maitland, as well as secular 'progressives' and socialists, including the Ford sisters, Bernard Shaw and Harold Cox's brother-in-law, Sydney Olivier, whose aesthetic and spiritual interests made him one of Carpenter's favoured Fabians. Carpenter's brother Alfred married Cox's sister, and, when he retired as a Captain from the Royal Navy in 1895, also joined the Humanitarian League.

When Salt had first proposed setting up the organisation Carpenter worried that the Salts were too unworldly to run a League, being, as he put it to Oates, 'quiet simple people'.[60] But Salt demonstrated redoubtable skills as a committee man and, as he presided over an eccentric collection of supporters, some of whom were excessively egotistical, these proved vital. Most trying was the mystical, anti-vivisectionist Edward Maitland. In February 1892 the long-suffering Salt grumbled to Carpenter that Maitland had gossiped so much about the 'esoteric Christ' it had been impossible to get through the business until Salt, in the chair, had considered 'invoking the services of the esoteric Pontius Pilate'.[61]

Though Carpenter also found Maitland opinioned, he collaborated on a Humanitarian League pamphlet with him against vivisection in 1893.[62] Pressure from the formidable anti-vivisectionist lobby had secured the Cruelty to Animals Act in 1876 which regulated vivisection. However it could be evaded by obtaining certificates from the Home Office, and anti-vivisectionist campaigners wanted to get rid of these loop holes. For Carpenter vivisection was a prime example of scientists abrogating ethical responsibility under the cloak of scientific necessity. He expanded on the theme of animal rights in the *Clarion* in 1894, insisting that it was 'Labour's' duty 'to defend the dumb animals and creatures weaker than itself against the horrible exploitation of so-called Science'.[63] Carpenter acted as a conduit between the ethical radicalism of the Humanitarian League and working-class socialists, sending Salt's rabbit-coursing pamphlets to Alf Mattison, when he was in the thick of union organising in May 1892, with a request to put one in the Free Library.[64]

In the first half of the 1890s contradictory approaches jostled on the left. The gains made in municipal elections inclined both the I.L.P. and the S.D.F. to stick to safe issues and avoid any outbreaks of utopian eccentricity. But utopianism continued to surface. After speaking for the S.D.F. in London in 1893, on 'How to Make a Living on the Land', Carpenter cheerily remarked to Alf Mattison, 'it is remarkable . . . how many people are wanting to escape from town life'.[65] Poor Hyndman would surely have been gnashing his teeth at the thought of his members hiking off to a myriad 'Crankie Farms'. Operating alongside the explicitly political structures and interacting with them, the Fellowship of the New Life and the Humanitarian League contrived to transplant patches of the utopianism of the 1880s into daily life and civil society. The growing strata of middle-class progressives who clustered around the two groupings were creating a culture in which it was becoming possible to be dissident, odd and yet semi-respectable. Carpenter's *Towards Democracy*, and his lifestyle politics, were gaining a new crop of adherents. As one of them, W.J. Jupp, put it in the Fellowship of the New Life journal, *Seed-Time*, Carpenter was 'absolutely free from the fetters of conventionality'.[66]

Carpenter might well have settled into this amiable humanitarian niche as the epitome of the gentlemanly rebel. He never did. One reason was his abhorrence of being bagged by any particular grouping, even if the Humanitarian League was a kind of organisational home from home for him. Another problem was that while he staunchly supported humanitarian causes, he found some humanitarians terrible bores. Salt was horrified on one occasion when he spotted Carpenter feigning deafness in order to avoid a conversation with a woman member.[67] Carpenter, the spokesman for the outcast and the horned god, was edgy in the company of the worthy and the good. Just as he had slipped oblique references to homosexuality into *Civilisation: Its Cause and Cure* and *From Adam's Peak to Elephanta*, 'the Body' and the bonds of love kept popping into his lectures during the early 1890s. A chance encounter on a train in the Spring of

1891, shortly after returning from India, had galvanised a sexual exuberance. This had carried him through all the political confusion, recriminations and trials, and empowered him to break the repressive silence imposed on his erotic feelings. In the early 1890s Carpenter made a brave decision to write about sex, including same-sex love.

10

Homogenic Love

Carpenter first spotted George Merrill on the Totley train with a group of young men 'chatting and chafing' among themselves. Two decades later, Carpenter retained a visual memory of his lover standing out amidst 'the perky conventionality' of his companions because of his 'somewhat free style of dress'. A photograph of Merrill taken shortly after they met shows a skinny, attractive man in a floppy jacket, one hand in the pocket of loose trousers, the other through Carpenter's arm, with one of his braces peeping out and a cap perched cockily on his head. Merrill sported Sheffield street fashion with innovative style, yet beneath the flash Carpenter detected a 'look of wistful sadness'. Carpenter's redeemer urges made him susceptible to wistfulness and it would be Merrill's trump. 'We exchanged a few words and a look of recognition.'[1]

Carpenter's habit of looking was ingrained. He loved to be the observer, detached from the accoutrements of any fixed status and identity. In *Towards Democracy* he had roamed in imagination between geographical vistas and the human condition, while on the actual journey relayed in *From Adam's Peak to Elephanta*, he had been in transit. Belonging neither to the Raj, nor to the vast sub-continent of India, he had been able to scrutinise freely. As the probing one, searching out and catching some inner undisclosed truth in those he surveyed, his eye for human character and behaviour produced his most graphic writing. In everyday life he scanned too for beauty – especially a male beauty that could be invested with that quality of transcendence he had seen in the faces of the two Italians on his fateful journey over the Alps in 1887 to join Olive Schreiner in Paris. Trains, like Whitman's trams, promised an arousing random anonymity – an in-between, dynamic space where conventions rooted in fixed places and specific times might be suspended.

When the train arrived at Totley station on that day in the spring of 1891 a group of people who were visiting Carpenter streamed out of the other carriage to join him on the platform. That could have been it – the eyes clinching, a dash of danger and the young man moving away from the clutch of recognition back into the anonymity of the crowd – if George Merrill had not acted with an accomplished decisiveness. Leaving his friends he got off the train and followed Carpenter and his walking companions. Carpenter strode on in the direction of Millthorpe, acutely aware of the desirable young man with his 'appealing look' shadowing him. When, after about a mile, with 'a little manoeuvring', Carpenter contrived to fall back so they could speak, Merrill told him he had seen him in Sheffield and noticed his absence that winter. In a 'state of tension and eagerness', Merrill wanted Carpenter 'to stop and let the others go on, to return with him towards Sheffield and so forth'. Carpenter was too gentlemanly, too dutiful and too circumspect to desert his guests, even for 'and so forth', but despite the surprising and disorientating circumstances, he retained a sufficiently meticulous presence of mind to secure the ardent young man's name and address before parting from him.[2]

The encounter with Merrill marked the beginning of a relationship which altered the pattern of Carpenter's hopeless loves for men whose sexual desires were ambiguous. For once Carpenter was the pursued not the pursuer; Merrill was in no doubt of his interest in men. Here, however, the similarity stopped, for this was an attraction between two men who were utterly different. Not only was there a large gap in their ages, Merrill's upbringing contrasted dramatically with Carpenter's childhood. He had grown up in the slums of Sheffield in a family of eight boys and one girl. His father was an alcoholic and his mother took over as the mainstay of the family. Carpenter depicted her as 'a big racy-tongued, good-hearted woman with stout voice and leg of mutton arms', who alternated between chastising her large brood with the clothes line and 'convulsing them with laughter at her witticisms'.[3] Mrs Merrill's approach to child rearing was the antithesis of the inner rectitude Carpenter had acquired from his mother's stern, undemonstrative Protestantism.

Merrill had drifted from job to job since he was thirteen; working in the public baths, fetching and carrying in a moulder's workshop, taking the horse and cart out for file-grinders, serving in a pub. A similar randomness characterised his sexual encounters with men. Carpenter's account of his lover's life gives a fascinating glimpse of the sexual interconnections between classes which could exist in the interstices of late Victorian society. Merrill had left Sheffield to work in a boys' Catholic school until his priest friend had to leave because of 'undue familiarities'[4] with the pupils. Whereupon he fell in with a commercial traveller with whom he toured. As Merrill moved about the country he attracted the attention of several aristocratic men who gave him presents which he sent home to be pawned by his father for drink. One of these men was in the entourage of Prince Edward on a visit to York and confided to Merrill how he disliked the 'shooting and cards' and longed for 'some real love and attraction', presenting him with grapes – a luxury that could not be pawned.[5]

So, despite his youth, Merrill had steered through social polarities and knew that allure was no respecter of class boundaries. Carpenter describes him as 'at ease and quite himself in any society, aristocratic or vagabond', and delighted in Merrill's lack of guilt about 'the seamy side of life'.[6] Merrill was utterly oblivious to Christianity; on hearing that Jesus had spent his last night at Gethsemane, his response was 'who with?'[7] He was equally unfamiliar with Carpenter's intellectual and cultural world. He liked dirty jokes, swore profusely, had known 'coarse experiences' and possessed 'a strong sexuality of temperament and habit'.[8] Merrill's noble-savage credentials were thus impeccable. With Merrill, Carpenter at last could enjoy angst-free pleasure. Carpenter took another pied-à-terre in Sheffield, at 56 Glover Road, and the two men stayed there or accompanied one another on long walks over the moors.

Through those fraught and busy years of the early 1890s, the splits and

Racy-looking Merrill with Carpenter

denunciations, the abandoned dreams and new movements, Carpenter
was sustained by this sexually sure young lover, and when the third part
of *Towards Democracy* was published in 1892, among the additions were
poems of passion and, at last, of fulfilment:

> O Thou whose form is ever in my heart,
> O flesh that holds me rent with terrible force,
> Dear limbs and lips that seize upon my life
> And in your fire consume it . . .[9]

In 'Love's Vision', Carpenter wrote:

> At night in each other's arms,
> Content, overjoyed, resting deep deep down in the darkness . . .[10]

And in 'All Night Long':

> All night long in love, in the darkness, passing through your lips, my
>   love –
> Breathing the same breath, being folded in the same sleep, losing
> sense of Me and Thee . . .[11]

The rush of sexual energy which accompanied the early years of Carpenter's
relationship with Merrill was not exclusive, spilling over into differing kinds
of vaguely amative friendships with other young men. Carpenter's attachment
to Shortland continued; he was frequently at Millthorpe during the 1890s,
signing himself 'Thy Love Jim'[12] and sending affectionate kisses when work
prevented him from being at Carpenter's birthday in 1896.[13] Then there
was Carpenter's intense friendship with Alf Mattison, who was among the
favoured few invited to Glover Road. In 1892, when the Hukins were
going on holiday to Morecambe, Carpenter proposed taking a room in a
separate house there and told Mattison, 'you cd. come and stay with me'.[14]
When George Adams wanted Mattison and Tom Maguire to visit Millthorpe
while Carpenter was going to be away he sighed that he felt 'rather jealous'.[15]
If Shortland was all sturdy masculinity, with the intellectual Mattison
Carpenter could assume the tutelary, protective role he enjoyed with a
subdued flirtatious banter. Throughout the 1890s, Carpenter read Mattison's
writing, consoled him when he was unemployed and sent regular postal
orders and books to support the young militant when he was victimised.
The loving, ambiguous comradeship with Carpenter helped Mattison to
blossom into a writer, historian and photographer.

Nor did Merrill replace the other George. While Carpenter's love for George Hukin mellowed into a resigned affection, the special intimacy between them persisted. Apologising in August 1894 for forgetting Carpenter's fiftieth birthday, Hukin assured him, 'I don't forget you dear Ted, and birthdays or no birthdays makes no difference.'[16] The following year, Carpenter wrote from Oates' home in Leeds, 'I think of you dear boy and feel that strange inner feeling of nearness to you wh. I always feel – so I doubt if you'll ever be able to shake me off.'[17] Carpenter's indissoluble love for Hukin co-existed with the entry of George Merrill into his life.

In the summer of 1892, both Georges, like Eros and Psyche, were taken to meet the Whitmanite, James William Wallace, and his friend, Dr John Johnston, when they travelled over to Sheffield by train from Bolton. Both men were professionals; Wallace was from a working-class background, but had moved up the social scale by becoming an assistant to an architect, while Johnston was a G.P. However their enthusiasm for Whitman had set them apart from other members of the Bolton middle class and the two men had created their own intense conviviality through the fellowship of the Eagle Street 'College', a band of like-minded male friends which included several artisans and clerks and eventually some advanced women. Inveterate networkers and international in outlook, Wallace and Johnston had first met Carpenter in 1891, when he had accompanied Dr Bucke on a visit to Bolton.

When Whitman died in spring 1892, the demonstrative Bucke exclaimed to Wallace, 'We have buried the Christ.'[18] The Bolton Whitmanites, being Northern Britishers, were rather more restrained, but they too had a strong propensity for hero-worship and were unselfconscious about exposing themselves to hostile ridicule. During 1892 letters flew to and fro across the Atlantic, with Carpenter urging patience and caution about publishing material by or on Whitman. When Wallace and Johnston decided to visit Millthorpe, Carpenter tried to tease them out of reverence by joking about Bucke who was 'blazing away like a runaway comet with Paul, Mahomet, W.W. and a host of others in his train' in a book on 'cosmic consciousness'. Fearful of being treated as one of the cosmics, Carpenter, tried to shuffle off the spiritual pedestal; 'I verily fear your advent, lest finding me out as only the goose that I am you slay me and discover not even a golden egg within.' Practically and tactfully he enquired, 'Do you and Johnston like to sleep together, or shall I arrange for you to have separate rooms?'[19]

Despite his efforts to be low key, the visit was a momentous one for Wallace. Adopting Traubel's fly-on-the wall style, he chronicled how Carpenter arrived at the station to meet them with Merrill, who Wallace found 'simple, natural and gentle' – all esteemed masculine qualities among the Bolton Whitmanites. After Merrill left for his job at a newspaper printing works, they were joined by Hukin. Though Wallace approved of Hukin's unaffected manner, he was puzzled by the razor-grinder's reserve; the shy Hukin was no doubt uncomfortable at being so closely examined. The wispy youth photographed in the late 1880s had clearly filled out as a result of Fannie's cooking; Wallace put him in his mid thirties, guessed him to be 5 foot 6 inches tall, and noted that he was 'fairly stout with florid round good natured face moustache and chin beard and longish curly hair. Dressed in blue serge with loose jacket, soft hat, woollen shirt and collar attached'.[20]

Carpenter found in the Bolton Whitmanites political soul mates who combined spiritual enthusiasm with open-minded tolerance, affirming: 'He was more of an Anarchist than anything else as regards government. But, one could not rest in abstractions. To descend into the practical arena it was necessary to work with people whose opinions differ from one's own.[21] The closeness in terms of outlook was strengthened because, among this sympathetic group of comrades, Carpenter encountered a young man called Charles Sixsmith, known as 'Charlie', who became one of his best friends. Their first contact was brief and formal, over tea at Dr Johnston's in the winter of 1892, when Sixsmith recalled that Carpenter spoke about John Addington Symonds. A chance to get to know one another better came in the spring of 1894 when Carpenter returned to speak for the Bolton Labour Church. Before the meeting they relaxed by walking on the Rivington Hills outside Bolton, and Sixsmith recalled how Carpenter seized hold of him and playfully pulled him down a bank, then walked arm in arm with him, talking about his fruit trees at Millthorpe. At the meeting Sixsmith listened in awe to Carpenter's talk on how modern industrialism was killing all joy in labour and beauty in daily life and was delighted when Carpenter came up to him later, 'had a sham box after which he caught hold of me and we went downstairs and stood at the door together'. Sixsmith, in true Bolton Whitmanite fashion, saw this as the great man revealing 'how sociable, comradely and natural he was'.[22] The following day, Sixsmith met Carpenter in Manchester at the Labour Press, the left-wing publishing group in which Carpenter had invested money, and the young devotee pressed him to produce a pocket edition of *Towards Democracy* which could be carried on walks in the Rivington Hills.

Sixsmith was nineteen and just starting off in the lower echelons of business at Bentincke's mill. Like Mattison a few years earlier, the young man felt flattered to be singled out and delighted in the easy familiarity which banished any feelings of inferiority. 'You feel inclined to get hold of him as boy would his mate',[23] wrote the young Sixsmith in 1894. Carpenter was clearly attracted to him too, inviting him to Millthorpe and telling Wallace how much he had enjoyed his visit and how glad he had been to 'chat with Charlie Sixsmith at M/c [sic]'.[24] Sixsmith, who became one of Carpenter's dearest comrades, rose to be a manager and then a director in the textile industry and an important local figure in the town's socialist movement. Many years later he remembered how impressed he had been as a youth by Carpenter's 'handsome appearance – his erect, lithe body, trim-bearded face, penetrating eyes and beautiful voice'.[25]

Leaves of Grass and Towards Democracy together shaped the Bolton Whitmanites' socialism. Carpenter enabled them to translate Whitman, who they celebrated faithfully with lilac and loving cup, into a comradeship of daily life, a loving fellowship without affectation, infused with spiritual yearning, in which relating was spontaneous, natural, boundless. For Carpenter this new link with like-minded comrades, and particularly his pleasure in Sixsmith's company, renewed and confirmed his belief that transforming society must include nature, the body and sexuality.

Among the Bolton Whitmanites' correspondents was the homosexual writer J.A. Symonds, who had outraged Whitman in 1890 when he tried to persuade the poet to make his feelings towards men explicit and oppose the laws against sex between men. In August 1890, Symonds remarked to the editor Ernest Rhys how he would like to meet Carpenter. He wanted to confer on the 'passion between people of the same sex' that appeared in Whitman's Calamus collection.[26] Despite the similarities between Carpenter and Symonds in their age, background and sexual attraction to working-class men, their paths had not crossed. Carpenter was more aware than the erotically effusive Symonds how difficult it would be for Whitman to make his feelings towards men explicit in the context of American society, where any discussion of homosexuality was even more taboo than in Britain. But after meeting Merrill, Carpenter too was seeking a more outright way of expressing male–male love than was possible under Whitman's cloak of comradeship, and J.A. Symonds would act as the decisive stimulus for Carpenter's work Homogenic Love.

It was Havelock Ellis who was responsible for Carpenter and Symonds making contact, writing to Symonds about Greek love in modern life in July 1891. 'I am not sure that I should completely agree with you, but the question is one that constantly forces itself on one's attention.'[27] 'The question' may have been pressing itself on Ellis in particular, because when he wrote this letter he was on holiday with his new love, Edith Lees. A tiny woman with tight curls and intense blue eyes, Lees was the secretary of the Fellowship of the New Life and had lived in the Fellowship commune in Bloomsbury, along with Ramsay MacDonald, who was already nursing grand political ambitions. Disillusioned with communal experimenting, Edith Lees had agreed to marry Ellis, even though she had never fancied a man apart from an oblivious Percival Chubb. As she believed in absolute sincerity and honesty, it is likely Ellis was aware that July of her sexual feelings. They married, nonetheless, in December 1891.

When Ellis' friend Arthur Symons informed him that J.A. Symonds was thinking of writing a book on sexual inversion, Ellis pricked up his ears, for, after being married to Edith for several months, he had been considering exactly the same idea. When Symonds wrote to enquire whether his proposed work could be included in the Contemporary Science Series Ellis was editing, Ellis replied by warning him that the topic might contain difficulties but that he was hoping to discuss the plan when Symonds was next in London.[28] The literary, romantic Symonds wanted to bring the forbidden topic of male–male love out into the open and get rid of the Labouchere amendment, which he described to Ellis as 'Labby's inexpansible legislation'.[29] In contrast Ellis, trained in medical science and intrigued by the new concept of criminal anthropology, took the stance of the expert. Yet, like Symonds, he too had a personal investment in writing on 'inversion' because of his new wife Edith, whose sexuality he sought to understand, and conceivably hoped to turn around.

Over the course of 1892 Symonds and Carpenter were also bonding through letters and sending one another books. Carpenter dispatched *Towards Democracy* and received Symonds' *In the Key of Blue*. Early in 1893, Symonds read *From Adam's Peak to Elephanta* with his wife, and wrote enthusiastically to Carpenter. Around this time the two men met briefly in Brighton, where Carpenter caught a tantalising glimpse of Symonds' gondolier lover, the dazzling Angel Fusato, on an omnibus.[30] Symonds related to Dr Johnston the Bolton Whitmanite how he wished he could have spent more time with Carpenter, who might have a reputation for being 'faddy', but whose personality was so compelling, a few fads hardly mattered.[31]

Meanwhile Ellis and Symonds had agreed to collaborate. In December 1892 Ellis informed Carpenter they were embarking on a project on 'sexual inversion – including the Greek form of psychic abnormality and that felt and advocated by Whitman'. He asked if Carpenter would send him some case notes. Ellis explained how he had been drawn to the topic by the realisation that it was widespread and treated with outrageous severity under British law. He hoped that the result would be a 'sympathetic recognition for sexual inversion as a psychic abnormality which may be regarded as the highest ideal, and to clear away many vulgar errors – preparing the way if possible for a change in the law'.[32] Next came a letter from Symonds in Davos saying he was glad Ellis had told Carpenter of their plan for a joint work. 'I never saw him. But I like his way of corresponding on this subject. And I need somebody of medical importance to collaborate with. Alone, I would make but little effect – the effect of an eccentric.' He believed they agreed on fundamental points. 'The only difference is that he is too much inclined to stick to the neuropathical theory of explanation. But I am whittling that away to a minimum.'[33]

However Symonds had no sooner agreed to work with Ellis when he became uneasy about his colleague's approach. He opposed Ellis' use of the term 'psychic abnormality', causing Ellis to assure him it was a neutral medical category comparable to 'colour blindness' or 'colour hearing' (synaesthesia).[34] All too aware of the power of punitive definitions, Symonds was not convinced. He wrote to Carpenter suggesting that he might send his case notes directly to himself in Davos.[35] Carpenter was thus caught rather uncomfortably between his old friend and New Life ally, Ellis, and his new friend Symonds, with whom he was more in sympathy. The case notes duly went both to Davos and to Ellis.

Though Symonds was committed to the distanced 'scientific' approach as a channel through which homosexual relations could be calmly considered, he fretted under the restrictions imposed by such a framework. He expressed Romantic ideals to Carpenter of a 'new chivalry' which would see the birth of an 'elevated form of human love'.[36] In a letter of January 21, 1893, he explained that he saw cross-class relations between men as a means of cutting through social distinctions. Symonds told Carpenter he believed that if 'acknowledged and extended', these new forms of personal relationships could further 'the right sort of Socialism'.[37]

Symonds, who stayed with aristocratic acquaintances on visits to Britain, viewed socialism through a somewhat long-distance lens. Nonetheless his admiration of Whitman and his own feelings for working-class men drew him towards the personal democracy which was so crucial to Carpenter's own socialist commitment. Unlike Carpenter, Symonds imagined that such friendships in themselves dissolved class distinctions. While being blithely ignorant about how the class system was experienced from its lower rungs, Symonds did struggle to understand Fusato's differing take on intimacy between men which, being outside the conventional male–female moral arena, was simply a matter between a man's soul and God. Ellis was intrigued by Symonds' experiences and by Carpenter's discovery of physical sex between working-class men who were not exclusively attracted to men.[38]

Symonds found reading the contemporary writers on sex that Ellis diligently perused a chore, though he was impressed by the pioneering Karl Ulrichs, a German lawyer who had argued in the 1860s that desire for the same sex was in-born. Arguing that masculinity and femininity should be regarded as a continuum, Ulrichs had pioneered the method of the case study in an attempt to classify sexual variations and had invented the term 'Urning' for those who were attracted to members of their own sex. Symonds had sought him out in Italy in 1891, describing to Carpenter how he had discovered Ulrichs living in extreme poverty and how the resplendent Fusato had been bewildered by his veneration for the ragged old man.[39]

The triangular correspondence between Carpenter, Ellis and Symonds during 1892 and 1893 documents a concentrated exchange of ideas. While Carpenter and Ellis could communicate about the latest sexual theories, Carpenter found in Symonds a fellow spirit he could trust with the most intimate of questions. In December 1892 he wondered whether Symonds thought that the absorption of semen modified the physique of the person who absorbs it.[40] Symonds was not sure but wrote a month later to ask if Carpenter had been reading Silvio Venturi's *La Degenerazioni Psico-Sexuali*. Symonds considered it a 'tedious and stupid book' but added that Venturi had injected his patients with semen and found it good for their nerves.[41] Carpenter's odd notion was in accord with a residual puritanism which inclined him to justify sex as health-enhancing.

In the course of their correspondence, Symonds put a startling and extremely suggestive idea to Carpenter when he criticised existing physiological assumptions that 'sexual instincts follow the build of the sexual organs'; an approach which effectively disembodied desire from biology.[42] Though Carpenter was more apt to seek materialist explanations than Symonds, his inclination to emphasise relationships and feelings was affirmed by the literary and historical scholar. In February 1893 he was inspired to begin writing notes himself, sending them to Symonds for comments. Symonds' reply to the first draft of what became Carpenter's pamphlet, *Homogenic Love*, was warm and supportive; their outlook was convergent.[43] In contrast Symonds had become agitated about the gap between his and Ellis' viewpoints. He really wanted to 'meet and exchange thoughts in quiet somewhere, before this book on Sexual Inversion is begun'.[44] Could Carpenter come and stay with him in May?

That April Symonds went to Rome to spend time with his family, caught influenza, and died suddenly of lung congestion. His friend and trustee Horatio Brown was left with the manuscript of an eloquent autobiography that Symonds had instructed him to preserve without embarrassing his wife and daughters. Over the years, prompted by Symonds' wife and by his friend, the Cambridge moral philosopher Henry Sidgwick, Brown became progressively more anxious to prevent any reference to Symonds' homosexuality and the 'Memoirs' remained unpublished until 1984. The book testifies to Symonds' belief that one day a time would come when frank discussion of sexual feelings would be possible.

A few days before news of Symonds' death reached Carpenter, a copy of his last work, *Walt Whitman: A Study*, came through the post. It contained a moving personal tribute to the American writer who had enabled Symonds 'to fraternize in comradeship with men of all classes'.[45] Carpenter, who had followed the same Whitmanite path, wrote to Alf Mattison about his grief in losing Symonds.[46] Symonds' death left the dilemmas he, Ellis and Carpenter had begun to explore hanging. Carpenter shared some of Symonds' feelings about the limits of a 'scientific' approach which assumed deviancy, and was more inclined than Ellis to detect implicit bias in apparently objective propositions. On the other hand he was uneasy about Symonds' 'erotic sentimentality' in *The Key of Blue* and embraced the assumption behind Ellis' project – the hope that looking at sexual behaviour openly with an objective tone would result in more enlightened attitudes and laws.[47] So Carpenter helped Ellis by compiling notes on existing sexual theory, while resolving that he too would write on sexuality in his own way.

When Carpenter and Ellis were debating how best to raise a challenge to conventional ideas about sexuality, other moves were afoot which, in quite different ways, were bringing sex out into the public domain. Social purity reformers, resolved to curb immorality and protect the vulnerable, were energetically campaigning against prostitution, while daring new women, along with tiny clusters of free lovers, were contesting the hypocrisy of existing moral standards. In this period too, several novelists, including Thomas Hardy, whose work Carpenter and Ellis admired, were also trying to write frankly and honestly about sexual relations, while the emphasis on extreme sensation in the cult of artistic decadence, which interested Arthur Symons, seemed to be dissolving any basis for sexual morality. Carpenter was intervening in an arena which was busy, confused and potentially explosive.

Over the period 1893 to 1894, Carpenter set to work on four pamphlets: *Woman and her Place in a Free Society*, *Marriage in a Free Society*, *Homogenic Love and its Place in a Free Society* and *Sex-love and its Place in a Free Society*. The decision to write about sexuality in general was consistent with Carpenter's tendency to seek out broad alliances rather than to isolate himself. Moreover the other pamphlets gave *Homogenic Love* a degree of cover. He could appear as a writer on sexual topics in general, rather than as a homosexual pleading a case. However, while the other three pamphlets were published by the Labour Press in Manchester in 1894, and eventually found their way into the collection *Love's Coming of Age* in 1896, *Homogenic Love* could be printed only for private circulation. Circumstances thus contrived to separate *Homogenic Love* from the others and it had to wait until 1906 before joining the others in a revised form in *Love's Coming of Age*. So, while the latter gathered a wide readership, *Homogenic Love*, the first British statement by a homosexual man, linking emancipation to social transformation, was destined only for friends and acquaintances.

Carpenter's subjective involvement enabled him to write with controlled passion; the result was a persuasive, informed polemic enhanced by his impressive propaganda skills and easy grace of style. The manuscript, in Carpenter's clear and flowing hand, begins with a dash which expresses the new sexual buoyancy he felt in the early 1890s: '— Of all the many forms that Love delights to take, perhaps none is more interesting (for the very reason that it has been so inadequately considered) than that special attachment which we sometimes call by the name of Comradeship.' The relief in writing about a theme he felt so nearly is evident. But knowing all too well the alarm it could provoke, he corrected the text to make it sound more elevated and removed. Hence the 'special attachment' came to be 'sometimes denoted by the word Comradeship'.[48] Regardless of self-conscious modification, his own engagement permeates *Homogenic Love*. At last he was able to unburden himself of all those private conversations, fill out the scraps of expression he had permitted himself in letters, and make more explicit the coded reflections he had slipped into books and lectures.

He chose his title carefully, rejecting 'homosexual' as a 'bastard' word because of its Greek and Latin derivations and opting for 'homogenic'.[49] Carpenter used classical texts selectively to demonstrate that attitudes to men's love for one another were culturally relative. Along with other nineteenth-century propagandists for same-sex love, he stressed literary and philosophic ideals rather than the actual restrictions placed upon homosexuality in Greek and Roman society. He drew heavily on J.A. Symonds' writing on Greece, and, like Symonds, was inspired by accounts of male friendships in ancient times, singling out Diocles, the Athenian warrior-lover who gave his life for Philolaus, a Corinthian who was the law-giver of Thebes. This was the story which many years later would inspire his love poem to Hukin, and there are echoes of Beck too in his

Biblical allusions to the friendship of David and Jonathan. A new discovery was the work of the fourteenth-century mystical Persian poet, Hafiz. Carpenter had read his odes, *Divan*, in 1893 and copied some lines: 'From the cheek of the cupbearer radiant as the moon I gather a rose.' His heart stolen by the cupbearer, the poet finds, he can 'no longer talk or listen to any other.'[50]

In *Homogenic Love* Carpenter displayed his wide-ranging knowledge of natural history, travel works and anthropology, all thrown together in an omnivorous melange to show how love between men has existed in many cultures. Equally, his fluency in German, French and Italian enabled him to read works on sexual theory before they were translated into English. Along with Ulrichs, who had so impressed Symonds, he cites Richard Krafft-Ebing's *Psychopathia Sexualis* (1886) and Albert Moll's *Perversions of the Sexual Instinct* (1891). He was critical of both writers, observing to Ellis in 1894 that Krafft-Ebing wrote as a medical man who 'sees chiefly sufferers and patients and studies the pathology of the subject', while Moll, steered by the police towards male prostitutes, was inclined to exaggerate effeminacy.[51] Nevertheless he derived two broad conclusions from these very different theorists: attraction to one's own sex was congenital, and far more common than was popularly assumed.

Carpenter was concerned to refute contemporary panic about a supposed 'degeneration' mysteriously emanating from a miasma of urban slum-dwellers, criminals, decadent artists, mystics and homosexuals, insisting that the nervous troubles of many homogenic men arose from their social predicament rather than from their sexual inclination. He informed his readers that all those tough Dorian Greeks, Polynesian Islanders, Normans and Albanian mountaineers, attracted to other men, were unlikely to have been 'troubled by nervous degeneration'.[52] A similar fuss surrounded 'morbidity', an ill-defined, disparaging term which was often linked to homosexuality. In Carpenter's view 'morbidity' arose when desire 'is checked along one channel' causing it 'to flow with the more vehemence along the other channels'.[53] Echoing Whitman, Carpenter connected morbidity with a lack of balance which might make the expression of love exclusively sensual. He also craftily located the reviled morbidity in what he classified as the non-congenital homogenic attractions, which appeared as a result of external circumstances in such places as all-boys' schools, because these evinced 'mere carnal curiosity'.[54]

Carpenter's long-term aim was to end the legal prohibition on sexual relations between men. However he did not overtly contest the law against what he calls in the manuscript version, 'venus aversa', altering this for clarity's sake, in the printed version, to the biblical word used in English law, 'sodomy'.[55] Instead he advanced arguments which were to recur in many subsequent pleas for the legalisation of homosexuality. Carpenter not only asserted that same-sex desire was congenital, he insisted private behaviour was beyond the province of the law – a view that the social purity campaign was intent on dismantling. He added, for good measure, the pragmatic point that the attempt to regulate homogenic sexuality was anyway unenforceable and simply opened up opportunities for blackmailers. Carpenter also claimed that the law could not stop 'natural' feelings, only hound the unfortunate individuals caught expressing them.[56]

Because Carpenter was making a polemical case and intent on breaking through a taboo, he was not able in *Homogenic Love* to stop and explore any of the painful complexities of desire, of which he had been made well aware in his relationships with Beck and Hukin. There is an interesting aside in the manuscript version of *Homogenic Love* on the love letters that working-class men wrote to one another, but this is crossed out in order to keep the momentum of his argument. One advantage of Ellis' more ponderous approach in *Sexual Inversion* was that its style and method allowed diverse kinds of material to be scrutinised and evidence to be considered from differing angles. On the other hand, the great strength of *Homogenic Love* was that Carpenter could draw on his personal observation and experience. Interestingly Carpenter came close to endorsing Symonds' view that Whitman would not have spoken with such authority on democratic comradeship if he had not had ample knowledge of its effects upon himself and others. This still begged the question, of course, as to just what Whitman's comradeship entailed and Carpenter, ever the slippery thinker, is roundabout and carefully qualified.

He does not, indeed could not, ever say 'I' in his pamphlet, yet subjectivity endows his writing with an impassioned emotion. In *Homogenic Love* he was also witnessing for others silenced because they felt same-sex desire – a silencing Ellis, the investigator, could only perceive from without. He described the strain of concealment initially as 'frightful', moderating this to the less emotive 'great', identifying most intensely with the lonely fears of boys growing into manhood, inserting 'from girl to womanhood' into the handwritten manuscript as a dutiful afterthought.[57] Nonetheless his own impressionistic observations caused him to remark on an increase in homogenic relationships among women – especially in the United States. His conclusion was that women's bid for emancipation had made them no longer willing to enter into unequal marriages and had put a strain on relations between the sexes. Women's sexual choices are thus explained culturally. So while for propaganda purposes Carpenter wanted to stress that homogenic desire was congenital, he recognised in *Homogenic*

Love that in practice it could also be culturally formed. Ellis came to the same conclusion in *Sexual Inversion*. The argument about which aspect to emphasise would echo down the decades.

Homogenic Love was sent off in bundles early in 1895. When Symonds' cautious friend Horatio Brown received his six copies, he recommended removing the word 'delights' from the opening sentence on the grounds that it might offend the 'prejudiced' and dissuade doctors and lawyers from taking up the subject.[58] Carpenter ignored his advice. Indeed he particularly wanted his working-class friends to read his pamphlet and was cheered at receiving supportive comments from Alf Mattison. Ever the optimist, Carpenter suggested to Mattison that he could not 'help thinking that Tom M. has better ideas about it than what he makes out'.[59] But it was too late to convince Maguire. Early that March, a distressed Mattison found him ill with pneumonia in a freezing room with no fire; he died a few days later.[60] Carpenter's hopes of his pamphlet finding a wider audience were doomed, for the timing of its printing was most ill fated. In the spring of 1895, Oscar Wilde's conflict with the Marquess of Queensbury, the father of his love, Lord Alfred Douglas, provoked Wilde into bringing a charge of libel against the Marquess which predictably Wilde lost. 'Oscar W. has been very foolish (and naughty)', Carpenter observed gloomily in a letter to Mattison, depressed to see the 'Philistines' triumphant.[61] Wilde himself was then arrested, standing trial during April and May 1895. In the courtroom the playwright made his brave defence of 'the Love that dare not speak its name', provoking humour and hatred in equal measure with his witty replies to the prosecution.[62] But all his skill with words could not refute the damning evidence, not merely of his relationship with Douglas, but with a flock of young male prostitutes.

While the case was still pending, Carpenter wrote an anonymous letter to the radical *Star* newspaper protesting against the removal of Wilde's name from the playbills of *The Importance of Being Earnest*. Carpenter argued that morality, not law, should be the judge of 'sexual errors', contending that immorality lay in sacrificing another person 'for the sake of one's own pleasure or profit'. By this rubric Wilde's offence had been no worse than the common sacrifice of women to the pleasure of men, an appropriation commonly regarded as 'quite pardonable and "natural."'[63] This was an ingenious tack, aimed at the more radical supporters of social purity. But the scandal surrounding Wilde was feeding a great froth of moral panic, led by an emergent popular press, which labelled him 'High Priest of the Decadents'.[64] On May 25th, Wilde was sentenced to two years' hard labour. His imprisonment left a vortex of fear in its wake.

194   EDWARD CARPENTER: A LIFE OF LIBERTY AND LOVE

One paradoxical consequence was that Carpenter, the nature-loving, health-seeking simplifier, who wanted frank, earnest openness, was stymied by the downfall of his antithesis, the metropolitan hedonist Wilde, who loathed exercise, loved masks and was at his most serious when he was joking. In June Carpenter sent a copy of *Homogenic Love* to the radical editor of the *Review of Reviews*, William Thomas Stead. Though Stead was linked to the social purity cause as a campaigner against child prostitution, unlike Labouchere, he considered the law on homosexuality too severe and had spoken out against the hypocrisy in singling out Wilde. However, he explained to Carpenter that he valued the non-sexual terrain of male friendship and thought open discussion of a sexual kind put it in danger.[65]

Carpenter drew another blank when he tried to publish an article about Ulrichs' ideas of 'Urnings' as a third sex who were neither emphatically male or female. In July 'The Unknown People' was turned down by a journal called *The Humanitarian*. Carpenter complained to Hukin that he had expected more from the editor, Victoria Woodhull Martin, who he had met in a 'swell house' earlier in the month.[66] An American, Woodhull Martin had been a free lover, spiritualist, feminist and socialist but she had married a British banker and been born again respectable. 'All is going very cussedly', Carpenter informed Hukin. 'After all Victoria's talk about what she did 25 years ago she hasn't pluck to take up an unpopular cause now.'[67] *The Humanitarian* did publish a wary review in August regretting the silence of men of science on the subject of *Homogenic Love* but disassociating themselves from its author's views.[68]

Carpenter was appalled by the timorous atmosphere in London that summer. In July, Fisher Unwin, who was going to publish the three other sex pamphlets, took a look at *Homogenic Love* and cancelled the contract. In August, Carpenter related to Oates how Fisher Unwin had even dropped *Towards Democracy* from his list, refusing to listen when Carpenter told him that the panic gripping literary London would die down.[69] He was right, it did, but Wilde's hard labour left a grim tide-mark which proved difficult to eradicate. Moreover his doppelgänger haunted subsequent debate.

The trials turned Wilde into the quintessential 'homosexual'; an archetype which triggered indignant moralism in the I.L.P.'s *Labour Leader* about the 'uncleanness' lurking amidst the idle rich with their lives of 'filthy abomination'.[70] The more rationalistic S.D.F.'s *Justice* conceded that the vice of which Wilde was accused did not merely affect the wealthy and neurotic artistic cliques. *Justice* analysed homosexuality as an 'addiction', encouraged by public schools and the armed forces, and which could only be eradicated by 'careful teaching of the physical basis of morality'. Staunchly materialist, *Justice* assured its readers that socialism would remove the evil of male prostitution.[71] *Clarion* simply maintained an eloquent silence.

Isolated on the socialist left, in adversity, Carpenter turned to his anarchist allies on *Freedom*. In an article headed 'Some Recent Criminal Cases' that July, he chose his ground carefully, for even anarchists were not necessarily sympathetic on this issue. First he assailed the law, which exposed homosexuals to blackmail. Then he appealed to the anarchists to break the 'cowardly silence' on sex, including relations between people of the same sex. Sketching in graphic terms the loneliness and ignorance of the homogenic young, he insisted that their feelings were natural and pure. It was time for a 'sane and impartial consideration' of the subject.[72] Yet Carpenter could not help be aware that an article in the beleaguered *Freedom* was a drop in the ocean. In Germany and France the situation was somewhat better in progressive circles. In Germany the leading Social Democrat, Eduard Bernstein, had defended Wilde, arguing that moral attitudes were 'historical phenomena' and that homosexuality had existed in many cultures.[73] *Homogenic Love* was translated into German in 1895 and appeared in the French journal, *La Société Nouvelle*, the following year. And the privately printed English edition travelled surprisingly far afield via a dissident underground of radical contacts. In the catalogue of New York's Tamiment Library, a copy belonging to Helena Born is listed as bearing an inscription from 'J.H.R.' – which sounds like John Harrison Riley. But while *Homogenic Love* eventually reached people in other countries, in Britain there was a real danger after the Wilde trial not simply of the whole topic being suppressed, but of those who tried to discuss and campaign around homosexuality being ostracised. This predicament impelled Carpenter towards ingenious and circuitous stratagems.

11

A Long Campaign

'There is another long campaign to fight', Carpenter announced to Mattison after Wilde's conviction.[1] In his 'long campaign' Carpenter would elaborate in a more conscious manner on what he had been doing implicitly before, by consolidating and extending his network of homogenic male friends and keeping the way open for links with potential sympathisers in artistic, intellectual and radical circles. Unlike his other causes, this one required the adoption of cultural guerrilla tactics within the most ordinary details of everyday life, and Carpenter proved far better at it than at serving on the parish council.

While writing on sexuality Carpenter had been extending his homo-erotic 'freemasonry' of intellectual and artistic young men, and in the early 1890s a new young 'Theban' from Cambridge University called George Ives had made contact. Ives, the illegitimate offspring of an aristocratic family, had a private income, and lived in modern bachelor style off Piccadilly, in an apartment at E4, The Albany, which Wilde mischievously made the address of Jack Worthing in *The Importance of Being Earnest*. Ives was charmed by Wilde and his circle, though fearful of their recklessness. His large network of acquaintances also included several men in Carpenter's milieu; Frank Deas, who Carpenter had tried to fix up with Oates; the botanist George E. Comerford Casey, who Carpenter knew from holidaying in Nice; Henry Salt and Charles Ashbee. Ives was extremely interested in Ashbee's Guild and School of Handicraft and would often visit the East End.

When in March 1894 George Ives wrote a letter to Carpenter about love, he was already an admirer of *Civilisation: Its Cause and Cure* and had been intrigued by its references to the Theban band.[2] About to come out with a passionate defence of Greek love in *The Humanitarian*, Ives shaved off his moustache to be more Hellenic and formed the 'Order of Chaeronea'

The Bolton Whitmanites (Sixsmith seated first on right,
Dalmas seated second on left)

in honour of the Thebans – as the poor Thebans had been annihilated
at Chaeronea, the name was redolent with tragic heroism. While Ives'
'Order' was the first named grouping of British homosexuals, it was so
highly secret that it is difficult to know to what extent it actually operated
as an organisation, though Ives certainly saw himself as part of a movement
he called 'the Cause'.[3] Personally he was an odd mixture of highly individualistic egocentricity and commitment to social service, especially prison
reform on which he would later write. Ives considered himself to be a
socialist, but believed in elaborate ritual rather than democracy, observing
to a sceptical Carpenter that this was a weapon recognised by the Roman
Catholic Church.[4] He was inclined to regard his Thebans as an elect
cadre, with a clear chain of command in which working-class members
had to be taught 'the Faith'. In August 1894, ruminating, in the voluminous
diaries he kept, on Carpenter's conviction that the working class were
the nicest of people, Ives remarked dubiously, 'no doubt he had some
ground for so saying'.[5] Moreover, unlike Carpenter, Ives, a sheep and
goats man, conceived 'the Cause' in terms of 'us' and 'them'.

In contrast, from amidst the vague democratic comradeship of the
Bolton Whitmanites, came another new arrival into Carpenter's circle, a

young American musician, Philip Dalmas. From an artistic Whitmanite
family near Philadelphia, Dalmas was the first of several drifting, aesthetic
young men who became protégés of Carpenter's. During 1894 the free-
flowing Dalmas had caused a great stir in Bolton, arousing intense feelings
in Johnston, Wallace and Sixsmith. He soon adhered to Carpenter and
Millthorpe, endearing himself by setting parts of *Towards Democracy* to
music – including Carpenter's passionate love poem 'All Night Long'.
Dalmas was handsome, charming and musical. Moreover he possessed an
acute sensitivity to colour, and when Dalmas heard music in a rainbow,
Bolton and Millthorpe assumed him to have a special spiritual power. In
fact he was synaesthetic, coincidentally a condition that harmonised with
Symbolism's connection of sound and image – making Dalmas appear
avant garde as well as mystical.

Ashbee met him at Millthorpe one evening in September 1895 when
Dalmas was living nearby, and was captivated by this 'most romantic
person'. He describes how Dalmas

> entered with his baize bay slung across his shoulder, it was a sort of
> lawyer's brief bag and he had stuffed it with beetroot, potatoes, a kettle
> and other purchases made in Chesterfield for his own little ménage.
> We soon fell in love with each other, and in Edward's presence there
> is no ice. Dalmas curled himself up before the fire, rested his head of
> hair against Edward's breast, and we carried on a running fire of banter
> and conversation till bed-time.[6]

The Carpenter–Ashbee network mobilised on behalf of the romantic
musician. Ashbee put him up at his home in Cheyne Walk, Chelsea;
Frank Deas sent letters of introduction to the well-known concert pianist,
Leonard Borwick; and Kate Salt took Dalmas to see Shaw, who wrote
music criticism as a sideline.[7] Wet-blanket Shaw pointed out to Dalmas
that his compositions closely resembled Beethoven, though he conceded
that the young musician had talent and a 'vigorous bass voice'.[8] When
Dalmas left for a bohemian life in Paris, Kate Salt interceded again with
Shaw to find him rich pupils.

Carpenter attempted to bring his working-class friends, Hukin and
Mattison into this artistic, mildly erotic milieu. He had a tendency to
enthuse to middle-class men friends about Hukin, reporting back expressions of interest and admiration, which evoked in Hukin a gruff, Northern
distrust of 'gush'. In April 1894 Hukin wrote saying that he was pleased
Carpenter still thought of him, but refused cult status. 'As for these Philips
and others I don't feel that I can quite reciprocate their "tender feelings"

altogether. I'm afraid my little heart is much too small to share amongst so many.'⁹ He was too tactful to add that he did not wear it on a sleeve. Eventually Carpenter did persuade his Northern young men to mingle and both Hukin and Mattison became friendly with Dalmas.

During the spring and summer of 1895 Mattison became involved in an affair with a man. A chuffed Carpenter sent invitations to Mattison to bring his friend to Glover Road and 'sleep there tog. [sic]'. Ever the pedagogue, he could not resist adding, 'And you understand "Calamus" better now Eh?'¹⁰ Carpenter, the indefatigable educator, assiduously disseminated informative literature among the little band of supportive young men in his circle. A socialist friend of Sixsmith's, a telegraph boy from Liverpool called William Young, wrote in February 1896 thanking Carpenter for *Phaedrus*. Young was clearly struggling with the intricacies of the text, telling Carpenter that he knew nothing of Plato and found the world of books so bewildering that it made his head ache. He was reading *Homogenic Love* and enquired what the Theban Band might be. 'Is it a band of Comrade-Lovers ready to sacrifice their lives for Love and Truth?'¹¹ Young was rather discouraged because many of the references in the pamphlet were to books in Latin. Could Carpenter recommend any books about the Thebans available to the ordinary person?

Young was one among many working-class and lower-middle-class people seeking a broader culture in the 1890s and feeling frustrated because there were so few opportunities for them in higher education. The classical allusions, so familiar to Oxbridge educated intellectuals such as Carpenter, were off-putting to them, and Young's request pointed to the need for popular translations of the classics. This was regarded with distaste by elitist scholars, but to Carpenter, the inveterate populariser, keen for the Greeks to be the symbol of a golden age of male friendship, it was evident that basic educational work had to be done. Accordingly he applauded Goldsworthy Lowes Dickinson's *The Greek View of Life*, when it was published under the auspices of the University Extension Movement in 1896, telling Oates it was 'an excellent little book with a good chapter on friendship.'¹²

The propagation of the classics as the source for an alternative homogenic ideal was not without problems. Carpenter's notes show that at least after the publication of *Homogenic Love*, he was aware of the penalties for homosexual acts which existed in Greece and Rome.¹³ There was the awkward truth too that Plato's observations about homogenic love affairs were confined to an elite. An alternative way of configuring male comradeship was being developed by Ashbee in his Guild and School of Handicraft and in his University Extension classes. Ashbee drew on the supposed communality of the Middle Ages to criticise the competitive individualism of modern capitalist production and the narrowness of existing types of vocational training. In 1894 the Guild had published his book *A Few Chapters in Workshop Re-construction and Citizenship*. This was ostensibly about changing the conditions of work and combining craft teaching with a humanistic vision of education for social citizenship, but Ashbee included a few Whitmanite comments on personal comradely relations in the Guild that Carpenter picked out and noted down.

From 1895 this kind of subterfuge was even more necessary and despite Carpenter's resolve to use any possible channel of communication, it was not easy for him to write about male–male sexual feelings in contexts which might reach a popular audience. He managed a plug for nude bathing in *Love's Coming of Age* in 1896 and in 1897 wrote two oblique articles on Walt Whitman in *The Progressive Review*, later to be published as *Days with Walt Whitman* (1906).[14] He was more frank in private correspondence with Havelock Ellis, describing Whitman's letters to the working-class youth, Pete Doyle, as 'very homogenic'.[15] Ingeniously Carpenter snuck Greek sculpture, Michelangelo and the body into his essays on art in relation to life, published as *Angels' Wings* (1898).

He found an outlet for his article on 'An Unknown People' in the freethinking *Reformer* in 1897, even though he had not always seen eye to eye with its sceptical and rationalistic editor, J.M. Robertson.[16] It was issued as a pamphlet the same year. In 'An Unknown People', Carpenter reiterated the pleas he had made in *Freedom* for sexual education for lonely young 'Urnings'. Concerned still to refute the contemporary association of degeneration and morbidity with homosexuality, he insisted that Urnings were 'fine healthy specimens', rather than the sensual decadents of popular imagination, explaining for good measure that their attachments were not necessarily sexual in a physical way. Drawing on the writer Otto de Joux, Carpenter went on to argue that Urnings possessed unique qualities of sensitivity and could be 'reconcilers and interpreters'; characteristics indeed which corresponded closely with Carpenter's ideal self-image.[17] He wanted a representation of the homosexual as both sensitive and manly; Whitman continued to be his model.

A further essay on 'Affection in Education' hung around for three years before finally appearing, tucked away in the respectable but dry *International Journal of Ethics* in 1899. Carpenter's recognition that affection plays a vital part in education was far-sighted, but his defence of 'intense and romantic' feelings between, not just schoolboys, but teachers and pupils, was skating on thin ice indeed. As usual he presented a controversial point as morally beneficial. His contention was that the 'coarse and licentious' liaisons which flourished in public schools should be replaced by Greek-style relations conducted with 'self-restraint and tenderness'. Braving what he called 'the panic terror' in England about such relationships, he envisaged schools as Platonic sites of fond enquiry between boys, adding as an after-thought an endorsement of co-education.[18] He did not consider how inequality of power might sour the fondness, or admit any danger of lapses occurring in the 'self-restraint and tenderness'.

As an evangelical, democratic communicator, Carpenter faced insuperable contradictions, for the cultural and political pressures of the 1890s meant that representations of homoeroticism required the cover of artistic, intel-lectual or scientific superiority. Up until 1895 Charles Kains Jackson, editor of *The Artist and Journal of Home Culture*, had managed to publish poems about naked youths bathing by invoking the Hellenic stalking-horse, while *The Studio: An Illustrated Magazine of Fine and Applied Arts* printed drawings and photographs of 'aesthetic' male nudes. Havelock Ellis' insistence on 'scientific' objectivity in discussing sex constituted a similar pitch for the high-ground. However after the Wilde trial even these lofty habitats did not always prove secure – the authorities being apt to miss the finer nuances between posh and filth. Carpenter was not quite in either camp. He had never felt comfortable with the aesthetic stance and when he read the manuscript of Ellis' *Sexual Inversion* some of the doubts about a scientific discourse he had shared with Symonds returned. Carpenter was troubled that Ellis' detachment made it impossible for him to express any inner emotional empathy for 'the kind of love wh. appears to me to want no mark of authenticity except the question of race-propagation and which yet has a quality all of its own'.[19]

Ironically it was to be Ellis, aiming at the opinion formers, rather than the campaigning Carpenter, who came under fire. Ellis wrote to Carpenter in some exasperation in April 1896, telling him that while *Sexual Inversion* could be published in Germany and France, England was presenting diffi-culties.[20] After the book was printed, Horatio Brown decided that Symonds' contribution should be eradicated and bought up all the copies on behalf of the Symonds family. Carpenter described the elimination of all trace of Symonds in a letter to Kate Salt as 'a sheer betrayal'.[21] He minded more than Ellis, who stoically reported that he was working on a second edition. The former home secretary under the Liberals, Herbert Henry Asquith, had advised Brown that Symonds' literary approach could go against the book, and Ellis was inclined to concur: 'In some ways the change will be an improvement and it certainly renders it safer from attacks of all kinds.'[22]

Ellis' publisher in Britain was called Roland de Villiers; his list included the free thinker J.M. Robertson and he also produced *The Adult*, a journal edited by George Bedborough, the secretary of the Legitimation League, a group committed to free love and sexual reform. The League, which had started in Leeds in 1895 and then moved to London, included the anarchist Henry Seymour, who had links to the individualist anarchists around *Liberty* in Boston, with whom Helena Born and Miriam Daniell were associated. A plain-clothes detective, John Sweeney, on the prowl for information about anarchists, bought Ellis' *Sexual Inversion* in Bedborough's bookshop and took it to his superior officer, who was none other than William Melville. Since the Walsall enquiry, Chief Inspector Melville had become fixated on hunting down anarchists and was gratified to have in his possession what was evidently a very dirty book to use against his old opponents and Bedborough.

Bedborough was arrested, de Villiers quickly vanished, and Ellis went into shock as his scientific masterpiece was derided in court by the judge as 'this filthy work'.[23] Henry Seymour mobilised in Bedborough's defence and a Free Press Defence Committee was formed which included Carpenter, Robertson, the novelist Grant Allen, and Shaw. Detective Sweeney, unimpressed by literary or intellectual credentials, regarded them as 'a nice little gang of Secularists, Socialists, Anarchists, Free-Lovers'.[24] After Bedborough was found guilty and fined £100, Carpenter penned an outraged letter to the *Saturday Review*, defending Ellis' efforts to deal 'decently, straightforwardly and scientifically' with sexual inversion. He also indicted the attempt to remove 'ladies' from the public gallery and the subsequent abuse of those who defiantly stayed.[25] Plucky ladies apart, the trial was far from heroic; Bedborough was desperate to avoid martyrdom, while de Villiers turned out to have a criminal record for fraud in Germany. One positive outcome occurred inadvertently, the formation of Seymour's Free Press Defence Committee established a significant precedent in shifting the question of sexual inversion onto the terrain of civil liberties.

In the second half of the 1890s the fear surrounding the illegality of homosexuality meant the danger of blackmail was ever present. This came too close for comfort in 1896 when Charles Oates' long-standing relationship with Arthur Coles was turning nasty. Carpenter was worried because he and his wife were paying unwanted visits to Meanwoodside and thought they might come to the Sheffield area. He warned Hukin against the Coles, falling back again on Hukin's loyalty and discretion.[26] Even so, the apprehension of danger after 1895 was greater than the actual threat, for despite the comparative severity of British law, the numbers of prosecutions and convictions did not rise dramatically.

Though after the Wilde trial, homosexual men began to be labelled as 'oscarwildes', men who did not fit the green carnation stereotype remained in the shadows, swathed in a cloak of ambiguity because Victorian culture still kept the discussion of any kind of sex under wraps. In socialist circles this opaqueness was compounded by the overlap between political and personal comradeship. In 1897 Charles Ashbee explained to his future wife, Janet Forbes, that she was the first woman for whom he had felt 'the same loyal reverence of affection' he had given to his men friends, declaring that she would be his 'comrade wife'.[27] To a sheltered and inexperienced young woman such a statement would not have carried any sexual undertow. Equally when the married Dr Johnston was surprised to find himself kissing Philip Dalmas, he puzzled over 'a strange and indescribable feeling', and when Wallace and Sixsmith succumbed to the same 'curious attraction', they all concluded that they were experiencing a form of Dr Bucke's 'cosmic consciousness'.[28]

Despite fear, ambivalence and mystification, an exploratory sexual culture was nevertheless defying conventional morality in private, unexpected places, outside the control of Sweeney and Melville and their ilk. The Bristol working-class socialist, Robert Allan Nicol, wrote enthusiastically to Carpenter about his sex pamphlets from Placer County, California in September 1894. Along with Daniell and Born, Nicol had emigrated to the US, persuading the two women to leave Boston to join him in a communal farm in the foothills of the Sierra Nevada. Tragedy followed when the farm burned down and Daniell died soon afterwards. Sending her unpublished poems to Carpenter, Nicol observed that Miriam was with him on every page of the sex pamphlets.[29] Nicol sought spiritual enlightenment through Theosophy while celebrating the body and nature.[30] 'You know I like women as much as men' he told Carpenter.[31] Though he formed a relationship with another Bristol new woman, the Fabian writer Gertrude Dix, he retained fond memories of 'Fox Lane and the road to Chesterfield for did not Edward C come home in the dusk with me from Chesterfield one summer evening his arm in mine. And it was sweet.'[32]

The intimate structures of sexual feeling forming in the 1890s were far more complex than any theories about sexuality could encompass. Carpenter's ethos of acceptance and humour encouraged people to talk and write to him about their most secret troubles and he played an important role as a confidant in this private realm. This personal nurturing which was an integral element of Carpenter's 'long campaign' extended into other aspects of sexuality as well. In a remarkable letter which probably dates from the late 1890s, Charlie Sixsmith reflected to Carpenter on his love affairs:

I have not found the true mate. Women attract me and yet full intercourse has not satisfied me, and I prefer the company of men and become attached to them also. But really I am the greatest puzzle to myself – a bundle of paradoxes and contradictions and tangles pulled different ways. A hopeless muddle which I cannot sort out. Most other men don't seem so and I do envy them or rather wish I had the same singleness.[33]

Alf Mattison did not experience 'singleness' either, and, like Sixsmith, was ambiguous about his sexual orientation. During 1898 Mattison began courting 'Miss Florence Foulds', known less formally as 'Florrie'. But she and Mattison had no sooner met when an opportunity arose to travel through Europe with the upper-class homosexual I.L.P. member, John Lister, and Oates offered to help pay.[34] It was an undreamed of chance to make the kind of cultural grand tour men of Carpenter's class took for granted but was impossible for a working-class person. As well as being improving, it was seen as a means for the frail Mattison to recover his health. Mattison seized his chance, but there was an awkwardness. Even though the socialist working-class intellectual might be embraced by upper-class democratic comrades, he remained uncomfortably beholden to them. Florence Foulds took a dim view of the expedition and resented the privileged power of upper-middle-class homosexuals like Lister and Carpenter.[35] Her suspicions would have been confirmed had she seen a jokey letter from Carpenter to Mattison in Marseilles asking if he had met any 'lovely people male or female' or whether his 'capacity in that direction' had 'dried up'.[36]

By writing *Homogenic Love*, and the sex pamphlets which were published together as *Love's Coming of Age* in 1896, Carpenter became the visible figure challenging conventional morality in a period when such alternative approaches were under siege. As a result, Carpenter's personal life became ineradicably connected to his politics. This had problematic and burdensome implications for a free spirit who deplored political correctness from any quarter. Being a homosexual man and a left-wing sexual rebel in a period of moral panic, he had limited space in which to manoeuvre. Yet manoeuvre he did. Despite there being compelling reasons for no deviation from an idealised democratic comradeship to pass into record, just occasionally there are little hints of another Carpenter. Because Oates was such an old friend and because his sexual relationships corresponded more to conventional cross-class liaisons, Carpenter would sometimes let his ideological guard drop in letters to Meanwoodside. In 1897, when

Oates met a new love, Arthur Dixon, who worked at the Post Office, Carpenter wrote wishing Oates a 'true and faithful friendship' and then suddenly came out with the worldly-wise remark, 'I believe PO employees are not infrequently of the right sort.'[37] Only a few years earlier, social purity reformers, including Labouchere, had indignantly exposed how upper-class men were paying post office boys for sex; Oates' relationship was not comparable, but nonetheless Carpenter's aside would have made their hair stand on end.

On holiday with Oates there had been the young Italian in 1887, and the following year, when Carpenter was going to visit the South of France, he had sounded interested rather than suitably shocked when he mentioned to Oates that his friend George E. Comerford Casey said Nice was 'a sink of corruption'.[38] Carpenter and Oates, like many other Northern European men, found their ingrained sense of rectitude mysteriously melted in the Mediterranean sun. In Sheffield too, Carpenter described in *My Days and Dreams* how he had managed to meet working-class men in the early 1880s.[39] First Scotland Street and later Glover Road made this easier. Merrill had seen him in Sheffield before they met on the train in 1891, and as Merrill was not part of the socialist milieu, it was unlikely to have been at meetings. It is conceivable that Merrill was not the first man with whom Carpenter exchanged a look of recognition, for Carpenter was always fascinated by men who were utterly unlike himself. Charlie Sixsmith thought this was because Carpenter could never quite shed his refinement and 'would have liked more of the ruder elements of human nature in his make-up. . . . He would laugh at a coarse joke, but never told one, and if at rare times he used an oath, it seemed forced and unnatural to him.'[40] Rough diamonds presented a foil to his own self-consciousness.

One intriguing figure pops up in Carpenter's circle of working-class acquaintances and then abruptly vanishes. In 1889 Hukin mentioned how Gascoigne, the man who had helped them set up the Temperance Hotel for meetings, was leaving his lodgings in Franklin Street and was about to take over the Ball Inn, in Charles Street. Hukin thought they should warn him that it had changed hands many times and was not a good proposition.[41] According to the family memory of Gascoigne's descendants, one day in 1893 the publican stepped out of the house, never to be seen again. Whereupon Mary Ann and the children concluded that he had taken a ship to America to join Mr Carpenter. Henceforth Mary Ann Gascoigne survived by selling pies. She is listed in the 1903 Ordnance Survey Maps as a shopkeeper at 391 Washford Road. The pie recipe was passed down through the generations, along with the story of Carpenter as a bogey-man who lured husbands away.[42] He might have been the sage of the simple life in socialist circles, but he was acquiring a more sinister persona in urban myth.

In Merrill, Carpenter found his ideal of the rude. Their love affair, however, presented Carpenter with a quandary; while hitherto he had managed to keep the most markedly contrary strands of his life apart, the strength of their passionate relationship threw this into question. Two years after they met, the Fearnehoughs left Millthorpe and Carpenter did consider living with his lover, putting the idea aside because Merrill liked town life so much it seemed unlikely he would be able to settle into the countryside or take over the housekeeping. Also Carpenter was busy with his lectures and writing, and had made a promise to George Adams who was desperate to leave the slums with his wife Lucy and young family. Carpenter must also have been aware that it would not be easy to integrate Merrill into his life. Not only were some of his middle-class friends uncomfortable and distrustful, but Adams detested him.[43] The diplomatic Hukin accepted Merrill and Carpenter was delighted about his 'two Gs' as he called them.[44] However the rancour of the third 'George' festered for he felt that he was being sidelined.

Merrill's letters to 'My Dear Faithful Dad' are direct and uncomplicated in expressing desire.[45] He tells how he had thought of Carpenter all night and how pleased he had been to receive his 'loving letter'.[46] But the clinging, affectionate sadness Carpenter had first noticed in him came increasingly to the fore; Merrill was needy and vulnerable as well. Predictably, as Merrill and Carpenter came to know one another better, the rough, insouciant, noble savage revealed, along with sexual passion and affection, a troubling capacity for angst. He worried about a speech impediment which prevented him from doing much good for the social cause. Then he was distressed by his inability to 'get some good and useful work'.[47] Carpenter managed to get him a job as a waiter at the Hydro in Baslow in 1896. Jim Shortland later wangled him into the armour-plating section of Vickers which was becoming one of the main suppliers of warships and armaments. Carpenter gazed in horrified wonder at this power-house of capitalism, as gigantic cranes lifted great masses of steel and huge chisels licked through steel plates as if they were butter.[48] In *Towards Democracy* Carpenter waxed poetic on the flame of the Bessemer cupola, the yellow hot iron and the brawny men half-visible through clouds of flying steam.[49] Merrill, however, could not cope with the relentless work discipline of Vickers. By 1897 he was becoming moody and ill; he felt insecure and hated his dependence. Carpenter told Oates he was concerned about Merrill's 'nervous depression and palpitations of the heart'.[50] Merrill was not simply the sensual 'rogue' Carpenter liked to portray, any more than Carpenter was just the saintly sage welcoming the admiring crowds at Millthorpe.

Despite his feelings for Merrill, Carpenter could not quite let go of his love for Hukin and all those affectionate, flirtatious friendships. When he sent Frank Deas his article on *Towards Democracy* in the *Labour Prophet* with a photograph in 1894, Deas teased him that it would lead 'to even more adventures than lately. I must tell George M. to keep a (reasonably) jealous eye on you.'[51] During Carpenter's affair with Hukin, Oates had decided that Carpenter was more faithful than he could ever be.[52] However, ten years later, and involved with Merrill, Carpenter confided to Oates that he felt quite overwhelmed with young men: Philip Dalmas had just departed, Bob Muirhead, now married, but experiencing 'matrimonial trouble', was about to arrive, while Jim Shortland, George Hukin and George Merrill had all appeared at once.

> My poor little heart is stretched out of all shape among them all – and
> I long to have just <u>one</u> companion and to retire with that one for ever!
> Yet they are all beautiful. Why have I not a hundred bodies. My destiny
> is such a strange one – I cannot deal with it, and sometimes feel as if
> I must let all the reins slip from my fingers.[53]

Carpenter in his fifties still had a proclivity for hopeless longings. The determining twist in his destiny was that, amidst all these beautiful ones, only George Merrill was not either flitting away or married.

Carpenter played a pivotal role in the cultural networks of homogenic men during the 1890s. He acted as an exemplar, a confidant and helpmate to a large circle, or, to be more precise, to several overlapping circles of men. Some, like himself and Oates, were convinced of their 'singleness' in desiring men; others like Hukin, Mattison, Nicol and Sixsmith were more divided. Carpenter's empathy enabled him to encourage a new kind of sexual consciousness among both his educated upper-middle class friends like Ashbee and Lowes Dickinson and among the working-class men. This personal culture of homoerotic comradeship, contradictory, convoluted and always in flux, interacted with Carpenter's efforts to write about same-sex love.

Like Ellis' own, Carpenter's theorising of the homogenic condition would contribute to a shift in how homosexuality was seen by people outside his immediate circle. Both men played their parts, albeit rather different ones, in a wider process by which male friendship was at once being sexualised and becoming visible on a public terrain. In his attempt to undo prejudice, Carpenter drew on theorists who were seeking to present sexual behaviour in terms of scientific study. This new field of sexology with its objective discourse provided a lens which could destabilise conventional morality, even though the sexologists introduced their own standpoints under the cover of 'science'. Recognising that the sexologists were a mixed bag, an instrumental Carpenter extracted from their tomes convenient points to back up his own arguments, tactfully hailing the work of his friend Havelock Ellis as the best 'scientific treatment' of homosexuality.[54] He was aware that in adversity especially, scientific expertise could have its uses, though personally he remained suspicious of the positioning of the 'invert' as a specimen to be examined by the expert.

Romanticism was as significant in the making of a homosexual identity in the 1890s as the sexologists. Rough and manly Whitman, doomed and languid Wilde, along with the effusive Symonds, were all in the Romantic tradition. Despite his affection for Symonds, Carpenter found some of his writing embarrassing. He muttered to Ellis in December 1896 how 'all that about the odour of soldiers and sailors, grooms and jockeys and the attraction of uniforms' came over as 'rather absurd'.[55] Nonetheless Symonds bequeathed influential cultural tropes. His 'new chivalry' was embraced by George Ives along with other homosexual writers. With its echoes of the Pre-Raphaelites, Ruskin and Morris, 'new chivalry' could merge with Ashbee's Guild and School of Handicraft, which embodied a romantic view of medieval communality, suitably democratised through Whitmanite comradeship. Then there was the Hellenism embraced by Carpenter, as well as Symonds, Lowes Dickinson and Ives. Along with Romanticism it provided yet another heroic myth through which the derogatory associations of homosexuality with 'degeneration' could be countered and the owlish investigations of sexologists sidelined. Both myths legitimated rebellion, though in recreating the outcast as hero they could result in a new elitism of heroic warriors and ultra-sensitive seers.

Nonetheless Sweeney and Melville were right to sniff social subversion around 'sexual inversion' – even if it did not manifest itself in a form the police mind could pin down and grasp. The social meanings woven into the emerging conceptualisations of homosexual identity carried far-reaching challenges to the existing order. Ashbee's Arts and Crafts Guild ideas, like Lowes Dickinson's Hellenism, contested contemporary commercialism. Whitman's poems, along with Plato's *Phaedrus*, provided ways of writing the body that circumnavigated the prohibitions of Christianity. As for sexology, while Ellis' classifications of abnormality rightly disturbed

Carpenter and Symonds, the other aspect of his project, the understanding of sexuality, was most radical in its implications and became a central tenet of a modern mentality during the twentieth century.

In the short term the 'naughty' Wilde's demise did constitute a setback to Carpenter's hopes of decriminalisation and open comprehension. Nonetheless the 1890s saw a culture of resistance that was both theoretical and lived against the grain; Carpenter and his little band of friends held together and defied isolation. And, equally important, Carpenter's socialism, along with his personal tendency to have a finger in every pie, helped to form alliances with people from other cultural and social movements. By writing his sex pamphlets alongside *Homogenic Love*, Carpenter fostered a connection between new sexual relations, the emancipation of women and the creation of a free society. This was a remarkable step because the affinity between them was by no means self-evident. Frank Deas told Carpenter he could easily identify with the 'Sex-Love' pamphlet but that the one on 'Woman' had been a revelation: 'I have never really thought out the woman question.' Carpenter had revealed the connection between women's emancipation and male comradeship, though Deas could not help wondering what Ives would say: 'How will he fit it in with "The Cause". I fear he will dub me a traitor and renegade.' Ives apart, Deas could only chortle about the irony of a supposed 'woman-hater' blowing the first blast for women, showing how the so-called woman-hating man treated women better than the 'other kind'.[56] Carpenter was not quite the first to blow the blast, but he was certainly innovative in bringing to his Theban forces a second line of defence – advanced women.

12

Defending Wild Women

'When are your sex-bombs going to be flung on our waiting heads?' enquired Edith Ellis in December 1893.[1] She was referring to Carpenter's pamphlets, *Woman, and her Place in a Free Society*, *Marriage in Free Society* and *Sex-Love and its Place in a Free Society*, which all appeared over the course of the following year. Edith Ellis was the most recent addition to the circle of Carpenter's close women friends, Isabella Ford, Olive Schreiner and Kate Salt, from whom he had gleaned so many insights about the relation between the sexes. Married to Havelock Ellis but sexually attracted to women, Edith quickly claimed Carpenter as her friend. Her letters, in contrast to Ellis' staid tone, bubble with affection and jokes, interspersed by frank observations. In her letter about the 'sex bombs', the defiant Edith exclaimed on how little doctors had faced what she called 'the real sex difficulties', adding, 'They dogmatise about the penis and the vagina as much as the missionary over the immortal souls of the heathen.'[2]

Edith's relationship with Carpenter brought out her liking for farming and the countryside as well as for the world of advanced ideas. To Carpenter's amusement, Edith could sit in the local pub with the farm men who remembered her as 'that little lady . . . with that curly hair, like a lad's and them blue eyes, what talked about pigs and cows'.[3] A darker side co-existed with Edith Ellis' animated personality. Carpenter ascribed this to the extreme contrasts in her temperament; 'democratic yet dominating, combative yet sympathetic, hasty yet tenacious; practical and imaginative, logical and intuitive, feminine and masculine all in one'.[4] In other words Edith completely blew Carpenter and Ellis' propensity to apportion humanity into types.

Carpenter's advanced women friends communicated the complexity of subjective conflicts as well as external social constraints. Isabella Ford was writing a novel in which two women living in a flat in London explore their dilemmas about men, marriage and freedom. *On the Threshold* was

Edith and Havelock Ellis

published in 1895. Edith Ellis sent him reports on her struggles with what later became *Seaweed: A Cornish Idyll* (1898), and he was inspired by Schreiner's allegory about woman's search for freedom, *Three Dreams in a Desert* (1890). Equally he knew about their private thoughts, for women, as well as men, were apt to confide in him feelings that were too raw and confusing to express openly. Olive Schreiner had written to Carpenter about Ellis and Karl Pearson during the 1880s, and later disclosed her attraction to Bob Muirhead. In 1893, explaining how she was drawn to men of action rather than intellectuals, she said she could never marry 'Bob' because 'He's too good.'[5]

Carpenter's most stormy female friendship would be with Kate Salt, who unlike the others never made a mark in the public sphere as a writer or speaker. Nonetheless, in the early 1890s, it was Kate who acted as his intelligent and helpful critic when he was struggling with the 'sex bombs'. In October 1893 he acknowledged what a contentious zone he was entering in writing about sex and women. 'Alas "fools rush in . . .".'[6] In February 1894, he wrote expressing gratitude for her comments on 'Woman', which had made him aware how some of his remarks were in 'the <u>clergyman vein</u>'.[7] Though he had suspected that something was wrong with his tone, he had not been able to put his finger on it and Kate's observations were the most useful he had received. By March *Marriage*, the one he found the worst to write, was nearly completed: 'Never did I have so much trouble with a rebellious infant as with this one.'[8] This may well have been because Carpenter was not personally engaged with the topic which was currently exercising new women, anarchists and free lovers. But it could also have been because, resistant as ever to absolute principles, he agreed with Havelock Ellis that marriage should not be dismissed out of hand, and was consequently steering between polarities. When Kate was unhappy with his acceptance of a marriage contract, he responded by asserting that he was 'conciliatory' because he could not see 'any definitive alternative'.[9] Olive Schreiner, recently married to the South African farmer, Samuel Cron Cronwright, sent her approval of his endorsement of marriage, while urging that women's financial independence and inner subjection needed greater stress. Schreiner compared the deep patterns of subordination between men and women to the internalised colonialism in the relation of whites and blacks.[10]

Sex-Love was showing signs of being a bestseller by the standards of the Labour Press – by March 1894, 2,000 copies had been sold.[11] 'All the women are delighted with my sex-pamphlet', announced a chuffed Carpenter to Hukin early in 1894, while informing Roger Fry that praise from women was 'good testimony'.[12] Carpenter was impressed by Fry's friend James McTaggart on the philosophy of love, commenting:

> Love is the nearest word we know for the last timeless relation, and as Love – even as we know it – is infinitely varied – so the timeless relations of each 'spirit' to all the others are infinitely various. These relations I believe are intuitively apprehended . . . – and the intuition only provoked or "recalled" by sense perceptions.[13]

Paradoxically Carpenter could muse on love in the abstract and appeal to women, even though he could not communicate the sexual cause closest to his own heart. Letters began to arrive from socialist women he did not know. Emma Brooke, who had clashed with Schreiner's love Karl Pearson in the Men and Women's Club, and whose own novel *A Superfluous Woman* appeared early in 1894, wrote in February to inform Carpenter that she had read his pamphlet on 'sex-love' with 'delight'. An active Fabian, Brooke believed that 'a great Love' could bring women satisfaction, rather than motherhood as was commonly supposed.[14] Another correspondent, Edith A. Macduff, announced: 'I have for a long time felt very strongly about the hollow and impure hypocrisy with which the conventional world surrounds the sacred and beautiful facts of the physical life.'[15] She wanted sex education for children, and birth control.

Individual responses could not completely make up for the lack of press notices, though the Whitmanite journal *The Conservator*, edited by Horace Traubel, did hail *Sex-Love* from across the Atlantic as the antidote to French novels: 'Let the subject be permeated by nature's antiseptics, daylight and fresh air.'[16] In Britain however, nature's antiseptics did not impress the publishers Carpenter approached to do a collection of the pamphlets minus *Homogenic Love*, after Fisher Unwin turned him down. Again he was prepared to compromise, telling Bertram Dobell he had not felt it possible to pass over a topic occupying so much attention among German scholars and that his *Homogenic Love* had unfortunately acquired 'meanings it was never intended to carry' as a result of the Wilde trial.[17] After failing to convince any London publisher, back he went to the Manchester Labour Press, and *Love's Coming of Age* appeared early in 1896. Though the climate for such a work was still inauspicious, the ever sanguine Carpenter predicted a winner to Mattison: 'I think *Love's Coming of Age* will score a success.'[18]

In *Love's Coming of Age* Carpenter paid his tribute to those new women of the 1890s who were refusing the restrictive gender destiny that he believed had crippled his sisters. In the early 1890s unattached women could be spotted, 'on the prowl all over the country, filling the theatres and concert-rooms . . . besetting the trains, swarming on the tops of the buses, dodging on bicycles under the horses' heads'.[19] Most men, ostrich-like, refused to acknowledge this restless mobility or the incipient ambitions women were displaying. They still expected women to suppress their own individuality to sustain the 'beefy self-satisfaction' of 'man, the ungrown'– the kind of man who organised the modern world.[20] On marriage the woman not only gave her body, she was expected 'to wipe her mind clear of all opinions in order that she may hold it up as a kind of mirror in which he may behold reflected his lordly self'. Carpenter detected women's survival strategies. 'She cultivates the gentle science of indirectness. While holding up a mirror for the Man to admire himself in, *behind that mirror* she goes her own way and carries out her own designs.' As a man himself he could perceive how the 'self-surrender' demanded of women perpetuated the incomprehension of the sexes. The man sensed that if he let go of his stance of coldness, 'The clinging dependent creature will infallibly overgrow and smother him.'[21] Carpenter had great fun in *Love's Coming of Age* with how the crunch came when 'man, the ungrown' fell in love. Pelting along on his hobby and career, forgetful of the human heart, such a man 'struggles frantically like a fly in treacle; and all the time hasn't the faintest idea whether he has been inveigled into the situation, or whether he got there of his own accord, or what he wants now that he is there'.[22]

Like Shaw, who played with these male fears of women's hidden power in his drama, Carpenter mainly bore perceptive witness to the gender wars of the middle classes rather than the working classes. But *Love's Coming of Age* did speak to some of the concerns of working-class and lower-middle-class women, who during the 1890s were beginning to participate in local government and taking a more active role in the co-operative movement and the trades unions. They too were nursing dreams of a fuller life. Carpenter's unusual lifestyle enabled him to be far more insightful than most men of his class about the domestic labour that an 1890s house entailed. He had learned from watching urban working-class and farm women doing housework, commenting that few men realised 'what monotonous drudgery it really means, and yet what incessant forethought and care; they forget that the woman has no eight hour day, that her work is always staring her in the face, and waiting for her, even on into the night . . . in a perpetual round of petty cares'.[23]

Not only was he pioneering in recognising that housework really *was* work, he also understood, after living at Scotland Street, how the overall environment affected domestic labour. Returning to the idea he had raised in *Civilisation: Its Cause and Cure* of an architecture arising from needs, in *Love's Coming of Age*, he called for improved house-construction, public bakeries and laundries as well as rational, simple and healthy approaches to food and furniture. And of course he invoked that old enemy of his, 'smoke'. When he was writing, the socialisation of domestic labour and the reorganisation of housework were being discussed not only among advanced middle-class women, but by members of the Women's Co-operative Guild as well as by a few male co-operators and socialists, including Tom Mann. Though an acceptance of separate spheres of male and female responsibility at work and in the home prevailed, a minority of socialist working-class 'new women' would have welcomed Carpenter's assertion that men too should 'assist in some part of the domestic work', enabling the women 'occasionally and when desirable to find salaried work outside, and so contribute to the maintenance of the family'.[24]

Love's Coming of Age is a perspicacious but not consistent work. This is partly because the assimilative Carpenter reproduces the contrary attitudes to the 'woman question' which were current at the time. On one side he elevated motherly feeling while endorsing the opposing 'advanced' position that motherhood was too important to leave to actual mothers and that 'training' was needed. From the 1890s socialist women were developing a concept of motherhood as not only an individual activity but one from which society benefited as a whole. A Carpenter version of this citizen-mother steps out of the pages of *Love's Coming of Age*:

> A woman capable at all points to bear children, to guard them, to teach them, to turn them out strong and healthy citizens of the great world, stands at the farthest remove from the finnikin doll or the meek drudge whom man by a kind of false sexual selection had through many centuries evolved as his ideal.[25]

Alongside these Spartan-sounding mothers are juxtaposed Carpenter's alternative ideal of Spartan ladettes; Whitman-style, they are into swimming, rowing, riding, wrestling, shooting, running, and they *fight*. The tomboy Amazon flits through his writing with the Social Mother in tow.

Some of the untidiness in *Love's Coming of Age* derived from a profound indecision in Carpenter's thinking; he could never reconcile his tendency to categorise with the theoretical dynamism that dissolved all his meticulous demarcations. Hence, while inclining towards androgyny, Carpenter also postulated that physiological differences gave rise to distinct kinds of sex instincts in women and men, and believed that women were more primitive, intuitive and emotional than men. Yet he qualified his assertions of essential differences by noting variations. Observing that 'Modern Women' appeared to have renounced conventional instincts of sex and mothering, Carpenter proceeded to comment on mannish temperaments and homogenic attachments evident among 'ultra-rationalising and brain-cultured' types. His startling conclusion was: 'Sometimes it seems possible that a new sex is on the make.'[26] This new sex followed the proposition Symonds had put to him of 'sexual instincts' being detached from biology. However, unlike Symonds, who simply assumed that women's sphere was the household, Carpenter admitted women into the 'new chivalry' of social service by melding them into a 'third sex'. This ploy, of a sex apart, provided Carpenter with exceptions to his own pronouncements on difference which enabled him to leave the patterns of gender open. Though the fluidity in Carpenter's thinking undermined his classification into types, it did not deter him from prejudiced typifications; 'The Jew and the Speculator' reappear in *Love's Coming of Age* as the 'money-grubbing interest' leading the public schoolboy by the nose.[27]

Love's Coming of Age displayed another contradiction prevalent not only in Carpenter's own thought but in the socialism of the period; the difficulty of combining an evolutionary perspective with an emphasis on human agency and action. Drawing on the work of the American evolutionary anthropologist Lewis Henry Morgan, which Engels had used in *The Origin of the Family*, Carpenter argued that the family had narrowed but would expand again in a communistic society. He also posited that new relationships between men and women would evolve. 'With the rise of the new society, which is already outlining itself within the structure of the old, many of the difficulties and bugbears, that at present stand in the way of a more healthy relation between the sexes will of themselves disappear.'[28] This was a conventional Second International approach and Engels too had envisaged freer relationships in the future.

Yet, unlike Engels, Carpenter, the radical individualist and anarchist, also called on the free woman to 'declare herself'. As the Sheffield anarchists had done, he proclaimed, 'Let her insist on her right to speak, dress, think, act, and above all use her sex, as she deems best, let her face the scorn and the ridicule.'[29] Only when the free woman had won honour would the prostitute cease to exist. Like his friend Olive Schreiner, Carpenter believed that men and women's destinies were bound together. One sex could not realise a full humanity without the other. Accordingly man must 'help her gain her feet' and respect women's right to psychological and bodily autonomy; 'Let him never by word or deed tempt her to grant as a bargain what can only be precious as a gift.'[30] Carpenter conceives agency mainly in individual rather than collective terms, though at one point he reverted to his 1870s vision of an alliance between women and workmen. However, his assumption was that as neither of these two groups were strong on intellectual and organisational work, they would have to thump the 'Middle-class Man' into organising the world for them.[31] Given what he had said about 'Man, the Unknown', this would seem a somewhat forlorn hope!

Carpenter's conviction that women and men could change sexual relationships along with his invocation of historical forces contributed to its appeal in the socialist movement and in his humanitarian constituency. Moreover by eschewing a dogmatic 'free love' position, *Love's Coming of Age* helped to stake out new ground in which critiques of existing sexual morality, institutions and relations could become part of a respectable progressive discourse. Endorsing the Fellowship of the New Life's Kantian moral code, Carpenter presented a sexual ethic which would be influential for generations to come: 'The object of love is a person, and cannot be used for private advantage without the most dire infringement of the law of equality.'[32] Like Engels, Carpenter saw monogamy as an historic advance for women, while being critical of the form it took in contemporary society. His defence of marriage contracts was based on the pragmatic recognition that women required a degree of protection. At the same time he wanted to reduce the role of the state in personal relations by making divorce much easier. Indeed he argued that the state should intervene only to protect children, which in his view included legislating away the disadvantages of illegitimacy. These changes in the law would take many years to achieve in practice.

Carpenter envisaged the ideal marriage as one based on mutuality and freedom: 'A marriage, so free, so spontaneous, that it would allow of wide excursions of the pair from each other.'[33] Such companionate marriage between equals was being sought by several of his friends, including Havelock Ellis, who praised Carpenter's comments on marriage as 'felicitous' and remarked on his 'calm and contemplative manner'.[34] Carpenter did have a certain advantage over his friend; he was not married to a woman who had no desire for him – nor was he likely to be. If Carpenter's homosexuality meant that he was necessarily an abstract theorist on heterosexual marriages, it alerted him to the need for an inner regulation in personal relationships as opposed to the authority of Church and State.

Carpenter's melodious prose gracefully muffled the startling modernity of many of his propositions. In *Love's Coming of Age* he advocated sex education and nudity, and slipped in the idea that there was an 'immense *variety* of love'.[35] He also asserted the 'self-dependence and self-ownership of women',[36] a concept which had appeared in the campaign against the Contagious Diseases Acts and was circulating in feminist and in free-love circles where an argument was under way about contraception. Carpenter was sceptical about 'artificial checks', a sniffiness which was consistent with his rejection of externality, though hardly practical.[37]

Despite his ingenious iconoclasm, Carpenter could still not quite decide whether to affirm the body or float off into cosmic consciousness. Hence he advocates a hardy temperance and suggests that as progress was made towards a more frank communal society, the sex act would become less important. Yet Carpenter argues with his own inclination towards ascetic control over the body:

The kiss of the senses is beautiful beyond all and every abstraction; the touch of the sunlight, the glory of form and color, the magic of sweet sound, the joy of human embraces, the passion of sex – all so much the more perfect because they are as it were something divine made actual and realisable. In such a mood asceticism in any form seems the grossest impiety and folly, and the pursuit of the Unseen a mere abandonment of the world for its shadow.[38]

Desiring to hold the two impulses together, he intimates that they were conjoined in the early Star and Sex worships. Over the next two decades Carpenter's interest in Paganism as a way of acknowledging body and spirit grew stronger.

Love's Coming of Age may not have been a work of philosophic rigour, but it was written with a light touch which acted as an effective antidote to the mood of moral panic that followed Wilde's trial in 1895. Carpenter's peculiar amalgam of sexual subversion, social hygiene and spirituality demonstrated its author's considerable skills as a propagandist. Though *Love's Coming of Age* implied far more than met the eye, Carpenter was at his most adroit when presenting extreme views in a moderate tone, an ability which enabled him to appeal to a broad constituency. Carpenter's sex bombs detonated on a long fuse which made them appear not too sexy. His guile cleared countless paths into the next century.

When *Love's Coming of Age* was first published an ominous silence fell: 'Is it a boycott in the press?' asked a solicitous Henry Salt in May 1896, adding, 'It is very odd that there are no notices.'[39] Many books that are not reviewed never sell, some that *are* reviewed never take off; *Love's Coming of Age* fell into a third category; it received little attention from reviewers and a great deal of word-of-mouth promotion. Over time it turned into one of Carpenter's most successful works, going into many editions in Britain and the US and being translated into German, Italian, Swedish, Dutch and French. In *My Days and Dreams* Carpenter was able to relate a blissful admission of error from a publisher at Swan Sonnenschein who had rejected *Love's Coming of Age*. The book had been praised in the man's church, and to his chagrin the congregation had eagerly noted its title down. 'I could not help smiling', purred its author, gratified by the thought of the publisher mentally totting up the sales from this one plug.[40]

It took a while, however, for the book to reach what Carpenter described as the wider literary and respectable readership. Predictably it met with a favourable response in Carpenter's own circle. The shy, inhibited Goldsworthy Lowes Dickinson wrote to express his thanks, particularly for the section on 'The Free Society' in which Carpenter argued for tolerance. 'You say many things that I feel more intimately than any others, and I always imagine myself to be almost alone in feeling.'[41] Carpenter had come to admire Tolstoy through Havelock Ellis, and in 1897 he persuaded Ellis to smuggle a gift of *Love's Coming of Age* into Russia for the novelist. The nervous Ellis, who was attending a medical congress in Moscow with Arthur Symons, stowed Carpenter's 'dynamite' into a slit he cut in his jacket lining, however he and Symons crossed the border from Poland without being searched. Unable to meet Tolstoy because his child was ill, they left *Love's Coming of Age* at Tolstoy's town house. What the prodigal turned ascetic made of it is unclear, though Tolstoy was an admirer of Carpenter's writings on science.

The initial market for *Love's Coming of Age* came through the expanding socialist movement, a few notices snowballing into a substantial readership. When Salt had written in May he enclosed one review from the broad and eclectic Leeds Independent Labour Party journal, the *New Age*, edited by Joseph Clayton. Then in June it was hailed with enthusiasm by 'Lily Bell' in the I.L.P.'s *Labour Leader*. 'Lily Bell' was the pseudonym of Isobella Bream Pearce, active in the Glasgow I.L.P., and an advocate of women's emancipation. She contrasted Carpenter's tone with that of other socialist men. 'Most men write with such an air of superiority, such an assumption of masculine authority and right to lay down the law as to what women may or may not do, what may or may not be her proper "sphere" in life . . .'.[42]

'The Sex Question' and 'The Woman Question' were hot topics bubbling away among socialists despite efforts among the leaders of all the groupings to keep a lid on them. Though the *Clarion* was prepared to countenance a degree of bohemianism, Robert Blatchford thought Carpenter should leave sex alone. Personally he found the whole subject of nudity 'nasty' and did not think the 'sexual parts' in either sex were beautiful. Politically, Blatchford admitted that 'sexual relations' were all wrong and must be altered, but against Carpenter's insistence that socialists must confront sexuality, he considered the main task was to bring about industrial change; sexual change would have to wait for the next generation.[43] The leadership of the Independent Labour Party too were keen to steer away from any suggestion of sexual dissidence and scandal; the last thing they wanted was to be tarred with the 'free-love' tag associated with the anarchists. However Carpenter's resolve to take the discussion out of what he called 'the free love box' gained him an enthusiastic readership among the young people who were coming into the socialist movement. *Love's Coming of Age* opened up an acceptable middle ground between convention and the free lovers.[44]

During the 1890s the utopian aspiration to live the future in the present tended to be couched in terms of spiritual enthusiasm. The fervid dedication of oneself to a cause seemed to dissolve all boundaries between individuals, and while this was not a sexual connection, it could generate a climate of intimacy in which customary moral codes seemed inadequate. Part of Carpenter's appeal lay in his ability to touch on this rapturous idealism. Alongside the ethereal gusts, went a desire among some socialists, influenced by Whitman and Carpenter, to affirm the body, the senses and nature. This too was apt to be expressed in spiritual terms. In 1896 the former Bristol trades union organiser Robert Allan Nicol reported from California that he had experienced a 'clear feeling' which for the first time had enabled him to 'distinguish myself as something apart from and superior to my brain and intellect. There swept thro' me a power of mastery over my body – not an attitude of rejection, but self-realisation – something I have long known and believed but never up till now realised.' He added, 'I want to realise my body and all its faculties.'[45]

In a more subdued manner socialists in Britain were articulating similar aspirations. In the late 1890s a nervous Charlie Sixsmith gave the first of what were to be several lectures over the years, on the man he admired so much. When he came to *Love's Coming of Age*, Sixsmith gingerly told his Lancashire audience: 'The physical, the animal is as sacred and important as any other part of man, it is the base of all and a sane and healthy spirituality and mentality can only flow out of a sane healthy animality.' Whitman with his 'fullness of life', and Carpenter, 'feminine, gentle, intuitive, thoughtful retiring', had enabled the Bolton I.L.P.er to accept sex and the body.[46]

Love's Coming of Age fostered an association between Carpenter and femininity which he had himself noted when writing about *Towards Democracy* in the *Labour Prophet*.[47] 'I believe you were a woman in some other incarnation', remarked Isabella Ford.[48] When Edith Ellis came to write her *Personal Impressions of Edward Carpenter*, she stated, 'In *Love's Coming of Age* he proves he can understand the passionate, bewildering, and mystical heart of a woman.'[49] Ideas were being exchanged internationally and Carpenter's fame reached across to the United States. Among his admirers was an American socialist, Charlotte Perkins Gilman, becoming known in Britain for poems and articles about what she termed 'The Art of Living'. Accordingly when Gilman visited Britain in 1896, she did not just do the radical rounds in London, but travelled north where she had a following among *Clarion* readers. After lecturing on the 'New Motherhood' for the Women's Labour Party and on 'Thou Shalt Love' for the Labour Church, on Monday September 28th Gilman took the train from Halifax to Sheffield. After getting lost she eventually arrived at Dore and Totley station and then travelled by cab to Millthorpe. Carpenter measured her feet for sandals and then it was on to her next appointment with women Theosophists and Quakers in Sheffield before returning to London. She recorded this rather rushed encounter with Carpenter, who seems to have been in sage-like mode: 'Most interesting visit. A beautiful soul',[50] wrote

Gilman in her diary. Carpenter never mentioned Gilman, though his ideas about housework and training for motherhood bore a resemblance to hers. Nonetheless her visit had put Millthorpe on the alternative heritage trail.

Somewhat bizarrely, Carpenter's writing on sex and women led to him being placed on the check list for alternative heterosexual relationships in America. About to marry for the second time in 1897, Gilman instructed her future husband Houghton Gilman to read Carpenter's pamphlets on '"Women" "Marriage" and "Sex Love"' carefully. As she informed him that she thought more highly of them 'than of any I ever read on those lines', the would-be suitor was under considerable pressure to concur.[51] In 1898, when Helena Born was starting a relationship with the former Manchester Socialist Leaguer and anarchist, William Bailie, who had emigrated to Boston, she was delighted by his comments on *Love's Coming of Age*. Born declared she saw things so much from Carpenter's 'point of view that your appreciation of his utterance will conduce greatly to our mutual understanding'. Undaunted that Bailie was already married with a family, Born, the free spirit, observed: 'It is so easy to let an absorbing love disturb and alienate other affectional relationships and I am convinced that it is not as it should be. It's an attempt to limit that which should be limitless, and exclusiveness defeats its own ends. A great love should be a central fire radiating its warmth and glow in all directions.'[52] This ideal of the great love was circulating internationally among advanced women during the 1890s and 1900s, countering conventional morality with its assertion of a higher passion.

In Britain, *Love's Coming of Age* resonated in the socialist movement because conflicting sexual cultures jostled one another. A new breed of young educated socialist women speakers, Enid Stacy, Katharine St John Conway, Caroline Martyn and Margaret McMillan, all of whom read Carpenter, were in a particularly exposed and precarious position. They were revered as prophetesses of a new dawn, which entailed a special purity, yet they found themselves, sotto voce, the objects of desire. On the outer rim of Carpenter's circle, and regarding him with a certain awe, all four of the socialist new women admired his writing. Stacy and St John Conway belonged to a group of young Fabians called the 'Magic Circle', who corresponded nationally on political and personal topics including free unions. Stacy disapproved, but St John Conway dithered when she became part of a domestic trio with a working-class socialist, Dan Irving. Irving made passes, while Mrs Irving made her do the housework. Later came a soul union with James William Wallace which linked Bristol and Bolton, and a passionate courtship with John Bruce Glasier, who she married in 1893 at Rough Firth, Dumfriesshire, according to the Scottish custom of declaring before two witnesses.

Carpenter also acquired a constituency among the growing numbers of literary 'new women' swelling the ranks of the pioneers of the 1880s. Initially their ideas had simply been ridiculed, but in the fallout after the Wilde trial, they found themselves being castigated as immoral and subversive, along with homosexuals and decadents. In 1896 Carpenter was asked to speak on science at London's most advanced women's club, 'The Pioneer'. Founded by the temperance supporter, Emily Massenbred, and named after Whitman's poem 'Pioneers O Pioneers', the club debated anti-vivisection, anti-vaccination, Theosophy and 'feminism' – a new term for women's rights advocates who considered women to be rather better than men. A prominent 'Pioneer' was the new woman writer, Mona Caird. Caird, who had attended meetings of the Men and Women's Club, wrote critiques of marriage that sent shivers of horror through polite society and provided Shaw with material for his sassy heroines. In 1892 Caird had written 'A Defence of Wild Women' in the Nineteenth Century, and, like Carpenter, was also involved in the animal rights and anti-vivisection causes. She may well have been the instigator of the summons which caused Carpenter to chuckle to Hukin in 1896, 'The wild women of the Pioneer Club have hunted me down at last.'[53]

Feminism found a political focus in 1897 when Millicent Fawcett brought together the existing groups under one umbrella in the National Union of Women's Suffrage Societies. The aim was the vote; Fawcett wanted no wild women – or men for that matter – to muddy the waters. A youthful Bertrand Russell, interested in Carpenter's writings on sex in the late 1890s, recalled the frosty atmosphere when Fawcett and Carpenter were both in Edinburgh, attending a conference on women's suffrage. She resolutely declined to speak to the author of Homogenic Love.[54]

There were some gulfs even Carpenter the great reconciler was not able to bridge. Nonetheless his fan club kept on growing. In 1898 Edith Ellis wrote asking for a copy of Homogenic Love for a woman acquaintance of hers who was an enthusiast of Love's Coming of Age. This admirer of Carpenter's had gazed at two photographs of him and pronounced, 'In the first he is a faun . . . in the second a man'; 'Lordy-lordy', commented Edith.[55]

While Carpenter gained a following among women through Love's Coming of Age, a dissident note was struck by Henry Salt who insisted that Olive Schreiner, Isabella Ford and 'the female friends that knew him best', believed that Carpenter did not understand women.[56] Salt is a somewhat hostile witness, but Carpenter certainly had his own presuppositions about how women should be. Foremost among his amiable women were the tomboys, like sister Ellen who could accompany him on long walks, and the responsive meditative types, such as Lizzie who faithfully read his works. These were the prototypes for the enlightened 'ladies' who could be relied upon to avert their eyes from youths bathing in Endcliffe Wood and sit tight during the Bedborough trial. For Carpenter they represented an alternative ethical force against 'man, the ungrown'. He also invested mothers, especially working-class mothers, with a redoubtable moral power. Marching down Leeds' dreary Kirkstall Road on May Day 1897, with thousands of people singing 'England Arise', Carpenter dilated to Mattison on the tragic faces of the working-class women holding babies at their breasts.[57] Mothers en masse embodied alternative principles of need and care against profit and competition for Carpenter. To be fair to him, this elevation of motherhood was not just iconographic, Carpenter was personally affectionate to the real mothers of his male friends, sending messages to Oates' and Mattison's mothers in his letters and expressing warmth towards the chaotic Mrs Merrill.

While they seem ostensibly dissimilar, Carpenter's ideal women have one overriding characteristic in common: they are not at all bothersome. The tomboys were self-sustaining; the receptive types possessed deep spiritual resources within their own souls; and other men's mothers were primarily the responsibility of their sons. Sister Sophy still lurked as the negative image of all things female, and a tacit rule imposed on his women friends was that on no account were they to boss, interrupt or otherwise inconvenience him. The implications of his approach could be upsetting. According to Salt, Isabella Ford was annoyed when Carpenter pressed her to visit Millthorpe for the weekend. She made the trek from Adel, only to find herself abandoned by her host who announced he was off with a friend for the day.[58] This would have been inconceivable in the well-ordered Ford household. Carpenter's cavalier rejection of the norms of sociability was not exclusively restricted to his women friends; however, without the romance of comradeship, his capacity to focus on them was considerably less sustained. The oscillation between attentiveness and indifference, which confused all his friends, was thus more marked. All the women in his close circle were familiar with Carpenter's fits of extraordinary comprehension followed by a sudden retreat under the cloak of absent-mindedness. At one moment they were stroking an empathic faun, at the next the man bolted.

The swings in Carpenter's response caused the most serious trouble in

Isabella Ford, as pictured in the *Yorkshire Factory Times*, 1889

his relations with Kate Salt. He had tried to warn her in March 1890 when the woolly shawl arrived that she must not idealise him, because he was such a 'humbug'.[59] Her early letters addressed to 'Chips' are full of demonstrative expressions of affection; it is evident that for Kate their friendship was of profound import; 'You are like a sign post Chips!', she declared in 1892 when her brother Jim Joynes was seriously ill.[60] She could tell him anything, knowing he would not judge her by conventional standards. He could comprehend how the barrier of reserve between her and Jim had made her brother's early death in 1893 even harder to bear. He could also accept her sexual feelings towards women and believed in her musical and literary gifts.

Kate was not able to take on the outer world, like Carpenter's other close women friends. She was dogged by feelings of inadequacy and an overwhelming sense of inferiority froze her own talents, surrounded as she was by busy achievers. Her reverence for Carpenter became an obstacle in their friendship. She was puzzled to discover herself feeling closer to him when they were apart; in real life she was never quite at ease in his presence. 'I wish Chips I could get over <u>being afraid of you</u>. I mean minding what you think of me', Kate wrote in January 1892. Kate knew this arose partly from her own paralysing self-doubt. 'I am always shamming and never really myself.'[61] But it was also coming from his response to her self-conscious fear which made him disgruntled and sharp with her. Her dread of annoying him pressed heavy on their relationship.

Intellectually, Carpenter could step back and observe how her sympathies were preyed upon by others, inhibiting her from assembling the self-esteem to fuel creativity. He genuinely longed for her to find something *she* wanted to do: 'It is not enough that you shd. be interested in us but we must be interested in <u>your work</u>.'[62] But the brutal truth was that he evaded the burden of insecurities she plied him with because he was not *that* interested. In 1894, when their friendship was in difficulty, Carpenter wondered why it was that they never seemed to get the chance to have a good talk.[63] The reason lay in his dread of her emotions; fearing her dependence caused him to duck intimate moments – just like 'man, the ungrown' in fact.

Shaw was still pursuing the passionate pianist of Crankie Farm days, and his company dazzled and distressed Kate. In 1896 she recounted to Carpenter: 'That blessed Shaw turns up here two or three times a week. Sometimes we have rapturous music – mounting on clouds till we touch high heavens – but sometimes bewildering whirlpools of talk – when I lose all hold and feel myself being dragged into an abyss.'[64] She confided that Shaw simply refused to acknowledge that 'the shuddering horror' he would feel if he were to be 'touched or fondled' by a man was exactly how she regarded his advances. When she had tried to explain, 'doubting Thomas went and wrote a play called "You Never Can Tell".'[65] Though the emancipated heroine Gloria informs her suitor Valentine that his talk of 'chemistry' is 'nonsense', in the play of course, it gets to her in the end. It was never so with Kate, who worked as Shaw's unpaid typist and secretary during 1898: 'In the absence of sentimental interruptions we get along famously', averred the playwright.[66] Shaw blamed Carpenter for Kate's lack of interest, and was still grumbling in his old age about how Carpenter had convinced her she was an Urning, leading her to refuse to consummate her marriage with Henry.[67] More likely it was the other way round; Carpenter, the signpost, indicated words for already existing inclinations.

Carpenter's teasing evasive friendship with Kate crunched into crisis in February 1897 when her need for him overspilled in a desperate letter. 'Edward! don't leave me altogether if you can help it. I have really tried hard – but it is <u>so</u> hard – and sometimes I feel as if I shall go down. You know, you know I don't want to torment you.'[68] She longed to be able to creep in, sit beside him and touch his hand.[69] In her moods of bleak despair, which Carpenter called her 'black blues', Kate resembled his troubled younger sister Dora, rather than Lizzie.[70]

The underlying reality in what appears as a relationship of inordinate emotional inequality was that Carpenter, like everyone else, actually relied on Kate a great deal. It was Kate who had a unique ability to 'blend' his diverse guests together at Millthorpe: 'I can't help wishing sometimes that destiny wd. throw you and H. up high and dry at Holmesfield – irretrievably stranded.'[71] Despite his realisation that Kate dedicated herself too much to the needs of others, nevertheless he depended on her to help the American musician Philip Dalmas or to accompany Max Flint when he was too ill to travel alone. It was Kate who provided furniture to make Millthorpe more aesthetic and a paraffin stove to make Glover Road less cold. And, when Carpenter was in the midst of a painful estrangement from George Adams in 1897, it was to Kate that he turned for approbation. So, regardless of his nervousness about their psychologically convoluted embroilment, he did not shy away from Kate entirely; she had a special place among his women friends.

Carpenter was more gruff towards the young women he met through the socialist movement during the 1890s. When Wallace prevailed upon him to see 'Miss McMillan and other friends' when he came over to lecture on 'The Future of Labor' [sic] in Bolton in April 1894, Carpenter agreed somewhat grudgingly.[72] The young women intruded on the male camaraderie. Bruce Glasier's decision to marry Katharine St John Conway in 1893 jolted his friendship with Carpenter. On hearing the news Carpenter wrote in a frolicsome fashion on June 4th, wondering whether the new couple would be 'Mr and Mrs Katharine Bruce St. John Johnny Conway-Glasier or Glasier-Conway.'[73] The smitten Glasier was offended and Carpenter had to apologise: 'Sincerely I think K.C. a true and noble woman'. He added a little snidely, 'It is only on the surface that we have been sometimes disappointed by her.'[74] Katharine St John Conway sensed disapproval and was fearful that gossip from Bristol was the cause. To Katharine, in her mid-twenties, the author she revered who was also the comrade of the man she loved was an intimidating figure, all the more so because his lack of sexual interest in women invested in him an apparent austerity. She was anxious to gain his approval.

Nervous women adherents were in a catch-22 because though Carpenter might be prone to vanity, he really did dislike sanctification. Henry Salt illustrates this with an amusing cameo of Carpenter telling a story about his Cambridge days in which he remarked,

'Once when I was drunk' only to be interrupted by a laugh from a woman admirer, 'I like that Edward Carpenter drunk!' 'When I was drunk . . . !' he continued sternly, and again the enthusiast intervened with some jocular comment. 'I say', he repeated, 'when I was drunk'; and this time there was something in his tone which froze even the worshipper into silence.[75]

The tone that froze belonged to the man, not the faun.

It was the man of course who had felt that terrible jealousy towards Fannie. Her occasional and careful letters to Carpenter reveal little: unlike the middle-class women friends, she did not confide. Painstakingly, as the years went by, the two knitted an amicable relationship because of their mutual love for George. But he at once united and divided them. The wariness between them had been there from the beginning, and, even though it became overlaid by familiarity, it lingered on. But the initial hostility Carpenter displayed towards Fannie was unique; in general he was not at all hostile to women, he simply preferred the company of his close men friends. As he put it in the autobiographical notes that he sent to Charlie Sixsmith: 'I have excellent and life-long friends among women; but the romance of friendship and love has always gone out with me, to companions of my own sex.'[76] Ever dutiful, Carpenter was scrupulous about doing the right thing. In September 1899, when the newly engaged Alf Mattison visited Millthorpe, Carpenter gallantly picked roses from the garden for his fiancé Florence Foulds, sending his congratulations to Mattison in October: 'I think you are quite right to "embark".'[77] Mattison's nervousness about the first meeting between Carpenter and Florrie comes sweetly through in his account of what clearly was for him a pivotal encounter. He planned it with care, bringing them together on the neutral ground of the 'Three Horse Shoes' pub in Meanwood. Visits to Millthorpe followed, but Florrie, like Fannie and Lucy, must have known that despite Carpenter's good manners, it was the men who were the real friends.

The working-class women in Carpenter's life were relegated to a place on the far horizon. Working-class mothers might be wonderful from a distance on Kirkstall Road, but as individuals they were outside Carpenter's emotional orbit. His potent empathy never stretched out to Mary Ann Fearnehough, always known as 'Mrs' and bereft of a first name, who spring-cleaned around him in the midst of the anarchist trials in 1892. 'My room has come out a fiery red', he cracked to Kate Salt.[78] Lucy Adams' zeal with the housework was reported to Kate in 1893, soon after the Adamses moved in. 'Lucy keeps turning out a lot of work.'[79] Their feelings were mentioned in passing, again mainly in his letters to Kate.

'Mrs F' was 'anxious' about leaving Millthorpe; 'Lucy' was pining for town life. Carpenter was similarly remote from the children around him, expressing a fondness for Harry Adams bubbling over the soap-blowing machine and remarking to Kate Salt on the prettiness of a little girl called Alice from the Greaves family in Glover Road, with whom he lodged when he stayed in Sheffield. He was deeply distressed when a drunken Willie Greaves attacked Mrs Greaves in front of Alice, yet he viewed the working-class women through a haze of psychological incomprehension.

As ever it was Kate Salt who acted as his helpmate in relationships he could not fathom. In 1890, regretful that she would not come into Sheffield to meet his working-class friends, he is sure Mrs Fearnehough would be cheered up if Kate could teach her some new dishes. This was Carpenterese for 'please instruct this woman to cook more varied food'. Then he is letting Kate know how Lucy Adams would be pleased that Kate was coming to stay. Carpenter knew that Kate could communicate with her.

The great seer's benign gaze swept over the working-class women and then put them out of mind, and though his middle-class women friends received devoted letters, they too were held very gently at bay. When their needs frightened him, he promptly withdrew. Yet inadvertently he fostered networks of friendship and support between the women in his overlapping circles. Isabella Ford, Olive Schreiner and Kate Salt met through Carpenter. Schreiner befriended Lucy Adams, as did Fannie Hukin. When the radical quarry-man John Furniss' wife was ill, Mary Ann Fearnehough cared for her. The Fearnehoughs' daughter Annie went to live with the Hukins. Florrie Mattison could rely on a welcome from Lucy Adams and Fannie Hukin when she and Alf visited Millthorpe. All these working-class women who appear only through tiny peep-holes, in scattered throwaway references in the correspondence of others, would have had tales to tell – some rather caustic for Carpenter's ears no doubt. More considerate and perceptive than the majority of men of his class and era, aware of the value of working-class women's labour, their views and sentiments remained, nonetheless, outside his compass. He barely discerned the tenuous women's world that grew gossamer-like about his own in the Cordwell Valley.

13

Millthorpe

By the 1890s, guests were arriving at Millthorpe as if they were entering the portals of the New Life. Bestowing deep symbolic meaning on the place, they transmuted Carpenter's mundane routines into rituals of great moment. An account by one of Carpenter's most faithful chroniclers, Charlie Sixsmith, reveals how the New Life was not for the faint-hearted or the shivery:

> Rising about seven, Edward would usually take a dip in the brook, a sunbath, and a gallop round the garden; or a sponge-down in a sheltered corner of the lawn. Then, after tidying up his room, a little work in the yard or garden, and breakfast, he settled down to his writing which he mostly did in the mornings and nearly always out of doors, winter and summer.[1]

When the Bolton Whitmanites, James William Wallace and Dr John Johnston visited in the summer of 1892, Wallace meticulously recorded how on Sunday, August 14th, Carpenter rose at 7.45 with water for Wallace and Johnston's bath; breakfast was at 8.30, followed by a stroll in the garden where Wallace took in the hut that looked like a sentry box and the 'clear stream at the bottom'. Scrutinising their host, Wallace thought that Carpenter lacked 'robustness and virility', noticing how his legs were extremely thin, but reckoned that his surroundings and lifestyle made him healthy. That August Carpenter had his coat thrown open, and the observant Wallace was interested to see that he wore no vest. Other items of clothing that caught his attention were Carpenter's sandals and 'slouch hat' – Carpenter had become attached to this soft felt hat during the late 1880s; it gave him a wandering wayfarer look.

Along with Carpenter's style of dress, Wallace carefully detailed the Millthorpe supper of porridge, cold ham, radishes, with brown and white bread, butter-milk and tea – the latter 'stimulant' a concession to the Bolton guests. He was more enthusiastic about a 'capital' Sunday 'dinner' in the middle of the day: meat, Yorkshire pudding, potatoes and the sweetest peas he had ever tasted, climaxing in a gooseberry and strawberry pie made by Mary Ann Fearnehough. Soul unions or no soul unions, Wallace clearly liked his food, remarking how Carpenter ate no meat. With some surprise he recorded how Fearnehough carved at the head of the table and, while displaying respect towards Carpenter, did not treat him with deference. In contrast to Carpenter, the Fearnehoughs, with their grown-up offspring, Annie and George, who were visiting from Sheffield, seemed elderly to Wallace; he regarded them as maintaining the house and garden for Carpenter, rather than as friends.

The magic of Millthorpe was in the relating. Wallace recounts how after supper in the evening he, Johnston, Carpenter and Hukin settled down to talk. Wallace smoked a pipe, Hukin and Johnston puffed away at their cigars, Carpenter lit a cigarette and they were away, ruminating about the socialist editor, Robert Blatchford, about Whitman, Emerson and Dr Bucke, who had brought them together. As the night sky cleared they all went out to look at the stars through Carpenter's telescope. The rest of Wallace and Johnston's stay was spent in more talk, along with walking, reading, listening to Carpenter play Beethoven and Schubert on the piano in the kitchen, and looking at photographs of Henry and Kate Salt, George Adams, Havelock Ellis, Olive Schreiner, Bessie and Isabella Ford. Carpenter's photographs provided a way of linking friends and celebrities, which complemented his assiduous arrangements for people to meet in person; photographs were constantly being sent in letters, borrowed and copied.

Wallace was charmed by the thoughtful touches; the pipe, especially ordered for him, and the roses Carpenter picked for them to take home for John Johnston's wife. Carpenter also measured the two men's feet for sandals. The precise Wallace records parting on the 3 o'clock train from Dore and Totley station on August 15th, taking the 4.15 from Sheffield and arriving at his home in Adlington, outside Bolton, at 7.10.[2] In a few years' time Carpenter could happily announce that a new train had been timetabled from Manchester to Dore and Totley directly in 1¼ hours, obligingly facilitating communication between Bolton and Millthorpe – the present journey-time beats this 1894 innovation by three minutes.[3] Reflecting on their expedition, Wallace concluded that the discussions, the pie, the astronomy, the delicate sensibility of Carpenter at the piano had all been wonderful. He was impressed too by the heady democratic comradeship: 'Pleasant to see how naturally and simply Carpenter and

(Left to right) Hukin, Carpenter, Sixsmith and Merrill (front) at Millthorpe

George Hukin intertwined arms round each other's waists like boys or lovers.'⁴ Were there flowers too for Fannie?

Millthorpe might be existentially delightful as a site for conversation and encounters; about the house itself Wallace was not at all sure. Unlike Ashbee and Unwin, he was not won over by the long narrow stone building with its slated roof and 'plain and simple design'. He took it in like the draughtsman he was, even drawing a plan: sitting room with stairs, kitchen, scullery, wash house and stable, all in line without a corridor. The sitting room, fifteen foot square and so plain he thought it resembled an office, was summarised with professional exactitude: 'Walls distempered in terra cotta colour, floorboards stained, with square centre carpet, stove in front of fireplace, plain-deal table polished, with drawers etc, chest of drawers and a few (20 or so) books on top of drawers.' When he asked Carpenter about the house, Carpenter said his architect had been influenced by the jerry-building of the early 1880s. The disadvantages of living in the acme of simplification were evidently becoming apparent, for Carpenter announced that he was planning to add another room which he wished to have some taste and beauty. A tactful Wallace wondered whether the plainness and even ugliness of the house might be regarded as displaying a 'unique fitness'. Carpenter remained silent and Wallace suspected his host was doubtful. The best aspect of Millthorpe, Wallace decided, was 'Beautiful views from the windows'.[5] Wallace's observation applied particularly to the back of the house which faced the undulating slopes of the Cordwell Valley. An idiosyncratic feature of Millthorpe was that whereas houses usually put their best face forwards, Carpenter's was built back to front, reticently confronting the road and luxuriating in the privacy of the back garden.

The friend of Charles Ashbee and Frank Deas, George Ives, who travelled north in April 1897, was particularly harsh on Millthorpe. 'It was a cottage (dreadfully like those buildings that the railway companies build for country-station masters) and in straight lines which I deplored.' He considered the building to be bare and hard, lacking the broken outlines or creeper coverings of a village cottage. While he approved of the rustic shed, the brook and the valley, it was thumbs down for Fearnehough's legacy, the 'rectilinear and hideous sort of kitchen garden, with the little fruit-trees planted all in straight rows'.[6] Nor did Carpenter's early rising and dips in the brook appeal; Ives was so cold at Millthorpe he slept in his coat. His idea of the bohemian life was urban bachelor comfort, not the Northern countryside.

Most guests were quite unconcerned about the architecture. When Wallace took Charlie Sixsmith for the first time he discovered paradise:

> It was a bright March day, clusters of daffodils and snowdrops bordered the brook and hedgerow; all around were hills, woods, and fields, and close by a stone-roofed hamlet and farmstead. Sitting at table, to a vegetarian meal, one looked through the open door down the sunlit garden to the hills.[7]

To Alf Mattison, who had never been in the countryside before, the contrast with the grey grime of Hunslet was heaven – a verdant wonder of hedgerows bursting with leaves, primroses by the brook, cherry blossom on the trees.

Millthorpe represented release and fun too for Mattison, who loved the walks and outings. On one marathon trek on Easter Saturday in 1895, Mattison came over with three of his Leeds comrades. Along with Shortland, Adams and Carpenter, they went from Dore and Totley station to Hathersage. The following day they walked down the River Derwent, through Grindleford and Bamford, which must have caused a minor stir as they were singing and giving out leaflets as they went. Then they climbed up Shivering Mountain (Mam Tor), which lived up to its name; they were caught in freezing hail before arriving back at Millthorpe.[8]

In *My Days and Dreams* Carpenter remarked that his account of Millthorpe made the place sound as if it were a perpetual garden-party with only the distance from the station and the winter snow securing any peace.[9] He might well have compared his home to an adult education summer school which ran on for most of the year, in which nature, outings, politics, talk, books, music and the extraordinary commingling of people constituted an education in itself. From his Millthorpe walks with Carpenter, Mattison acquired not only his liking for rambling, but a desire to learn about natural history, social history and folklore. Carpenter taught him about plants, the enclosure of the commons, and introduced him to the old custom of well-dressing at Barlow in 1893. In 1897 a proud, scholarly Mattison organised his own historical outing, escorting Bessie Joynes and Lucy Adams to the grand Chatsworth House and romantic Haddon Hall, with the help of a hired landau and George Adams with the horse and cart.[10]

Not everyone fell into Carpenter's schemes so happily. Henry Salt found Carpenter's expeditions over-regimented because their host was inclined to decree who should walk together, carefully moving from one set of walkers to another, while Olive Schreiner seems to have resisted hiking altogether, causing Carpenter, who disapproved of sedentary guests, to remark in 1893 to Kate Salt how Olive had hardly gone out.[11] But to young men familiar with the punitive regulation of board school and workplace, Carpenter's benign autocracy provided an alternative etiquette for their precious leisure days.

In the evenings, Carpenter shared his love of music with guests, perched on the piano stool playing Chopin, Beethoven and Schubert. Another Millthorpe pastime was reading books out loud – Isabella Ford's new woman novel, *On the Threshold*, or Thomas Hardy's controversial *Tess of the d'Urbervilles*. It was by no means all purposeful and improving. There were jaunts into Sheffield, not just to meetings or an I.L.P. social, but to the popular 'Nigger Minstrels' and the Empire Palace of Varieties. Carpenter enjoyed the music hall as much as his working-class friends. Politics were never far away; in 1897 Mattison describes Joe Potter, the young man Carpenter had met at the foot races, back from sea, joining them at the Empire and rushing off afterwards with a crowd who were chasing scabs brought in to break an engineering strike.[12]

The giddy mix of guests contributed to scenes of wild hilarity at Millthorpe. Carpenter, who took a mischievous delight in oddity, wrote in amusement to George Hukin about an evening he spent in October

1895 with Raymond Unwin, Kate Salt, Bessie Joynes, Jim Shortland, George Merrill and the new woman novelist from Bristol, Gertrude Dix, 'in ballet costume knickers'.[13]

Strong friendships formed among the visitors. 'Do you remember', Kate Salt asked Alf Mattison, 'how we sat and talked one evening in Carpenter's study, with the moonlight outside and Edward's Beethoven floating in from the other room?[14] Memories persisted over the years. 'I have often thought of the talk I had with you on the bridge at Dore and Totley station', reminisced Henry Salt to Mattison in 1919.[15] Sometimes this communion of spirits contained a sensuous undertow. George Adams and Alf Mattison both carried a flame for Olive Schreiner. On that 1893 visit when she upset Carpenter by not taking exercise, she was agonising over whether to marry her farmer Samuel Cron Cronwright. Mattison, who was holidaying at Millthorpe, would spend hours with her in the cottage she had rented in the village, arguing about politics. Eventually a gleeful Schreiner revealed she had been winding him up; she hated capitalism as much as he did. These fervent disputes resulted in them becoming what Mattison calls quite 'chummy', whereupon the watchful George Adams made it his business to inform Mattison how he happened to know that a young fellow at the Cape had asked Miss Schreiner to marry him. Schreiner gave the fateful telegram accepting Cronwright to Mattison to take to the Post Office, yet when she left for South Africa, she told Carpenter how she would have liked to kiss the shy young Leeds engineer goodbye, but did not know if he would have liked it. On learning of this, a rueful Mattison exclaimed in his letter book 'would I have liked it?'[16]

Millthorpe provided the setting for many desirous looks and unstated flutters. These thwarted romances smouldered away in secrecy – except that everyone tended to divulge their attachments in a euphemistic, round-about manner to Carpenter. Kate Salt was initially uneasy with the ailing Max Flint, conscious of his eyes hungrily trying to catch hers while he worked making sandals with George Adams.[17] He must have got the message and switched his attentions to Bessie Joynes, telling Carpenter how he was missing her in November 1893.[18] When Flint died in 1902, Bessie revealed how much she cared for him to Carpenter, saying his death brought back the pain of the loss of her brother Jim. It appears that Carpenter discreetly conveyed his guests' mutual affections, for she added, 'I'm so glad to think that he knew.'[19]

Visitors were not always harmonious. Katharine and John Bruce Glasier, honeymooning at Millthorpe in 1893, strenuously objected to Schreiner's views on the 'kaffirs' of South Africa and it was left to Carpenter to make sure the young couple parted in the glow of his approbation.[20] Carpenter could placate principled, argumentative honeymooners, but found his sisters impossibly difficult to accommodate. In 1894 there was a great commotion when three sisters, most probably Sophy, Dora and Alice, all unmarried, came to stay, along with a 'broken down worldly cousin'. Carpenter moaned to Kate Salt that there were 'Struggles into Dronfield and other places to get provisions – shriekings of pigs and lambs and fowls murdered for their support – arrival of drays with beer and wine.'[21] To make it worse, it was raining and cold every day. The younger sisters, Alice and Dora, visited Millthorpe on other occasions, but only brother Alfred could really adapt to Carpenter's odd friends and lifestyle. His contact with the Fellowship of the New Life enabled him to take Mattison the working-class socialist, Dalmas the bohemian, and Dix, the new woman writer, in his stride. Ida Hyett remarked how her Uncle Alfred contrived to harmonise his naval traditions with his brother Edward's ideas.[22]

The sheer volume of visitors created considerable logistic problems and, as Carpenter was in the position of tour manager, his letters frequently display an obsessive anxiety about arrangements. Henry Salt conceded that he was a good organiser, yet despite all his efforts, guests were wont to turn up in unexpected flocks.[23] As Robert Blatchford's *Clarion* sprouted recreational clubs in the 1890s, a great host of vigorous young socialists were doing what Carpenter and his friends had initiated ad hoc. Parties of *Clarion* ramblers and cyclists on jolly propaganda outings started stopping off at Millthorpe. During July 1897, one contingent of cyclists from Manchester and Sheffield came puffing in when Mattison, Dalmas and Bessie Joynes were all staying. Mattison recalled how Carpenter walked them round the garden conversing en route, because the house was so full there was nowhere else to put them.[24] The flows of visitors taxed Carpenter's mathematical and diplomatic skills. Guests could be annoyingly uncertain about their plans or overstay their welcome, and Salt remarks on Carpenter's dexterity at removing the unwanted ones.[25] When Millthorpe was bursting at the seams, overflows had to be found. Guests rented nearby cottages or stayed at the Keys' substantial Cordwell Farm across the road from Carpenter's house. An alternative was the Hukins, until they moved to Totley in 1897, perhaps to put some distance between themselves and Carpenter. In his role as the accommodator, Carpenter was inclined to incorporate close friends, leading even the devoted Hukin to comment to Salt, 'Edward's not content with making his own plans; he wants to make everyone else's as well.'[26]

Carpenter represented the charismatic hub of Millthorpe and his charm worked on the most dissimilar of guests. Roger Fry, who visited around

1890, was interested in the copies of Italian art stored in Ruskin's museum at Walkley, but puzzled by Millthorpe mores, reporting to his parents: 'The manner of life here is very curious and quite unlike anything I ever saw before.' Though Fry had rather feared Carpenter would live the life of a 'somewhat rampant and sensational Bohemian' he had been agreeably disappointed to find him 'a most delightful man and absolutely free from all affectation'.[27] Part of Carpenter's fascination lay not simply in what he said, but in how he looked. A nervous, newly wed Janet Ashbee, at Millthorpe on her honeymoon in October 1898, recorded in the joint journal she kept with her husband that she had at last met Edward Carpenter, remarking, as Ellis had done on his first encounter, on the 'magnetic brown eyes'.[28]

Guests and household members alike sought that special feeling of contact which Lowes Dickinson described as Carpenter's capacity to sink into the person with whom he was talking, evincing such empathy that it seemed as if 'a second half' were confronting one.[29] As resident sage and therapist, everyone confided in him and relied on receiving an individualised blessing. Kate Salt, disconsolate in 1894 because she had not been able to talk to Carpenter alone, observed to Alf Mattison, 'I wonder he is not torn to pieces by the hosts of people wanting to see him all the time; all tugging and pulling away at him by different strings.'[30] The perceptive Kate understood that Millthorpe absorbed a prodigious amount of emotional labour.

At the same time Millthorpe was the place where Carpenter did his writing, working outdoors or in the sentry-box, which was sometimes so cold that the ink froze in his pen. The decision to take pen and paper outside was probably not just an act of asceticism, but because the house itself was so often full of people and their needs. Moreover, as well as churning out his books, articles, lectures and letters, Carpenter was also contributing to the manual labour which, along with Charles Carpenter's careful investments, helped to maintain Millthorpe – gardening, sandal-making, cleaning, mending and sewing.

Millthorpe might be an intellectual and recreational location for guests, but for Carpenter and for other permanent residents it was a co-operative workplace. Albert Fearnehough ran the garden, looked after the horse, drove the cart and played a fiddle; Mary Ann Fearnehough, in her white apron, did the cooking and most of the cleaning. When George and Lucy Adams moved in, early in 1893, they took over from the Fearnehoughs. Adams proved quicker than the ponderous Fearnehough in the garden and also learned sandal-making from Carpenter, who tended to switch to handling distribution. They had innovated on Cox's original pair. 'Do

you wish "Cashmere" or Millthorpe pattern?' enquired Carpenter of Charlie Sixsmith in 1895.[31] Adams added bee-keeping to the domestic economy
of Millthorpe, contriving to find time for the landscape painting that was
his own real love. Lucy Adams' prodigious cleaning was a contribution
that became most evident on the occasions when she was ill in bed and
the men had to improvise. In July 1896 when she fell out of the trap and
hurt her leg, Carpenter told Oates he and George Adams were 'nurses,
cooks, housemaids and farm laborers [sic] all combined!'[32] Ashbee, alone,
noticed another Lucy when he visited in September 1895, 'a gentle sympathetic, sweet-natured woman who manages the household with quiet
dignity. She is not a drudge and has a gift for conversation.'[33] So Lucy too
may have had aspirations towards that world of ideas and the spirit pursued
so earnestly by those for whom she cooked and cleaned. She loved Hardy's
Jude the Obscure, which Alf Mattison loaned the household. However the
habit of ceaseless housework became ingrained; the socialist journalist Harold
Armitage remarked upon it many years later, when the Adamses had migrated
to the garden city Unwin helped to design at Letchworth.[34]

Carpenter's pragmatic utopianism inclined him towards adapting
whatever aptitudes his guests displayed. Thus Dalmas wrote sonatas, sang
and played the piano. Flint, frequently praised for his pluck by Carpenter,
played the piano with little Lucy and Harry Adams and kept them entertained. Too frail for heavy work, Flint did a little light dusting and his
tailoring skills came in handy; he made the sandals with Adams and later
took up basket making. Mattison was a particularly useful guest, being
good at carpentry and odd jobs, and when he took up photography would
be summonsed over to add to Carpenter's collection of pictures of friends
and of himself.

Millthorpe manifested Carpenter's theories about creative labour and
free association on a mini-scale; it also embodied his faith in loving
fellowship. It acted as an alternative workplace and home rolled into one
where countless guests felt they were glimpsing the new dawn of their
dreams. Carpenter was the alchemist in all this; without him the place
became sad and empty. Long after it was all over, the vast, sprawling
network of friends carried Millthorpe and his kindness in their memories.
Charlie Sixsmith spoke for many when he looked back fondly on
Carpenter's care and hospitality: 'no parent or elder brother could have
been more considerate both in big and little things for my welfare'.[35]

However, having sought the new life and made it in miniature at Millthorpe,
Carpenter discovered that wants and desires could be contradictory – even
in Arcadia. The unresolved tensions kept recurring. He wished to be

independent from familial ties, yet persisted in collecting far more people than usually dwell in any family, all of whom depended upon him psychologically and materially. He sought contemplative solitude, but then would grow lonely. At a loose end one night in the early 1890s while babysitting young Harry Adams, he asked the writer Robert Murray Gilchrist, who lived at Cartledge Hall in Holmesfield, to drop in and share a bottle of whiskey.[36] Longing to surround himself with an alternative, predominantly male, family, he would issue invitations to far-flung friends. Whereupon too many of them would come at once with the result that he would be falling over guests when he desired to be at peace. It was difficult to get the balance right and unconscionably complicated to ensure that he was in the company of congenial spirits.

Carpenter disliked making changes in his life and held on to old relationships out of loyalty and duty, even when he was fretting within them. Throughout the late 1880s and early 1890s, Albert Fearnehough's dour presence loomed heavily over festivities at Millthorpe. Fearnehough, who had thought he and his family were moving in with a lonely bachelor, found himself instead amidst crowds of Salts, Shortlands, Browns, Mattisons, and Bolton Whitmanites. Among these regular visitors only the Salts made any effort to befriend Albert and Mary Ann Fearnehough, the young men were either rattled or puzzled by their presence. In 1892 Carpenter began manoeuvring for the Adamses to replace the Fearnehoughs. George Adams was eager to come and Carpenter seems to have promised him a place at Millthorpe. The obstacles to the two men's plans were Lucy's resistance to country life and the Fearnehoughs' reluctance to leave. In October 1892 George Adams brought Lucy and the children to look at Millthorpe.[37] By March 1893 Carpenter was assuring Mattison, who felt intimidated by the clayey countryman, that he would not feel afraid of coming when the Adamses moved in.[38] Fearnehough, accepting the inevitable, found a place nearby. It was damp and needed a lot of work on it, but in March 1893 household goods acquired jointly over the years were divided and loaded onto a dray which Fearnehough and Carpenter, yoke-fellows to the last, pulled up to the new house. Carpenter told Kate Salt that while 'Mrs F' was anxious about the future, Albert had been very good and thoughtful about the move.[39] Fearnehough, never emotionally demonstrative, kept his feelings to himself.

Carpenter spent what he described to John Bruce Glasier as 'one ambrosial night alone' with Bruno the dog, who remained at Millthorpe, before the Adams arrived the following day.[40] His ears were instantly blasted by the quite unbelievable amount of noise that emanated from the two small Adams. Once the sociable George Adams was installed, the steady stream of visitors turned into a veritable flood, causing Carpenter periodically to issue 'full up' notices in his letters to friends. Sometimes he fled himself. 'I hope we shall not be very crowded at Xmas' he remarked to Alf Mattison in November 1893, 'if we are I shall return to Sheffd and leave you all to boil in yr. own juice'.[41] The tone of helplessness was absurd, after all it was he who had invited all the guests. Yet this plaintive protest was expressive of the psychological paradox of Millthorpe. At home, Carpenter found himself, once again, not really at home.

In theory he had made his own life part of his politics, however he discovered that an incontrovertible disadvantage of prefiguring the future in his own hearth and home was that the personal as politics invaded his private existence, leaving him without any individual retreat. So he could be putting guests at their ease, reassuring them with his calm confidence, and lifting their spirits so they could commune with the One, all the while feeling wretched himself. It was not even just a matter of ensuring that the visitors were people he really wanted to be with, the expectations of others made him feel trapped. He, who had cast off outer conventions, discovered there were less overt inward impositions. Not surprisingly, Henry Salt detected an irritability lurking below the surface of Carpenter's guru-like persona – a bad temper kept firmly under control.[42]

Carpenter's survival strategy was the emotional and sometimes physical withdrawal that so distressed his friends. He delighted in his bolt-hole at 56 Glover Road with the unjudgemental, indigent Greaves family, to which only specially chosen friends were invited. The elect were not always suitably impressed at being granted the privilege. Ives may have found Millthorpe unaesthetic in 1897, but the two small rooms at Glover Road completely appalled him – 'Such a crib'. The supper Carpenter gave him there was no better, 'pressed beef all gelatine, or the like, with tea, biscuits, and dried figs'.[43] It started to rain; various friends of Carpenter's who seemed to be factory workers dropped in. A frayed Ives was greatly relieved when the London express puffed into Sheffield station to return him to metropolitan bachelordom.

Carpenter had other kinds of decampment that were less ascetic. The foreign trips continued, for he longed to be in the sun, sighing to Kate Salt in the Spring of 1897, 'I wish someone wd. have a shanty in the Meditern. [sic] coast where one cd. go'.[44] Merrill introduced him to what would nowadays be called the 'short-break' holiday. Carpenter announced to Mattison in June 1895 that he and Merrill were alone together in Hornsea, on the East Yorkshire coast, 'to escape the Millthorpe visitors, and to rest a bit, bathe if possible'.[45] Merrill's liking for the bright lights was an eye-opener for Carpenter. In contrast to those village dances with

Joseph Sharpe and his son in the early 1880s, Carpenter recounted to Oates a new and startling vista of working-class pleasure at an Isle of Man dance hall in August 1895, where about 1,000 ''Arry and Jemimas' twirled around; boys in cricket flannels with coloured sashes and girls with straw hats.[46] Their trips away undid the sense of duty that hounded Carpenter; as Charlie Sixsmith discerned, Merrill 'protected Edward from the bores'.[47]

The substitution of the Adams family for the Fearnehoughs did not prove to be the felicitous solution Carpenter had envisaged. Adams had entered Millthorpe's alternative world with enthusiasm. He enjoyed the company of Carpenter's middle-class friends, Isabella Ford, Olive Schreiner, the Salts and the Ellises; moreover, he could at last paint, while knowing his children were safely out of the Sheffield slums. In contrast Lucy, reluctant to leave her life in the town, did not settle well. Her restlessness was already depressing Adams in July 1893. With Carpenter away, her resentment was assailing him, causing Hukin to observe to Carpenter, chap to chap, 'I imagine G. finds Lucy rather trying at times. (Oh these wives.)'[48]

Lucy appears to have adapted to being the domestic mainstay of a rural commune, but Adams' jealousy of George Merrill gnawed away. Hukin was in an awkward position as Adams' friend, nevertheless his loyalty to Carpenter and his characteristic kindness and diplomacy disposed him to befriend Merrill. In July 1893 when Merrill lay ill in bed with dysentery, Hukin dropped by in his dusty workshop clothes with a cornflower blancmange in a dinner basket, enquiring, '"How art ta lad?"'[49] Carpenter was profoundly touched, but Hukin earned Adams' animosity. During 1897 Carpenter was under heavy pressure from the two highly emotional Georges and by the summer such a crisis was looming that even he could play ostrich no longer. Adams' intransigent hostility preyed on Merrill, whose jauntiness was merely surface-deep. Carpenter told Oates in August he was very anxious about Merrill's nervous depression and palpitations of the heart.[50] That autumn Millthorpe was so unbearably tense Carpenter was thinking of selling the house. When Kate Salt sympathised with Adams' distress at the possibility of his life at Millthorpe coming to an end, Carpenter defended himself by saying that George's suffering was caused by his own capacity to hurt; 'His extraordinary tenacity comes out in a certain unforgivingness wh. is rather terrible – absolutely unrelenting.'[51]

In November, Carpenter complained to Oates that it was exasperating when one's friends played the watchdog and sought to drive off other people for one's own good. 'I suffered that from Albert F. and now the same with George Adams.' He had resorted to fleeing to Glover Road and London. 'I have been <u>thinking</u> and thinking over it till my head is almost turned.'[52] In fact he had already mentioned the proposition of Merrill moving in to Kate Salt the month before in October, saying, 'He has a talent for housekeeping and Max is devoted to him.'[53] Carpenter was inclined to depict himself as jockeyed by the wishes of the Adams, Merrill and Max; this spin of himself as the mediator was a cover for his uneasy conscience. He was still unable to shake off the hold of obligation towards Adams.

Carpenter's indecision was also partly because his own desires were not straightforward. Merrill had been his getaway love, living with him was quite another matter. Carpenter disclosed to Oates in November, 'G M is very sweet and twines himself round my heart more and more – but I do not want to let him monopolise or depend on me too much.' If Merrill was twining, Adams was 'stabbing' him with cruel remarks, Carpenter found Adams so 'dreadfully untrustworthy'. Only the 'large-heartedness' of George Hukin gave him any help through the emotional morass.[54] The morass persisted until early December when he informed Kate Salt that his neighbour, Mrs Doncaster, a kindly, broad-minded Quaker, had suggested that George Merrill should come and keep house for him.[55] Once Mrs Doncaster had made the decision it could at last be settled! Carpenter would stay at Millthorpe with Max Flint and George Merrill, the Adamses would move to a place nearby.

Over the Christmas period the atmosphere at Millthorpe was so tense that Carpenter planned to be mainly at Glover Road. January was no better; Lucy cracked and her bottled-up resentment resulted in a terrible row with Flint, which shocked Kate Salt when Carpenter relayed his report by letter.[56] Carpenter, consumed with suspicion that the Adams were spreading scandal about him to Robert Murray Gilchrist, kept building up moral capital in his letters to friends. Purporting to be quite bewildered about his wrecked relationship with George Adams, he maintained to Kate, 'I never know whether he is friendly or offended at some unknown something.'[57] Carpenter had too much spiritual pride to admit he might hurt anyone by pursuing his own interests. Adams, stubborn and wounded, saw the emotional variability as resting with Carpenter, divulging to Henry Salt, who knew very well what he meant, 'He first drives you away from him, and then draws you back again.'[58] Other friends including Kate Salt, Schreiner, Mattison and the Hukins, while sympathising with the Adams, valued Carpenter's friendship and attempted to remain neutral. Neither protagonist made it easy for them. 'I have done so much for him and without a grudge or thought – and he receives it all in so pettish a spirit', complained Carpenter to Kate Salt. George Adams had departed on February 1, 1898, like a 'great baby' refusing to even say good morning.[59] Carpenter considered that Lucy had taken it rather better. Maybe she was relieved to be running her own domain at Adamsfield on Fox Lane. Carpenter remained so aggrieved he was not willing to take a gift from Kate Salt round to the Adams' new home.

Carpenter's happiness when George Merrill arrived on February 2nd was palpable. The weather was so bad he feared his lover would never make it. But Merrill turned up with two Sheffield youths dragging all his belongings on a light porter's cart. All three, blue with cold, tumbled enthusiastically into the warmth of Millthorpe and proceeded to make their way through the whole contents of the larder. Carpenter sat amiable and at ease with this 'Bohemian crew'. He recalled in the manuscript notes he wrote on Merrill, 'The town lads mingled their joy at getting a decent meal with wonderment as to how we could possibly remain in such an outlandish place.' They enquired of Merrill, '"Art ta going to live out here"', and, when he replied that he was going to try, the astounded town lads declared him to be plucky indeed and trundled back to Sheffield with their pony cart.[60]

A cheerful Carpenter promptly issued statements to his friends about the new regime. Kate Salt was assured that Merrill was proving a most suitable domestic companion who had taken 'to the housework like a duck to water – everything clean and neat and with real pleasure in it'. Carpenter predicted, 'I believe it will do first rate.'[61] As a guilt-ridden Carpenter had given most of the furniture and crockery to the Adams, once again Kate Salt came to the rescue. Carpenter told her that her little brown table with two leaves stood under the window, her candlesticks were on the mantelpiece, her cupboard with green doors was hanging on the wall, her coconut matting was on the floor and her crockery was on a shelf. In a letter to Oates on February 10th he extolled Merrill's cooking and ironing and related how Flint, Merrill and himself were sitting 'snug by the fire'. Most important, Merrill had adapted to country life. 'G is so happy.'[62] Merrill was soon a regular at the local Royal Oak pub drinking his ale with the countrymen.

The shock-waves of Merrill's installation at Millthorpe resonated through the village and beyond. Friends who tried to bring peace between Adamsfield and Millthorpe encountered an obstinate and bitter Adams. To Hukin's exasperation, his old friend refused to see Fannie and Kate Salt when they attempted a visit.[63] Adams and Carpenter were never really reconciled and Carpenter's continuing unease about the breakdown of this relationship caused him to devote far more space to Adams than to Hukin in *My Days and Dreams*. Carpenter falsely depicted Adams' departure as the other man's choice, owing to ill-health; his comment that Adams was 'a good friend and a good hater' was nearer the mark.[64] This was one personal conflict Carpenter's charm could not smooth over.

More immediately, Merrill's proximity, combined with the relaxation in the tension and rage of the last few months, brought a powerful surge of released energy. His verse 'Two Gifts' which appeared in the Legitimation League's *The Adult* in February 1898, ended with lines of exultant defiance:

> So simple, so grand –
> The gifts of human love and the pure body –
> And all the rest may go to the devil![65]

14

Culture and Everyday Life

A sombre Carpenter, reflecting to Alf Mattison on the question 'Will there be a Revn.? [*sic*]', in October 1897, observed 'No such luck.'[1] He was feeling personally gloomy, anxious about Merrill's health and troubled by the antagonism between himself and Adams at Millthorpe, but his conclusion was not just a subjective one. Adverse external political and social circumstances could not be denied by the late 1890s. How differently the possibilities of change had appeared a decade before!

In 1897 Carpenter pitched towards the future with an edited collection, *Forecasts of the Coming Century*, published by the Labour Press and *Clarion*. It was a mixed bag of essays, written by friends and acquaintances with divergent views and bundled together in a haphazard manner. The forecasters included the theorist of evolution, Alfred Russel Wallace, on co-operative land colonies; Tom Mann on links between trades unions and the co-operative movement; Margaret McMillan on education; Enid Stacy on women's rights; William Morris on art (the article was reprinted), Henry Salt on literature; the individualistic novelist, Grant Allen, on 'Natural Inequality'; and an acerbic Shaw on 'Illusions of Socialism'. The editor's grand plan was undoubtedly to demonstrate unity amidst diversity, but the end result was simply muddle, as if his heart was not really in the project. Indeed the idea of the collection had originated with Tom Mann.[2]

Forecasts of the Coming Century did enable Carpenter to publish the thoughts about strategies he had been trying out with audiences in his lectures over the course of the decade. His contribution, 'Transitions to Freedom' – the original title was 'Transitions to Communism' – developed the theme that, regardless of their differing routes, Anarchists, Social Democrats, Labour parties, Fabians and Trades Unions shared the same aims. Returning to the old bugbear of the individual versus the collective, Carpenter attempted a reconciliation: 'If anyone will only think for a minute of his own inner nature he will see that the only society which would ever really satisfy him would be one in which he was perfectly free, and yet bound by ties of deepest trust to the other members.'[3] Carpenter also thought people could only be free when they cared for their neighbours as well as themselves.

Though Carpenter knew from his own experience how this utopia was far easier to articulate than to live, his resolve to keep individual rights and collective association simultaneously in view enabled him to home in on one of socialism's key dilemmas. Accepting an intermediate role for the state in certain areas such as the railways, Carpenter ingeniously proposed a 'double collectivism'.[4] Taking up Tom Mann's proposals for combinations of trades unions and co-operative societies to extend into production and distribution, Carpenter conceived of 'a voluntary collectivism working within and parallel with the official collectivism of the State'.[5]

Carpenter's conception of this 'voluntary' collectivism extended beyond work and economic life. He wanted to foster a counter-culture of co-operative association through which people would not simply apprehend the need for change intellectually, but would generate new values, habits and ways of behaving: 'The sentiment of the Common Life – the habit of acting together for common ends, the habit of acting together for common interests.'[6] His hope was that these would go beyond simply opposing capitalist society and grow into alternative ways of living and relating.

Like most books which purport to predict what is ahead, *Forecasts of the Coming Century* actually documented contemporary uncertainties; in so far as it contained foresights, these were for the nether distance. Falling between these two disparities of a dubious present and distant possibilities, it was one of Carpenter's less auspicious efforts and was not to reach many people at the time, or, indeed, subsequently. Over a hundred years later the copy that had been beautifully preserved in Manchester's John Rylands Library arrived on my desk with most of its pages still uncut.

Carpenter discovered the travails of editing while collecting his contributors' essays; Shaw had been particularly trying. Badgered during the summer of 1896, he had responded snootily, 'I decline to consider anything seriously.'[7] Shaw's testiness stemmed from having to pen an article every day from a 'confounded' International Socialist Congress and from Kate Salt's failure to show up at the music festival in Bayreuth. The resulting 'Illusions of Socialism', was a devastating onslaught against the psychological myths sustaining the socialist movement: the dream of a future of sunshine and rainbows, the drama of the virtuous worker as hero or heroine wrestling with evil, the religiosity of a judgement day when capital would be cast down in favour of honest labour. Brilliant Shaw cut right through

Carpenter's laborious efforts at fostering a transformative culture, insisting that socialists needed to shed their dreams. The new century required 'Acuteness of intellect, political experience, practical capacity, the strength of character which gives a man power to look unpleasant facts in the face.'[8] Typically, Carpenter, in his role as editor, muffled the difference between his approach and Shaw's. Both of them could, however, agree on the 'unpleasant facts' which were converging from all directions in the second half of the 1890s.

This period saw a regrouping of the forces of moralism. An odd combination of the old conservative establishment, a new populist press and some strands of social purity were castigating not only 'oscarwildes' but the aesthetes around the avant-garde journal, the *Yellow Book*, along with Thomas Hardy's frank criticisms of marriage in *Jude the Obscure*. Though the new women novelists continued to defy 'Mrs Grundyism' and wage a culture war against conventional mores, the rebellious intelligentsia was forced onto the defensive in the second half of the 1890s. The assault from without was compounded by a growing pessimism within their own ranks. The Hungarian Max Nordau's *Degeneration*, published in English in 1895 saw a creeping decadence reflected in increased disease, crime, madness and suicide. The utopias of the past acquired a dystopic edge when H.G. Wells' Time Traveller in *The Time Machine* (1895) boldly set off into the future by slipping via the Fourth Dimension, through the interstices of the universe, only to find the frolicking Eloi being bred as food by the bleached nocturnal Morlock. Both present and future were beginning to look equally out of joint.

Grundy and gloom on the cultural front were accompanied by new political contexts. Though the socialists and anarchists held the Liberals in contempt, the eclipse of the Liberal Party in 1895 and the subsequent ascendancy of the Conservatives made it harder for the I.L.P. and the S.D.F. to operate on the local and national electoral planes. Meanwhile the new Conservative Party was creating a grassroots base, flirting with social reform and playing the triumphalist imperial card for all it was worth. The grim truth for socialists was that this populist Toryism appealed to sections of the working class. As the evangelical optimism of the I.L.P.'s early days subsided, its leaders sought to distance the Party from any association with the militant rowdyism of new unionism and direct action on the streets. The employers meanwhile recovered their balance, mounting a sustained attack on the gains won by workers, using lock-outs, troops and the courts.

Consequently, by the time Carpenter's *Forecasts* appeared a series of closures had pushed his proposals for transition onto the extreme margins.

His hopes for a new libertarian–labour alliance received a setback shortly after the book was published. Bruce Glasier and MacDonald, now leading figures in the I.L.P., were manoeuvring to remove Tom Mann, who they regarded as too soft on anarchism, from the secretaryship. When Mann emigrated to Australia, Carpenter lost his labour movement ally. The insurrectionary anarchism which had foundered after Walsall was decimated in Britain by 1897, though it continued in Europe. After a bomb was thrown into a religious procession in Barcelona in Spain in 1897, the Spanish authorities tortured, exiled and executed anarchist suspects. Carpenter and Salt joined a small band of protesters at the Spanish embassy in London and Carpenter became a member of the Spanish Atrocities Committee, writing the preface for a leaflet which argued that the bomb was the work of an agent provocateur.[9] His support was of great significance for the beleaguered Spanish left, though he was privately uneasy, telling Kate Salt he was troubled about pledging himself for Spanish anarchist refugees he did not know.[10] In Britain the anarchist movement turned away from confrontation with the state and, inspired by Kropotkin and Tolstoy, concentrated on setting up small-scale utopian communities instead.

The country was undergoing extensive economic and social change. The 'Great Depression' with its insecurity and periodic bouts of unemployment finally came to an end in the mid 1890s. The relative prosperity this brought for the lower middle classes in trade or clerical work, and for sections of the skilled working class, was accompanied by a decrease in the hours of work. Music halls, dance halls, pubs, gambling, sport and holidays became extremely profitable as a mass leisure industry emerged. Communication was transformed in 1896 by a new kind of popular daily newspaper, the *Daily Mail*, which mixed news with recipes and society gossip. Read by some artisans, as well as the lower middle class, and popular among women as well as men, it propounded the virtues of Empire, becoming the mouthpiece for men like Cecil Rhodes who were pressing for overt territorial aggrandisement in Africa. It increased its circulation year by year.

In *Civilisation: Its Cause and Cure* Carpenter had contested the assumption that the superiority of British culture justified the domination of others. By the late 1890s eugenic claims were bolstering the Anglo-Saxon right to rule and this was accompanied by a potent myth of Empire as the cure for febrile degeneracy – physical and mental. Its appeal extended beyond the patriotic right. Several of Carpenter's friends were attracted to the vigour of 1890s popular imperialism. Goldsworthy Lowes Dickinson, influenced by his right-wing Hegelian philosopher friend, James McTaggart, thrilled momentarily at the pageant of Empire while watching a procession during the Queen's Jubilee. He described himself as 'a kind of Socialistic Tory' in this period.[11] Ashbee too hankered after the Empire as a regenerative cultural ideal. In South Africa, Olive Schreiner was initially fascinated by Cecil Rhodes' energy, before doing a U-turn and vehemently opposing him. From 1897, Schreiner's letters to Carpenter were warning that the greed and aggression of Rhodes and the capitalists would lead to war with the Boers.

The second half of the 1890s proved a difficult period for socialists, not merely because of the political setbacks which culminated in the Boer War of 1899, but because the standpoints and alignments of the 1880s and early '90s were disintegrating as the economy entered a new gear. The chiliastic sense of a coming conflagration was deferred, and socialists settled in for what was evidently going to be a protracted struggle. The Social Democratic Federation had carved out a base in London and, though the Independent Labour Party found victory in national elections elusive, they had acquired a recognised political identity in industry and in working-class communities. The broad reach of the 1890s labour move-ment extended well beyond the socialist groupings of the 1880s. Faced with a popular Imperialist culture, the creation of an alternative culture became more salient. This is reflected in Carpenter's preoccupation with 'culture' in the sense of nurturing alternative sentiments, habits and values, and his venture into aesthetic theory with an 'art of life' to counter the detachment of the fin-de-siècle's 'art for art's sake'. Morris' emphasis on culture increasingly seemed to hold the key to sustaining a broad movement of opposition and transforming everyday life and relationships.

William Morris died in 1896; paying tribute to him in *Freedom*, Carpenter wrote: 'In the early days of the Socialist League Morris had a hope, and a strong hope, that the little branches of the League, spreading and growing over the land, would before long reach hands to each other and form a network of free communal life over the whole country.'[12] When he had sought a contribution from the ailing Morris for *Forecasts of the Coming Century* in June 1896, a downbeat Carpenter had remarked, 'The movement goes on in a queer way of its own – but it does go on.'[13] Acknowledging that the transformatory vision of the Socialist League had failed, he wanted to transplant it into the new circumstances of the 1890s. While the League itself had not brought into being 'a network of free communal life', the utopian impulse still resonated in what Carpenter described as 'that very complex and far-reaching movement which we call by the name of modern Socialism'.[14] Just as he had theorised a labour *movement* from new unionism and the international agitation for the eight-hour day, Carpenter refused to confine socialism to the pursuit of power or the elaboration of policy. He could see how the socialist movement of the 1890s was developing a vibrant culture out of a mix of desire, need and a resolve to have fun and a fuller life in the here and now. He intimated that this constituted a formidable source of strength and was in empathetic accord with the longing he could hear and see expressed around him.

The socialist movement of the 1890s, no longer huddling in small clubs and cafes, responded by adopting 'England Arise' as its anthem. The Yorkshire Federation of the I.L.P. gathered in their thousands at Hardcastle Craggs near Hebden Bridge on Whit Monday 1896, and Carpenter's 'England Arise' echoed powerfully round the dell. The following year at Leeds' May Day on Woodhouse Moor, twenty-thousand voices called for England to arise, then, when Carpenter and Mattison went to join Oates at the Central I.L.P. club for tea after the demonstration, the rafters shook once more.[15] Four decades later the Labour politician, J.R. Clynes, remembered Carpenter in sandals and 'striking country dress', and the overflowing hope with which the delegates had sung 'England Arise' at the I.L.P.'s 1898 conference in Birmingham.[16] The song carried the vision of the 1880s towards the coming century, promising not just a better society but the transformation of 'slum-dwellers' into 'heroes, patriots, and lovers', who then climax together in the release of emotion in the millennial final verse, 'England is risen! – and the day is here.'[17]

In the meantime, just like the earlier working-class Chartist movement, the socialist movement of the 1890s generated alternative rituals and services out of daily needs. Labour babies could be brought to the Labour Church; Clarion Cinderella clubs fed and entertained poor children, Socialist Sunday Schools taught them precepts of love and co-operation. In 1895, Carpenter wrote a play for the Socialist Sunday Schools and I.L.P. youth clubs, 'St George and the Dragon', in which the patron saint was redeployed from services to the status quo to rescue the king's daughter from the dragon of capitalism.[18] He was in touch with the Clarion Glee Clubs and choirs which sometimes performed when he spoke. By the 1900s they were attracting talented young musicians like Gustav Holst and Rutland Boughton.

A new generation of socialist recruits who aspired to more than the common round and daily task were clustering round *Clarion*. Blatchford's journal provided a cultural fare of Ruskin, Morris, Whitman and Carpenter, interspersed with humour, while *Clarion*'s offshoots offered child care, choirs and, of course, cycling. Clarion cyclists took a quote from Morris' 'Dream of John Ball' as their motto: 'Fellowship is Life', and pedalled off with it to Derbyshire. The motto applied equally to the linked Clarion

Field Clubs which combined exercise with education. Leeds' Clarion Field Club was started by Alf Mattison, while the Sheffield Field Club was reconstituted in 1900 as the Clarion Ramblers, by a member of the Amalgamated Society of Engineers and Carpenter fan, George Herbert Bridges Ward. Known as 'Bert', Ward, who was sympathetic to anarchism, became a long-term political associate of Carpenter's and eventually the eminence grise among rambling organisers. The ramblers, staunch prop-agators of learning through doing, took in not only nature, but folklore, archaeology, astronomy and local history as they walked. They rediscovered lost footpaths, defended common land and defiantly trespassed if landowners denied them right of way, sometimes with secateurs and wire cutters.

Carpenter's close proximity to this culture, which was interwoven with socialism, enabled him to understand better than Shaw the need to sustain aspirations and create communal forms for daily activities. Nonetheless, a niggling scepticism prevented Carpenter from completely identifying with Kropotkin's anarchist-communism or from joining communes to prefigure the perfect future then and there. Some of the people he inspired were less restrained. The Norton Socialist Colony was founded near Millthorpe in the grounds of Norton Hall, owned by a retired lace-maker sympathetic to utopian schemes. It was initiated by an art student, Herbert H. Stansfield and a manager at the Home and Colonial Stores, Hugh Mapleton, who belonged to a new wave of anarchistic 'Return to Nature' enthusiasts. Stansfield had been a member of the Sheffield Field Club, while Mapleton had been on the committee with Carpenter of yet another attempt in the mid 1890s to re-establish a non-sectarian Sheffield Socialist Society. One of its pledges, along with transforming society as a whole, was to encourage 'social and industrial schemes'.[19]

The Norton Socialist Colony was one such scheme. Its seven members set about growing tomatoes, cucumbers and mushrooms, which they sold, not in the market as Carpenter had done, but door to door. Intent on living the ideals of the men who had inspired them – Carpenter, Thoreau and Kropotkin – the Norton Colonists had no rules; 'All business is discussed and work arranged over the communal breakfast table', stated Mapleton. They were, however, very strong on principles: 'Included in our "Return to Nature" principles is vegetarianism, teetotalism, non-smoking and abstention from salt, chemicals, drugs, and minerals, and all fermenting and decomposing foods.'[20] Exactly the same problem that had beset St George's Farm at Totley was repeated at Norton. In 1898 Mapleton admitted that because of being hampered by their 'inexperience in practical horticulture', they had added sandal-making.[21] The locals might regard the long-haired, bare-legged colonists in their sandals and cloaks as bizarre, but to Mapleton the Norton Socialist Colony was part of a wider project – a new order of society.[22] He was vindicated in a convoluted way, for after the Norton Colony folded in 1900 and its members scattered, Mapleton became a successful manufacturer of vegetarian food in Lancashire.

The Fellowship journal *Seed-Time* ceased publication in 1898, yet the desire to *live* the New Life continued through the projects it had fostered, progressive education, a tenants' co-operative housing venture, a typists' co-operative and the Croydon Ethical and Religious Fellowship.[23] These little pockets of utopianism were only loosely linked to 'politics' yet exercised a diffuse influence within daily life. So while the spectrum of mainstream politics shifted to the right in the second half of the 1890s, utopian dissidence in everyday life bubbled up in unexpected places. Even the British Museum Reading Room became a site of conflict; when a dress reformer was excluded for entering in sandals in 1897, Carpenter leapt to his defence.[24]

Carpenter bridged the culture that arose in the immediate environs of the socialist groups and the alternative views about lifestyle and personal relationships which were, in part, the legacy of the Fellowship of the New Life. The Fellowship's causes – ethical consumption, the emancipation of women, simplicity in art – were taken up by future generations of rebels. They adopted its Kantian morality of not using others and its valuing of a life close to nature, sincerity in personal relations and following the inner light on moral issues. Henry Salt described the Fellowship as pioneering 'Every-day Ethics' and the Humanitarian League took up the mantle, attracting socialists, anarchists, spiritualists, occultists, vegetarians, anti-vivisectionists and anti-vaccinationists.[25] Its loose structure enabled a myriad of minority projects to acquire a greater degree of space.

Carpenter was particularly involved with two Humanitarian League campaigns: the reform of prisons and the humane treatment of animals, propagating both causes within the Northern I.L.P. and Labour Church groups as well as in London lectures.[26] The combined impact of Kropotkin and Malatesta's critique of Lombroso's theories of criminal types, the Walsall campaign and the Wilde trial, had convinced Carpenter of the need for prison reform. Criticising imprisonment as a means of revenge or mere deterrence, he argued for a recognition that much crime arose because of social injustice, telling his I.L.P. and Labour Church audiences that the present prison system was both cruel and counterproductive.[27] While the authorities might boast of a lack of overt violence in British jails, the prisoners' spirits were broken nonetheless by the solitude and dull monotony of prison life, by a sense of abandonment and by the lack of humanity in how they were treated. His visits to Fred Charles had made him painfully aware of the psychological desolation, the dread of night-time memories, the longing for freedom. 'Society is surely strong enough not to be <u>afraid</u> of its criminals', he wrote in 1895.[28]

Carpenter's humanitarian objections to vivisection were integral to his critique of a science that negated emotion and denied the relevance of moral values. This, in turn, was linked to his rejection of the machine-view which he saw as permeating Western culture. His opposition to Western capitalism was not simply about the manner in which things were produced, distributed and consumed, but about an ontological assumption of superiority. He wanted to change how human beings inter-related with nature and how they perceived their own beings. By the second half of the 1890s his questioning of 'civilisation' no longer appeared so cranky; scientific paradigms were being overturned, the destructive aspects of technology were becoming evident, Eastern religion and Schopenhauer were in vogue, interest was growing in unconscious motivation, artists and writers were asserting that positive values were to be found in societies dismissed as 'primitive'.

Hence a large audience attended his lecture on 'The Need for a Rational and Humane Science' at St Martin's Hall, London, in October 1896. They included Henry Salt, the Fabian Sydney Olivier, the anarchist Charlotte Wilson and Bernard Shaw, a committed anti-vivisectionist and debunker of doctors. Henry W. Nevinson, the radical journalist who had briefly encountered Carpenter at Toynbee Hall in the late 1880s, was also present and was sufficiently impressed both by the man and by his speech to record the event.

> He is certainly a very beautiful and attractive person; tall, slim, and fairly straight; loose hair, and beard just grizzled; strong, dark eyebrows, dark eyes, straight nose and cheeks of palish brown; . . . [he] was dressed in loose greys, with a blue shirt, and tie in a large bow; voice soft but strong enough without effort; spoke from a few notes and went slowly ahead in almost perfect grammar, and with apparent composure . . .
> His main purpose was to show that Science, owing to its limitation, is apt to leave out many vital sides. The study of it should teach increased perception like that of savages; it should be intellectual, but also dwell on the moral or emotional relations of the object to ourselves.[29]

By the time Carpenter wrote up his lecture criticising the values of contemporary science for a collection published by the Humanitarian League in 1897, he had encountered the writings of Elisée Reclus, the French geographer and anarchist, whose work on human beings' kinship with animals Carpenter would later translate. Reclus' critique had grown out of a very different rationalist trajectory from Carpenter's, however they shared a mystical sense of the connection of life in nature. Reclus was arguing for a social and organic geography which took human needs and the environment into account. He was also part of a dissident band which included Kropotkin and the Scottish New Lifer, Patrick Geddes, who opposed the way in which Darwin's theories of evolution were being used by social theorists to justify capitalist competition, arguing that cooperation and nurturing could enable animals and human beings alike to survive.

Thinkers like Reclus, Kropotkin and Geddes ranged over a vast terrain without boundaries; geography, science, animal behaviour, psychology, civic planning and sociology. Carpenter, who was similarly all-embracing, was thus coming into contact with a welter of ideas, partly through his British networks and partly through his familiarity with European thought. He was acquiring an ever-wider intellectual basis for contesting the values underpinning 'civilisation'. As a result he was not only connecting human-itarian causes to his socialist activism, but stretching out into an intellectual world that extended beyond even the furthest reaches of British labour movement culture.

Hence, Carpenter, the epistemological rover, was understandably ruffled when Ellis' friend Arthur Symons asked for a few words on 'Simplification' in 1896 for his new journal the *Savoy*, which aimed to nudge the *Yellow Book* from its avant-garde perch. Carpenter complied, but grizzled at embodying the simple life. 'I should think it only a comparatively-speaking small part of my programme.'[30] The simple life had loosened up a little since his original formulation in the mid 1880s; Carpenter had been assailed by far too many people carrying 'reticules' who peered into his study and remarked, 'But I thought it was against your *principles* to have ornaments.' Whereupon he would explain 'for the hundredth time' that he had 'never set up duty as against beauty, and that anyhow, I have not the smallest intention of boxing my life, or that of others, within the four corners of any cut-and-dried principle'.[31] 'Simplification', Carpenter now declared, was but 'The first letter of the alphabet of the Art of Life'.[32]

In 1898 Carpenter included the essay he wrote for Symons on 'Simpli-fication' in his collection *Angels' Wings*, along with another piece 'The Return to Nature' which had been originally published in the *Humanitarian* in 1896. He defined 'Nature' as including simplicity in living, 'A kind of savagery' in dress and diet, the move to the country from the town, a celebration of open-air life, as well as paganism in religion and morals, orientalism in philosophy and nature-methods in art. He also interpreted it as an introspective psychological exploration, 'A return to the more primitive, indispensable and universal part of oneself.'[33] Like Schopenhauer, he held that art communicated directly to the emotions, making for a special kind of knowing.

Carpenter began *Angels' Wings* with the assertion that the 'Democratic idea' would affect both art and artistic methods. Inspired by Whitman's intense, empathetic 'consciousness of the Actual', he combined this with the socialist aesthetics of William Morris.[34] Carpenter wanted art to be engaged with life, simple and direct in form, yet suffused with an inner sense of the marvellous. In contrast to a pessimistic elitism that deplored the spread of mass education, Carpenter was convinced that the greatest works of art could communicate far beyond the small world of the connoisseur and bring an expansion of possibility. *Angels' Wings* itself carries the mark of the popularising skills he had acquired through all those University Extension classes and socialist meetings. Carpenter lists his points and categorises his artists into convenient bundles, tidily summarising the historical evolution of art, moving from an organic link with everyday culture, through individualism towards a co-operative commonwealth, in a manner that was well suited for intelligent artisans and lower-middle-class readers with patchy educational backgrounds.

In a letter to Henry Salt in the early 1890s Carpenter had said that he always thought a good deal about how he wrote, while avoiding anything that looked like a conscious literary effect. He considered that an open, free style required an open mind.[35] Such an approach inclined him to distrust the French Symbolists' delight in the enigmatic and their readiness to break completely with conventional forms of communication. Though in *Angel's Wings* he expressed interest in the evocation of rhythm, sound and colour which fascinated the Symbolists, he was sceptical about one art form borrowing from another. On the other hand he was not drawn to their rivals, the naturalists like Zola, who documented an everyday in which human beings were ineradicably caught. Eschewing grimy fatalism, Carpenter plumped for a romantic realism which depicted the external world, illuminated by the artist's subjective feeling. He identified this quality in Whitman, in the work of the French peasant artist, Jean François Millet, as well as in Richard Wagner's organic vision of art and his insistence on an inner necessity within human creativity. Wagner's desire to reconnect art with the social life of the people, along with his emphasis on the artist as an individual with exceptional insights, exerted considerable influence on socialist and anarchist artists, though Shaw in *The Perfect Wagnerite* (1898) did criticise his anti-Semitism.[36]

In *Angels' Wings* Carpenter returned to the Romantics' belief that the artist could be the agent of change. As the title of the book implied, he was still in pursuit of the utopian wish which had animated *Towards Democracy*. If politics disappointed, all the more important that art should convey harmony, amidst the 'jumble of the actual'.[37] It should be at once transcendent and integral to the culture of the everyday. Yet *Angels' Wings*, which went into seven editions between 1898 and 1923, owed its popularity to the fact that it looked forwards as well as backwards. Carpenter, whose interpretation of realism was broad, can be seen edging towards the 'moderns' of the twentieth century. He defined Impressionism as a 'Subtler Realism' capable of catching flux and compared its emergence to a parallel movement in modern literature 'towards the portrayal of emotion rather than action', and a trend in music to emphasise 'motive' rather than 'form or tonality'.[38] In examining a piece of art he wanted to know 'What contagion of *feeling* does it communicate?'[39] Intent on the artist's inner need to create, he insisted 'The Art of Life is to know that Life *is* Art, that it is Expression.'[40]

Moreover the angels' wings spanned both heaven and earth, the ideal and the real, and the angel represented the connection between body and soul denied within contemporary 'civilisation'.[41] In his essay on 'The Human Body in its Relation in Art', Carpenter rejected Tolstoy's dismissal of the senses, an asceticism currently influencing some free lovers, anarchists and commune-dwellers. Indeed in *Angels' Wings* the breakthrough into another realm of consciousness is equated with sex, a connection Carpenter had only made before poetically in *Towards Democracy* or in implicit comments on the lingam or on pagan religions. He describes Beethoven's Piano Sonata in C Sharp as 'a kind of orgasm in music . . . the rending of a veil which has long hemmed us in – the revelation of a new world'.[42] Carpenter is careful to distinguish himself from the 'Decadents'' delight in sensation: 'The maximum of enjoyment is not got by the *pursuit* of Pleasure; but rather by going your own way and letting the pleasure pursue you.'[43] Nonetheless his affirmation of life as primarily 'an expression of one's Self', and his assertion of 'Boldness and loving Acceptance', caught the contemporary preoccupation with personal identity and provided aspiring pagans with a slogan.[44] So there it was, the return to nature no longer meant struggling like Lowes Dickinson to milk a recalcitrant cow, but the release of psychological repression, a new ethic of life-tasting. This rendition proved to have a greater appeal in the new century than Ruskinian realisation through manual labour. Involuntarily *Angels' Wings* constituted a more accurate 'forecast' than *Forecasts of the Coming Century*; Carpenter had hit the zeitgeist on the spot.

During the 1890s and 1900s Carpenter's efforts to reconcile organic and iconoclastic approaches to art, along with his endorsement of both realism and the inner imagination of the artist, struck a chord among artists and critics not only in Britain but in the United States and Europe. Aesthetic boundaries which have rigidified in retrospect were being frequently crossed in this period, and Carpenter appealed to a widespread desire to allow for individual expression while retaining some kind of connection to a wider collectivity. Both Charles Ashbee with his social vision of transformed labour, and Roger Fry, intent on form and sensation, came under his spell. Carpenter's writings encouraged the efforts of Raymond Unwin, Patrick Geddes and A.J. Penty towards an organic architecture. For Alfred Orage and other writers, including Herbert Read, associated with the radical journal the *New Age* in the early years of the twentieth century, it was Carpenter's mix of organicism and vitalism which was attractive. In the United States several artists who discovered Carpenter's writing were pursuing similar connections from equally contrasting starting points. The romantic realist Edwin Markham's popular poem 'The Man with the Hoe' (1898) was written in response to Millet's famous picture, while the grimmer realism of the painter Robert Henri drew on a Whitmanite approach of simplicity.[45] The very different work of the eccentric Boston photographer F. Holland Day contrived to assimilate arts and crafts, the Belgian Symbolist Maurice Maeterlinck, as well as Carpenter in his portraits, which combined the spiritual and the erotic.[46] Around the time *Angels' Wings* was published, interest in the ideas of Whitman and Morris was growing in France and even more so in Belgium because these two writers seemed to promise ways through the impasse of Symbolism's introspective individual consciousness and Naturalism's pessimistic submergence in the world as it was. Left-wing artists from within this milieu who adopted the slogan 'art for all' as opposed to 'art for art's sake' would soon discover Carpenter's works.[47] In *Angels' Wings* Carpenter was tapping into incipient shifts in approaches to the relation of art to society which would take off in the early years of the twentieth century.

However *Angels' Wings* also grew out of his own predicament in the closing years of the century. Carpenter gives us a personal clue to his state of mind while writing the book right at the end when, linking the individual's experience with society, he remarks, 'One feels, say, that one's life is expanding pretty rapidly along a certain line. This goes on for some time; then comes a check. One calls it a disappointment.' Hukin, to whom *Angels' Wings* is dedicated, had been Carpenter's most painful disappointment. Was he at last able to put this pain behind him? The tardy revolution which he and many of his friends had pursued with such diligent passion since the early 1880s comprised another disappointment. Yet, the game, he tells us, is not over. As ever the unfolding is from the interior. One 'feels back within oneself for another point of departure farther down. New plans and a new growth arise.' Once again the animating 'sap' finds an 'outlet'.[48] In November 1898, when *Angels' Wings* came out, Carpenter was happily settled with George Merrill at Millthorpe and the book's decisive celebration of physicality echoes their partnership.

Merrill's arrival signalled a new era; Christmas 1898 contrasted pleasantly with the tensions of the previous year. In a letter to Kate Salt, Carpenter depicted himself and Merrill with Max Flint, now trying to make baskets, seated comfortably round the fire after all their guests had departed. He said that he was 'Floating along lazily, with scraps and bits of work like toy boats, made of green leaves, down the stream very happy and restful', and carefully enclosed a pressed dried flower for her.[49]

This mood of contented fulfilment filtered into the poem he wrote for Merrill, 'Hafiz to the Cup-Bearer', which appeared in the fourth and last section of *Towards Democracy*, 'Who Shall Command the Heart', in 1902. More elaborately and consciously written than the poignant, heart-felt poems to Hukin, 'Philolaus to Diocles' and 'In a Stone-Floored Workshop', Merrill is cast as the messenger of divine love who with hesitant step leaves 'the crowded footways of Shiráz' and lays his life at the feet of Hafiz. Carpenter – alias the Persian Sufi poet, Hafiz – receives his cupbearer who is 'Faint and ashamed, like one by some divine wine vanquished.'[50] When Merrill first came, Carpenter had indeed worried that his younger companion might miss the crowds of Sheffield and find life in the countryside too monotonous, anxiously arranging for Kate Salt and Bessie Joynes to come and keep Merrill company when Carpenter went away.[51] Charlie Sixsmith proved a more congenial alternative, and Merrill would decamp for short breaks in Lancashire. He adjusted to rural habits in his own way, casting off his flash Sheffield street-style for well-cut tweeds and a bohemian loose tie which accentuated his waif-like look. At night he headed off up the hill to the Royal Oak, more likely for several beers than divine wine, though he may well have returned to Carpenter, still writing away or reading into the night at home, suitably faint, ashamed and vanquished.

When Edith Ellis came to stay, Carpenter made one of his occasional visits to the Royal Oak's little parlour and impressed her by being on familiar terms with the locals. Carpenter would sip a ginger wine and play the piano in the Royal Oak, but he was not a pub-goer like Merrill.

Merrill and Carpenter at Millthorpe

It was an attraction of opposites and several of Carpenter's friends were full of gloomy prognostications about domestic life in an all-male household. However Edith Ellis presented an idyllic picture of Carpenter and Merrill in their early years together. When she visited Millthorpe, she sat happily between the two men, one mending his shirt and the other darning a pair of socks, noting approvingly how Carpenter took his share in the washing-up.[52] Carpenter had sewn himself a Saxon tunic of his own design, telling Kate Salt that after a morning sunbath he was living in it until dinnertime.[53] Friends mounted a campaign against him going out in the Saxon tunic, regarding beskirtedness as a step too far. But the little sewing basket, its colouring faded by the years, along with the pattern for the tunic, have survived and sit with the Carpenter Collection in the Sheffield archive.

Charles and Janet Ashbee visited in January 1903 and recorded in their shared *Memoirs* how impressed they were by George Merrill's culinary advances and sense of style. As he served salmon, steak pie and blackberry tart, doffing his apron as he sat down to eat, they congratulated him on 'Educating Edward up to a respectable diet'.[54] They also noted how the little kitchen was now firmly under his control. Despite all the shared mending when Edith Ellis stayed, the two men had established a complementary, but distinct modus vivendi. Charlie Sixsmith recalled Carpenter playing Schumann, Schubert or Rubinstein on the piano and Merrill accompanying him with a resounding baritone.[55]

Merrill's wandering life had equipped him to adapt to the unknown with aplomb. When Carpenter took him off on holiday to Monte Carlo in the summer of 1899, Merrill wanted to go to the casino, but when they appeared at the door dressed in their tweedy plus fours, loose shirts and sandals the doormen turned the odd-looking pair away. An American anarchist, T.H. Bell, produced a dress suit, but he was much taller than Carpenter who looked like an old-clothes man when he put it on. So Merrill, nature's gentleman, donned the black jacket and trousers and strode in straight-backed 'with the dignity of a duke', while Carpenter sneaked along behind him.[56] Carpenter later wrote a poem reflecting on the vanities of the gamblers, without any mention of his own elegant companion taking to the casino as to the manor born.[57]

They were off again the following year, accompanied by Charlie Sixsmith, to stay in the Swiss Alps with Carpenter's brother Alfred and his wife. 'I feel so happy directly I get out of England', Carpenter told Kate Salt.[58] He noted approvingly to George Hukin, toiling away at his razor-grinding, that 'G and Charlie have been walking splendidly'.[59] Merrill, who found letter-writing an even greater ordeal than Hukin, managed a few lines: 'Dear G. I am too full to say much (not all wine) so you must guess my feelings.'[60] Merrill's brashness and the 'saving sense of humour' that Charles Ashbee characterised as 'almost burlesque', served as a cover for his sensitivity.[61] Over the years it became internalised as part of his personality.

During the early 1900s Charlie Sixsmith accompanied Carpenter and Merrill on several more holidays in search of the sun in the South of France, as well as in Italy, Corsica and Sicily. In 1904 Carpenter took George Hukin, whose asthma was causing concern, along as well. Carpenter, ever the tour manager, steered the three younger men through Menton, Genoa, Bordighera and Florence. They had a wonderful time, though Carpenter grumbled mildly to Kate Salt because the two Georges and Charlie did not share his liking for bathing and climbing mountains.[62] Meanwhile Fannie, lonely at home in Totley, wrote to Carpenter, 'It will be nice to have George back', nobly adding that she was sure it was doing him good.[63] The previous year Carpenter and Merrill had taken an adventurous trip through Spain to Morocco at the instigation of a penniless artist friend of Havelock Ellis', called Harry Bishop who was living in

Morocco with his Arab lover. Merrill found this holiday rather more arduous than Monte Carlo. In the old town of Tetuan, in the wild Rif mountains, a rueful Merrill patted the Vaseline sent by Sixsmith on his nose and explained, without bothering about huffing his aitches, that 'The sun as [sic] fetched the skin of [sic] our noses.' One compensation was being 'chaffed' by their guide, a 'damn good looking Moor'.[64]

Carpenter's family and friends could not agree about Merrill. Carpenter's younger sisters, Dora and Alice, his niece, Dorothy, and his tolerant ex-sailor brother Alfred accepted him, while the older sisters appear to have endured the new development as yet another manifestation of their brother's obdurate eccentricity.[65] Carpenter's sister Emmie Daubeny surveyed the relationship from a lofty perch. She told her niece, 'Ted is sensitive, nervous and over-refined.' In Emmie Daubeny's opinion, as a highly civilised type, Carpenter drew strength and virility 'from the simple sons of the soil with whom he associates'.[66]

Henry Salt, who liked George Adams, made no effort towards such positive spins, considering Merrill to be 'the evil genius' of Carpenter's life.[67] Alf Mattison was far too loyal to Carpenter to oppose Merrill, but he too may have been ambivalent because he carefully preserved and notated Salt's hostile comments along with critical letters from Fannie Hukin. Moreover Fannie, and the Mattisons, scrupulously retained their friendships with George and Lucy Adams. Charlie Sixsmith, however, quickly became Merrill's buddy and ally, Edith Ellis was completely at ease with him, and Charles and Janet Ashbee also took him in their stride.

Carpenter was convinced that Merrill was popular in the village, marvelling at how young working-class women confided in him.[68] However George Hukin, who picked up rumours unlikely to reach Carpenter's ears, warned him of gossip against Merrill in 1902. Carpenter brushed this aside: 'I think the stories whatever they are are greatly exaggerated – but G will no doubt be on his guard in future.'[69] Carpenter felt protective towards Merrill, especially after his mother died in 1899, and in 'Hafiz to the Cup-Bearer' he addresses Merrill as 'Dear Son'. His 'simple Nature-child', his 'rose in winter', his 'ruby embedded in marl and clay', was beyond criticism, even by implication, and even from George Hukin.[70]

Merrill's down-to-earth attitudes and bawdy remarks delighted Carpenter as the antithesis to his own self-conscious unconventionality. Sixsmith recalled how when the affectionate, care-free, irresponsible Merrill 'Stepped over the line', Carpenter 'always excused him saying it was his childlike spontaneity'. Sixsmith knew the two men well enough to see that their protection of one another was mutual. Carpenter might appear to be tolerant of all-comers, but when he sniffed insincerity or respectability, the suffocating horrors of the Brighton society of his youth were evoked and he could be 'curtly rude'.[71] Merrill's bluff affability glided through these awkward social encounters Carpenter found so painful, and Sixsmith relates how his wit and fun would relieve tense or dull moments with the serious-minded visitors. As Charles Ashbee put it, the two men were 'as fitted as a hermit crab and his shell'.[72] After Merrill moved to Millthorpe, entry into Carpenter's close, inner circle depended on accepting him.

Carpenter did not present their life together as an ideal – he simply took it for granted as a fait accompli. But this did not prevent others from creating legends around the two men. To a new generation the two men's life at Millthorpe assumed mythical qualities of cross-class comradeship, ascetic self-sufficiency and utopian communal life. Countless more visitors trekked from Totley to Millthorpe, and among them were troubled young men, uncertain how to negotiate their desires for other men in an unfriendly, uncomprehending world. They made Carpenter and Merrill into culture heroes, the exemplars of a free union which transcended the grim externals of everyday codes and laws. The two men may not have been quite as the pilgrims perceived them; nonetheless they were indeed gifted in the 'art of life'. Carpenter possessed a knack of making the mundane glisten with an inexpressible meaning, while Merrill's charm lay in turning the everyday into rollicking fun.

PART 2

15

Who Shall Command the Heart?

In 1901, *Towards Democracy*, the book Carpenter regarded as the visionary source for his life's work, was in danger, for the tottering Labour Press in Manchester had finally been declared bankrupt. Determined to smuggle out the remaining copies he owned, Carpenter hired a dray and rode to the rescue like a veritable Don Quixote. He and the drayman bore the heavy load of books off, jogging through the fog and turmoil of the Manchester streets to unload them in a friendly City Councillor's office.

It was an act of faith; yet *Towards Democracy* was about to find its era. In 1902 Swan Sonnenschein published a fourth and final instalment, 'Who Shall Command the Heart'. Encouraged by rising sales, in 1905 they produced a complete version on India paper, slim enough to be tucked into a pocket, just as Charlie Sixsmith had suggested long ago.[1] From then on it went into reprint after reprint, causing Stanley Unwin, who later became Carpenter's publisher, to reflect that it was impossible to tell what would sell.[2]

Carpenter's prose poems spoke to a world in which the certainties of both Christianity and science were being assailed. Their declamatory prophetic tone, in which the subjective 'I' is abstracted to fuse with a pantheistic spirituality, resounded in a void of doubt. Readers in the 1900s responded with enthusiasm to his appeal to the heart and his counsel 'Be in truth thine own creator', for the anxieties which had troubled the upper middle class in Carpenter's Cambridge days had now reached much further afield.[3] Though a religious frame of mind persisted, the thinking members of non-conformist chapels were discovering Darwin. In small provincial towns and villages all over Britain, Genesis was being scrutinised with scepticism. Yet science in the early twentieth century did not offer a safe haven either. Darwin was being contested and the evolutionary ideas of Jean Baptiste Lamarck, which Carpenter had long preferred, were enjoying a brief revival. During the early 1900s neo-Lamarckians proposed a vital force distinct from biological matter, while profound upheavals in mathematics and physics seemed to challenge the axioms of materialistic approaches in science and, indeed, common-sense assumptions about the 'real' world.

When Carpenter's republican friend from Cambridge, William Kingdom Clifford, had translated the work of the German mathematician Georg Friedrich Bernhard Riemann back in the early 1870s, his non-Euclidian geometry with its theories of curved space with manifold dimensions had appeared esoteric. By the early twentieth century, however, mathematicians were adopting non-Euclidian geometries in an effort to comprehend space well before Einstein fully developed his theory of relativity. Speculation that our apprehension of space might be subjective was accompanied by the discovery of radio waves, X-rays, radioactivity and electrons which assailed conventional wisdom about the physical world. As matter dissolved into energy, the boundaries between outside and inside appeared to be caving in. The universe seemed to be full of intriguing mysteries, making telepathy, clairvoyance, extra-sensory perception and even spirits appear as valid topics for scientific investigation. During the late 1890s and early 1900s investigation into psychical research interacted with new thinking in physics and James Hinton's mathematician son Charles was propounding theories of a Fourth Dimension. This mathematical proposition caught the imagination of thinkers and artists alike; it extended into infinity and also suggested that an intense form of mystical introspection might be the means of glimpsing something beyond the beyond. Hinton's Fourth Dimension and Bucke's cosmic consciousness thus travelled in tandem.[4] Carpenter was aware of these debates, though he hedged his bets. In his poem 'In the British Museum Library', he refers wearily to the 'interminable discussions of modern science', mentioning 'the investigations into ghostly geometries of four or five dimensions'.[5] In another poem he has the mathematician tracking 'the hidden property of curves and closed figures'.[6]

One response to a loss of Christian faith was a surge of interest in mysticism and the occult, along with a wider respect for Eastern religious thought. Carpenter, who had added Taoism to his spiritual accoutrements, asked in 'Nothing Less Than All': 'Does the truth lie with the East or with the West – with Buddhists and the followers of Lao Tsze [sic], or with those who span seas and rivers by bridges and wing aerial flights by machinery?'[7] Was it to be harmony with nature or control over it? His own inclination was incontestably towards the former. However he did not completely abandon a 'Western' scientific outlook. Instead he tried to overcome the divide by drawing on contemporary science in his efforts to comprehend life, being and consciousness. His search was for an epistemological wholeness which could combine science and reason, meta-physics and mysticism. Moreover Carpenter articulates a wish to harmonise 'body and soul, the outer and the inner'.[8] He wanted to accept the lot as Whitman had done, rather than opting for one or the other, and the poems are infused with 'sweet enjoyment'.[9] The sensuous confidence of his own security with Merrill reaches outwards and Carpenter exalts the body in sun and sand; he celebrates 'the ocean of sex' and announces that the 'uranian', the outcast redeemer, is about to appear in glory from the 'mists of ages'.[10] The final part of Towards Democracy, 'Who Shall Command the Heart', connected with a new energy which was emerging out of the tumult of ideas; it spoke to a widespread desire to bury the old century along with the old Queen.

Notwithstanding, traces of doubt linger about hedonism and asceticism. In 'Nothing Less than All' he poses the question: 'Is it for pleasure and the world and the present, or for death and translation and spirituality, that we must live?'[11] The body is not only a source of delight, it is also presented as a hindrance; 'The Stupid Old Body' is to be left behind little by little.[12] He expressed another long-standing ambivalence in a poem called 'In An Old Quarry'; in this he returns to the boy who had wandered the Sussex Downs and intimates that the human condition is to be lost and estranged, with 'Each seeking his true mates'.[13] Then in another poem, and another mood, he discloses a desire to hold within the circle of his arms more friends 'than the universe holds'.[14] Carpenter's poetry intimates the possibility of direct human relationships defined by inner feelings and desire rather than convention. Uncannily, his personal intellectual and emotional ambiguities and angsts touched contemporary sensitivities, and he would return again and again to the questions he had posed poetically in the prodigious output of books, pamphlets and articles.

Nevertheless, not all Carpenter's old friends felt sympathetic towards the oceanic embrace. Edward Anthony Beck wrote from Cambridge to John Dalton at Windsor observing that no doubt he had seen the new edition of Towards Democracy, adding that Carpenter had also 'published some pamphlets of a not very savoury sort about Love in its more abnormal manifestations'. Indiscretion had been compounded when Carpenter had turned up in Cambridge dressed 'in a blue serge suit and flannel shirt'.[15] Beck was embedded in respectable academia, but criticism came also from the left. Robert Blatchford announced in Clarion that while he had liked Towards Democracy when he had first read it, he had changed and so had Carpenter. 'Edward Carpenter is not a young man; he is a scholar, and he knows the world. Why should he affront us by echoes of Walt Whitman's lubberly frankness about sex?'[16] John Bruce Glasier, now chairman of the

Independent Labour Party, which was affiliated to the newly formed Labour Party, was also embarrassed. Time and circumstance had distanced the organisation man from the ardent bohemian who had hoped for revolution and courted Katharine St John Conway so passionately. Glasier noted in his diary that though Blatchford's review might be somewhat rude, he, too, objected to Whitman and Carpenter's celebration of 'sexual sensation'.[17] In contrast Charles Ashbee, now ensconced with Janet Ashbee and his Guild of Handicraft at Chipping Campden in the Cotswolds, happily imbibed the new addition to *Towards Democracy* with his Christmas pudding in 1902.[18]

In the same year Carpenter edited an anthology celebrating same-sex love, entitled *Ioläus* after the warrior comrade of Hercules. *Ioläus* was an ingenious move on Carpenter's part. It adopted a reassuring, familiar form, the sentimental friendship miscellany, as a means of breaking the ban on any discussion in a popular idiom of homosexuality or lesbianism. It was exactly the kind of book the Liverpool postal worker Will Young had been looking for when he struggled with the classical references in *Homogenic Love*. Indeed in July 1902, when Carpenter sent £10 to Alf Mattison as a wedding present, he promised a copy of his new compilation would follow.[19] In *Ioläus* Carpenter the evangelical educator extended his embrace to a great crowd of historical 'friends'. Greek and Spartan warrior lovers and shepherd boys appear in procession along with Sir Thomas Browne, Michelangelo and the Persian poet Hafiz. From more recent times, Richard Wagner, Ludwig II, King of Prussia, Walt Whitman, Byron and Shelley present themselves in its pages. Nor were the women quite forgotten; Carpenter included Queen Anne and Lady Churchill as well as the resolute Lady Eleanor Butler and Sarah Ponsonby who eloped to live in Wales and became known as the 'Ladies of Llangollen' during the eighteenth century.[20]

Carpenter told Ellis that he was dealing with 'the <u>romance</u> of Friendship only; sex-things are not mentioned, tho they may here and there be read between the lines'.[21] Ambiguity provided Carpenter with a degree of cover reinforced by august acknowledgements. The message, nonetheless, was clear; the most eminent of personages had loved their own sex. The book was, on the whole, well-received. The I.L.P.'s *Labour Leader* commended Carpenter's 'tact and wisdom' on a subject that was difficult to present to a prudish and ignorant public.[22] Several reviewers in liberal and labour papers even ventured to suggest that the physical and erotic aspect of friendship had been underplayed.[23] However one voice from the past launched into vituperative attack. The anarchist David Nicoll, who was still producing *Commonweal*, denounced Carpenter as a part of a homosexual, reactionary, Jesuit plot which included Kropotkin's friend, now turned Fabian, Charlotte Wilson, and the leader of the I.L.P., Keir Hardie. Nicoll's paranoid charges of 'filth and dirt' were coming from a broken, isolated man, at loggerheads even with his anarchist comrades, and they could be ignored.[24]

Far more distressing for Carpenter in the early 1900s were two real-life friendships in which the idealised embrace was powerless to overcome acrimony. On the whole, Carpenter's friendships from the 1880s withstood the passing of time, but his relationship with George Adams remained unresolved and his closeness to Kate Salt was fraught with tension. By 1901 Adams felt so bitter towards Carpenter that he had fallen out with George Hukin. Carpenter tried pouring oil on troubled waters in a letter to Hukin in April 1901: 'He does care for you very much only it is stupid of him to make it a burden to you.'[25] Carpenter remarked that Adams was behaving with Hukin just like Kate Salt did with him. No decisive breach occurred between Carpenter and Kate Salt, though in December 1901 she mentioned a banishment imposed by Carpenter two years before. The 'banishment' was hardly effective for Kate continued to crash through the intricate psychological barriers Carpenter constructed to fend her off. She still yearned to be ever closer, appointing him as her therapeutic advisor and confiding in him with a raw honesty. What rejoinder could he offer to her confession that she and Henry Salt dwelt together only because of her pity for her husband? It must have been disturbing for Carpenter to read, 'No touch possible (Oh! the pity of it!) and no under-standing.'[26] He was, after all, meant to be a friend of Henry's too. But Kate's emotional distress was too acute to engage with Carpenter's reactions, though she did pause momentarily to wonder why it was that she talked to him when he never talked to her. Carpenter, holed in by the barrage of bottled-up emotion in the letters from Kate, found her intimacies alarming and invasive. His response was to withdraw, making her renew her efforts to evoke some comeback.

Despite feeling hounded, his old dependence on her persisted. It was Kate who sent the new translation of the *Bhagavad-Gita*, Kate who shared his interest in Persian poetry, telling him about a Sufi woman writer, Rabia, in the thirteenth century. And it was 'dear old Kate' to whom he could recount his ailments and confide practical worries. Kate might demand the impossible, yet she related to him with unstinting loving acceptance. Carpenter was never reconciled with Adams, but so long as Kate and he were apart, Carpenter could keep her intensity at bay with a teasing familiarity. He could be unguarded with Kate, as he was with the men he trusted implicitly, Hukin, Sixsmith and Mattison.

When Dr Bucke's long awaited *Cosmic Consciousness* was finally published in 1901, Carpenter confided to Kate Salt that it was 'rather a farrago'.[27] He was even franker with Charlie Sixsmith, declaring the book to be a mixture of 'bosh' and useful quotes and references.[28] Though the title of Bucke's book derived from Carpenter, he could not help but be somewhat embarrassed to find himself up with Buddha, Christ, Mohammed, Plotinus and Whitman as a key cosmic. Bucke's stakes were high, for his also-rans, classified as 'Additional – some of them Lesser, Imperfect and Doubtful Instances', included Moses, Socrates, Wordsworth and Thoreau.[29] Nevertheless Bucke's work acquired a cult status among cosmic questers and enhanced Carpenter's fame in some surprising places. There was, for example, the gold miner from the Sierra Nevada who arrived in Millthorpe after a long fast overwhelmed by ecstatic visions to whom Carpenter gave a cup of tea and the *Bhagavad-Gita*.[30] He corresponded with the mystical miner for many years, patiently acting as an unpaid long-distance therapist.

In *My Days and Dreams* in 1916, Carpenter was carefully tactful about Bucke's book, stating that while it might be 'a bit casual, hurried, doctrinaire, un-literary', it had acquired a following and exercised an influence 'beneath the surface'.[31] Bucke's idea of an evolving cosmic consciousness offered an attractive variant on mechanical materialism and his 'farrago' permeated the alternative religious, ethical and humanitarian milieu in the early years of the twentieth century. Carpenter identified with these underground currents of knowledge, though his own work actually *spanned* mainstream and alternative cultures. In the early 1900s he assumed an important role as a transmitter of a melange of heterodoxies which were being nurtured not only by Theosophists, or members of the Labour Churches and the Humanitarian League, but by the followers of 'Higher Thought', like his sister Emmie, who believed in the power of the mind over the body. Higher Thought was an American import, though it was known there as 'New Thought' or 'Harmonial Religion'. Founded by Phineas Parkhurst Quimby, it combined Swedenborg with Emerson. Carpenter was also popular with another high-minded group which derived from America, Stanton Coit's Ethical Movement which cultivated a secular ethics. Following their tenet of 'deed not creed', they were setting up Neighbourhood Guilds in the early 1900s which aimed to be more grassroots than settlements like Toynbee Hall.

In November 1902 Carpenter was invited into new territory when he addressed the London Spiritualist Alliance on 'The Dream World and the Real World'. Spiritualism too had crossed the Atlantic in the middle years of the nineteenth century; it had gained a considerable following in Britain by the 1900s, and a large crowd gathered. The lecture was reported in *Light: A Journal of Psychical, Occult and Mystical Research* amidst advertisements for Electricity Cures for Indigestion and Nervous Exhaustion and Animal Magnetism. Carpenter spoke as a friendly outsider, airing the scattered thoughts he had begun to intimate in his prose-poetry on reverie and consciousness. He linked spiritualism to a wider scepticism about materialism expressed in Theosophy and Mental Healing. He was becoming increasingly interested in the new field of psychology and, in his concluding remarks, mused that images had their birth in feelings, adding that where feelings came from was another question.[32]

This was one of the speculations which would germinate into his next book, *The Art of Creation* (1904). Its title surfaced in 1903 when Carpenter spoke for the William Morris Labour Church in Leek, but the key to its contents was the subtitle 'Essays on the Self and its Powers'.[33] A brochure from the publisher, George Allen, promised a reconciliation of Spirit and Matter, Plato and Darwin, Religion and Physiology, the Gods and Evolution, and puffed the message: 'Man himself, as soon as he understands can take part in the art of creation.'[34]

In *The Art of Creation* Carpenter reiterated his belief that the 'simple consciousness' of primitive man and the child could combine with the self-consciousness of alienated Western humanity in a new synthesis of cosmic consciousness. Ultimately he believed that this could only be through following the heart as Romanticism had indicated. Yet just as the British Idealist philosopher James McTaggart had sought to prove his thesis of love by logic, Carpenter suggested that thought could take the spiritual searcher to the brink of union with the cosmos.[35] Thus *The Art of Creation* enabled Carpenter to return to the Idealist philosophers his father had admired and search for that tantalisingly elusive state of unity with nature which had inspired the Romantics.

Carpenter embarked on a mighty effort to get behind his own self-conscious intellectual knowing by situating his approach to the 'Universal Self' within a long tradition. His trajectory begins with the Hindu sacred treatises, the *Upanishads*, Buddha, Lao-Tzu, then incorporates Plato, Plotinus and the Gnostic heretics. Arriving at fourteenth-century mysticism, he moves on to Spinoza, Berkeley, Kant, Hegel, Schopenhauer and the Scottish metaphysical philosopher, J.F. Ferrier, who coined the word 'epistemology'. Carpenter had already posited that a body of doctrine had been handed down from ancient times when he wrote about the Gnani in *From Adam's Peak to Elephanta* and in *The Art of Creation* he simply elaborates the map. His inclination is to stress what is similar in his 'tradition', without pausing to acknowledge the difficulties in tracing actual historical interactions between his early thinkers or philosophical discord among his

'Self in Porch', 1905, by Alf Mattison

later ones. Instead he is intent on marking out a theoretical trail which leads to a consciousness of being apart from and beyond the intellect. He places himself within a continuum.[36]

The Art of Creation is a work of extraordinary synthesis in which Carpenter is feeling his way towards a vision of countless selves expanding into infinity if only self-consciousness could be overcome. During the 1900s mysticism was very much in vogue, partly because of the search for an alternative to religious faith and partly because of the Symbolists' stress on inner revelation. So Carpenter's book was decidedly of the moment. His own experience with the Gnani had made him open to differing modes of knowing, and, by the time he wrote *The Art of Creation* he was aware of Sufism, as well as Taoism and the Japanese Buddhism which was being popularised in the West through the writings of the American Lafcadio Hearn. He suggests that 'flashes (or glimmers)' of cosmic union could be attained, as Plotinus and Eckhart had noted, through mysticism, or, as Schopenhauer had mooted, through art.[37]

In *Towards Democracy* he had hinted at a 'faint faint glamor here and there', and sensed, amidst the trees in the night, 'wavering dubious forms and presences'.[38] He put this less poetically in *The Art of Creation*, arguing that the riddle to the creation of the universe was insoluble without a transcendent factor, 'Will, Being, the Ego, a Fourth dimension, or whatever we may term it'.[39] Cambridge had trained him to be wary and so he proceeded cautiously, proposing that if the subject is '*more* thinkable by assuming say a fourth dimensional being than by following the ramifications of "matter and force" into infinite space and time, we are quite justified in adopting the former method'.[40] Under cover, he had contrived to transmogrify a mathematical theory into a spiritual presence in nature.

An underlying yearning for a syncretic wholeness led him to question the separation of spirit and matter. At the beginning of *The Art of Creation*, Carpenter quoted the Chinese Taoist Lao-Tzu, 'These two things, the spiritual and the material, though we call them by different names, in their Origins are one and the same.'[41] Perhaps not quite convinced that Lao-Tzu would persuade all his readers, and perhaps because he, himself, retained certain Victorian habits of thought, Carpenter invoked 'science' as well as art and mysticism in his exploration of forms of 'out-of-body' consciousness, launching out into psychiatry, a terrain which was relatively new to him. Though some strands of psychiatry, still closely linked to physiology, focused on the body as matter, an interest in dreams, hypnosis and the sub-conscious was contributing to a new field which incorporated insights from philosophy and the arts. Schopenhauer's awareness of the 'secret decisions' governing human emotions and actions,[42] and Symbolism's

274 EDWARD CARPENTER: A LIFE OF LIBERTY AND LOVE

acknowledgement of hidden messages dwelling within the overt and running counterpoint to the obvious, were particularly important in the understanding of neurosis.

Carpenter's wide reading in philosophy and literature as well as sexology, along with his ability to understand French, German and Italian, had equipped him to engage with European psychiatry. In *The Art of Creation* he cites Alfred Binet, who like many psychiatrists was interested in how hysteria suggested that states of consciousness could co-exist, and Theodule Ribot, whose stress on the dynamic contributed to the emergence of phenomenology. He also drew on an influential book by Frederic W. Myers, a lengthy two-volume treatise on the knowledge gleaned from a life's work studying psychical phenomena, entitled *Human Personality and its Survival of Bodily Death* (1903). Detailed analysis of claims of encounters with spirits, along with an early familiarity with Freud, led Myers to question a unitary self and to propose theories of subliminal mental activity.[43] This idea was familiar to Carpenter poetically through Whitman. But now he began to *theorise* that there might be potentially many selves and differing types of consciousness. He also inclined to the view that structures of feeling peculiar to differing races were passed on, invoking Lamarck, along with Plato and Bucke's views on biology.[44]

Dismissing epistemological boundaries, Carpenter ventured into the overlapping fields of physiology and psychiatry. Characteristically he had a thesis that he wanted to prove. In *Civilisation: Its Cause and Cure* he had suggested that the brain was 'transitional' between the nerves of sense and 'the great sympathetic nerve'.[45] This idea that the emotions were governed by the ganglionic nervous system rather than the brain had been put forward in Dr Bucke's *Man's Moral Nature* (1879). Bucke's proposition, first presented in a paper he gave in 1877, derived from research by J.G. Davey, a doctor who had worked in Ceylon during the 1850s.[46] The theory had been propounded in the late eighteenth century by Marie François Xavier Bichat and gained a following in the early part of the nineteenth century, but by the 1900s it was no longer accepted by most physiologists who disputed the independence of the cerebrospinal and the ganglionic.

Carpenter employed a former member of the Fellowship of the New Life, Henry Binns, to check out current thinking in physiology. Binns, who wrote on Whitman and mysticism, had no specialised knowledge but evidently needed the money, for he nervously requested 2s 6d an hour, explaining this was the rate paid by the philanthropist Joseph Rowntree. Binns did his best, valiantly ploughing through a long list of writers who had written on nerves and the brain. He found himself expanding into the experimental psychology of Wilhelm Wundt in

Germany, the influential social psychology of the neo-Lamarckian William McDougall which stressed instinctive drives, as well as the psychological theories of the American philosopher William James. In his lengthy report Binns mentioned in passing a review of the work of two somewhat wacky characters called Josef Breuer and Sigmund Freud, who 'uphold the sexual element in hysteria and cure it by demanding repeated confession of all the psychic shocks and morbidities'.[47] As the hours mounted up, the unfortunate Binns soon realised that it was impossible to 'get up embryology, physiology and psychology . . . in the course of a few days'.[48] His other problem was that he realised his paymaster wanted the Sympathetic Nervous System to be the autonomous site of emotions. Nevertheless Binns kept explaining that this was *not* the view of contemporary physiologists. 'Indeed the whole existence and function of the symp. [*sic*] is in doubt.'[49] Undeterred, Carpenter headed off into the British Museum to read J.G. Davey's *Ganglionic Nervous System* for himself.[50]

In *The Art of Creation* Carpenter was carefully qualified, stating that the Great Sympathetic autonomously co-operated with the brain, but that there was some support for it having a more primary role.[51] Binns' advice had just about prevailed. Carpenter's apparently arcane preoccupation with the physiological ideas of Bichat, Davey and Bucke about the ganglionic nervous system derived from his desire to assert an 'affective' life denied by modern Western society. The 'Great Sympathetic' seemed to provide the key to recovering an 'organic consciousness' which he had felt in India and Ceylon and explored in his reading of works on the Tantras and on yoga. 'The Hindus and other Orientals have in these directions, partly by deliberate practice, come into touch with the command of regions whose existence the Western peoples hardly suspect.'[52] However as a practised propagandist he knew that Eastern ideas alone would not carry sufficient authority, and sought to mainstream them by seeking scientific corroboration.

Carpenter was not alone in his search for an 'organic consciousness', and while the 'Great Sympathetic' was dismissed within scientific circles it lodged itself into Western occult thinking from whence it travelled down interesting subterranean tracks to surface in D.H. Lawrence's *Women in Love* in 1917. Lawrence does not acknowledge Carpenter as his source. However, he certainly knew of Carpenter's writings and gave *Towards Democracy* to his friend, Helen Corke, in Croydon.[53] An explanation might be Lawrence's disinclination to record his borrowings, on the other hand the similarities in his and Carpenter's writing could be accounted for by the cultural influences they shared rather than direct transmission. Like Carpenter, Lawrence was familiar with Whitman and Schopenhauer and he had read the Thoesophist Helena Blavatsky.

The theories about sexual energy in *Women in Love can* be traced to Lawrence's enthusiasm for *The Apocalypse Unsealed* by J.M. Pryse. Pryse asserted that according to ancient Indian neurological ideas, an energy, Kundalini, could be generated at the base of the spine which acted on the other ganglia or chakras and on the brain, charging the whole being with an illumination which was both sensual and spiritual.[54] Yet it appears that the concept was already familiar to the novelist in general terms before *The Apocalypse Unsealed* was published in 1910, for Lawrence told Bertrand Russell in a letter written in 1915 that he had believed since he was about twenty that there was a seat of consciousness apart from the brain or the nervous system.[55] Whether this notion came from reading *Civilisation: Its Cause and Cure* or *The Art of Creation* remains tantalisingly unverifiable.

The Art of Creation's sense of spirit in nature and Carpenter's distrust of all forms of mechanistic materialism also echo in E.M. Forster's *The Longest Journey* (1907). Poor Rickie Elliot frightens himself with the notion that the 'trees and coppices and summer fields of parsley were alive' and ends up doing a mile's detour just to evade the fauns, while the novel begins with an argument at Cambridge about whether a cow is real.[56] It is true that mind, matter and the reality of cows were hot topics at Cambridge during the early 1900s, and again it is not clear whether Forster had actually read *The Art of Creation* at this point. He would, however, have known of it through his friendship with G. Lowes Dickinson. Moreover he lists Carpenter among other authors in his Diary in 1907.[57]

These similarities are of interest not only in terms of the direct impact of Carpenter's writing on Lawrence and Forster, but because they indicate how he was addressing cultural and philosophical debates which were very much in the air. In *The Art of Creation* Carpenter was consciously aiming at opinion formers. By elaborating a mystical awareness in prose he aimed to reach an intellectual and political public that might have been inclined to dismiss his poetry. The former Sheffield socialist, David Thompson, who was working at Washington's Library of Congress, congratulated Carpenter on making the translation, saying he thought the book would appeal to university men and women because it was formulated in a language they understood better than *Towards Democracy*.[58]

Carpenter focuses on individual cosmic transcendence in *The Art of Creation*. 'The central life *is* and lives and – moves within us.'[59] However that other strand of the Romantic heritage, social community, present in so much of his writing, appears towards the end of the book with the redeeming promise of the 'Celestial City, Our Home' from which come our 'Dreams of Paradise and Cities of the Sun'.[60] Carpenter wanted to take his labour movement friends with him, observing to Sixsmith, 'A good deal of it – the oneself, the physiology, etcetera will seem new and puzzling to people but I hope and think the book will *wear* well; and justify its bold statements.'[61]

He was successful in appealing to Beatrice Webb who hailed *The Art of Creation* with delight as the metaphysics 'of the Socialist creed as to social relations – the Faith we Hold'.[62] She was less happy a few years later when she and Sidney visited another fan of *The Art of Creation*, the eccentric Maharaja of Chhatarpur, who demanded that the Webbs should deliver Carpenter in person forthwith.[63]

Carpenter did not, however, convince in Cambridge, where G.E. Moore's *Principia Ethica* had shifted the philosophical paradigms in 1903, making McTaggart's Idealist absolutes look distinctly dated. Lowes Dickinson, who was familiar with current philosophical debates, took issue with Carpenter in a new journal, the *Independent Review*, on the relationship between the subject knowing and the object known. Dickinson observed that when the object was known, there was of course a subject knowing it; but that was no reason to say the object did not exist, whether or not there was anyone there to know it. 'As a matter of fact, we do, most of us, habitually conceive a world of matter existing before there was any consciousness, The conception may be erroneous; but it is certainly not senseless or self-contradictory.'[64]

Carpenter was stung to reply that 'Mr. Dickinson' had missed the point. He said he did not 'deny that "matter" or the objective basis of external things' had an 'independent existence', but rejected the proposition 'that it has an independent non-mental existence, and I say that if it has then such existence cannot be known or even imagined'.[65] Carpenter added a special 'Note On Matter' for a new and enlarged edition of *The Art of Creation* in 1907. The critique was painful not simply because of his long association with Lowes Dickinson, but also because it appeared in the *Independent Review*. With its cover designed by Roger Fry, the journal was influential in exactly the liberal intellectual circles Carpenter had hoped to reach with his book.

Nevertheless the Fabian Sydney Olivier, now in the Colonial Office, enthusiastically sent a copy of *The Art of Creation* to William James. James' *The Varieties of Religious Experience* had appeared in 1902 and he was empathetic to all aspects of spirituality, including spiritualism and mental healing which were exceedingly popular in the United States. In many ways he and Carpenter had been going along parallel tracks. Like Carpenter, James was familiar with Friedrich von Schelling's attempt to get behind an alienated modern self-consciousness as well as with Whitman's celebration of immediate existence. He too had trawled through Myers and European dynamic psychiatry. Moreover, James had adopted the term 'cosmic consciousness', arguing that we screened ourselves from this dimension of perception in daily life, ignoring how it could become a source of psychological renewal.

The Art of Creation did indeed interest James, though he disagreed with the fusing of matter and spirit and considered that Carpenter over-did ancestral memory. James also balked at the assumption of mysticism as the voice of authority within Carpenter's writing, telling Olivier:

> I used to think that that authority was a staggerer to all forms of pluralistic belief, but now I feel less respectful – mysticism is authoritative as to *more unity* than which at first appears but it is 'passing to the limit' to erect it into an absolute philosophic authority, as excluding the 'other' completely.[66]

This was of course exactly the difficulty Carpenter had himself encountered with the Gnani's spiritual certainties. And James was echoing Olive Schreiner's objection to Carpenter's initial challenge to scientific knowing in Civilisation: Its Cause and Cure. Reason could be a means of contesting cultural assumptions rooted in tradition. As Schreiner had remarked, this could be to the advantage of those who were disenfranchised and excluded. Carpenter's apparent openness could disguise the strength of his inner certainties. Even though he rejected occult forms of spirituality and favoured Whitman's democratic vista of a union open to all with the cosmos, by privileging a knowing beyond reason Carpenter put his assertions outside any terrain that could be contested by reasoning. The inveterate reconciler of opposites was unable to resolve this dilemma. Nor could he resolve the contradiction that E.M. Forster spotted many years later: 'Like most mystics, he wanted to both merge in the universe and to retain his identity, and since he was neither a strong nor a wary thinker he brought forward no plausible solution of the contradiction.'[67] Forster was writing in 1931 when he had come to question his youthful esteem for Carpenter.

In the early 1900s, however, Carpenter expressed a contemporaneous aspiration for spiritual perceptions outside conventional Christianity. He was part of a wider trend in which Theosophy and the chakras gained recruits, pagans were all the rage and myths and fertility symbols were being eagerly discovered. When Carpenter spoke on 'Deities and Devils in the Light of Race Memory', at the Leeds Arts Club in April 1904, the enthusiastic crowd who piled in to hear him were ready to be reassured that the old Gods were but the projections of human fears and aspirations and not inclined to quibble over theoretical contradictions.[68] The club brought together his devoted old friends Alf Mattison and Isabella Ford, along with the newly emergent local avant-garde, led by the charismatic Theosophist and schoolteacher Alfred Orage and the Nietzschean journalist Holbrook Jackson. Both men were committed to individual growth as well as to new forms of collectivity. They belonged to a burgeoning provincial intelligentsia which bypassed the metropolis and Oxbridge. They were iconoclastic moderns looking for connections between apparent opposites. *The Art of Creation* offered a convenient reconciliation between the dichotomies troubling them; science and mysticism, mind and matter, sex and spirit, individual and community. Carpenter's optimism about the potential of human beings to evolve held considerable attraction, for it transferred the nineteenth century's faith in progress into the inner psyche. There were to be no shibboleths, no boundaries in the new epoch of the infinite self.

The Art of Creation stayed in print in Britain until the early 1920s and was also published in the United States and translated into German, Italian and Japanese. It did not 'wear' quite as Carpenter had wished, instead it is very much a book of its time, a chaotic treasure trove of currents of opinion which have faded from view. Like Carpenter, *The Art of Creation* has dated in style, yet, as so often with his writing, the questions at the heart of his enquiry are as pertinent and mysterious as when he asked them. What is consciousness? Where does it come from? Could there be dimensions beyond the ones we inhabit? What is identity and just how many selves can a body contain?

16

Body and Spirit

The divide which touched Carpenter's own life most personally was the abiding split between body and spirit. His homosexuality meant this could never be just a philosophic issue or even a matter of personal ethics. In 1898 the Vagrancy Act's ban on 'importuning' had been strengthened and it was mainly used against homosexuals. The application of legislation was, in fact, variable and arbitrary, nonetheless, along with periodic press scandals and the threat of blackmail, it contributed to an atmosphere edged with fear. Even Carpenter in the seclusion of the countryside did not escape entirely. Charles Oates died in 1901, leaving an estate valued at what was then the vast sum of £119,280, whereupon Arthur Cole, Oates' former lover, started to haunt Millthorpe because Carpenter was Oates' executor. In the spring of 1904 matters came to a head when Cole parked himself outside the gate and refused to leave. Finally, in the middle of the night, Carpenter and Hukin, who happened to be visiting, marched Cole off to the police station. Confronted by the local policeman, Cole crumpled and, amidst abject apologies, the crisis was averted. The incident however left Carpenter shaken, angry and fearful.[1]

In this context it is not surprising to find Carpenter moving in a crab-like manner, though his resolve to write on homosexuality never faltered. In 1903 he confided to Charles Ashbee it was 'The question of homogenic love-fellowship . . . as the basis, or at least one of the motors of social reconstruction' that really interested him, adding that his socialist friends were angry with him for playing with a subject they saw as 'a red herring trailed in the path of democracy'.[2] Dismissing prejudice against homosexuality as 'fossilization', he continued to draw inspiration from Walt Whitman.[3] In his 1902 article on 'Walt Whitman's Children' he had suggested warily that Whitman was attracted, at least in thought, to men as well as women,[4] and in 1906 he celebrated Whitman as the prophet of 'The universal soul, rediscovering itself in all forms, in the healthy and beautiful human body, in sex and fraternity, in the life with the earth and the open air'.[5] Whitman's affirmation of the body and physicality enabled Carpenter to countervail the asceticism within Christianity and some strands of Eastern religion. This combination of sex and spirit became his hallmark. When Havelock Ellis' fifth volume in his *Studies in the Psychology of Sex, Sexual Selection in Man*, appeared in 1905, Carpenter congratulated his friend on indicating the 'telephone wires between the visible forms of the world and the invisible forms of the celestial and Platonic ideas!'[6] Though Carpenter joked about his own incurable idealism, in fact he saw the material and the spiritual as intertwined.

The publication of an enlarged edition of *Love's Coming of Age* by Swan Sonnenschein in 1906 enabled him to modify his notes 'On Preventive Checks to Population' by adding his endorsement of the 'soul-union' without ejaculation advocated by the American writer Alice B. Stockham in her book *Karezza* (1896). Still impractically dismissive of contraceptives, Carpenter contrived to bundle in far-reaching ideas by proposing that the sexual practices which predominated in the West could be subject to cultural change and distinguishing between 'Sexual intercourse for the definite purpose of race-propagation and sexual intercourse for simple union'.[7] By undermining the emphasis within the Christian church on sex for procreation, Carpenter opened the way for an acceptance of sexual pleasure for its own sake which negated one of the objections to homosexuality. Carpenter's elevation of the spiritual-sounding soul-union thus acted as a stalking horse for a celebration of homogenic, non-procreative sex. This was deft indeed.

Moreover this 1906 edition at last included a reworked version of his 1897 article, 'An Unknown People', entitled 'The Intermediate Sex'. Still drawing on K.H. Ulrichs, Carpenter argued that while there were polarities of masculinity and femininity in both men and women, there were also 'intermediate' types who balanced the characteristics associated with 'male' and 'female' and indicated new cultural possibilities. Carpenter also claimed that the physical and mental aspects of love were conjoined regardless of one's sexual preference.[8] By downplaying a distinct physical desire, while avowing the body and nature, Carpenter sought to subvert the pervasive image of homosexuality as a furtive degenerate sensuality. He was recasting male–male love by presenting a continuum of sexual characteristics and of sexuality, nimbly recruiting a wider constituency by association.

Carpenter's impulse to reach out to a broad audience, including women, contrasted with the ethos surrounding other key literary and intellectual homosexual figures in Britain. In the 1900s the 'new chivalry' network around Charles Kains Jackson continued to produce artistic portrayals of nudes, slim volumes of poetry, and novels, often for private circulation. Reviews would appear in little magazines and a few small presses continued to take the risk of publication. Most of the energy went into surviving. It was an introverted, defensive, carefully coded culture which took cover behind classical and biblical allusions. Secrecy was accentuated because several of the writers were attracted to young men or boys. Carpenter knew some of the men in this circle; Marc-André Raffalovich, the son of a wealthy banker, who wrote poems exalting sundry Ganymedes; John Gambril Nicholson, a schoolteacher, who published *A Garland of Ladslove* in 1911; and Charles Sayle, a poet, literary scholar and librarian at Cambridge. At Cambridge, especially, homosexuality was an open secret. Lytton Strachey, who was influenced by both McTaggart and Lowes Dickinson, turned the criminal connotations of 'sodomy' around in his Platonic concept of the 'Higher Sodomy', a form of love he regarded as superior to male–female desire. Officially the 'Higher Sodomy' was not physical, though Strachey and his circle of male friends, which included the economist, John Maynard Keynes, did not follow the ascetic ideal too rigidly.

Outside these small elitist literary and intellectual circles the communication of ideas about homosexuality continued to be conducted through the 'scientific' discourse which had been initiated by the German and Austrian sexual theorists and Havelock Ellis in the late nineteenth century. By the 1900s medical and psychiatric texts were being augmented by anthropological and sociological works. While these brought the topic out for discussion and demonstrated that a variety of sexual practices and institutions existed, they tended still to retain assumptions about abnormality and degeneracy. Moreover, like the medical works, they were couched in academic language and aimed at the educated, though in Britain this was still not a guarantee that they would escape censorship.

When Carpenter managed to find a German publisher for a collection of his essays on homosexuality, a pessimistic Havelock Ellis reflected that given the intensive level of sexual debate in Germany and Austria the essays were actually more needed in English, though he did not consider England ripe yet for such a project.[9] Nevertheless, the resolute Carpenter persuaded Swan Sonnenschein to publish *The Intermediate Sex: A Study of Some Transitional Types of Men and Women* in 1908. He was so determined to get his ideas out to the public at large that he appears to have funded the book's publication. For though it was distributed by Swan Sonnenschein, it was actually owned by Carpenter. The book was remarkable in addressing a general readership and thus breaking the taboo on how ideas about homosexuality could be communicated. Carpenter's commitment to fusing body and spirit afforded some protection, along with the fact that since much of the book had appeared already its contents might be regarded as being already in the public domain. Carpenter also spattered references to untranslated European texts throughout and included a long bibliographical appendix. Quite apart from his enthusiasm to educate, these enabled him to couch his most passionate beliefs in scholarly terms. Though the language he used was free of the jargon weighing down the scientific texts, he was adept at a diffuse turn of phrase which made it exceedingly difficult to pin down his precise meaning. What he said might appear perfectly clear; what he *meant* was frequently opaque. Moreover the papers in *The Intermediate Sex* were written over several years and express subtly shifting perspectives

In using the term the 'intermediate sex' Carpenter was adapting a concept which was already in circulation. Carpenter aimed to assert a distinctness without enclosing homosexuals within a definition of differ-ence; he was, however, confronted by a dilemma, for European sexual theorists and campaigners were divided over biology and culture. The founder of the German Scientific Humanitarian Committee, Magnus Hirschfeld, clung to his conviction that homosexuality was congenital and adopted this stance in defending people who faced legal prosecutions and social prejudice. But from 1902 an assertive new German homosexual grouping, the Community of the Special, was bringing an added twist to the debate, rejecting the inborn thesis while presenting men who desired men as a cultural elect.

Carpenter inclined to the view that homosexuality was innate while presenting a cultural vision of his intermediates as harbingers of the new age. Rejecting elitism, he tempered his chosen ones with a Uranian Spirit which embodied humanitarian values. Adopting Otto de Joux's idea of Uranians as 'Idealists',[10] Carpenter endowed them with a capacity for direct bonds of personal affection which he saw as negating the capitalist alienation of money and law. This promotion of 'intermediates' into the cultural advance guard of socialism exasperated Bernard Shaw, who refused to sign a manifesto calling for the legalisation of homosexuality in December 1909. He sympathised with Carpenter's attempts to stop criminalisation but was enraged by the idea that 'intermediacy' should be recommended to 'the normal' as the desired way to be.[11]

At the beginning of *The Intermediate Sex* Carpenter quotes the Viennese writer Otto Weininger on transitional forms in chemistry, physics and biology in support of a continuum in which every living being was too complex to be put 'wholly on one side, or wholly on the other'.[12] Weininger was beset by contradictions, for he asserted variety while holding on to ideas of male and female types, reproducing within supposedly abstract categories his own misogynist attitudes. Carpenter remarked to Ellis in 1906 that it was a pity the 'rash and dogmatic' author of *Sex and Character* (1903) did not balance his depiction of the 'Absolute Female' with the 'absurdities of the Absolute Male'. Nevertheless he thought the book opened up 'new veins of thought' and felt a theoretical affinity with Weininger's vitalism.[13] It was important to Carpenter that Weininger did not pathologise homosexuality, and in *The Intermediate Sex*, partly under his influence, the fixed essential types that still linger in Carpenter's outlook are subjected to meltdown, while the Uranian 'temperament' is depicted dynamically in swift and constant interaction between 'masculine' and 'feminine' elements.

When Carpenter had written *Homogenic Love* in 1894 he had drawn on European sexual theory, and in 1908 he continued to shore up his arguments with the latest works. Despite fretting under the constraints, Carpenter was careful to release copies for review first to medical and scientific journals, nudging Ellis for a review with suitable scholarly gravitas.[14] Ellis, as usual, tended towards gloom and caution. Telling his friend he might be able to get a 'little notice' into the *Journal of Mental Science*, Ellis warned Carpenter that he had to 'be careful with them and it may be necessary to throw the notice into a somewhat critical form'.[15] In the event *The Intermediate Sex* received sympathetic reviews from several scholarly publications. 'There is nothing nasty here' pronounced *The Medical Times*, while the *Journal of Education* and *The Schoolmaster* were similarly impressed.[16]

Not so the *British Medical Journal*; the reviewer quoted great chunks of text and trounced any claim to 'scientific or literary merit'. Pressing home the book's dangerously low price, the article closed with the contemptuous comment, 'The author has definitely unbuttoned himself to anyone who likes to pay 3s 6d for this book.'[17] The *B.M.J.* by implication was branding his work as obscene. Carpenter knew that such an attack in the *B.M.J.* could have serious consequences. Though he had used the cloak of scholarly references he had eschewed the distanced approach which discussed homosexuality in pathological terms. His book was pushing at the boundaries, for he hoped to persuade as well as to inform. Anxiously Carpenter wrote a letter to the *B.M.J.* insisting that at no point in the book did he advocate sexual intercourse between people of the same sex, simply 'sincere attachment and warm friendship'.[18]

Troubled by the 'nasty review', Carpenter told Sixsmith in July that he was gathering his allies in the medical profession in defence, adding that he thought the book would 'hold its own – not without storms'.[19]

The Intermediate Sex did rather better than holding its own; it sold extremely well, going into many editions, first with Swan Sonnenschein and later with Allen and Unwin. Carpenter was particularly pleased to receive a letter praising the book from Edith How-Martyn, a member of the feminist group the Women's Freedom League. He responded by explaining how much the book was needed: 'I find so many people who are really <u>suffering</u> from the general ignorance on the subject; and of course it is good to feel that one can be of use to them.' Carpenter related how the *B.M.J.* had refused to print his letter and mentioned some other 'spiteful attacks' from people who wanted to damage the socialist cause.[20]

Despite his lofty stance of *noblesse oblige*, Carpenter was feeling vulnerable and exposed when he wrote to How-Martyn, for the *B.M.J.* was not his only antagonist. He was being hounded by a member of the right-wing Liberty and Property Defence League, called M.D. O'Brien, who lived at nearby Dronfield. In 1908, O'Brien, who was obsessively hostile to both socialism and homosexuality, had accused Carpenter of 'vice' when he was speaking on 'Socialism and State Interference' in Sheffield and Chesterfield. Then, in the spring of 1909, when Carpenter and Merrill were away on holiday at the villa of the American socialist George Herron in Florence, O'Brien had turned up at the Hukins' back door with a satchel of pamphlets entitled, 'Socialism and Infamy: The Homogenic or Comrade Love Exposed: An Open Letter in Plain Words for a Socialist Prophet to Edward Carpenter M.A.' Referring to the great hosts of visitors to Millthorpe, O'Brien accused Carpenter and his 'Homogenic Comrades' of morbid appetites, naked dancing, corruption of youth, paganism and socialism.[21] After calling at the Hukins he had proceeded to distribute his pamphlets throughout the village. Hukin was worried, but strove to calm any anxiety Carpenter might feel: 'I think if he has nothing more than your writings to base his accusations upon he may well be ignored.'[22] Charlie Sixsmith rushed over to support Hukin, reassuring Carpenter that the pamphlet was so 'obviously malicious and damned foolish' that no sensible person would be convinced by it.[23] Carpenter despatched a diplomatic letter to the local newspaper, but Merrill's response was more forthright; denouncing that '<u>rotter</u> of <u>cur</u>' to Sixsmith, he added, 'It would be a pleasure to just twist such vermons [*sic*] necks.'[24]

Both Sixsmith and Hukin regarded Merrill as Carpenter's Achilles' Heel and were intent on preventing him from blustering about in the village. Sixsmith resolved that on their return from Florence, Merrill should come and stay with him and his new wife Lucy at Anderton, near Bolton.

Aware that any implied criticism of Merrill had to be phrased carefully to Carpenter, Sixsmith wrote,

> I really shall talk very strongly to him. His very foolish inclinations will land him into serious trouble if he goes on and will bring harm to you indirectly. Of course we know he means well enough, but people don't understand and misunderstand him. I should like to have a talk with you as soon as you come back.[25]

O'Brien did stir up feeling against Carpenter. By April 11th, Fannie was reporting that women in Dronfield were threatening to waylay and mob Carpenter when he came back home. Hukin warned, 'G. is the real problem with all the stories going about concerning him. I think it would be wise to keep him away for the present. Of course one does not know how much O'Brien knows.'[26] When Carpenter arrived back from Italy he felt apprehensive about his reception in the village and particularly concerned about attitudes to Merrill. Married friends, the Sixsmiths and the Salts were imported as guests to provide further respectability, parading rather self-consciously through the village with their anxious host. The following year the Salts moved up to Millthorpe, though as they were living with Kate's woman lover, O'Brien, if he had only known, might have questioned them as respectable ballast.

Carpenter was advised by his solicitor against taking legal action, even though O'Brien's pamphlet was libellous and defamatory, because a jury might be prejudiced against Carpenter's opinions. He counselled Carpenter to secure support from people whose names commanded respect locally, and Carpenter turned to his old ally, the Quaker Mrs Doncaster, who was enlisted to praise his books to the vicar, Reverend Bradshaw.[27] O'Brien had broadened his attack to put pressure on the Holmesfield schoolmaster and the vicar, leading Bradshaw to retort indignantly that he had known Carpenter for twenty years and was convinced of the cleanliness of his life. All those parish council meetings with the somnolent vicar had after all not been in vain. The local establishment had come on side.

Carpenter kept up a brave front in public, dealing with O'Brien's intervention at a Women's Suffrage meeting with apparent serenity; privately however, he was rattled and distressed, snapping at an I.L.P. friend, Richard Hawkin, for writing a supportive letter to the *Sheffield Daily Telegraph*. The last thing he wanted was a heroic battle and martyrdom *à la* Wilde. Instead Carpenter's strategy was to dampen the publicity with a gentlemanly personal letter to the *Telegraph*'s editor suggesting that the correspondence be closed, along with a gift of *The Intermediate Sex*. He apologised to the well-meaning Hawkin later,[28] but confided to Alf Mattison that the 'beastly attack' had confused his brain, putting everything else out of his head.[29] Most upsetting was the inner discord that had arisen among his nearest and dearest. 'I am sorry to say G.H. is a little "off" about "G.M."' Carpenter blamed the influence of his literary neighbour Murray Gilchrist, who he had suspected of being in league with Adams against Merrill. Nevertheless, despite his staunch loyalty towards Merrill, Carpenter did concede that 'The fright has done G.M. a lot of good.'[30]

In September 1909 O'Brien renewed his attacks. Most alarming, he had got hold of *The Intermediate Sex* and the *B.M.J.* review. It began to look as if Carpenter's worst fears were about to be realised. However luck was on his side. O'Brien made a fatal mistake in accusing the vicar of colluding with Carpenter. An indignant Bradshaw wrote to say that the whole parish was up in arms because O'Brien was calling 'Holmesfield the "Sodom of Derbyshire".'[31] O'Brien's efforts at populist revolt had misfired, instead the inept fanatic had contrived to unite the village in support of Carpenter. Splutters from O'Brien continued over the next few years, however he was imploding. His wife, exasperated because he spent all his time out denouncing speakers at socialist meetings, left him, declaring that he was not in his right mind and making off with the household beds and bedding. O'Brien was outraged, but his daughters and his mother supported Mrs O'Brien. In 1913 O'Brien issued a diatribe against the women in his family, castigating them along with 'The Socialist Prophet of Sodom and Gomorrah Edward Carpenter' and was later charged with attacking a woman who had sheltered his mother and wife.[32]

Carpenter had escaped, though O'Brien's onslaught was not without consequences. There were no more meetings with the Reverend Bradshaw, for Carpenter came bottom of the poll in the parish council elections in 1910. Instead, George Merrill and Carpenter busied themselves with community relations by setting up a youth club in a local barn. They lured Alf Mattison over in 1911 to show improving lantern slides and acted in a performance there of Carpenter's socialist play for children, 'St George and the Dragon', in January 1913. Carpenter looked the part as a Druid-like priest in a white robe and staff, while George Merrill played the cat with protruding whiskers.[33] Among the children in the audience were Kathleen and Mary Bunting, and many years later Kathleen Bunting remembered the irrepressible Merrill in his brown cat suit and whiskers 'rubbing round peoples' legs'.[34] Clearly Merrill had forgotten any fright caused by the O'Brien affair. Mary Bunting declared 'Mr Merrill had a name it was openly spoken about. . . . we knew there was something queer about Mr Merrill.'[35] Carpenter, in contrast was remembered by the

Buntings as a kindly old gentleman who had a remarkable number of gentlemen to visit at Millthorpe. 'More than that we didn't know',[36] Kathleen Bunting declared. Adults in the village presumably knew more. Nonetheless the crisis had been averted.

During the 1900s Carpenter was becoming a celebrity – albeit an alternative one. His growing fame endowed him with an aura of glamour and brought ever more letters and visits from admirers. Carpenter acted as a father figure, reading their poems and dispensing advice. In one 1906 letter to a young Russian, Constantine Sarantchoft – who Carpenter met through Vladimir Tchertkoff, the exiled Tolstoyan defender of the religious sect, the Dukhobors – there is an implicit reference to George Hukin. Responding with tenderness to Sarantchoft's distress about a thwarted love for another man, Carpenter wrote:

> I understand it so well, and know what you must have suffered. I have been through similar storms and trials myself. I suppose we gain something from them. Would the person one loves ever seem *divine* if there were no difficulty in winning their love? How wonderful when the Gods appear to us poor mortals – even in the faces and figures of those who say Farewell to us! 'Tis better to have loved and lost than never to have loved at all.'[37]

While the lover who got away is invested with godlike qualities, the young men who hiked to Millthorpe brought more mundane assurances to the bronzed, white-haired Carpenter. One shy visitor, a journalist on the I.L.P.'s *Labour Leader*, C. Langdon Everard, who arrived from Manchester in 1908 having read *Ioläus*, did not see the Bunting girls' 'old gentleman'. He assured Carpenter, 'You were all I expected you to be and more. As to your being old – To me fair friend, you can never be old!'[38] Such flattery was heartening and alluring. Nor were all Carpenter's dealings on a purely fatherly plane. Some of the young men were attracted physically as well as spiritually to the sage who seemed to defy time. In Gilbert Beith's collection of memorial essays, *Edward Carpenter: In Appreciation* (1931), Walter Seward describes an 'intimate friendship'.[39] Though the phrase is ambiguous, Seward's letters, which Carpenter kept, reveal a love affair. They met in 1909 when Carpenter and Merrill were holidaying in Lyme Regis with a couple who had translated *Towards Democracy* into German, Lilly Nadler-Nuellens and her Hungarian husband, the Tolstoyan Count Ervin Batthyány. Seward describes himself as drifting, a socialistic butterfly, unhappily chained to a job in the City. On meeting Carpenter, Seward was drawn, as many other people had been, to the penetrating

Carpenter in 1910, by Elliot and Fry

gaze. Then in June 1910 he read *Love's Coming of Age* and *Towards Democracy* and was overwhelmed. 'You've opened the gates for me', he declared in a letter to Carpenter, signing himself, 'Your devoted W.' Carpenter had called him a 'wounded pigeon', but Seward insisted he was not wounded, he had been 'frozen' and Carpenter had 'thawed' him.[40] In an undated letter, Seward wrote, 'I believe you said one couldn't reason about the love which has sprung up between us. If this is so why should I feel any qualms of unworthiness?'[41]

They met in Millthorpe and in London, where Carpenter stayed at the Batthyány's Hampstead home. For Seward the space apart seemed agonisingly long. He felt insecure and woefully inadequate in relation to Carpenter, considering himself 'Not fit to be a Diocles to a Philolaus'.[42] But by April 1911 a more confident Seward is arranging to meet Carpenter en route from Chesterfield, and declaring, 'I'm a lucky man to be your number three! (at least I suppose it's number three but I don't care what number it is I'm there.)'[43] Despite opposition from his parents, under Carpenter's tutelage, Seward gave up his job in the City, met Carpenter's bohemian friends who hovered around George Herron in Italy, read 'The

Visit to a Gnani' and started writing for the *Clarion* under the pseudonym of 'Rochester Raggles'. His connection to Carpenter redefined the course of his life.

While Seward was spending those idyllic days at Millthorpe in the years before the First World War, bathing in the brook, feeling the garden turf beneath his bare feet and walking with Carpenter, he does not appear to have noticed the effect of his presence upon Merrill. In a disgruntled letter to Charlie Sixsmith during one of Seward's visits, Merrill complained that he was exhausted with spring cleaning and tidying up after joiners and painters who were fixing a new wainscoting. 'My quill is full' exclaimed a grumpy Merrill, adding that he was particularly fed up with 'W. Seaward [*sic*], who the more I see of the less I like'.[44] Merrill had accommodated to Hukin, the divine and unattainable, but he was not happy about accepting this upstart number three.

Nonetheless Seward and Carpenter saw one another quite frequently until the First World War, when Seward enlisted in the army, and they remained good friends after desire faded. There were other encounters too. Albert Löwy, a trainee solicitor, sympathetic to feminism, wrote a fan letter enthusing about *Towards Democracy* in 1911. He was duly invited to Millthorpe and taken for a walk. His meeting with Carpenter convinced him that love was a religion and sympathy a passion. He poured out his thanks in a letter: 'In the marvel of your touch I learned the magic secrets of love.' Löwy declared he had experienced 'a life condensed in a moment's joy', and signed himself 'Your cup-bearer'.[45] He was echoing the poem 'Hafiz to the Cup-bearer', which Carpenter had written to Merrill, just as Seward had evoked the poem to Hukin. The young devotees were grafting themselves onto the romance of Carpenter's life.

Carpenter, though profoundly protective of and loyal to Merrill, had never committed himself to an exclusive sexual relationship. In his poem 'Mightier than Mammon' he celebrated the unbounded 'Liberation of Love, and with it of Sex'.[46] In 'Nothing Less than All' he had posed the question

Shall I give my life (how gladly!) to my one my only lover,
absorbed, we two, our days in single devotion to each other –
Or shall I pour it out upon a hundred and a thousand beautiful
forms to spread from them in an ever-widening ring to others?[47]

When Seward and Löwy were visiting the question still hung unresolved. Seward felt a particular connection to the book Carpenter was writing in the early part of their relationship, *The Drama of Love and Death* (1912), in which Carpenter quotes the influential Swedish feminist Ellen Key as saying that fidelity in love could never be promised, but had to be won afresh every day. By 1912 Merrill and Carpenter had been together for around twenty years and the book contains an interesting reflection on long-term relationships.

> Two people, after years, cease to exchange their views and opinions with the same vitality as at first; they lose their snap and crackle with regard to each other. . . . If something has been lost in respect of the physical rush and torrent, and something in respect of the mental breeze and sparkle, great things have been gained in the ever-widening assurance and confidence of spiritual unity, and a kind of lake-like calm which indeed reflects the heavens.[48]

Carpenter also declared, 'Regeneration is the key to the meaning of love.'[49] Did he find regeneration in his young visitors' love and admiration? He certainly considered that 'continence' was needed in long-term relationships. By this he meant an openness to others. 'New subjects of interest, and points of contact, must be sought; temporary absences rather encouraged than deprecated; and lesser loves, as we have already hinted, not turned into gages of battle.'[50] Was he admonishing Merrill? There are indeed hints that the two men did go their separate ways while remaining close partners in this period. What is not clear however are Merrill's views on how Carpenter went about this. Did he too aspire to 'lake-like calm'? Was he happy cleaning up after the unpractical public school young men accustomed to servants? 'Few things, in fact, endear one to a partner so much as the sense that one can freely confide to him or her one's *affaires de coeur*', observed Carpenter in *The Drama of Love and Death*.[51] This had been the ethic devised by the Fellowship of the New Life – openness and honesty. But it did not necessarily accord with Merrill's past of quick, snatched encounters, or with the mysterious indiscretions which led to so many local rumours. Impossible to know, but a good guess would be that while Carpenter worked out the theory of their relationship, Merrill ducked and dived making the best of circumstances as they presented themselves.

Carpenter was reworking the late nineteenth-century progressive ideal of democratic comradeship, but he was also expressing an early twentieth-century search for an honest comprehension of personal relationships. New attitudes to the personal as well as to sexuality were unfolding in the years immediately preceding the First World War. Open discussion of sexual experience, a conviction of the significance of desire, a belief that the intimate aspects of the self were organic elements in personality, and a wish that equality and democracy should extend to personal life marked out a new modernity. Such rationalism was suffused with a Romantic tinge of self-expression which Carpenter was also to embody. He believed that intense emotions, however fleeting, hinted at a connection to the 'cosmic', an attitude to loving which he helped to diffuse in bohemia. Initially affecting the intelligentsia, some of these assumptions about sex later percolated into society at large.

Thus Carpenter contrived to articulate the emerging mood and played a key role in shaping 'modern' attitudes to sex. The irony was, of course, that while his commitment to honesty inspired others, he, himself, was not able to be completely open. In 1911 he sent some autobiographical notes to Charlie Sixsmith in which he regretted the lack of frankness about 'love and sex' in the biographies of 'respectable persons';[52] Carpenter was thinking particularly of Tchaikovsky, but it was his subjective dilemma too. Though he would excise this observation from the published version of My Days and Dreams in 1916, given contemporary attitudes, Carpenter was remarkably explicit about his sexual feelings in his autobiography. Moreover his preservation of the letters from young men describing physical relations and erotic friendship is a testimony to his faith that one day body and spirit would be reconciled in all forms of love.

On the other hand, Carpenter in his sixties was perhaps reminding himself not to set too much store by the flattering adulation of the young when he wrote in The Drama of Love and Death:

When people – I would say – come (not without clatter) and offer you their hearts, do not pay too much attention. What they offer may be genuine, or it may not – they themselves probably do not know. Nor do you also fall into a like mistake, offering something which you have not the power to give – or to withhold. Silence and Time alone avail.[53]

Silence and time were with Merrill, and, if any prying neighbours were wondering about Seward, Löwy and the rest, there was a multitude of multifarious others arriving in Millthorpe. The socialist Countess of Warwick, a former mistress of Edward VII, would have confused even O'Brien. She graciously invited her hosts for a return visit: 'Our household is as simple as your own – but our "cook" is not nearly as good!! So you must be forbearing.'[54] Any simplicity at Warwick Castle was the result of 'Daisy' Warwick's large debts, incurred not only through personal extravagance but through enthusiastic social projects. And what would O'Brien have made of the Dowager Countess of Carnarvon who was there in the autumn of 1913 with her sister? She had no sooner left when Alf Mattison arrived and a troupe of Clarion campers were ensconced in the Royal Oak eating rabbit pie.[55] As Charles Ashbee remarked while visiting Millthorpe in March 1913, 'One never knows whom one may meet here, a plough boy, a patrician, a philosopher, but it is always aristocracy.'[56] The promiscuous muddle of Millthorpe camouflaged its subversive sexy sage. When a 'Special Correspondent' arrived at Millthorpe in 1912 to interview Carpenter for the *Christian Commonwealth*, the organ of R.J. Campbell's progressive New Theology movement which endowed all human beings with divinity, the journalist was struck by the grave, worn face, dreamy eyes and tempered spirit. 'Special Correspondent' assumed that these derived from 'A life of almost spartan simplicity and starkness, and years of thinking upon the essential problems of human destiny.'[57] A closer inspection would have revealed that life at Millthorpe was not quite as it seemed.

During the 1900s Carpenter appeared to be taking a mischievous delight in confusing people in his writings as well as in his lifestyle. *The Drama of Love and Death* begins with a promise of providing instruction on love for the young. Carpenter did indeed apply his interest in Tantric approaches to love-making by rebuking the 'young man, husband or lover' for 'hurried completion' and admonishing spending a long time in magnetic diffusion, merging, suffering, even pain.[58] However apart from telling his lovers that sex was best in the open air, Carpenter was not strong on details. Instead the hopeful young person was referred to 'the Pagan conception of the world' and Plato's *Phaedrus*.[59]

By way of the classics we arrive at the protozoa. Drawing partly on Patrick Geddes and Arthur J. Thomson's *The Evolution of Sex*, Carpenter argued that resemblances could be found between the attraction of cells and 'the great human problems of Love and Death'.[60] Carpenter is still intent on verifying his metaphysics through contemporary science, though behind the scientific frontage on the conjunction of cells lay an earlier Romantic assumption that all life possessed a 'yearning' to move to a higher phase of existence. Once again the message is embedded in the subtitle: 'A Study of Human Evolution and Transfiguration'. Intent on showing that consciousness could evolve, Carpenter hurtles us off towards Schopenhauer and the *Upanishads*.

Carpenter had been disgruntled when critics noted similarities between *The Art of Creation* and the French philosopher Henri Bergson, denying familiarity with his work; but by the time he was writing *The Drama of Love and Death* he had read Bergson's *Creative Evolution*. Carpenter carefully marked his 1911 French edition, noting Bergson's assertion that a fixed notion of the ego was an illusion[61] along with Bergson's criticism of the neo-Darwinians for dismissing 'an impulsion which passes from germ to germ across the individuals'.[62] Both men shared common influences in Plotinus, Schopenhauer and the late nineteenth-century milieu of Symbolism and dynamic psychiatry, and both were searching for an alternative to what they considered as mechanistic and fatalistic theories of evolution. Like Carpenter, Bergson supported his philosophical ideas about consciousness with references to contemporary science and was similarly fascinated by the protozoa's resemblance to the higher organisms. Bergson's *élan vital* resembles Carpenter's collective energy, while his concept of a 'double direction of individuality and association' in 'the evolution of life' expressed the dialectical knot in Carpenter's approach.[63] Recognising an affinity in their outlook, Carpenter jotted 'See Art of Creation' alongside Bergson's observation that the form of thought could be said to define the shape of what is perceived.[64]

In 1912 in Britain, Bergson was as up to the minute as you could get. Alfred Orage had migrated from the Leeds Arts Club to London, turning Joseph Clayton's I.L.P. periodical the *New Age* into an avant-garde journal which propagated Bergson, along with Nietzsche and the French philosopher of action and the will, Georges Sorel. Open to iconoclastic European theory, the *New Age* stimulated powerful waves of radical thinking from its office in Tooks Court near Chancery Lane, not because it had a large readership, but because it attracted an intense one. Once again Carpenter demonstrated his ability to straddle the Zeitgeist.

Carpenter's ability to read German, French and Italian enabled him to assimilate not only vitalist philosophy but the new field of psychoanalysis. By 1912, when he produced *The Drama of Love and Death*, he was conversant with Freud on dreams, as well as the critique of Freud articulated by Roberto Assagioli, who Carpenter had met through the American émigré, George Herron, in Florence. Assagioli studied with Freud but struggled to bring a spiritual wholeness to psychoanalytic ideas of the unconscious. Like many people in the 1900s Assagioli was influenced by Frederic Myers; Carpenter carefully marked a reference to Myers in an early paper by Assagioli, 'Il Subcosciente'. Assagioli's search for a higher consciousness marked his life's work.[65] After working with Jung, Assagioli would devise an approach he called 'psychosynthesis' which sought to harmonise the sub-conscious, the conscious and supra (or cosmic) consciousness.

Carpenter also keep abreast of new work in science, marvelling in *The Drama of Love and Death* at the energy within electrons revealed by the physicist J.J. Thomson. His interest had been aroused by Sir Oliver Lodge's *Electrons* (1910), which had proposed that electro-magnetic radiation indicated some interconnection between matter and spirit, and Carpenter had struggled to explain the exciting implications of electrons to a bewildered Alf Mattison.[66] In *The Drama of Love and Death* Carpenter suggested that Lodge's 'electrical charges' were 'analogous to mental states', and made a further jump to spirit photography and telepathy, which Frederic Myers had studied.[67] Such a leap was less odd in 1912 than it might appear today. In an era when the telephone and the wireless were still miraculous, leading physicists such as Lodge were members, as Myers had been, of the Society for Psychical Research. Scientists pursued isotopes *and* ghosts; wondering about a spirit behind the universe in the strange parabola they believed they could detect.[68] Carpenter too was intrigued enough to show Alf Mattison 'spirit photographs' in 1913, and, in the same year, when the Bolton Whitmanite Dr Johnston arrived in his modern motor car, Carpenter discussed telepathy with him, noting how animals possessed sensory perceptions that humans lacked.[69]

Carpenter bundled Bergson, Swedenborg, psychoanalysis, modern science and the Theosophical writings of his old friend from Aligarh, Bhagavan Das, into *The Drama of Love and Death*, assuring his readers that the evolution of human consciousness would equip them to shed their petty selves, while death would be simply a return to the 'All-Self'.[70] He speculates that the soul could be conceived as an ultra-microscopic or 'fourth dimensional' entity pushing forward even before birth 'towards its manifestation in the visible'.[71] Writing in an era which seemed over-charged with life energy, Carpenter asked why should death, the last barrier, not also dissolve? 'Man is the Magician who whether in dreams or in trance or in actual life can, if he wills it, raise up and give reality to the forms of his desire and his love.'[72]

His book appeared in an extraordinary year when it seemed as if new frontiers had been reached. In 1912 the restless self was seeking infinite expansion, even while its core was in molten flux. Direct action seethed among workers and women; Ireland was in ferment; writers and artists were rejecting realism and young women at the Slade were beginning to cut their hair and shorten their skirts. Carpenter's destabilised self flowing along 'streams of memory and experience', his dissolving 'Man' and 'Woman', his acceptance of manifold sexual attractions, and his Paganism appeared credible and curiously in accord with new trends in left politics, the visual arts and literature. By the end of *The Drama of Love and Death* the self had splintered into many selves; the soul had transposed into the psyche and the Victorian sage had renewed his modernity with the moon.

The year after *The Drama of Love and Death* was published Charles Ashbee thought he could detect 'a curious aura' growing up about Carpenter.[73] This may have been a result of contemplating mortality and immortality, but equally it could have had a simpler explanation. Carpenter's hearing was deteriorating. Ashbee also noted that his hand was a little shaky. These marks of ageing suggested that even he could not escape the passing of time. Carpenter had also been forced to recognise that his urge to embrace all his friends was necessarily curtailed by the restricting three dimensions of bodily being. Charles Oates' death in 1901 had been followed by Max Flint's in February 1902. When Bessie Joynes, a frequent visitor to Millthorpe, died in autumn 1905, another link with the 1880s was gone. She had never been a close friend of Carpenter's, even so, Kate Salt wrote saying how much he had helped her sister-in-law.[74] Most troubling for Carpenter was the news in December 1910 that his old antagonist George Adams had died. The Adamses had moved from Millthorpe to the new garden city at Letchworth, where Adams continued to make his sandals for the resident garden city settlers. Carpenter and he had never been reconciled and a troubled Carpenter hastened to Letchworth to see what he could do for Lucy and the children.[75] Shortly afterwards he composed a 'Farewell Message' which he wanted to be read over his own grave. He assured his future mourners that leaving the body behind was of no great consequence, for whatever lay beyond, the ties of love would hold. Indeed true lovers were already joined in 'a world far beyond and behind the visible', all that was needed was for 'the real soul or self' to escape in order to 'reach it'.[76] Though Carpenter sometimes conceived immortality as an organic union with the One, he could not quite abandon notions of individual immortality.

In 1912 his younger sister Dora, who suffered from depression, took her own life, leaving a note explaining 'Something within my brain never ceases to drive and drive and drive.'[77] Carpenter told Charlie Sixsmith that she had given herself too much to others; the others being Carpenter's imperious older sister Sophy and the mentally backward Alice. Both had depended on the brilliant Dora. Now they were left alone in the house at 8, St Albans Road, St John's Wood. Carpenter tried to make sense of Dora's suicide in his letter to Sixsmith; somehow Dora had known 'The time had come for her spirit to wing in flight.'[78] His niece Ida Hyett later gave a more down to earth explanation. She suspected that Dora was attracted to women but had never resolved her sexuality.[79]

Shortly after Dora's suicide, death filled the news when the Titanic sank. Carpenter had been expecting a visit at Millthorpe from the doughty campaigner against child prostitution, W.T. Stead, now deeply involved in spiritualism. Busier even than Carpenter, Stead had postponed coming until he returned from a trip to America. Fatally he happened to sail on the Titanic and was drowned. 'Poor old Stead will not get to Millthorpe now – only in the spirit',[80] Carpenter reflected in a letter to Sixsmith. The following spring another public tragedy assumed a personal dimension when Charles Oates' nephew perished on Captain Scott's Antarctic expedition; Carpenter observed gloomily to Mattison that the family seemed doomed by fatality.[81]

Though an awareness of mortality and his own ageing was inevitably impinging, Carpenter's youthful appetite for new intellectual, cultural and political perspectives continued unabated. The radical journalist Henry Nevinson records bumping into Carpenter at Roger Fry's controversial Post-Impressionist Exhibition on December 21, 1910. Nevinson was accompanied by a group of modern-minded literary friends, S.K and Katie Ratcliffe, H.N. and Jane Brailsford, who he duly introduced to Carpenter, remarking in his diary how the older man was 'benign and wise and still open to new light'.[82]

This openness to 'new light' encouraged a new generation of rebels to adopt Carpenter as their Pagan prophet of modern love. One morning at Millthorpe, Carpenter noticed something crawling out of a sack. It turned out to be a Cambridge student, Ben Keeling, who had arrived unannounced late at night and decided to sleep outside rather than wake the household. *Love's Coming of Age* had convinced the young Keeling of the need to abolish the family and confirmed his belief that sex was at the root of everything – a view which was gaining purchase among the radical Cambridge young around the Fabian Society.[83] The Cambridge Fabian Society – which included Keeling, Hugh Dalton, the son of Carpenter's university friend, John, and the dazzling poet Rupert Brooke, along with the daughters of Sydney and Margaret Olivier, Bryn and Noel – valued emotion, the senses and the primitive over reason and 'civilisation'. 'Back to nature' at Cambridge was partly a matter of style, but it did also contain values of honesty in personal relations, commitment to inner feelings of authenticity, and social and sexual tolerance. In 1912 Bryn Olivier's fiancé Hugh Popham asked her whether she was shocked by the 'homosexual love' of the men in their circle, including Keynes. He added, 'I imagine you have read your Uncle Edward Carpenter's books on the subject.' She replied she had guessed that 'these charming people' were all attracted to men, and though originally wondering whether 'there was some nice feeling wanting', had decided that it was not. 'Homosexuality is, after all such a Fact that sentiment has nothing to do with it.'[84]

The frankness of the young Fabians upset Beatrice Webb, who rather unfairly blamed it all on Goldsworthy Lowes Dickinson for encouraging comradely informality at Cambridge.[85] In contrast the novelist Virginia Stephens (later Woolf) delighted in their anti-intellectual ethos. Here was 'Sunshine, nature, primitive art, cakes with sugar on the top, love, lust, paganism, general bawdiness.'[86] Bloomsbury nicknamed the new young set 'Neo-Pagans'. Carpenter had generated spiritual offspring.

In May 1910 Henry Nevinson was struggling away over an article on 'Paganism' and felt immediately dissatisfied with his effort.[87] 'Paganism' defied neat definitions, encompassing diverse attitudes and crossing over quite different cultural sets. Roger Fry wrote to Virginia Stephens' sister Vanessa Bell from sun-drenched Poitiers in August 1911 declaring, 'My dear I am a queer Pagan creature.'[88] Fry's Pagans were Hellenic moderns who defied 'Victorianism' and promised an aesthetic spirituality without sin and its attendant guilt, but Paganism was also woven into a nostalgia for rural life, enthusiasm for the 'folk', a Romantic yearning for an organic community, along with efforts to create alternative national identities and democratic popular cultures. Delight in the spontaneous and respect for 'primitive' societies were part of the Pagan mix too. Carpenter manages to waft in and out of these Paganisms, as well as Fry's.

From the 1890s Carpenter's critique of civilisation resonated with a sense that much was being lost in the rapid migration from the countryside. A desire to catch and conserve a vanishing England was a common theme in the novels and poetry of the early twentieth century; other manifestations were the rural crafts encouraged by the High Church sandal-wearing socialist, Conrad Noel, as vicar of Thaxted, with the Countess of Warwick's support. A conserving socialism also permeated the widespread interest in folk music, dance and customs. Carpenter knew the early folk-song collector and Christian Socialist, Charles Marson, from Bristol, and he corresponded with the Fabian Cecil Sharp, who dedicated his life to folk song and dance. The pioneer of the folk dance revival, the feminist and socialist Mary Neal, was also a staunch admirer of Carpenter.

Along with the retrieval of 'authenticity' went a celebration of an imagined lost golden age of collectivity which fed into the reworking of national identities. The search for English traditions was paralleled by a corresponding upsurge of interest in Celtic culture. Carpenter, who had a long-standing interest in folklore, was in touch with key figures in the Celtic National revival, Patrick Geddes and W.B. Yeats. This search for roots and national identity was not exclusive; the Celts mingled with Yeats' interest in Theosophy, while Whitman, socialism and feminism all influenced Irish radical culture before the First World War. When the socialist James Cousins came to discuss the Irish literary revival with Carpenter at Millthorpe in 1914, he wrote up his interview with Carpenter not only in the *Irish Citizen*, but in *The Herald of the Star*, a journal edited by the Indian Theosophist, J. Krishnamurti.[89]

Like the writers, musicians who sought out the folk as sources for a better future were inclined to mix and elaborate on the raw material. Carpenter's friend, the composer Rutland Boughton, wanted to create a choral drama which drew on folk-music and the choral singing popular with both *Clarion* socialists and the patriotic King and Country choirs. Steeped in Celtic myths and Arthurian legends, along with Wagner, Boughton was also a committed Carpenterian socialist. In 1908, Boughton, who was working at the Birmingham Midland Institute, wrote to Carpenter praising his early drama of a people's deliverance, *Moses*, and saying that he was planning 'A Democratic Society with the object of bringing the arts and the lives of the people closer'.[90] In 1909 Carpenter and Boughton collaborated closely on a musical adaptation of some of Carpenter's poetry from *Towards Democracy*; 'Midnight' was performed with municipal pride at the first civic festival in Birmingham in 1910.[91] In 1914 Boughton started the first Glastonbury music festival which aimed to change the content, form and audience for classical music. Through Boughton, Carpenter came into contact with a group of composers who drew on a mix of folk traditions and Eastern influences, including Granville Bantock, who was also based in Birmingham and at the height of his fame. He felt a special affinity to them, partly because he greatly respected their musical skills as superior to his own and experienced a profound personal joy from working with them, but also because their music, being both rooted and transcendent, expressed in sound what he sought in his own life and thought. Writing on Boughton in 'Music Drama in the Future' for the *New Age* in 1908, Carpenter suggested that a democratic music drama might contest the darker sadistic passions Wagner aroused. Carpenter wanted organic connection without the baggage of blood, soil, family, race and nation. The wizard in the Millthorpe barn who was inclined to take off into the Mediterranean sun loathed enclosure and boundaries. Reflecting on the implications of Boughton's music, Carpenter stated, 'The modern spirit will demand absolutely fluent transition from form to form and from passage to passage without any barriers or breaks.'[92]

In *The Drama of Love and Death*, Carpenter had set out to blend physiology, zoology and physics into his metaphysical search for union with Nature. This was no sooner finished than he was combing through sociology and anthropology for a new work, *Intermediate Types Among Primitive Folk*

(1914), which linked a defence of homosexuality to a wider critique of dominant ideas about morality and civilisation. *The Origin and Development of Moral Ideas* (1906–8) by his friend the Finnish academic Edvard Westermarck furnished monumental support for the old Hintonian heresy that vice and virtue should be regarded as culturally relative as well as evidence on how different cultures had cast homosexuals as both shamans and heretics.[93] The anarchist Élisée Reclus' *Primitive Folk* (1890) challenged Western contempt towards 'primitive' peoples and provided fascinating material about cultures in which boys and girls appeared to take on different gender identities without becoming outsiders. Carpenter was also able to use the work of the German sex reformer, Hirschfeld, to demonstrate how in many cultures men who were seen as neither male or female could be prophets, priests or wizards. Contesting the sexual theorist Iwan Bloch's view that this was simply a mistake on the part of the 'primitives', Carpenter maintained that the 'homosexual temperament' *did* often display 'divinatory or unusual psychic powers'.[94]

Carpenter's 'intermediates' in 'primitive' cultures are drawn to creative and spiritual roles partly through innate gifts, but he also introduces culture into the equation. He speculates that the men who did not want to fight composed songs or observed the effects of herbs and the movement of the stars; an awareness of their difference then forced them to think and as their minds turned inwards, they became the first thinkers, dreamers, discoverers. Carpenter suggests that such prophetic figures tended to be cast as wizards when one religion was superseded by another. By extending into anthropology Carpenter found a means of subverting conventional assumptions of appropriate behaviour by proposing that his pagan intermediate shamans, artists and healers were the far-sighted ones who pushed society onwards. He had rendered his outcasts heroes.

When Carpenter was writing his *Intermediate Types Among Primitive Folk*, anthropology was just beginning to take shape as an academic discipline in Britain. While one strand emerged from studies of mental illness and criminology, another arose alongside the fascination with legends, folklore and myths which derived from Romanticism and was closely allied to the study of ancient religions. Anthropologists' pursuit of universal human origins in ancient times was turning up innumerable variations in which they searched for patterns. The great inspiration was the work of the Scottish anthropologist Sir James Frazer. Frazer's epic *The Golden Bough*, published in twelve volumes between 1890 and 1915, combined scholarship in the classics with anthropology. Carpenter adopted Frazer's method of comparing customs in a wide range of societies, past and present, by drawing together accounts of the 'intermediates'.

Carpenter had been interested in comparative religion since his Cambridge days and was familiar with studies arguing that Christianity had borrowed from the pagans. Indeed it had been his lectures on sun-worship, deities and devils during the 1900s which had contributed to his reputation as a modern Pagan. Aware of sexual interpretations of primitive religion in terms of fertility and of the phallus as a symbol of both physical potency and spiritual love, Carpenter innovated in *Intermediate Types* by proposing that the tendency in many religions to make the Gods encompass both sexes might be interpreted as a deep psychological recognition that 'the sex temperament *is* undifferentiated.'[95] This marks an interesting shift from his previous views of fixed characteristics. Emotionally however, he still considered that representations of the mixed God/Goddess were not beautiful. He mentions Siva who had upset him in the caves of Elephanta along with the bearded Egyptian Isis and the Syrian Aphrodite.[96]

The second part of *Intermediate Types* focuses on warriors. Carpenter knew from his classical studies that love between men had flourished among warriors and had long carried a torch for his Thebans. He had been excited to discover Suyewo-Iwaya on 'Comrade-Love in Japan', showing how Japanese warriors had valued the love between men over male/female love.[97] Stumbling into this new territory, he began to extend his knowledge of the history of homosexuality in Japan through a growing circle of young radical Japanese friends.

Carpenter's enthusiasms went off in several directions at once and he hardly bothered if they undermined his own case. As Havelock Ellis pointed out in *The Occult Review* Carpenter's homosexual warriors could not be interpreted in terms of 'intermediacy' any more than the Greeks or Japanese could be classed as 'primitive'.[98] Carpenter's insights are indeed often contradictory and his arguments circumlocutory. In his writing on homosexuality Carpenter oscillated between congenital approaches and appeals to culture, nor could he decide between a case for explicit difference and theories of a shared bisexuality. While being emotionally sure of his own congenital attraction to men rather than women, his politics led him to believe that every particular experience of oppression carried an alternative possibility for universal enfranchisement and intellectually he inclined to a dynamism without boundaries.

Intermediate Types Among Primitive Folk proved the last straw for John Bruce Glasier. In a review for the *Socialist Review* which was never printed, Glasier declared, 'I cannot follow him in these later mystical and sex speculations.'[99] For Glasier paganism and the primitive phallus were leading Carpenter onto dangerous ground. In contrast, in 1910 Edith Ellis had dubbed him 'a prophet of the soul and the body'[100] and, in 1913, trying to explain how the connection between the two was integral to Carpenter's whole outlook, the American Whitmanite, Horace Traubel remarked, 'Some people suppose that sex things are always physiological . . . But sex is omnipresent and omnipotent.'[101] This might have been an alarming idea for some of Carpenter's contemporaries but a new generation of 'moderns' scampered happily onto the newly mapped terrain. Carpenter's idiosyncratic combination of body and soul enabled him to skirt round taboos and contrived to fox his opponents. Indeed the lawyer and sex reformer E.S.P. Haynes wondered whether Carpenter was not 'quite as simple as he appeared', concluding that the mysticism 'gave him a certain detachment which protected him against prosecution as a heretic'.[102] As for the non-mystical Merrill, he just tried out the idealistic admirers. The radical American writer J. William Lloyd relates how he held an affectionate Merrill at bay as they returned from the pub in 1913. The alternative-living Lloyd took beery advances in his stride but was shocked to find a not-so-simple Carpenter smoking a cigarette when they reached Millthorpe.[103]

17

The Larger Socialism

Carpenter may have grown more contemplative in his late fifties and sixties, dreamily watching the mayfly grubs in the brook at the bottom of his garden transmogrify into 'aerial fairy' beings 'with pearl-green wings' and pondering on the connection between sex and spirit, but this did not mean he abandoned his political engagement.[1] Throughout the 1900s he was writing and speaking on the key political and social issues of the day, while developing the combination of socialism, anarchism, humanitarianism and experimental lifestyle he had initiated during the 1880s.

When the century began the jingoism unleashed by the Boer War led him to focus on imperialism. In his poem 'Empire' he lambasted 'England' as an old hypocrite, a sham, a bully of weak nations. For Carpenter, not only had English imperialism reduced countries such as Ireland and India to rags, it had corroded the conqueror too. He declared that England's 'heart was dead/Withered within the body, and all the veins/Were choked with yellow dirt'. Only brotherhood and love could 'stay the greed of gold'.[2] In an article in Henry Salt's *Humane Review* in 1900, Carpenter turned to India. Drawing on the S.D.F. leader Hyndman's research on the Salt Taxes imposed by the British, Carpenter argued that rather than assuming famines were acts of God or Nature, human intervention should be seen as a major factor.[3] This insight led Arunachalam to write approvingly, 'One of the things that makes me not despondent about England is that there still is a small minority of good men not afraid to tell the truth and struggle for the right.'[4]

Carpenter also displayed an understanding of the contradictions of the 'modernisation' which imperialism brought in its wake. The story Harold Cox had told him of two boys' love for one another at Aligarh left a deep impression and, in December 1899 writing for the *New Age*, Carpenter adapted it in his tale of Ganesh and Narayan's experiences as rural migrants in Bombay. As well as draining colonised countries of their resources, imperialism was taking the factory system around the globe and Carpenter describes how, after Ganesh died as a result of an accident in a textile mill, Narayan was caught between two worlds. He felt unable to return to the narrowness of village life, yet he loathed the system that killed his friend. Carpenter brings Ganesh and Narayan's suffering home; employers' search for cheap labour would pull wages down in Britain.[5]

Yet he was all too aware that the Empire and the Boer War – which he, like many socialists and liberals, opposed – were popular; patriotic crowds were shouting down speakers at 'Stop the War' meetings and even attacking them. Inspired by Olive Schreiner's letters and writings, Carpenter produced a leaflet, 'Boer and Briton', through the Labour Press in January 1900 and busily bundled copies off to friends. Even the ailing Charles Oates, who was complaining of pain and numbness, was sent a pile of leaflets along with brisk advice that he needed more sun and rest.[6] Oates was to die of a heart attack the following year. The flag-waving jingoism of the Boer War intensified Carpenter's feelings of alienation towards his own country. The exasperated author of 'England Arise' declared to Oates, 'The English (with the exception of the working classes), make me sick.'[7]

Yet his response to the estrangement of the anti-war lobby within Britain was to scapegoat the Jews. The Afrikaner farmers epitomised the rural virtue of an imagined organic society while Johannesburg was a veritable personification of cosmopolitan evil: 'A hell of Jews, financiers, greedy speculators, adventurers, prostitutes, bars, banks, gaming saloons and every invention of the devil.' He told his readers that the British generals were 'being led by the nose by the Jews'.[8] The Jews Carpenter attacked were rhetorical categories, embodying forces he opposed rather than individual Jewish people towards whom he was perfectly friendly. He was not alone; thoughtless anti-Semitic attitudes were common in this period, appearing among liberals and socialists as well as on the right. Nevertheless there were alternative standpoints and this anti-Semitism on the left did not go unopposed. The socialist James Connolly was sensitive to ethnic and racial prejudice and attacked references to 'Jewish plots' and 'Jewish-controlled newspapers', insisting the target should be capitalist greed rather than race or religion.[9]

Carpenter's anti-Semitism was associated with his continuing propensity to typecast on the basis of his own prejudices. After his holiday with Merrill and the artist Harry Bishop in Morocco he wrote a series of articles for the New Age in which the 'Manly and straightforward Berbers' came out on top, followed by the Arabs, 'Romantic, imaginative, fickle, more subtle and intellectual'.[10] At the bottom were the 'Shop-keeping Moors' who he thought had 'the same greasy-commercial look about them that one associates with trade at home'.[11] That old Cambridge snobbery against trade was still alive and kicking and had converged with racial prejudices. Carpenter's attitudes to race were not consistent, for during the 1900s he was also contesting anti-Chinese stereotypes in articles and lectures on China's civilisation, attacking the racist behaviour of the British in India and demanding the extension of democracy to all the colonised peoples.[12]

Carpenter's anti-imperialism did contain traces of a subtle sense of superiority. Like many people on the left at the time, Carpenter was inclined to keep England at the hub of a humanitarian world order. Thus in his 'Boer and Briton' leaflet Carpenter called for a more glorious patriotism in which England would relinquish exploitative imperialism for an 'Empire of Humanity' in the 'hearts of the lesser races of the world'.[13] It remains ambiguous whether he meant they were 'lesser' in terms of power or 'lesser' innately. Nevertheless amidst the imperial hubris of the era his 'Empire of Humanity' kept shifting leftwards. In 1906 Carpenter wrote a remarkable 'Message to India' hailing the Indian National Congress and declaring that the liberation and self-expression of the Indian people would benefit the world. He proposed that the Humanitarian League should bypass the politicians and send an independent mission to India which would open up 'a channel of friendly communication' and discover what was 'really going on among the people of India'. F.D. Maurice's advocacy of direct personal contact, the inspiration for the college at Aligarh, is translated into a new person-to-person internationalism: 'The peoples of the various countries must join hands and work out their own destinies.'[14] Three years later, looking back on the Anglo-Boer war in a lecture in Chesterfield, Carpenter contended that if there had been a network of societies doing research and educational work on international affairs it would have been easier to put the case against war. He thought the time had come to set up these anti-militarist committees and to make international links.[15] These far-sighted suggestions resulting from anti-war action in the Boer War planted seeds which grew into efforts to democratise foreign policy and develop internationalism, culminating in the creation of the League of Nations.

Carpenter was in touch with the centre of both the Social Democratic Federation and the Independent Labour Party, having kept on friendly terms with Hyndman, MacDonald, Bruce Glasier and Hardie regardless of political differences. His extensive round of lectures also took him into the nooks and crannies of the labour movement. A letter from 'A Friend of Labour' in a local newspaper graphically evokes a Croydon Labour

Church where Carpenter spoke on China in 1901 as 'a cross between a mission hall and a dancing saloon'. Labour Church hymn-books were on the bookstall and Carpenter shared the platform with a few potted shrubs and 'an energetic musician . . . seated at a grand piano'.[16] The letter writer was amazed at how long the audience of thoughtful workers and 'Hindoo gentlemen' regaled Carpenter with questions.[17] Interest in Carpenter spanned labour, progressive and ethical milieux. Between 1900 and 1910 he not only addressed local branches of the Labour Churches, the Independent Labour Party and the Fabians, but the Theosophists, sundry Ethical Societies, the University Extension Movement, the National Federation of Head Teachers, the Christian Social Union and the Progressive League. His topics ranged from 'Matter and Consciousness', 'Sun-Worship and Christianity', 'Deities and Devils' to the sweated trades, the land question and the role of the state. His meetings could attract intellectuals like Holbrook Jackson, J.L. Hammond and J.M. Keynes,[18] or labour militants like Alf Barton, a former anarchist, who was active on Sheffield Trades Council.[19] A fiery young railwayman, C.T. Cramp, known as 'Charley', was so inspired by hearing Carpenter, he arranged for him to address 3,000 railway workers in 1907 at Sheffield Corn Exchange. They were indicative of a new mood within the trade unions.

With a reforming Liberal Government in power from 1906 there seemed at last hope for the old and for low-paid 'sweated' workers. Carpenter still imagined that in an ideal future the fear of poverty would be removed by everyone receiving the basic means of living, but more immediately he believed that a legal minimum wage was necessary. After a national campaign against 'sweating' had started, Carpenter began to give talks on the subject he had discussed for many years with George Hukin. In October 1907, along with Ramsay Macdonald, he was one of the speakers at 'The Minimum Wage Sweated Industries National Conference' in Glasgow, arguing that higher wages would not harm industries and asserting, amidst applause, the need for concerted international action.[20] Though the minimum wage agitation was not successful, it did result in a compromise – the Trade Boards Act of 1909 which established minimum rates in specific low-paid sections.

The Liberals' legislative reforms backed by the newly formed Labour Party presented Carpenter with a dilemma. When defending the minimum wage he had added the proviso that legislation and inspection were needed because society was not yet sufficiently prepared inwardly for voluntary change. On the same grounds, addressing a huge meeting of over 2,000 people in Manchester in November 1908, he called for state ownership of the mines and the milk supply, approving public administration of gas, water and transport. But he remained uneasy about relying on state interference, voicing his fears in talks for the Fabians in Sheffield, the Social Democrats in Chesterfield, and the Didsbury Socialist Society in Manchester over the course of 1908. He deemed that state control could foster non-competitive sentiments and improve workers' conditions, but believed it must be an interim measure.[21] Carpenter might have viewed the state as socially and culturally necessary, but his political libertarianism led him to suspect it as inherently coercive and he looked around for voluntary social alternatives which could foster opposing collective values to capitalism.

Land nationalisation, labour colonies and co-operatives were all being mooted in the early 1900s, while groups of unemployed men had resorted to direct action and were farming on squatted land. From 1905, in a series of lectures and articles on unemployment and the land question Carpenter put forward proposals for the unemployed to find work through colonies in the countryside and by becoming small-holders.[22] Ashbee's Guild and School of Handicraft in Chipping Campden was Carpenter's ideal, and in 1905 he spoke for the Oxford University Extension movement at Chipping Campden, while staying with the Ashbees, on 'Small Holdings and Life on the Land'.[23] Inspired by experimental projects in Europe, Carpenter proposed co-operative small-holdings and co-operative agricultural associations.[24] In 1907 he brought his ideas together in an article in the prestigious *Albany Review*, which later became a Fabian tract entitled 'The Village and the Landlord'. Carpenter envisaged a rural economy transformed by co-operative banks, along with a network of co-operatives for egg collecting, the buying of foodstuffs and selling products. Though Carpenter accepted that land should be publicly owned, both nationally and by local authorities, he wanted state ownership to be *combined* with co-operative ventures and private small-holdings. This was partly because of his dislike of state intervention and also because he was convinced, like Kropotkin, that small-holdings encouraged enterprise, attention to detail and all-round skills.[25]

Carpenter's proposals were attacked on all sides of the political spectrum. On the left some I.L.P. activists accused him of advocating a form of self-imposed slavery, to which Carpenter replied that collectivist state-owned farms would not be appropriate for all kinds of agriculture.[26] Carpenter's land schemes led the *Sheffield Daily Telegraph* to comment that 'Socialism has no more eloquent exponent', while pouring scorn on the impracticability of his ideas from the right.[27] Carpenter's support of tenants' rights and his onslaught on wealthy landowners were particularly controversial at a time when the aristocracy were under pressure to pay more in taxation.

The depression in agricultural prices and the imposition of death duties had left them somewhat less secure than they had been when Carpenter had mounted his first attack on the Duke of Rutland in 1889. Inclined to live as grandly as ever, some of the old aristocracy were speculating while turning their noses up at the nouveaux riches gaining titles, donning ermine and buying landed estates.

Carpenter returned to the fray in the *Albany Review* in 1908, denouncing the aristocracy as an inbred, useless set who perpetuated deference. Instead of innovating on their estates, Carpenter accused them of turning their property into game reserves. The power of the aristocracy was wielded politically through the 'reactionary institution' of the House of Lords which Carpenter described as a 'dead-weight'. Hereditary peers should be phased out and the Second Chamber be filled, like the Chinese Academy, with 'Scholars and Savants', along with people who had given 'useful service' to society.[28]

Carpenter hoped that his article on the 'British Aristocracy and the House of Lords' would be taken up by the Fabians like his previous one on 'The Village and the Landlord', though he sensed that it might not exactly express their views.[29] Its vehemence of tone made it un-Fabian, though radical Liberals liked it well enough. However these were sensitive political times. In 1909 Lloyd George's social reforming budget aroused lordly rebellion and they rejected it, forcing a constitutional crisis and an election in January 1910. In attacking the House of Lords, Carpenter had hit on the hottest of hot potatoes and his pamphlet was not taken up by the Fabians. Instead it was issued by a small progressive London publisher, Arthur C. Fifield, to the fury of the *British Empire Review* which shuddered at a Carpenter-style 'House of Lords' full of manual workers and 'advanced women'. Taking a swipe below the belt, the reviewer suggested that when Carpenter referred to 'advanced women' he might be meaning 'old women', and hence 'we might look forward to finding Mr. Carpenter there himself'.[30] Carpenter was, by innuendo, being warned; attacking the 'House of Lords' was taboo.

The criminalisation of homosexuality and the imprisonment of his anarchist friends had prompted Carpenter's 1890s lectures on humanitarian approaches to law and prison. When the 1903–4 'Report of the Commissioners of Prisons and the Director of Convict Prisons' indicated that some reforms might be in the offing, Carpenter decided to elaborate his earlier lectures into an ingenious little book, *Prisons, Police and Punishment* (1905). In this Carpenter contested the view that fear of harsh punishment curbed crime, arguing that most crime had social and economic causes.

His position was not deterministic, for, as he pointed out, the majority of unemployed people did not commit crimes. Nor did he claim like Kropotkin and Tolstoy that laws and prisons were completely unnecessary. Instead he challenged the cultural bias in how crime was defined and exposed the power relations embedded within the practice of the legal system. Those who dispensed justice knew the world of Eton and Oxbridge, not that of the workers, tramps, seamen, farm labourers or tradesmen they condemned. As for the police and their spies and informers, corruption permeated their work. Rather than prioritising offences against the property of the rich, Carpenter recommended that crimes against the vulnerable, children and animals should be regarded as most heinous. He also put anti-social crimes such as polluting factory chimneys high on his list.

Carpenter carefully compiled newspaper cuttings on cases and read up on criminology, including new work from the United States. He put forward specific demands for better food, more exercise and education to prevent re-offending, and expressed approval of the introduction of gardening, as well as proposals for gymnastic exercises, skills training and education for citizenship, noting hopefully how one New York reformatory had tried music. Yet Carpenter, whose libertarianism was sometimes annealed with a flash of his admiral grandfather, also believed there could be times when 'a good hiding' might considerably benefit a man – in the 1900s this meant flogging.[31] His scheme for sending prisoners to colonies on the land is ominously redolent of labour camps to a modern eye, though, to be fair, he was more probably thinking of the benefits of fresh air and manual work. Some propositions were not well thought through, nonetheless *Prisons, Police and Punishment* did not simply criticise the system in the abstract but came up with proposals that were, on the whole, both radical and practicable. Moreover, Carpenter's book is suffused with empathetic insights into just how the legal system was rigged against underdogs and outcasts. Though he maintained a studied silence on homosexual cases, it was preceded by Oscar Wilde's 'Ballad of Reading Gaol'. Wilde's name is not, however, mentioned, except in an Appendix, 'The Solitary System', at the end of the book.

Carpenter's book appeared when the Humanitarian League was campaigning for prison reform along with a welter of other causes that ranged from protests at the treatment of colonised peoples and attempts to reduce the arms trade, to opposition towards enforced vaccination and medical experiments on the poor and insane. The League's agitation against cruelty to animals involved criticism of the fur and feather trades, exposure of the conditions in slaughterhouses and cattle ships, and disapproval of both hunting and vivisection. Carpenter, who had a personal grudge against hunting after his beloved spaniel Bruno narrowly escaped being devoured by hounds, knew that country people were divided on the issue. He pointed out how it damaged farmers' fences and crops and caused extra work for farmers' wives when the pups were farmed out to them. He grumbled about the danger of the gamekeepers' traps set to catch grouse and about the devastating effect for tenant farmers' crops of the rabbits bred by Derbyshire landowners for hunting. Legally, the small farmers had the right to shoot rabbits on their land, but in practice this meant confronting gamekeepers and their powerful masters. Despite Carpenter's vegetarianism and support for what Henry Salt termed 'animal rights', Carpenter did accept the shooting of animals for food or if they threatened farming.[32]

On vivisection however he was adamant. Since the 1880s he had been accumulating pamphlets and newspaper cuttings on vivisection and he was still insisting in his lectures and articles that it violated not only the tortured victims but any claim to humanity. Moreover, agreeing for once with Bernard Shaw, he was convinced that it was invariably not necessary.[33] Like Shaw, Carpenter's protest against the overweening claims of science extended to vaccination as well.[34] Membership of these two vigorous campaigns was quite often intertwined; anti-vaccinationists pointed out the dangers of vaccination and animal lovers decried the use of calf lymph. Carpenter chaired a meeting in Sheffield for the fiery Dr Walter Hadwen, who protested against both vivisection and vaccination. Putting forward his view that healthy lives were the answer, not the torture of animals, Carpenter asserted 'our divine relation to animals'.[35]

In 1906 Carpenter's translation of the anarchist Elisée Reclus' 'La Grande Famille' appeared as 'The Great Kinship' in the *Humane Review*. Like Reclus, Carpenter believed that a loss of connection with animals and the land had contributed to the ascendancy of values of domination. And, like Reclus, he shared a dream of the forest doe and the birds trusting human beings.[36] He did register a hiccup in this benign communion in his article 'Sport and Agriculture' in *The Humanitarian* in 1913, with the observation that hunting appeared to be a survival of the primitive instinct.[37] Clearly there were aspects of the primitive, along with the Wagnerian darker passions, that the resolute critic of civilisation would prefer to discard.

Though a vegetarian, he was carefully pragmatic on the subject – rather too pragmatic for vegetarian friends such as Henry Salt. Nonetheless Carpenter was elected President of the Vegetarian Congress in 1909. Speaking at the Congress that year in Manchester, he could not resist joking about the prevalence of patriarchs with long white hair and beards.

He redeemed himself by hailing the proliferation of vegetarian restaurants and commending a vegetarian diet. Giving up meat resulted in a 'new lightness and brightness of body and mind, a greater activity, a greater mental clearness, a greater serenity of mind, more power of enduring fatigue, more hardihood with regard to cold and pain'.[38]

The bronzed, lithe man who looked much younger than his years was a good advertisement for the nut croquettes which supplemented his humanitarianism. Instead of 'mutton-chops and port wine, mufflers and medicine bottles', it was to be exercise, fewer clothes and mind control.[39] Carpenter was, of course, simply repeating what he had said twenty years before; however in the early twentieth century growing cohorts of young moderns were prepared to take up alternative health, alternative diets, alternative clothes and alternative restaurants. Carpenter, sipping his ginger wine in the Royal Oak, even extended it to alternative pubs. He envisioned them selling only the purest of beers produced by state breweries, complemented by 'Teas and temperance drinks'.[40]

Carpenter's visionary plans for a Royal Oak in which real ale met the juice bar may have gained adherents among the idealistic Clarion ramblers from Sheffield who used to gather with George Herbert Bridges Ward in a thatched-roofed shed by the pub, for, as Ward remarked, while their feet were on the heather, their 'hearts and hopes were with the stars'.[41] The local farmers, in contrast, took more convincing, requiring practical demonstrations that new schemes actually worked before they would try them. They remained stolidly unimpressed by Carpenter's co-operative proposals, though the youth club he and George Merrill had started in the barn of a silversmith in Holmesfield proved a success. Whist drives, dances, socials and a billiard table livened up the village and provided a gathering point for first the boys and then boys and girls. Along with Merrill and his cat whiskers, the outings Carpenter organised for the young farm labourers were still remembered over half a century later.

Carpenter's life at Millthorpe had taught him that change had to be acceptable to local people and this meant it must grow out of existing roots. Nonetheless he still dreamed of a transformed co-operative rural community with allotments, public playgrounds and public cricket grounds. He imagined afforestation schemes and proposed that 'the wilder moors and mountains' should be preserved by County Councils or by the state as animal and bird sanctuaries, nature reserves where everyone could wander.[42] His campaigns against Sheffield's 'smoke pall' had brought home the damaging impact the city could have on the countryside and led him to think up positive ways in which people from the towns and cities could relate to the countryside.[43] Carpenter suggested large open-air swimming pools combined with running tracks on the outskirts of towns. In a period when many working-class homes did not have baths, he envisaged that these municipal leisure centres should include bathrooms. He had not given up on his battle against bathing costumes, announcing that clothing would be either not necessary or of the 'slightest'.[44] Along with the ramblers, runners and swimmers, he suggested bringing school children out to conservation areas to study real squirrels and rabbits.[45]

To an extent Carpenter was in accord with the mood of the times; a range of groupings were moving on similar lines. A conservation movement, influenced by the American National Parks was under way in the 1900s, while Raymond Unwin's Garden City at Letchworth and his Hampstead Garden suburb sought to link the city with the countryside. The Clarion cyclists and ramblers were bringing wave upon wave of young townspeople out to discover forgotten footpaths and the beauty of nature. Hence Carpenter's ideas resonated both among those concerned to conserve the countryside and with those who wanted to foster a better relationship between town and country. However these divergent lobbies did not automatically recognise a common cause. Conservationists were not necessarily sympathetic to working-class ramblers, though G.H.B. Ward was connected to both movements. Vegetarians were not all socialists and many socialists scoffed at them and at anti-vivisectionists. Just as he had admonished the I.L.P. on its foundation to 'keep it broad', Carpenter tried to patch together alliances, upbraiding socialists for not showing themselves to be 'The most humane and generous of all the peoples of the earth'.[46] While Machiavellian Carpenter considered that this would afford an opportunity to persuade the members of the 'Society for the Protection of Animals' of the virtues of socialism, idealistic Carpenter divined a connection between all creation in a common life. At a packed meeting of the Sheffield Ethical Society in 1910, he urged an inner change of heart alongside new institutions and a recognition that 'Each self was united with the self of all human beings'.[47]

Again Carpenter was articulating a widespread aspiration within a progressive milieu. Stanton Coit's Ethical Societies, modelled on American circles of ethical culture, had grown since the 1890s and, along with their grassroots projects, had taken over from the Labour Church in offering alternative services for marriages, funerals and the naming of children. Because the Ethical Movement sought to transcend creed they could provide a neutral space regardless of religious belief and often hosted Carpenter's lectures in the early 1900s, attracting tolerant, intellectual audiences. Radical Christians could be equally sympathetic to his message of inner and outer change. R.J. Campbell's 'New Theology' and 'League of Progressive Thought and Social Service' were attracting many socialists and feminists. As well as pronouncing all human beings divine and taking a rational approach to biblical miracles and the Virgin Birth, Campbell endorsed ethical socialism; Fenner Brockway worked for his journal *The Christian Commonwealth* as a young I.L.P. member. Then there were sympathetic Anglican Christian Socialists like Percy Dearmer and Conrad Noel who favoured arts and crafts, simplification and an end to class divisions.[48] Some dissidents turned to the old Gods. The cleric Edward Lewis, Carpenter's first biographer, shared his interest in the pagan roots of Christianity and left the Anglican Church to launch his alternative faith, the 'New Paganism'.[49] Ethical secularists, heterodox Christians and Pagans thus dwelt in a high-minded progressive cosmos alongside the Theosophists and their offshoots.

The socialist movement, too, was far from being an homogenous entity; many socialists were looking for various forms of spirituality, as well as change in the here and now. As Carpenter's Bristol socialist friend Robert Gilliard put it in 1910, 'There was what might be called the bread and cheese side of socialism and there was also a much deeper and broader side.'[50] 'Deeper and broader' could have various manifestations. For Christian Socialists and members of Labour Churches it was a mix of humanitarian ethics and a longing for transcendence. For Alfred Orage at the Leeds Art Club and later in the journal the *New Age*, it was an avant-garde fusion of Carpenter with Theosophy, Neo-Platonism and Nietzsche. For George Newton, who went to hear Carpenter lecture for the Fabians in Sheffield on 'Rest', it represented a precious moment of inner peace. He was seventeen and training to be a butcher when he heard Carpenter telling the audience to seek out a quiet spot at lunchtime and really rest. Meditation for young working-class men like Newton was a matter of sitting down outside the shop, but he remembered Carpenter's advice all his life.[51]

Carpenter appealed both to the interest many socialists expressed in a diffuse spirituality and to the habits of reverence they brought to their politics – the religion of socialism. Fenner Brockway observed how they no longer believed in dogmatic theology and that Carpenter gave them the spiritual food they still needed: '*Towards Democracy* was our bible. We read it at those moments when we wanted to retire from the excitement of our socialist work, and in quietude seek the calm and power that alone gives sustaining strength.'[52] As the detours to the celestial city seemed to grow longer and ever more convoluted, many socialists sought inner guidance from Carpenter about how to be and how to live, for the utopian conviction that socialism implied new human beings, new relationships and styles of life lingered on. George Newton considered that Carpenter was a real socialist because he 'lived out' his beliefs.[53]

All over Britain in the early twentieth century, clusters of Carpenter-type socialists were living out their beliefs. Carpenter often visited the communal house in Wallosey where Will Young, now rising in the postal service and married to Lily, daughter of the former Bristol Christian Socialist, Robert Weare, lived with his in-laws. The Young children grew up surrounded by activism, talk and political guests, who included Charlie Sixsmith and the Glasiers as well as Carpenter.[54] Carpenter also dropped in at Fenner Brockway's I.L.P. commune in Myddelton Square, Islington, London. The commune was daringly mixed. Though Brockway insists that 'sexual correctness' was maintained, romance was clearly in the air, for he met his future wife there.[55] In old age, Brockway paid tribute to the effect of Carpenter's enlightened attitudes to sex and women's emancipation on him.[56] In his novel *Mr Noon*, D.H. Lawrence wrote with affection and humour of his two unconventional shopkeeping socialist friends in Eastwood, Willie and Sallie Hopkin, staunch readers of the *New Statesman* and Orage's *New Age*. On Sundays, the one day when their shop closed, they had time for books, journals and walks. Being vegetarians they could dispense with Sunday joints to tramp off into the countryside.[57] Sallie Hopkin, whose refusal to put up lace curtains shocked local respectability, was the sister of the young runner and marine engineer, Joe Potter, who Carpenter had met in the early 1880s and Carpenter used to visit the Hopkins at Eastwood. Whether Carpenter and Lawrence ever encountered one another in person is unclear, but they certainly knew of each other's doings through the Hopkins.

Before the First World War, left politics and lifestyle were inclined to fuse. Letchworth Garden City, designed by Raymond Unwin, was packed with 'deeper and broader' alternative lifers – socialists, anarchists, Theosophists, vegetarians. According to one contemporary account a typical (male) garden citizen sported far and near spectacles, knickerbockers and sandals. 'Over his fire-place – which is a hole in the wall lined with brick – is . . . a large photo of Madame Blavatsky, some charming old furniture, several Persian rugs.'[58] The books on the shelf would include works by Carpenter as well as Morris, Tolstoy and the writer on Japanese religion and culture, Lafcadio Hearn.

It was of course possible to pursue spirituality and politics without adopting an alternative lifestyle in its entirety. Charlie Sixsmith, now a worthy parish councillor, kept *The Art of Creation* on a chair by his bedside; while two new acquaintances of Carpenter's, the Reverend Charles Grinling and his wife Ethel in Woolwich, mixed labour politics with Christianity and remained open to heterodoxies spiritual and secular. Both Whitman enthusiasts, they read *Ioläus* and Carpenter's 'An Unknown People' in pamphlet form as well as his socialist writings.[59]

Around 1909 Carpenter found a name for his approach –'The Larger Socialism'. He wanted a socialism which would not simply end material inequality but would bring new forms of associating and relating, a new aesthetic of the everyday in harmony with nature. In 1910 he elaborated these ideas in 'A Thought for May-Day' for the readers of the *Labour Leader*. In this he said that socialism must make all aspects of life 'sacred and beautiful', bringing 'loving companionship and mutual helpfulness'. It must 'clear our skies and purify our streams, and secure for us great tracts of public land in which the life of the people may develop. It must teach us to sing once more at our work, and to rejoice in it; to make our workshops healthful, and bright, and cheery.' By 1910 simplification had really got its glad rags on. Carpenter swept his socialists, adorned in delightful clothes, into a whirl of festivals, play-acting, dances, music and frequent holidays. What is more, the prophet who had been heading towards democracy and waiting for England to arise for several decades, wanted change soon. In 'A Thought for May-Day' he stressed the 'soon'. Otherwise he feared they would all 'perish of dullness and despair in this colourless, soul-less, uninspired life of the present day'.[60]

I.L.P. members, Fabians, Clarion Scouts, trades unionists and spiritual searchers turned up to hear him speak on this 'Larger Socialism' in Chesterfield, Sheffield, Liverpool, Bristol, Manchester, Stockport, Blackburn and Glasgow between 1909 and 1910.[61] In Chesterfield the local newspaper related how Unionists sat side-by-side with 'red-hot' socialists and Liberals, agnostics next to preachers. Carpenter told them that socialism was not about doctrines or parties but an oceanic rise of human feeling. This appeared to have a soothing effect, for people of the most divergent opinions mysteriously seemed to agree with the speaker. They cheered when he called for internationalism and applauded his call for the 'Religion of Socialism', a democracy of personal relationships based on respect for all human beings and a solidarity which embraced all living creatures.[62] Reviewing a book by Robert Gardner called *In the Heart of Democracy*, in the *New Age* in 1909, Carpenter had praised its author for going 'beyond and back' of social and political theories.[63] This was, of course, exactly what he himself sought to do.

18

New Movements; New Transitions

An amiable characteristic of the larger socialism was that it wafted over the kind of political affiliations Carpenter found so constraining. He was inclined to deploy his multiple selves in order to dodge the nitty-gritty of alignment. Throughout the 1900s he continued to send goodwill messages to Labour in parliament, but his heart remained with the utopianism of the 1880s and he was jubilant when a sharp-dressing young revolutionary, Victor Grayson, was elected as an independent socialist M.P. for Colne Valley in Yorkshire in 1907. Boycotted by the Labour M.P.s in the Commons, Grayson became the defender of old-age pensions, the unemployed, feminists, rebel Irish workers and anarchists. Briefly, between 1907 and 1910 a dissident libertarian left gravitated towards Grayson, who personified their dissatisfaction with Labour representatives at Westminster. The pallid, charismatic young man was soon burnt out and already in alcoholic auto-destruct when he was defeated in the General Election of 1910. Yet Grayson proved a forerunner. New forms of anarchism and libertarian socialism along with militant movements among workers and women were emerging. For Carpenter, these extra-parliamentary rebels were creative evolution made manifest. He was drawn towards them, regardless of his ties with the Labour leadership.

The shift in consciousness was not restricted to Britain. Amidst the big bundles of post delivered at Millthorpe, two versions of an article entitled 'Work's Coming of Age' published in American left journals arrived in 1909. Their author was a young Hungarian revolutionary, Odon Por, whose Byronic good looks smouldered out of the accompanying photograph. His views were endorsed by Carpenter's friend in Florence, George Herron, who urged Americans to take note of the upsurge of the new European syndicalist movement, with its stress on direct action.[1] Por showed a familiarity with theorists on syndicalism, such as the German sociologist Robert Michels.[2] But it was Por's observations on the moral solidarity of the Italian workers that caught Carpenter's attention. He marked a passage in the text in which Por asserted that the workers' rebellion was 'freeing and elevating their consciousness'. In the course of struggle Por argued that a 'mutation of personality' occurred.[3]

Carpenter had never quite shed his Morris-style suspicion of parliament as a means of securing change. In 1905, writing in the journal of the Amalgamated Society of Engineers, he had urged building 'a real Labour Party' while branding the House of Commons as 'a dilatory monster'.[4] He encouraged the engineers to take up a proposal made by the land nationaliser Alfred Russel Wallace to establish their own self-managed works. This distrust of parliament was paralleled by his long-standing suspicion of the state. In *Prisons, Police and Punishment* in 1905, Carpenter had reasserted his concept of a 'double collectivism' of voluntary organisations and the state, in a slightly modified version of the essay 'Transitions to Communism' which had been in his collection *Forecasts of the Coming Century* (1897). Instead of describing the aim as being 'Anarchist-Communism', as he had during the 1890s, he used the term 'Non-Governmental Society'. Still fascinated by Herman Melville's novel *Typee* (1846), which portrayed the 'easy communism' of the Marquesas Islanders in the Pacific, Carpenter dreamed of dispensing with the state altogether.[5] Over the next few years he took hope from new anti-statist movements, syndicalism and guild socialism, hoping that direct democracy could both replace the existing form of the state and intimate the alternative values of a future free communal society.[6]

Guild socialism originated in the aesthetic and spiritual critique of capitalism articulated in A.J. Penty's *The Restoration of the Gild System* (1906). Penty, who proposed the revival of the medieval guilds as a means of bringing craftsmen and artists together to recover 'a language of expression', presented his book as a sequel to Carpenter's *Civilisation: Its Cause and Cure*, which had influenced him profoundly.[7] A Fabian architect, Penty had lived the simple life, making furniture with the former secretary of the 1896 Sheffield Socialist Society, Albert Waddington. Both men had come to regard existing socialist thinking as too materialistic. Involved in Theosophy, and the Church Socialist League, Penty began with a broad vision of human association as a means of transforming social relationships, later coming to see trades unions and workers as the agents of change and elaborating guild socialist ideas in the *New Age*.

Concurrent concepts of 'industrial unionism', or workers' power concentrated in 'One Big Union', had been developing among groups of militant workers internationally. The return of Tom Mann from Australia, full of the new theories of syndicalism in 1910, acted as a catalyst.

The Social Democratic Party (formerly the Social Democratic Federation) and the I.L.P. held a meeting in the Albert Hall in August for Mann, at which Carpenter took the chair and the I.L.P. orchestra played.[8] But Mann and his Industrial Syndicalist Education League (I.S.E.L.) were soon at odds with both organisations.

In September 1910 Carpenter was still hoping that unions, the Labour Party and the socialist groups might act in combination, telling a young correspondent, William Goodwin – who was not only the secretary of the Lincoln Trades Council, the I.L.P. *and* the S.D.P., but about to set up a new paper – that 'a strong move' by the unions could be 'the starting point of all sorts of new developments'.[9] Over the course of 1910 and 1911 mounting unrest among seamen, dockers, railway workers and miners inclined him to put emphasis on workers' direct action. By the autumn of 1911 an excited Carpenter was proposing to the Sheffield I.L.P. that the miners should learn the lesson of the railway workers and extend their strike by taking over the mines, either by means of nationalisation or direct action. He wanted the unions 'Not only to disorganise but to reorganise'.[10] This proactive role seemed possible in the tumultuous context of 1911. Speaking to the Leeds Arts Club in October, Carpenter advocated the revival of craft guilds, explained how French syndicalists believed 'workers should carry on their industries co-operatively' and assured his listeners that workers' control would result in production which was artistic and craft-based.[11] Shortly afterwards, when he addressed a meeting of the Leeds Clarion Scouts and had an audience of young activists who were happy to denounce the older I.L.P. generation, Carpenter let rip in an enthusiastic defence of Tom Mann's industrial syndicalism.[12]

In May 1912 Carpenter wrote 'Long Live Syndicalism' for Tom Mann's paper *The Syndicalist*, and also wrote in similar vein on syndicalism for a new Scottish paper, *The Anarchist*. In his usual eclectic manner he linked syndicalism and Penty's idea of a renewal of craft guilds. The amalgam brought a protest from Thomas Johnston in the Scottish I.L.P. paper *Forward*. Was Carpenter not aware that the guilds he idealised had been tyrannical monopolistic institutions?[13] Carpenter, however, was not one for the niceties of historical detail.

Carpenter's support for syndicalism meant that he was no longer associated with a transcendent 'Larger Socialism', but instead was a participant in a fierce political affray. An incensed John Bruce Glasier accused him of displaying feet of clay, declaring that Carpenter was a bizarre mix of 'superman' and 'fool' who showed 'amazing indiscretion' in defending the syndicalists.[14] Glasier wrote as a loyal I.L.P. member, disturbed, along with Ramsay MacDonald and Philip Snowden, by the strikes and the apparent impact of syndicalist ideas. But indiscretion was a misnomer, for Carpenter had never been a party man. Nor was syndicalism ever an organisation in the manner of the I.L.P. It existed rather as a tendency around Tom Mann and as a more diffuse spirit of rebellion among left-wingers disenchanted with the slow pace of change through parliament. From April 1912 rebels inside and outside the Labour Party acquired their own paper when George Lansbury's *Daily Herald* was launched. Its columns were open to deviant left currents and in June Odon Por was calling for syndicalists to combine a 'new society with the creation of a new man'. It was a definition of syndicalism with which Carpenter could concur.[15]

Under the mild-sounding title 'Beauty in Civic Life', Carpenter took his syndicalist and guild socialist ideas to such bodies as the Beautiful Sheffield League, the Humanitarian League, the Progressive League, the Bolton Housing and Town Planning League, and the Oxford University Fabian Society.[16] The Fabians were under pressure from dissidents like Penty and Orage, while at Oxford a young, and still poetic G.D.H. Cole, was suggesting that syndicalism pointed the way to creative labour and an end to servility and bureaucracy. Cole had been reading the criticisms of state socialism which were being penned by Hilaire Belloc and G.K. Chesterton from the anti-bureaucratic right. He was also guided by the political theorist A.D. Lindsay who emphasised economic and social voluntary organisations alongside state collectivism. The state was no longer the apogee of associational life for pluralist thinkers like Lindsay who were breaking with the Idealist equation of the state and the collective which had influenced the previous generation of Liberals and socialists.

A.D. Lindsay was President of the Oxford University Fabian Society when Carpenter came to speak on 'Beauty in Civic Life' in May 1912, and he chaired the meeting. Carpenter declared that he 'looked to Syndicalism to restore a free and voluntary co-operation of workers . . . in countless guilds'. These would be 'self determining' but federated together to exchange products. He was careful to add that he imagined not only guilds of manual workers; they might be 'clerical, artistic or what not' – the Oxford audience could be assured of a place among the what-nots.[17] Interviewed in the *Co-operative News* the following month, Carpenter insisted that workers should organise their own industries. Syndicalism, he suggested, should be seen as an alternative to the stultifying bureaucracy of a socialist state. He did not envisage that syndicalism in Britain would bowl 'the central Government completely over – not at any rate, at present'. Instead he foresaw an encroachment of workers' control in industry over the conditions of work and wages, along with the survival of central government 'to watch the total interests of the

nation, to harmonise the claims of the various trades and to represent a
certain public right in such things as the land, the railways, the mines,
the docks and other national property'.[18]

Carpenter's commitment to a medium-term role for the state-as-it-
might-be, differed from those strands in syndicalism which saw the state
simply as an appendage of capitalism. Carpenter was closer to the approach
G.D.H. Cole would soon adopt in the process of breaking away from
Fabianism to theorise Guild Socialism. However much Carpenter wanted
the state to float away he kept having to haul it back to legislate for
unpolluted air or shorter hours, to nationalise or municipalise gas and
electricity services or combine with co-operatives or social housing to
improve living conditions.

When Odon Por sent Carpenter his articles on 'Work's Coming of
Age', he scribbled next to the title, 'Will inevitably Bring Love's coming
of Age'.[19] Carpenter, however, retained the holistic utopianism of the
1880s and was not inclined to concentrate on one sphere alone in the
hope that broader change would follow, nor was he prepared to be
confined by syndicalism's focus on the workplace. Instead, as he trundled
about the country delivering his lectures on 'Beauty in Civic Life', he
kept extending the scope of syndicalism to include the making of beautiful
things, the creation of beautiful surroundings, beautiful clothes and beautiful
people.

Just what beauty was and how exactly it linked to a new social order
remained unclear, but Carpenter was not alone in seeking their association.
Charles Ashbee's Guild had collapsed in 1907, nonetheless when he wrote
The Building of Thelema in 1910, he sent his joiner's apprentice hero Ralfe,
the embodiment of the Industrial Democracy, off to the City of Thelema,
a utopia which bore an uncanny resemblance to Millthorpe.[20] Though
arts and crafts were on the wane, a desire for beauty in the everyday was
manifesting itself in many ways, through anti-smoke campaigns, through
conservation, through Boughton's music festivals, through folk dance and
folk music. From 1910 local 'Beauty in Civic Life' groups started to sprout
around the country; Patrick Geddes was theorising Carpenter's vision of
an architecture based on need into an organic approach to town planning;
Unwin was designing his garden cities; while Roger Fry was seeking to
transform the interior design of what he called 'Bird's Custard Island'.[21]

Kropotkin, the great theorist of democratising daily life, was seventy
in 1912 and Carpenter was one of the 'English friends' who sent him
their thanks for teaching them to rely on the voluntary principle in social
life.[22] Kropotkin too had come to accept a combination of municipal
ownership and voluntary projects set up by trades unions and co-operative

societies. His hope was that these experimental measures would enable people to imagine the forms an anarcho-communist society might take.[23] The voluntary principle was being conceptualised in new ways. In 1913 Carpenter was approached by a young man called Stephen Reynolds who was trying to extend democratisation into the actual process of investigating the everyday.[24] Reynolds' 1911 study of the Devon fishing industry, *Seems So! A Working-Class View of Politics*, had presented a challenge to top-down research. Reynolds, who was part of the *New Age* circle, had lived and worked with two fishermen, the Woolley brothers, and the book was their joint effort. It was a reminder that what might look like a reform to the privileged could smack of the reformatory to recipients: 'The poor man knows his own life better than anyone else can know it for him' insisted Reynolds and the Woolleys.[25] Reynolds' homosexuality accentuated his empathy with the fishermen and, on hearing from Havelock Ellis that Carpenter liked his book, Reynolds confided his plan for a fishing co-operative to offset the bureaucracy of the Department of Fisheries.[26] It was the start of a long friendship, though the fishing co-operative, like so many other dreams, would be overwhelmed by the First World War.

While the syndicalists were disputing the efficacy of political action and Reynolds was criticising Fabian-style social reform, many of Carpenter's women friends were demanding the most basic of political rights – the suffrage. Carpenter had followed the fortunes of the National Union of Women's Suffrage Societies (N.U.W.S.S.), established in 1897 by Millicent Fawcett and Isabella Ford. He was aware too that working-class women in the trades unions and in women's labour organisations such as the Women's Labour League and the Women's Co-operative Guild were making the connection between the vote and economic and social reforms.[27] However, socialists put extending the franchise low on their list of priorities. When Carpenter took the chair for Isabella Ford at Attercliffe I.L.P., in October 1903, she was preoccupied with her efforts to persuade the leadership to accept women's suffrage as a demand. Apart from Keir Hardie, they were decidedly lukewarm.[28] In the same month, Emmeline Pankhurst brought a small group of I.L.P. women together at her home at 62, Nelson Street, Manchester, to act as a pressure group, and the Women's Social and Political Union (W.S.P.U.) was born. Henceforth the National Union of Women's Suffrage Societies would have an increasingly vocal and militant gad-fly: 'Males getting alarmed for their supremacy. And sometimes I think a good thing. They <u>should</u> be alarmed – stir them up a bit', noted Carpenter.[29]

The women Carpenter knew in the suffrage movement tended to have been part of a wider milieu of reform politics. Isabella Ford had been involved with women workers' struggles in Yorkshire and active in the I.L.P. Her Manchester counterparts in the North of England Society for Women's Suffrage were liberal social reformers radicalised by the movement for the vote and, in October 1908, they unwittingly presented Carpenter with a cast-iron alibi for not attending Charlie Sixsmith's wedding by inviting him to speak on 'Prison Reform' at a huge demonstration for the vote.[30] Assembling at Manchester Town Hall in Albert Square, the suffrage procession marched out to Alexandra Park, watched by a great crowd of onlookers. A *Manchester Evening News* photographer snapped Carpenter at the front, wearing one of the soft felt hats he favoured and carrying his umbrella – it was Manchester after all. He was flanked by North of England Society for Women's Suffrage members, Margaret Ashton, Helena Swanwick and Kathleen Courtney, along with Dr Helen Wilson from Sheffield, the daughter of the Liberal M.P., H.J. Wilson, who had helped Carpenter to defend both the Walsall anarchists and the Spanish anarchist Francisco Ferrer executed in 1909. The socialist feminists were represented by Isabella Ford with Charlotte Despard and Teresa Billington-Greig. It was a broad sweep of the feminist movement.[31]

Charlotte Despard and Teresa Billington-Greig had recently broken with the Pankhursts' Women's Social and Political Union and formed a new organisation, the Women's Freedom League, to which Carpenter had sent a £1 donation. A vegetarian, a spiritualist and a Theosophist, Despard took a wide view of socialism and of the suffrage movement. She felt intuitively that Carpenter understood that it was about 'Freedom. Women's Freedom to live and act and express that which is in her'.[32] She told him it was a great joy to have his support because he recognised 'that which lies behind – our love of the new and better world – that Democracy which is to recreate society'.[33]

Over the course of 1909 Carpenter spoke around the country on women's suffrage, telling Sixsmith that a great crowd had come to hear him in Nottingham in July.[34] He was back in Lancashire at Pendleton Town Hall in the autumn at the invitation of the North of England Society for Women's Suffrage. Kathleen Courtney explained that 'Mrs Cooper' would talk about the industrial aspects of which she had personal experience.[35] This was the former cotton-worker Selina Cooper who was active in the socialist and the suffrage movements and, like Isabella Ford, keen to develop support in labour circles for women's enfranchisement.

Carpenter's empathy with women's claims to freedom led him into the Men's League for Women's Suffrage, an organisation founded in 1907 which focused on educational and propaganda work. Carpenter spoke for the League in Trafalgar Square alongside the writer Laurence Housman and the Christian Socialist, Joseph Clayton, who had edited the *New Age* in Leeds before Orage relaunched it.[36] In 1909 Carpenter was among a long list of distinguished men which included Bernard Shaw, John Galsworthy, Thomas Hardy and John Masefield, who signed 'A Declaration of Representative Men in Favour of Women's Suffrage'.[37] The League gave its support to all wings of the Women's Suffrage Movement.

As tension mounted between moderates and militants this became somewhat difficult, but Carpenter pursued his usual approach of trying to rise above faction. Differing aspects of his personality could extend to the divergent wings. Close to the socialist humanitarianism of his old friend Isabella Ford, he could connect with Charlotte Despard's mix of non-violent direct action and spirituality, while respecting the social reformers, Margaret Ashton and Helen Wilson. Yet he could also feel a sympathy for the young militants in the Women's Social and Political Union, some of whom had been nurtured in the northern radical labour politics in which he was himself deeply embedded. The former mill-worker turned suffragette organiser, Annie Kenney, had been introduced to Ruskin, Morris, Whitman and Carpenter through Blatchford's *Clarion* and credited them, along with the Persian poet, Omar Khayam, for having kept 'Labour clean, fresh, upright and virile'! While recruiting for the W.S.P.U. in the remote moorland areas outside Halifax, she used to discuss Carpenter's books late into the night with her hosts.[38] Another W.S.P.U. member, Mary Gawthorpe, from Leeds, recalled her Labour Church on Dewsbury Road, singing 'England Arise' amidst 'trails of Edward Carpentarian glory'.[39] Though closely associated with Isabella Ford in the Leeds Arts Club and the I.L.P., Gawthorpe was drawn like many other young women to the W.S.P.U. by the charismatic Christabel Pankhurst. When the W.S.P.U. set up a branch in Sheffield in 1906 she went off to help organise and made the journey to Millthorpe. Carpenter was not there, perhaps he was up to his old evasive dodges. However Mary Gawthorpe bought her first pair of sandals.[40]

Ill-health soon forced Gawthorpe to drop out of militant action but in 1912 she was circulating a petition against the forced feeding of imprisoned suffragettes on hunger strike. The atmosphere was very tense; Mary Leigh, a W.S.P.U. bandswoman, had set fire to a box in Dublin Theatre Royal and she and Gladys Evans had hurled a hatchet into the carriage of the Prime Minister Herbert Asquith and the Irish Nationalist Leader John Redmond. Havelock Ellis adamantly refused to sign, but Carpenter was prepared to support the militants. A few years later when Gawthorpe was down on her luck and applying for a typewriting course at Kensington College, London, he provided a reference.[41]

From the opposite end of the social spectrum, the daughter of Queen Victoria's lady-in-waiting, Lady Constance Lytton, was recruited into the W.S.P.U. by Emmeline Pethick Lawrence and Annie Kenney in 1909. She wrote to Carpenter shortly after she joined mentioning the friends they had in common – Olive Schreiner, the folk-dancing feminist, Mary Neal, and the publisher Arthur Fifield. Shyly commenting on Carpenter's pamphlet on the House of Lords, she assured him that the aristocracy did have a few good points and described herself as 'an whole-hogger' for the suffrage cause.[42] A few months later she was in prison and writing to say how relevant his *Prisons, Police and Punishment* seemed from Holloway. Having viewed prison from the inside, she wondered that it did not create even more prisoners than it did already.[43] As a result of her treatment in prison Constance Lytton suffered two strokes, leaving her right arm paralysed, inadvertently becoming a suffrage heroine.

If Gawthorpe and Lytton were forced to retire, new recruits were coming eagerly forward to take their place. Molly Morris from Manchester became the W.S.P.U. organiser in Sheffield at the high pitch of militancy towards the end of 1912. Nevertheless she made time to join the Ethical Society, along with several other W.S.P.U. members, and accompanied Bert Ward and the Clarion Ramblers on walks down the Rivelin Valley or over the Pennines. On one occasion they went to visit Carpenter and were greeted graciously.[44] Locally radicals tended to interact regardless of organisational affiliation, and the bravery of the W.S.P.U. won the admiration and solidarity of members of the syndicalist left, despite their contempt for parliament and the vote. A young Sheffield worker, Jack Murphy, bought a copy of *The Suffragette* one evening at the Queen's Monument in 1913 from Molly. His preferred reading was really the *New Age*, but Murphy was smitten by the dedicated W.S.P.U. paper-seller. In 1921, when the pair, having hastily married, were heading off to revolutionary Russia, she was surprised to hear her communist shop-steward husband reciting poems by Carpenter, Whitman and Omar Khayam.[45]

Carpenter's support for women's suffrage reinforced his Northern networks which spanned Liberalism, Labour and the revolutionary left. The Men's League for Women's Suffrage also extended his contacts in literary and journalistic circles resulting in friendships which would deepen over the next two decades. A key figure in the group was the journalist Henry W. Nevinson. However in 1910 Nevinson left the League to found the more radical Men's Political Union for Women's Enfranchisement, which supported the militants in the W.S.P.U. He was joined by his friend the poet and journalist, Gerald Gould, who was married to the W.S.P.U. feminist, Barbara Gould. Over the course of 1913, amidst the increasingly desperate militancy of the W.S.P.U., relations with the autocratic Christabel Pankhurst became strained, and Nevinson and the Goulds broke with the W.S.P.U. to form the United Suffragists which included men as well as women. Laurence Housman and the editor of the new left paper the *Daily Herald*, George Lansbury, were among the members, who also included Mary Neal and Cecil Sharp's sister, Evelyn.[46] Though Carpenter was not a member of the United Suffragists, through Nevinson he became closely associated with the group on a personal basis.

Nevinson had met Carpenter briefly back in the 1880s at Toynbee Hall and been impressed by his lecture on science in 1896. After a chance meeting at the Post-Impressionists exhibition at the end of 1910, they had come across one another again at a gathering in Havelock Ellis' home in West Drayton in August 1912, and Nevinson was soon introduced to a 'blue-eyed George Merrill' who he presumed initially was Carpenter's servant.[47] Nevinson and Carpenter quickly discovered that they enjoyed conversing about syndicalism, shorter working hours, and the censoring of books in the British Museum. They had many friends in common and Nevinson was a keen networker who kept in with the London literary

Evelyn Sharp

swim. Conveniently he enabled Carpenter to dip in and out of a world he found stimulating in short doses. He also began writing about Carpenter, who was particularly delighted by his review of *Intermediate Types Among Primitive Folk* in 1914.[48] In Nevinson Carpenter found an articulate and well-connected ally in the world of journalism.

Nevinson, who was unhappily married, had a penchant for falling in love with women of extreme views. Among them was the feminist writer Evelyn Sharp who experienced an immediate rapport on her first encounter with Carpenter in 1914. She was impressed by the matter-of-fact equality in Carpenter's manner, which contrasted with the patronage she often encountered from men. Sharp felt that they could meet on the common ground of their humanity and that Carpenter's homosexuality made for a more direct contact. It seemed as if she already knew him, having read his books, heard about him from friends and worn Millthorpe sandals for many years.[49] In her autobiography, *Unfinished Adventure* (1933), Sharp remarked that two lines of approach could be delineated in the women's suffrage movement. 'Either you saw the vote as a political influence, or you saw it as a symbol of freedom.'[50] She, without doubt, was in the latter camp, and so, of course, was Carpenter. The exponent of the 'Larger Socialism' embraced the 'Larger Feminism'.

Ideas about women's personal emancipation were running counterpoint with the suffrage movement. Some solutions reached back into nineteenth-century sexual utopianism, like the group families, free love and Neo-Malthusianism put forward by a veteran of the Men and Women's Club, Jane Clapperton, in her *A Vision of the Future* (1904). Carpenter reviewed her book somewhat sceptically. His close observation of several surges of new womanhood had inclined him to stress inner psychological and spiritual shifts over alterations in the outer structures of society and politics.[51] Clapperton did recognise the need to change attitudes but her 'scientific meliorism' tended towards sweeping external reconstruction.[52] Instead Carpenter offered an alternative culture of sexual relations based on mutuality, tolerance and comradely love in which guilt and possessiveness were smoothly eradicated. Morality was 'not a code, but simply the realisation of the common life'.[53] This avoided the prescriptive pitfalls of the free-love libertarians. Moreover it contrasted with the suspicion of sex evident in some other strands of radical culture from the Tolstoyans to the social purity feminists. Carpenter's outlook was decidedly more cheery too than Weininger's pessimistic contention that only denial of intercourse would emancipate women from the overwhelming sexuality that constituted their 'nature'. Carpenter's refusal to dogmatise held out a pleasing possibility of exploration in personal relations. Along with his commitment to sexual pleasure and freedom, this gained him adherents among yet another crop of new women. Carpenterian emanations flowed outwards into a reconfiguration of intimacy and lifestyle.

Their reach was surprisingly far-flung. Constance Annesley, born into the Irish aristocracy, read *Towards Democracy* in Ireland, surrounded by the far-right rebels against Home Rule, Sir Edward Carson and F.E. Smith. Her personal revolt against her background was to marry Miles Malleson, a left-wing drama student, and live with him in a tiny Bloomsbury flat. In her autobiography, *After Ten Years* (1931), she testified how Edward Carpenter led the couple into an open, unpossessive marriage and seven years later to an amiable divorce.[54]

Though rebellion appeared among the upper classes, it was more characteristic among those 'in-between' women whose social status was indeterminate because they were neither exactly working class nor properly part of the respectable middle classes. D.H. Lawrence wrote about women like these from his own milieu who were cutting themselves adrift from the old ways of being women. Sallie Hopkin's friend in Eastwood, Alice Dax, attracted him and troubled him enough for her to be an influence on his emancipated Clara in *Sons and Lovers* (1913). Alice Dax's father was a clerk; she had worked in the Post Office before marrying a dispensing chemist and optician. She read widely, attended the Congregational Literary Society and kept Carpenter's books on her shelves. Moreover, she designed her domestic space according to the uncluttered clarity of simplification; she put up few pictures, no knick-knacks and, like Sallie Hopkin, abolished net curtains. The feminist Dax's floors were polished wood or linoleum for easy cleaning and she allowed only one rug. The sparse décor suggested a woman ready for take-off. But this was not to be. Unlike Lawrence, with whom she had an affair, and like many other edgy in-between women, Alice Dax stayed put, frightening Willie Hopkin with her intelligent, acerbic questions.[55]

Around the country, clusters of socialist and feminist women were rejecting conventions, wondering about sexuality and questing for intellectual and spiritual fulfilment. Carpenter offered them an exciting bundle of startling alternatives, expressed in a reassuringly moderate tone. Some had rather more leeway than Sallie Hopkin and Alice Dax. Two women from Manor Park in North East London have left an intense account of how they moved from Methodism through R.J. Campbell's 'New Theology' towards personal and political heterodoxy; Ruth Slate and Eva Slawson's letters, along with Slawson's diary, reveal two young women clerical workers attracted to the suffrage movement and socialism. Both women wanted a mingling of soul and body and were searching for a sense of identity which was not bounded by existing presuppositions. *Love's Coming of Age* and *Towards Democracy* indicated ways of being for which a language hardly existed. The two women belonged to a circle of lower middle class dissidents experimenting with differing interpretations of 'intermediacy'.[56]

In December 1911, Eva Slawson was sent the first issue of a new magazine called the *Freewoman*, which quickly became the mouthpiece of the rebellious 'in-between' women.[57] It was founded by Mary Gawthorpe, rapidly moving out of her working-class background through her involvement in politics, and Dora Marsden, the daughter of a Huddersfield woollen-waste dealer who had deserted the family when she was a child. Marsden, who had also been a pupil teacher and W.S.P.U. member, wanted to create a forum for a feminism that went beyond the vote. The *Freewoman* tackled free unions, divorce law reform, the family, co-operative housekeeping, nurseries and prostitution. Like the *New Age*, it was politically and intellectually adventurous, ranging over German sexual theory as well as Havelock Ellis and Carpenter's own writings. Pounding against taboos, the magazine exploded the powerful social myth that women were the natural guardians of conservative personal values.

Unlike *The Times* which regarded the *Freewoman* as degenerate, W.H. Smith's shops which banned it, and the police who harassed its office, Carpenter was a staunch supporter. After the magazine went bankrupt in 1913 and was re-launched as the *New Freewoman*, he praised it as 'broad-minded and courageous'.[58] Marsden was driven by her conviction that women (and men) needed not simply political or even social reform but an inner release of creative power. Though her outlook resembled aspects of Carpenter's thinking, in Marsden's case the individualist will prevailed and the *New Freewoman* transmogrified into the *Egoist*, a literary magazine linked to Ezra Pound's Vorticist movement.

Even the redoubtable Dora Marsden had moved cautiously on the question of homosexuality and lesbianism. The subject was raised by an architect, Harry Birnstingl, a friend of Marsden and her companion Grace Jardine. When she received Birnstingl's article, Marsden consulted a socialist doctor, Charles Whitby, who advised publication with a reply by himself.[59] Birnstingl argued that 'Uranians' possessed positive male and female qualities and cited Carpenter's *The Intermediate Sex*. He also came out with the politically explosive observation that the agitators of the women's freedom movement should not be seen as 'sexless' for they often formed 'romantic – nay sometimes passionate – attachments with each other'.[60] In his refutation of Birnstingl, Whitby singled out Carpenter's *Intermediate Sex* which he clearly considered to be the main source of contamination. Describing Carpenter as a 'democratic anarchist of the school of Whitman and Rousseau', Whitby scorned Carpenter's efforts to challenge the degeneracy tag, comparing homosexuals to 'imbeciles, dwarfs and monsters'.[61] Homosexuality was a regretful condition rather than a cultural intimation of an androgynous future; Whitby thought homosexuals should be tolerated, not emulated. Birnstingl replied, and Albert Löwy, the young man who had been so transfixed by his visit to Carpenter the previous year, entered the fray with 'The Intellectual Limitations of the Normal'.[62] Though Charles Whitby stuck to his guns, the *Freewoman* had broken yet another taboo. The strategic Carpenter later offered Marsden an article called 'The Status of Women in Early Greek Times'. Its political message was tucked inside the classical history: 'It is the Uranian *classes* of men or those at least who are touched by the Uranian temperament, who chiefly support the women's movement.'[63] As ever, he was making alliances.

Any overt *movement* of lesbians or homosexuals was out of the question, but Carpenter contrived a covert organisational role through his correspondence, becoming a focal point for isolated women and men troubled about their sexuality who treated him as a mentor and informal therapist in whom they would confide. They drew on his writing in order to comprehend their own sexual feelings and to contest ideas of normality. Thus Amy Tasker told how she had always liked wearing boys' clothing and felt 'masculine' in her relations with women, and Winifred Moore wrote from Brisbane, Australia, to say she had not recognised her feelings towards women until she had found herself reflected in the chapter on 'The Intermediate Sex' in *Love's Coming of Age*.[64] A similar process of realisation and identification affected other correspondents. The woman to whom D.H. Lawrence had given *Towards Democracy*, Helen Corke, read *Love's Coming of Age* after their relationship ended and began a correspondence with Carpenter. Many years later she expressed her gratitude 'for his simple and logical explanation of what in my own nature had seemed inexplicable – only to be classed as abnormality'.[65]

Carpenter as the visible figure was constantly helping to link people up. In 1910 he responded to a letter from the Cambridge librarian Augustus Theodore Bartholomew saying he had mentioned his name to Magnus Hirschfeld who was heading to Cambridge from Millthorpe.[66] Edith Vance, who had been involved in the Legitimation League's free-love debates in the 1890s, wrote asking for his pamphlet 'An Unknown People' in 1913.[67] The following year she sought Carpenter's help in defending a man accused of homosexuality. Carpenter sent her his copy of Otto Weininger's *Sex*

and Character (1903) with the relevant page references marked and directed
her to friendly bookshops: Rebman's at 125, Shaftesbury Avenue and
Henderson's at 66, Charing Cross Road – known as the 'Bomb Shop'
because of its anarchist stock. He also recommended *The Sexual Question*
by Auguste Forel, which he described as a 'useful book'. While Forel was
unsympathetic to homosexuality, he argued prosecution was pointless.
Again Carpenter carefully noted the page references and suggested that
Vance should consult Harold Benjamin K.C.[68] After the man was acquitted,
Carpenter followed up with Kains Jackson's address so he could get in
touch.[69]

Another correspondent was a socialist and feminist, Kathlyn Oliver,
who enquired whether Carpenter knew of any organisation of Urnings
through which one could meet kindred spirits.[70] Carpenter's correspondence reveals him taking considerable trouble in advising and connecting
his burgeoning contacts. Friends testified to the 'help' he had given. By
1911 Roger Fry had become a distinguished art critic, but he remembered
the responsive older man who had made him sandals with fondness and
gratitude. 'You helped me ever so much', he wrote.[71] Remarkably
Carpenter's 'helping' extended to those he hardly knew. By the 1900s
he had acquired a gratifying collection of disconsolate aspiring writers. 'I
feel now sure that you <u>could</u> <u>help</u> <u>me</u> a <u>lot</u>', wrote Siegfried Sassoon.[72]
Towards Democracy and *The Intermediate Sex* had made him understand an
antipathy he felt towards young women. Sassoon had dropped out of
Cambridge to the disapproval of his sculptor uncle, Harold Cox's brother-
in-law, Hamo Thornycroft, who, despite a radical youth in the arts and
crafts movement, had turned into an establishment artist. Under a cloud,
and mooching about on the family estate, Sassoon was ostensibly
preoccupied with cricket, riding and hunting, but he was writing poetry,
and slipped some sonnets and a photograph into the letter to Carpenter.[73]
Carpenter's advice on the poems, which simulated Masefield, was that
Sassoon must search for his own voice. Carpenter informed the indolent,
wealthy whippersnapper it was time he wrote 'something solid', adding,
'only I expect you ought to go and do something solid first!'[74] Neither
of them could have imagined in 1913 what Sassoon was to do.

An even younger would-be poet, Robert Graves, was still at Charter-
house when he wrote thanking Carpenter for *Ioläus* and *The Intermediate
Sex*, which had 'absolutely taken the scales' from his eyes. Graves found
Carpenter's advocacy of Platonic attachments at school relieved his 'doubts
and suspicions'.[75] Graves had been caught up in disturbing circumstances.
After being rebuked by the choirmaster for his attraction to a boy at
school, Graves, indignant at the homosexual master's hypocrisy, had

exposed the man to the head, but then felt guilty and troubled.[76] Now he resolved to visit Abbotsholme, meet Reddie, and see what the attitude there was to emotional attachments. Already interested in myths and legends, Graves told Carpenter he should have included the Irish Cuchulain saga in *The Intermediate Sex* for 'There you have another Theban band in the boy-troop of Ulster.'[77] In a few months' time Graves himself would be in uniform.

Unlike Sassoon and Graves, E.M. Forster was a well-known author by the time he made personal contact with Carpenter in 1913. Yet they already seemed to be acquainted, through Carpenter's books, mutual friends and a shared attachment to India. By coincidence Forster had tutored Syed Ross Masoud, grandson of the founder of the Anglo-Oriental College at Aligarh, Sir Syed Ahmed Khan, and his Platonic love for his pupil drew him towards India. Forster approached the older man full of reverence, regarding Carpenter 'a saviour'.[78] George Merrill, who was familiar with the syndrome of nervous devotees visiting, intuitively broke through Forster's self-conscious reticence:

> George Merrill – touched my backside – gently and just above the buttocks. I believe he touched most peoples. The sensation was unusual and I still remember it, as I remember the position of a long-vanished tooth. It was as much psychological as physical. It seemed to go straight through the small of my back into my ideas, without involving any thought.[79]

Forster interpreted his response as in 'accordance with Carpenter's yogified mysticism'.[80] The chakras worked; Merrill's touch and Millthorpe acted as a release. Forster exclaimed in his diary, 'Forward rather than back, Edward Carpenter! Edward Carpenter! Edward Carpenter!'[81]

On his return Forster sat down and wrote *Maurice*, a novel about love between men, and sent it to Carpenter in August 1914. He also showed it to Lytton Strachey, who appears in the book as the clever Risley. In Strachey's opinion working-class Alec and middle-class Maurice's relationship rested upon 'lust and sentiment' and would only last six weeks;[82] Carpenter however liked the denouement of romantic reunion which he described as 'improbable but not impossible'. Instructed to call Carpenter 'Chips', Forster was admitted into Carpenter's inner circle and urged to provide a proper name: 'Why do you always hide behind initials?'[83] In Carpenter Forster had alighted upon an inspirational and nurturing energy. Though more cautious in temperament than Carpenter, he acquired from him and Lowes Dickinson the habit of travelling hopefully. And, through

Forster's novels, the Cambridge nineteenth-century theologian F.D. Maurice's faith in personal relationships passed on into the wider culture of the twentieth century.

Carpenter had not abandoned hope of consolidating the spider's web of comradely networks growing around him. In *The Intermediate Sex* he had conceived of the 'Guild' idea extending into intimate personal relations. And indeed in October 1912 Walter Seward reported that he was attending meetings of 'The Octave', a group formed by Charles Kains Jackson and George Ives. Officially they were discussing literary, musical and socio-logical subjects; in fact Seward, who was ill-suited to secrecy, revealed that they met once a month to talk about 'the higher Uranianism'. Along with its intellectual role, the Octave acted as a friendly society, therapy group and dating agency. Seward described it as 'A masonic kind of body working to assist the mentally distressed in the Uranian world.'[84] Kains Jackson put it more directly – the aim of the Octave was 'to get hold of Uranians and make them happy'.[85] The bluff Seward was flitting from love to love, glad to be in touch with such 'nice chaps'.[86]

However Carpenter had met a thoughtful I.L.P. member, a friend of the Salts called E. Bertram Lloyd, who loved music, shared his political and intellectual interests and was, moreover, an extremely capable organiser. Ashbee met Lloyd at Millthorpe with the poet Sidney Lomer in March 1913, and found him a 'charming fellow.' He noted that Lloyd was 'chafing in some paternal business'.[87] The paternal business was Lloyd's Royal Exchange, the insurance firm; Lloyd, or 'Wolf', as Carpenter called him, had to toil in finance in order to pursue his radical causes outside office hours. Lloyd was interested in German sexual theory, and Carpenter, the networker, gave him a letter of introduction to Magnus Hirschfeld in August 1913. When he got to Berlin, Lloyd was amused and delighted by Hirschfeld's open house, an 'International Club and Auskamptsbureau of Homo-sex'.[88] He was warmly welcomed by Hirschfeld who told him Carpenter would receive a fine reception if he were to visit Germany. In Lloyd, Carpenter found a younger friend who shared his interests, approached serious ideas with irony and, most importantly, wanted to help him. Lloyd wrangled with Carpenter's German publisher Eugen Diederichs, who was cooling on translating further books. Diederichs informed Lloyd that he was only planning '"national" stuff at present.'[89] It was an ominous flicker which they both ignored. Letters from Lloyd arrived encouraging Carpenter to write on 'love-religion worship', offering to help with footnotes, commenting on articles in the *Freewoman*, remarking on Futurism and reporting on performances of Wagner's *Faust* and

Beethoven's Eighth Symphony. An added bonus was that this new political and intellectual companion liked George Merrill, making jokes about Merrill's performance in 'St George and Dragon' and his attempt at a caraway seed diet.[90] Carpenter enjoyed 'Wolf's' company so much he became quite resentful if the Salts came along.[91] Relations between the two households had deteriorated since the Salts had moved nearby in 1910 and were made more tense as both Carpenter and Kate Salt claimed Lloyd.

During 1913 Carpenter was designing a scheme in which Lloyd was a key player. That August Magnus Hirschfeld delivered a lecture at the Fourteenth International Medical Congress in London and Carpenter got in via Ellis.[92] Hirschfeld's address impressed many of the doctors but they argued there would not be any public support for his views. Carpenter was resolved to demonstrate that such support did exist. He had alerted Laurence Housman that Hirschfeld was speaking at the congress and, with Housman, arranged a meeting on August 12th at the Hotel Cecil, for Hirschfeld to speak with men interested in reforming the laws on homosexuality. The ad hoc committee of a new organisation, the British Society of Psychiatry, came out of this gathering; it included Carpenter, Housman, Ives, Kains Jackson and Lloyd.[93] The aristocratic Francis Walter Jekyll, a keen collector of Jamaican folklore, who was then working in the British Museum, also attended the Hotel Cecil meeting. He was strategically placed, for the campaigners aimed to end the censoring of books in the Reading Room.[94]

On November 12th Lloyd wrote to Carpenter saying Housman had been round to visit and seemed 'very keen about your new society'.[95] However, since Housman was often out of London and Carpenter was in Millthorpe, the new society clearly needed a backroom organiser who would worry about details. Sure enough, by March 1914 a harassed Lloyd was reporting to Carpenter that the publicity material had been printed in red and brown rather than black, and looked as if it were advertising a gentleman's club.[96] Nevertheless women were not put off from the new group, which took the name 'British Society for the Study of Sex Psychology' (B.S.S.S.P.) at its inaugural meeting on July 8, 1914, held at the Medical Society of London. Several women joined, including the first British woman psychiatrist, Jessie Murray, the psychoanalyst and friend of D.H. Lawrence, Barbara Low, along with the socialist feminist Stella Browne who, with Lloyd and George Ives became the organisational hub of the B.S.S.S.P.[97] Carpenter and Housman were trying to extend the space for discussion of topics which had been taboo; the July meeting was chaired by an eminent magistrate, Cecil Chapman, and the society attracted lawyers, doctors, and clergymen in a phalanx of respectability. It included men and women concerned about social purity and sex hygiene, along with campaigners for homosexual law reform, divorce law reform, birth control, abortion and sex education in schools. The society sought to apply an open-minded approach to sexuality rather than take up positions. Housman signalled its remit: 'We are a note of interrogation.'[98]

There did seem to be some signs of new openings for frank debate. Lloyd reported a crowd of interested women at his lecture on prostitution and syphilis in 1913.[99] An incipient lobby against censorship was also emerging. In the prestigious *English Review*, in December 1913, Carpenter and the radical lawyer E.S.P. Haynes protested against the special catalogue in the British Museum, which excluded from the public works deemed to be subversive to religion and the throne or improper and obscene.[100]

International developments seemed similarly encouraging. Carpenter was invited by Albert Moll to speak on a subject of his choice at the First International Congress for Sex Research to be held in Berlin during autumn 1914 and offered a paper on 'The Exclusion of Homosexuality from Cultural History', though he was persuaded by Moll to change the title to the more neutral 'Homosexuality in Cultural History'.[101] At Carpenter's suggestion it was agreed that Bertram Lloyd should be one of the speakers on 'Prostitution'.[102] So thanks mainly to Carpenter, the rising sexual theorist found himself not only addressing the B.S.S.S.P. in London but speaking at an international congress in Berlin. However, Carpenter had hitched them both to the less radical wing of the German sex-reform movement and Hirschfeld, the outspoken advocate of homosexuality, was left to discover that Carpenter was speaking for the group which rivalled his own. Though somewhat offended, he assured Carpenter politely that he would be very pleased to see him and Lloyd, enquiring how the project they had initiated in London was going.[103]

Carpenter had his congress paper ready in manuscript that summer. Based on *Intermediate Types Among Primitive Folk*, it stressed the valuable role of homosexuals in culture. However the wise men and healers, the Samurai and the Thebans, were not destined to make it to Berlin. By autumn 1914 the suppositions of the previous summer had been blasted into the nether distance.

19

Image and Impact

Carpenter's resolve to follow his heart had a fortuitous consequence; the wide scope of his work broadened his audience well beyond his initial socialist constituency. Word of mouth, interviews and visual images, as well as his writings, contributed to his reputation. In the period before the First World War Carpenter became well known without ever being quite mainstream, his prestige vested in a series of ever extending niche circles. The dashing wayfarer look of his 1887 photograph was being over-taken by a prophetic persona. Unconventional prophets were in vogue and Carpenter was distilled as myth. He came to symbolise the mystical shadow of the ebullient materialistic era, the spiritual searcher oblivious to worldly concerns and in union with nature, who assumed a modern, democratic guise. The *Sheffield Independent* proudly dubbed him the 'Sage of Holmesfield', while the American radical J. William Lloyd extolled the 'Christ-Spirit' of 'the greatest man in England' and pronounced Carpenter to be 'the Social Conscience Incarnate'.[1] Carpenter was growing old grace-fully and his arresting appearance in his late fifties and sixties fitted the part of contemporary sage; Edith Ellis' *Three Modern Seers* (1910) crystallised the image of Carpenter as 'seer'.[2]

Ever more fans and followers, journalists and photographers arrived at his door, coming not only from Britain but from further afield. Harry Beswick, one of the many journalists to seek out the 'prophet', depicted a 'spare, scholarly figure clad in tweeds, with sandals on his feet instead of shoes; skin covered with a dark grizzled beard, and hair a silver sable'.[3] Carpenter developed his own style of dress, but he was careful about sartorial details. When J. William Lloyd walked down the hill from Dore and Totley station to visit the man he regarded as the greatest in England, he was greeted by Carpenter in a simple soft suit, knee breeches, stockings, sandals and 'a silken sash' around his waist.[4] The idealistic Russian socialist, Constantine Sarantchoft remarked on Carpenter's elegance in an 'artistic ensemble' of long, navy blue cloak, soft hat and sandals.[5] Edward Lewis, Carpenter's New Pagan friend, arrived while researching the biography he was writing of Carpenter. As he walked along, carrying his knapsack from Chesterfield, he spotted Carpenter in the distance, 'erect, lithe, athletic in appearance, sandalled with free stride and high step . . . a soft felt hat tilted to one side in the half-rakish fashion of Walt Whitman'.[6]

This was simplification with style, but it was not just the style that captivated so many of the people who met Carpenter. In struggling to articulate the impact of Carpenter's charisma, people frequently mention the warm empathy he communicated through touch and eye-contact. Lloyd was charmed by the affectionate greeting he received: 'He took me by the hands; his manner was nervous, almost to a slight tremulousness.'[7] The Italian socialist and university professor, Guido Ferrando, who became a close friend, met Carpenter at George Herron's villa in Florence in 1909 and experienced 'a sense of elation, of blissful peace', when Carpenter took his hand in a warm grasp, recalling the 'vivid, piercing eyes looking deep into mine, the noble luminous smile'.[8] For the railwayman, C.T. Cramp, it was Carpenter's way of concentrating intensely on the person he encountered and his blend of inner certainty with a refusal to dogmatise that was so compelling.[9]

Numerous accounts from people of all classes and many cultures testify to a fusion of grace and power in Carpenter's capacity for empathetic communication. E.M. Forster best expresses the impact of Carpenter's magnetic personality which he compared to that of a religious teacher: 'it depended on contact and couldn't be written down on paper, and its effect was to increase one's vitality, so that one went away better able to do one's work. One's own work not his; it was an influence, not a doctrine. It suggested the direct transference of power.'[10]

While the psychological strength Carpenter transferred to others partly came from within, it must, of course, have been enhanced by the expectations of those who sought him out. Moreover it was homoerotically charged. While women liked and admired him, turning to him for help, especially after a close friend or relative died, those who encountered him most dramatically were men – and often young men. Their meetings with the ineluctably sexy sage were part spiritual transcendence, part sensuous infusions.

Carpenter's pan-sexual charm did not seduce everyone. The Cambridge Higher Sodomite, Lytton Strachey, always greeted Carpenter's name 'with a series of little squeaks'.[11] Strachey disdained the Carpenterian simple life nearly as much as heterosexual copulation, and when his two bête noirs combined at the 1904 marriage of George Trevelyan and Janet Ward, daughter of the social-reforming novelist Mrs Humphrey Ward, he found the whole event insufferable. The bride and groom planned to live the simple life, sniffed Strachey in a letter to his sister Pippa.[12]

Though close to Goldsworthy Lowes Dickinson and friendly with Fry and Forster, Carpenter did not go down well with other Bloomsburies. In 1911, when Carpenter visited Fry in Guildford, Vanessa Bell simply could not understand why Fry still admired him so much. She saw only a sentimental and rather silly old man with Victorian attitudes to child rearing – Carpenter had been shocked when her three-year-old son Julian poured earth over her hair and neck without being reprimanded.[13] The glamorous Rupert Brooke threw down a glove of defiance in a 1909 lecture for the Cambridge University Fabians, 'Democracy and the Arts', assuring his listeners, 'I am not going to rhapsodise about the Spirit of Democracy as dawning in the operas of Wagner or the anarchic prose of Whitman or Carpenter.' Nor was he going to mention brotherhood, comrade or 'cumrade'.[14] Even the New Age took a jab at Carpenter in 1910 when he revamped his cherished Moses as The Promised Land. The acerbic critic, A.E. Randall, pronounced it a 'dramatic disaster', adding in a snide swipe, 'Just as Edward Carpenter journeyed "Towards Democracy" and never got there, so he now journeys towards "The Promised Land" only to see the curtain lowered as Joshua gives the command "Forward ever more".'[15]

Carpenter's personal utopianism, earnestly emulated by some, made him a figure of fun to others. Edith Nesbit, the socialist children's writer who had clattered away when Carpenter spoke for the Fabians all those years ago, took delight in teasing Carpenter in The New Treasure Seekers in 1904. One of her characters, Eustace Sandal, is described as 'a vegetarian and a primitive social something, and an all-wooler'. He believed in 'The Life Beautiful', was extremely good and 'awfully dull', and survived on a diet of bread and cheese.[16] His equally ascetic sister, Miss Sandal, dwelt in a house without ornaments, in which the walls were all white plaster, the furniture white deal, and the only carpets were white matting. Only at the end of the book do the visiting children learn that the décor was chosen rather than the result of dire poverty.

Amidst the mirth, Carpenter attempted to assert that the modern drive for ever greater productivity with its rush of trams and motor cars was making simplification a new common-sense alternative. Dressed in a brown frieze suit and turn-down collar, he insisted in his 1906 lecture for the Humanitarian League at Essex Hall in London that advocates of the simple life were no longer regarded as 'Diogenes who enjoyed life in a tub'.[17]

MORNING LEADER CARTOON, 13 MARCH, 1906.

"If Society people had to make their own clothes there would be some curious scenes in the streets, and many would go about attired in simply an Indian blanket."—Mr. EDWD. CARPENTER at the meeting of the Humanitarian League at Essex Hall.

(By courtesy of the *Daily News*.)

Morning Leader Cartoon 13 March 1906

He spoke too soon! A cartoonist in the *Morning Leader* picked up on his remark: 'If society people had to make their own clothes there would be some curious scenes in the streets, and many would go about attired in simply an Indian blanket.'[18] It appeared as the caption beneath a drawing of two top-hatted men in sandals, one wearing a blanket, the other a sack. Part of Carpenter's charm was his sense of humour and he reproduced the sketch in *My Days and Dreams*.

He might be able to see the funny side, but Janet Ashbee was beset by people who took the simple life very seriously indeed. Less inclined to reverence than her husband, Janet contended that it always rained at Millthorpe and was incredulous to find that a 'School of the Simple Life' had opened in Chelsea.[19] In May 1906 she suffered from a simple life overdose when she went to stay with the Bolton architect Charles Holden and his wife Margaret in Hertfordshire. Holden, now mainly remembered for his work on the London Underground, was trying to design in the simplified spirit of Carpenter, and Bristol Public Library was one of his projects. The Holdens also emulated the Carpenter lifestyle at home, causing Janet Ashbee to groan about whitewashed walls, brown bread, bananas and no hot water.

She puzzled over the differing versions, 'Roger Fry five or six years ago told me he had tried the simple life, but had found it so complex that he had to give it up.'[20] Her conclusion was that the simple life was actually within the individual; a view Holbrook Jackson was also propounding at the time to the readers of the *Yorkshire Weekly Post*. According to Jackson, Carpenter's message was not about décor, but an inner Nietzschean drive towards a consciously directed intensity which scrapped etiquette and headed towards a new future combining 'the tonic wildness of barbaric peoples with the exalted ethics of communal life'.[21]

Carpenter, meanwhile, lived as he wished to live; the guru of simplification departed on his pleasurable holidays in Switzerland, Spain, Morocco and Italy, dressed in his artistic ensembles, attended performances of Maurice Maeterlinck's fashionable *The Blue Bird* and Ibsen's *Hedda Gabler* with George Merrill, dined with Henry Nevinson in London and was welcome at John Masefield's 'At Homes'. Diogenes was not much in evidence, yet the image of the unworldly, retiring sage continued to accrue around him. 'Don't you find it lonely here sometimes?' enquired the Christian Socialist, Conrad Noel, in an interview at Millthorpe during the summer of 1905.[22] Extolling his rural neighbours, the 'hermit' admitted that occasionally an intellectual artisan friend from Manchester or Sheffield would visit!

If Carpenter casually contributed to his myth, friends and admirers were also partly responsible. Charlie Sixsmith reasserted Edith Ellis' version of Carpenter as a 'seer' in his lectures on Carpenter, adding a Calvinist twist. Sixsmith depicted Carpenter as spending many years speaking in drab rooms to tiny groups, writing in defunct journals and being cherished 'in the hearts and minds of a few elect'. Proudly naturalising Carpenter as a Northerner, Sixsmith's lecture notes pronounced that his hero 'was not the man to boom it or advertise himself', despite being hailed by artists, reformers, philosophers and leaders of thought.[23] Eventually, Sixsmith was convinced that Carpenter would influence the multitude. It was not quite the whole truth, but Sixsmith was using broad brushstrokes. A suitably modest Carpenter was grateful: 'It is too, too . . . of course; still it is pleasant to be well spoken of – and the lecture seems to have been well received.'[24]

For Carpenter's first biographer, the New Pagan, Edward Lewis, Carpenter was 'a wayside sower of seed', a Bergsonian super-tramp who believed sufficiently in himself and his message to disregard 'on what soil it may be flung'. Lewis stressed how the spiritual entwined with the affirmation of the body in Carpenter's writing and referred to Carpenter's homosexuality. 'To him has fallen the lot of the Urning to be misunderstood, and his heart has known the tragedy of a brooding love apparently rendered ineffectual because of the aloofness and unbelief of the world.'[25]

This was carefully worded but it affirmed Carpenter as the sexual outsider. Versions of Carpenter as the unworldly sage and nature man, the misunderstood and neglected outsider, were replayed over and over again. Not only were they over-simplifications, they assumed he was insouciant of image and reputation. This was far from the truth. The B.S.S.S.P. lawyer E.S.P. Haynes was right, despite his emperor-has-no-clothes approach. Carpenter was not 'quite as simple as he appeared'.[26]

Carpenter – who spent so much time pouring over the photographs he exchanged with friends – was acutely aware of the power of the visual image, and always interested in how he was being represented. He had his own personal photographers on tap because both Alf Mattison and George Hukin were keen amateurs. Mattison used to stagger up from Totley station to Millthorpe with his heavy camera to photograph Carpenter and Merrill. In 1905 he took a picture of Carpenter standing by the porch in sandals, cummerbund, plus fours and Walt Whitman hat, which Carpenter thought was excellent and jocularly decreed 'ought to be a standard photo of the animal'.[27] And so it proved; 'Self in Porch (1905)' was featured in *My Days and Dreams* and reproduced many times. On the other hand Carpenter took against two portraits of Merrill and himself wearing the velvet jacket that Salt remembered as natty; Mattison was instructed to destroy the plates.

Mattison had some high-powered rivals. Two American photographers, the wealthy Bostonian Frederick Holland Day, and his distant cousin, Alvin Langdon Coburn, took Carpenter's photograph in the early 1900s. Day's 1900 study portrays a handsome bearded man in a beautiful white shirt with a short floppy tie. It reveals a smooth, unwrinkled face and one work-worn hand. Carpenter looks out, away from the photographer gazing into the distance with a detached contemplative gaze. But it was the young Coburn who succeeded best in catching the elusive charisma on camera. He took Carpenter's picture in 1905, after reading *Towards Democracy* over and over again and being inspired by *The Art of Creation*. Coburn commented many years later that 'it is the eyes which have the most to say in a portrait; they are the "windows of the soul".'[28] His compelling portrait does indeed convey

Carpenter in 1905, by Alvin Langdon Coburn

the extraordinary communicative power of Carpenter's eyes far better than any words, intimating the rapport so many admirers and friends struggled to articulate. Coburn's image of Carpenter was one of a series of portraits of British literary figures, which included Bernard Shaw, published in *Men of Mark* (1913). It was Shaw who inadvertently provided another gifted photographer. Like Carpenter, always ready to help young talent, he fell for Lena Connell, one of Fenner Brockway's fellow communards, and launched her on a successful career by allowing her to take eighty photographs of him. Lena Connell took a picture of Carpenter resplendent in his cloak and chain, sporting an artistic floppy tie, which accompanied the interview by a 'Special Correspondent' in the *Christian Commonwealth* in 1912. When Connell's photograph was shown in an exhibition in Sheffield in 1913, Carpenter went to survey himself, reporting to Charlie Sixsmith that she had done 'a really fine portrait'.[29] He was quite aware that artistic photographs were a crucial component of literary celebrity.

Carpenter was as engaged with the fortunes of his written works as he was with his visual image. He sent out notices and copies himself and conducted a lengthy correspondence with publishers displaying the know-how about publicity, covers, types of paper and bindings he had acquired from his experience with the Manchester Labour Press. As a political animal propagating minority causes, Carpenter's relationship with publishers was never simply commercial. In Britain and in other countries, the political and the personal affected his dealings with both small political presses and larger publishing concerns. Arthur C. Fifield's The Simple Life Press took the place of the defunct Labour Press, publishing some of Carpenter's pamphlets along with *Prisons, Police and Punishment*.

In his dealings with mainstream publishers, Carpenter the mathematician kept a sharp eye on his royalty statements and bargained with publishers over the terms of his contracts. However his royalties were never completely secure. Swan Sonnenschein had done some of his books in the late 1880s and 1890s and continued to publish his new books in the 1900s. After a fire in their warehouse destroyed a lot of stock, they were absorbed by George Allen's, a firm with an imposing reputation as the publishers of Ruskin. They did Carpenter's *The Art of Creation* (1904), his *Days with Walt Whitman* (1906) and *Sketches from Life in Town and Country* (1908). All seemed to be going well, but George Allen's son, William, was not able to keep the firm in profit. Though *The Drama of Love and Death* was selling vigorously in 1912, payment was slow in coming and troubled letters were exchanged. Finally, in 1914, the ambitious Stanley Unwin, a former Abbotsholmian, stepped in to form Allen and Unwin's. Carpenter was initially uneasy because it had been Stanley Unwin's uncle, T. Fisher Unwin who had cancelled his contract for *Love's Coming of Age* in the wake of the Wilde trial. But he and Stanley Unwin got on well personally and in Unwin he found a publisher who combined commercial aptitude with an interest in his authors' ideas. Unwin was clear that Carpenter had to be promoted as a total package. 'Thanks to our handling all his books, and thus being able to make one sell another, and to list them all together, we were able to build up his income for him most agreeably.'[30]

When it came to publication in other countries, Carpenter's work tended to be launched by small presses who took him up for purely ideological reasons. While these were valuable in terms of gaining him entry points, communications were slow and royalties often delayed. In 1900 *Love's Coming of Age* was produced in the expanding American book market by Stockham Publishing Co., owned by Alice B. Stockham. Stockham and Carpenter were in affinity. She moved in Whitmanite and free-love circles, shared Carpenter's interest in Eastern religion and loved *Towards Democracy*.[31] She came to see him at Millthorpe in 1910 when George Merrill won her heart by putting lavender under her pillow.[32]

The socialist Charles H. Kerr took over *Love's Coming of Age* in 1905. Then, in 1911, two adventurous small publishers, Boni and Liveright and Mitchell Kennerley, issued editions of the same work. Both publishers carried a certain kudos. Albert and Charles Boni had established the famous Washington Square Bookshop on Macdougall Street, a popular bohemian hangout, before Albert went into publishing with Charles Liveright, while Kennerley was highly esteemed for his avant-garde list which included Bergson, Freud, Wells, Yeats and Ellis. In 1912 Kennerley also did *Towards Democracy* – however Carpenter was soon enlisting the help of the newly formed Society of Authors in pursuit of unpaid royalties. Stanley Unwin's hard-headed advice was to get out of Kennerley's hands and persuade a mainstream publisher such as Macmillan's or Scribner's to take the whole list.[33] Macmillan's already had some of Carpenter's works, *The Art of Creation*, *Days with Walt Whitman*, *Sketches from Life in Town and Country*, while Scribner's, who were adopting an approach similar to Unwin's, later took Carpenter's autobiography. In theory this policy would have been simpler, but though Carpenter put out feelers to mainstream American publishers, he did not completely break with Kennerley who did pay a massive £165 in 1915.[34] His foreign publishers in America and elsewhere remained a variegated patchwork of alternative, left and advanced presses along with more commercial firms. These oddly assorted outlets fostered his outsider image, though the mix of politics, personal contact and salesmanship did not always work so harmoniously as it did with Stanley Unwin.

Carpenter became an international figure between 1900 and 1914. His search for a larger socialism, his opposition to imperialism, his support for women's rights, homosexual freedom and humanitarian causes resonated in many countries. Moreover his assertion of the heart and experience, his desire for harmony with nature, his desire to balance body and spirit and link mysticism with science were issues preoccupying sections of the intelligentsia around the world.

As in Britain his initial promoters were small coteries outside the mainstream, and several translators were fans who became close personal friends. Among them was George Herron, who performed a central role in launching Carpenter in Italy. A Christian Socialist, Herron had worked as a professor at Grinnell College in Iowa until he divorced his wife to marry the heiress Carrie Rand, whose family endowed his professorship, causing a scandal in the conservative Western town of Burlington. As a result, Herron, his new wife and mother-in-law, had gone into a congenial exile in Florence. By the early 1900s the beautiful old city had become a gathering point for artistic bohemians and unconventional aristocrats, many of whom converged at the Herrons' villa, La Primola, 15, Via Benedetto da Maiano.[35]

Unlike many of the expatriates, Herron was in touch with Italian intellectuals. Philosophic idealism, William James, Paganism and Bergson were all being discussed in the cafés and salons of Florence, interest in Whitman had developed and Carpenter's work was just being discovered. Herron wrote to Carpenter in 1908 telling him that the Whitman enthusiast Professor Guido Ferrando was starting to translate The Art of Creation and Love's Coming of Age. Promising Carpenter Italian disciples, Herron characterised Ferrando's associates as philosophers, socialists and anarchists who were opposed to the restrictions of the Catholic Church in Italy.[36] Rejecting the fin de siècle decadence espoused by Gabriele D'Annunzio, they wanted to connect back to the radical idealism of Mazzini. Ferrando's friends included the art historian Ricardo Nobili, Professor of Modern Art at the University of Florence and the psychoanalyst Roberto Assagioli, whose unusual therapeutic approach combining Whitman, Carpenter, Freud and Jung was popular with the advanced women who congregated in Florence.[37] Carpenter met these sympathetic Italians when he and George Merrill stayed with the Herrons early in 1909, while O'Brien was distributing his denunciations around Derbyshire.

Ferrando's translation of Love's Coming of Age went down particularly well in Italy. Its success was remarkable as it was not reviewed, but commended solely by word of mouth, for the hold of Catholicism was still stifling open discussion of sexuality in the media. Ferrando however had aroused interest through an article in the leading spiritual journal La Nuova Parola on Carpenter's work. A group of young people formed a 'Union of Young Men' to discuss sexuality from a moral and religious perspective after reading Love's Coming of Age. The Art of Creation had a more restricted readership, though Nobili was an enthusiast.[38]

Carpenter met the anarchistic Teresina Bagnoli through the Florentine group when he visited Herron again in 1911, and she took on the task of translating Part I of *Towards Democracy*. Carpenter also encountered in Florence a student of Ferrando's, Biagio di Paulo, who had translated an extract from *Towards Democracy* in 1909. To the demonstrative di Paulo Carpenter was another Francesco d'Assisi, a Tolstoy.[39] The two men wrote to one another at length, poems were posted to Millthorpe and di Paulo was added to the list of indigent young men who received postal orders from Carpenter.

Carpenter's work became particularly popular in Germany, but here too he was first promoted by enthusiasts. The Tolstoyan aristocrat Count Ervin Batthyány came from Hungary to stay in Millthorpe in 1901, trundling a wheelbarrow about with Carpenter and relating the reforms he was planning to initiate on his estates. Batthyány took a copy of *Towards Democracy* back with him and began to translate it into German with a married friend, Lilly Nadler-Nuellens. In the process the couple fell in love. When Batthyány set up a school, workshops and a reading room for the peasants who were still living in a state of partial serfdom, his horrified aristocratic relatives incarcerated him in a mental asylum and his lands were sequestered. Lilly Nadler-Nuellens campaigned energetically for his release. The couple migrated to Britain, where they settled in Hampstead.[40] After a legal battle which lasted several years, Batthyány's inheritance was restored; according to an announcement in the *Daily Telegraph* in March 1913, the Count planned to devote his wealth to causes in keeping with his socialistic beliefs.[41] The Batthyánys became close personal friends of Carpenter's and he and Merrill often stayed with them in London and in Lyme Regis where they took their holidays. Like his Italian translators, they were in close harmony with Carpenter's intellectual and political outlook.

Shared convictions also led Karl Federn in Germany, and Marcelle Senard in France, to translate Carpenter's work. They acted informally as his agent in their respective countries, prodding publishers and reviewers and writing about him themselves. Federn was sympathetic to the left and feminism but uneasy with mechanistic interpretations of materialism and searching for an alternative to Tolstoy's sexual asceticism.[42] His translations of *Love's Coming of Age* (1902) and *Civilisation: Its Cause and Cure* (1903) both sold extremely well, partly because the large German women's movement contained currents interested in sexual politics. In 1904 an amused Federn told Carpenter that *Love's Coming of Age* had divided the International Woman Suffrage Alliance's conference in Berlin.[43] Carpenter also had an enthusiastic following among the socialists. By 1912 Federn was able to report sales of forty thousand copies, adding that he could not think of any other English work achieving a comparable success in Germany. 'Good isn't it' pencilled Carpenter on the margin of Federn's letter.[44]

More diffusely, Carpenter's writing on sex and his critique of civilisation were in accord with the counter-cultural youth movement 'Wandervogel', which was challenging the stiff formality of German society. Hiking all over the countryside in bright shirts, carrying rucksacks, sleeping rough in barns and bathing naked, Wandervogel was an existential defiance of industrialisation and an assertion of a powerful Romantic impulse towards self-expression and Volksgemeinschaft. Carpenter could appeal to this mix of desire for a new culture and rejection of modern commerce. In 1908 Federn persuaded the mainstream house of Eugen Diederichs to take on Carpenter's *The Art of Creation*. Diederichs was sympathetic to the anti-rational protest and the celebration of the body Wandervogel represented and prepared to take a chance with Carpenter's book. However *The Art of Creation* moved very slowly. This, along with the more nationalistic ethos which appropriated 'des Volkes', no doubt explains Lloyd's problems in arousing any interest in *The Drama of Love and Death* in 1913. Diederichs himself reflected the shift – in post-war Germany he edited the right-wing journal *Die Tat*.[45]

Marcelle Senard, who translated *Towards Democracy* into French, was committed, like Federn, to Carpenter's ideas. She spent two months with him at Millthorpe while translating Parts III and IV of *Towards Democracy* into *Vers l'affranchissement*, making sure that every phrase was precisely nuanced.[46] Senard was from a Burgundian aristocratic family but had gravitated towards the international bohemians who passed through Paris and Florence like the American Mabel Dodge.[47] Aware that Carpenter's mode of thinking was alien to the French rationalist tradition, she made it her mission to explain him, producing a small book of extraordinary clarity summarising his thought. Her *Edward Carpenter et sa Philosophie* was published in 1914, along with *Towards Democracy*.[48]

Carpenter's ideas appealed to overlapping circles in Europe; as in Britain, his readers crossed over spiritual and political milieux. Romain Rolland, the French novelist who was influenced by Tolstoy, yearned for more direct and sincere human relationships. He believed that the means adopted for changing society affected consciousness and thus the outcome of political actions. Like Carpenter he was interested in Eastern religion and wanted a synthesis of reason and intuition. The two men shared an admiration for Beethoven, and Carpenter wrote an introduction for Rolland's book on the composer which eventually came out in 1917.[49] Rolland was part of a small literary grouping in France who looked towards the Anglo-Saxons for a new spirit of directness. The group included the Whitmanite Léon Bazalgette, who translated *Leaves of Grass* into French and corresponded with Carpenter as well as 'les "College" boys de Bolton'.[50] In Belgium a congenial non-sectarian radical culture flourished in the environs of the Workers' Party. Carpenter's connection between art and life was an important source of inspiration for the Belgian architect Henry Van de Velde. A friend of Elisée Reclus, and influenced by Kropotkin and Nietzsche as well as Carpenter and Morris, Van de Velde was instrumental in transforming Arts and Crafts (or art nouveau) into a new kind of social art which could reach beyond a wealthy elite. He set out to crack the problem which had forced Ashbee's Guild of Handicraft in Chipping Campden to close in 1907. Combining craft and machine and incorporating simplification into his new aesthetic, Van de Velde's Weimar School of Arts and Crafts in Germany was the precursor of Bauhaus modernism.[51]

These European intellectuals and artists moved freely over national borders. In 1904 Karl Federn mentioned in a letter to Carpenter that the French journalist, Jacques Mesnil, was about to visit Vienna and hoped to meet Carpenter in Italy.[52] The anarchist Mesnil was friendly with Bazalgette and Rolland and admired Elisée Reclus, sending Carpenter an article he had written on Reclus in 1905. He had read most of Carpenter's writings and was commissioned to write an account of Carpenter's work by the sociologist Robert Michels in 1914 for the *Encyclopédie Sociologique*.[53] By the time Michels was editing his *Encyclopédie* in 1914, his outlook had grown more pessimistic and elitist, but his early interests had spanned sex, women's emancipation and syndicalism and he too was familiar with Carpenter's books.[54]

Carpenter's ideas spread ever further afield through Dutch, Danish and Swedish translations. He was particularly proud of his Bulgarian fans, Charles Dosseff and Ivan Vaptzaroft, who translated several chapters of *Civilisation: Its Cause and Cure*, along with all of *England's Ideal*, in their magazine *Renaissans* just before the First World War.[55] The editors of *Renaissans* were in close contact with their Russian counterparts. In Russia, Carpenter's work had first become known to small groups of idealistic Tolstoyans through Tolstoy's interest in his critique of science during the late 1890s. In 1905 Tolstoy was seeking more information about Carpenter's work from his British translator, Aylmer Maude.[56] *Civilisation: Its Cause and Cure* was translated into Russian in the following year by Ivan Najivin, a novelist interested in Tolstoy's theories of the simple life and in Eastern religious thought.[57]

Various forms of esoteric groupings including spiritualism and Theosophy were gaining adherents in Russia. One of these intense seekers after the miraculous, the mathematician and mystic, Pyötr Demianovitch Ouspensky, became one of the most popular lecturers for the Russian Theosophists. Ouspensky believed that the evolution of consciousness to a higher level could be short-circuited by Nietzschean Supermen who could attain an ecstatic perception. In his book *Tertium Organum* (1911), Ouspensky cited Richard Maurice Bucke along with William James and incorporated Charles

Hinton's argument that it was simply our three-dimensional make-up that prevented us from perceiving a fourth dimension. Ouspensky, echoing Plotinus and Bergson, proposed that this could be conceptualised as time outside a linear chronology, glimpsed in those instances when a past experience usurps the present, and that a higher space could be perceived by opening one's receptivity to other forms of consciousness.[58]

A visit to Millthorpe was clearly over-determined. Ouspensky arrived in 1913 while he was on a long trek for enlightenment. Much in awe of Carpenter, he wrote saying that he had forgotten everything he had wanted to ask, but was nevertheless content because he had 'felt very much'.[59] Excited by Carpenter's interest in combining spirit and matter, Ouspensky translated Carpenter's *Drama of Love and Death* into Russian. However, by the time it came out in 1915, he had moved on to become a disciple of George Ivanovich Gurdjieff, whose demanding methods of eliminating individuality as a means of intensifying perception later attracted Orage.

More congenial to Carpenter personally was Constantine Sarantchoft. When they first met the young Russian was working on the Tolstoyan exile Vladimir Tchertkoff's printing press in Christchurch and wandering around dreamily with a light rug over his shoulder sketching and endeavouring to write.[60] He sent his efforts to Carpenter along with accounts of his sexual woes. By 1910 Sarantchoft had moved to 6, Clapton Square, Hackney, a Social Democratic household which Lenin visited.[61] In the Spring of 1914 he was back in Christchurch and Carpenter was consulting him on the prospects for secluded beaches away from civilisation with a bathing van for Lucy Sixsmith.[62] Carpenter's Tolstoyans, mystics and socialists reflected the kaleidoscopic responses evoked by Russia's mix of archaic autocracy and brutal industrialisation.

Russia's rival Japan was also rapidly industrialising and here too an intense debate about modernisation was under way. From the 1890s some Japanese intellectuals had turned to John Ruskin and William Morris' protests against the social impact of industrialisation, finding echoes of their own concerns. Parts of Carpenter's *Civilisation: Its Cause and Cure* had appeared in a Japanese magazine in Los Angeles, and the whole book was issued in Japan by a group called Minyusha (The Friends of the People) in 1893 as part of a series of 'Books for the Common People'.

By the 1900s Whitman, Tolstoy, Bergson and the Belgian mystical writer Maurice Maeterlinck were all being read in Japan. Cognisant of Western avant-garde ideas, Japanese intellectuals were searching for cultural alternatives to imperialism and the ideology of their ruling oligarchy. The journalist Lafcadio Hearn's version of a mystical Japan was not only popular in Letchworth Garden City, it also had an impact within Japan itself. By the time Japan and Russia went to war in 1904, a complex mix of old and new, national and international, Eastern and Western ideas were co-existing in Japanese culture. Ethical socialism, Marxism, syndicalism and anarchism were soon added to the potpourri, and, as in Europe, Carpenter's ideas travelled down all these tracks. A small group of socialists who opposed the war started a magazine called the *Plebs Newspaper* (*Heimin-shinbun*). This 'Plebs' grouping included two young leftists, Toshihiko Sakai and Sanshiro Ishikawa, both of whom were drawn to Carpenter's work. Toshihiko Sakai, who became keen on free love, began to translate *Love's Coming of Age*.[63] Sanshiro Ishikawa, being a Christian Socialist, did not approve of free love, though he thought highly of both *Love's Coming of Age* and *Civilisation: Its Cause and Cure*. When he came across a pamphlet by the American Tolstoyan, Ernest Crosby, on Carpenter, Ishikawa, who was searching for an alternative to 'mere mechanical materialistic socialism', wrote to Millthorpe, filled with an evangelical enthusiasm to spread the Carpenter 'gospel over the country'.[64]

Events, and the Japanese authorities, intervened to prevent this. When the idealistic Sanshiro Ishikawa helped socialist women launch a journal called *Sekai Fujin* (*World Women*) he was put in prison. Carpenter parcelled up *Angels' Wings* for the prisoner and a friend, Iso Abé (also Isoo Abe), sent thanks on his behalf.[65] Jail turned out to be a safe haven, for, while Ishikawa was incarcerated, a group of anarchists were accused of a plot to assassinate the Emperor Meiji and this resulted in the execution of twelve of his friends.[66] On his release in 1910 Ishikawa wrote to tell Carpenter how he was reading *Prisons, Police and Punishment* with heartfelt recognition.[67] His own study of 'Carpenter sage' made a deep impression in radical circles in Japan and even reached the migrant community on the west coast of the United States.[68]

As repression mounted in Japan, Sanshiro Ishikawa had to flee. He was smuggled to Europe in 1913 as an attendant of the wife of the sympathetic Belgian consul and, in November 1913, Carpenter met him in London and took him up North. There the young Japanese got the full Millthorpe treatment. Carpenter and Merrill took him to their village club in the evening. The next morning Carpenter and he went for a walk. Later in the day Carpenter played the piano and Merrill sang 'England Arise', then Sanshiro Ishikawa was introduced to Henry Salt who told him about the Humanitarian League. With Carpenter there were long exciting discussions about Kropotkin, Oscar Wilde, Lafcadio Hearn, Shintoism, Zen Buddhism and Saikaku Ihara's novels on homosexuality; a lifelong friendship began that autumn.[69]

Sanshiro Ishikawa was delighted with all this talk, but completely penniless. Carpenter swung into action, writing to friends for help. Bertram Lloyd offered to put up the young Japanese visitor but feared it would be hard for him to find work because his English was not very good.[70] When Stephen Reynolds needed a secretary to help with his investigation into the fishing industry, Carpenter proposed Sanshiro Ishikawa, but a testy Reynolds responded, 'The Japanese chap would scarcely do for a secretary and handyman with indifferent English.'[71] So Carpenter kept sending postal orders and enlisted the help of faithful Charlie Sixsmith and Kate Salt on his new friend's behalf.[72] 'Please be not so much anxious about me. I am used to be a wanderer', wrote Sanshiro Ishikawa, whose English might have been 'indifferent', but was nevertheless endearing.[73] Paul Reclus, the nephew of Elisée, eventually gave Sanshiro Ishikawa a home in Brussels. He settled there early in 1914, earning a living as a decorator and becoming an anarchist. Regardless of exile, he wrote for a newspaper in Japan about suffrage demonstrations, syndicalist-led strikes in Europe *and* his 'Pilgrimage to Sheffield'. He told Carpenter with pride that the newspaper had a circulation of five hundred thousand readers and that his friends had read about Millthorpe 'with so much interesting [sic] that they felt much jealous for me'.[74] Stories of a utopian sandal factory in the English countryside and a musical philosopher of the simple life wafted through Japan, along with sections of *Towards Democracy* and *The Art of Creation*, translated by Carpenter's other close Japanese friend, the Tolstoyan, Saikwa Tomita.

The vast territories under British Imperial rule were seething with ethnic conflicts, labour organising, and anti-colonial movements in the years before the First World War. Olive Schreiner had made the connection between workers and racial prejudice while also defending Jewish immigrants in South Africa in 1905. In the 1900s attempts were being made to exclude Jews on the grounds that Yiddish was not a European language. Though they were able to defeat these arguments, some members of the Jewish community made common cause with Hindu and Muslim immigrants from India who faced more severe restrictions and prejudice. Among them was Hermann Kallenbach, a wealthy architect who established Tolstoy Farm about twenty miles from Johannesburg as a refuge for the movement of non-violent resistance led by an Indian lawyer, Mohandâs Karamchand Gandhi. Both men wore sandals, were vegetarians and were influenced by Theosophy as well as Tolstoy.[75] A letter dated July 29, 1911 from Gandhi, addressed 'Tolstoy Farm, Lawley Station, Transvaal' asked Carpenter if he would be able to meet with a friend of his, Mr Kallenbach.[76] Whether Carpenter actually met Gandhi or Kallenbach is not clear, though they certainly had friends in common. Gandhi admired Salt, who he had met through the Vegetarian Society in the 1890s, and Charlotte Despard, with whom he discussed non-violent resistance on a visit to England in

1909. Subsequent connections would be made through the Cousinses from Ireland and the Youngs from Liverpool.

In Sri Lanka and India new social movements were emerging around labour conditions and women's rights, while the relationship between East and West which had troubled Arunachalam was being addressed politically in the Nationalist movement. Annie Besant, who remained on good terms with Carpenter, played a prominent role in both Nationalism and Theosophy in India, and Bhagavan Das was also involved with the Theosophists and appreciative of his English friend's efforts 'to spiritualise the materialistic thought of this age'.[77] Support from the Theosophists was not to be sniffed at; in 1913 they distributed 5,000 circulars advertising Carpenter's *Intermediate Types Among Primitive Folk*, partly paid for by Carpenter himself.[78]

Alongside the campaigns for national self-determination, a vision of cultural revival in art and literature was emerging. Ajit Kumar Chakravarti (also Chakraverti Chakraborty), wrote in excitement to Carpenter in 1911 from Shantiniketan, Bolpur, Bengal, about a great poet, Rabindranath Tagore, whose poetry, he believed, was not simply of national significance. Chakravarti, who was a teacher at the school Tagore had founded, translated the poems with Arunachalam's cousin, the artist and writer, Ananda Coomaraswamy. He told Carpenter that Tagore's writing contained international implications because he sought to 'harmonise the conflicting race-cultures and ideals and to weld them together into a spiritual whole'.[79] The affinity was obvious and Carpenter and Tagore did subsequently make contact with one another.[80] The translations became *Gitanjali*, Tagore's first collection in English, and Chakravarti's 'burning desire' to introduce Tagore to Western readers was more than realised. Amidst the newly awakened enthusiasm for Eastern art, and assisted by keen promotion on the part of the artist William Rothenstein and of Yeats, Tagore became a celebrity in the West and was given the Nobel Prize for Literature in 1913.

The British Empire presented writers in India and elsewhere with an acute dilemma of language, for English offered a wide readership but belonged to the colonial masters. In Jamaica during the early 1900s the folklorist Francis Walter Jekyll, who was later to support Carpenter's campaign against the censoring of the books in the British Museum library catalogue, encouraged his eighteen-year-old protégé Claude McKay to draw on local vernacular culture in his writings. He undertook McKay's education, introducing him to works by Oscar Wilde, Whitman and Carpenter, and later financed him at university.[81] McKay, who became a socialist, travelled to Britain and Russia, eventually taking part in New York's creative upsurge of black artists and intellectuals after the First World War, the Harlem Renaissance.

★   ★   ★

Along with Germany, it was the United States that gave Carpenter his most avid reception. In the early twentieth century, the United States, with its vast, modern factories and expendable supply of young immigrant labour, was rapidly overtaking the European powers. This ruthless economic expansion and the growing urban crisis it produced greatly troubled American rebels. Some hoped for a craft revival and the return to idylls of a simple life, while others looked to social reform or socialist revolution. Some dissident Americans, appalled by the rampant victory of materialism, turned to various forms of esoteric spirituality or aestheticism. Carpenter's American constituency was composed of people from all these groupings, but he enjoyed a particular popularity with networks which cut across several causes.

When the century began Carpenter's following consisted of the tiniest of groupuscules. In 1901 when George Herron's friend, Leonard D. Abbott wrote on Carpenter's poetry in a small magazine, *The Comrade*, he conceded that readers of Carpenter's work in America were few and far between.[82] The Ashbees encountered a few traces when they visited in 1900. They saw Philip Dalmas, back in America by the early 1900s, drifting between his Whitmanite family in Philadelphia and New York. Then, at Hull House, the Chicago Social Settlement founded by the reformer Jane Addams, they encountered a 'young Carpenterian socialist', romantically beflannelled, with big brown eyes all aglow with enthusiasm, who asked them for a donation to the *International Socialist Review*.[83] Janet Ashbee spent some time at Elbert Hubbard's Roycraft Arts and Crafts Community in New York State, which sought to bring craftsmen back to the countryside. The diet of buckwheat and apples reminded her of Millthorpe and she described the place to Ashbee as a 'Brook Farm Carpenter flannel shirt felt hat long hair community.'[84]

By 1913 these small clusters of 'Carpenterians' were to become a much broader constituency: Leonard Abbott, along with a group of his friends, Ernest Crosby, J. William Lloyd and the poet Edwin Markham, who formed a Whitman–Tolstoy nexus, open to both socialist and anarchist ideas, acted as the catalyst. Crosby's enthusiastic pamphlet *Edward Carpenter: Poet and Prophet*, which had found its way to Sanshiro Ishikawa in Japan, was published by the Whitmanite journal, *The Conservator*, in 1901.[85] Crosby, born into the New York intellectual elite, was like Carpenter a rebel against his class. He had trained as a lawyer succeeding his friend, Theodore Roosevelt, in the New York legislature. But his appointment as a judge in the International Court in Egypt in 1889 prompted a migration from privilege. Crosby's experience of British imperialism and his reading of Tolstoy turned him into an anti-imperialist and an advocate of non-violent resistance. Like Carpenter, he disliked sectarianism and took on many causes, opposing war and supporting civil liberties. Between 1902 and 1905 he helped to produce a little magazine, *The Whim*, which announced itself on the masthead as 'A periodical without a tendency'. In *The Whim* in 1903 Crosby hailed Carpenter as 'a spiritual son of Whitman and hence a sort of grandson of transcendentalism';[86] Carpenter had been adopted by the other America.

Leonard D. Abbott, like his close friend Crosby, consciously sought to connect across causes and bridge the anarchist/socialist divide. He opposed militarism, campaigned for free thought and free speech, supported birth control and libertarian education. He also wanted greater freedom in sexual relationships, advocating paganism and the simple life. For Abbott, Carpenter in his 'sunny Yorkshire dale' epitomised 'Simplicity in food, dress and material things; intellectual and bodily strength; passionate comradeship and clean sex-relationship; sympathy and love for all life human and animal alike; free living close to the woods and the fields and the open sea.'[87] Even though any discussion of sex was still perilous in puritanical America, Abbott made his protest against the society which had driven his friend George Herron into exile in an article on 'The Renaissance of Paganism', in which he tentatively asserted the needs of the flesh and 'the natural play of affections'.[88] He referred to Carpenter's writing on marriage in this article, and in 1911 wrote on 'Homosexual Love' in *The Free Comrade*, mentioning *The Intermediate Sex*.[89]

The self-educated intellectual, J. William Lloyd, who helped Abbott to edit *The Free Comrade*, had been influenced by Whitman and by the individualist anarchist in Boston, Benjamin R. Tucker. After reading Carpenter in 1900, Lloyd along with his friend Abbott, would seek to publicise Carpenter's writings in America. He was interested in Carpenter's acceptance of 'every kind of love';[90] Lloyd wanted a larger loving, a larger openness to others in which relationships were not exclusive. He also strove to imagine new kinds of human relating through utopian fiction. In Lloyd's *The Dwellers in Vale Sunrise: How They Got Together and Lived Happy Ever After* (1904), the 'Dwellers' call themselves 'Simplicists', dress in artistic brilliant colours, wear strange barbaric jewellery and grow their hair long. Local people called them 'The Tribe'.[91]

Lloyd and Abbott shared a faith, like Carpenter, that glimpses of a new future could be seen within the social movements of the time, identifying industrial unionism, free thought and sexual emancipation as the keys to change. They, too, espoused a Larger Socialism. In 1910 Abbott and Lloyd wanted their revived version of *The Free Comrade: An Utterance of the Free Spirit* to be 'the organ of the larger Socialism, of the Free comradeship of all who liberate, of all workers and dreamers of the New Times'.[92]

Though Abbott busied himself with a series of small magazines, he was a skilful networker, capable of pulling in an impressive selection of celebrities to pay tribute to the executed Spanish anarchist, Francisco Ferrer; among those appearing with Carpenter in *Francisco Ferrer: His Life, Work and Martyrdom* (1910) were the popular novelists Upton Sinclair and Jack London.[93] Abbott produced the book with Helena Born's friend, Helen Tufts Bailie.[94] After the Ferrer Modern School was set up in New York in memory of the anarchist, it too benefited from Abbott's wide-ranging contacts. London and Sinclair, both Carpenter enthusiasts, read their work there, along with the transcendental realist Edwin Markham, who had become very well-known through his poem 'The Man with the Hoe' in 1899.[95] Markham, who Abbott described as 'the Laureate of Labour', held Carpenter in great esteem, declaring to Henry Binns that Carpenter was 'the bravest man alive'.[96] Many other Carpenter admirers passed through the Modern School; the radical lawyer Clarence Darrow who visited Millthorpe in 1902;[97] the realist artist Robert Henri; and Mabel Dodge's friend, Max Weber, who was breaking with realism in his painting and questing for a fourth dimension.[98]

Carpenter appealed to the bohemians who gravitated towards Mabel Dodge's informal salon in Greenwich Village, which buzzed with talk of spontaneity, socialism, Eastern religion, Paganism and sexual freedom. Greenwich Village was the apogee of the dissident bohemias spilling over from the Arts and Crafts colonies into the towns and cities of America. Carpenter was on the reading list, along with Whitman and Tolstoy.[99] 'New women' and 'new men' were experimenting with alternative ways of living and challenging conventional assumptions about femininity and masculinity. Perception and emotion were rated over reason and logic among intellectual bohemians, and were personified in the free expression dancing of Isadora Duncan. Duncan, who may have met Carpenter in Florence, wrote from the Savoy hotel in London in 1912 saying she would love to see him and talk about Walt Whitman.[100] Their admiration for one another was mutual. Carpenter delighted in Duncan's dancing and listed her in *My Days and Dreams* as one of his inspirational encouragers.[101]

Along with Dodge and Duncan, the anarchist Emma Goldman was a pivotal female figure in Greenwich Village and her journal *Mother Earth* linked workers' struggles with sexual freedom, including homosexuality and lesbianism. In 1912, *Mother Earth* carried a special offer. For five dollars readers could obtain the anarchist communist Alexander Berkman's *Prison Memoirs*, the French utopian socialist Proudhon's *What is Property*, Frank Harris' *The Bomb* along with Carpenter's *Love's Coming of Age*.[102]

As well as being promoted through America's bohemians, Carpenter was popular in the Arts and Crafts movement which also had Whitmanite connections. The Whitmanite, Oscar Lovell Triggs, a teacher in the English department at the University of Chicago, wrote a book in 1905 praising Carpenter's approach to democracy and his connection of art with life.[103] Triggs, who had founded the Industrial Art League and the Morris Society, was involved in the large Arts and Crafts movement in America. Gustav Stickley's journal *The Craftsman: An Illustrated Monthly Magazine for the Simplification of Life* frequently mentioned Carpenter and printed six articles on him between 1905 and 1909.[104] Not all were completely adulatory, the socialist John Spargo joked about meeting a Glaswegian worker who summed Carpenter up as 'just brotherly love, clean water and no fun'.[105]

On the whole though, Carpenter's message of simplification and direct personal communion with nature chimed well with the outlook of radical Americans in the early 1900s. Tales of the great English philosopher living by the labour of his hands in 'a small cottage in the country near Manchester' began to be relayed from coast to coast.[106] In 1905 a happy Leonard Abbott could tell Carpenter that his name was frequently in the American papers and that his circle of readers was widening all the time.[107] Carpenter's fame rode partly on the rising wave of American socialism which was inclined to stress personal life, and partly on a parallel search for a spiritual alternative to materialism. The 1909 edition of *Current Literature* hailed 'The New Spiritual America Emerging', claiming Carpenter as one of its influences.[108] The spiritual preoccupation with consciousness was soon to be stimulated by the combined influences of Symbolism, Bergson and Nietzsche on avant-garde America. Consequently Carpenter's *The Art of Creation* and *The Drama of Love and Death* could slot into a market fostered by this rather attenuated alternative to the mainstream triumph of materialism. Carpenter, who had taken so many ideas and attitudes from Whitman and the Transcendentalists, contrived to export them back to America.

Some strands within these spiritual groupings tended towards the occult. The architect Claude Bragdon, who had been reared in a Theosophical family, conceived an organic architecture in harmony with the cosmic consciousness he had discovered in Bucke and Carpenter. Then he came across P.D. Ouspensky's *Tertium Organum* (1911) and began to translate it. Excited by the combination of esoteric spirituality and mathematics in Ouspensky's idea of a new kind of space, the Fourth Dimension, Bragdon sent a copy of his own book *A Primer of Higher Space* (1913) to Carpenter in 1914 explaining he felt a connection despite not knowing him personally.[109] In replying to Bragdon, Carpenter enquired if he was familiar with Charles Hinton's 'elaborate models and illustrations of the

Tesseract'.[110] Hinton's 'Tesseract' consisted of painted cubes designed to exercise the brain to envision a four-dimensional realm. Consciousness seemed to be infinitely expanding, and especially so in optimistic America.

Already in 1903 Charles Ashbee had come to the conclusion that Carpenter's true greatness was existential. 'Edward is always more convincing than his writings.'[111] Carpenter's personal presence clearly did affect people so profoundly that they became devoted propagators of his ideas, yet a capacity for absorbent empathy in one-to-one encounters does not explain his impact upon readers in Britain and other lands who never met him in person. Carpenter's writings were convincing to his contemporaries not because of their logic or even their originality, but because they voiced intimations already rippling within differing milieux. It was this ability which made him, in Forster's words, 'a rebel appropriate to his age', a comment which is applicable internationally, not just to Britain.[112]

Carpenter's knack of expressing ideas just before they surfaced stayed with him, as did his ability to steer political, cultural and sexual heterodoxies out on to wider terrains. He would craftily insinuate a reassuring and familiar riff just before he launched into an unknown tune, presenting the latest iconoclasm as common sense. This made him a most effective campaigner, all the more so because he was not simply a propagandist badgering from the outside but was able to enter the mindsets of the people around him and meet their concerns. Moreover, Carpenter could effect a series of lightning changes: sexual radical, noble savage, sage, simplifier, socialist, anarchist, artistic commentator, market gardener and mystic mathematician. He never seemed to settle in any one guise, with the result that he was puzzling but peculiarly pervasive.

Carpenter's adherents were inclined to forgive his theoretical inconsistencies because they recognised the impulses which he personified and saw their own aspirations mirrored in the man of many selves. In the process they partially invented him. He became a myth, not only through the stories of the sandal-maker in the idyllic vale, but because he seemed to embody qualities which were being shed in the world as it was, while at the same time heralding a new modernity. 'The twentieth century is on us and a new world is preparing', announced Carpenter in the *New Age* in 1910.[113] And so it was, though sadly not the kind of world he had in mind.

20

Healer of Nations

In the summer of 1914 Charlie Sixsmith was hatching a plan. Carpenter would be seventy on August 29th, and Sixsmith, along with Henry Salt, had decided to collect signatures for a birthday address in honour of their old friend. Carpenter responded with appropriate bashfulness in a letter to Sixsmith on June 7th:

> I really do much hope that you and he will give up this 70th birthday affair, and let it slide on to 75! By this time a quite natural EC boom will have taken place, of itself so to speak, with no trouble in getting it up; and I shall have five years respite to do some much needed work. I really dread the hundreds of tiresome people that you are going to let loose upon me.

Faced with their resolve he yielded. It seemed so much trouble, but he would not stand in their way. They were all so bent on it. 'Perhaps as you say it will be good for the Cause.'[1]

Carpenter was still carrying his years lightly. The Irish writer James H. Cousins, who visited just before the birthday, remarked on Carpenter sitting down on the sofa to discuss the Irish literary movement, tucking his legs under him like a tailor. Even more amazing, Carpenter stepped out that evening at a dance at the youth club in the barn, leading off 'with a suffragette who had twice done time'.[2]

Nonetheless seventy years were still seventy years of accumulated happenings and people. The letters and signatures that poured in for Sixsmith and Salt's address read like an archaeological geo-phys of Carpenter's wide-ranging circles. From the early days of school, Cambridge and University Extension came the explorer Henry Cotterill, Edward Anthony Beck, who had become Master of Trinity Hall, the Ford sisters, and Carpenter's fellow lodger in Leeds, the economist Herbert Somerton

Foxwell, who praised his old friend's poetic and prophetic powers.[3] Carpenter's socialist and anarchist networks of the 1880s and 1890s brought in Bernard Shaw, H.M. Hyndman, Ramsay MacDonald and the Webbs. His participation in the suffrage movement produced a similarly eclectic response. Feminist signatories included Margaret Ashton, Charlotte Despard and Lady Constance Lytton, as well as the Lancashire campaigner for homeless women, Mary Higgs. The literary and artistic figures who signed ranged from those in regular contact, Henry Nevinson, Holbrook Jackson, Gerald Gould, John Gambril Nicholson, George Ives, to those who knew him through friends or by reputation, John Masefield, H.G. Wells, W.B. Yeats, William Rothenstein and Gwen John. Among the international contingent were Olive Schreiner, the Batthyánys, Magnus Hirschfeld, Guido and Ella Ferrando, George Herron, Horace Traubel, John Burroughs, Jane Addams, Jack London and two poets from India, Rabindranath Tagore and Sorofini Naidu.[4]

Alf Mattison walked from Totley on the 29th to find Carpenter, visibly moved, surrounded by piles of letters and telegrams. Throughout the day local boys were kept busy bringing more and more. Carpenter read out extracts to him, chuckling over the promise of a present from the eccentric Maharajah Chhatarpur who had so discomfited the Webbs by demanding that Carpenter and Merrill be sent out to him from England. 'I hope it's not an elephant', joked Carpenter.[5]

Two hundred and ninety-seven names made it onto the address. Carpenter marvelled at how Sixsmith and Salt had got hold of so many people and loved its 'varied character'.[6] It was fitting that an address to Carpenter was signed by so many friends who were not part of the celebrated great and the good: the Hukins, Albert Fearnehough, Lucy Adams, former lovers Joe Potter and Jim Shortland, the Millthorpe handyman Charlie Roughton and a socialist migrant to New Zealand, Joseph Kirkpatrick, who sent news of John Furniss, the Christian Socialist quarry-man and communitarian farmer. Carpenter had given him money to help him emigrate and he was now farming in the wilderness near Huntly.[7] Some were too old to respond with ease; Joseph Friedenson, Max Flint and Alf Mattison's friend from the Leeds Jewish Socialist League, wrote in a shaky hand, sending greetings to their 'Dear Comrade'.[8] Bundles of letters continued to arrive after the birthday from people who had been away on holiday or on long ocean journeys to give speaking tours in far flung parts.

All these loving testimonies had been eclipsed before they reached Carpenter by Britain's declaration of war with Germany on August 4th. 'One can think of little else', Carpenter wrote to Sixsmith on August 31st.[9] Emotionally overwhelmed by the extraordinary response to the

Henry W. Nevinson, 1914

birthday address, he found it hard to grasp how so much warm, human feeling could be accompanied by bloodshed. In London the following week, Carpenter sought out Henry Nevinson to talk about the war. Nevinson gave a dinner for Carpenter at one of his favourite restaurants, Brice's in Old Compton Street. Among the guests were other United Suffragists, Evelyn Sharp and Barbara Gould. After dinner Carpenter and Nevinson went to Evelyn Sharp's rooms, still talking about the war.[10]

These discussions were vital to Carpenter, who was struggling to find his bearings. An event as decisive as war made his predilection for staying on the fence difficult indeed. Later that month he started writing in an effort to comprehend the madness that had engulfed them. Though it had seemed to happen so suddenly, he wanted to stand back and trace its roots. Drawing on lectures given by the historian H.A.L. Fisher, the Vice-Chancellor of Sheffield University, Carpenter came to the conclusion that Germany had been the aggressor. Though he was careful to qualify this verdict with the assertion that no nation was a homogeneous entity.[11]

Carpenter noticed how the attitudes of local people hardened over the next few months. Initially there had been little support for war with

Germany, however reports of atrocities committed by German soldiers in the invasion of Belgium fanned a hatred of all Germans.[12] Carpenter tried to counter this hostility; Kathleen Bunting remembered him visiting her mother in Holmesfield and insisting 'It's not the people. It's not the people.'[13] Carpenter maintained a sceptical attitude to the veracity of the reports of brutality, but he did respond with profound emotion to the suffering of Belgium. When asked to contribute to a book produced by the *Daily Telegraph* for the Belgians from 'representative' global figures, he tried to bring solace by intimating that their 'devotion and heroism' could contribute to a new, better Europe.[14]

Carpenter set out to understand not only the diplomatic, but the emotional and psychological factors which contributed to war. In December 1914, writing in the now weekly *Herald* which was edited by the United Suffragist Gerald Gould, with George Lansbury, Carpenter engaged with patriotism. Describing himself as 'International' by temperament, he nonetheless suggested that such cosmopolitanism could be 'empty and arid'.[15] Most people were not to be jumped out of a narrow circle of life, which consisted of their families and neighbourhoods, into internationalism. He thought that socialists needed to distinguish between the external corrupt manifestations of a flag-waving patriotism and a deep love of country. This 'deeper' patriotism contained a positive core in its sense of attachment to particular places while extending ideas of service outwards beyond kin and friends. He saw it as an interim phase which could constitute a basis for the wider values of internationalism based on 'our common humanity'.[16] Coincidentally Carpenter's article appeared a few days before the German and British soldiers sang carols, played football and exchanged food on the battlefront that Christmas.

Early in 1915 he was attempting to apply his reading of the recent literature on crowd psychology to the causes of war. People went along with their leaders because of powerful emotions, habits, instincts, myths. It was necessary to get down to these deep roots in order to tackle warlike feelings; the process of healing had to arise from the base of the 'Tree of Life'. He did not think 'Peace societies and Nobel Prizes and Hague Tribunals and reforms of the Diplomatic Service and democratic control of Foreign Secretaries and Quaker and Tolstoyan preachments' were sufficient to plumb such depths.[17] Carpenter was referring to the pacifist movement and to the Union of Democratic Control (U.D.C.) formed by E.D. Morel, Charles Trevelyan and Ramsay MacDonald, which was critical of the undemocratic diplomacy which had preceded the war.

Carpenter's efforts to stand back and maintain space for thinking without supporting or opposing the war, appealed to many other troubled and indecisive people in Britain. His essays were published as *The Healing of Nations and the Hidden Sources of their Strife* in March 1915. Stanley Unwin selected a quote, 'The Tree of Life . . . whose leaves are for the Healing of Nations', and put it on the austere wartime cover. Unwin had to reprint the following month. He continued to reprint the collection until 1918, and Charles Scribner's produced an American edition in 1915. In an Appendix, Carpenter included an extract from the French novelist Romain Rolland's declaration 'Above the Battlefield' which had been produced in pamphlet form in English in 1914. Carpenter was in accord with Rolland's interpretation of nationalism: 'Love of my country does not demand that I shall hate and slay those noble and faithful souls who also love their country, but rather that I should honour them, and seek to unite myself with them.'[18]

Rolland, who hated barriers between peoples, was compelled to voice his opposition from neutral Switzerland, and, in Britain as well as in France, it was becoming more and more difficult to stay above the combat. Carpenter's *Healing of Nations* was rejected by a London bookseller who equated its tolerant tone with being pro-German.[19] Even the devoted Sixsmith was upset by Carpenter's remarks about the responsibility of the commercial classes for the war.[20] The war pushed some people towards polarised certainties. Several of Carpenter's literary acquaintances – Alfred Orage, John Galsworthy, John Masefield, G.K. Chesterton and Israel Zangwell – signed up to promote the war effort, along with the historian George Trevelyan. Laurence Housman, like Carpenter, did not oppose the war initially, but was disturbed by the manner in which political events began to permeate personal responses and relationships. He regretted how the outlook on the war became the determinant, pushing other allegiances into the background and pulling people who were for or against it apart.[21] But division was hard to avoid. Henry Nevinson was exasperated with his friend Israel Zangwell for agreeing to help the war effort. Nevinson disliked militarism and what he called 'patriot slush'.[22] In some cases families were split; George Trevelyan's brother Charles left the Liberal government when war was declared, resulting in a painful estrangement between the two brothers. Over time some people's attitudes shifted. Patriotic Ashbee and sceptical Lowes Dickinson, at loggerheads in 1914 on the war, set off with Housman in 1916 to the US to campaign for a League of Nations. Several of Carpenter's friends were decisively opposed to the war, including E. Bertram Lloyd, Isabella Ford, Fenner Brockway, Richard Hawkin and Olive Schreiner. Schreiner was disappointed that Carpenter did not side more strongly with the anti-war groups, however he was unsympathetic to both religious and left pacifism.[23] He was not at all purist in temperament and wanted to direct any criticisms of the war at a great swathe of decent, tolerant compatriots. Psychologically averse to isolation, Carpenter's inclination was towards union, nevertheless political circumstances were making his usual strategies for avoiding polarised conflict more and more convoluted.

It was Bertram Lloyd who managed to draw Carpenter towards the outer reaches of the anti-war milieu. Lloyd, being a great joiner, belonged not only to the British Society for the Study of Sex Psychology, the I.L.P. and the Humanitarian League, but to a group initiated by Fenner Brockway's wife Lilla in November 1914, the No-Conscription Fellowship (N.C.F.).[24] In June 1915, Lloyd related to Carpenter how he had stepped in to organise a 'Conference on Pacifist Philosophy' because he foresaw a muddle and could not bear waste. Neither could Carpenter, and he found it impossible to say no to Lloyd, who gently mooted that Carpenter might be one of the speakers. Carpenter had initially spluttered over the term 'Pacifist Philosophy' but the diplomatic Lloyd persuaded him that the event would help people 'clarify their minds on the underlying issues'.[25] Lloyd accomplished a minor coup; when Carpenter spoke at Caxton Hall on 'War and Peace in Human Happiness: A Backward and a Forward Glance', he attracted the largest attendance in a distinguished line-up. Around five hundred people crowded in to hear Carpenter tell them that a new era of mutual aid would arise from the misery of war. The Conference on Pacifist Philosophy brought together many of his old friends and acquaintances, including Isabella Ford, Patrick Geddes, Laurence Housman, along with G. Lowes Dickinson who was already envisioning how a League of Nations might arise from the ashes of war. Two formidable anti-war intellectuals, Bertrand Russell and J.A. Hobson, who would be on the fringes of Carpenter's circle during the war, were also present.[26]

Carpenter's position as a visible figure, nationally and internationally, along with the political and intellectual circles in which he moved, made it difficult for him to maintain his stance of transcendent neutrality. Throughout the summer and autumn requests to speak kept arriving. He confessed to Charlie Sixsmith that he was extremely reluctant to pronounce either way on the war; in August 1915 it seemed too early for a definitive view.[27] While he found it difficult to express his thoughts on the war in general, he was adamantly opposed to proposals to introduce conscription which he equated with Prussianism.[28] Carpenter's fulminations earned him a stiff rebuke from the Conservative *Morning Post* which accused him of insulting Britain's allies and soldiers. 'Does Mr Carpenter uphold our cause or does he condemn it?'[29]

The question was ominous and carried a concealed threat. Those who were not fervent warmongers started to be branded as pro-German. Nonetheless, Carpenter dutifully responded to requests to speak on 'War and Peace' in the autumn of 1915, giving his vague spiritual sustenance, sometimes accompanied by anthems, hymns and Handel, to the Sheffield and South Place Ethical Societies, the Croydon Humanitarian League and to the Leeds and Folkestone Theosophists.[30] That October all men of military age were required to 'attest' that they were willing to serve. Faced with huge losses of men in the war and an excess of enthusiastic volunteers from essential areas of the labour market, the new coalition government was seeking to rationalise recruitment. Carpenter, like many other people, regarded this as a first step on the way to conscription, towards which he adopted a stand of decisive resistance.

Carpenter's approach differed from that of Romain Rolland, who opposed the war but was of the view that if one accepted a war, state-enforced conscription was reasonable.[31] Carpenter maintained Rolland had been deceived by the Northcliffe newspapers, an odd interpretation of Rolland's French conception of the citizen and the state.[32] For the Englishman individual conscience must always be the supreme authority: 'If there is one thing which we all, I think, believe in it is that every man and woman should be free to act according to the dictates of his or her conscience', Carpenter declared in November 1915.[33] This was his message to the No-Conscription Fellowship Convention in December. The *Labour Leader* reported it being received with 'particular warmth' when it was read along with greetings from Charles Trevelyan, Ramsay MacDonald and Philip Snowden.[34] In the 'no-conscription' cause Carpenter had found his issue. From this point he was drawn politically towards the opposition to the war.

In December 1915 Carpenter received disturbing information from Stanley Unwin. An Inspector from the Criminal Investigation Department had called to say they had received a complaint about *The Intermediate Sex* and, having bought a copy, CID were agreed that its contents were indecent and unfit for publication. Thinking on his feet Unwin asked the police to mark the passages and bring the book round.[35] There was an oppressive feel in the air. D.H. Lawrence's *The Rainbow* had been suppressed that November, and the magistrate, who regarded Lawrence's views on the war as disgraceful as the 'filth' in his novel, had specifically mentioned the chapter in which Lawrence alluded to a lesbian encounter. As the chapter is entitled 'Shame', Lawrence was not exactly proselytising.[36] The situation was dangerous for Carpenter. The stock of books were his property as well as his copyright, consequently the cost of a prosecution would have to be borne by him. Carpenter was well aware that if a case were brought it could easily go against him and told Unwin that as a last resort they should agree to sell *The Intermediate Sex* under a medical or magisterial endorsement.[37] However to limit sales in this way would be a tremendous setback, a political defeat as much as a commercial loss. It must have seemed as if the wartime mind-set was reaching into every crevice of consciousness.

Carpenter responded to this brush with the state by composing a formal letter in defence of *The Intermediate Sex*, pointing out that the book had been in circulation since 1909 as well as being in the Bodleian, Cambridge University Library, the British Museum Reading Room and many provincial libraries. Moreover it had been praised by 'school masters, medical and legal men, ladies, even mothers'.[38] He also enclosed a leaflet containing extracts from the reviews. In a private letter to Unwin on December 10, 1915 Carpenter suggested explaining to the police that these topics were now 'talked about quite freely at Oxford and elsewhere', and, for good measure, provided his publisher with a list of eminent people who could testify to his respectability.[39] Carpenter's intriguing bevy of 'referees' included the Head of Eton, three Liberal politicians, Lord Haldane, Augustine Birrell and Sir W.P. Byles, along with his Fabian friend, Sir Sydney Olivier. Professor Gilbert Murray, Sir Oliver Lodge and G. Lowes Dickinson represented the academy. From the medical profession came two Red Cross doctors, Hector Munro and Haden Guest. Then there was Cecil Chapman, the prominent London magistrate who supported the B.S.S.S.P. Carpenter also put down the name of Sir Edmund Gosse whose poems he and Charles Oates had admired in the early 1890s. Now an establishment figure, Gosse had an honorary post as librarian to the House of Lords. The folklorist Francis Walter Jekyll appeared too. After returning from Jamaica Jekyll had worked in the Department of Printed Books at the British Library until 1914. Then he served in the Ministry of Information from 1917–20. However next to Jekyll's name, Carpenter pencilled in 'H.O.' Either Carpenter muddled the dates or Jekyll did have some connection to the Home Office in 1915 which was not put on record.[40] Anyway Carpenter clearly considered that the well-connected Jekyll's name would carry weight with CID.

The fierce B.S.S.S.P. activist Stella Browne told Havelock Ellis she had wanted to write a letter to the *New Age* but Carpenter had forbidden her, saying they were trying to find out who had instigated the prosecution. She had to console herself that at least Unwin had 'played up about it'.[41] Unwin had gone in gentlemanly fashion, directly to the Assistant Commissioner of Police, Sir Basil Thomson.[42] For Thomson subversives grew like 'toadstools' and spouted like 'geysers', his anxious eye scrutinised anarchists, syndicalists, socialists and pacifists along with members of the N.C.F., the

U.D.C. and the National Council for Civil Liberties.[43] Unwin's 'battle-royal' with the Assistant Commissioner consisted of two strategic prongs.[44] He sought to establish Carpenter's respectable credentials with explanations of the contested phrases and references to illustrious friends, while flattering Thomson's literary aspirations. Thomson had earlier been Prime Minister of the Friendly Islands (Tonga), a colonial outpost Unwin had happened to visit himself. He also happened to consider Thomson's *The Diversion of a Prime Minister* one of the best books ever written on Tonga.[45] Whether it was Unwin, Tonga or the respectables who saved Carpenter is uncertain, but Sir Basil backed down and a triumphant Unwin was able to wave the eminences of the birthday list at the Assistant Commissioner. In a letter to Ellis, an irreverent Stella Browne wondered whether the Home Office had feared that *The Intermediate Sex* might endanger the innocence and virtue of the conscripts.[46]

A bill for compulsory military service was introduced in January 1916. But the non-conformist Liberal conscience being a mighty force to be reckoned with, Herbert Asquith conceded exemptions on the grounds of family or business, ill-health or conscientious objection. Bertram Lloyd, who understood Carpenter most cannily, never pushed the No-Conscription Fellowship overtly. Instead he sent Carpenter personal accounts of how objectors were being treated.[47] Carpenter, who loathed conscription and censorship in equal measure, was troubled by a raid on the office of the Russian Seamen and Firemen instigated by the Tsar's intelligence service, and by the news blackout when Charles Trevelyan came up to Sheffield to speak for the U.D.C. in March.[48] He sent a message of support to the Sheffield No-Conscription Fellowship and received reports that the large April N.C.F. Convention in London had 'passed off all right'.[49] 'NCF looming large', Carpenter noted in his diary on April 20th.[50] In May, Miles Malleson, the left-wing playwright and actor, wrote to him about seventeen conscientious objectors being sent to France where they could have been shot. In this dramatic instance the N.C.F. managed to get a deputation to meet with Asquith.[51] The draconian powers of the wartime state were sometimes offset by such bizarre personal interventions because some of the opposition and some of the pro-war politicians knew one another through Liberal and Labour Party contacts.

'I wonder how you feel about the war', wrote an evidently uneasy Sydney Olivier, back from being Governor of Jamaica, and now Secretary of the Board of Agriculture and Fisheries. His hopes of socialism dashed, Olivier had become a 'fight-to-the-finisher'.[52] Carpenter was moving in a quite different direction in response to conscription, censorship and the ban on exporting written or printed material not only to enemy countries, but to neutral ones too. In 1916 there were police raids on the offices of the Independent Labour Party, the Union of Democratic Control and the Women's Labour League. When Fred Henderson's radical bookshop in Charing Cross Road was also raided, copies of Miles Malleson's anti-war plays were seized, one of which included an introduction by Carpenter.[53]

In these overtly repressive circumstances Carpenter's benign, gentlemanly style would no longer wash. In a lecture in Sheffield he recounted how his niece, a nurse in Serbia, had been taken prisoner and treated with chivalry by Austrian and Hungarian officers. This personal anecdote was deemed subversive and his lecture was not reported in the local papers that had always covered his meetings. He had to resort to *War and Peace*, the journal edited by the pacifist Norman Angell.[54] Carpenter no longer spoke vaguely about alternative interpretations of patriotism. On June 11th, in a letter to a soldier in the King's Royal Rifles, called George Clemas, he exploded in exasperation, 'Oh when will this idiotic nonsense cease.'[55]

This was his mood as he began work on a passionate protest against war, *Never Again*, which described the bodies of the soldiers on the beach at Gallipoli and evoked the sufferings of the Jews of the Russian Pale, 'hounded homeless in winter', along with the 'cry of the black and coloured peoples of the earth'. Carpenter decried the waste of war. 'Great Britain has already spent on the war enough to provide *every* family in the whole kingdom with a comfortable cottage and an acre of land.' He now believed the point of no return had been reached; 'Construction', a new international solidarity based on love, was the only hope for the future.[56] Though *Never Again* was his declaration of emotional revulsion, Carpenter could bolster his polemic by drawing on his extensive collection of news cuttings and pamphlets. His library included material by H.A.L. Fisher, Charles Trevelyan, E.D. Morel and G. Lowes Dickinson, and an account by the American reformer, Jane Addams, of her interviews with the foreign ministers of Europe as part of an international women's peace mission. As ever, his friendship networks were a vital resource. Constantine Sarantchoft supplied him with E.L. Minsky's translation of Russian Duma speeches published by the Jewish Labour League.[57] The horrors of Gallipoli came first hand; Nevinson had been there as the *Manchester Guardian*'s correspondent. The question was how could *Never Again* be wriggled past the censor? Carpenter sought the advice that July of both Unwin and Nevinson. Nevinson not only know about battlefields, he understood the politics of the London literary scene. He advised Carpenter not to publish *Never Again* as a supplement to the left-wing *Herald* and also proposed some changes.[58]

Over the summer and autumn of 1916 the political climate polarised. When Nevinson and Carpenter met, the journalist was distraught about the imminent execution of the Irish patriot Roger Casement who had been charged with treason.[59] Nevinson admired Casement's stand against slavery in Africa and mobilised friends to protest, including Carpenter, who received a formal reply on behalf of the Prime Minister from M. Bonham Carter dated July 18th, containing the hollow promise that his letter would be considered.[60] None of the pleas for Casement was, of any avail, including one entreating mercy on the grounds of his 'mental irresponsibility', organised by the novelist Arthur Conan Doyle.[61] Carpenter declined to sign Conan Doyle's memorial on the grounds that he had already written on Casement's behalf.[62] When the government released information from Casement's diaries which recorded homosexual relations with men and 'native boys', controversy raged over whether these were genuine or British intelligence dirty tricks. Nevinson took the position that the revelations were not relevant to Casement's trial.[63] Rumours of Casement's homosexuality had apparently already reached Carpenter, for an enigmatic entry in Carpenter's diary dated November 7, 1915 records that a friend of Casement's, Sidney Parry, came to see him at Millthorpe. 'Talk about Casement (? homogenic)'.[64] On August 3, 1916, Carpenter wrote simply 'Roger Casement hanged!'[65]

In the autumn of 1916 *Never Again* was passed by the censor and published by Allen and Unwin. It circulated internationally and was translated into Norwegian, Swedish and Japanese. [66] Marcelle Senard did a French translation under the pseudonym of 'A. Marsen', but because dissent was tightly controlled, it was published in Switzerland. Carpenter's scepticism about the war reached those who were caught up in it and those who opposed outright. Léon Bazalgette read *Never Again* just before he departed for the front.[67] The popularity of *Never Again* appears to have disturbed the authorities; the anti-war Jacques Mesnil suspected Carpenter's letters were being intercepted because of long delays.[68] Despite his initial caution, as 1916 drew to a close, Carpenter had moved into the anti-war camp.

From autumn 1916 Carpenter began to press for peace negotiations. In a letter to the Liberal *Daily Chronicle* in October he challenged Lloyd George's reported resolve to fight to the finish. The German people, announced Carpenter, were swinging away from jingoism towards distrust of their government.[69] It is not clear on what basis he came to this conclusion, though it was true that President Woodrow Wilson's peace moves seemed to be received sympathetically in Germany, but then the Germans had been doing rather better than the allies in the conflict. G. Lowes

Dickinson, Ashbee and the U.D.C. all had high hopes of Wilson in 1916. In an article in the *Nation* in February 1917, Carpenter argued that the Straits should be internationalised, a proposal that was one of Wilson's fourteen peace points.[70] Early in 1917 Carpenter was not only in touch with the radical editor of the *Nation*, Nevinson's colleague H.W. Massingham, he was also calling on Bertrand Russell, whose opposition to the war and participation in the No-Conscription Fellowship meant he was being closely monitored by the government.[71]

While the Labour Party supported a fight to the finish, Lloyd George's government faced opposition, not only from the peace movement but from workers. Sheffield, in the winter of 1916–17, was at the centre of resistance to the 'combing out' of skilled engineers which fed into a wider mood of industrial unrest. Motorcyclists spread the strike message to munitions centres all over the country and the thoughtful Jack Murphy emerged as a leader of the rank-and-file shop-stewards movement. The Ministry of Munitions countered with an intelligence network of informers, who sometimes acted as provocateurs. Among these was the shadowy figure of Alex Gordon, a spiritualist and former member of the British Socialist Party, who went under several pseudonyms. Posing as a conscientious objector, Gordon made contact with one of the Sheffield shop-stewards, Walter Hill, who invited him to a meeting, put him up for the night and gave him money to get to Glasgow. In his report to the Ministry of Munitions, Gordon described Hill as a 'follower of the prophet Edward Carpenter, a socialist "head-light"'. He also asserted that Hill was an advocate of the Homogenic or Comrade Love preached by Carpenter. Gordon claimed that Hill had threatened King George and Lloyd George and that Carpenter was 'a menace to morality and recruiting'.[72] Early in 1917 when the left-wing Labour MP, W.C. Anderson (also under surveillance by the Ministry of Munitions) tried to persuade Hill to speak out against the dubious Alex Gordon, Hill was afraid of something else in his own character being exploited – presumably his homosexuality.[73]

Industrial militancy combined with revolution in Russia. 'Wonderful Week', wrote Carpenter in his diary in March 1917, rejoicing in the rise of the Duma.[74] That June, he recorded a 'Pro-Russian Conference in Leeds'.[75] This was the extraordinary occasion when excited delegates, including such unlikely figures as Ramsay MacDonald, called for Workers and Soldiers Councils or soviets in Britain. The stirring of hope on the left was accompanied by a wider suspicion in the country at large of the political leaders, especially Lloyd George, who seemed so intent on maintaining the conflict.

The poet Siegfried Sassoon voiced these pervasive doubts in his celebrated letter of defiance in July 1917. Instead of a war of defence, they had become embroiled in one of 'aggression and conquest'.[76] Addressed to his commanding officer, Sassoon's letter also went to Carpenter, along with a small group of other people whose opinions Sassoon respected, including Thomas Hardy, Uncle Hamo Thornycroft and Harold Cox. Carpenter responded enthusiastically: 'Well done good and faithful! Let me know if I can be of any use in the matter. I shall be in London for a few days or so, and could see you if feasible.'[77]

In contrast, most of Sassoon's friends, including Robert Graves, regarded his letter as a betrayal of his fellow soldiers. Graves contrived to get Sassoon before a Medical Board and the rebel was sent up to Scotland for treatment at Craiglockhart War Hospital by the psychoanalyst Dr Rivers. Sassoon wrote to Carpenter in August from Craiglockhart saying he did not know how long he would be there. 'I am glad you think I have done a little good.'[78] But Sassoon brooded on the men still fighting and dying. In October he was in better spirits, joking about the 'elephantine RAMC Colonels' at his Medical Board. He assured Carpenter that he had only consented to go to Craiglockhart because 'I should otherwise have been sent to a proper lunatic place.'[79]

Events continued to push Carpenter into protests against the government. The U.D.C. activist E.D. Morel was arrested under the Defence of the Realm Act (DORA) for sending two of his publications to Romain Rolland in Switzerland. Carpenter responded angrily with a doggerel verse, 'Ballad of the Bodkin and the Musket', satirising Morel's prosecutors, and made copies for Sassoon, Nevinson, Lloyd and Mrs Morel.[80] When neither the *Labour Leader* nor the anti-war *Cambridge Review* would publish his satirical rhyme, Carpenter had it printed at his own expense. He also wrote to the Home Secretary contesting Morel's imprisonment.[81] As the wartime state edged closer and closer towards individuals' lives and actions, Carpenter became increasingly rebellious. The all-pervasive Leviathan must have evoked the treatment of Wilde and the anarchists.

But alongside the libertarianism which flared up in response to injustices, Carpenter still inclined towards broad initiatives. Towards the end of 1917, when the Unionist Lord Lansdowne sent a letter to the *Daily Telegraph* arguing for a negotiated peace, Carpenter's hopes of a settlement were renewed. Though Lansdowne's intervention did not alter government policy, it did establish a basis for a broader group beyond the anti-war movement to gather behind the vague slogan of a 'negotiated peace'. On December 28th the Parliamentary Committee of the T.U.C. and the National Executive Committee of the Labour Party held a joint conference.

A sub-committee produced a memorandum on war aims, calling for the democratisation of foreign policy, an end to secret diplomacy, international limitations on armaments and the establishment of a League of Nations.[82] Carpenter, who attended the conference, was delighted that the demands of the U.D.C. and Lowes Dickinson's dream of a League had been taken on by the official Labour movement. He wrote to his soldier confidant, George Clemas, declaring what an interesting conference it had been and asserting that the Labour men were the only sensible politicians going at the present.[83] Ironically Lloyd George, who sorely needed Labour support, was quite happy to fudge any differences.

Yet still the war went on. Carpenter took heart from revolutionary Russia's decision to give up fighting. What could be more sensible than putting the needs of the people for food above war? he asked in the *Herald* in March 1918. He thought Russia's action proved the point he had made in *The Healing of Nations*; social conflict within combatant countries could be a force for peace; this 'rising democracy' carried the seeds of a new global order.[84] This was exactly the kind of message the readers of the *Herald* wanted to hear, but it cut no ice with Carpenter's friend George Clemas in his Winchester barracks. Now a sergeant, Clemas wrote saying that he could see no signs of the rising tide of protest of which Carpenter wrote. Nor did he believe that the high death toll would have any impact on the politicians.[85]

In the spring of 1918 the state landed metaphorically on Millthorpe's porch. On April 12th Carpenter recorded in his diary that the age of call-up had been extended to the age of fifty-one.[86] This meant George Merrill was liable for military service. Carpenter, appalled that 'the dirty paw of the state' was reaching out for his friend, sought advice from Harry Doncaster, a member of the local wealthy Quaker family which had protected Carpenter in the past.[87] Harry Doncaster was now a magistrate and familiar with the procedures for appealing. An agitated Carpenter wrote Doncaster's instructions out carefully twice in his diary: 'Appeal to be written by G.M. on ground of agricult' [sic] work at Millthorpe extent of fruit farm absence of assistance. Health not good. 20 years helping me run the place.'[88]

Doncaster advised against seeking conscientious-objector status. When it came to Merrill there were to be no political heroics. Somewhat illogically, given what he had observed of the wartime state over the last few years, Carpenter took it personally. 'The very idea of our little oasis being broken up is intolerable.'[89] Instead of the lofty higher patriotism of 1914, Carpenter simply wanted to hang on to George. On July 24th the two men went to Derby for Merrill's medical examination full of dread.

After three agonising hours of suspense, he was pronounced Grade IV and discharged on health grounds.[90] All those nights in the Royal Oak had stood George Merrill in good stead.

That summer a letter came from Sassoon. After Dr Rivers' therapy he had returned to his regiment, the Royal Welch Fusiliers, in Palestine and then been sent to France where he had received a head wound. 'I don't think I shall be allowed to go to the Front again; and apart from my craving to be with the men, I can't see that it would do much good.' He had been offered a desk job in munitions but wanted to be an ordinary worker, ideally in a Sheffield factory. Inspired by the close comradeship he had experienced with other soldiers in the army, he had found the means of expressing the union Whitman and Carpenter intimated in his own poetic idiom. Carpenter's emphasis on emotional and experiential knowing over the intellect appealed to Sassoon: 'I know nothing about Labour, except that the whole world depends on it. And I'm one of those people who can only learn things by coming in the closest possible contact with them. Books tell me nothing.'[91] Sassoon was puzzled to find that all sorts of obstacles were put in the way of his scheme to work in a Sheffield factory.[92] The powers-that-be no doubt considered that the now celebrated war poet and the militant shop-steward, Jack Murphy, would be an undesirable combination. Instead Sassoon was given six months' 'home service' with the Ministry of Information and lionised by such lions as Winston Churchill, T.E. Lawrence and Thomas Hardy. In between the pomp and circumstance, he did contrive to escape into the arms of a young soldier in a Margate hotel, pouring out all his long-suppressed feelings into the poem 'Lovers'.[93]

Sassoon's longing for personal union, along with his ambiguities about duty, service and loyalty, were all profoundly comprehensible to Carpenter, who was moved by the sense of comradeship which many soldiers expressed. He had met the two Walter brothers, Karl and Wilfred, friends of the Woolwich I.L.P. Grinlings and the Russian Tolstoyan Tchertkoff before the war.[94] Anarchist Karl, declared medically unfit, ran a small magazine, but Wilfred was in uniform and a sergeant by 1916 when he described this personal comradeship graphically in a letter to Carpenter. He marvelled at the extraordinary mix of men he found himself amongst. 'Sharp humorous Cockneys . . . superb big grousing Highlanders . . . sweet spoken lads from the Western Counties . . . burly miners . . . East County farm hands.'[95] Soldiering broke down class distinctions and a solidarity emerged amidst the misery and horrors of trench warfare.

Carpenter's patriotism was emotionally charged by the readiness of such men to sacrifice their lives for a remote collectivity. Moreover, he was attracted to soldiers, and strong hints of Theban romance infused his good works during the war. In 1915, on an obligatory familial visit to Gloucestershire, Carpenter spent a week in a Y.M.C.A. tent at a local barracks with George Merrill. This enabled him to meet up with soldiers and go on walks with them.[96] Then there were the wounded, loyally attended by compassionate citizens at Sheffield's King Edward VII Hospital. Carpenter's visits to the sick there went beyond the norms of charity. One man to whom he gave his photograph sent 'heaps of love and kisses' and mentioned a 'Malcolm' who had visited Millthorpe. 'I hope you enjoyed him coming to see you.'[97] This was not quite what the authorities envisaged from patriotic visits.

Carpenter developed two new intimate relationships with men in the army. The correspondence he had begun in 1915 with the former board school teacher, George Clemas, who he nicknamed 'Clem', briefly flared as a physical attraction and mellowed into a lifetime's friendship. Another close soldier friend was a socialist from Leeds, Joseph Hobson, whose letters hint at something more than a political friendship. In 1917 Hobson asks whether Carpenter would prefer him not to attend his lecture for the Leeds Theosophists and says he is thinking of visiting Millthorpe again, 'Just to have a look at you, and the remainder will have to be sweet memories and pleasurable anticipations.'[98] Hobson, a miner's son, had volunteered for the army, though he was repulsed by the drinking and swaggering of his companions, observing that they appeared to have a mistaken idea of manhood.[99]

Carpenter had gone to great efforts to detach himself from his family and had little in common with them apart from Alfred. Still he must have felt gratified when Ellen (Nelly), now Lady Hyett, wrote from Painswick House, Gloucestershire, to congratulate him on *Never Again* in October 1916. She, too, felt a revulsion against the indiscriminate hatred of the German people.[100] Even so, Carpenter's family traditions exerted an unspoken pull towards patriotism. The strength of the naval heritage became more pronounced in wartime. Ellen's husband Francis worked for the Admiralty during the war. Then there was brother Alfred's son, Captain Alfred Francis Carpenter, who as Commander of the *Vindictive*, became a hero in 1916 when his cruiser filled with concrete was sunk, leading a flotilla of vessels to block the U-boat base at the Zeebrugge canal. Holmesfield was bursting with pride when the *Daily Sketch* did an article on 'The Fighting Carpenters' which featured the rather weedy-looking young nephew, Alfred Francis, in naval cap, brother Alfred, stern and impressive as a veteran of the Sudan, father Charles Carpenter, vaguely lauded for his 'eventful career', and a broad-faced Admiral James Carpenter who the paper described as renowned for his exploits under Rodney in Dominique.[101] Carpenter approached the 'Fighting Carpenters' with jocularity; nonetheless he offered to send Alf Mattison a copy of the *Daily Sketch*.[102]

Loyal to the men fighting, yet feeling a growing revulsion towards the war, Carpenter tried to empathise with the contrasting choices made by friends, family and political associates. This was not so easy for they were very much at variance. If Olive Schreiner, Isabella Ford, the Glasiers, Ramsay MacDonald, Margaret Ashton and Bertram Lloyd lined up in the anti-war movement, there was Olivier in the government along with the trades unionists, C.T. Cramp, George Barnes and J.R. Clynes, all three of whom revered Carpenter. Even the intransigent Hyndman was serving on the Food Committee, while Tom Mann opposed conscription but wanted Britain to win the war, and Stephen Reynolds had been given a job he loved as a Fisheries inspector.[103] Outside Britain there were similarly divergent and confused responses. Sanshiro Ishikawa, following Kropotkin, sided with the allies against Prussian militarism.[104] In Italy Biagio di Paulo resisted heroically, but eventually went into the army where oddly he found a calm he had not known in civilian life.[105] George Herron's pacifism had transmuted into a steadfast support for the Allies against the Prussian state. He wanted America to engage and from 1916 began writing articles in this vein in *Clarion* and the *New Age*, as well as in the French press. Towards the end of 1917 the American Ambassador in Paris asked him to send reports to the State Department, and Herron became Wilson's negotiator in Europe.[106] In contrast Romain Rolland was a vocal opponent of the war, and so too was Jacques Mesnil.[107] Marcelle Senard eventually moved to Switzerland, but when war broke out she threw herself with aristocratic verve into running a hospital for the wounded and suggested that Merrill and Carpenter might come over to help.[108] Writing to Sanshiro Ishikawa, who was thinking about nursing in June 1915, Carpenter announced that he and Merrill were having similar thoughts!

Carpenter was inclined to invest both soldiers and protestors with heroic status, but this did not prevent him accepting the decisions of friends who devised strategies for hiding from the war, carrying on as if it were not happening. The artist Harry Bishop, tucked away in Tunisia in 1915, wrote bemoaning 'the infernal war'.[109] Roger Fry, for whom the war seemed like a bad dream, concentrated on keeping his Omega craft workshops going and finding jobs for conscientious objectors.[110] E.M. Forster hid for a while in the National Gallery, cataloguing, until he wangled his way to Egypt as a 'searcher', finding out the names and addresses of dying soldiers.[111]

Though Carpenter felt uneasy when he met Bertram Lloyd's friend, the B.S.S.S.P. member, Harold Picton, who he thought was pro-German, he loyally sustained conscientious objectors as outcast anti-hero types.[112] Characteristically he did not distinguish between those like Count Ervin Batthyány and Bertram Lloyd, who were prepared to do alternative forms of work, and the absolutists who refused to help the war effort and were put in prison. Carpenter was sympathetic to Lloyd when he sought exemption from a London Military Tribunal in March 1916, while the absolutist Richard Hawkin, the Sheffield I.L.P. supporter who had tried to defend Carpenter from O'Brien, could also rely on Carpenter's support.[113] For Hawkin refusing to fight was to bear moral witness; a defiance of the few against the many. He told the Sheffield No-Conscription Convention in March 1916, that those who resisted conscription would never receive applause from the multitude or be remembered.[114] Called up in April, Hawkin went on the run, often turning up at Millthorpe which was a popular port of call for conscientious objectors.[115] In the summer of 1917, when Hawkin was imprisoned in Wormwood Scrubbs, Carpenter wrote in sympathy.[116] When the letter was returned he forwarded it to the writer Alison Uttley, with a broad hint, 'I see that Dick can have a letter and a visit.'[117] He also spoke out in support of Fenner Brockway, put in solitary confinement in 1918 for smuggling out an article to the *Manchester Guardian* and encouraging other prisoners to resist.[118]

Despite his respect for those who believed it their duty to fight, over the course of the war Carpenter abandoned his initial ideal of a higher patriotism carrying social values. He told Harold Picton, whose oppositionist views had come to seem less extreme, 'It's time is past; it begins to stink.'[119] But Carpenter was not a pacifist, nor did he share the absolute opposition to the war expressed by a minority of socialist C.O.s like Hawkin and Brockway; his ferocity was aroused in defence of liberties.

Carpenter's response to the war was not politically consistent, and like many others, he shifted over time. By April 1918 he was describing it as 'this abomination of desolation'.[120] His ambiguous reaction is emotionally intelligible and was shared by others. Above all he wanted to remain connected to his 'mass people' and they, by and large, supported the war effort and died for reasons unclear. Carpenter struggled to maintain a space for dialogue through his writings, his lectures, and by opening Millthorpe to combatants and non-combatants alike. Through those four long years Carpenter clung on to two amorphous hopes. Somehow an oasis of alternative sentiments and values was to be preserved and somehow a new era of humanity would arise from the mud and blood of the battlefields.

21

Hope Against Hope

The war was not confined to battles and diplomacy, or even to the lives of those directly affected through military service. It suppressed cultural expression, not simply through external censorship, but through an internal paring down of what could be imagined. The wartime mentality wrenched its way inexorably into the psyche and into personal relations, bringing its harsh 'joy of hatred', and corroding hope.[1] Carpenter recognised this penetration of being and existence from the start, observing to Charlie Sixsmith in August 1914 how hard it was to 'clean the slate of one's mind' and write on anything 'except battle and bloodshed'.[2] Carpenter responded by trying to preserve Millthorpe as an oasis of comradely continuity and openness. He countered the war's reach through his friendships and political networks by persisting with his discussions and lectures and by struggling to write on sexual and social liberation. Dreams of alternatives and wry humour were mustered from his arsenal of psychological resistance. It was a Canute-like defiance; circumstances beyond any individual's control kept sweeping his efforts away. Yet, somehow, amidst death, grief and despair, he kept raising his small symbolic islands of lifestyle, politics and ideas. As year followed year, these became especially precious to the war-weary.

Millthorpe survived as a refuge for old friends like Bob Muirhead, Robert Sharland from the Bristol Socialists, Jim Shortland, Alf Mattison, Charlie Sixsmith and Joe Potter along with his brother-in-law, Willie Hopkin, who had somehow managed to become chairman of his local tribunal while supporting his friend D.H. Lawrence's opposition to the war.[3] Among Carpenter's newer friends were George Clemas, Sidney Lomer and Gilbert Beith, a shy, admiring Red Cross ambulance driver who became one of Carpenter's literary executors. Another new contact who would figure in Carpenter's life over the next decade was the Norwegian translator of *Towards Democracy*, a bespectacled Illit Gröndahl.

If any spies from the Ministry of Munitions had been lurking by the

Millthorpe

gate they would have been confused to see men in uniform along with conscientious objectors like Bertram Lloyd and Richard Hawkin. The promiscuous mix of visitors to Millthorpe persisted: academics, musicians, artists, literary figures, birth-control campaigners, local people and eccentrics. Sometimes they all appeared at once. On June 20, 1915, the Vice-Chancellor of Sheffield University, H.A.L. Fisher, came to tea, when a local woman, Mrs Lumby, and her three children dropped in to tell Carpenter of their problems. Carpenter's neighbour, Harry Doncaster, Professor Geldart, an advocate of women's higher education from Oxford, and a young man from Holmesfield, Charlie Nield, also crammed into Millthorpe that day.[4]

Carpenter could adapt to diversity and was well practised at being the considerate host, even though he found some guests a little difficult. His relationship with Florrie Mattison was somewhat uneasy, but when she paid a rare visit in 1918, Carpenter made a gallant effort and complimented her on the new costume she had just made, much to the delight of Alf.[5] He was less tolerant when his sister Alice appeared, burdened with clothes. An irritated Carpenter managed to divert her to Fannie Hukin's and vanish to London for part of her stay.[6] Millthorpe still acted as a magnet for bizarre folk towards whom he remained genially benign. One night in June 1915, Carpenter and Merrill were flummoxed to discover a young woman asleep under the lilac; she had walked from the South Midlands to pay homage, sleeping out along the way.[7] Then there was a follower of Thomas Davidson, the inspirational force behind the Fellowship of the New Life, who seemed quite mad.[8]

The behaviour of the hosts too could be unusual. A reverential group from a Nottinghamshire mining town were bemused to see George Merrill dancing a jig in the road as they left and telling them to leave a drop of ale for him at the pub.[9] Merrill also startled Henry Nevinson by leaping naked over the grass one sunny morning in May 1917, announcing blithely he was going to wash his feet.[10] Millthorpe's back garden continued to serve as a mini-nudist colony; Carpenter at 73 still enjoyed his sunbaths and cold sponge-downs on the lawn, blithely unaware that young Mary and Kathleen Bunting, along with other village children, were in the habit of peeping at the strange goings-on with inquisitive interest.[11] Nevertheless, as he grew older some of the practical disadvantages of the slightly damp, hastily built house did affect him. When the boiler broke down he would head off to the Hukins in Holmesfield or the Potters in Sheffield for a hot bath. Though his market gardening enabled him to sell and exchange vegetables, fruit and eggs, he had to hire a local man to help. Maintaining Millthorpe as a place of resuscitation for others required considerable effort, even though Carpenter always insisted that he lived as he lived simply in order to please himself.

His emotional attachment to the villagers had deepened over time. It was important to him that he was asked to chair the meetings of the Farmers' Association, and attend the ploughing contests. Local people depended on him too; he gave advice, witnessed will, Daddy Key's bought baby clothes with Merrill for Mabel Key's baby girl, Margaret Annie in 1917, and loyally visited an ailing Arnold Allcard, whose name appears in his Common Place Book, alongside a quotation from Plutarch about the 'Chaste Desire' of the Thebans.[12] These everyday bonds and continuities assumed a precious significance in wartime. Nonetheless the war did affect life at Holmesfield and Millthorpe. Mabel Key now collected Henry Nevinson in the pony and trap from Dore and Totley station, because the young men in the family were fighting in the war; and George Croft, who helped Carpenter with the fruit and vegetables, waited apprehensively for news of a missing son.[13] In July 1917 young Charlie Nield, home on leave, came to visit with a local girl, Nellie, full of tales of soldiers throwing down their rifles and being fired on by order of the officers. He and Nellie sat by the brook making daisy chains.[14] By October Charlie Nield had been wounded; on November 2nd Carpenter recorded his death.[15]

The surfeit of grief over the thousands dying in combat blanched out ordinary emotions. Two members of Carpenter's family died during the war. First his brother George, and then his sister Sophy. He was not close to either of them, regarding George as a rather seedy and pathetic figure and Sophy as domineering.[16] However her death, aged 83, in January 1918, was particularly distressing because it was preceded by a long-drawn-out period in which she had been 'silent and wandering'.[17] 'Sophie oblivious', Carpenter recorded in his diary on August 1, 1916.[18] His older sister's bleak isolation was evident at her funeral; few came to mourn her.[19] Carpenter adopted his familial role as financial organiser, telling the musician Granville Bantock that he was 'torn about (like everyone else these days) with endless affairs and complications'.[20] The numbness extended to his own old friends; despite having been concerned about Edith Ellis' undeniable mental distress, her death in September 1916 evoked little emotional response, though of course he sent condolences to Havelock who was wracked with guilt because he and Edith had become estranged.[21] Edith Ellis had wanted Carpenter to speak at her funeral, but Carpenter told Ellis he was booked to address socialist children in Sheffield and could not get to London.[22] He did, however, send Ellis a Preface for her book, *The New Horizon in Love and Life* (1921).[23] When Carpenter's unfulfilled Cambridge love of long ago, Edward Anthony Beck, died in the same year, something did stir. Carpenter had kept his youthful poems, etched in pain and frustrated desire, and started revising them during the war.[24] Time ineradicably was passing.

One searing loss, however, burned right through the protective psychological lethargy induced by the war. It changed Carpenter's life and profoundly affected his relationship to Millthorpe. On Tuesday March 13, 1917, the day after Carpenter hailed the rise of the Russian Duma, George Hukin visited Carpenter who was ill in bed with a severe bronchial complaint, caused by a visit to Sarantchoft in an arctic Bournemouth.[25] On returning home, Hukin found the steep hill from Millthorpe to Holmesfield hard going.[26] He suffered an asthma attack and four days later, when George Merrill called, Hukin, too, was sick in bed with bronchitis.[27] Self-effacing and considerate as ever, Hukin sent a message on March 20th telling Merrill not to leave 'Ted'.[28] But a day later he was weaker and desperately asking for them both.[29] Carpenter could not get out because a heavy snowstorm was raging, but Merrill got through with some grapes and flowers that Charlie Sixsmith had sent for Carpenter. Merrill found Hukin very weak but overjoyed to see him and left one of Sixsmith's carnations with the grapes.[30] On Thursday 22nd Carpenter struggled out of bed and reached the Hukins' home. He was too late; George was already unconscious.[31] At 11 p.m., in a frail hand, Carpenter wrote a postcard to Sixsmith: 'Grieved to say that G. H. passed away an hour ago.' The doctor's diagnosis was poignant; Hukin's heart at fifty-seven was 'worn out'.[32]

The following day Carpenter stayed at home, unable to move, 'suffused with the thoughts of 30 years'. George Merrill, always emotionally direct and demonstrative, wept through the night; he too had come to love and depend on George Hukin's calm unassuming integrity. Over the next few days Carpenter and Merrill huddled together with Fannie, the Sixsmiths and the Salts united by their grief.[33] Though Carpenter and the Salts' relationship was strained, Kate knew intuitively what Carpenter needed to hear and he cherished her words. 'I feel all the time that you have gathered him into your arms forever – and he, you! Nothing can ever disentwine you now.'[34]

On March 26th in the snow, with a cold wind blowing, they buried George Hukin in a grave nestling by the hedge at the outer edge of the churchyard in Holmesfield.[35] Carpenter delivered a short statement, written in a trembling hand. Retreating behind distanced phrases, he described Hukin as a 'well-known and much loved resident of the village', and explained how he had retired from razor-grinding in 1910, earning a living by gardening and taking photographs of local people.[36] Carpenter and a few other mourners knew how the carefully chosen words were replete with inner meanings which could not be disclosed. After the funeral he sifted through his precious bundle of letters from George Hukin, while George Merrill kept looking out over the fields, expecting the man who had shared his love of Carpenter to appear. But Hukin would never take the short cut from Holmesfield again.

Old habits died hard. When Carpenter returned from his trips to London he used to call in at Fannie's, just as he had done when George was alive. Yet, the ache of Hukin's absence was everywhere, in the familiar places around Millthorpe and within himself. Hukin's photograph on the wall looked shyly down, the visible memorial of all those years of love. Before the war Carpenter had been inclined to doubt a personal immortality, regardless of his hope of lover's meeting. Though aware of research into psychic phenomenon, he had kept his distance. However, the mass bereavement of wartime was boosting the popularity of spiritualism and, after Hukin's death, the yearning for contact proved stronger than any theory. When a shell-shocked soldier friend, Herbert Mills, described his experiences with mediums, Carpenter's interest was aroused.[37] To the envy of a curious George Ives, Carpenter attended several séances early in 1918, including one that was incongruously disrupted by a Zeppelin raid, before he finally felt that he had reached Hukin.[38] He may also have glimpsed the spirit of his former love in the two sympathetic young soldiers who became part of his intimate circle. Joseph Hobson, the Leeds socialist, went straight to his heart when he admired Hukin's photograph, and George Clemas echoed one of Carpenter's deepest sentiments when he wrote saying 'Life without affection is nothing worth.'[39] Nonetheless, Millthorpe, without Hukin nearby, would never be the same.

During the war Carpenter's family responsibilities kept taking him to London, and he accrued a growing number of friends in the area for whom he felt a close affection. Among them was a young man called Harold Coxeter, who Carpenter entrusted with the statement he wanted to be read at his funeral. Coxeter used to drive Carpenter and Merrill from the station to their rooms at 18, Cartwright Gardens, a crescent off the Euston Road between St Pancras and King's Cross. Carpenter's London base, which faced onto a communal garden, was a friendly companionable place, popular with I.L.P. members and trades unionists visiting London on political business.[40] To Henry Nevinson's sophisticated eye, number 18 'resembled a shabby boarding house', but Carpenter, allergic to luxurious surroundings, considered it quite smart once a bit of new paper and paint were applied.[41] He and Merrill did explore a house in Golders Green in December 1917, but decided it was too dreary; Cartwright Gardens was anyway far more convenient than the new West London suburbs.[42]

Carpenter grumbled about the fog, filth and smells of London and complained that Zeppelin raids made continuous work impossible, nevertheless, he enjoyed the random encounters of a big city. He would wander down to Trafalgar Square to observe the Canadian soldiers. On one occasion he chanced upon two soulful 'fitters' under Waterloo Bridge who had read *Towards Democracy* and, on a summer day in 1916, met a delightful 'frisky' bus conductor.[43] Surprises lurked within London's smog including a moment of bohemian sybaritic glamour, a jolly champagne supper in Chelsea where most of the guests stripped off and jumped into a big bath. Carpenter was careful to assure 'Clem', confined to barracks at Winchester, that Merrill and he had not leapt in.[44]

Henry Nevinson's worldly know-how about the journalistic and literary scene, along with his stimulating conversation and networks, comprised another attraction drawing Carpenter to London. On Carpenter's part there may have been more than just pleasure in their mental compatibility, for as they walked back from St James's Park one evening in July 1916, Nevinson sensed that when Carpenter suggested they sit down some kind of 'affectionate display' might ensue and hurried Carpenter back to Cartwright Gardens. However the formality of their political, literary friendship had been breached, enabling them to talk more intimately of homosexuality. When Carpenter confided that he was 'heavily weighted' on that 'side', Nevinson replied how he liked the world of men, but all his passionate friendships, since his school days, had been with women.[45] Then he related an anecdote he had heard as a war correspondent of an Albanian custom of male marriage; just the kind of story that intrigued Carpenter.

Any physical consummation of their close friendship was laid to rest that July evening; Nevinson henceforth was simply 'a splendid chap' for Carpenter.[46] The straight-backed, manly Nevinson, whose war wound and persistent ailments, combined with his sensitivity, endowed him with the requisite touch of erotic vulnerability, remained a favourite with Carpenter. Moreover Nevinson and the radical intellectuals in his network helped Carpenter to work out his ideas and provided him with new outlets for his writing in the war. The United Suffragists constituted the core of this loose circle which spanned out into left journalism and a web of radical groupings. Gerald Gould, George Lansbury and Evelyn Sharp on the *Herald* voiced the opinions of a broad anti-war left. Nevinson's friend, S.K. Ratcliffe, who Carpenter had met at Fry's exhibition, was in the sceptical South Place Ethical Society, which included other Nevinson associates: J.A. Hobson, the anti-imperialist writer, Delisle Burns, a radical academic, who Carpenter described to Charlie Sixsmith as 'an interesting fellow', and Norman Angell, the pacifist editor of *War and Peace*. Then there was H.W. Massingham editing the *Nation*, which took a more cautious approach to the war.

Carpenter enjoyed hobnobbing with Massingham, Gould and Lansbury in the offices of the *Nation* and the *Herald*.[47] It was a throwback to those animated discussions during the 1880s in the offices of left journals. He was finding all kinds of welcome oases within London, dining with Nevinson at Brice's in Old Compton Street or patronising a coffee-house popular with the literary down-at-heel called St George's, round the corner from Cecil Court, in St Martin's Lane, where the coffee was good and cheap and games of chess were played in a smoking room upstairs.[48] In January 1918 Carpenter recorded visiting a stylish haunt of the radical intelligentsia, the 1917 Club in Gerrard Street, Soho, and he often made his way to Fred Henderson's Charing Cross Road anarchist bookshop, the 'Bomb Shop', to see how his books were selling and add to his already extensive library.[49] *Love's Coming of Age* and *The Intermediate Sex* went down particularly well with Bomb Shoppers.

Another congenial port of call was 'The Attic', Miles and Constance Malleson's little flat in Bernard Street, decorated in simplified style with whitewashed walls, green paint on the floors and curtains made from cheap, vivid East African cloth.[50] When they decamped to 6, Mecklenburg Square in 1917, they were still conveniently close to Cartwright Gardens.[51] The Mallesons' open marriage was based on their interpretation of *Love's Coming of Age* and they had put up Carpenter's photograph in pride of place in the flat. Their friends included another Carpenter fan, the long-legged bohemian, Captain Jack White. White, an outspoken supporter of the Irish Citizen Army as well as free love, was an escapee from an illustrious military family. The Mallesons' networks crossed the N.C.F. and the U.D.C.; they were in touch with Bertrand Russell as well as Charles Trevelyan and his brother Robert, E.D. Morel and Arthur Ponsonby, all of whom moved into the outer rim of Carpenter's acquaintances during the war.

Bertram Lloyd, Carpenter's other connection to the N.C.F., was also his main informant on the doings of the British Society for the Study of Sex Psychology. The B.S.S.S.P. was an important source of intellectual contacts for Carpenter, and the discussions on sexual questions at its meetings served as a buffer against the consuming exigencies of war.[52] Its membership overlapped with other societies, the 1917 Club, the Malthusian League, and the Eugenics Society. The Society contained a strong contingent who wanted to change attitudes and laws relating to homosexuality which included George Ives, Charles Kains Jackson, Laurence Housman and the conscientious objector, Harold Picton, along with new sexual theorists like Eden Paul and psychoanalysts such as Barbara Low and Ernest Jones. Several of Carpenter's old acquaintances attended meetings, among them were Cecil Reddie from Abbotsholme and, until her death in 1916, Edith Ellis. Havelock Ellis was not a member; he preferred to emanate approval from a distance. Stella Browne, the doughty Canadian campaigner for women's sexual freedom, kept him informed of the B.S.S.S.P.'s doings. She along with Bertram Lloyd and George Ives continued to form an informal triumvirate who ran the day-to-day business of the Society.

Carpenter, like Ellis, had never been a joiner, yet he did come down for B.S.S.S.P. meetings quite frequently, attending one on 'War Babies' with E.M. Forster in April 1915.[53] Later that year he celebrated the death of the censor Comstock, the bane of American free lovers, birth controllers and sex reformers, by going to hear a paper by Stella Browne arguing for the diversity of women's sexual desires.[54] Like Carpenter, Browne believed that the transformation of sex and society was integrally linked. And, like him, she was aware of the need for new forms of cultural expression, noting the lack of a 'sexual vocabulary' to articulate women's feelings.[55]

B.S.S.S.P. meetings were sociable as well as intellectual occasions. In July 1916 Carpenter took George Clemas to one addressed by E.S.P. Haynes; George Ives and Edith Ellis were also there, along with a young man called Leonard Green, who later became one of Carpenter's literary executors.[56] Green's first collection of short stories, Dream Comrades (1916), featured a comely homoerotic Christ as a Pagan symbol.[57] However, the prevailing ethos of the B.S.S.S.P was one of no-nonsense earnest rationality. Bertram Lloyd recounted with pride a particularly frank debate on masturbation at one meeting.[58] Carpenter missed that one, but he did go to Eden Paul's paper on 'The Child' in 1918, which crashed through another taboo, childhood sexuality.[59] Eden Paul, a member of the I.L.P., was a friend of Stella Browne's and, like her, later joined the Communist Party. He did not accept Carpenter's assumptions of congenital homosexuality, believing instead that everyone was potentially bisexual, an approach Carpenter shifted towards during the 1920s. Regardless of their disagreements, Eden Paul generously acknowledged the older man's contribution to dispersing 'a fog of prejudice which still obscures our views of sex'.[60]

B.S.S.S.P. members saw themselves very much as fog-dispersers too, but beyond the fog their views were too diverse for concerted action on the lines of Hirschfeld's Committee. They did put pressure as a Society on the British Museum for greater public access to the proscribed books tucked away in the library's 'cupboard', but this had minimal effect. In 1917, Stella Browne, with support from Carpenter and Barbara Low, pushed for a meeting on sex instruction in schools. In February Carpenter drafted a submission to the Minister of Education and Barbara Low headed a B.S.S.S.P. study group on the topic.[61] On this, as on many other issues, the Society could not agree; the B.S.S.S.P.'s strength lay in raising issues for public debate rather than lobbying for change.

Intense internal wrangles occurred within the Society over how to disseminate their ideas. George Ives, who had been shaken to the core by the Wilde trial, was inclined to be cautious and highly secretive. Bertram Lloyd clashed with him in 1915 over whether the names of the committee members should be printed.[62] They were at loggerheads again in 1916 because Ives wanted B.S.S.S.P. pamphlets to be sold only to members of the legal, medical and clerical professions.[63] In contrast, Stella

Browne was always in favour of militant evangelism as well as action. Bertram Lloyd tended to act as the mediating go-between.

In general Carpenter was in broad agreement with his dear 'Wolf', except on the birth-control advocate Marie Stopes. When Carpenter read the manuscript of *Married Love* in May 1916, he responded enthusiastically: 'You certainly get in a lot of important points – menstruation, positions, ejaculation without penetration, birth control, insemination etc – which will terrify Mrs Grundy; but she poor thing, is in a very moribund condition already so the book may only hasten her end.'[64] A protective and slightly startled Carpenter even wondered whether all these important points might best be published initially in French. Early in June he was quite charmed by the arrival at Millthorpe of 'Mrs Stopes with Rücksack', and sat in the garden reading *Married Love* with her. Carpenter approved not only of the manuscript but of this light-travelling advanced woman's 'eager quick mind'.[65] He presented her with his *Visit to a Gnani*, a copy of *Intermediate Types* and an introduction to Bertram Lloyd. Stopes and Lloyd's meeting proved disastrous; Lloyd found Stopes' high opinion of her own scientific credentials to be arrogant, and her disdain towards the B.S.S.S.P. as amateurs utterly exasperating.[66] Carpenter, nevertheless, was happy to endorse *Married Love* when it was published in 1918.[67]

A moment of thought might have made Carpenter realise that the individualistic Marie Stopes was unlikely to cohabit happily in the same organisation as the individualistic and left-wing Stella Browne. But Carpenter studiously disregarded factional disputes among the birth controllers by being benignly even-handed to Browne, meeting her for supper at the Espresso, bailing her out financially when she was in crisis, and reading her manuscript on the French novelist Colette.[68] Carpenter was similarly amicable towards Browne's friend Margaret Sanger. In 1914, on trial in the United States for giving birth-control advice, Sanger had jumped bail and fled to Liverpool. From there she made contact with Carpenter in a roundabout way through his old Whitmanite networks; a recommendation from Horace Traubel had resulted in a letter from Charlie Sixsmith to Havelock Ellis. Ellis was entranced by the pretty modern woman from across the Atlantic and he, in turn, wrote to Carpenter about the fugitive who had worked with the 'advanced socialists'.[69] They met in the Egyptian room at the British Museum in January 1915 where Sanger poured out her plans for research into birth control and sexuality.[70] That September, before she returned to the United States to face trial, Carpenter signed a statement to President Wilson defending Sanger's work.[71] When Sanger asked Carpenter to contribute to her *Birth Control Review* in 1918 she referred to the 'great strides' made in the birth-control movement, insisting,

'Much of this success we owe to you for the seeds that you have sown in opening the minds of the people through your books and articles on the sex subject.'[72]

Though Carpenter did not write any new books explicitly on sexuality during the war, he did contrive to smuggle sex into his other writings. In *The Healing of Nations* (1915) he opposed the heartless justification of war as a means of reducing population. Instead he supported 'family limitation'. While Carpenter had advocated Karezza-style lovemaking without the male orgasm, he came to accept the practical need for the 'preventative checks' of contraception. In *The Healing of Nations* he linked birth control with 'Eugenic and healthy conditions of child-rearing and nurture' which he said demanded small families.[73] In early twentieth-century Britain eugenics was gaining adherents not only among those on the right who wanted to prevent the poor from breeding supposedly unfit stock, but among socialists, feminists, sexual reformers and birth controllers who saw it as the key to new model people for their new model world. Carpenter adopted this approach when he urged the working class not 'to play into the hands of the dividend-hunting rich by increasing the supply of cheap labour, while at the same time the general standard of the population becomes more and more degraded'.[74] Like many people at the time he did not stop to consider the repressive or elitist aspects of theories of reproductive perfectibility.

When Carpenter published *My Days and Dreams* in 1916 he slipped in a little vignette of zany paganism. The emancipated future would see 'the freeing of Woman to equality with Man, the extension of the monogamic Marriage into some kind of group-alliance, the restoration and full recognition of the heroic friendships of Greek and primitive times'.[75] He also edged towards a personal statement of his sexual feelings in his observation on the pernicious consequences for a person of his 'temperament' of 'the absence of marriage or its equivalent'.[76] Reviewing *My Days and Dreams* in the *Herald*, Gerald Gould remarked on Carpenter's 'quiet, unconscious courage' in tackling sexual questions.[77] This courage, combined with his refusal to judge, encouraged confidences. A Miss Fairbanks wondered in 1917 whether he could find a 'helpmate' (sex unspecified) for her.[78] Sydney Lomer expressed his distress at being separated from his orderly 'Georgie' with whom he was smitten.[79] E.M. Forster despatched a photograph of his love Mustapha, an Egyptian tram driver.[80]

The sexual politics of war were contradictory. Officially 'acts of indecency' and 'sodomy' were severely punished in the armed forces, but the unusual circumstances of military life enlarged the crevices for relationships between men flung together in circumstances which mocked conventional notions of morality.

The authorities responded with sex information which was surrounded by dread and fear, rather than the erotic happiness propagated by Carpenter and other optimistic libertarian sexual reformers. After George Clemas saw one of the social hygienists' melodramatic propaganda films, *Damaged Goods*, in 1917, he panicked and decided he had caught V.D. Carpenter, characteristically bland about bodily ailments, reassured him that it was just a touch of eczema which had flared up in response to the repression of his physical feelings for his fellow soldier, Joe.[81] Carpenter was perhaps not the best of medical advisers but his unflinching commitment to expelling guilt was a key element in the therapeutic role he assumed within his circle. 'I could not tell this to another man except you, dear Edward – no other would understand', wrote Clemas when his love Joe was sent to the front. 'Others do not know my real self at all, they see only the mask that covers me.'[82] As the Conscientious Objector, Harold Picton, put it, 'Edward helped many to understand themselves.'[83]

Carpenter's tenacity in thinking about pleasure and freedom, his personal courage and his readiness to listen and help, encouraged idealisation, and his relationship with Merrill was often construed by journalists who did not know the couple well as a romantic union between the man of Nature and the spiritual, intellectual sage. Both Merrill and Carpenter gave credence to this notion of mutual complementarity. When Carpenter told the Irish writer James Cousins that George Merrill never read his works, Merrill chipped in 'I am like the boy who would not eat jam because he worked where it was made.' Cousins cast Merrill as the passive muse, concluding that the key to their relationship was that Merrill *lived* Carpenter's writings.[84] This idealised picture contrasted with the reputation that continued to hover around Merrill in the village and among some of Carpenter's close friends. Henry Salt was particularly hostile, regarding Merrill as a crude, overbearing schemer.[85] According to Salt, Merrill spoiled their friendship, a breach which Kate felt particularly deeply.[86] In 1917, after a long period of tension between the two households, the Salts sold up and went back down South.

Between the two extremes, E.M. Forster and Henry Nevinson provide the most insightful assessments, being well-disposed to Merrill but sufficiently close not to idealise Carpenter and Merrill as a couple. Forster, who remembered the inspirational touch which had released *Maurice* with affection, told his confidant Florence Barger that despite Merrill's lack of education, he had a great respect for him, adding wryly that he had never taken to

Merrill's much-praised cooking which always made him ill.[87] The sharp-eyed Nevinson noted Merrill's mixture of 'knowledge and ignorance' and was impressed by his intuitive quickness as well as his enthusiastic singing.[88] Their comments indicate the psychological acuity which led local work-ing-class women to confide in Merrill and made Carpenter dependent on him in everyday dealings with people. Merrill's perceptive capacity appeared too in a responsiveness to music, drama and novels. While Merrill may not have read Carpenter, he was happy to go to plays by Maeterlinck and Ibsen, and enjoyed reading Thomas Hardy and Jack London. Carpenter borrowed D.H. Lawrence's *The Rainbow* for Merrill from Willie Hopkin in 1916. There was more to the Nature man than met the eye.

Carpenter, the great revealer, was scrupulously discreet about Merrill, and only a few short notes and letters by Merrill himself survive. They confirm Nevinson's impression that he was devoted to Carpenter. But just a few hints suggest that their relationship was more complicated than it appeared on the surface. 'All right again with G.M.,' Carpenter noted in his diary on March 27, 1916.[89] As the two men had been together for twenty years, some quarrelling was hardly surprising. However, Merrill had been jealous of Walter Seward who had been visiting the previous month, and may well have resented George Clemas in whom Carpenter was becom-ing so interested. Clemas had sent his photograph in January with an admiring letter, and that spring he enclosed primroses, picked on a long walk in Dorset in which he had been thinking of Carpenter. Expressing his happiness in meeting Carpenter in the flesh, the young soldier avowed, 'Now I have known your body, and I am very glad. I was not disappointed.'[90] He felt the hours spent with Carpenter had been the most precious in his life. Clemas posted his sonnets to Carpenter and was soon being addressed affectionately as 'Clem' and elevated to 'dearest boy'.[91] Carpenter discussed their mutual attraction, tickling his jealousy with tales of other young men like Biagio di Paulo. They exchanged rings. By July a flirtatious, teasing Carpenter was telling the young soldier, 'I am wearing your ring now; but of course I like to wear G's sometimes.'[92] Clem proved more diplomatic than Walter Seward, tactfully negotiating a connection to Merrill by request-ing photographs of both of them. Nonetheless an inquisitive Dr Johnston 'Perceived a change in George', in October 1916.[93] Merrill need not have feared. The initially physical passionate relationship between Carpenter and Clem transmuted into an intimate friendship and before long Carpenter had assumed a tutelary role, introducing Clem to *Phaedrus* and integrating his love Joe into the Millthorpe inner circle.

Through his encounter with Carpenter George Clemas came to recog-nise his own sexual feelings. Shy and in awe of Carpenter at first, he became more confident, though he was alarmed by the frankness of *Intermediate Types Among Primitive Folk*, *Ioläus* and *Towards Democracy*. While prejudice existed, a nervous Clemas wondered if it was wise to hand them to just anybody.[94] The reticent Clem found a special place in Carpenter's affection because he could be confidently at ease with him. He trusted Clem emotionally, expressing his sadness and psychological need when George Hukin died by urging Clem not to forget 'your loving friend'.[95] This new loving friendship had the effect of demoting Walter Seward; Carpenter was dismissing him as 'queer but honest' by September 1918.[96]

While Carpenter's sage-like demeanour tended to be equated with a transcendental spirituality which some contemporaries contrasted with the earthy Merrill, the division was misleading. The self-conscious and spiritual Carpenter was also sensuous and romantic. Resolutely untroubled by guilt about sexual encounters and with a discreetly roving eye, he was quite capable of being a bit of a flirt. At seventy-three he declared cheerily to Clem, 'I confess I always find my indulgences (wh.[*sic*] are rare) exhilarating and fortifying.'[97] Sex, being healthy and good for you, was beyond reproach.

Although Carpenter preserved the evidence of his relationships with various young men, George Merrill's response to their open relationship remains unknown. Carpenter did, however, leave several scattered hints about Merrill's independent friendships which indicate that during the war he and Carpenter went their separate ways more than in the past. Merrill visited not only the Sixsmiths but friends in other parts of the country. Then there was a sailor friend in Sheffield who the Leeds socialist and soldier, Joseph Hobson, teased Merrill about in a letter to Carpenter, 'I think he knows I would like to meet him.'[98] The sociable and resourceful Merrill acquired his own London network; the aristocratic Francis Walter Jekyll took him out to dinner in style at Simpson's. He was entertained by the friend of Ellis and Bishop, the Finnish academic and author of learned tomes on the family, Edvard Westermarck.[99] And in July 1916 Carpenter told Clem 'George is very happy in Harold Coxeter's warm affection.'[100]

Beyond these faint suggestions of George Merrill finding his own way, his private feelings about Carpenter's 'indulgences', or indeed of living always in the shadow of George Hukin, are uncertain. Apart from the short spurts of jealousy, outwardly he appears to have made do with whatever life turned up, including any opportunities for passing sex. Merrill's early life had induced pragmatism and he undoubtedly noted how the young men came and went, while he remained the bird in the bush. Merrill would be aware that he, and sometimes members of his family, were completely dependent on Carpenter economically. However, Merrill was both resourceful at getting by and freedom-loving; it was not merely

practical necessity which bound him to Carpenter. Whatever he felt about
Carpenter's romancing he never revealed any hurt or humiliation to the
people who idealised their relationship. The love between the two companions at Millthorpe may have been more complicated than the myth, but
it was deep and real enough. On the surface Merrill may have been reliant
on Carpenter but, when confronted with the possibility of losing Merrill
to the army, Carpenter's own need and dependence on Merrill came
through.

Somehow Carpenter managed to hang on to his broad utopianism throughout the First World War. In *My Days and Dreams* a vision of transformed
sexual relations is integrally connected to a fundamentally different social
order. He lambasted the Victorian era for its

> Commercialism in public life . . . cant in religion, pure materialism in
> science, futility in social conventions, the worship of stocks and shares,
> the starving of the human heart, the denial of the body and its needs,
> the huddling concealment of the body in clothes, the 'impure hush'
> on matters of sex, class-division, contempt of manual labour, and the
> cruel banning of women from every natural and useful expression of
> their lives.[101]

His autobiography reiterated the schemes for industrial villages, co-operatives
and local markets, the hopes of unpolluted air and rivers and dreams of
a radical new internationalism expounded in his earlier works. His accounts
of the odd people who trooped to Millthorpe displayed the ironic skill
in portraying people he had revealed in *Sketches of Life from Town and
Country*. Carpenter joked too about his anthology on friendship, *Ioläus*,
being mistaken for an oil firm. The humour was quite conscious. Carpenter
confided to Clem in 1917 that the actualities of wartime life were so
depressing, 'one has either to make fun of them or to dream oneself into
another world'.[102] The self-depreciating charm in *My Days and Dreams*
contributed to his following, but it also evoked scorn. In a review of the
book for the *New Age*, the hollow-cheeked Nietzschean, A.E. Randall,
who had jeered at *The Promised Land*, commented archly on Carpenter's
'quiet English chuckle at all fanaticism'.[103] This was a caricatured dismissal
of a man who had extolled outlaws, held forth on the meaning of pain,
and shown remarkable courage in his writings on homosexuality; nonetheless it resonated. The contempt was mutual; Carpenter referred to the
New Age critic as 'that ass Randall'.[104]

Carpenter acquired two more formidable antagonists than Randall:

D.H. Lawrence and Bertrand Russell, both of whom were willing their own alternatives to a war-torn world into being. Carpenter and Lawrence shared common influences and friends, but if Carpenter ever met Lawrence he did not remember, observing to Helen Corke, 'I have never met D.H.L. but should think he would be a rather "difficult" person.'[105] The two men, aware of one another through mutual friends, shadow-boxed around the edges of their overlapping circles during the war. Carpenter makes only a few scattered references to Lawrence. When he read *The Rainbow* he told Willie Hopkin he found the style forced, but regarded its censoring as ridiculous.[106] If he noticed that Lawrence named both Chapter X and Chapter XIV 'The Widening Circle', an odd echo of the poem 'Widening Circles' in the last section of *Towards Democracy*, he made no reference to it. The phrase is, after all, a general one and its use may well be coincidental.[107] A brief diary reference indicates that Carpenter was sufficiently interested in Lawrence's work to read his poems.[108] Carpenter did meet Russell through the anti-war movement and they moved in similar circles, though they were acquaintances rather than friends. Despite the tangential nature of Carpenter's contact with the two men a ferocious intensity was spluttering on the sidelines.

Early in 1915 Lawrence struck up a somewhat hectoring friendship with E.M. Forster and briefly grew close to Russell. Russell, increasingly alienated from Cambridge, was planning a series of lectures that summer on 'Social Reconstruction', a term which was coming into usage among radical Quakers and other opponents of the war. Lawrence, who was nursing his own schemes for social revolution and utopian communities, scrawled contemptuous amendments and comments on the synopsis Russell sent him in July. He attacked Russell for not accepting that 'hate and conflict' acted as a crucial catalyst for change. Evoking Whitman and Carpenter's 'exfoliation', Lawrence insisted 'every bud must burst its cover, and the cover doesn't want to burst'.[109] On September 25th Lawrence sent Russell a devastating letter declaring he was living a lie.[110] On the same day he announced to Willie Hopkin that he had had a violent split with 'Bertie Russell' because he could not stand the things Russell said.[111] Lawrence wanted Hopkin to help find subscribers for his anti-war magazine *The Signature*. Could Hopkin bring together the people around Sheffield who really cared, and would he make contact with Lawrence's ex-loves, Alice Dax and Jessie Chambers, to enlist their support?[112] Hopkin, who had been at Millthorpe with his brother-in-law Joe Potter that May and would go again in November, suggested approaching Carpenter. Lawrence replied on September 25, 1915: 'If you will send Edward Carpenter a leaflet, I shall be glad; though he is not in my line. But he may give the paper to some young creature.'[113] Lawrence's 'not in my line' is ambiguous; he could be referring to Carpenter's less clear-cut attitudes to the war, his patrician desire for union with workers, or his homosexuality.

An elliptic note in E.M. Forster's diary on September 9th suggests that Lawrence's response to Carpenter was not as detached as he implied in the letter to Hopkin: 'After Lawrence's remarks about Carpenter realise with regret that I cannot know him.'[114] Whatever Lawrence said to Forster struck so hurtfully that it is most likely to have been about homosexuality. Lawrence's feelings of attraction to men as well as to women, his conviction that sexual love between men and women was creative, whereas homosexuality was disintegratory, along with his recoil from the upper-class homosexual milieu at Cambridge, resulted in an explosive turmoil. Amidst such conflicting perceptions and reactions, he kept erupting with furious vehemence. So while the extent to which Lawrence was influenced consciously or unconsciously by Carpenter remains a matter for speculation, by 1915 it is evident that Lawrence wanted to cauterise any traces of the older man's thinking that may have remained.

Russell delivered his lectures in London during the spring of 1916, incorporating Lawrence's catalysts of hate and conflict in the printed version of *Principles of Social Reconstruction*. Russell had been edging towards an intellectual pessimism already, but Lawrence left his imprint emotionally. Lawrentian ideas of pain and cruelty resurfaced in the course of Russell's passionate courtship of Constance Malleson, which involved a philosophical assault on Carpenter's influence upon her. Constance Malleson had just begun her career in theatre and film under the stage name, Colette O'Niel, and was active in the anti-war movement. The two lovers met through their work in the No-Conscription Fellowship. After an N.C.F. convention in September 1916, Russell invited the beautiful twenty-one-year-old, defiantly committed to her politics and her acting, out to dinner. She, in turn, asked him back to the Attic.[115] They talked through the night, or rather Russell talked, sitting stiffly by the fire, prodding her assumptions. Love must be like the fire, not a timid refuge of tolerant mutuality. Life was not simple, nor was the spirit of socialism likeable. 'One lived with the pain of the world and with all the cruelty of it.'[116] Only by understanding the wild pain at the centre would one be able to search for something beyond what the world contained – something transfigured.

When he left, Constance Malleson looked at Carpenter's picture. 'Everything I had believed in had fallen away. Everything I had known and loved. I felt stunted and torn. I was crying.' Amidst her tears she realised 'Nothing was any good but courage. Soft things had no place in this world.'[117] It was not quite the end of Carpenter; in September 1917

Russell tried to convey to his 'heart's love' what he described as 'my religion'. He feared he had taken away from her something she had got from Carpenter. 'I feel you haven't yet quite got anything to take its place. I believe that together we could find something that would be truer and deeper, and take more account of what's grim in the world, but would be equally sustaining.'[118] In January 1918 Russell referred once again rather ruefully to her anguish in giving up Carpenter. By then the contrary philosopher had decided it was the humanitarian idealism he had assailed which had made him love her, as opposed to the more boisterous, ruthless aspect he was beginning to detect in the aspiring film star.[119] Their love was beginning to seem impossible.

In the summer and autumn of 1917, Carpenter, unaware of the dramatic imbroglios in which he featured off-stage, and fleeing the memories of Hukin at home, was back on the road with a new lecture topic. In his talks on 'The Liberation of Industry' he was full of praise for Bertrand Russell's *Principles of Social Reconstruction* lectures. 'Reconstruction' for both Russell and Carpenter spanned personal life as well as economics and politics. Ignoring Russell's solipsistic remark that men needed loving relationships that led to paternity, Carpenter expressed approval of his comments on creative versus possessive love.[120] The term 'Social Reconstruction' also encompassed the ideas Carpenter had been pursuing of a combination of unions, co-operatives and National Guilds as a means of extending and complementing parliamentary democracy. This current of thought had survived regardless of the war. Odon Por had written to Carpenter in May 1915 outlining similar plans of linking syndicalism with wider social 'reconstruction', and the National Guilds League was working on the same lines.[121] By 1917 local National Guilds groups were arguing for self-government at work instead of accepting that the role of unions would be purely defensive. Theories of direct action at work instead of a reliance on the state were being debated on the left and various versions of syndicalism and Guild Socialism were being aired in the *Daily Herald*.

Carpenter's views on 'The Liberation of Industry' consequently struck home, and his lectures for the Workers' Educational Association and the University in Sheffield, the Adult School in Chesterfield and, that haunt of the libertarian left, the Brotherhood Church in Southgate Road, Hackney, London, all met with an enthusiastic response. He recorded in his diary on July 22nd how an audience of three hundred people at the Brotherhood Church pelted him with questions.[122] He got off lightly; the following week a Pacifist conference held there was attacked by a patriotic mob! In September Carpenter took 'The Liberation of Industry' to another crowded meeting organised by the Leicester Independent Labour Party, gaining three new recruits for the I.L.P., and meetings at Manchester and Sheffield followed.[123] Early in November 1917, Granville Bantock, his composer friend who had become a Professor at Birmingham University, organised a triple bill in which Carpenter spoke on 'The Liberation of Industry' for the I.L.P., did 'Art and Life' for the Workers' Educational Association and expounded on 'The True Self' to a grander gathering at the University which included Bantock, the scientist Sir Oliver Lodge and the philosopher J.H. Muirhead. Questions had been raised in the Senate about Carpenter's visit, causing an anxious Bantock to enquire whether Carpenter would be dealing with the sex-problem. An amenable Carpenter had reassured him that sex was 'quite outside' the topics he would discuss.[124] He felt a special debt to Bantock, who had provided him with invaluable help on the music of his beloved choral composition 'City of the Sun'. Ironically Carpenter's next gig was a lecture on 'Rest' for the Leeds Theosophists, which attracted an over-flowing audience of five hundred people. By November 14th, a protective Bertram Lloyd was growing worried that the busy sage might be getting 'fagged out'.[125]

However Carpenter took his speaking engagements in trouper-like style. As well as being a means of assuaging his grief about Hukin, the lectures were dog and pony promotional events for his new book, published by Stanley Unwin in 1917, *Towards Industrial Freedom*. In this collection of essays, Carpenter grappled with the power of global capitalism which was enabling the combatant countries to sustain the war. Carpenter, like many socialists, thought the Moloch of international capitalism would eventually annihilate from within. But more immediately the spread of 'Taylorised' large-scale industry was devouring hopes of reviving creative crafts and local industries, leading him to the view that mechanical systems of mass-production may have to be retained for the interim because of their liberatory potential for greater leisure.

Carpenter's awareness of the need to develop transitions towards his utopian City of the Sun forced him to consider once again the vexed question of the state. Wartime conscription, censorship and surveillance had fostered his anarchic distrust of the state and emotionally he wanted a non-governmental society, free, communal and without fear. However, unlike many of the anti-state left, Carpenter's Fabian-like attention to specifics meant that the state kept moving back in. He needed it for the public ownership of the transport system, to secure shorter hours and the regulation of child labour, as well as for his afforestation and land-reclamation schemes. How else would the school-leaving age be raised and the farm colonies and training schemes which were to end unemployment be established? Indeed, as these projects for the unemployed were to be 'compulsory in some cases', Carpenter's non-governmental society needed some force to ensure that people did what they might not want to do.[126] Inclining increasingly to the Guild Socialists because they sought to counter the state by strengthening industrial and community-based forms of democracy, in *Towards Industrial Freedom*, Carpenter again proposed 'a *voluntary* collectivism working within and parallel with the official collectivism of the State'.[127] The essays in the book, mostly written before the war, were assembled in yet another attempt to signal what might be. He envisaged unions and co-operative societies producing and distributing goods, creating social forms of wealth; still believing that dreams could sustain alternative imaginative possibilities, he tried to indicate the intermediary shapes that change could take as well.

Ideas of social reconstruction, industrial democracy and a desire for the democratisation of international relations were flowing back and forth across the Atlantic. They appealed to American progressives, battered by the harsh suppression of dissent after the U.S. entered the war in 1917, but uncomfortable with revolutionary anarcho-syndicalism. In 1917 Charles Scribner's issued *Towards Industrial Freedom* in the States where it stayed in circulation into the 1920s. But after the brief spurt of hope for the left that accompanied the Russian Revolution, cynicism set in quite quickly on both sides of the ocean. Already in November 1918 Stephen Reynolds was remarking bitterly to Carpenter that they would only be able to reconstruct on 'lines dictated by the capitalist and governing classes'.[128] Notwithstanding, others, including the ever-sanguine Carpenter, hoped on.

Carpenter compared his books to old moles in *My Days and Dreams*, observing how they threw up heaps in the most unlikely places.[129] During the war they were circulating vigorously not only in the U.S. but in France and Italy, while Scandinavia was opening up, partly thanks to Illit Gröndahl. Enthusiasts still created his markets. Saikwa Tomita had translated *Towards Democracy* into Japanese in 1915, while Sanshiro Ishikawa translated *Never Again* the following year. The old moles were doing well in Britain during the First World War. Fourteen of Carpenter's titles were listed on the back of *The Healing of Nations* as still in circulation in 1915, and ten books were reissued between 1915 and 1916.[130] The birthday address and two eulogistic studies, Edward Lewis' *Edward Carpenter: An Exposition and an Appreciation* (1915) and A.H. Moncure Sime's *Edward Carpenter: His Ideas and Ideals* (1916), along with the numerous articles and reviews, assisted Unwin's promotional efforts.[131] The bibliography in *My Days and Dreams* records that the complete edition of *Towards Democracy* had sold 16,000 copies, *England's Ideal* 13,000 and *Love's Coming of Age* 14,000 by 1916.[132] Worldwide, *Love's Coming of Age* reached around 100,000.[133] Carpenter could afford one of his chuckles when a dismissive A.E. Randall sought to puncture the halo of praise by maintaining that Carpenter had only 'made publicly accessible trends of thought'.[134] Randall was right, though the sneer was unnecessary; Carpenter was an impressive synthetic thinker, and indeed, this was how he had reached a wide readership among workers as well as the educated middle classes. One of his skills lay in engaging with what constituted the current common sense and then steering what was assumed deftly leftwards. He possessed a redoubtable knack too of sliding subversion through the narrowest slits, a cunning diplomatic ability that Harold Picton noted him applying when arguing the cause of the intermediate sex.[135]

Carpenter's resolve to carry on thinking outside the bounds of war was remarkable. He kept on seeking his oases in the turmoil. In May 1918 he was confiding to Granville Bantock, whose music seemed so evocative of Pan, how he was trying to get together something on Paganism and Christianity, 'to the credit of the former'.[136] Nevertheless, he found working on this Pagan book difficult. 'One can only move slowly and fitfully, impeded and broken up at every step by distressing and hampering events.'[137] All he could do was to take heart from the spring blossoms and hope for real life in the future. Papton Adult School came to visit Millthorpe in June 1918, and Carpenter addressed them on the lawn on 'War and Reconstruction'; literature was distributed along with red poppies.[138] These Millthorpe poppies were symbols of a grassroots patriotism, for the mighty wartime state had overlooked the wounded men discharged from the forces, and two left-wing organisations had taken on their welfare: the National Association of Discharged Soldiers and Sailors (N.A.D.S.S.) and the National Federation of Discharged and Demobilised Soldiers and Sailors (N.F.D.D.S.S.). Only after the war would they merge into the more conservative British Legion, which institutionalised the red poppies as a support for ex-servicemen and their families.[139]

That last year of the war dragged painfully on, straining even Carpenter's sanguinity and resources for hope in reconstruction. At the end, on November 11th, he was numb with exhaustion, writing in the tiny handwriting he used in his small diaries, 'Armistice signed at 5 am. Fighting ceased at 11.0.'[140]

22

Reconstruction and Revolution?

The war might be over; its unravelling took rather longer. Demobilisation was slow and beset with bureaucratic muddles, while demoralisation and unrest among the men still in uniform was widespread. 'I wish you 200 men had all gone wild and wrecked the whole show', wrote an incendiary Carpenter to George Clemas in spring 1919, on hearing that they had been discharged without food.[1] German prisoners, still incarcerated, were equally desperate to return home and Carpenter characteristically tried to help them.

Slowly however, the khaki faded from the streets as the war transmuted into memory. One response to its lurking shadows was to make an individual break. Joseph Hobson left Leeds for South Africa where he became active in the trades union movement. George Clemas made the less dramatic, though personally significant, move to a place at Cambridge, through the Government University Scheme for War Veterans, aided by Carpenter. Yet an aspiration for a wider collective change also persisted in a yearning for democracy and social justice internationally and at home.

When the Peace Talks began in January 1919, Woodrow Wilson's support for the League of Nations and desire to resume trade with Germany without severe reparations, raised hopes that a new kind of diplomacy might prevail. In the Spring of 1919 Carpenter signed a statement in the *Westminster Gazette* urging that Germany should not be treated in a punitive manner; among his co-signatories were Henry Nevinson and Ramsay MacDonald.[2] However, Wilson's approach met opposition from the Allies at the Peace Conference as well as in America, where both the right and left, for differing reasons, disliked his liberal internationalism. The League of Nations did, of course, emerge, though in the translation of dream to institution many of the formative ideas fell away.

Throughout 1919 and 1920 the left internationally was agitating against intervention in Russia. In Britain a National Hands Off Russia Committee was formed, supported by, among others, 'Charley' Cramp and Tom Mann. Carpenter missed signing the *Nation*'s letter of support for Maxim Gorky's appeal from Russian intellectuals for an end to intervention because he was away in London. So he sent his own statement calling for a resumption of 'mutual relations' between Britain and the Soviet Union and international action by European intellectuals in support of the Russians. Carpenter also sent a letter to the *Daily Herald*, asserting that intervention was motivated by a desire to secure the interest on loans contracted under the Tsar and designs on Russia's rich ore fields and mines.[3]

At home, parliamentary democracy had been extended in February 1918 with the passing of the Representation of the People Act which gave men over twenty-one and women over thirty the vote. But on the left ideas about democracy increasingly focused on work and daily life rather than parliament. Indeed it seemed that the pre-war questioning of clear demarcations between politics, economics and society was being confirmed by events. The election of Lloyd George's post-war Coalition Government blocked hopes of fundamental socialist reforms in parliament and strengthened Carpenter's association with the *Daily Herald*, which became the hub of left-wing dissent in the immediate post-war era. Now a daily with a circulation of around three hundred thousand, Lansbury's lively, combative paper spawned local 'Herald Leagues', formed by readers. The newspaper, with its rallies and its Leagues, provided an eclectic platform for debating ethical international relations and anti-imperialism, along with syndicalism, guild socialism, direct action and nationalisation. George Lansbury as editor was open to a range of left currents while Gerald Gould's intellectual and literary connections brought in journalists like Nevinson, Sharp and Brailsford, along with poets such as Siegfried Sassoon and Robert Graves. Other contributors included Havelock Ellis and Carpenter himself.

A combination of radical ideas and rising prices were resulting in an explosion of industrial conflicts in which workers' demands extended beyond pay. By 1919 the miners were pushing for the nationalisation of the collieries, and, that April, a group of about forty miners and their wives arrived at Millthorpe to discuss union affairs and Bolshevism in the garden.[4] A few days later Carpenter reported to Clem on the militant mood of the miners' Southport conference, adding a little wistfully of the Millthorpe visitors that it had not been possible to get on closer terms with any of the miners in particular.[5] In June, Carpenter's friend Charley Cramp, now President of the National Union of Railwaymen, argued that the Triple Alliance of miners, railway and transport workers, should aim at the 'control of industry'.[6] Carpenter hailed the Triple Alliance as a move to guild socialism in the *Daily Herald* on September 22nd and, at a rally called by the Herald League in Holborn on September 26th, his advice to workers was 'Do it Yourselves'.[7] Nevinson, who was at the rally, noted approvingly in his diary that Carpenter's anarchism was coming to the fore.[8]

After the heady fervour of the Herald rally, Carpenter stayed on in London, meeting Charley Cramp and the secretary of the N.U.R., J.H. Thomas, before returning north on October 8th.[9] However both men were under intense pressure from Lloyd George to stop calls for nationalisation and workers' control from the N.U.R.; they settled instead for participation on wages boards which dealt with pay and conditions.

Meanwhile, an undeterred Carpenter was calling for workers' control in the police and the army, as well as the mines, predicting that these extensions of direct democracy would mean that the police would no longer regard the defence of property and government power as their main business and that the army would refuse to fight for capitalist exploitation and jingoism.[10] This was wild talk, but 1919 was a wild year. Men in the army were in such a mutinous mood that they forced their officers to negotiate over conditions, while the National Federation of Discharged Soldiers and Sailors had fought the police in May for the right to march on parliament. Then in July, the police, who had themselves formed a union, went on strike in London and Liverpool. By the time Carpenter was writing, the strike had been defeated and its supporters blacklisted; despite J.H. Thomas' efforts to get them reinstated they never worked in the police force again. If resistance was fierce in 1919, so was the government's retaliation.

Lloyd George was more sympathetic to social housing and land reform than he was to labour disputes. Wartime exigencies had enabled Raymond Unwin to develop public housing and his insistence on design and standards influenced post-war reconstruction. In 1919 Town Planning legislation encouraged local authorities to build housing by providing a subsidy. Briefly it seemed as if collaboration between the Building Guilds and local authorities on these projects might be possible, a connection Unwin favoured. Carpenter had a do-it-yourself proposal he put before a large meeting in Kentish Town, chaired by Sydney Olivier early in 1920. To further 'Art and Beauty in Actual Life' and alleviate unemployment, he suggested that builders should form co-operatives and offer their services door to door.[11]

Carpenter still visited the Land Nationalisation Society when in London, however its influence was receding, and a consensus on mixed forms of ownership was appearing in Fabian and Labour Party circles. Lloyd George also supported changes in rural land ownership and the Land Settlement (Facilities) Act of 1919 provided for small-holdings, farm colonies, profit-sharing farms and co-operative marketing – all long espoused by Carpenter. Along with pre-war death duties and the death of so many heirs in the war, the Act resulted in land changing hands on an unprecedented scale; however the small-holders who tried to farm without any experience often failed. Carpenter hoped that small private holdings might benefit from a central farm and various forms of craft work, urging unions and co-operatives to establish farm colonies.[12]

The post-war enthusiasm for rural regeneration was not just economic; simplification somehow contrived to be born again in each new era, and some settlers were inspired by a back-to-the-land culture of communal living, natural food and dress, folk songs and dances. Carpenter's articles on the land in the *Daily Herald* resulted in a letter from Edward Reeves, a member of the Land Colonisation and Industrial Guild, telling Carpenter of a Christian Socialist vegetarian settlement at Kelling in Norfolk and allotments in Lowestoft, Wroxham, Cromer and Boston which he described as 'Colonies of Revolution'.[13] Then there was a young man called H. Carson Scott who wrote from the trendy 1917 Club to say that he, along with three musical, literary and philosophic friends, wanted to abandon their modern civilised lives for a poultry farm. Could Carpenter advise them?[14]

Back-to-the-land ideas were not confined to Britain. Reeves reported that he was just back from helping to set up the first European colony supported by his Land Colonization and Industrial Guild in the Maritime Alps.[15] And far away in Japan, artists and intellectuals who recoiled from the impact of rapid industrialisation turned to Carpenter, along with Ruskin, Morris and Tolstoy, and formed colonies. One settlement grew into Atarashiki Mura (New Village) where everyone worked on the land as equals. Nagashima Naoki, one of the settlers there, produced a partial translation of *England's Ideal* and *Angel's Wings*.[16] Sanshiro Ishikawa paid his last visit to Millthorpe in August 1920. At last able to return home, he participated in the Japanese anarchist movement, formed a Japanese Fabian Society, worked on the land in a village outside Tokyo and advocated nudity.[17]

However in Britain the Guild Socialist movement on which Carpenter had pinned his hopes soon fragmented. G.D.H. Cole inclined towards the Bolsheviks, but in 1920, A.J. Penty, whose vision of the 'Gilds' had been partly inspired by Carpenter, insisted that an organic society could not be brought into being in a 'catastrophic way'.[18] He, along with other anti-communist Guild members, began to move towards the 'social credit' ideas of Major Clifford Hugh Douglas, who was convinced that the money supply held the key to prosperity. Gradually Penty's politics shifted towards the extreme right, as did Odon Por's. Carpenter stuck to his abstract ideas of anarchist-communism, a vision of release from the cash nexus through associative commonality. He used the term 'communism' in conscious defiance of its branding as 'a bogey', adamant that bogeys were utilised to frighten the 'innocent and ignorant' and thus 'to prevent people thinking and to keep things just as they are'.[19]

During 1919 and 1920, amidst the swirling schemes for reconstruction and revolution, Carpenter was intensely busy. Once the war was over he had resumed work on his Pagan project, travelling to Sheffield University Library and Manchester's John Rylands in search of books. His vast friendship network and family commitments kept him going back and forth between Millthorpe and London. His diaries for these years record a welter of encounters with old friends, including Havelock Ellis, Isabella Ford, Olive Schreiner, Henry Nevinson, George Ives, E.M. Forster and Annie Besant along with newer names, among them the Indian poet Sarojini Naidu, a friend of Besant, Tagore and Gandhi, who had signed his birthday address. He was in close intellectual collaboration with Bertram Lloyd who shared his growing interest in anthropology as well as sex psychology. In 1920 Bertram Lloyd was negotiating for the German sex-reformer Magnus Hirschfeld's books to be placed in the British Museum's public catalogue and asking if Carpenter could persuade Bertrand Russell to speak for the B.S.S.S.P.[20] In June Carpenter promised he would chair Edvard Westermarck's talk on 'The Evolution of Modesty'.[21] Then there were publishers, editors, lectures and meetings.

On top of all his other activities, he maintained his extensive correspondence, not simply with friends in Britain but with people in many parts of the world. In June 1920 the American architect, Claude Bragdon, made contact again by sending Carpenter his translation of P.D. Ouspensky's *Tertium Organum*. Carpenter was in accord with Ouspensky's critique of materialistic intellectual frameworks and with his treatment of time and motion as an illusion which Carpenter saw as reminiscent of Einstein. However he grumbled that the last section was 'rather "fuzzy wuzzy"!'[22] Carpenter did not share the Russian's preoccupation with arcana.

Somehow Carpenter, now in his mid seventies, found time for personal assignations and outings. In spring 1920 he recorded with evident pride a long ramble in Derbyshire of twenty miles in the company of a young artist friend of Harry Bishop's called Ted Earle. 'Not a bit tired!'[23] As well as his customary Derbyshire walks, he was visiting friends all over the south during 1919 and 1920, recording in his diaries expeditions to Exmouth, Sidmouth, Margate, Lyme Regis and Brighton, where Henry Salt had settled. He also paid a trip to Windsor where he renewed his connection with Canon John Dalton, the Cambridge friend who had become royal tutor in his stead.[24]

However even Carpenter could not entirely defeat time and materiality. By 1919 he had grown so deaf he was consulting a doctor and buying an ear trumpet; some disturbing spasms of forgetfulness were evident too.[25] Then, in December 1919, while writing at his standing desk, Carpenter fainted. An alarmed Merrill called a doctor, but Carpenter made light of it and was up and about in a few days.[26] The 'faint' may have been a result of exhaustion, or perhaps a mild stroke. But he simply resumed his hectic regime. Professing surprise that he lived in a 'whirlpool', he told Clem in January 1920 that he had just done four lectures in London and would do four more the following week. 'Why do I do it? Well I am bombarded with requests, and for the sake of calm and peace I live in storm.'[27] In 1920 Unwin published two of Carpenter's lectures, 'Rest' and 'The Teaching of the Upanishads'; those who knew him well must have smiled wryly at his protest against the rush of modern life – telegrams, telephones, motor-cars and aeroplanes – for it was indeed characteristic of Carpenter to seek peace by navigating straight into the storm.[28] He needed the whirlpool as much as space for periodic withdrawal. In some notes on 'Self-Consciousness' written around this time he described life as a dance, 'an everlasting outflow of energy whose mere existence justifies itself'.[29]

Family troubles were, however, excluded from the energy dance; again Carpenter's frequent visits to London entailed caring for a sister. This time it was Alice, who had never been able to look after herself and was starting to behave wildly and erratically. On one visit in January 1919 she proposed to charge Carpenter and Merrill for their keep until the blunt-spoken Yorkshireman protested.[30] Again Carpenter described her to Clem as fretful and jumpy when he visited in May. He and his brother Alfred managed to move her into a flat in Richmond with a companion.[31] But seeing Alice was not easy. She rebelled against Richmond. In August he wrote in his diary, 'A. very wearying'; she was disorientated, confused and lonely, begging him not to leave her when he paid his dutiful visits.[32] Her world had crumbled with the loss of first Dora and then Sophy. When Alice too died in 1921, Isabella Ford consoled Carpenter that at least she would be in peace.[33] Dora, Sophy, George and then Alice's last years had all been troubled.

The death of several old friends confirmed that time, at least in familiar dimensions, was real enough. Kate Salt seemed weak and depressed when Carpenter saw her early in 1919. He observed in his diary that Henry was worried, but concluded, with his usual mind-over-matter approach, that Kate was not seeing enough people. Given that he, Merrill, the Batthyánys and Sassoon's sculptor uncle, Hamo Thorneycroft, were all at Lyme Regis, this was an odd diagnosis.[34] Kate wrote in frail handwriting on February 7th, 'Must confess I'm chiefly asleep.'[35] She was dead within a few days. A sobered Carpenter wrote to Florrie Mattison, 'All other thoughts are now discounted by the sad news of Kate Salt's death.'[36] He was finally focusing on the woman he had evaded so deftly when she was alive. Kate's only legacy, apart from the personal memories of those who loved her, was her correspondence. When Henry Salt began the task of going through her letters, he suggested to Carpenter that perhaps some should be destroyed.[37] It is not clear whether Carpenter did this, though there are some long gaps in his letters from Kate and some parts appear to be missing.

Bessie Ford died too that summer of a brain haemorrhage. Isabella, who had been so close to her sister, felt as if part of herself had gone. She turned to Carpenter in her grief, describing how she kept thinking she would consult Bessie or show her something. Like Carpenter when Hukin died, she could not accept that souls could just be snuffed out. Isabella Ford wrote with the intense, raw feeling of bereavement, 'Dear Edward, I am glad you have George and I hope he is very very good to you.'[38] Carpenter visited the Mattisons on August 27th and called at Adel Grange the following day, where he found Isabella and Emily Ford with their friend Violet Paget, the novelist who wrote under the pseudonym of 'Vernon Lee'. Isabella took him up to Bessie's bedroom and presented him with her sister's copy of The Trojan Women and a brass candlestick. He returned home to Millthorpe in pelting rain, clutching these bizarre remnants of an old friendship. The following day was his seventy-fifth birthday.[39]

Carpenter paid his last visit to John Bruce Glasier who was terminally ill in Manchester in June 1920. Glasier, pale and in pain, was being nursed by Katherine, in between her editing of the Labour Leader. He was propped up on pillows and finishing his book on William Morris. Carpenter shared Glasier's admiration for Morris, but otherwise they had become politically estranged. However, at the end, Carpenter tried to bury the animosities, writing an affectionate account of their last meeting for the Labour Leader.[40] The man who had introduced Katherine Bruce Glasier to Carpenter's work, Robert Weare, also died in 1920. Never a national figure, he had played a vital role in the rank and file of the socialist groupings in Bristol, Liverpool and Wallasey.[41] Olive Schreiner visited Britain for the last time in 1920. She left for South Africa that August bidding Carpenter farewell with the hope that one day a new world without hate and dominance would rise.[42] She died that December.

Continuities seemed all the more precious to those who survived. Isabella Ford's visit to Millthorpe in October 1919 helped her grief to heal. The peace and familiarity of the place, walks with Carpenter talking about Whitman, meeting Fannie Hukin, brought solace. 'I feel as if I can put on my harness more easily and be less cross and horrid here since I have been with you. The peace and loveliness of it all, still hangs round me.' Back at Adel Grange she wrote 'I feel so sad without you and George and the stream.'[43] Alf Mattison also kept up his visits to Millthorpe with its restorative peace and its memories. So many links to the past were embedded in the place. Carpenter was still in close contact with Fannie Hukin and the Keys and still visiting Arnold Allcard. Joe Potter and Jim Shortland, along with their wives, would come for tea, and Carpenter used to stay with them when in Sheffield. Loyal to his working-class friends from the past, he was still finding jobs for members of the chaotic Greaves family with whom he had lodged in Sheffield, and he collected £5 from John Bingham, now an august local dignitary, for Fred Charles, the sensitive anarchist whose life had been so scarred by impossible illusions and a scheming state. Three new additions in Carpenter's daily life were Tom Nicholson and his wife Annie, who now helped with the work at Millthorpe along with the handyman, Charlie Roughton.

The young men still rolled up at Millthorpe, which continued to be prone to congestion. Early in 1919 Clem was informed, 'I am afraid, dear boy, that we cannot keep you a week, as the stream of visitors and other engagements is too great, and garden and correspondence all behind hand.'[44] Clem was no longer quite such a favourite. In April they had a tiff about Clem's lack of interest in politics and when he visited in June, Carpenter wrote disapprovingly of signs of 'finesse', though he conceded that the young man remained sincere underneath.[45] By March 1920 'Clemas', now at Cambridge, was being described as 'prim and correct as ever'.[46]

Carpenter's flightiness in relation to young men became more pronounced during his seventies. In 1919 the former Red Cross ambulance driver, Gilbert Beith, is mentioned in letters and in Carpenter's diary. In March that year, Carpenter recorded that Beith was 'pathetically loving' when he visited Millthorpe; like Harold Coxeter, the obliging Beith was prepared to transport Carpenter and Merrill in his motor car.[47] The name of a

Sheffield man, Jack Burton, appears too, as does that of Ted Earle, the London artist with whom Carpenter went on the twenty-mile hike. Carpenter met Earle several times when he was in London during 1919 and he had acquired a sufficiently privileged status to be invited for Christmas and introduced to the Mattisons and Fannie Hukin. He was even shown Carpenter's 'Sicilian photos' and ones of the Gnani. Merrill was not happy. On December 24th the precious photographs of Walt Whitman were brought out and on Christmas Day a fond Carpenter looked at the stars with Earle through his telescope, an all too familiar indication of deep intimacy. 'G. jealous' noted Carpenter in his diary.[48] On Monday 29th Carpenter registered 'Climax of G. and scene.'[49] The following day he jotted 'G. better' – perhaps Merrill was taking comfort from the knowledge that Earle was departing on Wednesday in the cart with Will Key for Chesterfield station.[50] Merrill's anger once expressed, quickly blew over and on Friday January 2nd Carpenter announced in his diary 'G. sorry about Ted and Jack B.'[51] Carpenter simply circumvented Merrill's jealousy by seeing Earle in London.

Around the same time he was seeing Earle and Jack Burton, he also met up with Herbert Mills, the shell-shocked soldier who had introduced him to séances. Mills was now working in a drapers and gentlemen's outfitters in Hereford. Carpenter visited him in Hereford in October 1919 and they spent several days walking and talking.[52] In February 1920 Herbert Mills appeared at Millthorpe with Jack Burton and stayed for a few days. On February 15th he was declared to be 'amusing and useful in house'.[53] By March 11th he was 'very quaint and affte. [sic]' and on the 19th Carpenter confided in his diary 'H J Mills in aftn. [sic] slept with me.'[54] Carpenter and the handy Mills planted cabbages contentedly together, happily bathing in the brook and sowing small seeds in the garden. It was an easy, light, congenial relationship. Mills had no sooner departed when Ted Earle came to stay – this was the occasion of the long walk.[55] Carpenter, following his no-jealousy maxim, went out in Gilbert Beith's car with Herbert Mills, Ted Earle and another new friend, Guy Bernard.[56] He and Carpenter had shared what Carpenter called 'confessions' that February.[57] By March the Sicilian photographs were being displayed and an intellectual friendship commenced which later resulted in their collaboration on a book about Shelley.[58] A wistful and confused Herbert Mills wrote from the Sheffield Y.M.C.A., thanking Carpenter for the 'sponging' and confiding how they all wanted indications of Carpenter's special attention. Assuring the seventy-five-year-old Carpenter that he valued not only his body and intellect but his spirit, Mills added, 'You can do without me or Earle or B or anyone and that is where I admire you.'[59]

Carpenter's serene detachment amidst this bevy of young admirers did not derive from a purely spiritual transcendence – he was, after all, secure in his loving relationship with George Merrill. Mutual trust was its bedrock, enabling them to muddle through their various liaisons. Merrill's jealous resentments might erupt quickly, but they dissipated just as fast and he too seems to have found erotic diversions. In his diary in February 1920 Carpenter recounted how a devoted friend of Merrill's had arrived from Oldham, as well as a Mancunian with a scented handkerchief who Carpenter pronounced 'too too'.[60] The flamboyant dandyism Carpenter had always disdained was back in vogue in the post-war era though the majority of homosexual men avoided such overt display. Over the years Merrill could observe how Carpenter's flirtatious friendships waxed and waned. By July 1921 poor Beith was being dismissed in a letter to Clem as too much of a 'piffler and a casual to be interesting' – wonderful eyes and a motor car could take you only so far in Carpenter's affections.[61] In contrast Merrill was the constant figure, secure after all these years, incongruously licensed as a 'male servant' from January 1920.[62]

While Carpenter's intimacies were lived ad hoc amidst a cloud of emotional confusion, to others he appeared as a fount of clarity, the great explainer of sex's mysteries. The fan mail continued to arrive, claiming him as kin and requesting signed photographs. His advice was sought by Enid M. Chambers who was thinking of setting up a group of Uranian women to overcome their isolation. She had already participated in one-to-one counselling but felt there was a need to involve more women and she believed that only a Uranian could understand a Uranian.[63] Carpenter's male friends turned to him too. Sidney Lomer's wartime love Georgie had got married, now had a son, and wrote only occasionally. An ill and anguished Lomer wrote from Falmouth saying he was convinced that Georgie seemed very melancholy and wondering if Carpenter could go and see the young man to ascertain the situation? Lomer wanted Georgie to come and live with him and bring his son, even though another part of him knew there was 'no solution'.[64] E.M. Forster's emotional troubles were more easily sorted; in August 1920 he recorded in his diary that Carpenter had explained that Forster liked 'the lower classes' because they were not self-conscious. 'I am and therefore need them.'[65]

The illegality and scandal surrounding homosexual and lesbian love meant that the recognition, the 'confession', the honesty, possible with Carpenter assumed an intense emotional value for friends and correspondents alike. Even for people who had no contact with him personally, he had become the touchstone of a freer sexuality. The very mention of his name served as an oblique way of saying what could not be said openly in a hostile culture. Around the world his books were being exchanged as billets doux: a leading figure in the Harlem Renaissance, the African American writer Alain Locke, presented the poet Countée Cullen with a copy of *Ioläus*.[66]

Though Carpenter, writing to Marie Stopes in 1918, welcomed 'the landslide of general opinion' which was making it possible to talk more freely about sex, the new sexual freedom remained skin deep.[67] Illegitimacy was still a stigma, male chauvinism lingered on, and same-sex love was inclined to be acknowledged sotto voce. The gains of the new frankness were also somewhat precarious, moral panics were apt to boomerang back on the sex-reformers. Nonetheless the reformers' trench of scientific academic study which legitimated free enquiry continued to hold fast, and a new generation were eagerly stepping in to extend it. A psychology student called Beatrice Sergeant who was writing her PhD on homosexuality came to Millthorpe for tea and counsel in June 1919 and Carpenter lent her some books.[68] She must have enjoyed herself because she came back in August with a friend. A puzzled Carpenter recorded in his diary how his two guests spent Sunday doing gymnastic exercises on the lawn.[69] It was all very modern and emancipated. However, on Monday, when the two 'girls' came 'prancing in at 11 am', the great sex guru suddenly turned into a Victorian papa. 'Explosion on my part.'[70] The two young women had clearly assumed that in loco parentis would not apply with the author of *Love's Coming of Age*! How could they comprehend Carpenter's complicated mix of abandon and restraint?

They must have been particularly confused because by the early 1920s Carpenter seemed to epitomise the modern, educated, rational outlook on sex. His Fellowship of the New Life values of democracy, mutuality and non-possessiveness were grafted onto the contemporary progressive causes of open, companionate marriage, planned parenthood and sex education in schools. Accordingly he was asked to sponsor Marie Stopes' birth-control clinic at 61 Marlborough Road, Holloway, North London, which opened in 1921 providing diaphragms to its anxious clientele.[71] And, when Stopes' rival, Stella Browne wrote a panegyric to Carpenter in Margaret Sanger's *Birth Control Review* in 1921, she singled out his ideas about sex education in schools for special praise. Browne noted how Carpenter envisaged not only the practicalities of 'sex hygiene', but the 'expansion of emotional possibilities' through 'humane understanding'.[72] Both the practicalities and the emotional expansion proved rather too much for the London County Council, even though they were lobbied by sexual reformers throughout the 1920s.

While the sunny-side-up elements in Carpenter were adopted by the

Margaret Sanger

progressive, humanitarian wing of the sex-reform movement, their stress on sexual enlightenment and honesty about the body and relationships represented only one of his slants. Carpenter's writing also intimated a darker path of ecstasy and the moon. Despite Lawrence's repudiation, the older man would have understood Lawrence's words written for a foreword to the American edition of *Women in Love*: 'Let us hesitate no longer to announce that the sensual passions and mysteries are equally sacred with the spiritual mysteries and passions.' Carpenter's style was to beat more around the bush, but like Lawrence, and of course Whitman, he too wanted this tangling of sex and spirit. He too wished to chart 'New unfoldings . . . the passionate struggle into conscious being.'[73]

Intent on shaking sexuality free of its Christian connotations with sin, yet inclined to be oblique, as Carpenter grew older he buttressed his subversion with more and more learned references. His *Pagan and Christian Creeds* published by Stanley Unwin in 1920 was replete with sources. He still picked up ideas magpie-like from old friends like Cotterill and new ones like the Freudian Ernest Jones, but he had also been reading widely: Jane

Harrison and Gilbert Murray on ancient history, Salamon Reinach on religion, Wilhelm Wundt and Carl Jung on psychology and myths, Sir James George Frazer on anthropology and folklore. Nonetheless the scholarship of *Pagan and Christian Creeds* really served as rococo decoration for Carpenter's resolve to dislodge Christianity, which he associated with the self-conscious preoccupation with individual salvation, from its claims of spiritual superiority. Carpenter demonstrated how Christianity had reproduced many aspects of earlier faiths – an idea which had engaged him while still at Cambridge – and that the Bible was untrustworthy as a literal document. Making adept use of the telling anecdote, Carpenter recounted how the Zulus, familiar with the long marches of large numbers of people, had pointed out to Bishop Colenso that the crossing of the Red Sea in a single night would have been impossible. He also stressed the spiritual and ethical values of other religions, mentioning the Jewish 'Testament of the Twelve Patriarchs'.[74]

Despite all the new learning, *Pagan and Christian Creeds* reiterated the critique of 'civilisation' Carpenter had been putting forward since the 1880s. The familiar three stages of consciousness appear too, along with Carpenter's Lamarckian theories of evolution. Lamarck's ideas had enjoyed a brief revival in the early twentieth century because they seemed to be in accord with the philosophical interest in inner vital agency, though they were soon to lose credibility in the face of mounting evidence which supported Darwin's theories. Carpenter's spiritual evolutionary perspective still inclined him to Lamarck because he believed this allowed for a non-material impetus for transformation. His critique of civilisation also led him towards a dialectical rejection of linear progress. He wanted to present the 'primitive' phase as having been overlaid rather than completely discarded. Hence the pre-civilised past could provide alternative sources of feelings and values which could indicate the synthesis of cosmic consciousness. In *Pagan and Christian Creeds*, Carpenter relaunched his effort to ensure that understandings beyond Western 'civilisation' should be acknowledged and respected, setting out to vindicate paganism and rescue primitive societies from what he regarded as the condescension of the anthropologists.

Carpenter's book was published on the cusp of a major paradigm shift in anthropology which was beginning to move away from nineteenth-century postulates of a series of universal stages towards fieldwork within specific cultures. Instead of single causes or origins this new anthropology stressed the distinct context of customs and myths. Carpenter retained many of the assumptions and approaches of nineteenth-century anthro-pology, however, characteristically, *Pagan and Christian Creeds* contained contradictory elements. Carpenter undermined the idea of absolute phases with observations of how cultural facets could be found running side by side and in some cases might fuse. He admired the works of A.E. Crawley in which religion was intertwined in the fabric of social life. Crawley's relativistic argument that to primitive peoples religion would seem as real as science did to inhabitants of the early twentieth century appealed to Carpenter, and in his conclusion to *Pagan and Christian Creeds* he suggested early religious beliefs contained profound psychological insights.

The book was, on the whole, received well by reviewers, though a few thought Carpenter was too harsh on Christianity and the ultra-modern *Athenaeum* sniffed that he was out of date on phallic cults.[75] Nobody suggested that the elevation of so-called 'primitives' might contain an ambivalent condescension. Respect for the 'primitive', an assertion of paganism, the challenge to 'civilisation' and a dismissal of purely intellectual ways of knowing were very much in accord with the mood of the early 1920s, and Stanley Unwin seized the time by bringing out a new enlarged edition of *Civilisation: Its Cause and Cure*.

In his introduction to the new edition, dated December 1920, Carpenter referred with a shudder to the attack mounted on his talk all those years ago by the Fabians. While admitting that his critique of civilisation had been based on 'imaginative *élan*' rather than solid data, he was rather pleased at how the essays had stood the test of time. His scepticism about scientific laws had been borne out; the atom had 'exploded of itself' and the 'fixed Chemical Elements' had 'dissolved into protean vapours and emanations, ions and electrons, impossible to follow through their endless transformations'. He summed up the impulse of *Civilisation: Its Cause and Cure* in the phrase, 'the true field of science is to be found in Life, and the best way to *know* things is to *experience* their meaning and to identify oneself with them through Action'.[76]

The new edition included an Appendix on 'pre-civilised' peoples, a collection of interesting extracts which included Carpenter's favourite, Herman Melville's *Typee*. E. Bertram Lloyd is thanked for compiling this material on cultures which ranged from Africa to the North Pole. Carpenter's assumption was that these examples of 'the many admirable virtues of the early peoples' could be read as evidence of a previous phase of human existence, though he was sufficiently wary to add that not all the practices of 'primitive folk' were to be admired.[77]

Carpenter added an essay, 'The New Morality', which elaborated on the points he had made in 'The Defence of Criminals' and 'Custom'. Arguing that Nietzsche had been a healthy reaction to 'spooney Altruism', Carpenter nevertheless thought that his 'Will to Power' denied the possibility of a social alternative. Nietzsche's contempt for the 'knock-kneed and the humbug' might be entertaining but 'His blonde beasts and his laughing lions' gave us no clear direction other than 'the worship of Force as a Formula'.[78] Carpenter in contrast rejected formulaic moralities, of both the spooney and Nietzschean varieties. He wanted an organic sentiment of 'the Common Life' combined with 'the recognition of Individual Affection and Expression'; his morality was one of 'acceptance and recognition and wide-reaching redemption'.[79]

Carpenter's vision of his new order in touch with nature and satisfying the heart – free from domination and imbued with values of association while allowing space for self-expression, sex and the inner life – was articulated when the glimpse of social transformation which had appeared after the war was rapidly slipping into the nether distance. An economic downturn set in towards the end of 1920 and placed the left and the labour movement, already beset by internal divisions, on the defensive. The miners took the brunt first. Other countries in Europe were re-establishing their mining industries and competition was driving down the price of coal. The government, which had directed industry nationally during the war, brought forward the date when the mines would be back in private hands to April 1, 1921. When the colliery owners announced wages would be decreased the miners resisted and were locked out. The Miners' Federation was prepared to accept some reductions but wanted a national wages board to determine rates and a national pool which would enable the richer coalfields to subsidise the less profitable areas.

Carpenter wrote to Ramsay MacDonald in April 1921, expressing support for the national pool, but regretting the growing divisions among the trades union leaders.[80] Indeed the slump had made trades unionists cautious. Carpenter's friend Charley Cramp was moving to the right and J.H. Thomas suspected that a national pool constituted a step towards nationalisation which the railway workers had abandoned. Under pressure from a hostile press and with lukewarm support from Labour M.P.s, many of whom were opposed to trades unions making political proposals, the Triple Alliance of miners, railway and transport workers disintegrated.

Carpenter responded with a vehement defence of the miners in their adversity. In the Liberal *Daily News* on May 3rd he praised the 'constructive' scheme of the national pool. The atmosphere was tense, a twitchy government had troops positioned in the London parks ready for trouble and the *Daily News*, with its progressive but nervous readership in mind, took care to give Carpenter a strapline of indubitable respectability, announcing how he had been 10th Wrangler in 1868 and a former fellow of Trinity

Hall. Carpenter argued that capital consolidated in its own interests and asked why it was not permissible for labour to do the same. He knew the men on strike and they were 'steadfast, hard-working, practical-minded'. Moreover they were showing themselves willing to suffer privation for a principle in their support for the national pool. It was a proposal that deserved to be extended to other industries which he believed would 'hasten the day when industry generally will be handled by those who are most directly concerned in it'. Critics of workers' control such as Ramsay MacDonald had objected that each craft or industry could not incorporate and represent wider social interests; Carpenter simply swept these objections under the carpet, declaring that industrial organisation 'built up from below' would necessarily be 'for the general benefit of the nation', rather than for the financial interests that held sway under present conditions. The miners were to be congratulated for having the foresight to act in the public interest.[81]

Carpenter returned to the fray on May 28th in the *Daily News*, pointing out that the dispute was undoubtedly contributing to the good weather by reducing air pollution. National regulation was clearly necessary because the colliery owners could not be relied upon to introduce environmental methods of utilising coal.[82] In June he was back again on 'Cold and Wet Weather,' pointing out how pollution contributed to grey skies and rain.[83]

Class struggle might bring out the sun, but the old pagan sun gods were not able to defend their miner allies. The dispute dragged on through the boiling hot summer to defeat for the miners, breaking the proud sense of entitlement which was the heritage of the war years. Overall union membership declined while a minority of the militants gravitated to the new Communist left. Its formation reconfigured radical politics; the Communist thrust towards decisive clarity accentuated the dividing lines in the labour movement already evident in defeat.

Carpenter, removed from the day-to-day wrangles, lunged to the defence of 'Communistic doctrines' as akin to those of the early Christian church, endorsing in the *Daily News* a proposition of Bernard Shaw's that free bread should be distributed for the unemployed whose numbers were rapidly mounting.[84] The mathematically minded Bob Muirhead sent him a counter-proposal. Why not scrap unemployment doles and old-age pensions in favour of a universal benefit, a 'National Dividend' of around £1 a week. This 'Citizen's Income' would serve as a good half-way house to communism and take the sting out of capitalism without entailing large-scale nationalisation.[85] But the attack on the miners and the repressive climate of police raids and prosecutions had aroused Carpenter's ire. Though the *Daily News* printed a reassuring photograph of a white-bearded

Carpenter, he was resolute that any social reconstruction worth having would have to be 'revolutionary'.[86]

Carpenter's revolution of course included bodily delight, an acceptance of individuality and, above all intense personal comradeship. That July he had escaped the fraught arena of class solidarity for a holiday in Dorset, meeting Clem in Shaftesbury and then driving down to Yeovil and Chard with Gilbert Beith and Ted Earle, arriving at a deserted beach to the west of Lyme Regis where they splashed naked in the waves and fried in the sun under a huge boulder for several wonderful hours.[87] An inspired Carpenter penned an article defending nudism, called 'Back to the Wild', which was rejected by the *Daily News*, the *Manchester Guardian* and the *Sheffield Daily Telegraph*. When an Oxford undergraduate, Arthur Reade, heard about this censorship he wrote to ask Carpenter if he could print 'Back to the Wild' in his communist youth journal, *Free Oxford*.[88] Carpenter duly sent his article celebrating various signs of pagan subversion he had spotted in daily life, from the proliferation of scantily-clad sunbathers to dissidence in the Boy Scouts – a disgruntled Scout had written enquiring whether Carpenter was going to head an alternative Scout camp. This must have been a reference to John Hargrave's 'Kibbo Kift Kindred', a 1920 breakaway from the Scouts inspired by Carpenter, Morris and 'Red Indianism' which eventually morphed into the Woodcraft Folk.[89]

Free Oxford considered Carpenter's outlook to be most humane, comparing him to the Bolshevik sexual reformer Alexandra Kollontai.[90] In contrast a magazine called *Plain English* signalled out Carpenter's article for stern criticism; under the heading 'Naked and Unashamed', his views on birth control, along with his advocacy of manly embraces and nudism were castigated.[91] Irony of ironies, *Plain English* was edited by Wilde's downfall, Lord Alfred Douglas! *Free Oxford* was rejected by Blackwell's bookshop. 'As rank bourgeois . . . we feel that we ought not to hasten the collapse of our class by assisting in the distribution of this paper.'[92] Then the unfortunate Reade was sent down from the University. In defiance of repressive, unfree Oxford, Carpenter energetically distributed the fifty copies he had received in lieu of payment.

A letter came from Henry Salt in December 1921, teasing Carpenter for having a hand in the proscription of that 'Oxford Bolshevist Journal'. In the same communiqué Salt expressed interest in the 'Guildford Plan'.[93] As the news spread from Salt to Mattison, to Isabella Ford, northerners were left gasping.[94] Carpenter and Merrill were moving from Millthorpe, to settle in suburban Surrey. There were some, Charlie Sixsmith included, who never reconciled themselves to the Guildford plan. But Guildford it was to be; social reconstruction and revolution might have to be deferred; one fundamental change was to be acted upon.

23

Guildford

Northern friends might have been shocked about the move south, but Harold Coxeter, with a place in Surbiton as well as on St Pancras Road, was delighted, confidently guaranteeing that Surrey was definitely the place to be. By 1921, Guildford, accessible by rail from London and close to the Downs, was highly desirable and new villas were rapidly being built.

The move was not quite as sudden as it seemed. For some time Carpenter and Merrill had been looking at flats in London and early in 1921 had rented a tiny one in Chelsea. But London exhausted Carpenter and his fits of forgetfulness and difficulties in walking were becoming impossible to ignore. Harold Coxeter assured him that once he was in Guildford and out of 'the rush and strain of London', all would be well.[1] Carpenter's brother Alfred had also been urging him to move closer for health reasons.[2] Alfred's home in Croydon was in striking distance of Guildford, while Gilbert Beith lived in nearby Gomshall and Harold Picton had a cottage near Godalming. E.M. Forster also lived in Surrey, so friends were nearby and Guildford was big enough to have its own Trades Council as well as an I.L.P. branch and holiday centre.

Charlie Sixsmith suspected it was really Merrill who was keen to move.[3] While Merrill may have found village life too constraining, Carpenter had been developing his own closer attachments to the south, which loyalty to Sixsmith would make him reluctant to reveal. Notable among these was the artist Ted Earle, to whom Carpenter had become deeply devoted. The immediate impetus for the 'Guildford Plan' was the offer by Earle's uncle, Frank Chapman, to buy Millthorpe and preserve it as a memorial guest house run by Tom and Annie Nicholson.[4]

Over the winter of 1921–2 Carpenter's health deteriorated dramatically. He was, moreover, aware that he was growing increasingly forgetful and was psychologically distressed, telling Havelock Ellis on February 27, 1922, 'I feel rather lost and stranded at present, and one's friends all evaporated!'[5]

Carpenter with Merrill on porch at 'Millthorpe', Mountside Road

It is not clear whether this was caused by the strain of Alice's mental illness and death, the prolonged stay in London, or the trauma of such a momentous move, but when he paid a short visit to Millthorpe in May 1922, a shocked Fannie Hukin recounted to Alf Mattison, 'He has changed into quite an old man – no memory, and falls asleep anytime if more than one person is talking. George Merrill says Edward cannot bear him out of his sight. He also seems very uncertain on his feet.'[6]

Characteristically Carpenter tried to ignore his infirmities and once in Guildford persisted in setting off on his customary walks. Forced to sit down to rest by the path, he was inclined to doze off, causing Merrill to become anxious when he did not return home. The new house they had chosen on Mountside Road was conveniently close to the station, but it was at the top of a steep hill. Friends were not overly impressed by the 'new highly varnished villa', though most were inclined to praise the vista from the Hog's Back, apart from E.M. Forster who disdained what he called the 'large crude view'.[7] He had decided that Carpenter in Guildford no longer held any 'mystery' for him.

Carpenter announced to Alf Mattison on July 1st that Guildford was charming and the people friendly. They had named the new house 'Millthorpe'.[8] Though nothing would replace the original Millthorpe for Isabella Ford, Mattison persuaded her that Carpenter was happy enough.[9] Fannie Hukin proved harder to convince. While she conceded in a letter to Mattison that this new Guildford Millthorpe might be more convenient, she did not think it was prettier than the old one. Moreover, Carpenter's new household puzzled her. She noted that 'Mr. Earle, the artist' was painting Carpenter's portrait, occupying a large upstairs room as his studio and bedroom. 'George Merrill rules the roost and does a lot of talking.' Meanwhile Charlie Roughton, who had moved down with Merrill and Carpenter, just worked quietly away. Carpenter looked better than he had in May, though he was still forgetful and seemed restless. 'Edward likes to have lots of people about him now-a-days. He is very much changed.'[10] Fannie sensed that there was something odd about the atmosphere, referring to the way the men chaffed each other all the time. She was familiar enough to recognise forced jocularity, though she had no idea what it might conceal. Carpenter's dependency had certainly enabled Merrill's ethos to prevail. E.M. Forster noted his ebullient mood on a visit in May, recording in his diary, 'G.M. skittish and very plain, invited me, politely refused he transferred giving details afterwards.'[11] When Charlie Sixsmith called in November he informed Alf Mattison that Merrill was enjoying a good time and getting quite fat in Guildford. He, too, observed that Charlie Roughton seemed to be doing all the work.[12]

On July 7th, Millthorpe and its four and a half acres were sold to Frances William Chapman for £1,500.[13] Initially Carpenter was delighted with the 'kind friend', and the idea of Millthorpe as a house of rest and culture for the socialist movement.[14] Then on September 3rd, Chapman's wife, Helen, wrote to Carpenter in some distress explaining that her husband's mental state had become disturbed, he was suffering from paranoia and acting violently. It also appeared that Chapman was not as rich as he had implied and wanted his family to leave Newcastle and settle at Millthorpe.[15] A shaken Carpenter replied in pencil, apologising that he did not feel up to pen and ink. Gallantly he returned Chapman's cheque, making him the 'beneficial owner' in consideration of his affection – an ambiguous arrangement that was arguable in law.[16]

Over the next year Carpenter's relationship with Chapman grew progressively less affectionate and he became extremely worried about Millthorpe and his own financial position. In October 1923 Harold Coxeter sent him a cheque for £700, saying that Carpenter could pay it back at his convenience. Jokingly, Coxeter appointed himself as 'Business Adviser in Chief' as well as loving friend.[17] The muddle with Chapman continued to dog Carpenter until June 1924 when Chapman was persuaded to sell Millthorpe for £100 to Tom Nicholson and Charlie Roughton, who had been maintaining it.[18]

Despite all this agitation, Carpenter recovered somewhat over the autumn of 1922. Though still unsteady on his feet, the spasms of forgetfulness receded and he began to fantasise about a trip to Sicily to see Biagio di Paulo.[19] While visiting brother Alfred, he even went up in an aeroplane and enjoyed it greatly.[20] By the end of 1922, Carpenter had recovered from his uprooting sufficiently to speak on 'Some Friends of Walt Whitman: A Study in Sex Psychology' at Caxton Hall, London, stating that he believed Whitman had loved both men and women but was 'before all a lover of the Male'. Carpenter observed that Whitman, who he described as the most candid and cautious of men, could never admit this publicly in late nineteenth-century America, as the press would have been 'at his heels, snarling and slandering'.[21]

While ostensibly lecturing on Whitman, Carpenter reaffirmed his support for modern women and non-reproductive sex. Challenging the equation of femininity with inferiority, he queried whether 'the continuation of the race should be regarded as the main object of love and sex'. Carpenter said that offspring were a beautiful 'bye-product [sic]', but asserted it was the 'consolidation of a new form of life – the double life' of a loving couple, fused into oneness, which moved humanity on to a 'new order of evolution'.[22] It was an odd combination, the idea of the 'great love' popular among some emancipated women in the early 1900s and an ultra-modern defence of non-reproductive sexual pleasure, hitched to his version of Lamarckian theories of evolution propelled by an inner vitalism. In the early 1920s Carpenter still adhered to Lamarck, as did Shaw whose *Back to Methuselah* (1921) had caused him to send a sharp reminder to the dramatist saying that the theories were all there in his recently reissued *Civilisation: Its Cause and Cure*.[23] On the other hand, the eclectic Carpenter appreciated any kind of scientific endorsement and carefully kept a newspaper cutting of a talk by Julian Huxley on 'The Determination of Sex' for the Royal Society of Arts in 1922. Huxley, who was sympathetic to the B.S.S.S.P., argued that 'blind hereditary forces' determined sexual preferences and predicted artificial insemination.[24]

When *Love's Coming of Age* was reissued by Allen and Unwin in 1923, Carpenter still recommended physical control to keep the sexual encounter on an emotional plane, but he did concede that contraceptives were necessary.[25] On April 11th Carpenter's eclectic melange of old and new concepts attracted a mainly young audience, including a large number of

Japanese followers, to a meeting organised by the League of Peace and Freedom at the Mortimer Hall, London. The following week, Bertram Lloyd, who was busy ensuring that Carpenter's Whitman talk became a B.S.S.S.P. pamphlet, acted as impresario for an elaborate event in the same hall. Carpenter spoke on Beethoven and read from *Angel's Wings* and *Never Again*, while two friends of Lloyd's, Irene and Syliva Colenso, played the violin and the piano.[26]

Sylvia Colenso proved a precious find. Carpenter still loved to play the piano, but he could no longer always recall the music, and she started to visit Guildford and play for him. He also took great delight in the gramophone records Nevinson was bringing him as presents. Music, always so important in his life as a source of inspiration and peace, in these last years became even more so. In old age he cherished his musical friends, Rutland Boughton, Granville Bantock, the writer J.D.M. Rorke and the Norwegian composer and pianist Fridjof Backer-Gröndhal, with a special reverence. When Backer-Gröndhal performed in Guildford, he came to Mountside Road to play for the writer whose work he admired.

When Carpenter's Norwegian translator, Illit Gröndahl came to stay in the early summer of 1923, he was shocked at the rapid decline of his mentor. Carpenter now struggled to climb the steep winding road to the house and, on one occasion, half sitting and half lying on the ground, had to ask the young Norwegian for a hand up.[27] Henry Nevinson and Evelyn Sharp made a trip to Mountside in May, and Nevinson noted in his diary that Carpenter was 'ageing and deaf and rather shaky'. He accompanied them outside on to the Hog's Back, but was unable to join them on their walk to Compton. His sister Nellie, now Lady Hyett, was looking after him and Nevinson was impressed by this refined, intellectual lady who was so alert and up-to-date. When she chaffed Carpenter about his socialism, Nevinson sprang to Carpenter's defence, declaring him to be the 'complete Anarchist'.[28]

The 'Complete Anarchist' received a visit from an up-and-coming labour politician that June, when Hugh Dalton drove his father John over from Windsor. Hugh Dalton had discovered Carpenter's writings while a rebellious Cambridge Fabian; now he wanted to leave his lecturing at the London School of Economics and was looking for a parliamentary seat, dithering between Chesterfield and Huddersfield. While young Hugh wanted to sound Carpenter out on labour movement contacts, inconvenient trains and shaky legs made his father grateful to have a driver. The two old men, connected by Hugh's socialism, fondly renewed their college friendship.[29] Despite deploring the motor car, Carpenter appreciated the convenience of this modern form of transport in his advancing years.

An idealistic young American appeared at the Mountside house later that summer. Chester Alan Arthur III came from a wealthy elite family and was the grandson of the twenty-first President. Galvanised by the romantic nationalism of A.E. Russell, Arthur had decided he had a special mission in Ireland and must help the Irish Republicans. Whilst staying at the Republican rendezvous, Roebuck House, near Dublin – a vast Victorian mansion bought by Charlotte Despard for Maude Gonne and her children – Despard encouraged him to seek out Carpenter. Arthur, interested in Carpenter and Whitman, was troubled about his sexuality and looking for help.

To Chester Arthur's romantic eyes the Mountside suburban villa appeared as a rose-covered cottage and the man who 'held out his arms as if welcoming a long-gone son' looked physically beautiful.[30] Many years later he recalled the bronzed copper face and the shining silver hair; Carpenter's clothes also remained imprinted on his memory, a plain wool shirt and unpressed tweed trousers.

In a letter to Carpenter on September 8th Arthur poured out his feelings about the visit which had released the pent-up yearning for emotional contact with his remote millionaire father; 'If only I had been young when you were young, I know that we would have loved and done great work together.' Arthur wanted Carpenter to come to Ireland and stay with him and meet his wife, a niece of the writer Edmund Wilson. He promised to introduce Carpenter to 'the beautiful young rebels from the hills'.[31] But Carpenter was not up to meeting warriors. Another youthful admirer who came searching around this time for the fount of Greek agape and German Freundschaft, was Michael Davidson, then a journalist in Norwich and involved in a chaste affair with the schoolboy W.H. Auden. Davidson was dismayed to find 'a feeble old man, beyond conversation, who coquettishly pinched my behind'.[32] Only the revolving summer house in the garden lived up to expectations.

As the days lengthened that autumn, Carpenter's spirits sank. He felt frustrated because he could not get through much work any more, and on October 28th he confided to Nevinson that he had begun to realise the world was a sad and wicked place.[33] It was as if all the negativity he had held at bay was boomeranging back. His mood of dejection was not only a result of personal infirmities; the libertarian political ideals he had lived for were being assailed on all sides. Friends in other countries who had dreamed of personal and political democracy were also disconsolate. In 1923 Marcelle Senard was working for the International Labour Organisation as a translator in Switzerland. Without any illusions that her work could contribute to international understanding, Senard contented herself by farming a peasant plot. She reported that George Herron was seriously afflicted with neurasthenia and torturing himself with the thought that his faith in Woodrow Wilson and the League of Nations had deceived others. Guido Ferrando too was 'discouraged and depressed'.[34] Assagioli was rather more cheerful, but then his energies were focused on devising psychological and spiritual theories about how to treat depression.[35] The problems of his progressive clientele were not purely subjective; ineluctably space for the idealistic socialism of the pre-war era was closing in, pressed by the Fascists on the right and the Communists on the left. In France Romain Rolland had become embroiled in a furious controversy with the Communist writer, Henri Barbusse, over the relationship of means and ends. Bazalgette and Mesnil sympathised with Rolland who was turning towards Gandhi's ideas of non-violent resistance. The acrimonious conflict divided the French intellectual left and carried sobering implications for the future.[36]

Within Britain the labour movement had suffered a series of defeats and unemployment remained high. 'Such misery all around and being able to do so little to alleviate it', Carpenter wrote sadly to Evelyn Sharp in November.[37] A general election was imminent in December 1923 but a pessimistic Carpenter remarked to Charles Ashbee, back from Palestine and visiting Guildford, 'Ramsay MacDonald – Clynes and the rest of them – he had known these men as boys – what will they do? Not much, – they have the brains and they are good men – but we are in an age when little can be done by politics – what is wanted is the change of heart.'[38] The first Labour government was elected and MacDonald became Prime Minister, however he was dependent on Asquith's support and his room for manoeuvre was indeed restricted. Labour no sooner took power when members of the Associated Society of Locomotive Engineers and Firemen went on strike for better terms than those agreed by the N.U.R. with the National Railway Wages Board. Carpenter summoned the Guild-ford engine-driver, Jim Godfrey, to Millthorpe, Mountside, to explain the dispute to him. It was the start of a good friendship which brought Carpenter into closer contact with the Guildford labour movement and into the orbit of the left-wing National Council for Labour Colleges and the Plebs League.[39]

At the beginning of 1924 Carpenter decided to change his will. In 1917 Bertram Lloyd and Harold Coxeter had been named as his literary executors, but he and Lloyd had begun to drift apart, and now he appointed Walter Seward and George Clemas along with Coxeter.[40] On February 18th he revealed to Clemas, who was teaching at nearby Kingston upon Thames, that his heart was 'rather shaky'.[41] His doctors advised him to stop living at the top of a hill and to avoid all mental exertion. Dr James Laing of Harley Street (recommended by Havelock Ellis) ordered twelve hours in bed each day and a diet of rusks, oatmeal, chicken, fish and milk – a relatively luxurious regime for one who survived mainly on eggs![42] Carpenter played it down, casually mentioning a little heart weakness in his correspondence.[43] Nevinson was more direct; Carpenter had suffered 'two sharp attacks of heart failure'. Carpenter had pressed his cheek next to Nevinson's when they parted in April with such 'deep emotion' that the journalist left convinced it was their last meeting.[44] Despite maintaining a stiff upper lip in everyday parlance, distrust and despair permeate the poem 'At the Very Edge of Death' which appeared in *The English Review* that May, in which he wrote of the 'tangle of cross-purposes and misunder-standings which we call existence'. Carpenter refers sourly to 'These unworthy suspicions, these malicious innuendoes, those stifled revenges and hatreds which constitute human life.' In contrast death and 'the aroma of another world' seemed welcome; the green graveyard on the Mount seemed so close.[45]

Then, in May, the depression began to lift. Carpenter received a cheery letter from a medical student called Alec West about an idealistic commu-nity, 'The Sanctuary' near Storrington on the South Downs. Vera Pragnell, a wealthy textile heiress, had bought land and announced anyone could build on it. Down and outs, bohemians and leftists of all persuasions were living in huts at 'The Sanctuary'. West told Carpenter that friends of his, the Woolwich I.L.P. supporter Ethel Grinling, along with the former soldier, Wilfred Walter, and his wife Margaret were there, and that Carpen-ter's books were on every shelf.[46] A new utopia beckoned.

A few days later another utopia came knocking on Carpenter's door. Chester Arthur was back, bursting with passion about Ireland, Whitman and Carpenter. Arthur's buoyant confidence, sustained by a sense of invul-nerability which derived partly from privilege and partly from his own youthful exuberance, denied all boundaries, obstacles and taboos. He had been carefully looking out for signs of physical 'comrade-love' among the men he met in the Irish Republican Army, and, despite finding no overt indications, was convinced that in their communion of spirit they comprised a true Theban band.[47] *Towards Democracy* and the Kerry mountains merged in Arthur's imagination.

In his letter dated May 14th Arthur thanked Carpenter from his inner-most heart for the kindness shown to him 'by the dear old man who was so very gentle in my unhappiness, and whose songs are my inspiration and my comfort'.[48] Envious of Merrill and Ted Inigan because they could always be near Carpenter, Arthur declared he would keep Carpenter's photograph with him to remind him of his visit. True to his word, Chester Arthur did remember Carpenter. Many years later, Arthur, who became something of a guru for American beats and hippies, wrote two accounts of visiting Carpenter. The first was published in a book called *The Circle of Sex* under the pseudonym he adopted, 'Gavin Arthur' in 1966; the other was a private manuscript written in 1967 which he gave to the beat poet Allen Ginsberg. It was published posthumously in the magazine *Gay Sunshine* in 1978 and reprinted in Winston Leyland's collection, *Gay Roots*, in 1991.[49]

The two versions are perplexing. Arthur fuses the visits into one; in *The Circle of Sex* Arthur says he visited Carpenter in 1923, returning on several subsequent occasions, but there is no evidence of more than two trips to Guildford.[50] The dates are unclear; the editor in the 1978 *Gay Sunshine* version dates the meeting in 1923 too, but the later reprint has it as 1924.[51] In *The Circle of Sex* Arthur says that it was on his 1923 visit that Inigan suggested he should sleep with Carpenter. 'A young man's electricity is so good for recharging the batteries of the old.'[52] However, this is more likely to have occurred on the second encounter in 1924: Ted Inigan does not appear to have been at Guildford in 1923. Chester Arthur's second letter to Carpenter hints at intimacy rather than the first, while Arthur wrote to his mother on May 13, 1924, with an account of a momentous meeting with Carpenter who gave him a letter of introduction to Havelock Ellis.[53]

Hazy on dates, Arthur retained a graphic recall on sex. In his 1966 account Arthur describes Carpenter's 'stroking fingers' as they lay together, an 'electric build-up' and an 'intense orgasm of the whole nervous system'.[54] The statement Arthur gave to Ginsberg was more explicit, detailing Carpenter's skill in slowly arousing him by burying his face in the hair of his chest, gently touching his nipple with his tongue. 'At last his hand was moving between my legs and his tongue was in my belly-button. And then when he was tickling my fundament just behind the balls and I could not hold it any longer, his mouth closed just over the head of my penis and I could feel my young vitality flowing into his old age.'[55] After he came there was no drained exhaustion, just a great peacefulness in which he fell asleep dreaming of the seminal smell of autumn woods. The following morning Carpenter made love 'rapturously'[56] to him again, after which, in *The Circle of Sex* version, an admiring George Merrill appeared with two cups of tea, declaring, with a nod to Arthur's adopted Irishness, 'What a broth of a boy', and Ted Inigan sponged them down with a wet towel.[57] Arthur says that over breakfast Carpenter related how he had slept with Whitman, insisting on the physical and spiritual expression of comrade love.[58]

These are memories from long afterwards. Not only are the two visits blurred into one, Arthur probably freely invented some of the direct speech. Nevertheless the gist rings true; Carpenter did hold theories of semen and energy, he did have sexual encounters with young men, he was familiar with ways of prolonging intercourse. As for Carpenter's announcement of sleeping with Walt Whitman, while we know from his letter to 'Benjamin' that their encounter was intense and passionate, this has to remain in the realm of hearsay. Two things are certain however. Firstly, in the second half of May 1924 Carpenter cheered up. Secondly, meeting Carpenter proved a turning point for the drifting, disconsolate Arthur. He went on to learn about the sexual theories of Havelock Ellis and Magnus Hirschfeld, become familiar with Eastern religion, practised as an astrologer and energetically pursued both mysticism and sex, including an affair with Neal Cassady, the inspiration for Jack Kerouac's Dean Moriarty in *On the Road*.[59] Metaphorically at least, Walt Whitman lived on. By a strange coincidence Ruth Stafford Goldy, the sister of the young man Harry Stafford who Carpenter had met when he visited Whitman, wrote on May 28th to say how her brother had continued to speak of Carpenter until his death in 1918.[60] Her letter and the photograph of Harry Stafford she enclosed must have evoked powerful memories.

Carpenter's buoyancy was tested by two major shocks that summer. In June the dreamy Russian socialist and protégé of the Tolstoyan Tchertkoff, Constantine Sarantchoft, came to stay in Guildford.[61] He was translating for the Russian delegation who were in Britain to negotiate a trade treaty with the Labour Government. Sarantchoft now shared a small flat in Chelsea with Ted Earle; Carpenter had introduced the two younger men and a rough draft of an undated letter reveals this had led to an uneasy threesome. Assuring Sarantchoft of his continuing affection and respect, Carpenter told the Russian in this draft, 'Of course I understand yr. [*sic*] devotion to Ted, because I have felt and feel the same – quite the same – tho' I have not said much about it.' Carpenter added 'I sometimes indeed think dear Con, that you have never quite understood how devoted Ted and I are to each other, and how a third person coming in has caused us a little dislocation and embarrassment.'[62] This was Carpenter hurt and angry; the no-jealousy policy was coming home to roost, though, of course, he insists he did not want Sarantchoft to stop loving Ted. The entanglement of the three men may have contributed to Carpenter's depressed pessimism in the second half of 1923 and the first few months of 1924. Had there been 'unworthy suspicions' and 'malicious innuendoes'? It seems that by 1924 relations between Sarantchoft and Earle too had run into difficulty. While staying at Guildford in June the unhappy Russian left the house, saying he was going to post a letter. Sarantchoft flung himself in front of the Waterloo to Portsmouth train and died in hospital saying his mind was going and he could endure life no longer. He had sought out Carpenter and chosen to die at Guildford. A newspaper cutting, carefully preserved, records Ted Inigan stonewalling the press.[63] Carpenter was sufficiently troubled to write notes on 'Constantine's' life in which he attributed his suicide to disappointment in love.[64] He wrote with detachment, distancing himself from the violent event. It was as if he had to ration emotion.

The following month Isabella Ford died. She had fallen ill campaigning for the Labour Party that winter and had been unable to go to Washington for the Women's International League for Peace and Freedom that spring because she was bed-ridden.[65] Finally, despite her powerful sense of duty, she had been no longer able to take up her harness and drive herself on. The *Yorkshire Evening Post* carried a report on July 5, 1924 stating, 'Shortly before her death she said, "I feel I should like a little sleep and to be left alone." '[66] The resolute old friend was gone.

Regardless of both these personal blows, Carpenter penned a letter of support to the beleaguered Labour Government which produced a warm reply from Sydney Olivier, about to become Secretary of State for India, expressing his grief over Isabella Ford's death.[67] Ramsay MacDonald also wrote, bemoaning the burdens of office: 'I can but turn my face in the right direction and stagger on a few steps; then a rest and on again.'[68] He was under pressure from the labour movement to establish links with Russia and introduce reforms at home, while facing the bitter hostility of the establishment which would soon contrive to force Labour out of power.

Carpenter was still prepared to back new organisations. The Humanitarian League had folded after the First World War. Though Henry Salt retired from the fray to write his memoirs, other former members of the League ensured that it had many offshoots. The publisher Ernest Bell set up one of these, the League for the Prohibition of Cruel Sports, in 1924, backed by Carpenter, Salt and Shaw.[69]

During the summer of 1924 Carpenter's hope and vigour returned somewhat. He was greatly cheered by meeting up with Goldsworthy Lowes Dickinson at Robert Trevelyan's home, and entertained S.L. Cronwright Schreiner who had just completed his collection of Olive Schreiner's letters.[70] His interest in India was as strong as ever and he welcomed Annie Besant back to Britain, eagerly reading Romain Rolland's book on Gandhi.[71] During August, Carpenter was happily wrapped up in E.M. Forster's new novel, *A Passage to India*, writing a letter in which the teasing tone he usually adopted with Forster was replaced by one of profound respect for what his younger friend had achieved and an admiring acknowledgement that he could never have written such a book. *A Passage to India*, with its title taken from a Whitman poem, evoked Carpenter's own long involvement with South Asia, from F.D. Maurice's faith in personal relations, to Aligarh and Cox's sandals, to Arunachalam, the Theosophists and on to Tagore, Naidu and tangentially to Gandhi. He observed wryly that the only problem was his own slowness of apprehension – he had to keep turning back the pages to remember the characters.[72]

This forgetfulness was evident when Henry Nevinson paid a visit with Katie Ratcliffe, the Quaker wife of the journalist S.K. Ratcliffe, on August 10th; Carpenter did not recall that they had met and ignored her while inquiring about Evelyn Sharp who he was evidently disappointed not to see. An embarrassed Nevinson was made all the more uncomfortable by two Wigan 'disciples', down for the Wembley football match. Not only were they heavy going conversationally, they were excruciating singers. Nevinson concluded tersely in his diary, 'The visit was not a success.' He managed, however, to snatch a word with Carpenter who imparted the news that he was planning a new book on Shelley's 'sex problems'.[73]

It was the lull before the storm; Carpenter was about to be eighty.

24

Last Years

With a Labour Government in office the 'Complete Anarchist's' birthday became an alternative state occasion. Tom Nicholson and G.H.B. Ward proposed an album signed by the Labour Cabinet which the former trades union organiser, Margaret Bondfield, now Parliamentary Secretary to the Ministry of Labour, put into effect.[1] Such an illustrious album greatly helped Walter Seward in his role as press officer for the birthday, and he did such a zealous job that a flustered George Merrill announced to Tom and Annie Nicholson that reporters were 'waiting in long queys [sic]', while Millthorpe, Mountside, looked like a 'flower and fruit store'. He declared 'Edward is a little tired but bearing up very well.'[2] Surrounded by letters, telegrams and parcels, Carpenter smiled at the flock of reporters and proclaimed, 'I am still surviving.'[3]

Tributes appeared in the socialist papers, the *Daily Herald*, *Clarion*, the *New Statesman*, and Hyndman's *Justice* as well as in the *Manchester Guardian*, the *Observer* and the *Evening Standard*. Even the *Egyptian Gazette* reported on Carpenter at eighty.[4] The philosopher, C.E.M. Joad, who had been associated with the National Guilds League, hailed the eighty-year-old as the harbinger of modernity.

> Carpenter denounced the Victorians for hypocrisy, held up their conventions to ridicule, and called their civilisation a disease. He was like a man coming into a stuffy sitting room in a seaside boarding house, and opening the window to let in light and air. . . .[5]

It is a lovely image and it catches figuratively the emotional release Carpenter offered to those who regarded themselves as escapees from the nineteenth century. In 1924 this could still resonate.

Meanwhile, the man himself issued a rather rambling response denouncing the commercial age as a 'Mad Hatter's Tea Party', and struggled to sort

EDWARD CARPENTER: A LIFE OF LIBERTY AND LOVE

out his vast correspondence.[6] From the 1880s came Roger Fry, Annie Besant and the Russian tailor he had befriended in the Leeds Socialist League, John Dyche. From more recent times there was the birth controller, Norman Haire, who knew him through the B.S.S.S.P. and new friends from the Sanctuary. In between there were hundreds of other names. Merrill was particularly chuffed by such celebrities as the Countess of Warwick, Sybil Thorndike and the popular novelist Hall Caine.[7] But Carpenter proudly showed Jim Godfrey the tribute from the T.U.C.[8] He was undoubtedly also moved by the list of Sheffield I.L.P. members, which included J.H. Bingham, collected by R.H. Minshall, bearing witness to how he had taught them to 'look beyond personal success and power', and by the Sheffield Clarion Club, who had so often bicycled to Millthorpe and the Royal Oak, and who now thanked him for 'his warm heart and sincere friendship'. But most remarkable of all were the 109 signatures gathered by Tom Nicholson and Charlie Roughton from the 'Neighbours and Friends of Millthorpe'.[9] Along with the vicar, the Gilchrists and the Wards, were a great host of Keys, Kays, Buntings, Greaveses, Pearsons and Allcards, not forgetting Fannie Hukin as well as Harriet Haslam and Kate Webster from the Royal Oak. The country people united in a collective expression of affection for the eccentric neighbour who had helped so many of them. Late missives were still arriving with good wishes and thanks in September, including one from E.D. Morel thanking Carpenter for a letter commending him for a Nobel Peace Prize.[10] Carpenter had helped so many people in such diverse ways and now their gratitude flowed towards him in a great wave of feeling.

It was overwhelming; Charlie Roughton observed to Sixsmith on September 7th that he expected Carpenter 'will be glad that he is not 80 years old often'.[11] E.M. Forster, who went to Guildford on September 30th, concluded that the birthday had shattered Carpenter. He noted in his diary that his old friend 'retrospects' much.[12] It was understandable, for every letter and every name must have evoked memories and wonder at the destiny which had cast some for the Cabinet and others for the cowshed. Carpenter groaned to Clem early in October about being annihilated by incessant letter writing after 'the Birthday'.[13] He, Merrill and Inigan then departed for a holiday in Bournemouth to recover.

The hubbub of 'the Birthday' interrupted Carpenter's work on *The Psychology of the Poet Shelley* with Guy Barnard, who adopted the pseudonym 'George Barnefield'. Carpenter transferred the copyright to Barnard, saying that the younger man had written most of the book.[14] Then Carpenter pushed a sceptical Stanley Unwin to increase the royalties; this brought a riposte: 'I fear that none of us is likely to make a fortune out of the two papers on "The Psychology of the Poet Shelley" for the thesis is not likely to be a popular one however correct it might be.'[15] Nonetheless he yielded; Unwin had a soft spot for Carpenter, whose works he collected, even though in these later years Carpenter's loss of memory made him 'apt to blame us for doing something he had instructed us to do only the day before'.[16]

In *The Psychology of the Poet Shelley*, which came out early in 1925, Barnard argued that Shelley was bisexual with repressed homosexual feelings for James Hogg. A more guarded Carpenter intimated that Shelley did not quite share the temperament of those whose predominant love-attraction was to the opposite sex. He suggested that Shelley was a fore-runner of a love which transcended the 'mere sexual urge'.[17] Carpenter proposed that humanity was now evolving towards this less excitable future in which everyone would possess elements of the masculine and the feminine. Nevinson was unconvinced, ruminating in his diary, 'that sex idea has grown upon the man with age'.[18]

In his contribution to the book Carpenter denied any specialist knowledge of 'Modern Psychology'.[19] This was disingenuous, for he had read far more than he was admitting. It was a device which enabled him to bypass the current framework of thinking in order to assert direct experience. He persisted in drawing on his own life and the lives of homosexual friends. He also had a personal source – the lonely people whose confessional letters still came. 'Although I am known as Bob, physically I am a girl', wrote 'Bob Rodgers' who described the mockery and scoffing which had resulted. 'Perhaps if I were a real man, I should be less sensitive. As it is, I assume a show of bravado which I am often far from feeling. Your encouragement stimulates and gives strength to fight on.'[20] Carpenter was sufficiently intrigued by this letter to copy it out in his now shaky handwriting.

If Carpenter in old age inclined to peaceful androgyny, he was still quietly and steadfastly unconventional in living his ideals. Since Ted Inigan had moved in Carpenter had been living as part of a trio instead of a couple. Forster called them 'the family' in a letter to his friend Florence Barger in October 1924, imparting the information that all three residents at Millthorpe, Mountside, had enjoyed her shortbread, while insisting on referring to her formally as 'Mrs Barger'.[21] Proprieties were maintained by the unusual family. The American anarchist and sex radical, Emma Goldman, who went to Mountside in May 1925, was utterly mystified. She wrote telling her former lover, Alexander Berkman, that Carpenter lived with a man he had 'picked up from the gutter 35 years ago' – a somewhat melodramatic depiction of Dore and Totley railway station!

Unfamiliar with Carpenter's disregard for style while at home, she was shocked by the contrast between his shabby dress and the fashionable suit and fine shirt of a man she calls 'Goe'. She observed that this 'Goe' – George Merrill – had a ring on his finger and was full of his own importance, and that Carpenter treated him like a man would treat 'a younger wife'. Her confusion was compounded when she detected that 'the cook seems to be the lover of Goe, or at least the younger friend to compensate him for the old age of E.C.'[22] A disorientated Goldman muddled her 'Goes' and 'Georges', relating to Berkman how the Shelley book was under 'Goe's' name.

The 'Goe' character, suspicious of her motives in calling, bewildered her with protective admonitions about all the claims on 'poor Ed' for money and favours, insisting that 'poor Ed' had to be looked after.[23] Goldman, who was in Britain campaigning against the imprisonment of left oppositionists in Russia, had indeed written to Carpenter in December 1924 angling for his support and a donation towards a hall.[24] But her reason for the Guildford trip was to pay homage to the 'great Libertarian' she had long admired and persuade him to write an introduction to a new edition of Berkman's *Prison Memoirs*.[25] The book contained sympathetic and thoughtful accounts of male prisoners' love for one another, which both Carpenter and Merrill admired, and Carpenter agreed to write a short introduction for the 1926 version, alluding in code to friendships. Though Goldman had lectured on homosexuality and lesbianism, becoming herself a focus for many private confessional letters, she did not take to Merrill and the Mountside household disturbed her. Sighing about Carpenter's domestic arrangements, she reflected to Berkman that the main thing was for him to have a happy old age.[26]

Carpenter, with his oatmeal porridge, omelettes and stewed fruit, was hardly a big spender, though despite Merrill's efforts, money dribbled away to causes and individuals fallen on hard times. It went to Clem, to Biagio di Paulo, as well as to various young men Carpenter hardly knew. When he had money he gave it away. But early in 1925 he panicked. Nevinson was dryly amused on February 27th when he took Carpenter one of his son Richard's etchings, to find that Harold Coxeter was 'having some trouble with the great and simple advocate of poverty' who was convinced he would end up in the workhouse.[27]

Despite anxieties about money, the holidays (Aix-le Bains in June 1925) and excursions continued.[28] Enjoying the immediacy of life had always been a vital feature in Carpenter and Merrill's relationship, from the trip to the Isle of Man, through to the exotic holidays abroad. Merrill with

Carpenter and Merrill on a boating expedition at Guildford, 1925

his great feeling for occasion enjoyed dressing up. Photographs of the two men on a boating expedition while at Guildford reveal the naturally elegant Carpenter in a tweed suit, with a walking stick and hat tilted at the Walt Whitman angle beside Merrill who is holding himself like a burgher of substance and sporting a beer belly.

Merrill's zest for outings is evident in his account of a visit to Thomas Hardy in the autumn of 1925, when the novelist was 85. He recounted affectionately to Sixsmith how 'T.H. and Edward swung along the road looking very happy', though Hardy proved the better walker.[29] The sociable Merrill, with his hankering after celebrity, loved meeting the famous writer, but the event was undoubtedly special because the private imaginative self Merrill tended to cover with bluster had long delighted in Hardy's plots and characters. Such excitement, however, was fast becoming the exception. Carpenter's loss of mobility was making it harder to do the external things which had been so crucial in his and Merrill's partnership. Merrill, who had always liked a drink, turned to the pub more and more for diversion.

Carpenter still attended B.S.S.S.P. meetings, vainly attempting to entice

Ellis to one on 'Incest' in March 1925, after which he stayed with George Ives.[30] He needed the intellectual and political stimulation of these forays, though he could no longer take off to London so easily as in the past. He did, however, make some new contacts in Guildford. In January 1925 the Trades and Labour Council had invited Carpenter to be their 'Honoured Guest' when George Lansbury came to speak in Guildford.[31] This brought him back in touch with Lansbury, who, though billed as 'General Manager' of the *Daily Herald*, had under pressure from the Labour establishment just resigned. He was about to launch the lively left-wing *Lansbury's Labour Weekly*, which issued a supplementary song book bringing 'England Arise' to the inter-war generation.[32] When the left-wing railway man, Jim Godfrey, was branded a communist by the local papers in November 1925, Carpenter sturdily signed his nomination papers to be a councillor. Nonetheless, Carpenter felt lonely at Guildford, marooned on his Mountside. After all those years of being so busy, in the mid 1920s he finally had time on his hands and his world was shrinking. As the wider public realm receded, the microcosm of the personal assumed more significance; friends became all the more important to him and so did music. He was gratified when Nevinson sent a gramophone record in autumn 1926, confessing 'I seem to come very near you when it is being played', and relating how he had been living 'quite out of the world in dreams'.[33] Listening to the music he loved he could wander into reveries, telling Evelyn Sharp that 'In some hours, when life turns its face away from us, we realise how necessary Beauty is.'[34]

He was constantly urging Havelock Ellis to visit, though a little troubled when Ellis proposed coming with his new love in the autumn of 1926. 'I shd. [*sic*] like also to see Madame Cyon, but she must excuse me if (among numberless demands on my time) I prove to be rather distrait and ineffectual.'[35] It was the old, familiar friends he needed, for with them he did not need to present a front. For some time Carpenter had been hurt that Bertram Lloyd did not visit him more often.[36] Clem continued to visit loyally, though the needy older man was dismayed when Clem, who was teaching, was unable to stay the night in autumn 1925.[37] Their relationship was gradually being transformed. Instead of Carpenter being the all-knowing counsellor, he had become dependent on the younger man, begging him to visit early in August 1926. 'I am left high and dry with George and Ted – both angelic in their way but still one wants an occasional change!'[38] On August 2nd Carpenter wrote to Charlie Sixsmith in great excitement; Biagio di Paulo had arrived from Italy where Benito Mussolini's rise had resulted in the brutal suppression of the left. Carpenter immediately set about making plans for di Paulo's stay in Britain. Inigan would bring him to the Sixsmiths, 'I do not feel equal to much travelling myself and have to conserve my power.'[39] Initially all went well, though by August 17th Carpenter was intimating that their visitor needed to find some employment. Over the next two months, however, the relationship with Biagio di Paulo declined. When he departed in October Carpenter confided to Sixsmith that the Italian's ways had not been altogether satisfactory during the latter part of his stay.[40] Biagio had fallen from grace and yet another romantic fantasy been shattered.

Carpenter's constant tussle against his forgetfulness absorbed a good deal of his energy. He had to focus his consciousness on the details of everyday life. Touched by Nevinson's gifts of Chopin and Bach records in September 1926, he observed to Evelyn Sharp that Nevinson must have 'a secret latch key to my heart. He seems to know by instinct what . . . I <u>need</u>.'[41] Yet Carpenter could not quite remember exactly what pieces were on the records. During 1926 he was so cocooned that even the dramatic events of the General Strike did not really impinge. Interviewed by the *Daily News* for his eighty-second birthday he remarked that the 'Trade unions have rather shot their bolt.'[42]

As the hardship caused by the lock-out intensified during the autumn, however, he girded himself up to defend the miners in the *Manchester Guardian*. His old combative spirit was aroused, though his argument meandered in 'The Miners As I Have Known Them'. With evident respect for the miners' skill and courage he contended that their working practices prefigured values of co-operation. He went on to elaborate a theory that the miners sub-consciously retained 'in their minds much of the primitive mentality of pre-civilisation days'.[43] It is unlikely the men and women who had discussed unions and Bolshevism on his lawn a few years before up north in Derbyshire would have accepted this primordial tag, but mining communities were being hammered so much they most probably concluded the strange old man meant well.

Shortly after 'The Miners As I have Known Them' appeared, Carpenter wrote to Canon John Dalton, announcing, 'My friend Gilbert Beith (brother of Ian Hay Beith) proposes to drive over to Windsor one day in the motor car. I am wondering whether <u>you are at home</u> and whether you would spare me a half-hour for a walk in the Park with Beith and perhaps with George Merrill.' Gilbert Beith's brother was enjoying some success as a playwright and Carpenter could not resist impressing with a tinge of literary fame. He described Merrill to Dalton as his 'faithful friend'.[44] The expedition was arranged for October 20th and Ted Inigan was added to the party as Merrill had a cold. Dalton sent them elaborate instructions about how to gain entrance.[45] George V would no doubt have been somewhat dismayed had he known that a subversive friend of the miners and of his bête noir, the wild George Lansbury, was strolling through his park.

E.M. Forster was pleased that Carpenter seemed remarkably fit when he called in December, and early in 1927 Carpenter was fantasising of an excursion with Clem up Melbury Hill and down to Dorchester to call on Hardy.[46] Satyrs, pagan deities and a wild dance among the cowslips and primroses on the Dorset hill flitted before him until, 'wiser counsels prevailed, and all the difficulties rose up and gave me pause'.[47] When Henry Nevinson and Evelyn Sharp visited in April 1927, they found Carpenter still in surprisingly fine fettle. They sat out in the garden drinking tea with him talking, just like the old days, about Lowes Dickinson, China, the trades unions, until George Merrill's ominous return 'smelling horribly of drink'.[48] Nevinson was far from being a teetotaller, but was troubled to note Carpenter's anxiety. Without Tom Nicholson's watchful eye and without the exercise involved at the original Millthorpe, alcohol was getting a hold over Merrill. Carpenter's concern may have been partly because of Evelyn Sharp's presence, for in a letter after the incident he made a point of telling her how Merrill identified with her latest book, *The London Child*.[49] Carpenter, ever protective of his faithful friend, wanted to ensure he was not typecast as loutish.

In practice however, he was depending increasingly on the Norwegian, Illit Gröndahl and on Merrill's love, Ted Inigan. Gröndahl came to work as Carpenter's researcher and amanuensis in December 1925 and stayed for two years, going up and down stairs to fetch books so Carpenter could write.[50] He and Carpenter would drink glasses of lemon-water and eat biscuits together while they worked and occasionally went on little walks along the Hog's Back. Sometimes, when Carpenter was going to bed, he would change his mind and go outside with Ted Inigan in the vain hope of hearing a nightingale. He became restless indoors, 'Come on, let's get out; I must have some air', he would say to Inigan.[51] It was Inigan who helped Carpenter to visit Henry Salt in Brighton in May 1927, accompanying the two old men to a concert on the pier. For Carpenter the trip was a nostalgic return to his childhood and he found himself pondering on why both he and Salt had such intimate connections to Brighton. On the train journey back, as he gazed out of the window at his beloved Downs, the hill named after St Martha, the dutiful saint of active spirituality, suddenly sprang into view.[52] Had she been watching him all those years?

Just before his eighty-third birthday that August, Carpenter wrote ruefully to the Moorhay and Totley farmer and friend of John Furniss,

George Pearson, 'I am a rare old croc now.'[53] Not only was he feeling
his age, a disconcerting conjecture that life was without any pattern had
been flickering into his mind. He tended to confide such doubts to Clem
who had never placed much faith in Carpenter's earlier uplifting panaceas.[54]
Instead of the grand harmonies Carpenter had lived by, in old age he
began to suspect that nature was likely to leave humanity 'in the lurch
with ineffectual boots and snow trickling down our backs!'[55] He was
acutely aware of the insecurity of existence, reflecting to Clem, 'I begin
to realise how precarious life is and how impossible to depend on. Theoretically, I knew this before. Practically I know it now.'[56]

However his moods swung this way and that; the day after writing
this letter he wrote again, his feathers fluffed up in delight. Clem had
sent carnations for his eighty-third birthday, 'the very incarnation of love
and affection', purred Carpenter. Friendship now seemed the main thing.[57]

Yet Carpenter was working on a new book in 1927. When Charley
Cramp came to take him for a drive through the Surrey heather, Carpenter
portrayed this as being about 'Eastern religions'.[58] *Light from the East* (1927)
was an edited collection of Ponnambalam Arunachalam's letters to him.
These ranged beyond the spiritual. During the First World War, Arunachalam had become more critical of British rule, hailing the Russian withdrawal
from the war in one letter in August 1917.[59] After retiring from the Civil
Service, Arunachalam had founded the Ceylon Social Service League in
1915, to encourage village industries and co-operative credit and, in 1919,
he helped the friend of Tagore and Gandhi, Charles Freer Andrews, to
create the Ceylon Workers' League among the exploited tea plantation
workers. That year he was elected the first President of the Ceylon
National Congress which he had helped to found. He resigned in 1923
because the Sinhalese rejected a separate Tamil seat. Concerned to preserve
Tamil history and literature, Arunachalam formed the Ceylon Tamil
League. However, when he died in 1924, his hopes of Tamil and Sinhalese
co-operation on the basis of distinct cultural identities were being negated
by a growing division between the two groups. Arunachalam's contribution
to his country seemed in danger of being sidelined and his widow, Svarnam
Arunachalam, started nudging Carpenter to write his life. Carpenter
arranged for Arunachalam's letters to be typed but tried to wiggle out of
writing a biography, suggesting that perhaps she might do something.
This produced a steely reply; Svarnam Arunachalam made it known that
it was not customary for Hindu ladies to write biographies of their
husbands. When she reminded him that he was her husband's dearest
friend, promised to send him the necessary information and offset any

strain on his resources by covering clerical and printing costs, Carpenter gave in.[60]

In the introduction he wrote to Arunachalam's letters, Carpenter insisted that Western science could never plumb the being at the root of experience. It was not a matter of discovering the causes of things; the key was the ability to 'dismiss Thought' and to perceive without struggling.[61] Of course he had spent his life plumbing and struggling and indeed, like Arunachalam, could not entirely give up on the endeavour to bring the contrasting ways of knowing into a closer affinity.

Arunachalam had regarded the spiritual and the erotic in Hindu thinking as integrally connected. The lingam, the smooth cylindrical stone which was the sign of the God Siva, symbolised for Arunachalam union, solidarity and human fellowship.[62] Carpenter, too, universalised the lingam, though his nuance differed. It was 'prophetic of a new Man (or Woman) already appearing in our midst – a type which is destined to unite the qualities of both sexes (the tenderness and adaptability of the female with the strength and reliability of the male) and to be the herald of the reunion of Eros and Psyche'.[63] He suppressed, as he had done all his life, the tensions within this willed reunion of sex and gender, sex and spirit. Though Carpenter did acknowledge the emphasis on control over desire in Hindu religion, he was personally drawn to what he saw as an acceptance of sexuality and eroticism in the popular manifestations of the religion. Along with a long line of European commentators from the seventeenth century, he interpreted the lingam as originating as a phallic symbol, while the God Siva's male and female aspects suggested a potential bisexuality to him.[64] He could remember the sensuousness of the procession in the religious festival he had witnessed and an echo of Kalua flickers across the page as the dancer 'throwing out forms of grace without ceasing and creating beauty by merely liberating his own energies'.[65] Carpenter in old age still believed the instant of sexual fusion constituted a glimmer of transcendence. In Light from the East he maintained that spiritual revelation was reminiscent of the (male) orgasm in 'its burning withering intensity – the fixed almost rigid condition which precedes its culmination, the threads like lightning, streaming from all parts of the organism to their fulfilment, and the ecstatic deliverance'.[66] In 1928 he equates sex and spirit more overtly than when he had travelled through Ceylon and India in 1890–91. Moreover he had taken on board psychological theories of bisexuality – albeit with an emphasis on the masculine.

Carpenter appended a manuscript on 'Birth Control and Bisexuality', written a little earlier, to Light from the East. In this he expressed his fascination with 'cross-types' and praised the wonders of modern girls, who seemed to signify a new androgyny. These 1920s boyish young women were hailed as an evolutionary step forwards and contrasted with the dependent, subservient females he had regarded with dread ever since he was a young man; 'I find that they sap and deplete us – many of us – to an almost fatal extent.' With the energy-sappers out of the way, human beings of indeterminate gender, 'neither excessively male nor excessively female', could predominate.[67] Estrangement between men and women, sexual difference, inequality, repressed or discordant desires all floated away in *Light from the East*.

It is not clear what Svarnam Arunachalam made of this surprising testimony to her husband's life and work. By the time the book was finished towards the end of 1927 Carpenter's own existence was growing too fragile for him to register reactions. When Henry Salt visited that autumn he thought Merrill was looking 'out of sorts'.[68] And on September 24th, Henry Nevinson and Evelyn Sharp were troubled to find Carpenter mentally slow and repeating himself. He was consumed by distress at the death of Isadora Duncan, strangled by one of the scarves she used for her free-expression dancing; in the old man's mind the androgynous creativity of the dance which unified sex and spirit had been broken. Carpenter kept saying it was a horrible world, holding onto the hand of the man he regarded as close to the Ancient Greeks, the 'manly' war correspondent with the 'womanly' sensibility.[69]

The curious, subversive amalgam, *Light from the East*, Carpenter's final work, expresses the contradictory explorations of his own life. His old friend Goldsworthy Lowes Dickinson had long puzzled how Carpenter had managed to confound the popular view of homosexuals as decadent sensualists, while believing in and practising 'the physical relation very frankly'. It was profoundly mysterious to Lowes Dickinson how it was 'that popular opinion hasn't managed to put him into prison and murder him . . . We must be thankful for small mercies.'[70] But the sexy sage did not always waft away reaction. Chester (Gavin) Arthur recounts how a banker he met expressed disgust at 'that socialist faggot',[71] and, when Carpenter's name was put forward for the Freedom of the City in December 1927, Sheffield Tories took a similar view. To the distress of Carpenter's socialist friends in Sheffield, the right managed to defeat the proposal by a narrow majority.[72]

Carpenter himself was beyond noticing the slight. In January 1928 the unthinkable happened. George Merrill died. Henry Salt's 'out of sorts' had been an understatement, Merrill had been ill for several months. Fannie Hukin only found out by chance on January 18th, when she bumped into Tom Nicholson on the Sheffield bus heading down to the funeral. She immediately wrote to Alf Mattison and Florrie.[73] Regardless of the ambivalence of their feelings for Merrill, all three could imagine the impact on Carpenter. And indeed he was completely overwhelmed with grief, unable to respond to visitors or letters. A fortnight after Merrill died, Mattison managed to get to Guildford. Carpenter, bent over, walking with a stick, sat and stared vacantly at the carpet. Mattison was so shocked by the strange unfamiliarity of his bleak outlook on life that he felt unable to record what Carpenter said. Yet it was evident how pleased Carpenter was to see him. The two dear friends went out into the garden together, even though the rain was gently falling and, just as Mattison was about to leave, Carpenter leant on his arm, saying, 'He was the light of my eyes.'[74]

The loss of Merrill defeated Carpenter. As Ted Inigan observed, 'Things were not the same afterwards.'[75] Vera Pragnell produced six hundred copies of a little book, *The Story of the Sanctuary*, with a fellow Carpenter enthusiast, Victor Neuburg, at the Vine Press in Steyning. It was dedicated to Carpenter as 'Love's pilgrim, sage and bard' and the 'Master ever young'.[76] Bob Muirhead put it more bluntly; Carpenter had entered a 'second childhood'.[77] He was suffering from dementia.

The steep ascent up Mountside was now impossible for Carpenter and the long overdue decision to move was taken. He and Inigan stayed for a while in rooms nearby with a Mr and Mrs Corbyn at 72, Woodland Avenue, while waiting for their new bungalow, Inglenook, in Josephs Road, on the outskirts of Guildford.[78] But Carpenter had no sooner completed the purchase when he suffered another 'seizure' and Inigan had to take him to his new home in an ambulance.

Nevinson, rather unkindly, dismissed Inglenook as 'a poor little place on the flats near the river'.[79] Josephs Road might not have been grand but it was a pleasant road. However this final stroke had left Carpenter unable to stand or walk, he spoke slowly and could hardly hear. When Nevinson and Sharp called at Inglenook, his artistic niece Dorothea Clements was helping to care for him. Though he looked the same, Nevinson felt he was no longer E.C. A newspaper report on 'Edward Carpenter at Eighty-Four' reported on how this was the first birthday when Carpenter could not respond to friends and disciples.[80] Another stated that he was so shy he had three escape exits from his work room.[81] This was surely exaggerated but he was indeed restless. It was as if his youthful fear of being trapped in unwanted social situations had grown more pronounced with his virtual immobility. Inigan relates how Carpenter became tired when friends talked too much and would refuse to see people.[82] Moreover he was unable to recognise even those he knew well,

Carpenter in wheelchair at Josephs Road, with Birgit Gröndahl and Ted Inigan

including the Nicholsons, who returned, most distressed, to Millthorpe.[83] Yet in flashes of lucidity Carpenter jested about his infirmities and he formed an attachment to two neighbours, Miss Long and Miss Hamblin, who he dubbed, 'The long and the short of it.'[84]

When his mind cleared he was aware of his condition. In January 1929, Gröndahl's sister, Birgit, came over from Norway, and Carpenter, alert and cognizant, remarked 'This is a red-letter day for me.'[85] The recognition that his understanding was often clouded must have been especially galling for one so set on psychological and emotional control, and the humiliation and suffering are evident on his face in a photograph with Ted Inigan and Birgit Gröndahl taken in the back garden. Carpenter sits hunched in his chair, covered with a plaid rug, staring at the camera with fear and outrage. The contrast with the composure and power evident in earlier photographs is marked. Many years later, in 1944, when giving a radio broadcast on Carpenter, E.M. Forster still shuddered at the memory of his friend towards the end, containing his distress in carefully studied humdrum, 'Life can be and usually is pretty cruel in spots.'[86]

Carpenter camouflaged his feelings in irony. 'I am disastrously well', he quipped to Henry Nevinson and Evelyn Sharp in June as he was being drawn in his wheelchair by Inigan and a new helper, Percy Barker, from Sheffield. Even while Nevinson and Sharp were there though, he was slipping in and out of oblivion. When Evelyn Sharp told him of a huge labour rally at the Albert Hall where ten thousand people had sung 'England Arise' and remembered him, an uncomprehending Carpenter replied airily, 'They could not help but think of me.'[87] The involuntary remark contained an inner lucidity. He had, after all, been waiting long indeed for the comrades, patriots and lovers to arise.

If Carpenter was characteristically optimistic about his medical condition, this time his doctor was emphatic; there could be no partial recovery. On June 19th he could still recognise Henry Nevinson, and Gilbert Beith reported to a Labour Party man close to Ramsay MacDonald, A. Luckhurst Scott, that Carpenter seemed easier and more tranquil. However when Luckhurst Scott went to Guildford on June 22nd, Carpenter was comatose. Beith and Dorothea Clements asked Luckhurst Scott to intercede with Ramsay MacDonald who they hoped might speak at Carpenter's funeral. But MacDonald, in election gear, declined.[88] On June 28th Charlie Sixsmith received a telegram from Percy Barker saying Carpenter had passed peacefully away.[89] Nevinson, who had been out of the country, found out from a report in the Observer on the 30th and wrote sadly in his diary that their shy friendship was over.[90]

Ted Inigan telegrammed Charlie Sixsmith on July 1st: 'Funeral 3 o'clock today.'[91] It was not much notice, but Inigan and Barker were no doubt exhausted and overwhelmed. Nonetheless, Charlie Sixsmith, along with Alf Mattison, who caught an early train from Leeds, were there among the mourners at Carpenter's funeral. Henry Nevinson and Evelyn Sharp also travelled to Guildford. Ironically the pagan was buried with conventional Church of England rites, though Captain Leonard Green, now a literary executor with Beith and Clemas, read Carpenter's poem 'Into the Region of the Sun' at the grave high on the hill next to George Merrill.[92] Nevinson made an impromptu speech in tribute to Carpenter's courage. His voice breaking as he said the word, he repeated it more emphatically, 'courage to challenge conventional standards to live among the common people, honouring those who worked with their hands'.[93]

This was the romantic Nevinson speaking; nevertheless his sharp journalistic eye had scanned the two hundred or so mourners, registering there was 'no one of great distinction'.[94] His friends S.K. and Katie Ratcliffe were there, he recognised Raymond and Ethel Unwin, Beith, Coxeter, Clemas and Seward, along with Captain Green. A.L. Scott and Jim

Middleton represented the National Labour Party, R.H. Minshall, the Sheffield I.L.P., the left-winger J.F. Horrabin came from the National Council of Labour Colleges, and Charley Cramp sent a wreath from the N.U.R. A large contingent from the Guildford labour movement turned up; the Labour Party, the Trades Council, the Bakers' Union, the Workers' Union, the Adult School and the Women's Co-operative Guild, were there in force. Carpenter's relatives included General C.H. Carpenter and Colonel George Carpenter, as well as Carpenter's nieces, Dorothea Clements and the independent Ida Hyett who Carpenter had helped to acquire a flat in London at 24, Highbury Place.[95]

Ida Hyett took charge of the distribution of Carpenter's rather meagre possessions. Alf Mattison requested his watch and pen, but they had already been allocated, and Carpenter's barometer was despatched instead. John Dalton meekly enquired if he could purchase one of Carpenter's books but was told that all those at Inglenook had been given away.[96] Despite the anxieties about money, Carpenter left £5,214, most of which went to his nephews and nieces and to Ted Inigan. Fannie Hukin was remembered with a legacy of £100.[97]

Over the next few months the obituary writers struggled to sum up a man whose life defied categorisation. *The Times* remarked on his quest for self-knowledge, the *Manchester Guardian* on his influence on individuals, the *Telegraph* on his mysticism and brilliant eyes. *Cruel Sports* elaborated on Carpenter's opposition to rabbit coursing and stag hunting. The *Daily Herald* referred to his defence of homosexuality and printed special tributes from central Labour Party figures: Prime Minister, Ramsay MacDonald; Home Secretary, J.R. Clynes; and the Lord Privy Seal, J.H. Thomas. Fenner Brockway wrote with passion in the *New Leader* of Carpenter's defiance of convention. The I.L.P. was at loggerheads with MacDonald, but in death Carpenter miraculously united the socialist movement. *Forward*, *Clarion*, *The Social Democrat* and *Plebs* all remembered him with affection. In J.F. Horrabin's sketch in *Plebs*, of 'Carpenter on the moon', he strides forward in broad-brimmed hat and floppy tie, and the *Singer and Sower* declared that while the Fabians might be 'gas-and-water' socialists, Carpenter embodied 'sandal-and-song socialism'.[98] For the *Healthy Life* he was 'the fiery socialist, the gentle mystic and graceful pagan seer'.[99]

In August Alf Mattison paid a visit to Millthorpe and was depressed at its decline; Tom Nicholson appeared to have lost heart and the practical Mattison noticed that repairs needed doing.[100] Early in September, Nevinson, who had discovered Carpenter lingered on in his mind, drove up to Millthorpe to metaphorically lay the spirit. He did not detect the disrepair, 'Everything was just the same; only the soul has gone.'[101] But he did learn that Tom Nicholson, who had taken out a mortgage in January 1929, was having difficulty paying off the ten shillings a week and was worried that Millthorpe would have to be sold. Nevinson then made his way to visit George Pearson. Now badly crippled by rheumatism, Pearson had finally managed to purchase the Moorhay farm, close to the quarries where John Furniss had worked, and the family were also growing fruit and vegetables at Totley. The Pearsons, prospering at last, had even acquired a motor car.

Early in 1930, the statement Carpenter had written in 1910 to be read at his funeral turned up. He had entrusted the address to Harold Coxeter who had deposited it in the bank and forgotten about it. An indignant Clemas pronounced this 'a neglect of duty' when he posted a copy to Charlie Sixsmith, while a Cassandra-like Salt opined to Alf Mattison from Brighton that 'disastrous confusion' had surrounded Carpenter's death. It had all been 'a tragedy and a muddle'.[102] An edginess surrounded Carpenter's memory as friends vied to occupy the position of being his true intimates.

Towards the end of 1929 a volume of recollections in which Carpenter's thwarted funeral address could be published was being mooted. Some demurred: Alf Mattison because he did not feel up to the task, Bertram Lloyd because he disliked the idea of a book of crowded tributes, and Shaw because he preferred to imagine the Noble Savage in his happy hunting ground with all his faculties restored.[103] Several hiccups ensued. Mattison was dismayed by what he called the 'levity' of Salt's contribution – a tactful depiction of the resentment which spurted from Salt's ambivalent recollections of Carpenter. Clemas was despatched to talk it over with Salt, who refused any modifications.[104] E.M. Forster was crucial in seeing the project through, mollifying Clemas when Beith was named as editor of *Edward Carpenter: In Appreciation*, and persuading Evelyn Sharp of the special need for the collection. 'E.C. won't survive (I think) in his books, but in the testimonies of his friends. He was so much more important in himself than in his printed words.'[105]

Yet even Forster, the wordsmith, found Carpenter's gift for evoking affection elusive. Ted Inigan caught it, his Lancashire intonation in the rhythm of his homage; 'Sometimes he would say he was a great trouble to me, but he was not, as it was only pleasure for me to do anything for him, and I would have willingly kept on doing so if only he had lived. He was like a father to me. God rest his soul.'[106]

25

Bearing the Memory

While E.M. Forster was so assiduously prodding the contributors to *In Appreciation*, he was torn by an inner uncertainty. After a meeting with Carpenter's Literary Executors, Beith, Green and Clemas, in December 1929, Forster puzzled in his *Commonplace Book* over the man who had affected him so deeply. 'Astonishing how he drains away . . . I suppose there was something there, but as soon as one touches it it's gone. Slow but steady decline of power.' This disturbing personal sense of Carpenter dissolving propelled Forster's struggle to define the magnetic transference of vitality, the feeling of peacefulness and power, Carpenter had communicated. 'He touched everyone, everywhere. Even when he wasn't intimate he was in direct contact.'[1] Forster was reminding himself of the extraordinary gift he had received from Carpenter in that surge of creativity which, in 1929, seemed somehow incongruous and hardly conceivable.

Several of the contributors conjured up images of Carpenter, as if they too feared his dissolution. For Ramsay MacDonald he was forever leaning on the gate at Millthorpe. Goldsworthy Lowes Dickinson summonsed the 'tallish spare figure, bearded with a sensitive and beautiful head'. Laurence Housman recalled his first impression of the 'beauty and refinement' of the man he saw sliding up to the front for a meeting on crime and punishment, while the American J. William Lloyd testified to Carpenter's presence, 'a little bashful' yet 'spiritual and sweet with the slight subtle suggestion of a rebel'.[2]

But what did these flickering recollections amount to for the future? A troubled Forster suspected that Carpenter had been overtaken by time. His libertarian utopianism seemed to have no message for the 1930s.

The two things he admired most on earth were manual work and the fresh air, and he dreamed like William Morris that civilization would be cured by their union. The Labour movement took another course, and advanced by committee meetings and statistics towards a State-owned factory attached to State-supervised recreation grounds. Edward's heart beat no warmer at such joys. He felt no enthusiasm over municipal baths and municipally provided bathing-drawers. What he wanted was News from Nowhere and the place that is still nowhere, wildness, the rapture of unpolluted streams, sunrise and sunset over the moors, and in the midst of these the working people whom he loved, passionately in touch with one another and with the natural glories around them.[3]

Carpenter may have wanted to do away with bathing-drawers, but he was more municipally minded than Forster concedes. Yet Forster's delightful passage accurately evokes the seismic shifts occurring in the labour movement between the wars. Mass unemployment, the rise of fascism, the murky compromises of Labour in power and the growing significance of the Communist Party on the left with its strategic approach to means, all contributed to Carpenter's utopian connection of the personal and the political, body and spirit, creative work and union with nature appearing dated. Some of those who had shared his ethical vision, among them Ramsay MacDonald and Charley Cramp, moved to the right, while A.J. Penty and Odon Por from the guild socialist and syndicalist camps flirted with fascism.

Forster's apprehension seemed to be confirmed by those on the 1930s left who were anxious to put a line between themselves and the people they saw as the dithering utopians of an earlier era. Unemployment, class inequality, fascism, bred a desire for clarity, a sense of urgency. In *The Road to Wigan Pier* (1936), George Orwell expressed exasperation at the left's tendency to attract every 'fruit-juice drinker, nudist, sandal-wearer, sex-maniac, Quaker, "Nature Cure" quack, pacifist and feminist in England'.[4] In a letter to the working-class intellectual, Jack Common, Orwell took a stance of 'proletarian' manliness and signalled out Carpenter's influence on middle-class socialists, 'the sort of eunuch type with a vegetarian smell, who go about spreading sweetness and light . . . readers of Edward Carpenter or some other pious sodomite'.[5]

Changes in the economy and culture were also sidelining Carpenter's outlook by the 1930s. The ideas about alternative forms of work and consumption, so central to Carpenter's socialism, were being overridden by the mass production which made cheaper goods possible for working-class people. Efficient productivity and more things seemed to make sense to socialists struggling against the Depression. Modernist design sought to utilise technology, leaving arts and crafts, divested of its critical edge, to become a creative flourish confined to small highly priced workshops or passed in a diluted form into the schools as 'handicrafts'. Intellectual paradigms shifted too. The diffuse spirituality which had accompanied nineteenth-century dynamic psychology was tending to give way to a practically oriented psychology on the one hand and psychoanalytic theories on the other. Mainstream anthropology had cut its connection with an evolutionary perspective, philosophy had decisively dumped idealism.

Yet Forster was not quite confirmed in his prediction that Carpenter's impulse and ethos were draining away, for the processes of transition did not flow down a single channel. Carpenter's ideas, enthusiasms and causes continued along winding streams that took surprising routes. Writing in *The Adelphi*, a politically exploratory left journal which was open to mysticism, Rayner Heppenstall argued in 1934 that Carpenter's emphasis on inner feeling was a necessary spiritual complement to Marxism.[6] In Germany, Carpenter's translator Karl Federn was similarly critical of a narrow interpretation of materialism that denied the human spirit in his *The Materialist Conception of History* published in 1939.[7]

Carpenter himself had noticed shifts in scientific thinking during the 1920s, and Harold Picton suggested in his contribution to *Edward Carpenter: In Appreciation* in 1930 that as assumptions about the 'indestructibility of matter, invariability of mass, indivisibility of the atom' had 'gone by the board', the way was open for Carpenter's scepticism about scientific laws and a recognition of how much remained unknown and unpredictable.[8] Claude Bragdon's mathematical questioning of time, motion and materiality, even the elusive fourth dimension, on which Carpenter had maintained a careful neutrality, could seem less bizarre in the light of Einstein's theories of space and time. In the late 1920s and early 1930s 'vitalist' ideas of nature as organic and dynamic exerted an influence on physiology and bio-chemistry, while 'mechanists' and 'vitalists' alike were prepared to acknowledge that scientific hypotheses were approximations rather than finalities.

Carpenter's notion of an evolving spiritual consciousness, his hankering after a non-intellectual form of perception and an organic connection between art and life flowed on within a series of esoteric and avant-garde movements. Bragdon's vision of an organic architecture unfolding from a sub-conscious inner desire influenced the American art critic Sheldon Cheney. Cheney, who had discovered Carpenter's works in the 1920s, went on to celebrate expressionism which he saw as a form of art which intensified perception. The British anarchist, Herbert Read, who had been inspired by Carpenter's non-governmental society, developed an aesthetic in which art expressed a possibility of redemption in daily life, an approach which influenced progressive education and therapists. Carpenter's human-centred critique of technology's social purposes were elaborated by Patrick Geddes and passed through him to the influential American writer on machines and planning, Lewis Mumford.[9] The connecting theme was that external change was not enough.

The new life continued to foster communal educational experiments. In the US, the Ferrer Modern School relocated to a co-operative in New Jersey where it survived until 1953. Guido Ferrando helped Aldous Huxley and the former Theosophist, Krishnamurti, to set up the Happy Valley School in California on land bought by Annie Besant. It was one of many spiritual settlements.[10] Carpenter's hopes for change in the countryside were taken up by two British land reclaimers and pioneer organic farmers, Balfour Gardiner and his nephew Rolf, at Springhead in Dorset. Along with organic husbandry and a mystical feel for nature, Rolf Gardiner, who had trained in silviculture, pioneered ecological ideas of an interconnected agriculture and countryside in which trees were both shelter for livestock and defence against erosion. He favoured a mix of agriculture and rural industry, rural universities, folk songs, folk dances, hiking and, more ominously was rumoured to have a romantic attachment to a Dorset version of Nazism. Springhead survived to become a residential centre for green causes from crop-circlers to the Soil Association (founded in 1945). Throughout its permutations Edward Carpenter's 'Art of Creation' and 'Pagan and Christian Creeds' sat upstairs in the library.[11]

Between the wars conservation movements took off; the Council for the Preservation (later Protection) of Rural England along with the Association for the Protection of Local Scenery lobbied busily. The ramblers meanwhile grew more militant, taking direct action to defend the old rights of way. They might be wage slaves on weekdays, at the weekends they wanted to be free to roam. The Dartington Hall experiment in Devon sought to take the benefits of the city to the countryside, through rural regeneration, while dreams of the city beautiful were turning into bricks and mortar; Raymond Unwin's garden cities were being municipalised into vast housing estates like Wythenshawe in Manchester. Like the suburbs sprouting on the edges of the cities, council estates were designed to connect the rural with the urban, though the results were not to be quite what Carpenter or Unwin had had in mind.

The 1920s and 1930s saw continuing humanitarian campaigns around differing aspects of animal welfare, along with prison reform and agitation about the rights of mental patients. Ronald Kidd, the founder of the National Council for Civil Liberties (N.C.C.L.) in 1934 had been influenced by Carpenter and Ellis as a young man. Nevinson was the first choice for President; he declined on account of health but proposed Forster who accepted. Originally established in response to police harassment of the unemployed hunger marchers, after the war the N.C.C.L. went on to defend mental patients, travellers and immigrants, establishing a Gay Rights Committee in 1974.[12]

Some of Carpenter's heterodoxies reverberated down several generations and travelled far afield. Doreen Young, the granddaughter of Robert Weare and the daughter of Will and Lily Young, was educated, at Carpenter's suggestion, at the Theosophists' progressive school at Letchworth Garden City. As a student at the London School of Economics she met S.A. Wickremansinghe, also educated at a Theosophist school in Ceylon. Doreen Young went out to Ceylon, became the principal of a girls' school, and married Wickremansinghe. The Wickremansinghes, who became Communists, travelled through India with the Youngs in 1932, visiting Gandhi in prison and meeting Tagore and an ageing Annie Besant.[13] There were many other links between Carpenter and Gandhi, among them Charlotte Despard, James and Margaret Cousins, Sarojini Naidu, Romain Rolland and, of course, Henry Salt. When Gandhi visited the London Vegetarian Society in 1931 he related how Salt's 'A Plea for Vegetarianism' had strengthened his vegetarianism – a cause in which it must be said Carpenter was sometimes a backslider.[14] The interaction between East and West persisted after the Second World War when Gandhi's social thought, his interest in village co-operatives, his example of non-violent direct action, and his approach to politics, which had impressed Rolland, exercised considerable influence in the West as well as in India.

Between the wars innumerable interpretations of Eastern religion found a growing number of devotees in the West. They too grappled with dilemmas which echo Carpenter's; how to celebrate the individual while merging into the cosmos and how to at once affirm and detach oneself from the body. The poet Christopher Isherwood sought a reconciliation, like his mentor E.M. Forster, by following the heart. E.M. Forster, himself, despite his doubts, carried this Carpenterian insight in his fiction. His belief in an inner integrity of personal relations exerted a profound, if diffuse, effect, right through the second half of the twentieth century.[15]

Individual self-expression and alternative lifestyles proved to be the most popular of Carpenter's bequests to posterity. Regardless of Orwell's strictures, the simple life gained adherents who formed progressive schools, settled in country cottages and communes, went camping, became vegetarians, joined the ramblers on their mass trespasses and collected folk songs. Some wore sandals and some, in the nudist camps which were becoming popular between the wars, wore nothing at all. Philip Heseltine (Peter Warlock), the musician who had been influenced by Carpenter as a student, did not even bother to find a camp, stripping off in Piccadilly and riding around naked on his motorbike. Bizarre versions of the simple life manifested themselves in between-the-wars bohemia. The artist Eric Gill actually adopted the Saxon tunic Carpenter had been discouraged from wearing in Holmesfield.[16]

Aspects of the culture of simplification and self-expression adopted by bohemians and radicals gradually permeated the wider society, creating new norms. Ironically fragments of Carpenter's iconoclasm folded neatly into modernist design, labour saving suburban villas, D.I.Y. and companionate marriage. And, in 1944 the journalist Desmond MacCarthy argued that it had been Carpenter's challenge to social customs and mental habits which had really survived.[17] In the same year E.M. Forster suggested that Carpenter's reputation had waned precisely because so many of his proposals and attitudes had passed into the 'common stock'.[18]

This was not, however, the case when it came to Carpenter's passionate defence of 'intermediates'. On same-sex love the cultural closures he had resisted held fast. When Virginia Woolf published her novel *Orlando* in 1928 it proved possible to intimate lesbianism so long as the allusions appeared in the context of fantasy. However the following year Radclyffe Hall's *The Well of Loneliness* with its broad middle-brow appeal evoked a horrified reaction. The case exposed the contradictory assumption that knowledge of lesbian love was acceptable for an elect but impermissible for the general public. As a consequence of the furore around the book being banned, Radclyffe Hall became at once notorious and celebrated, establishing her tailored jackets and plus fours as an image of 'the lesbian'. Radclyffe Hall, who was friendly with Havelock Ellis, acknowledged the influence of his work, however there are clear echoes of Carpenter in her conviction that those who desired members of their own sex were exemplars of a new human possibility.[19] The greater visibility of women in same sex relationships after 1928 may have reduced the isolation communicated by Carpenter's female correspondents, however it eroded the ambivalent non-sexual space for women who lived together.

Male homosexuality, always more visible because it was criminalised, was also affected by the psychological scrutiny which cut through ambiguities of 'friendship' or 'comradeship'. Support for the legalisation of homosexuality could combine with assumptions that it was a psychological disorder to be cured – though Jungians tended to be somewhat more sympathetic than Freudians. In less liberal circles, homosexual men were still treated as outcasts, branded as a type and periodically rounded up in vice raids. Between 1930 and 1950 prosecutions rose sharply partly through the use of 'decoys'. Repression was, however, never absolute; Forster after all fell in love with a policeman and some of the decoys were famously seduced.[20] Nevertheless, because homosexuality remained a criminal offence in Britain until 1967, and because sympathetic works on homosexuality were not easy to obtain, Carpenter's writings continued to bring reassurance and validation to the generation of men born towards the end of the nineteenth century and in the first few years of the twentieth. The author of the 1928 paean to Carpenter as 'our youth's doyen' in Vera Pragnell's *The Story of the Sanctuary*, Victor Neuburg was recovering from a destructive relationship with the occultist Aleister Crowley, when he met Carpenter. Carpenter's books along with Pragnell and her husband Dennis Earle, who had worked as Carpenter's secretary, helped in his recovery. The bisexual Neuburg later became a literary critic, a friend of Ellis' biographer, Arthur Calder-Marshall and the early champion of Dylan Thomas.[21]

Traces of Carpenter's influence are evident in Kevin Porter and Jeff Weeks' collection of reminiscences, *Between the Acts: Lives of Homosexual Men*, in which several men mention Carpenter's books. One upper-middle-class man, 'Gregory', who had attended meetings of the B.S.S.S.P. and met Carpenter, describes reading *The Intermediate Sex* along with Havelock Ellis' work. A younger man, Trevor Thomas, born in 1907 in a South Wales mining village, went to university and worked in a museum in Liverpool during the 1920s. Carpenter was important because he linked male comradeship with socialism; Thomas eventually became involved in the Campaign for Homosexual Equality (C.H.E.) in the early 1970s.[22]

The link between the left and homosexual rights which Carpenter had sought to foster continued to be ambivalent. After the revolution the Bolsheviks had abolished the laws against homosexuality, however, under Stalin in 1934, it became illegal once again and homosexual men were among those sent to labour camps. Nonetheless in other countries homo-sexual men did gravitate to the Communist Party where they were tolerated but expected to keep their sex lives private because scandal was politically damaging.[23]

In the United States it happened that the Communist Party was inadver-tently linked to the formation of the movement for homosexual civil rights, through Mattachine, founded in the late 1940s by the Communist Harry Hay.[24] Hay's participation in the Communist Party provided him with ideas about the rights of 'minorities' to equality, while his involvement in Pete Seeger's 'People's Songs' movement stimulated his interest in folk lore and led to his discovery of the male Mattachine troupes, associated with festivals of misrule when social conventions of class and gender were briefly turned upside down.

Hay's personal rebellion had begun early. Aged eleven in 1925, he had spotted *The Intermediate Sex* locked in a glass case in the local library. The word 'sex' caught his attention and he contrived to persuade the librarian to go out to the hairdressers, by promising to look after the books. On returning coiffured with her new marcel wave perm, she discovered, to her horror, the schoolboy still eagerly devouring Carpenter's prohibited book. Partly through Carpenter, Harry Hay developed a long-standing interest in anthropology. Like Carpenter he was intrigued by Native American, cross-dressing, all-male 'Berdache' households, linked customs across cultures, and saw aspects of 'the primitive' as sources for subversion.

Nineteen-fifties McCarthyite America was not a propitious time for either Leninism, homosexual freedoms or jovial misrule. However in the early sixties Hay came across Gerald Heard, the British friend of Forster and Isherwood who set little store by Carpenter, but did believe that homosexuals constituted an evolutionary prototype for future humanity. Rejecting Heard's elitism, Hay extracted the challenge to cultural hegemony and began to explore theories which went beyond protesting against discrimination. His thinking was in accord with the times; in 1966 Hay attended the North American Conference of Homophile Organizations in San Francisco, and, by 1969 Gay Liberation had emerged as a movement. To Hay the West Coaster, the East Coast scene appeared assimilationist and he conceived the 'Radical Faeries' as an alternative gay identity. Their first meeting was at the Sri Ram Ashram in Arizona in 1979, which resulted in the creation of non-hierarchical Faerie Circles. Adopting an emblem of the horned God, the Faeries with their shawls and sanctuaries cheerily embraced New Age neo-paganism. Hay developed an ideology of a 'Third Sex', distinct psychologically and culturally from heterosexuals, and argued that these differences carried potential benefits for society as a whole. He addressed the utopian dilemma with which Carpenter was so familiar. How can sources for an alternative culture be found and nurtured within the world as it is?

Carpenterian traces appeared too among the American beats from the late 1940s. Spiritual and sexual rapture was their hallmark and in their search for intense revelations they drew on Romanticism, Transcendentalism and Eastern religions. Rejecting American society, the beats celebrated outcasts as heroes and, regardless of McCarthyism, homosexuality was a strong undercurrent in the beat fraternity. The poet Allen Ginsberg was profoundly influenced by Whitman, friendly with Gavin (Chester) Arthur and knew of Carpenter's work. Moreover, along with Arthur, he, too, had a sexual relationship with Neal Cassady, the youth who inspired the Dean Moriarty character in Kerouac's *On the Road*. Ginsberg remained obsessively fascinated by this mainly heterosexual child of nature who was yet another manifestation of the unselfconscious 'primitive'. Intrigued by 'the line of transmission' which he felt connected him to Arthur, Carpenter and Whitman, Ginsberg claimed them as physical as well as spiritual forebears.[25] Another line of transmission into the beat milieu was theoretical – the critique of what Aldous Huxley called the 'scientific world picture' which he saw as geared to mass-production and the concentration of power in society rather than human emancipation. Huxley recommended *Civilisation: Its Cause and Cure* in his book *Science, Liberty and Peace* in 1947.[26] His influence on Arthur's friend Alan Watts helped to put Carpenter onto the beat reading list.

While Carpenter's influence meandered down all these faraway streams, vanishing underground and then resurfacing in unexpected ways, a group of friends and admirers were staunchly keeping his memory alive in the place most closely associated with him, Millthorpe. In 1930 around nine hundred of them gathered at the back of the house to listen to speeches by Henry Nevinson, Evelyn Sharp and E.M. Forster.[27] However political conflict in the labour movement quickly impinged. Ramsay MacDonald sent a letter for the service but a decision was made not to invite him, because the Prime Minister was already so unpopular with the left that demonstrations were likely.[28] Still, initially hopes were high and local socialists, R.H. Minshall, Richard Hawkin, J.H. Bingham, Bert Ward and Alf and Eleanor Barton combined with the Mattisons, Gilbert Beith, Raymond Unwin, Charley Cramp, Jim Middleton from the Labour Party, Ted Inigan and Ida Hyett in a Carpenter-inspired united front. The Kays provided their barn when it rained, the Nicholsons did the teas and admonished memorialists not to leave litter, the National Clarion Vocal Union choir offered musical interludes of Carpenter's songs and poems.[29] Kathleen Bunting, who had peeped at the naked bathers in the back garden and signed the eightieth birthday address, could recall the 'hymn singing' long after the words of the speakers had faded from memory.[30]

In 1932 the Edward Carpenter International Memorial Trust was established with the aim of raising £5,000 to buy Millthorpe and maintain it as an international guest house in Carpenter's memory. Underneath Alf Mattison's photograph of Carpenter on their Appeal were J.H. Bingham's words: 'It is good that we should hold in remembrance those who have given us their friendship. And those who have unstintingly given their service in the cause of humanity.'[31] However the times were hard, and unfortunately more stinting than they thought. The Trust was unable to raise the money and Tom Nicholson was growing increasingly desperate. The Trust appealed to the Workers' Travel Association which agreed to buy the property for the £1,000 Nicholson was asking. Their representative arrived at Millthorpe on December 12, 1933, to find Nicholson had just sold Millthorpe to Henry David Hoult for £1,700. The W.T.A. had been gazumped.[32]

Support for the Carpenter Memorial Trust then dwindled and it was replaced by the Carpenter Service Fellowship in 1935. Despite some tension between the northern socialists and Leonard Green and Gilbert Beith, the Fellowship continued to organise meetings at Millthorpe until the war.[33] At the 1937 gathering Florence Mattison, who was now a member of the Leeds Education Committee, spoke on 'My Memories of Carpenter' – how many of her memories were ones she could never voice in public![34]

The Fellowship remembered the socialist and humanitarian Carpenter and maintained a somewhat distant connection with Beith and Green in their southern middle-class milieu. In the autumn of 1943, Stanley Unwin, aware that the centenary of Carpenter's birth was in the offing, put out a feeler to test the market by advertising *Towards Democracy*, *The Intermediate Sex* and *Ioläus* in the *Times Literary Supplement*. Disappointingly, the response was nil.[35] Nevertheless, that November, Leonard Green lunched with Unwin and they decided to try and get E.M. Forster to do a radio broadcast and Charles Morgan to write a piece for the *T.L.S.*[36]

In March, Forster, the peacemaker once more, urged Beith to contact the northerners even if he had experienced difficulties in the past. Forster acknowledged that while an attempt to co-operate might be troublesome, the aim should be to get as much done by different people as possible.[37] By June an ailing and anxious Charlie Sixsmith was on the case, asking Beith to report on what was happening.[38] He need not have worried; Forster, Beith and Green had set about nobbling acquaintances in the press. Despite Unwin's view that there had been a falling off in interest in Carpenter's work, the result was an impressive burst of accolades: S.K. Ratcliffe in the *Manchester Guardian*, Charles Morgan in the *Times Literary Supplement*, Desmond MacCarthy in *The Listener*, along with a cluster of local papers, the *Evening Standard*, the *Bolton Journal* (Sixsmith), the *Yorkshire Post*, the *Southport Announcer* and the *Sheffield Telegraph*. *Tribune*, *Health and Life* and *The Countryman* also remembered Carpenter and, when E.M. Forster did his broadcast on Carpenter's life and work, a delighted Charlie Sixsmith wrote to the B.B.C. to congratulate them, receiving a polite reply from Mary P. Ussher on behalf of the Director.[39]

Beith held an informal event in his garden at 'Hollywood', Gomshall, Surrey, arranged by the Hurtwood Branch of the League of Nations. Over fifty people attended, including Forster who was the main speaker. Evelyn Sharp, now Mrs. H.W. Nevinson and having trouble with her eyesight, also spoke briefly along with C.H. Grinling, Beith and Green. Afterwards there was a swim in Beith's pool and a dinner attended by Beith, Green and Philip Unwin (of Allen and Unwin).[40]

When travel became easier after the war the Carpenter Memorial Fellowship resumed its gatherings in Holmesfield. As the years went by the memory-keepers found themselves remembering one another as well as Carpenter. In 1946 they paid tribute to Eleanor Barton's husband Alf, the old friend of John Furniss and George Pearson, who had been the councillor behind the move to grant Carpenter the freedom of the City.[41] Then in 1947 the Fellowship sadly marked the death of Alf Mattison. Yet Eleanor Barton, Florence Mattison, J.H. Bingham, G.H.B. Ward and Fenner Brockway still faithfully turned up. In 1947 the small boy who had deafened Carpenter when the Adams' moved to Millthorpe, came back to give the address; Harry Adams, the former conscientious objector, was now a PhD and on the executive of the National Union of Teachers.[42]

When Carpenter's house came up for sale again in 1955 the ageing memorial Fellowship, which numbered one hundred members, longed once again to buy it. But Bert Ward who was 79, told the *Sheffield Telegraph*, 'We just have not got the money – and we can't do anything about it.'[43] They had to settle for an exhibition in Sheffield Central Library of books and photographs. The Fellowship itself disbanded in 1962.

The Fellowship was not, however, the only means by which Carpenter's memory was conserved. Carpenter's staunch custodians, Alf Mattison and Charlie Sixsmith had both been carefully storing a record of his life and thought. Mattison had made approaches to the Chief Librarian in Sheffield, R.J. Gordon, as early as 1925 about his papers.[44] In 1929 a regretful J.P. Lamb wrote from Sheffield Public Library saying that it was a pity that Labour had not gained power in the city in time to secure Mattison's Carpenter material and added that Councillor Alf Barton would be disappointed to hear it was going instead to Leeds University.[45]

Sheffield City Library did acquire the papers and books left at Millthorpe when Tom Nicholson sold the house. This provoked an irate Leonard Green to protest to the Town Clark, E.B. Gibson, that Carpenter's will had specified all books and letters belonged to the trustees along with the royalties from his sales. Gibson managed to assure Green that they were in safe hands and friends began donating letters and books.[46] In 1949 J.P.

Lamb compiled *A Bibliography of Edward Carpenter*, listing his books and works about him. Whereupon Charlie Sixsmith combed through his collection noting additional material.[47]

Sixsmith was suffering from bad health but retained sufficient vigour to pursue librarians, complaining that not enough was being done to publicise the collection. A somewhat harassed Lamb assured Sixsmith that they compiled a list each year for the Commemoration Service and urged Sixsmith to push J.H. Bingham to use his influence as an Alderman. Lamb took the archival long view:

> Although those who knew Carpenter are naturally disappointed at the present neglect of his works, I think they should regard it as no more than the temporary eclipse which the reputations of even the greatest of writers have almost invariably suffered during the first fifty years after their deaths.[48]

Sixsmith's ire then fell on Harold Hamer, the Chief Librarian of Bolton Library. The cause of the contretemps was Walt Whitman's stuffed canary, sent many years before to J.W. Wallace by an American Whitmanite, Harriet Sprague. After Wallace's death his housekeeper Minnie Whiteside had looked after the stuffed canary. By 1950, elderly and suffering from angina, she had presented the canary to the library on condition that it would be displayed as her gift; this outraged Charlie Sixsmith who did not consider it to be her property. He was still grumbling about Minnie Whiteside's appropriation of the canary in 1953, and, despite Hamer's efforts to smooth the waters, made the decision to withdraw the offer of his papers to Bolton. Accordingly the Whitman/Sixsmith/Carpenter Collection was deposited in the John Rylands Library at Manchester.[49]

Meanwhile Gilbert Beith had been rounding up more letters and papers and these were duly deposited at Sheffield in 1958.[50] And there they sat awaiting the chroniclers.

Fortunately, Carpenter did not have to wait the full fifty years. From the mid 1950s Carpenter started to make his appearance through the emerging fields of labour and cultural history.[51] He became a topic for theses, being especially well served by Dilip Kumar Barua's comprehensive study *The Life and Work of Edward Carpenter* (1966), which situated him within Indian as well as European intellectual currents.[52]

Carpenter, meanwhile, continued to be remembered locally. *Derbyshire Life and Countryside* paid tribute in 1969 to 'The Sage of Cordwell'.[53] In 1973 Wendy Hill unearthed vivid memories in her interviews for the

Morning Telegraph. Local people recalled the visitors, the outings, the talks, the plays and dances in the barn. Kathleen Bunting spoke fondly of the kind man on her paper round, with his store of nuts and sweets, who felt sympathy for a child's cold hands. 'One day he gave me a hand-warmer with charcoal inside and he said, "Put this in your muff and it will keep your hands warm". It was a wonderful little thing.'[54]

After I wrote on Carpenter in *Socialism and the New Life* in 1977, a Rotherham man called Arthur Bruce sent a letter describing the Sheffield Clarion Cycling Club's gatherings at the Royal Oak pub. Though only a boy at the time he could recall their earnest discussions about politics, remarking sadly that fellow members of his local Labour Party had not heard of Carpenter.[55] If the more traditional socialist memory of Carpenter was fading, the 1970s saw a new left politics which linked sex and socialism, the personal and the political, body and spirit, nature and ecology. Carpenter began to be rediscovered. Rony Robinson, a playwright from Totley, whose grandmother had known Carpenter, wrote *Edward Carpenter Lives*, and the play was put on at the Crucible Theatre in Sheffield. The gay liberation movement generated an interest in Carpenter which resulted in books and plays including Noel Greig's *Dear Love of Comrades* (1979). Based on material about Carpenter's life in the Carpenter Collection in Sheffield, it was performed by the Gay Sweatshop drama group.[56] In 1980 a group of gay men in Leeds set up the Wild-Lavender Housing Co-operative in a utopian spirit to promote co-operative living among gay men. In 1984 they hosted a Gay Men's week at the commune Lauriston Hall in Scotland and went on to form the 'Edward Carpenter Community', a group which is still committed to nurturing personal spiritual growth and loving community.[57] Guildford Labour Party members also remembered Carpenter, naming a room in their building after him in 1986 and singing 'England Arise' at his grave, where Jonathan Cutbill, his literary executor, startled the Conservative Mayor and Lady Mayoress by booming passionately, 'Edward Carpenter was an extremely sexy man.'[58] Then, in 1994 the local labour movement celebrated Carpenter's 150th in a Guildford garden in the company of a few of his younger relations. So while some of the rivulets of dissent which had borne Carpenter along silted over, new channels appeared.

And, by fortuitous coincidence, in the 1990s Millthorpe, now called 'Carpenter House', happened to be opened as a guesthouse. Some guests stay there for the fishing, others to sell goods to local farmers, but some search out Carpenter's house to remember. Another 'Carpenter House' exists in North London – a late 1930s council block on Brecknock Road Estate, appropriately close to the Bumble Bee alternative health shops. In

2004, one of the residents, the writer Judith Williamson initiated the Community and Garden Project to transform an empty piece of tarmac into gardens, a football pitch and playground. Young people from the estate were among the diggers returning Londoners to the land in true Carpenter fashion.[59]

In the twenty-first century, with much proverbial water under the bridge, Carpenter would no doubt have been surprised to see how so many of his utopian speculations had enmeshed themselves in the everyday, become divested of politics and recreated as lifestyle, from organic food in supermarkets to nature cures turning over huge profits. The impact of consumer pressure for 'fair trade', along with the widespread awareness of ecology and sustainable development, would have delighted him. Recycling, the revival of small-holdings by organic farmers, the spread of farmers' markets and local sourcing are all unwittingly Carpenterian, and so are conservationists' plans for 're-wilding' and the Countryside and Rights of Way Act (2004) which extended ramblers' rights to roam. Perhaps the great sandal-wearer might even have felt a little outpaced by the foundation of the Society for Barefoot Living in 1994.[60]

Though Carpenter's affirmation of sexual diversity continues to be bitterly contested, changes in sexual attitudes, the acceptance of birth control, along with the global impact of the gay movement since the 1960s, have resulted in the kind of openness he wanted. His brown eyes would surely have twinkled at police contingents marching at Gay Pride demonstrations and he might well have raised an amused pagan eyebrow over the fracas about gay bishops.

On the other hand he would have been aghast at how pollution has damaged the environment globally, angry that land and capital have remained in the hands of a few, and distressed to note how even the mildest Fabian sort of gas-and-water socialism has turned into a pipe dream, while the City of the Sun appears to be permanently on hold. Even though he possessed a strong sense of the meantime, recognising like his friend from the Leicester socialist movement of the 1880s, Tom Barclay, 'how many swallows it takes to make a summer', Carpenter's utopianism sought transcendent transformation.[61] He would surely hail the new left-libertarian movements of dissenters and the disinherited while regretting how they have been severed from the utopian alternatives of the past, for the dilemmas faced by radical movements are perennial. Carpenter's tussles over how to create a new culture within the old without falling into prescription, how to establish collectivities which allow space for the personal and the spiritual aspirations of individuals are of contemporary not just historical interest. If some new unifying vision of what might be is to be devised these are knots which need unravelling. Carpenter lived long enough to observe how hard it was to ensure that grass roots pressure remained linked with the new institutional structures of labour or indeed of humanitarian internationalism. He developed a pragmatic approach to strategies for change, proposing that accepting there could be differing ways of journeying to a broadly similar destination would save a great deal of fruitless argument about *how* to bring about change.

Carpenter's mode of expressing his ideas has dated, but his quests are as theoretically pertinent now as ever. His attempt to map 'intermediacy' as both distinctive and yet within the spectrum of human sexuality, his speculations about the self and selves, his interest in experience as a source of knowing, his preoccupation with the inner spirit as the agent of transformation, his belief in a human kinship with animals, still resonate. Many of the questions he posed about science, consciousness, spirit and matter, remain in the realm of what is not known, though they are being reconsidered. In recent times some neuro-psychologists would acknowledge that our extended knowledge of the brain does not necessarily involve a deeper understanding of mind and consciousness, while some mathematicians have conceptualised new constituents of matter and dimensions in space invisible to us.[62] As physicists have found more strange particles, they too are prepared to wonder about 'dimensions in nature beyond the three space and one time that we currently experience'.[63] In knowing more, science has increasingly opened to imponderable uncertainties and, as we gaze with awe at Hubble's images of ancient exploding stars, some of Carpenter's intuitions about nature no longer appear so wacky.

While Carpenter has not left a coherent body of thought, the orientation of his thinking is a vital legacy. He struggled to connect his strong convictions with a dislike of fixed categories and an openness to a range of interpretations. Moreover he suggests, by example, an alertness to possibilities budding and bursting from unexpected places. Over the years he began to suspect that there was no ultimate destination, simply new contingencies accompanying every apparent gain. 'What is to be done?' he asked Clemas in 1927 after so many of his hopes had been defeated. 'Though I have written on the Cure of Civilisation generally I grieve to say I have no panacea for the present mass of human ills.'[64]

Carpenter provides no neat answers. Following his trajectory is like embarking on a ramble to Grindleford, only to find oneself re-routed to Tokyo, Colombo or anywhere. The journey becomes the exploration and the quest is for that fleeting glimpse of the 'free open life' in the face of a slum child emerging from the crowd.[65] He knew from the start that radical insights and upsurges could fade, 'The dream goes by, touches men's hearts, and floats and fades again.'[66] Over the years he became less convinced that redemption was imminent. 'History is a difficult horse to ride', he remarked to Henry Nevinson in relation to Russia.[67] And, when he wrote *My Days and Dreams*, during the dark years of war, he referred his readers to the Chinese Taoist thinker Lao-Tzu: 'The thirty spokes of a carriage-wheel uniting at the nave are made useful by the hole in the centre.'[68] Carpenter sits invisibly hobnobbing with his 'one' in the hole in the centre, deceptively modest, for who is to deny that spokes require holes? Now, as in his lifetime, he is apt to pop out from time to time, touch this and that and then float and fade away again. Now you see him; now you don't. One thing is certain, this complicated, confusing, contradictory, yet courageous man is not going to vanish entirely from view.

Notes

Introduction

1   G. Lowes Dickinson, 'Edward Carpenter as a Friend', in Gilbert Beith, ed., *Edward Carpenter: In Appreciation* (London: George Allen and Unwin, 1931), p. 36.

2   Edward Carpenter, 'The Drawing Room Table Literature', *New Age 20*, March 17, 1910 (C.C., CPer 84).

3   Arthur Calder-Marshall, *Havelock Ellis: A Biography* (London: Rupert Hart-Davis, 1959).

4   E.P. Thompson, *William Morris: Romantic to Revolutionary* (London: Merlin Press 1955, 1977).

5   Sheila Rowbotham and Jeffrey Weeks, *Socialism and the New Life: The Personal and Sexual Politics of Edward Carpenter and Havelock Ellis* (London: Pluto Press, 1977); Sheila Rowbotham, 'In Search of Carpenter', *History Workshop Journal* 3, Spring 1977; Sheila Rowbotham, '"Commanding the Heart": Edward Carpenter and Friends', *History Today* 37, September 1987, reprinted in Gordon Marsden, ed., *Victorian Values, Personalities and Perspectives in Nine-teenth-Century Society* (London: Longman 1990, 1998).

6   Carpenter to Fry, February 27, 1894, The Papers of Roger Fry, R.E.F. (Kings); E.S.P. Haynes, *The Lawyer, A Conversation. Pieces Selected from The Lawyer's Notebooks and Other Writings' by Renée Haynes* (London: Eyre and Spottiswood, 1951), p. 160.

7   Edward Carpenter, *My Days and Dreams* (London: George Allen and Unwin, 1916), p. 208.

8   Ibid., p. 167.

9   Ibid., p. 321.

10 Henry Salt, *Seventy Years Among Savages* (London: George Allen and Unwin 1921), p. 76.

11 Henry S. Salt, in Beith, ed., *Edward Carpenter*, p. 185.

12 George Bernard Shaw quoted in Anne Fremantle, *This Little Band of Prophets: The Story of the Gentle Fabians* (London: George Allen and Unwin 1960), p. 74.

13 George Bernard Shaw to Henry S. Salt, August 19, 1903, in Dan H. Laurence, ed., *Bernard Shaw, Collected Letters 1898–1910* (London: Max Reinhardt, 1972), p. 348.

14 Thompson, *William Morris*, Postscript 1976 (1977), p. 792.
15 Terry Eagleton, 'Reach-Me-Down Romantic' (on E.P. Thompson), *London Review of Books*, June 19, 2003, p. 8.

1 'At home I never really felt at home'

1 Carpenter, *My Days and Dreams*, p. 13.
2 Ida G. Hyett, in Beith, ed.,*Edward Carpenter*, p. 114.
3 Cuthbert Bede quoted in Clifford Musgrove, *Life in Brighton* (London: Faber and Faber, 1970), p. 296.
4 Hyett, in Beith, ed., *Edward Carpenter*, p. 114.
5 Carpenter, *My Days and Dreams*, p. 42.
6 Ibid.
7 Ibid., p. 43.
8 Carpenter in J.W. Wallace, Notes of Visit to Edward Carpenter, no page numbers, August 13-15, 1892, B.W.F.L.
9 Edward Carpenter, 'Out of the Home of Childhood', *Towards Democracy* (London: George Allen and Unwin, 1921), p. 501.
10 Carpenter in Wallace, Notes of Visit, B.W.F.L.
11 Millicent Garrett Fawcett, *What I Remember* (London: T. Fisher Unwin, 1924), p. 89.
12 Carpenter to Haynes, July 4, 1916, J.C; Haynes, *The Lawyer*, p. 48.
13 Carpenter, *My Days and Dreams*, p. 13.
14 Carpenter to Hukin, November 1, 1886, C.C. 361/1.
15 Hyett, in Beith, ed., *Edward Carpenter*, p. 115.
16 Carpenter, *My Days and Dreams*, pp. 15-16.
17 Ibid., p. 116.
18 Carpenter, *My Days and Dreams*, p. 96.
19 Edward Carpenter, 'Self-Analysis for Havelock Ellis', in Noël Greig, ed., *Edward Carpenter: Selected Writings, Volume 1: Sex* (London: GMP Publishers, 1984), p. 289
20 G.P. Burston, Typescript extracts from the Brighton College Register, C.C. Mss. 314.
21 Carpenter, *My Days and Dreams*, p. 18.
22 Ibid., p. 29.
23 John Addington Symonds, *The Memoirs of J.A. Symonds* ed., Phyllis Grosskurth (New York: Random House, 1984), p. 73.
24 Edward Carpenter, Poems, C.C. 3/15.
25 Hyett in Beith, ed., *Edward Carpenter*, pp. 114, 116-117.
26 Edward Carpenter, Notes on Janet McNair, C.C. 250/2, and Carpenter, *My Days and Dreams*, p. 31.
27 Lizzie Carpenter to Carpenter, no date, C.C. 342-43.
28 Carpenter to Sophia Carpenter, May 1, 1864, C.C. 339/2; Carpenter to Sophia Carpenter, July 1, 1864, C.C. 339/3.
29 Edward Carpenter, Notebook, no date, C.C. Mss. 335.
30 Carpenter to Charles Carpenter, July 13, 1864, C.C. 339/4.
31 Ibid., July 23, 1864, C.C. 339/5.

2 The Cambridge Radical

1 A section of 'Senate House Hill: Degree Morning 1863' is reprinted in Charles Crawley, *Trinity Hall: The History of a Cambridge College* (Cambridge: Printed for the College, 1976), illustration 13.

2 Fawcett, *What I Remember*, pp. 83–84.

3 Carpenter, *My Days and Dreams*, p. 13.

4 Henry Sidgwick in Arthur Sidgwick and Eleanor Mildred Sidgwick, *Henry Sidgwick: A Memoir* (London, Macmillan, 1906), p. 174.

5 Henry Sidgwick in Peter Allen, *The Cambridge Apostles: The Early Years* (Cambridge: Cambridge University Press, 1978). p. 208.

6 Carpenter, *My Days and Dreams*, p. 56.

7 Edward Carpenter, *On the Continuance of Modern Civilisation*, 1866, Mss. C.C. 1, p. 1.

8 McNair to Carpenter, no date, C.C. 386–421.

9 Carpenter to Charles Carpenter, May 28, 1867 (?), C.C. 339/7.

10 Ibid.

11 Carpenter, *My Days and Dreams*, p. 53.

12 Edward Carpenter, *The Religious Influence of Art* (Cambridge: Deighton Bell and Co., 1870), pp. 44, 18.

13 Ibid., pp. 34, 32, 38.

14 Carpenter, *My Days and Dreams*, pp. 56–57.

15 Edward Carpenter, Sermons, 1870–1871, no page numbers, Mss. C.C. 2/1.

16 Ibid.

17 John Ruskin, *Fors Clavigera: Letters to the Workmen and Labourers of Great Britain*, Vol. I, Letter VII, in E.T. Cook and Alexander Wedderburn, ed., *The Works of John Ruskin* (London: George Allen, 1907), p. 121.

18 Carpenter, Sermons 1870–1871, Mss. C.C. 2/1.

19 See Linda Dalrymple Henderson, *The Fourth Dimension and Non-Euclidean Geometry in Modern Art* (Princeton: Princeton University Press, 1983), p. 20.

20 Carpenter, *My Days and Dreams*, p. 60.

21 See Dilip Kumar Barua, *The Life and Work of Edward Carpenter in the Light of Religious, Political and Literary Movements of the Later Half of the Nineteenth Century*, University of Sheffield PhD, 1966, p. 32.

22 Lizzie Carpenter to Carpenter, no date, C.C. 342/26.

23 Carpenter to Dalton, October 29, 1871, D.P.

24 Carpenter Sermons 1870–1871, Mss. C.C. 2/9.

25 Dalton to Carpenter, November 6, 1870, C.C. 386/6.

26 Carpenter, *My Days and Dreams*, pp. 58–59.

27 Sophia Carpenter to Carpenter, no date, C.C. 340/12.

28 Carpenter, Ioläus' Manuscript letter and notes c. June 1865, with notes on homosexuality, C.C. Mss. 93.

29 Ibid., May 23–24, 1868.

30 Beck to Carpenter, March 17, 1871, C.C. 386/7.

31 See Edward Carpenter, 'Saved by a Nose,' in *Sketches from Life in Town and Country* (London: George Allen and Unwin, 1908), pp. 213–219.

32 Beck to Carpenter, September 1, 1871, C.C. 386/8.

33 Carpenter to Oates, September 5, 1871, C.C. 351/3.

34 Beck to Carpenter, September 23, 1872, C.C. 386/9.

35 Edward Carpenter, Love Unfulfilled, Mss. from c. 1873 revised 1915, C.C. 3/23.

36 Carpenter, *My Days and Dreams*, p. 62.

37 'The Late Master of Trinity Mr. Edward Beck', *Cambridge Chronicle*, April 19, 1916, C.C. Box 4, 63.

38 Carpenter to Oates, September 12, 1869, C.C. 351/1.

39 Carpenter, *My Days and Dreams*, p. 63.

40 Carpenter to Oates, December 19, 1870, C.C. 351/2.

41 Plato, *Phaedrus*, Translation and commentary by C.J. Rowe (Warminster, Wiltshire: Aris and Phillips, 1986), p. 71. See A.W. Price, *Love and Friendship in Plato and Aristotle* (Oxford: The Clarendon Press, 1989), pp. 61, 89.

42 Carpenter, *My Days and Dreams*, pp. 64–65.

43 Symonds, *Memoirs of J.A. Symonds*, p. 189.

44 Walt Whitman in David S. Reynolds, *Walt Whitman's America: A Cultural Biography* (New York: Alfred A. Knopf, 1995), p. 396.

45 Ibid., pp. 476–480.

46 Carpenter, 'Francesca', in *Sketches from Life in Town and Country*, p. 101.

47 Carpenter, *My Days and Dreams*, p. 69.

48 Daubeney to Carpenter, no date, c. 1872, C.C. 350/1.

49 Carpenter to Oates, April 2, 1873, C.C. 351/12.

50 Chushichi Tsuzuki, *Edward Carpenter, 1844–1929, Prophet of Human Fellowship*, (Cambridge: Cambridge University Press, 1980), pp. 25–6.

51 Edward Carpenter, *Narcissus and Other Poems* (London: Henry S. King, 1973).

52 Carpenter to Oates, March 23, 1873, C.C. 351/9.

53 Carpenter to Oates, February 2, 1874, C.C. 351/6. Edward Carpenter, *Moses: A Drama in Five Acts* (London: Henry S. King, 1875)

54 Carpenter, *My Days and Dreams*, p. 251. On Ponnambalam Arunachalam see Kumari Jayawardena, *Nobodies to Somebodies: The Rise of the Colonial Bourgeoisie in Sri Lanka* (London: Zed Books, 2002), pp. 215–217, 276; A. Jeyaratnam Wilson, *Sri Lankan Tamil, Nationalism: Its Origins and Development in the 19th and 20th Centuries* (London: Hurst and Company, 2000).

55 Sophy Carpenter to Edward Carpenter, no date, C.C. 342/11.

56 Carpenter to Oates, July 20, 1874, C.C. 351/17.

57 Ibid.

58 Carpenter to Whitman, July 12, 1874 in Horace Traubel, ed., *With Walt Whitman in Camden*, Vol. I (New York: Rowman and Littlefield, 1961), p. 158.

59 Ibid., p. 159

60 Ibid., p. 160.

61 Ibid., p. 161.

62 Ibid.

63 Whitman, May 15, 1888, in ibid., p. 158.

64 Carpenter, *My Days and Dreams*, p. 79.

3 Discovering the North

1 Carpenter to Oates, December 30, 1874, C.C. 351/18.

2 Edward Carpenter, 'Materialism', Lecture to the Leeds Co-operative Society, November 22, 1874, Mss. C.C. 7.

3 Carpenter to Dalton, February 28, no date, D.P.

4 On H.S. Foxwell see J. Bonar, 'H.S. Foxwell', Reprinted from the *Journal of the Royal Statistical Society*, Vol. XCIX, Part IV, 1936 (for Private Circulation), pp. 837–840 and J.M. Keynes, 'Herbert Somerton Foxwell', *The Economic Journal*, Vol. XLVI, No. 184, December 1936, pp. 589–614.

5 Carpenter, *My Days and Dreams*, p. 82.

6 Ibid., p. 81; Edward Carpenter, Address Book, no page numbers, C.C. Mss. 304.

7 June Hannam, *Isabella Ford* (Oxford: Basil Blackwell, 1989), pp. 7–26.

8 Carpenter to Joseph Estlin Carpenter, July 4, 1875, J.E.C.

9 William Henry Channing in David E. Shi, *The Simple Life: Plain Living and High Thinking in American Culture* (New York: Oxford University Press, 1985), p. 128.

10 Carpenter, *My Days and Dreams*, p. 83.

11 Carpenter to Oates, December 30, 1874, C.C. 351/18.

12 Beck to Dalton, February 25, 1901, D.P.

13 Carpenter to Oates, August 28, 1875, C.C. 351/21.

14 Carpenter to Oates, August 28, 1876. C.C. 351/23

15 Carpenter to Whitman, January 3, 1876, in Horace Traubel, ed., *With Walt Whitman in Camden*, Vol. 3 (New York: Rowman and Littlefield, 1961), p. 414.

16 Ibid., pp. 415–416.

17 Whitman, December 29, 1888, in ibid., p. 410.

18 Carpenter to Whitman, January 3, 1876, in ibid., p. 416.

19 Ibid.

20 Walt Whitman, December 29, 1888, in ibid., p. 418.

21 *West Jersey Press*, January 26, 1876, in Reynolds, *Walt Whitman's America*, p. 516.

22 Carpenter to Joseph Estlin Carpenter, November 30, 1875; March 5, 1876, J.E.C.

23 Extract from the *Pioneer*, Allahabad, March 7, 1876, C.C. N.C. 2/153.

24 Carpenter to Sophia Carpenter, March 29, 1876, C.C. 339/9.

25 Carpenter to Oates, March 28, 1876, C.C. 351/22.

26 Carpenter to Sophia Carpenter, April 5, 1876, C.C. 339/10.

27 Lizzie Carpenter to Carpenter, no date, 1876, C.C. 342/25.

28 Charles Carpenter to Carpenter, March 9, 1873, C.C. 340/1.

29 Tim Hilton, *John Ruskin* (New Haven: Yale University Press, 2002), pp. 534–536.

30 Carpenter to Charles Carpenter, November 28, 1873, C.C. 339/8.

31 Carpenter to Charles Carpenter, June 13, 1877, C.C. 339/11.

32 Carpenter, *My Days and Dreams,* p. 89. On John Burroughs, see Shi, *The Simple Life*, pp. 195, 198–202, 208.

33 Ralph Waldo Emerson in Perry Miller, ed., *The American Transcendentalists: Their Prose and Poetry* (New York: Doubleday, 1957), p. 18.

34 Carpenter, *My Days and Dreams*, pp. 81–88, Carpenter refers to Emerson's Over Soul in his Commonplace Book, 1865, Mss. C.C. 301.

35 Carpenter to Benjamin, May 4, 1877, Bayley-Whitman Collection, Ohio, Wesleyan University.

36 Edward Carpenter, *Days with Walt Whitman: With Some Notes On His Life and Work* (London: George Allen, 1906), pp. 4, 18. Carpenter dates his first visit to Whitman May 2, 1877; ibid., pp. 3–4. But he met Whitman on May 1st 1877. Walt Whitman to Anne Gilchrist, May 1st 1877, in Edwin Haviland Miller, ed., *Walt Whitman, The Correspondence, Vol. III 1876–1885* (New York: New York University Press, 1964), note 27, pp. 82–83.

37 Richard Maurice Bucke in Reynolds, *Walt Whitman's America*, p. 530.

38 Carpenter, *Days with Walt Whitman*, p. 32.

39 Gavin Arthur (pseudonym of Chester Arthur), 'The Gay Succession', in Winston Leyland, ed., *Gay Sunshine Interviews*, Vol. 1 (San Francisco: Gay Sunshine Press, 1991), p. 324.

40 Carpenter to Whitman, 'Friday Morning', no date, S.C.R.C. Syracuse University.

41 On Harry Stafford see Carpenter, *Days with Walt Whitman*, p. 11; Jonathan Ned Katz, *Love Stories: Sex Between Men Before Homosexuality* (Chicago: University of Chicago Press, 2001), pp. 224–231; Gary Schmidgell, *Walt Whitman: A Gay Life* (New York: Penguin, 1997), pp. 215–219.

42 On Whitman and Doyle see Carpenter, *Days with Walt Whitman*, pp. 147–150; Katz, *Love Stories*, pp. 165–175; Reynolds, *Walt Whitman's America*, pp. 247–251.

43 Carpenter, *My Days and Dreams*, p. 86; see Caroline Sarracino, 'Redrawing Whitman's Circle', in *Walt Whitman Quarterly Review*, Vol. 14, Nos. 2/3, Fall 1996/Winter 1997, pp. 120–124.

44 Carpenter, *Days with Walt Whitman*, p. 18.

45 Carpenter to Oates, August 22, 1877, C.C. 351/25.

46 Walt Whitman, August 1, 1889, in Horace Traubel, ed., *With Walt Whitman in Camden*, Vol. 5 (Carbondale, Illinois: Southern Illinois University Press, 1964), p. 405.

47 Carpenter to Whitman, January 3, 1876, in Traubel, ed., *With Walt Whitman in Camden*, Vol. 3, p. 417.

48 R.D. Roberts, *Eighteen Years of University Extension* (Cambridge: Cambridge University Press, 1891), p. 97.

49 James Stuart in ibid., p. 75. Carpenter, *My Days and Dreams*, p. 93.

50 Carpenter to Oates, October 3, 1879, C.C. 351/27.

51 Carpenter, *My Days and Dreams*, p. 94.

52 Lizzie Carpenter to Edward Carpenter, February 20, 1879, C.C. 342/18.

53 Edward Carpenter, *Homogenic Love, and its Place in a Free Society* (Manchester: The Labour Press Society, 1894, for private circulation), p. 28.

54 Symonds, *Memoirs of J.A. Symonds*, pp. 187, 253–254.

55 Edward Carpenter, Autobiographical Notes, July 11, 1911, Mss. p. 61, C.F.S./W.W./E.C.

56 Carpenter to Whitman, January 3, 1876 in Traubel, ed., *With Walt Whitman in Camden*, Vol. 3, p. 415.

57 Ibid.

58 Carpenter to Oates, August 22, 1877, C.C. 351/25.

59 Edward Carpenter, Beautiful Sheffield, Outline of an Address, Mss. C.F.S./W.W./E.C.

60 Ruskin, *Fors Clavigera*, in Cook and Wedderburn, eds, *The Works of John Ruskin*, p. 142.

61 Carpenter to Dalton, April 27, no date, D.P.
62 Carpenter, *My Days and Dreams*, pp. 101–102.
63 Carpenter to Whitman, Easter Sunday, 1880, C.F.S./W.W./E.C.
64 Carpenter to Whitman, July 1, 1880, C.F.S./W.W./E.C.
65 Carpenter, *My Days and Dreams*, pp. 101–102. On the possibility of a physical relationship, see David Goodway, *Anarchist Seeds Beneath the Snow: Left Libertarian Thought and British Writers from William Morris to Colin Ward* (Liverpool: Liverpool University Press, 2006), fn. 26, p. 42.
66 Fearnehough to Carpenter, September, no date, 1880; June 4, 1882; April, no date, 1882; C.C. 250/2.
67 Edward Carpenter, Albert Fearnehough, 1924, Mss. 250/2 C.C.
68 Carpenter to Whitman, July 1, 1881, W.W. L.O.C.
69 Carpenter, *My Days and Dreams*, p. 102.
70 Carpenter, 'Martin Turner', *Sketches from Life*, pp. 10–13.
71 Ibid., p. 14.
72 Fox to Carpenter, July 23, 1879, C.C. 386/15.
73 Carpenter to Oates, March 18, 1881, C.C. 351/29.
74 Arunachalam to Carpenter, July 18, 1880, C.C. 271/30.
75 Arunachalam to Edward Carpenter, no date, 1880, C.C. 271/28.
76 Ibid.
77 Carpenter, *My Days and Dreams*, p. 104.
78 Edward Carpenter, Pioneers of Science, 1879, 1881, Cambridge University Extension Lectures, Lectures, C.C. Mss. 13/11.

4 Becoming a Socialist

1 Ruskin to Riley, no date, R.P.
2 Hilton, *John Ruskin*, pp. 721–722; E.T. Cook and Alexander Wedderburn, eds., *The Guild and Museum of St. George; Reports, Catalogues and Other Papers* (London: George Allen, 1907), pp. xxiv–xxvii, pp. 116–126.
3 Arunachalam to Carpenter, July 18, 1880, C.C. 271/30.
4 Edward Carpenter, 'A Minstrel Communist', *Commonweal*, March 9, 1889.
5 Ruskin to Carpenter, May 18, 1880, C.C. 386/16.
6 Ruskin to Carpenter, July 27, 1880, C.C. 386/18.
7 M.A. Maloy, 'St. George's Farm', *Commonweal*, May 25, 1889.
8 Carpenter, *My Days and Dreams*, p. 133; John Hoyle, John Furniss, Typescript, W.C.M.; Sheila Rowbotham, '"Our Party is the People": Edward Carpenter and Radicalism in Sheffield', in John Rule and Robert Malcolmson, eds., *Protest and Survival; The Historical Experience. Essays for E.P. Thompson* (London: Merlin Press, 1993), pp. 265-270.
9 George Hendrick, *Henry Salt: Humanitarian Reformer and Man of Letters* (Urbana, Chicago: University of Illinois Press, 1977), p. 16.
10 Peter Kropotkin, *Memoirs of a Revolutionist* (New York: Grove Press, 1968), p. 492.
11 Emily Carpenter to Carpenter, February, no date, 1881, C.C. 342/9.
12 Ellen (Nelly) Hyett to Carpenter, January 24, 1881, C.C. 342/2.
13 Carpenter to Ellis, May 2, 1888, H.R.C.
14 Carpenter, *My Days and Dreams*, p. 106.
15 Carpenter to Whitman, July 1, 1881, W.W. L.O.C.

16 Edward Carpenter, Beethoven: The Symphony, Lecture XXII, Science and History of Music, Printed Syllabus, Cambridge University Extension Scheme, 1881, p. 29, C.C. Mss. 11.

17 Carpenter, *My Days and Dreams*, p. 105.

18 Edward Carpenter, Part 1 'Towards Democracy' (1881-2) XI in *Towards Democracy*, XI p. 17.

19 Ibid. XLI, p. 63.

20 Carpenter, *My Days and Dreams*, p. 190.

21 Carpenter to Whitman, March 16, 1882, in Traubel, ed., *With Walt Whitman in Camden*, Vol. I, p. 252.

22 Edward Aveling, 'Review of Towards Democracy', *Progress*, September 1881, C.C., N.C. 6/3.

23 Havelock Ellis, *My Life* (London: Heinemann, 1940), p. 163.

24 J.W. Wallace, Notes of visit to Edward Carpenter, August 13-15, 1892, Mss. No page numbers, B.A.

25 Edward Carpenter, 'A Note on "Towards Democracy"', reprinted from the *Labour Prophet*, May 1894, in *Towards Democracy*, p. 518.

26 Whitman in Horace Traubel, ed., *With Walt Whitman in Camden*, Vol. 4 (Philadelphia: University of Pennsylvania Press 1953), p. 278.

27 Carpenter, 'A Note on "Towards Democracy"', *Towards Democracy*, p. 519.

28 Carpenter to Whitman, March 16, 1882, in Traubel, ed., *With Walt Whitman in Camden*, Vol. I, p. 252.

29 Edward Carpenter, Poems, Mss. C.C. 3/8.

30 Carpenter, *Towards Democracy*, Part I. XXXIV, p. 50.

31 Ibid., XIV, p. 20; XIII, p. 19.

32 Fawcett, *What I Remember*, p. 89.

33 Aveling, 'Review of Towards Democracy', C.C. N.C. 6/3.

34 Carpenter, 'After Long Ages' (1883-1884), in *Towards Democracy*, Part II, p. 222.

35 Carpenter, *Towards Democracy*, III, p. 5.

36 Ibid. XI, p. 18.

37 Carpenter, *My Days and Dreams*, p. 107.

38 Carpenter, 'Self-analysis for Havelock Ellis', in Greig, *Edward Carpenter*, p. 290.

39 Carpenter to Oates, January 21, 1882, C.C. 351/31.

40 Edward Carpenter, Reminiscences, C.C. Mss. 253.

41 Carpenter, 'Self-Analysis for Havelock Ellis', p. 290.

42 Carpenter, *My Days and Dreams*, p. 110.

43 Whitman, December 6, 1888, in Traubel, ed., *With Walt Whitman in Camden*, Vol. 3, p. 247.

44 Carpenter, *My Days and Dreams*, p. 113.

45 Edward Carpenter, *Co-operative Production with References to the Experiment of Leclaire*, A lecture given at the Hall of Science, Sheffield, Sunday, March 18, 1883 (London: John Heywood, 1883), p. 24, Pamphlet, A.M.

46 Ibid.

47 H.M. Hyndman, *England for All: The Text Book of Democracy* (Brighton: The Harvester Press, 1973), p. 1.

48 Carpenter, *My Days and Dreams*, p. 114.

49 Tsuzuki, *Edward Carpenter*, p. 53.

50 Carpenter, *My Days and Dreams*, p. 246.

51 Tom Mann, *Memoirs* (London: MacGibbon and Kee, 1967), p. 25.

52 Carpenter, *My Days and Dreams*, p. 132. On Taylor, see J.H. Snainton, *The Making of Sheffield* (Sheffield: E. Weston and Sons, 1924), pp. 346–347.

53 Phyllis Grosskurth, *Havelock Ellis: A Biography* (New York: New York University Press), pp. 60–61.

54 Carpenter, *Towards Democracy*, XXXI, p. 45.

55 Whitman, December 6, 1888, in Traubel, ed., *With Walt Whitman in Camden*, Vol. 3, p. 247.

56 Edward Carpenter, 'On an Atlantic Steamship', *Towards Democracy*, Part II, p. 205.

57 Carpenter to Whitman, July 1, 1881, W.W. L.O.C.

58 Unwin to Parker in Mark Swenarton, *Artisans and Architects: The Ruskinian Tradition in Architectural Thought* (London: Macmillan, 1989), p. 132.

59 Unwin in ibid., pp. 132–133.

60 Morris to Mrs Burne-Jones, December 24, 1884, in Philip Henderson ed., *The Letters of William Morris to His Family and Friends* (London: Longmans Green and Co., 1950), p. 223.

61 Ibid.

62 Carpenter to Sharland, January 22, 1885, quoted in Tsuzuki, *Edward Carpenter*, p. 58.

63 Morris to Carpenter, May 2, 1885, C.C. 365/20.

64 Ibid.

65 Carpenter, 'Self-Analysis for Havelock Ellis', p. 290.

66 Salt, 'A Sage at Close Quarters', in Beith, ed., *Edward Carpenter*, p. 194.

67 Founders Day Ceremony, Honorary Degrees conferred by Manchester University; Raymond Unwin, *Manchester Guardian*, May 16, 1935, N.C; R.U.P.

68 Morris to Carpenter, September 13, 1885, C.C. 365/21.

69 John Furniss in *Sheffield Weekly Echo*, November 14, 1885.

70 William Morris, *Commonweal*, March 1886.

71 The Sheffield Socialist Society, 1886, Mss. pp. 1–2, A.M.

72 'Edward Carpenter Among the Sheffield Socialists', *Sheffield Weekly Echo*, July 17, 1886.

5 Widening Circles

1 Edward Carpenter, 'The Cause of Poverty', *Justice*, February 14, 1885, and *A Letter to the Employees of the Midland and Other Railway Companies* (Sheffield: John Fillingham, 1886), Edward Carpenter, Railway Natn. [sic], C.C. Mss. 32.

2 Edward Carpenter, 'Justice Before Charity: A Plea for Socialism', Openshawe Socialist League, *Manchester Guardian*, no date, C.C. N.C. 2/149; Edward Carpenter, 'Private Property: A Lecture Given in London and in Edinburgh' (1886), in Edward Carpenter, *England's Ideal and Other Papers on Social Subjects* (London: Swan Sonnenschein, 1895), pp. 139–165.

3 Carpenter, 'Desirable Mansions', *Progress*, June 1883, in ibid., p. 86.

4 Ibid., p. 87.

5 Carpenter, 'England's Ideal', *To-Day*, May 1884, in ibid., p. 15, fn. 1, p. 2.

6 Carpenter, 'Social Progress and Individual Effort: A Lecture given at Sheffield, February 1885', in ibid., p. 61.

7 Carpenter, 'England's Ideal', in ibid., fn. 1, p. 2.

8 Carpenter, 'Social Progress and Individual Effort', in ibid., p. 61.

9 Carpenter to Chubb, March 19, 1884, Chubb Papers, L.S.E.

10 Fabian Society's Meetings, Minutes, October 24, 1883, L.S.E.

11 Fabian Society's Meetings, Minutes, December 7, 1883, L.S.E.

12 George Bernard Shaw in W.H.G. Armytage, *Heavens Below: Utopian Experiments in England 1560–1960* (London: Routledge and Kegan Paul 1961), p. 332.

13 Havelock Ellis, Notes from Hinton's diaries, 10–2–72, H.E.P.

14 James Hinton in Mrs Havelock Ellis, *Three Modern Seers* (London: Stanley Paul & Co., no date, c. 1910), p. 73.

15 Havelock Ellis in Beith, ed., *Edward Carpenter*, p. 48.

16 Schreiner to Ellis, May 2, 1884, in S.C. Cronwright-Schreiner, ed., *The Letters of Olive Schreiner 1876–1920* (London: T. Fisher Unwin, 1924), p. 17.

17 Joseph Bristow, 'Symonds's History, Ellis's Heredity: Sexual Inversion', in Lucy Bland and Laura Doan, eds., *Sexology in Culture: Labelling Bodies and Desires* (Cambridge: Polity Press, 1998), p. 93.

18 Ellis to Carpenter, October 30, 1885, H.E.P.

19 Ibid.

20 Carpenter, *My Days and Dreams*, p. 227.

21 Schreiner to Carpenter, January 13, 1887, C.C. 359/2.

22 Ellis to Carpenter, December 2, 1887, H.E.P.

23 Carpenter to Ellis, December 14, 1885, enclosed in Schreiner to Pearson, no date, December 1885, K.P.C.

24 Carpenter, *My Days and Dreams*, p. 225.

25 Carpenter to Pease, December 1, 1885, Fabian Papers, L.S.E.

26 George Bernard Shaw report on Fabian meeting, January 1, 1886, quoted in Julia Briggs, *A Woman of Passion: The Life of E. Nesbit 1858–1924* (London: Penguin Books, 1987), p. 70.

27 Carpenter to Ellis, December 7, 1885, H.R.C.

28 Edward Carpenter, 'Simplification of Life: A Paper Read Before the Fellowship of the New Life', January 1886, in Carpenter, *England's Ideal*, p. 114.

29 Henry Page to Schreiner, January 7, 1886, Chubb Papers, L.S.E.

30 Ellis to Carpenter, January 13, 1886, H.E.P.

31 Carpenter to Ellis, January 16, 1886, H.R.C.

32 Shaw to Archibald Henderson, January 3, 1903, in Laurence, ed., *Bernard Shaw: Collected Letters*, p. 490.

33 Edward Carpenter, 'Does It Pay?', reprinted from *To-Day*, October 1886 in Carpenter, *England's Ideal*, p. 124.

34 Salt, *Seventy Years Among Savages*, p. 73.

35 Carpenter, *My Days and Dreams*, p. 237.

36 Salt, *Seventy Years Among Savages*, p. 65.

37 Salt in Hendrick, *Henry Salt*, p. 52.

38 George Bernard Shaw, Preface, Stephen Winsten, *Salt and his Circle* (London: Hutchinson & Co, 1951), pp. 9–10.

39 H.M. Hyndman, in ibid., p. 64.

40 G. Lowes Dickinson to C.R. Ashbee, J., May 12, 1885.
41 Ibid.
42 Carpenter, *My Days and Dreams*, p. 124; Harold Cox to Edward Carpenter, November 1, 1885, C.C. 250/2.
43 Harold Cox entry in D.N.B. 1949, pp. 196.
44 Cox to Carpenter, November 1, 1885, C.C. 250/2.
45 Carpenter to Goldsworthy Lowes Dickinson, July 2, 1887, R.E.F. 3/28.
46 Dickinson, in ed. Beith, *Edward Carpenter*, p. 36.
47 Dickinson in Alan Crawford, *C.R. Ashbee: Architect, Designer and Romantic Socialist* (New Haven: Yale University Press, 1985), p. 10.
48 Ashbee, J. December 11, 1885.
49 C.R. Ashbee, M. January 4, 1886
50 Lowes Dickinson to Ashbee, J. January 28, 1886.
51 Lowes Dickinson to Ashbee J. February 15, 1886.
52 Ashbee, M. April 2, 1886.
53 Ashbee, J. March 31, 1886.
54 Ashbee, J. April 1, 1886.
55 Fry to Ashbee, April 24, 1886, in Denys Sutton, ed., *Letters of Roger Fry* (London: Chatto and Windus, 1972), p. 109.
56 Virginia Woolf, *Roger Fry: A Biography* (London: The Hogarth Press, 1940), pp. 46–47.
57 Ashbee, J. July 20, 1886.
58 Ashbee, J. July 22, 1886.
59 Carpenter to Ashbee, M. July 29, 1886.
60 Ashbee, M. July 3, 1886.
61 Ashbee, M. Introduction (1938).
62 Ashbee, M. September 4, 1886.
63 Fry to Ashbee, J. September 2, 1886.
64 Ashbee to Fry, J. September 5, 1886.
65 Lowes Dickinson to Carpenter, no date, C.C. 386/413.
66 Ashbee, M. November 22, 1886.
67 Woolf, *Roger Fry*, pp. 47, 57.
68 Fry to Lady Fry, November 9, 1887, in Denys Sutton, ed., *Letters of Roger Fry*, (London: Chatto and Windus, 1972), p. 116; Roger Fry to Edward Carpenter, August 22, 1890, C.C. 386/33.
69 Havelock Ellis, 'Towards Democracy', *Papers for the Times*, February 1886, reprinted in Havelock Ellis, *Views and Reviews: A Selection of Uncollected Articles 1884–1932*, First Series: 1884–1919 (London: Desmond Harmsworth, 1932), p. 43.

6 Love and Loss

1 Edward Carpenter, 'In the Stoned-floored Workshop', *Towards Democracy*, Part IV, p. 419.
2 Hukin to Carpenter, July 8, 1886, C.C. 362/1.
3 *Sheffield Weekly Echo*, July 17, 1886.
4 Hukin to Carpenter, July 23, 1886, C.C. 362/2.
5 Hukin to Carpenter, October 28, 1886, C.C. 362/5.
6 Carpenter to Oates, December 20, 1886, C.C. 351/31.

7 Carpenter to Oates, October 28, 1886, C.C. 351/36.

8 Carpenter to Hukin, July 8, 1886, C.C. 362/1.

9 Carpenter to Oates, December 20, 1886, C.C. 351/37.

10 Ibid.

11 Carpenter to Ellis, no date (1887), H.R.C.

12 Carpenter, *My Days and Dreams*, p. 135.

13 Carpenter, 'Self-Analysis for Havelock Ellis', in Greig, *Edward Carpenter*, p. 290; see Graham Robb, *Strangers: Homosexual Love in the Nineteenth Century* (Basingstoke and Oxford: Picador, 2003), p. 21.

14 Hukin to Carpenter, January 7, 1887, C.C. 362/7.

15 Carpenter, 'Self-Analysis is for Havelock Ellis', p. 290.

16 *Sheffield Weekly Echo*, February 26, 1886; *Sheffield and Rotherham Independent*, February 23, 1887.

17 John Furniss in *Sheffield Weekly Echo*, February 26, 1887.

18 Charlotte Wilson, *Freedom*, April 1887.

19 Edward Carpenter, *Sheffield and Rotherham Independent*, February 23, 1887.

20 Edward Carpenter, letter to *Commonweal*, May 4, 1889.

21 Raymond Unwin, 'Social Experiments', *Commonweal*, March 5, 1887.

22 Carpenter to Charles Oates, April 10, 1887, C.C. 351/38.

23 Hukin to Carpenter, May 21, 1887, C.C. 362/10.

24 Hukin to Carpenter, May 15, 1887, C.C. 362/9.

25 Carpenter to Whitman, April 20, 1887, W.W. L.O.C.

26 Hukin to Carpenter, May 15, 1887, C.C. 362/9.

27 Hukin to Carpenter, May 21, 1887, C.C. 362/10.

28 Edward Carpenter, 'Edward Carpenter in Italy', letter from Nuove Tèrme, Acqui, North Italy, *Yorkshire Free Press*, May 28, 1887, C.C. C3015.

29 Hukin to Carpenter, May 24, 1887, C.C. 362/11.

30 Ibid.

31 Carpenter to Hukin, June 3, 1887, C.C. 361/5.

32 Carpenter to Hukin, Whit Monday, 1887, C.C. 361/3.

33 Hukin to Carpenter, Whit Sunday, 1887, C.C. 362/12.

34 Carpenter to Hukin, June 1, 1887, C.C. 361/4.

35 Carpenter to Oates, June 3, 1887, C.C. 351/40.

36 Ibid.

37 Carpenter to Hukin, June 3, 1887, C.C. 361/5.

38 Carpenter to Oates, July 27, 1887, C.C. 351/41.

39 Oates to Carpenter, November 17, 1887, C.C. 352/7.

40 Oates to Carpenter, October 15, 1887, C.C. 352/6.

41 Carpenter to Oates, April 15, 1888, C.C. 351-50.

42 Schreiner to Carpenter, June 8, 1887, C.C. 359/8.

43 Schreiner to Carpenter, September 10, 1887, C.C. 359/12.

44 Ibid.

45 Raymond Unwin, Diary, July 19, 1887, R.U.P.

46 Carpenter, *My Days and Dreams*, pp. 156–157.

47 Carpenter to Oates, August 9, 1887, C.C. 351/42.

48 Schreiner to Carpenter, September 10, 1887, C.C. 359/12.

49 Harold Armitage, 'George Adams: A Garden City Pioneer', *The Citizen*, January 15, 1932.

50 Adams to Carpenter, no date, C.C. 271/5.
51 Ellis to Carpenter, December 2, 1887, H.E.P.
52 Schreiner to Carpenter, December 25, 1887, C.C. 359/13.
53 Adams to Carpenter, no date, C.C. 271/5.
54 Raymond Unwin, Diary, September 6, 1887, R.U.P.
55 Ibid.
56 Lowes Dickinson to Carpenter, October 22, 1887, C.C. 386/23.
57 Ed. Dennis Proctor, *The Autobiography of G. Lowes Dickinson and Other Published Writings* (London: Duckworth 1973), p. 92.
58 Carpenter to Ashbee, October 9, 1887, Journal, C.R.A.
59 Hukin to Carpenter, November 21, 1887, C.C. 262/16; Adams to Carpenter, November 17, 1887, C.C. 271/35.
60 Henry W. Nevinson, *Changes and Chances* (London: Nisbet and Co., 1923), p. 85.
61 Carpenter to Oates, December 19, 1887, C.C. 351/43.
62 Hukin to Carpenter, November 21, 1887, C.C. 362/16.
63 Carpenter to Oates, December 19, 1887, C.C. 351/43.
64 Carpenter to Oates, January 4, 1888, 351/44.
65 Carpenter to Oates, February 19, 1888, C.C. 351/45.
66 Hukin to Carpenter, November 21, 1887, C.C. 362/16; May 11, 1888, C.C. 362/20.
67 Schreiner to Carpenter, March 12 or 26, 1888, C.C. 359/16.
68 Edward Carpenter, 'Philolaus to Diocles', *Towards Democracy*, Part IV, p. 415.

7 Political Dilemmas

1 Carpenter to (?) [Edith Nesbit], no date, B.
2 Carpenter to Oates, February 19, 1888, C.C. 351/45.
3 Hukin to Carpenter, March 15, 1888, C.C. 362/18; April 3, 1888, C.C. 362/19; January 27, 1889, C.C. 362/26.
4 Oscar Wilde quoted in Richard Ellmann, *Oscar Wilde* (London: Penguin, 1988), p. 274.
5 Carpenter to Brown, June 3, 1889, C.C. 372/1.
6 Carpenter, *My Days and Dreams*, p. 131.
7 Alf Mattison, Notes on Edward Carpenter, C.C. Mss. 388. On Alf Mattison see 'How ILP Rose from Small Beginnings. Interesting Reminiscences of Leeds Stalwart', *Evening News*, April 23, 1929. N.C. in Alf Mattison, *Letters Addressed to Alf Mattison of Leeds*, p. 326. A.M.
8 Alf Mattison, 'Edward Carpenter: A Reminiscence', *Leeds Weekly Citizen*, January 9, 1925.
9 Mattison, Notes on Edward Carpenter, C.C. Mss. 388.
10 Carpenter to Mattison, December, no date, 1889, A.M.
11 Carpenter to Whitman, May 18, 1889, in Traubel, ed., *With Walt Whitman in Camden*, Vol. 5, p. 256.
12 Helen Tufts, Biographical Introduction in Helen Tufts, ed., *Helena Born: Whitman's Ideal Democracy* (Boston, Mass; Everitt Press, 1902), pp. xvi–xvii.
13 Edward Carpenter, 'Does it Pay?', *England's Ideal*, p. 124.
14 Raymond Unwin, Diary, August 3, 1887, R.U.P.

15 Edward Carpenter, 'Bathing in Endcliffe Wood', *Sheffield Independent*, June 21, 1888, C.C. N.C. 1/75.

16 Edward Carpenter, 'Our Parish and Our Duke', Mss. Lecture Notes, 1888, C.C. Mss. 38; Edward Carpenter, *Our Parish and Our Duke: A Letter to the Parishioners of Holmesfield in Derbyshire* (Sheffield: John Fillingham, pamphlet, 1889).

17 Ed. Colin Ward, *Peter Kropotkin's Fields, Factories and Workshops of Tomorrow* (London: Freedom Press, 1983), pp. 135–136; Tsuzuki, *Edward Carpenter*, p. 92.

18 Edward Carpenter, Notes on Smoke Abatement, Mss. Notes for Lectures, C.C. 331/1; Edward Carpenter, *Report of a Lecture: The Smoke Nuisance and Smoke-Preventing Appliances*, reprinted with a few alterations from the Sheffield Daily Newspapers, October 28, 1889 (Sheffield: Leader and Sons, 1889), C.C. C0425; Edward Carpenter, 'Smoke', undated letter, no reference, N.C. in CFS/W.W./E.C.

19 Hukin to Carpenter, November 6, 1890, C.C. 362/38.

20 See B.W. Clapp, *An Environmental History of Britain since the Industrial Revolution* (London: Longman, 1994), pp. 40–41.

21 Carpenter to Reddie, December 21, 1887 in B.M. Ward, *Reddie of Abbotsholme* (London: George Allen and Unwin, 1934), p. 53. On Reddie see also J.H.G.I. Giesbers, *Cecil Reddie and Abbotsholme* (Druk: Centrale Drukkerij N.V. Nijamegen, 1970).

22 Fannie Hukin to Edward Carpenter, August 8, 1888, C.C. 363/123.

23 R.E., 'A Fellowship School', *The Sower: The Organ of the Fellowship of the New Life*, No. 1, July 1889.

24 Muirhead to Glasier, December 4, 1889, G.P.

25 Edward Carpenter, note on letter from Robert F. Muirhead, February, no date, 1925, C.C. Mss. 250/2.

26 Carpenter to Brown, April 23, 1889, C.C. 372/1.

27 Carpenter to Brown, June 3, 1889, C.C. 372/2.

28 Schreiner to Carpenter, July 28, 1889, C.C. 359/40.

29 Alf Mattison, Note in 'Olive Schreiner', *Letters Presented to Alf Mattison*, August 16, 1893, p. 8. See also Note in 'R.F. (Bob) Muirhead', in ibid., June 2, 1928, p. 365.

30 Brown to Glasier, November 10, 1889 (Wrongly catalogued 1888), G.P.

31 Carpenter to Brown, January 16, 1890, C.C. 372/5.

32 Carpenter, note on letter from Robert F. Muirhead, February, no date, 1925, C.C. Mss. 250/2.

33 Carpenter to Oates, February 23, 1890, C.C. 351/53.

34 Carpenter to Brown, March 2, 1890, C.C. 372/6.

35 Muirhead to Carpenter, February, no date, 1925, C.C. Mss. 250/2.

36 Schreiner to Carpenter, September 4, 1889, C.C. 359/42.

37 Carpenter to Mattison, March 12, 1890, A.M.

38 See Laurence Thompson, *The Enthusiasts: A Biography of John and Katharine Bruce Glasier* (London: Victor Gollancz, 1971), pp. 65–66.

39 Hukin to Carpenter, December 5, 1889, C.C. 362/33.

40 Edward Carpenter, 'An International Socialist Congress, Paris 1889', in Carpenter, *Sketches from Life in Town and Country*, p. 193.

41 Edward Carpenter, Breakdown of Our Industrial System, Bristol, January 1890, Mss. Notes, C.C. Mss. 258.

42 Stuart Uttley, *Third Report from the Select Committee of the House of Lords on the Sweating System* (London: Henry Hansard, 1889), p. 591.

43 George Hukin in ibid., p. 615.

44 Edward Carpenter, Socialism and the Foreigner, Sheffield, March 1890, Mss. Notes, C.C. 50/1.

45 See Hannam, *Isabella Ford*, pp. 55–56; John Battle, *Tom Maguire: Socialist and Poet* (Leeds: The Ford Maguire Society, 1997), p. 20; Alf Mattison in Edward Carpenter and Alf Mattison, eds., *Tom Maguire: A Remembrance* (Manchester: Manchester Labour Press Society, 1895), p. xv; Anon. 'Jacob Wolf Friedenson', Rank and File Personalities, No. 8. *The Socialist Review*, January 1927, N.C. in *Letters Addressed to Alf Mattison*, A.M.

46 Dyche to Carpenter, October 5, 1924, C.C. 313/44.

47 Carpenter, *My Days and Dreams*, pp. 176.

48 Hukin to Carpenter, July 7, 1889, C.C. 362/31.

49 'Sheffield', *Commonweal*, December 21, 1889. On its divisiveness, see Bruce Glasier to Brown, December 23, 1889, G.P.

50 Carpenter to Brown, January 16, 1890, C.C. 372/5.

51 *Manifesto of the Sheffield Socialists: An Appeal to Workers*, Sheffield Socialists Club, Lady's Bridge Buildings, 63 Blonk St, Sheffield, no date (1890), no page numbers. C.C. 372/6.

52 Maguire to Carpenter, July 30, 1890, in Carpenter and Mattison, *Tom Maguire*, p. xi.

53 Carpenter to Glasier, May 2, 1890, G.P.

54 Edward Carpenter, The Future Society, C.C. Mss. 48, no page numbers.

55 Carpenter to Oates, February 23, 1890, C.C. 351/53.

56 G. Lowes Dickinson in ed. Proctor, *The Autobiography of G. Lowes Dickinson*, p. 156.

57 Carpenter to Oates, February 23, 1890, C.C. 351/53.

58 Carpenter, *My Days and Dreams*, p. 7.

8 Challenging Civilisation

1 Anon, Fabiana, *To-day*, February 1889, C.C. CPer 131.

2 Bernard Shaw, January 1889, in Stanley Weintraub, ed., *Bernard Shaw: The Diaries 1885–1897* (University Park: Pennsylvania State University Press, 1986), p. 455.

3 Anon, Fabiana, *To-day*, February 1889, C.C. CPer 131.

4 Edward Carpenter, *Civilisation: Its Cause and Cure* (London: Swan Sonnenschein, 1893), pp. 48–49.

5 Ibid., p. 43.

6 Ibid., p. 25.

7 Ibid., p. 34.

8 Ibid., p. 35.

9 Ibid.

10 Ibid., p. 130.

11 Ibid., p. 140.

12 Ibid., p. 133.

13 Ibid., p. 41.
14 Ibid., p. 100.
15 Ibid., pp. 112–114.
16 Ibid., p. 12.
17 Ibid., p. 51.
18 Ibid., p. 87.
19 Edward Carpenter, 'The Value of the Value Theory', *To-day*, June 1889, C.C. CPer 131.
20 Carpenter, *Civilisation: Its Cause and Cure*, p. 85.
21 Carpenter to Ellis, March 27, 1890, H.R.C.
22 Carpenter, *Civilisation: Its Cause and Cure*, p. 146.
23 Carpenter to Bruce Glasier, January 19, 1892, G.P.
24 Schreiner to Carpenter, January 21, 1889, C.C. 359/35.
25 Helena Born in Tufts, *Helena Born*, p. xvii.
26 Tsuzuki, *Edward Carpenter*, p. 83.
27 Brown to Glasier, October 8, 1889, G.P.
28 James Brown, 'Some Objections to Socialism', *Commonweal*, January 4, 1891.
29 Edward Carpenter, *From Adam's Peak to Elephanta; Sketches in Ceylon and India* (London: George Allen and Unwin, 1921), pp. 139–147.
30 Antony Copley, *A Spiritual Bloomsbury: Hinduism and Homosexuality in the Lives and Writing of Edward Carpenter, E.M. Forster and Christopher Isherwood* (Lanham: Rowman and Littlefield, 2006), pp. 39–48; Jayawardena, *Nobodies to Somebodies*, pp. 215–217.
31 Arunachalam to Carpenter, November 25, 1888, C.C. 271/37, in Edward Carpenter, ed., *Light from the East: Being Letters on Gnanam, The Divine Knowledge by the Hon. P. Arunachalam* (London: George Allen and Unwin, 1927), p. 33.
32 Arunachalam to Carpenter, December 17, 1889, C.C. 271/39.
33 Carpenter, *My Days and Dreams*, pp. 250–251.
34 Ibid., p. 143.
35 H.P. Blavatsky to Mr. Sinnett, January 28, 1886, in A.T. Barker, ed., *The Letters of H.P. Blavatsky to A.P. Sinnett and other Miscellaneous Letters* (Pasadena, California: Theosophical University Press, 1973), first edition 1925, p. 178.
36 Carpenter, *My Days and Dreams*, pp. 240–245.
37 Edward Carpenter, 'Underneath and After All', *Lucifer*, Vol. VI, No. 37, May 15, 1890, p. 248.
38 Salt to Carpenter, October 17, 1890, C.C. 356/2.
39 Carpenter, *From Adam's Peak*, pp. 350–352.
40 Edward Carpenter, Mss. Letters and Notes on Homosexuality, C.C. Mss. 93.
41 Carpenter to Oates, February 23, 1890, C.C. 351/53.
42 Carpenter to Brown, July 17, 1890, C.C. 372/8.
43 Obituary of Charles Carpenter, Extract from the *Pioneer*, Allahabadad Newspaper, March 7, 1876, C.C. N.C. 2/153; Alfred Carpenter in C.F. Buckland, *Dictionary of Indian Biography* (New York: Haskell House Publishers, 1968), p. 74.
44 Carpenter to Oates, October 8, 1890, C.C. 351/55.
45 Kate Salt to Carpenter, December 3, 1912, C.C. 355/49.
46 Carpenter to Oates, December 7, 1890, C.C. 351/56.

47 Carpenter to Kate Salt, November 24, 1890, C.C. 354/11.
48 Carpenter to Oates, December 7, 1890, C.C. 351/56.
49 Carpenter, *From Adam's Peak*, pp. 57–58.
50 Ibid., p. 27.
51 Ibid., pp. 58–59.
52 Henry Salt, 'To Edward Carpenter in Ceylon', Winsten, *Salt and His Circle*, p. 76.
53 Carpenter, *From Adam's Peak*, p. 74.
54 Ibid., p. 58.
55 Ibid., pp. 117.
56 Ibid., pp. 122–123.
57 Ibid., p. 123.
58 Ibid., pp. 136, 151.
59 Arunachalam to Carpenter, March 18, 1898, C.C. 271/59, in Carpenter, ed., *Light from the East*, p. 73.
60 Carpenter, *From Adam's Peak*, p. 149.
61 Carpenter to Whitman, December 11, 1890, L.O.C.
62 Carpenter, *From Adam's Peak*, p. 200.
63 Carpenter to Whitman, December 11, 1890, L.O.C.
64 Carpenter, *From Adam's Peak*, pp. 169–170.
65 Ibid., pp. 157, 163.
66 Carpenter to Kate Salt, November 24, 1890, C.C. 354/11.
67 Carpenter, *From Adam's Peak*, pp. 177–178.
68 Carpenter to Kate Salt, November 24, 1890, C.C. 354/11.
69 Carpenter, *From Adam's Peak*, pp. 208–210.
70 Ibid., p. 228.
71 Carpenter to Kate Salt, February 22, 1891, C.C. 354/12.
72 Carpenter, *From Adam's Peak*, pp. 271–274.
73 Bhagavan Das to Edward Carpenter, January 16, 1893, C.C. 378/18. On Bhagavan (or Bhagawan) Das see Dilip Kumar Barua, *Edward Carpenter, 1844–1929: An Apostle of Freedom* (Burdwan, India: The University of Burdwan, 1991), p. 141.
74 Carpenter, *From Adam's Peak*, pp. 288–290.
75 Carpenter to Mattison, December 23, 1890, A.M.
76 Carpenter, *From Adam's Peak*, 1892 edition, p. 47. In the 1921 revised edition 'the despised darkie' becomes 'these brothers and sisters whose skins are dark by nature rather than by art' (p. 46).
77 Edward Carpenter, Social Movements in India, Mss. Notes for a Lecture given at the Sheffield Hall of Science, October 4, 1890, and at Hammersmith, November 1891, C.C. Mss. 52.
78 Carpenter, *From Adam's Peak*, p. 37.
79 Ibid., p. 14.
80 Ibid., p. 34.
81 Ibid., p. 27; See Parminder Kaur Bakshi, 'Homosexuality and Orientalism: Edward Carpenter's Journey to the East', in Tony Brown, ed., *Edward Carpenter and Late Victorian Radicalism* (London: Frank Cass, 1990), pp. 161–166.
82 Edward Carpenter, Autobiographical Notes, July 1911, C.F.S./W.W./E.C. p. 48; see Tariq Rahman, 'The Literary Treatment of Indian Themes in

the Works of Edward Carpenter', *Durham University Review*, 80, 1987, pp. 78–79.

83 Carpenter, *From Adam's Peak*, pp. 13, 219.

84 Ibid., p. 308.

85 Carpenter, Social Movements in India, C.C. Mss. 52.

86 Carpenter to Mattison, October 5, 1891, A.M; Fannie Hukin to Carpenter, January 29, 1891, C.C. 362/124.

87 Das to Carpenter, January 16, 1893, C.C. 378/18.

88 'A Socialist's View of India', *Pioneer*, January 10, 1893, C.C. N.C. 6/111.

89 'An Original Globe Trotter', *The Times of India*, January 28, 1893, C.C. N.C. 6/113.

90 C.E. Crawford to Carpenter, August 19, 1891, C.C. 386/36 and October 20, 1891, C.C. 386/37.

91 *The Athenaeum*, January 7, 1893, C.C. N.C. 6/115.

92 *Tribune*, New York, February 5, 1893, C.C. N.C. 6/122.

93 'Review of From Adam's Peak to Elephanta', *Lucifer*, Vol. xi, No. 66, February 15, 1893, pp. 508, 510.

9 Utopian Mutations

1 William Morris, 'Where Are We Now?', *Commonweal*, November 15, 1890.

2 John Creaghe, Letter, *Commonweal*, November 29, 1890.

3 Hukin to Carpenter, November 20, 1890, C.C. 362/39.

4 Hukin to Carpenter, January 15, 1891, C.C. 362/43.

5 Hukin to Carpenter, January 22, 1891, C.C. 362/44.

6 Glasier to Brown, April 23, 1891, G.P.

7 Brown to Glasier, Wednesday, no date, 1891, G.P.

8 'Sheffield Propaganda', *Commonweal*, June 6, 1891; see D.J. Nicoll, *Stanley's Exploits or, Civilising Africa* (London: Kate Sharpley Library, BM Hurricane, 2001), pamphlet, third edition.

9 'Sheffield', *Commonweal*, August 29, 1891.

10 Ibid., September 5, 1891.

11 *The Sheffield Anarchist*, July 19, 1891; October 4, 1891; August 27, 1891.

12 Cyril Bell, *Commonweal*, December 26, 1891.

13 John Creaghe, 'Correspondence', *Commonweal*, November 28, 1891.

14 Carpenter to Mattison, November 29, 1891, A.M.

15 Edward Carpenter, 'Correspondence', *Commonweal*, December 5, 1891.

16 John Creaghe, 'Correspondence', *Commonweal*, December 19, 1891.

17 Thomas Barclay, 'Correspondence', *Commonweal*, December 12, 1891. On Barclay see Bill Lancaster, *Radicalism, Cooperation and Socialism: Leicester working class politics, 1860–1906* (Leicester: Leicester University Press, 1987), pp. 111–115.

18 John Creaghe, 'Correspondence', *Commonweal*, December 19, 1891.

19 Ibid., December 26, 1891.

20 David Nicoll, *Life in English Prisons* (London: Kate Sharpley Library, BM Hurricane, 1992), pamphlet, p. 9.

21 John Quail, *The Slow Burning Fuse: The Lost History of the British Anarchists* (London: Paladin, 1978), p. 106.

22 Carpenter to Glasier, January 19, 1892, G.P.

23 Carpenter to Glasier, March 31, 1892, G.P.

24 Glasier to Brown, April 20, 1892, G.P.; Glasier to Brown, March 24, 1892, G.P.; Carpenter to Glasier, May 2, 1890, G.P.

25 *The Times*, April 5, 1892, and *Saturday Review*, April 9, 1892, quoted in Tsuzuki, *Edward Carpenter*, p. 101.

26 Brown to Glasier, March 23, 1892, G.P.; Carpenter to Glasier, March 31, 1892, G.P.; Glasier to Brown, March 24, 1892, G.P.

27 Edward Carpenter, 'A Letter Relating to the Walsall Anarchists', reprinted from *Freedom* of December 1892 (written November 25, 1892), C.C. Mss. 22.

28 Carpenter to Henderson, November 25, 1896, H.E.N. 43/78,561X3.

29 Ford to Carpenter, July 24, 1899, C.C. 271/61.

30 Edward Carpenter, *Defensa de los Criminales: Critica de la Moralidad* (Buenos Aires: P. Tonini, 1901), pamphlet, C.C. Co425.

31 Glasier to Carpenter, March 21, 1893, G.P.

32 Carpenter to Glasier, March 25, 1893.

33 John Bruce Glasier, 'James Brown', *Freedom*, May 1893; Edward Carpenter and John Bruce Glasier, eds., 'Prefatory Note' in *Verses by James M. Brown of Glasgow* (Glasgow: Labour Literature Society, 1893).

34 Fry to Lady Fry, January 14, 1894, in ed. Sutton, *Letters of Roger Fry*, p. 156.

35 Edward Carpenter, The Way Out, 1893–1896, C.C. Mss. 58; Edward Carpenter, The Changed Ideal of Society, 1894, C.C. Mss. 61; Edward Carpenter, Parties in the Labor Movement, 1893, C.C. Mss. 57.

36 Carpenter to Mattison, July 8, 1892, A.M.

37 Carpenter to Mattison, October 20, 1892, A.M.

38 Maguire to Carpenter, November 26, 1892 in Carpenter and Mattison, eds., *Tom Maguire*, p. xii.

39 Carpenter to Wallace, December 6, 1892, B.W.F.C.

40 Edward Carpenter, Parties in the Labour Movement, Glasgow, February 13, 1893, and Halifax, March 5, 1893, Mss. 57.

41 Arunachalam to Edward Carpenter, September 17, 1893, C.C. 271/47.

42 Isabella Ford quoted in Hannam, *Isabella Ford*, p. 54.

43 Edward Carpenter, The Future Society, February 1890, C.C. Mss. 48, on Frank Smith see Armytage, *Heavens Below*, pp. 281, 317, 320.

44 John Trevor, *My Quest for God* (London: 'Labour Prophet' Office, 1897), pp. 219–242; K.S. Inglis, *Churches and the Working Class in Victorian England* (London: Routledge and Kegan Paul, 1963), pp. 215–222.

45 *The Labour Prophet*, The Organ of the Labour Church, Vol. 1, No. 12, December 1892.

46 Edward Carpenter, 'The Thirsk Accident', Letter, *Sheffield Independent*, November 7, 1892, C.C. N.C.1/69.

47 Alf Mattison, Note-book B, April 1894, p. 6.; Barlow and Cowley (near Chesterfield), Unemployed Miners Relief Fund, November 1893, C.C. 269/52.

48 Carpenter to Hukin, March 7, 1892, C.C. 361/10.

49 Edward Carpenter, The Way Out, 1893–1894, C.C. Mss. 58.

50 Edward Carpenter, 'A Note on "Towards Democracy"', reprinted from the *Labour Prophet*, May 1894, in *Towards Democracy*, p. 512.

51 Carpenter to Mattison, January 27, 1893, A.M.
52 Edward Carpenter, 'Democracy and the Delegate Theory', *Clarion*, November 24, 1894, N.C. C.F.S./W.W./E.C.
53 Ibid.
54 Ibid.
55 John Lister, Letter, *Clarion*, January 5, 1895, N.C. C.F.S./W.W./E.C.
56 Edward Carpenter, Parish Councils (December 1894), Mss. Notes for a speech to parish meeting, C.C. Mss. 62; Edward Carpenter's Lecture Engagements; Alf Mattison, Note-book B, p. 93, A.M.
57 The Fabian Society, *Parish and District Councils: What They Are and What They Can Do* (London: The Fabian Society, 1893).
58 Eds. Norman and Jeanne MacKenzie, *The Diaries of Beatrice Webb* (London: Virago, 2000), October 11, 1894, p. 188.
59 Carpenter, *My Days and Dreams*, p. 291.
60 Carpenter to Oates, June 7, 1891, C.C. 351/57.
61 Salt to Carpenter, February 9, 1892, C.C. 356/8.
62 Edward Carpenter and Edward Maitland, *Vivisection*, The Humanitarian League's Publications, No. 6 (London: William Reeves, 1893), pamphlet.
63 Edward Carpenter, 'Vivisection', *Clarion*, December 1, 1894, N.C. C.F.S./W.W./E.C.
64 Carpenter to Mattison, May 7, 1892, A.M.
65 Carpenter to Mattison, January 13, 1893, A.M.
66 W.J. Jupp, 'Towards Democracy', *Seed-Time*, No. 16, April 1893, L.S.E.
67 Salt in Beith, ed., *Edward Carpenter*, p. 191.

10 Homogenic Love

1 Edward Carpenter, *George Merrill: A True History, and Study in Psychology*, March 5, 1913, typed Mss., p. 22, C.C. 363/17.
2 Ibid.
3 Ibid., p. 2.
4 Ibid., p. 15.
5 Ibid., p. 19.
6 Ibid., pp. 17, 6.
7 Ibid., p. 2.
8 Ibid., p. 6.
9 Edward Carpenter, 'O Thou Whose Form', *Towards Democracy*, p. 276.
10 Edward Carpenter, 'Love's Vision', *Towards Democracy*, p. 275.
11 Edward Carpenter, 'All Night Long', *Towards Democracy*, p. 274.
12 Shortland to Carpenter, no date, C.C. 386/425.
13 Shortland to Carpenter, August 25, 1896, C.C. 386/72.
14 Carpenter to Mattison, August 31, 1892, A.M.
15 Carpenter to Mattison, July 4, 1893. A.M.
16 Hukin to Carpenter, August 21, 1894, C.C. 362/63.
17 Carpenter to Hukin, March 7, 1895, C.C. 361/19.
18 Bucke to Wallace, April 10, 1892, B.W.F.C.
19 Carpenter to Wallace, July 19, 1892, B.W.F.C.
20 Wallace, Notes of Visit to Edward Carpenter, August 13–15, 1892 (no page numbers), B.W.F.C.

21 Ibid.

22 Charles Sixsmith, Notes on Edward Carpenter, Mss. April 11, 1894, C.F.S./W.W./E.C.

23 Ibid.

24 Carpenter to Wallace, April 11, 1894, B.W.F.C.

25 Sixsmith in Beith, ed., *Edward Carpenter*, p. 216.

26 Symonds to Rhys, August 27, 1890, in Herbert M. Schueller and Robert L. Peters, eds., *The Letters of John Addington Symonds, Vol. III, 1885–1893* (Detroit: Wayne State University Press, 1969), p. 490.

27 Ellis to Symonds, July 10, 1891, H.E.P.

28 Ellis to Symonds, June 18, 1892, H.E.P.

29 Symonds to Ellis, July, no date, 1891, in Schueller and Peters, eds., *The Letters of John Addington Symonds*, p. 587.

30 Symonds to Johnston, January 21, 1893, in ibid., pp. 809–810; Symonds to Carpenter, February 7, 1893, in ibid., pp. 814–815. On Fusato see Katz, *Love Stories*, pp. 259–261.

31 Symonds to Johnston, January 21, 1893 in Schueller and Peters, eds., *The Letters of John Addington Symonds*, p. 809.

32 Ellis to Carpenter, December 17, 1892, H.E.P.

33 Symonds to Carpenter, December 29, 1892, in Schueller and Peters, eds., *The Letters of John Addington Symonds*, p. 797.

34 Ellis to Symonds, January 3, 1893, H.E.P.

35 Symonds to Carpenter, January 21, 1893, in Schueller and Peters, eds., *The Letters of John Addington Symonds*, p. 808.

36 Symonds to Carpenter, December 29, 1892, in ibid., p. 799.

37 Symonds to Carpenter, January 21, 1893, in ibid., p. 808.

38 Havelock Ellis, *Studies in the Psychology of Sex*, Vol. 2 (Philadelphia: F.A. Davis, 1923), third edition, pp. 23–26.

39 Symonds to Carpenter, February 7, 1893, in Schueller and Peters, *The Letters of John Addington Symonds*, pp. 814–815.

40 Symonds to Carpenter, December 29, 1892, in ibid., p. 798.

41 Symonds to Carpenter, January 29, 1893, in ibid., pp. 810–811.

42 Symonds to Carpenter, December 29, 1892, in ibid., p. 798.

43 Symonds to Carpenter, February 5, 1893, in ibid., p. 813.

44 Symonds to Carpenter, February 7, 1893, in ibid., p. 815.

45 J.A. Symonds, *Walt Whitman: A Study* (London: George Routledge and Sons, 1893), pp. 159–160.

46 Carpenter to Mattison, April 22, 1893, A. M.

47 Carpenter to Ellis, December 4, 1896, H.R.C.

48 Edward Carpenter, Homogenic Love, Manuscript, C.C. Mss. 60, p. 1.

49 Ibid., p. 2.

50 Hafiz quoted in Edward Carpenter, Mss. Notes on Homosexuality, C.C. Mss. 93.

51 Carpenter to Ellis, January 19, 1894, H.R.C.

52 Carpenter, Homogenic Love, Manuscript, C.C. Mss. 60, p. 34.

53 Ibid., p. 46.

54 Ibid., p. 23.

55 Ibid., p. 68. Carpenter, *Homogenic Love, and its Place in a Free Society*, p. 50.

56 Carpenter, Homogenic Love, Manuscript, C.C. Mss. 60, pp. 68–70.

57 Ibid., p. 36.

58 Brown to Carpenter, February 27, 1895, C.C. 386/53.

59 Carpenter to Mattison, February 10, 1895, A.M.

60 Alf Mattison, Note-book A, March 8, 1895, pp. 21–22.

61 Carpenter to Mattison, April 9, 1895, A.M.

62 Ellmann, Oscar Wilde, pp. 414–35.

63 'Helvellyn', 'Oscar Wilde, Two Views of the Present Position', Star, no date, no reference, C.C. N.C. 1/66.

64 Ellmann, Oscar Wilde, p. 446.

65 Stead to Carpenter, June 22, 1895, C.C. 386/54.

66 Carpenter to Hukin, July 23, 1895, C.C. 361/20; July 31, 1895, C.C. 361/21.

67 Carpenter to Hukin, July 31, 1895, C.C. 361/21.

68 Anon, 'Edward Carpenter's Tracts on Sex', The Humanitarian, Vol. II, No. 2, August 1895, pp. 150–155.

69 Carpenter to Oates, August 26, 1895, C.C. 351/64. See also T. Fisher Unwin to Carpenter, August 16, 1895, 268/51.

70 Labour Leader, April 13, 1895.

71 Justice, April 13, 1895.

72 Edward Carpenter, 'Some Recent Criminal Cases', Freedom, July 1895.

73 Edward Bernstein, Die Neue Zeit, April–May 1895, quoted in John Lauritsen and David Thorstad, The Early Homosexual Rights Movement (1864–1935) (New York: Times Change Press, 1974), p. 59.

11 A Long Campaign

1 Carpenter to Mattison, June 1, 1895, A.M.

2 Ives to Carpenter, March 28, 1894, C.C. 386/47.

3 See Deas to Carpenter, May 17, 1894, C.C. 386/51.

4 Ives to Carpenter, April 16, 1894, C.C. 386/48.

5 George Ives quoted in John Stokes, Oscar Wilde: Myths, Miracles, and Limitations, (Cambridge: Cambridge University Press 1996), p. 70.

6 Ashbee, September 14, 15, 16, 1895. M.

7 Dalmas to Carpenter, February 13, 1896, C.C. 386/66; Deas to Carpenter, All Fools Day, 1896, C.C. 386/69.

8 Shaw to Charlotte Payne-Towshend, October 31, 1897, in Laurence, ed., Bernard Shaw: Collected Letters, p. 818.

9 Hukin to Carpenter, April 8, 1895, C.C. 362/69.

10 Carpenter to Mattison, April 29, 1895, A.M.

11 Young to Carpenter, February 11, 1896, C.C. 386/65.

12 Carpenter to Oates, October 3, 1896, C.C. 351/71.

13 Carpenter, Ioläus: Manuscript Notes on Homosexuality, C.C. Mss 93.

14 Edward Carpenter, Love's Coming of Age: A Series of Papers on the Relations of the Sexes (Manchester: Labour Press, 1896), p. 18; Edward Carpenter, 'A Visit to Walt Whitman in 1877', The Progressive Review, February 1897, pp. 407–417; 'Walt Whitman in 1884', The Progressive Review, April 1897, pp. 9–19. Reprinted in Carpenter, Days with Walt Whitman.

15 Carpenter to Ellis, January 15, 1896, H.R.C.

16 Edward Carpenter, 'An Unknown People', *The Reformer*, July 1897 and August 1897, N.C: C.F.S./W.W./E.C.

17 Ibid., pamphlet (London: A. and H. E. Bonner, 1897), p. 20, C.C. Co425, pp. 16, 37.

18 Edward Carpenter, 'Affection in Education', *International Journal of Ethics*, Vol. IX, No. 4, July 1899, pp. 483, 485, C.C. C Per 60.

19 Carpenter to Ellis, November 28, no date, H.R.C.

20 Ellis to Carpenter, April 24, 1896, H.E.P.

21 Carpenter to Kate Salt, August 31, 1897, C.C. 354/49.

22 Ellis to Carpenter, August 3, 1897, H.E.P.

23 Grosskurth, *Havelock Ellis*, p. 201.

24 John Sweeney quoted in Vincent Brome, *Havelock Ellis: Philosopher of Sex* (London: Routledge and Kegan Paul, 1979), p. 102.

25 Edward Carpenter, 'The Bedborough Case', *Saturday Review*, no date, 1898, C.C. NC1/74.

26 Carpenter to Oates, October 3, 1896, C.C. 351/71; Carpenter to Hukin, May 20, 1896, C.C. 361/25.

27 Ashbee to Forbes, September 2, 1897, in Felicity Ashbee, *Janet Ashbee: Love, Marriage and the Arts and Crafts Movement* (New York: Syracuse University Press, 2002), p. 25.

28 Johnston in H.G. Cocks, *Nameless Offences: Homosexual Desire in the 19th Century* (London: I.B. Tauris, 2003), pp. 190, 188.

29 Nicol to Carpenter, September 16, 1894, C.C. 271/53.

30 Nicol to Carpenter, December 28, 1894, C.C. 271/54; July 2, 1895, C.C. 271/55; March 6, 1896, C.C. 271/56; November, no date, C.C. 375/25.

31 Nicol to Carpenter, no date, C.C. 375/26.

32 Nicol to Carpenter, December 28, 1894, C.C. 271/54.

33 Sixsmith to Carpenter, no date, C.C. 386/427.

34 Alf Mattison, Note-book A, August 17, 1898, p. 70; November 19, 1898, p. 74, A.M.

35 I am grateful to Dorothy and E.P. Thompson for this information.

36 Carpenter to Mattison, January 15, 1899(?), A.M.

37 Carpenter to Oates, March 3, 1897, C.C. 351/72.

38 Carpenter to Oates, March 31, 1888, C.C. 351/49.

39 Carpenter, *My Days and Dreams*, p. 107.

40 Sixsmith in Beith, ed., *Edward Carpenter*, p. 226.

41 Hukin to Carpenter, January 16, 1889, C.C. 362/25.

42 I am grateful to a former student from the Gascoigne/Colyer/Parker family for this information. For Mrs Mary Ann Gascoigne's shop see ed. Alan Godfrey, *Old Ordnance Survey Maps Surveyed: 1889–91*, Revised in 1903 (Gateshead: Godfrey, 1985), Sheffield Central Reference Library.

43 Carpenter, *George Merrill*, Typed Mss p. 27, C.C. 363/17.

44 Carpenter to Sixsmith, April 19, 1912, C.F.S./W.W./E.C.

45 Merrill to Carpenter, no date, C.C. 386/2.

46 Merrill to Carpenter, October 26, 1896, C.C. 386/3; November 11, 1896, C.C. 386/5.

47 Merrill to Carpenter, October 26, 1896, C.C. 386/3; ibid. February 12, 1897, C.C. 386/7.
48 Carpenter, *George Merrill*, Typed Mss pp. 29–31, C.C. 363/17.
49 Carpenter, 'A Voice Over the Earth', *Towards Democracy*, Part III, pp. 298–299.
50 Carpenter to Oates, August 29, 1897, C.C. 351/76.
51 Deas to Carpenter, May 17, 1894, C.C. 386/51.
52 Oates to Carpenter, November 24–25, 1887, C.C. 352/8.
53 Carpenter to Oates, May 17, 1897, C.C. 351/74.
54 Carpenter to Ellis, November 28, 1897, H.R.C.
55 Carpenter to Ellis, December 4, 1896, H.R.C.
56 Deas to Carpenter, May 17, 1894, C.C. 386/51.

12 Defending Wild Women

1 Edith Ellis to Carpenter, December 27, 1893, C.C. 358/1.
2 Ibid.
3 Carpenter, *My Days and Dreams*, p. 226.
4 Edward Carpenter, Memoir of Edith Ellis, Mss. Notes for the Preface to *The New Horizon*, p. 6. H.E.P.
5 Schreiner to Carpenter, August 1, 1893, C.C. 359/63.
6 Carpenter to Kate Salt, October 15, 1893, C.C. 354/28.
7 Carpenter to Kate Salt, February 21, 1894, C.C. 354/29.
8 Carpenter to Kate Salt, March 17, 1894, C.C. 354/30.
9 Carpenter to Kate Salt, April 9, 1894, C.C. 354/31.
10 Schreiner to Carpenter, no date, C.C. 359/73.
11 Carpenter to Kate Salt, March 17, 1894, C.C. 354/30.
12 Carpenter to Hukin, January 31, 1894, C.C. 361/12, and Carpenter to Fry, February 27, 1894, R.E.F./3/28 Kings.
13 Carpenter to Fry, February 27, 1894, R.E.F./3/28 Kings.
14 Author of *A Superfluous Woman* to Edward Carpenter, February 4, 1894, C.C. 271/49. On Emma Brooke see Lucy Bland, *Banishing the Beast: English Feminism and Sexual Morality 1885–1914* (London: Penguin, 1995), pp. 21–22, 28–30.
15 Macduff to Carpenter, April 7, 1894, C.C. 271/51.
16 Isaac Hull Platt, 'Sex-Love and Its Place in a Free Society by Edward Carpenter', *The Conservator* 5: 29, April 1894, in Gary Schmidgall, ed., *Conserving Walt Whitman's Fame: Selections from Horace Traubel's Conservator, 1890–1919* (Iowa City: University of Iowa Press, 2006), p. 325.
17 Carpenter to Dobell, March 12, 1896, Ms. Dobell, 183, B.
18 Carpenter to Mattison, January 17, 1896, A.M.
19 Carpenter, *Love's Coming of Age*, p. 70.
20 Ibid., p. 29.
21 Ibid., pp. 81–82.
22 Ibid., p. 26.
23 Ibid., p. 46.
24 Ibid., p. 59.
25 Ibid., p. 55.
26 Ibid., pp. 66–67.
27 Ibid., pp. 33–34.

28 Ibid., p. 111.
29 Ibid., p. 61.
30 Ibid.
31 Ibid., p. 33.
32 Ibid., p. 5.
33 Ibid., p. 103.
34 Ellis to Carpenter, January 22, 1894, H.E.P.
35 Carpenter, *Love's Coming-of-Age*, pp. 104–105.
36 Ibid., p. 101.
37 'Remarks and Notes on Preventive Checks to Population', in ibid., p. 150.
38 'Some Remarks on the Early Star and Sex Worships', in ibid., p. 137.
39 Salt to Carpenter, May 22, 1896, C.C. 356/15.
40 Carpenter, *My Days and Dreams*, p. 198.
41 Lowes Dickinson to Carpenter, May 22, 1896, 386/70.
42 Lily Bell, 'Matrons and Maidens', *Labour Leader*, June 27, 1896. On Lily Bell/Isabella Bream Pearce see June Hannam and Karen Hunt, *Socialist Women, Britain, 1880s to 1920s* (London: Routledge, 2002), p. 35.
43 Blatchford to Edward Carpenter, January 11, 1894, C.C. 386/46.
44 Edward Carpenter, 'A Reply', *Free Review*, October 1896, p. 93.
45 Nicol to Carpenter, March 6, 1896, C.C. 271/56.
46 Charles Sixsmith, Edward Carpenter Poet and Reformer (Note-book, lecture on Edward Carpenter); manuscript dated 1898 but this is crossed out and January 25, 1899 added, C.F.S./W.W./E.C., no page numbers.
47 Carpenter, 'A Note on "Towards Democracy"', in *Towards Democracy*, pp. 518–519
48 Ford to Carpenter, January 28, no date, quoted in Hannam, *Isabella Ford*, p. 29.
49 Mrs Havelock Ellis, *Personal Impressions of Edward Carpenter* (Berkeley Heights, New Jersey: The Free Spirit Press, 1922), pp. 8–10.
50 Charlotte Perkins Gilman, Diary, September 28, 1896, C.P.G.
51 Charlotte Perkins Stetson to Houghton Gilman, June 4, 1897, C.P.G.
52 Born to Bailie, May 3, 1898, H.B.
53 Carpenter to Hukin, November 8, 1896, C.C. 361/26.
54 Bertrand Russell in Barua, *The Life and Work of Edward Carpenter*, PhD Thesis, p. 223.
55 Edith Ellis to Carpenter, November 15, 1898, H.E.P.
56 Salt in Beith, ed., *Edward Carpenter*, p. 188.
57 Mattison, Note-book A, May Day 1897, p. 44, A.M.
58 Salt in Beith, ed., *Edward Carpenter*, p. 190.
59 Carpenter to Kate Salt, March 1, 1890, C.C. 354/8.
60 Kate Salt to Carpenter, December 16, 1892, C.C. 355/8.
61 Kate Salt to Carpenter, January 4, 1892, C.C. 355/6.
62 Carpenter to Kate Salt, February 16, 1896, C.C. 354/40.
63 Carpenter to Kate Salt, no date, 1894, C.C. 354/36.
64 Kate Salt to Carpenter, March 11, 1896, C.C. 355/13.
65 Kate Salt to Carpenter, January 28, 1898, C.C. 355/19.
66 Bernard Shaw to Charlotte Payne-Townshend, March 16, 1898, in Laurence, *Bernard Shaw: Collected Letters*, p. 16.

67 Bernard Shaw, Preface to Winsten, *Salt and his Circle*, p. 9.
68 Kate Salt to Carpenter, February 17, 1897, C.C. 355/15.
69 Ibid. September 2, 1897, C.C. 355/18.
70 Carpenter to Kate Salt, March 10, 1897, C.C. 354/46.
71 Ibid., October 11, 1892, C.C. 354/18.
72 Carpenter to Wallace, March 30, 1894, B.W.F.C.
73 Carpenter to Bruce Glasier, June 4, 1893, G.P.
74 Carpenter to Bruce Glasier, June 13, 1893, G.P.
75 Salt in ed. Beith, *Edward Carpenter*, p. 194.
76 Edward Carpenter, Autobiographical Notes, Mss. July 1911, p. 62, C.F.S./W.W./E.C.
77 Carpenter to Mattison, October 17, 1899, A.M.
78 Carpenter to Kate Salt, May 6, 1892, C.C. 354/15.
79 Carpenter to Kate Salt, October 15, 1893, C.C. 354/28.

13 Millthorpe

1   Sixsmith in ed. Beith, *Edward Carpenter*, p. 218.
2   Wallace, Notes of Visit, Mss. No page numbers, B.A.
3   Carpenter to Wallace, July 22, 1894, B.A.
4   Wallace, Notes of Visit, Mss. No page numbers, B.A.
5   Ibid.
6   George Ives, in Beith, ed., *Edward Carpenter*, pp. 125, 127
7   Sixsmith in ibid., pp. 216–217.
8   See Mattison, Note-book A, Easter Saturday, 1895, p. 25, A.M.
9   Carpenter, *My Days and Dreams*, p. 167.
10 Mattison, Note-book A, July 17th 1897, p. 49, A.M.
11 Salt in ed. Beith, *Edward Carpenter*, p. 195; Carpenter to Kate Salt, August 28, 1893, C.C. 354/27.
12 Mattison, Note-book A, October 18, 1897, pp. 51–52, A.M.
13 Carpenter to Hukin, October 8, 1895, C.C. 361/22.
14 Kate Salt to Mattison, December 30, 1893, Mattison, *Letters Addressed to Alf Mattison*, p. 14, A.M.
15 Salt to Mattison, February 24, 1919, in ibid., pp. 16, 7, A.M.
16 Mattison, Note on foregoing letters, in ibid., p. 8, A.M.
17 Kate Salt to Carpenter, February 18, 1902, C.C. 355/25.
18 Flint to Carpenter, November 30, 1893, C.C. 364/1.
19 Bessie Joynes to Carpenter, February 20, 1902, C.C. 386/95.
20 Thompson, *The Enthusiasts*, p. 84.
21 Carpenter to Kate Salt, June 12, 1894, 354/32.
22 Hyett in Beith, ed., *Edward Carpenter*, p. 117.
23 Salt, *Seventy Years Among Savages*, p. 87.
24 Mattison, Note-book A, July 17, 1897, p. 48, A.M.
25 Salt in Beith, ed., *Edward Carpenter*, p. 193.
26 Ibid., p. 188.
27 Roger Fry, in Woolf, *Roger Fry*, p. 47. The later edited version dates the letter from Fry to Lady Fry as July 25, 1886 (ed. Diane F. Gillespie, *Roger Fry* [Oxford: Blackwell, 1995], pp. 38, 273).
28 Janet Ashbee, in Ashbee, *Janet Ashbee*, p. 34.

29 Ed. Proctor, *The Autobiography of G. Lowes Dickinson*, p. 156.

30 Kate Salt to Mattison, January 14, 1894, *Letters Addressed to Alf Mattison*, p. 15, A.M.

31 Carpenter to Sixsmith, February 19, 1895, C.F.S./W.W./E.C.

32 Carpenter to Oates, July 7, 1896, C.C. 351/69.

33 Ashbee, M., September 14, 15, 16, 1895.

34 Carpenter to Mattison, January 27, 1896, A.M.; Harold Armytage, 'George Adams: A Garden City Pioneer', *The Citizen*, Letchworth, January 15, 1932.

35 Sixsmith in Beith, ed., *Edward Carpenter*, p. 227.

36 Carpenter to Gilchrist, no date, C.C. M.D. 3545-3-9, 136.

37 Carpenter to Kate Salt, October 11, 1892, C.C. 354/13.

38 Carpenter to Mattison, March 26, 1893, A.M.

39 Carpenter to Kate Salt, March 22, 1893, C.C. 354/26.

40 Carpenter to Bruce Glasier, March 25, 1893, G.P.

41 Carpenter to Mattison, November 30, 1893, A.M.

42 Salt in Beith, ed., *Edward Carpenter*, p. 186.

43 Ives in ibid., p. 128.

44 Carpenter to Kate Salt, March 10, 1897, C.C. 354/46.

45 Carpenter to Mattison, June 1, 1895, A.M.

46 Carpenter to Oates, August 26, 1895, C.C. 351/64.

47 Sixsmith in Beith, ed., *Edward Carpenter*, p. 218.

48 Hukin to Carpenter, July 25, 1893, C.C. 362/59.

49 Hukin to Carpenter, July 20, 1893, C.C. 362/58; Carpenter, *George Merrill*, Mss. p. 28, C.C. 363/17.

50 Carpenter to Oates, August 29, 1897, C.C. 351/76.

51 Carpenter to Salt, October 12, 1897, C.C. 354/50.

52 Carpenter to Oates, November 4, 1897, C.C. 351/77.

53 Carpenter to Kate Salt, October 12, 1897, C.C. 354/50.

54 Carpenter to Oates, November 4, 1897, C.C. 351/77.

55 Carpenter to Kate Salt, December 10, 1897, C.C. 354/52.

56 Kate Salt to Carpenter, January 28, 1898, C.C. 355/19.

57 Carpenter to Kate Salt, Weds. evg. [*sic*], no date (but early 1898), C.C. 354/53.

58 George Adams quoted in Salt in Beith, ed., *Edward Carpenter*, p. 190.

59 Carpenter to Kate Salt, February 4, 1898, C.C. 354/54.

60 Carpenter, *George Merrill*, Mss. p. 33, C.C. 363/17.

61 Carpenter to Kate Salt, February 4, 1898, 354/54.

62 Carpenter to Oates, February 10, 1898, C.C. 351/80.

63 Hukin to Carpenter, June 28, 1898, C.C 362/78.

64 Carpenter, *My Days and Dreams*, pp. 158–159, 131.

65 Edward Carpenter, 'Two Gifts', *The Adult*, Vol. 2, No. 1, February 1898, p. 18.

14 Culture and Everyday Life

1 Carpenter to Mattison, October 3, 1897, A.M.

2 Carpenter to Mann, October 21, 1895, I.L.P. Papers, L.S.E.

3 Edward Carpenter, 'Transitions to Freedom', *Forecasts of the Coming Century* (Manchester: The Labour Press, 1897), p. 186.

4 Ibid., p. 188.

5 Ibid.

6 Ibid., p. 190.

7 Shaw to Carpenter, July 29, 1896, in Laurence, *Bernard Shaw: Collected Letters*, p. 637.

8 Shaw, 'Illusions of Socialism', in Carpenter, ed., *Forecasts of the Coming Century*, p. 161.

9 Edward Carpenter, Prefatory Note in The Spanish Atrocities Committee, ed., *Revival of the Inquisition* (London: J. Perry, 1897, Reprinted from *Freedom*), pamphlet, C.C. Co42S, No. 7.

10 Carpenter to Kate Salt, August 31, 1897, C.C. 354/49.

11 Ed. Proctor, *The Autobiography of G. Lowes Dickinson*, p. 144.

12 Edward Carpenter, 'Williams Morris', *Freedom*, December 1896, C.F.S./W.W./E.C.

13 Edward Carpenter to William Morris, June 12, 1896 in Robert Bridges, ed., *English Handwriting* (Oxford: The Clarendon Press, 1927), V. and A.

14 Carpenter, 'William Morris', *Freedom*, December 1896, C.F.S./W.W./E.C.

15 Alf Mattison, Note-book A, May 7, 1896, p. 33; May-Day Sunday 1897, p. 43, A.M.

16 The Rt. Hon. J.R. Clynes, *Memoirs* (London: Hutchinson, 1937), p. 86.

17 Edward Carpenter, 'England Arise', *Chants of Labour: A Song Book of the People* (London: George Allen and Unwin, 1888), p. 19.

18 Edward Carpenter, *St. George and the Dragon. A Play in Three Acts for Children and Young Folk*. Dedicated to the I.L.P. Clubs and Socialist Sunday Schools (London: I.L.P. 1908; first edition, Manchester: Labour Press Society, 1895), pamphlet, C.C. Co42S.

19 Sheffield Socialist Society, no date, C.C. 335/2.

20 Hugh Mapleton, in Dennis Hardy, *Alternative Communities in Nineteenth-Century England* (London: Faber and Faber, 1964) p. 185.

21 Ibid.

22 Ibid., p. 186.

23 *Seed-Time: The Organ of the New Fellowship*, No. 12, April 1892; No. 32, April 1897, L.S.E. On the Croydon Fellowship see Armytage, *Heavens Below*, pp. 335-339.

24 Edward Carpenter, 'The British Museum and Sandals', *Westminster Gazette*, April 1897, C.C. N.C.1/73.

25 Henry Salt, 'Every-day Ethics', *Seed-Time: The Organ of the New Fellowship*, No. 9, July 1891, L.S.E.

26 Edward Carpenter, 'The Humanising of Our Prisons', *Labour Leader*, May 11, 1895, C.F.S./W.W./E.C. Edward Carpenter, Prison Methods Lectures 1897-1898, C.C. Mss. 75; Edward Carpenter, 'The Need for a Rational and Humane Science', in The Humanitarian League, ed., *Lectures by Various Authors* (London: George Bell, 1897).

27 Carpenter, Prison Methods, C.C. Mss. 75.

28 Carpenter, 'The Humanising of Our Prisons', *Labour Leader*, May 11, 1895, C.F.S./W.W./E.C.

29 Nevinson, *Changes and Chances*, p. 129.

30 Edward Carpenter, 'The Simplification of Life' (reprinted from the *Savoy*

of July 1896) in Edward Carpenter, *Angels' Wings* (London: George Allen and Unwin, first edition 1899, sixth edition 1920), p. 237.

31 Ibid., pp. 237–238.
32 Ibid., p. 242.
33 Ibid., pp. 246, 247.
34 Ibid., pp. 1, 11.
35 Extract from a letter by Carpenter to Salt, March 12, no date, c. 1891, C.F.S./W.W./E.C.
36 See A.M. Gibbs, *Bernard Shaw: A Life* (Gainesville, Florida: University Press of Florida, 2005), pp. 217–218.
37 Carpenter, *Angels' Wings*, p. 134.
38 Ibid., pp. 134–135.
39 Ibid., p. 45
40 Ibid., p. 219.
41 M. Wynn Thomas, *Transatlantic Connections: Whitman U.S., Whitman U.K.* (Iowa City: University of Iowa Press, 2005), p. 182.
42 Carpenter, *Angels' Wings*, p. 161.
43 Ibid. p. 213.
44 Ibid. pp. 211, 221.
45 Linda Dalrymple Henderson, 'Mysticism as the "Tie that Binds": The Case of Edward Carpenter and Modernism', in *Art Journal*, Vol. 46, No. 1, Spring 1987, pp. 32, 34; William Innes Homer, *Robert Henri and his Circle* (Ithaca: Cornell University Press, 1969), p. 76.
46 Ed. Pam Roberts, *F. Holland Day* (Amsterdam: Waanders publishers, no date), pp. 13, 55–56; eds. Helmut and Alison Gernscheim, *Alvin Langdon Coburn: Photographer. An Autobiography* (New York: Dover, 1978), p. 14.
47 Eugenia W. Herbert, *The Artist and Social Reform: France and Belgium, 1885–1898* (New Haven: Yale University Press, 1961), pp. 207–209; Donald Drew Egbert, *Social Radicalism and the Arts* (London: Gerald Duckworth and Co. 1970) pp. 609–616; Dalrymple Henderson, 'Mysticism as the "Tie That Binds"', p. 34.
48 Carpenter, *Angels' Wings*, p. 247.
49 Carpenter to Kate Salt, December 30, 1898, C.C. 354/57.
50 Edward Carpenter, 'Hafiz to the Cup-Bearer', *Towards Democracy*, p. 416.
51 Carpenter to Kate Salt, June 3, 1898, C.C. 354/56.
52 Ellis in Beith, ed., *Edward Carpenter*, pp. 57–60.
53 Carpenter to Kate Salt, July 28, 1900, C.C. 354/69.
54 Ashbee, M. January, no date, 1903.
55 Sixsmith in Beith, ed., *Edward Carpenter*, p. 219.
56 T.H. Bell, *Edward Carpenter: The English Tolstoi* (Los Angeles: The Libertarian Group, 1932), pamphlet, p. 20.
57 Edward Carpenter, 'Monte Carlo', *Towards Democracy*, pp. 435–440.
58 Carpenter to Kate Salt, July 28, 1900, C.C. 354/69.
59 Carpenter to Hukin, August 22, 1900, C.C. 361/32.
60 Merrill to Hukin, August 22, 1900 (enclosed), C.C. 361/32.
61 Ashbee, M. January, no date, 1903.
62 Carpenter to Kate Salt, May 30, 1904, C.C. 354/85; June 22, 1904, C.C. 354/86.

63 Fannie Hukin to Carpenter, May 25, 1904, C.C. 362/125.

64 Merrill to Sixsmith, March 14, 1903, C.F.S./W.W./E.C.

65 Hyett in ed. Beith, *Edward Carpenter*, p. 116.

66 Ibid., p. 115.

67 Salt to Mattison, August 26, 1929, *Letters Addressed to Alf Mattison*, p. 394, A.M.

68 Carpenter, *George Merrill*, C.C. 363/17, p. 35.

69 Carpenter to Hukin, June 20, 1902, C.C. 361/39.

70 Edward Carpenter, 'Hafiz to the Cup-Bearer', *Towards Democracy*, pp. 416–417.

71 Sixsmith in Beith, ed., *Edward Carpenter*, pp. 218, 227.

72 Ashbee, M. January, no date, 1903.

15 Who Shall Command the Heart?

1 Carpenter, *My Days and Dreams*, p. 199.

2 Stanley Unwin, *The Truth About Publishing* (London: George Allen and Unwin, 1926), p. 54.

3 Edward Carpenter, 'To Become a Creator', *Towards Democracy*, p. 498.

4 Linda Dalrymple Henderson, *The Fourth Dimension and Non-Euclidean Geometry in Modern Art* (Princeton, New Jersey: Princeton University Press, 1983), pp. 5–27, 165.

5 Edward Carpenter, 'In the British Museum Library', *Towards Democracy*, pp. 459–460.

6 Edward Carpenter, 'Nothing Less Than All', *Towards Democracy*, p. 489.

7 Ibid., p. 488.

8 Carpenter, *My Days and Dreams*, p. 144.

9 Edward Carpenter, 'Nothing Less Than All', *Towards Democracy*, p. 488.

10 Edward Carpenter, 'The Ocean of Sex', ibid., p. 383; Edward Carpenter, 'O Child of Uranus', ibid., p. 411.

11 Edward Carpenter, 'Nothing Less Than All', ibid., p. 488.

12 Edward Carpenter, 'The Stupid Old Body', ibid., p. 484–485.

13 Edward Carpenter, 'In An Old Quarry', ibid., p. 494.

14 Edward Carpenter, 'O Joy Divine of Friends', ibid., p. 409.

15 Beck to Dalton, February 25, 1901, D.P.

16 Robert Blatchford, *Clarion*, December 19, 1902, quoted in Tsuzuki, *Edward Carpenter*, p. 381.

17 John Bruce Glasier, Diary, January 25, 1903, quoted in ibid.

18 Ashbee, J. Xmas 1902.

19 Carpenter to Mattison, July 5, 1902, A.M.

20 See ed. Edward Carpenter, *Ioläus: An Anthology of Friendship* (London: Swan Sonnenschein, 1902), pp. 15, 90, 109, 113–114, 129, 144, 153, 160–166, 177–179.

21 Carpenter to Ellis, February 27, 1901, H.R.C.

22 *Labour Leader*, April 12, 1902, C.C. N.C. 6/56.

23 *Daily Chronicle*, April 22, 1902, C.C. N.C. 6/55; *New Age*, May 23, 1907, C.C. N.C. 5/45.

24 David Nicoll, 'The Crimes of the Priests', *Commonweal*, October 1902.

25 Carpenter to Hukin, April 15, 1901, C.C. 361/34.

26 Kate Salt to Carpenter, December 27, 1901, C.C. 255/23.

27 Carpenter to Kate Salt, September 26, 1901, C.C. 354/77.

28 Carpenter to Sixsmith, September 4, 1901, C.F.S./W.W./E.C.

29 Richard Maurice Bucke, *Cosmic Consciousness: A Study of the Evolution of the Human Mind* (London: The Olympia Press 1972), p. 207; see Michael Robertson, *Worshipping Walt: The Whitman Disciples* (Princeton: Princeton University Press, 2008), pp. 128–137, 183.

30 Carpenter, *My Days and Dreams*, pp. 183–189.

31 Ibid., p. 206.

32 Edward Carpenter, 'The Dream World and the Real World', *Light: A Journal of Psychical, Occult and Mystical Research*, Vol. xxii, No. 1, 143, December 16, 1902, p. 583, C.C. C.Per 71.

33 Edward Carpenter, 'The Art of Creation', being the second anniversary lecture of the Larner Sugden Memorial delivered at the William Morris Labour Church at Leek. (Pamphlet) (Hanley, Potteries and Newcastle Cripples' Guild Press, 1903); Barua, *The Life and Work of Edward Carpenter*, p. 207.

34 *New Books by Edward Carpenter*, Brochure, May 1905, C.C. N.C. 5/63.

35 Edward Carpenter, *The Art of Creation* (London: George Allen, 1907), first edition 1904, pp. 54–58, 60–61, 90.

36 Edward Carpenter, Preface in ibid., p. vii.

37 Ibid., p. 67.

38 Edward Carpenter, 'Night', *Towards Democracy*, p. 381.

39 Carpenter, *The Art of Creation*, p. 7.

40 Ibid., p. 8.

41 Lao-Tzu quoted in Carpenter, *The Art of Creation*, p. v.

42 Schopenhauer quoted in Christopher Janaway, *Schopenhauer: A Very Short Introduction* (Oxford: Oxford University Press, 2004), p. 59.

43 Frederic W. Myers, *Human Personality and its Survival of Bodily Death* (London: Longmans Green and Co., 1903), Vol. 1, p. 13.

44 Carpenter, *The Art of Creation*, p. 202. See Peter Bowler, *The Eclipse of Darwinism: Anti-Darwinian Evolution Theories in the Decades Around 1900* (Baltimore: John Hopkins University Press, 1983), pp. 102–103. On the application of Lamarck in relation to a racial hierarchy, see ibid. p. 19.

45 Carpenter, *Civilisation: Its Cause and Cure*, p. 85.

46 Carpenter to Whitman, July 1, 1881, W.W.; Binns to Carpenter, April 12, 1904, C.C. 271/84; see Stanley Finger, *Origins of Neuroscience: A History of Exploration into Brain Function* (New York: Oxford University Press, 1994), pp. 266, 282–283; Edwin Clarke and L.S. Jacyna, *Nineteenth-Century Origins of Neuroscientific Concepts* (Berkeley and Los Angeles: University of California Press, 1987), pp. 29–57, 308–370.

47 Binns to Carpenter, February 3, 1904, C.C. 271/82.

48 Binns to Carpenter, April 12, 1904, C.C. 271/84.

49 Ibid.

50 Edward Carpenter, British Museum application for J.G. Davey, *Ganglionic Nervous System*, enclosed in ibid.

51 Carpenter, *The Art of Creation*, pp. 115–116.

52 Ibid., p. 109.

53 Mark Kinkead-Weekes, *D.H. Lawrence, Triumph to Exile 1912–1922* (Cambridge: Cambridge University Press, 1996), p. 394; Emile Delavenay, *D.H. Lawrence and Edward Carpenter: A Study in Edwardian Transition* (London: Heinemann 1971), pp. 69-72; Edward Nehls, *D.H. Lawrence: A Composite Biography*, Volume 1, 1885–1919 (Wisconsin: University of Wisconsin Press, 1957), p. 135; Helen Corke to Emile Delavenay, October 9, 1968, E.D.

54 Kinkead-Weekes, *D.H. Lawrence: Triumph to Exile*, pp. 388–389, 395; J.H. Pryse, *The Apocalypse Unsealed* (London: John M. Watkins, 1910), pp. 14–16.

55 D.H. Lawrence in Delavenay, *D.H. Lawrence and Edward Carpenter*, p. 70.

56 E.M. Forster, *The Longest Journey* (London: Penguin Books, 1964), first edition 1907, pp. 7–9, 77. See Tariq Rahman, 'Edward Carpenter and E.M. Forster', *Durham University Journal*, Vol. 89, No.1, December 1986, p. 62.

57 Anthony David Brown, *A Consideration of Some Parallels in the Personal and Social Ideals of E.M. Forster and Edward Carpenter*, PhD Thesis, University of Warwick, 1982, p. 141.

58 Thompson to Carpenter, March 27, 1905, C.C. 375/35.

59 Carpenter, *The Art of Creation*, p. 206.

60 Ibid.

61 Carpenter to Sixsmith, December 14, 1904, C.F.S./W.W./E.C.

62 Beatrice Webb to Mary Playne, June 21, 1907 in Norman MacKenzie, ed., *The Letters of Sidney and Beatrice Webb, Volume II. Partnership 1892–1912* (Cambridge and London: Cambridge University Press and L.S.E., 1978), p. 267.

63 Beatrice Webb to Forster, April 24, 1934, in Norman MacKenzie, ed., *The Letters of Sidney and Beatrice Webb, Volume III, Pilgrimage 1912–1947* (Cambridge and London: Cambridge University Press and L.S.E., 1978), p. 393.

64 G. Lowes Dickinson, 'The Art of Creation', *Independent Review*, Vol. IV, October 1904–January 1905, p. 638, C.C. C.Per 56.

65 Edward Carpenter, Reply to G. Lowes Dickinson, Mss. Notes, C.C. Mss. 105.

66 James to Olivier, February 10, 1905, in Margaret Olivier, ed., *Sydney Olivier: Letters and Selected Writings* (London: George Allen and Unwin, 1948), p. 125.

67 E.M. Forster in Beith, ed., *Edward Carpenter*, p. 77.

68 Edward Carpenter, Deities and Devils, Lecture Notes, 1906, C.C. Mss. 106. (The lecture was also given to the Sheffield Theosophists); Tom Steele, *Alfred Orage and the Leeds Arts Club 1893–1923* (Aldershot: Scolar Press, 1990), p. 75.

16 Body and Spirit

1 Undated newspaper cuttings in Charles Oates to Alf Mattison, *Letters Presented to Alf Mattison*, p. 42, A.M.; Edward Carpenter to Charles Sixsmith, May 12, 1904, C.F.S./W.W./E.C.

2 Ashbee, Ms. January 24, 1903.

3 Carpenter to Mr. Wilkeson, March 6, 1905, J.C.

4 Edward Carpenter, 'Walt Whitman's Children', *The Reformer*, February 1902 reprinted in Carpenter, *Days with Walt Whitman*, p. 139.

5 Edward Carpenter, 'Whitman as Prophet', in *Days with Walt Whitman*, p. 88.

6 Carpenter to Ellis, April 18, 1905, H.R.C.

7 Edward Carpenter, *Love's Coming of Age* (1906 edition), in Greig, ed., *Edward Carpenter*, p. 182.

8 Edward Carpenter, 'The Intermediate Sex', in *Love's Coming of Age* (1906 edition), in ibid., pp. 199–200, 190.

9 Ellis to Carpenter, April 8, 1907, H.E.P.

10 Edward Carpenter, *The Intermediate Sex: A Study of Some Transitional Types of Men and Women*, Appendix (London: George Allen and Unwin, 1981), first edition 1908, p. 172.

11 Shaw to Louis Wilkinson, December 20, 1909 in Laurence, ed., *Bernard Shaw: Collected Letters*, p. 890.

12 Otto Weininger in Carpenter, *The Intermediate Sex*, p. 5.

13 Carpenter to Ellis, October 8, 1906, H.R.C.

14 Carpenter to Ellis, January 11, 1909, H.R.C.

15 Ellis to Carpenter, January 17, 1909, H.E.P.

16 *The Medical Times*, February 27, 1909, C.C. N.C. 5/5; *Journal of Education*, June 1909, C.C. N.C. 6/23; *The Schoolmaster*, July 3, 1909, C.C. N.C. 6/25.

17 *British Medical Journal*, June 26, 1909, C.C. NC6/73.

18 Carpenter, letter to the *British Medical Journal*, July 6, 1909, C.C. Ms. 184/20.

19 Carpenter to Sixsmith, July 6, 1909, C.F.S./W.W./E.C.

20 Carpenter to How-Martyn, September 25, 1909, W.C.

21 M.D. O'Brien, Socialism and Infamy: The Homogenic or Comrade Love Exposed. An Open Letter in Plain Words for a Socialist Prophet, 1909, C.C. N.C. 2/104-108.

22 Hukin to Carpenter, March 26, 1909, C.C. 362/99.

23 Sixsmith to Carpenter, April 5, 1909, C.C. 386/165.

24 Merrill to Sixsmith, no date (1909), C.F.S./W.W./E.C.

25 Sixsmith to Carpenter, April 5, 1909, C.C. 386/165.

26 Hukin to Carpenter, April 11, 1909, 362/101.

27 E. Bramley to Carpenter, May 24, 1909, C.C. 272/2; Carpenter to Kate Salt, September 9, 1909, C.C. 354/98.

28 Carpenter to Hawkin, April 27, 1909; May 4, 1909, J.R.L.

29 Carpenter to Mattison, April 30, 1909, A.M.

30 Carpenter to Sixsmith, no date (1909).

31 Rev. C. Bradshaw to Carpenter, September 7, 1909, C.C. 272/3.

32 M.D. O'Brien, An Unnatural Mother, May 11, 1913, C.C. 386/214; M.D. O'Brien, Hiding the Truth to Defeat the Ends of Justice, no date, C.C. 386/214.

33 Reviews in the *Sheffield Guardian*, no date and January 31, 1913, C.C. N.C. 2/78–79.

34 Kathleen Bunting in Wendy Hill, 'Edward Carpenter, Memories of a "True Socialist"', *Morning Telegraph*, February 28, 1973.

35 Mary Bunting interviewed by Rony Robinson, c.1980.

36 Kathleen Bunting interviewed by Rony Robinson, c.1980.

37 Edward Carpenter to Constantine Sarantchoff, October 6, 1906, C.S.

38 C. Langdon Everard to Edward Carpenter, September 12, 1908, C.C. 386/160.

39 Walter Seward in Beith, ed., *Edward Carpenter*, p. 203.

40 Seward to Carpenter, June 30, 1910, C.C. 370/1.

41 Seward to Carpenter, no date, C.C. 370/10.

42 Ibid.

43 Seward to Carpenter, April 8, 1911, C.C. 370/2.

44 Merrill to Charles and Lucy Sixsmith, no date, C.F.S./W.W./E.C.

45 Löwy to Carpenter, October 9, 1911, C.C. 386/196.

46 Edward Carpenter, 'Mightier than Mammon', *Towards Democracy*, p. 403.

47 Edward Carpenter, 'Nothing Less Than All', *Towards Democracy*, p. 488. A misprint turns 'lover' into 'lever'.

48 Edward Carpenter, *The Drama of Love and Death* (London: George Allen and Unwin, 1912), pp. 65–66.

49 Ibid., p. 59.

50 Ibid., p. 66

51 Ibid.

52 Carpenter, Autobiographical Notes, July 1911, Mss. C.F.S./W.W./E.C., pp. 62–63.

53 Carpenter, *The Drama of Love and Death*, pp. 67–8.

54 Warwick to Carpenter, July 31, 1911(?), C.C. 386/180.

55 Alf Mattison, Note-book B, October, no date, 1913, p. 29; Mattison to Florrie Mattison, September 27, 1913 (in Carpenter to Mattison Letters), A.M.

56 Ashbee, M. March 1913.

57 Our Special Correspondent, 'Towards Freedom and Equality. Interview with Mr. Edward Carpenter', *Christian Commonwealth*, December 11, 1912, C.C. N.C. 2/1.

58 Carpenter, *The Drama of Love and Death*, pp. 39–40.

59 Ibid., p. 31.

60 Ibid., p. 5.

61 Henri Bergson, *L'Évolution Créatrice* (Paris: Félix Alcan et Guillaumin Réunis, 1911), p. 4. Henri Bergson, *Creative Evolution* (London: Macmillan, 1964), pp. 3–4.

62 Bergson, *L'Évolution Créatrice*, p. 93. Bergson, *Creative Evolution*, p. 90.

63 Bergson, *Creative Evolution*, p. 275.

64 Ibid., p. 389.

65 On Assagioli's work in Florence see Carolyn Burke, *Becoming Modern: The Life of Mina Loy* (New York: Farrar, Strauss and Giroux, 1996), pp. 146–147.

66 Mattison to Florrie Mattison, November, no date, 1911, in Mattison, Note-book B, pp. 4–5. A.M.

67 Carpenter, *The Drama of Love and Death*, p. 195.

68 See Jeff Hughes, 'Occultism and the Atom: The Curious Story of Isotopes', *Physics World*, September 2003, p. 33.

69 Mattison, Note-book B, October, no date, 1913, p. 29; J. Johnston, *Visit to Edward Carpenter*, May 27–29, 1911, Mss. no page numbers, B.W.F.C.

70 Carpenter, *The Drama of Love and Death*, p. 272.

71 Ibid., pp. 125–126.

72 Ibid., p. 261.

73 Ashbee, M. March, no date, 1913.

74 Kate Salt to Carpenter, November 17, 1905, C.C. 355/35.

75 Carpenter to Mattison, December 16, 1910, A.M.

76 'Farewell Message left by Edward Carpenter to be read over his Grave', December 30, 1910, in ed. Beith, *Edward Carpenter*, p. 246.

77 Dora Carpenter Suicide Note, C.C. 343/40.

78 Carpenter to Sixsmith, no date (Postmark March 12, 1912), C.F.S./W.W./E.C.

79 Hyett in ed. Beith, *Edward Carpenter*, p. 117.

80 Carpenter to Sixsmith, April 19, 1912, C.F.S./W.W./E.C.

81 Carpenter to Mattison, February 12, 1913, A.M.

82 Nevinson, Diary, December 21, 1910, H.N.D.; B.Mss.Eng.misc.e.616.

83 On Keeling see Alf Mattison, Journal, November 10, 1925, p. 89, Leeds Reference Library; Ben Pimlott, *Hugh Dalton* (London: Macmillan, 1985), pp. 48–49; ed. E. T.[owshend]. *Keeling: Letters and Recollections* (London: George Allen and Unwin, 1918), pp. 19, 62.

84 Bryn Olivier in Paul Delany, *The Neo-Pagans: Rupert Brooke and the Ordeal of Youth* (New York: The Free Press, Macmillan 1987), fn. 36, p. 252.

85 Ibid., p. 50.

86 Virginia Stephens (Woolf), in Nigel Jones, *Rupert Brooke, Life, Death and Myth* (London: Richard Cohen Books, 1999), p. 180.

87 Nevinson, *Diary*, May 4, 1910, H.N.D; B.Mss.Eng.misc.e.616.

88 Fry to Vanessa Bell, August, no date, 1911, in ed. Sutton, *Letters of Roger Fry*, p. 350.

89 James Cousins, 'Edward Carpenter as I Found Him', *Irish Citizen*, June 12, 1915, C.C. N.C. 2/50. James Cousins, 'Edward Carpenter: Prophet of Democracy', *The Herald of the Star*, August 11, 1915, C.C. N.C. 2/150.

90 Boughton to Carpenter, January 5, 1908, C.C. 271/108.

91 Reginald R. Buckley, 'Edward Carpenter Prophet and Poet', *T.P.s Weekly*, August 26, 1910, C.C. N.C. 2/2.

92 Edward Carpenter, 'Music Drama in the Future', *New Age*, August 15, 1908.

93 Edward Carpenter, *Intermediate Types Among Primitive Folk: A Study in Social Evolution* (London: George Allen and Co., 1914), pp. 16–17, 22, 31, 36, 50.

94 Ibid., p. 48.

95 Ibid., p. 82.

96 Ibid., p. 81.

97 Ibid., pp. 147–148.

98 Havelock Ellis, 'The Intermediate Types Among Primitive Folk', *Occult Review*, 1914, Reprinted in Ellis, *Views and Reviews*, p. 259.

99 John Bruce Glasier, Edward Carpenter, Proofs from *Socialist Review*, Mss. (this is dated wrongly as 1908), C.F.S./W.W./E.C.

100 Ellis, *Three Modern Seers*, p. 205.

101 Horace Traubel, 'The Intermediate Sex', *The Conservator*, February 1913; http://www.micklestreet.rutgers.edu/pages/Documents/Conservator/February1913.htm

102 Haynes, *The Lawyer*, p. 161.
103 J. William Lloyd, 'Four Months Overseas', unpublished typescript, 1913, p. 135. I owe this reference to D.A. Sachs.

17 The Larger Socialism

1 Edward Carpenter, 'The May-Fly', *Humane Review*, April 1903, reprinted in Carpenter, *The Art of Creation*, pp. 253, 237.
2 Edward Carpenter, 'Empire', *The Ethical World, An Organ of Democracy in Religion, Art, Industry and Politics*, June 16, 1900, reprinted in J. Bruce Glasier, ed., *The Minstrelsy of Peace* (Manchester: National Labour Press, no date, c. 1918), pp. 134–135.
3 Edward Carpenter, 'Empire in India and Elsewhere', *Humane Review*, October 1900 (reprinted London: Humanitarian League and A.C. Fifield, 1906), pp. 6–12, C.F.S./W.W./E.C.
4 Arunachalam to Carpenter, February, no date, 1901, C.C. 271/75, also in ed. Carpenter, *Light from the East*, p. 75.
5 Edward Carpenter, 'Narayan: A Tale of Indian Life', *New Age*, November 16, 23, 30, December 7, 1899. N.C. C.F.S./W.W./E.C.
6 Edward Carpenter, *Boer and Briton* (Manchester: Manchester Labour Press, Leaflet), C.C. C042S; Carpenter to Oates, January 5, 1900, C.C. 351/86.
7 Carpenter to Oates, April 25, 1901, C.C. 351/89.
8 Carpenter, *Boer and Briton*, p. 3. See Vincent Geoghegan, 'Edward Carpenter's England Revisited', *History of Political Thought*, Vol. xxiv, No. 3, August 2003.
9 James Connolly, *The Socialist*, May 1903, in Raymond Challinor, *The Origins of British Bolshevism* (London: Croom Helm, 1977), pp. 14–15.
10 Edward Carpenter, 'Tangier', *New Age*, February 14, 1907, N.C. C.F.S./W.W./E.C.
11 Edward Carpenter, 'Tangier', *New Age*, January 31, 1907, N.C.C.F.S./W.W./E.C.
12 See Edward Carpenter, Lecture on Social and Political Life: China, Manchester Ruskin Society, November 6, 1901; *Manchester Guardian*, November 7, 1901, C.C. N.C. 2/149; Carpenter, 'Empire in India and Elsewhere', p. 12; Edward Carpenter, 'The New South African Union', *Labour Leader*, August 27, 1909; September 3, 1909, C.C. N.C. 1/35–36.
13 Carpenter, *Boer and Briton*, p. 4.
14 Edward Carpenter, 'A Message to India', *New International Review*, Vol. 4, No. 2, December 1906, p. 49.
15 Edward Carpenter, The Larger Socialism, Lecture at Chesterfield, Newspaper report, no reference, October 1909, C.C. N.C. 1/84.
16 A Friend of Labour, Labour Church, Croydon, no reference, no date, 1901, C.C. N.C. 4/80.
17 Ibid.
18 Edward Carpenter, The Chinese Academy, Fabian Arts Group, February 21, 1907, Lecture notice and syllabus, C.C. N.C. 4/76 and N.C. 1/62.
19 Cramp to Carpenter, January 9, 1908, C.C. 386/144; C.T. Cramp in Beith, ed., *Edward Carpenter*, pp. 20–23. On Alf Barton see George Cores, *Personal Recollections of the Anarchist Past* (London: The Kate Sharpley Library), pp. 8–9.

20 Edward Carpenter, 'Sweated Industries National Conference in Glasgow', *Glasgow Herald*, October 2, 1907, C.C. N.C. 2/97; National Conference on Sweated Industries, Glasgow, October 11 and 12, 1907. Programme Mr. Edward Carpenter, 'The Minimum Wage: a benefit to Employers as well as to workers, with some remarks on its effects on Foreign Trade', C.C. N.C. 2/96.

21 Edward Carpenter, 'Socialism and Industry', *Manchester Guardian*, November 9, 1908, C.C. N.C. 1/94; Edward Carpenter, Socialism and State Interference, Sheffield Fabian Society Syllabus 1908–9, October 16, 1908, C.C. N.C. 4/71; Chesterfield, S.D.F. October 18, 1908, C.C. N.C. 4/70; Didsbury Socialist Society, November 7, 1908, C.C. N.C. 4/70.

22 Edward Carpenter, 'Small-holdings and Co-operation in Agriculture', Glasgow Fabian Society, February 10, 1905, C.C. N.C. 4/94; Sheffield Ethical Society, February 12, 1905, C.C. N.C. 1/41; Edward Carpenter, 'The Unemployed and the Land', Glasgow Clarion Scouts, February 11, 1905, C.C. N.C. 4/94; Borough of Woolwich Labour Representation Association, March 9, 1906, C.C. N.C. 2/42; North Sheffield I.L.P., C.C. N.C. 2/41; Sheffield Socialists, no date, C.C. N.C. 2/40.

23 Carpenter to Ashbee and Janet Ashbee, March 29, 1905 in Crawford, *C.R. Ashbee*, p. 127.

24 Edward Carpenter, 'Small Holdings and Life on the Land', Newspaper Report of Meeting of Sheffield Ethical Society, no reference, February 12, 1905, C.C. N.C. 1/89; Edward Carpenter, 'Message to the Land Nationalisation Society', in *Land and Labour: The Organ of the Land Nationalisation Movement*, Vol. xviii, No. 6, June 1906, p. 63.

25 Edward Carpenter, *The Village and the Landlord*, Reprinted from the *Albany Review*, April 1907, Fabian Tracts, No. 136 (London: The Fabian Society, 1907), pp. 10–11.

26 The Men of Kent, 'Socialism and Small Holdings', *Labour Leader*, July 17, 1908, C.C. N.C. 1/61; Edward Carpenter, 'The I.L.P. and Small Holdings' in ibid.

27 Anon, 'Current Topics', *Sheffield Daily Telegraph*, March 6, 1906, C.C. N.C. 1/58.

28 Edward Carpenter, *British Aristocracy and The House of Lords*, reprinted from the *Albany Review*, April 1908 (London: A.C. Fifield, 1908), pp. 6, 22–23, C.C. C0425.

29 Carpenter to Pease, May 12, 1908, F.P.

30 *British Empire Review*, no date, 1906, C.C. N.C. 6/27.

31 Edward Carpenter, *Prisons, Police and Punishment: An Enquiry into the Causes and Treatment of Crime and Criminals* (London: A.C. Fifield, 1905), p. 37. See Ian Taylor, 'A Social Role for the Prison: Edward Carpenter's "Prisons, Police and Punishment" (1905)', *International Journal for the Sociology of Law*, 19, 1991.

32 Carpenter, *My Days and Dreams*, pp. 153–154; Edward Carpenter, 'Sport and Agriculture', *The Humanitarian*, Vol. VI, No. 141, November 1913, pp. 179–180.

33 'Anti-Vivisection Meeting in Sheffield'. Speech by Mr. Edward Carpenter, no reference, no date, C.C. N.C. 1/88.

34 Edward Carpenter, 'Is Vaccination a Fraud? Sanitation v. Serum', no reference, no date, C.C. N.C. 1/95.

35 Dr. Walter Hadwen, 'Vivisection Criticised. Sheffield Branch of the British Union for the Abolition of Vivisection', no reference, no date, C.C. N.C. 1/95.

36 Elisée Reclus, 'La Grande Famille', *Le Magazine Internationale*, Janvier 1896, translated by Edward Carpenter, 'The Great Kinship', *Humane Review*, January 1906, p. 214.

37 Carpenter, 'Sport and Agriculture', *The Humanitarian*, Vol. VI, No. 141, November 1913, p. 178.

38 Report of Public Meeting presided over by Carpenter at the sixty-second anniversary of the Vegetarian Society. Cutting from the *Vegetarian Messenger and Health Review*, October 18, 1909, p. 315, C.C. N.C. 1/85.

39 Edward Carpenter, 'Health a Conquest', *The Commonwealth: A Christian Social Magazine*, Vol. X, No. 3, March 1905, p. 71, C. C.Per 19.

40 Carpenter, *My Days and Dreams*, p. 299.

41 George Herbert Bridges Ward in Ann Holt, *G.H.B. Ward, 1876-1957: His Lifelong Campaign for Access to the Countryside* (London: The Ramblers Association, 1985), pamphlet, p. 3.

42 Carpenter, *The Village and the Landlord*, p. 11, C.C. C0425.

43 Edward Carpenter, 'The Smoke Pall; A Plea for More Sunshine', *Sheffield Daily Telegraph*, June 2, 1910, N.C. C.F.S./W.W./E.C.; Edward Carpenter, 'The Smoke Pall; How to Cleanse Sheffield's Air', *Sheffield Daily Telegraph*, June 27, 1910, N.C. C.F.S./W.W./E.C.

44 Edward Carpenter, 'An Open-Air Gymnasium', *Sandow's Magazine*, January 1900, p. 80, C.F.S./W.W./E.C.

45 Carpenter, *The Village and the Landlord*, p. 10.

46 Edward Carpenter, 'Social Reform and the Protection of Animals', *The Humanitarian*, Vol. III, No. 56, October 1906, p. 77, C.F.S./W.W./E.C.

47 Edward Carpenter, 'Philosophy of Social Life: Report of address to the Sheffield Ethical Society', *Sheffield Daily Telegraph*, January 11, 1910, C.C. N.C. 1/91.

48 Conrad Noel, 'The Art of Living, A Chat with Edward Carpenter', *The Hindu*, July 13, 1905, C.C. N.C. 2/8.

49 Carpenter, *My Days and Dreams*, pp. 265-266.

50 Robert Gilliard chairing Edward Carpenter, 'The Larger Socialism', Bristol, no reference, no date, C.C. March 21, 1910, C.C: N.C. 1/84.

51 George Newton in Wendy Hill, 'Edward Carpenter: Memories of a "True Socialist"', *Morning Telegraph*, February 28, 1973.

52 Fenner Brockway, 'Edward Carpenter', *New Leader*, July 5, 1929, quoted in Stanley Pierson, 'Edward Carpenter: Prophet of a Socialist Millennium', *Victorian Studies*, Vol. XII, No. 3, March 1970, p. 301.

53 George Newton in Hill, 'Edward Carpenter: Memories of a "True Socialist"'.

54 Kumari Jayawardena, *Doreen Wickremasinghe, A Western Radical in Sri Lanka* (Colombo: Women's Education and Research Centre, 1991), pp. 7-11.

55 Fenner Brockway, *Towards Tomorrow: The Autobiography of Fenner Brockway* (London: Hart-Davis, 1977), p. 25.

56 Sheila Rowbotham, Interview with Fenner Brockway, 1986.

57 D.H. Lawrence, *Mr. Noon* (London: Granada Publishing, 1985), pp. 3–6.
58 Charles Lee in Swenarton, *Artisans and Architects*, p. 152.
59 Sixsmith to Carpenter, April 7, 1910, C.C. 386/171; Edward Carpenter to Ethel Grinling, May 30, 1902, C.C. 402/10, September 16, 1902, C.C. 402/11, October 1, 1902, C.C. 402/13.
60 Edward Carpenter, 'A Thought for May-Day', *Labour Leader*, May Day Supplement, April 29, 1910, C.C. N.C. 1/2.
61 Edward Carpenter, The Larger Socialism, Mss. Notes for Lecture, October 1909, C.C: N.C. 1/84; Assembly Rooms, Chesterfield, no reference, no date, C.C. N.C. 1/87; Meersbrook Vestry Hall, Sheffield, no reference, no date, C.C. N.C. 1/86; Engineers' Hall, Mount Pleasant, Liverpool Fabian Society, February 21, 1910 (Notice of Meeting), C.C. N.C. 4/99 and *Liverpool Daily Courier*, February 22, 1910, C.C. N.C. 2/93; The Shepherds' Hall, Old Market Street, Bristol Socialist Society, *Western Daily Press*, March 21, 1910, C.C. N.C. 1/84, Manchester Grand Theatre, November 7, 1909; Labour Church, Stockport, February 30, 1910; Blackburn I.L.P. Princess Theatre, October 16, 1910; Glasgow Clarion Scouts, Metropolitan, November 13, 1910, C.C. Mss. 160.
62 Carpenter, The Larger Socialism, Assembly Rooms, Chesterfield, no reference, no date, C.C. N.C. 1/87.
63 Edward Carpenter, 'Review, Robert Gardner *In The Heart of Democracy*', *New Age*, September 9, 1909, p. 368, N.C. C.F.S./W.W./E.C.

18 New Movements; New Transitions

1 Odon Por, 'Work's Coming-of-Age: Revolutionary Unionism in Europe', cutting, no reference, C.C. C.Per 62, p. 237.
2 Ibid., pp. 243, 245.
3 Odon Por, 'Work's Coming-of-Age: Revolutionary Unionism in Europe', *International Socialist Review*, Vol. X, No. 4, October 1909, C.C. C.Per 62, pp. 333, 338. (Despite having the same title the two articles differ in content.)
4 Edward Carpenter, 'Letter on the Proposal that the A.S.E. Should Start Works of its own', *Amalgamated Engineers' Monthly Journal*, April 1895, p. 43, C.C. C.Per 3.
5 Carpenter, *Prisons, Police and Punishment*, pp. 103, 108.
6 See the later version of 'Non-Governmental Society' in Edward Carpenter, *Towards Industrial Freedom* (London: George Allen and Unwin, 1918), first edition 1917, p. 93. See also Marie-Françoise Cachin, '"Non-governmental Society": Edward Carpenter's Position in the British Socialist Movement' in ed. Brown, *Edward Carpenter and Late Victorian Radicalism*, pp. 58–73.
7 A.J. Penty, *The Restoration of the Gild System* (London: Swan Sonnenschein, 1906), pp. viii, 51.
8 S.D.P. and I.L.P: Tom Mann the world famous orator (just back from Australia) will speak Thursday August 11th at the Albert Hall. 8 p.m. Mr. Edward Carpenter will preside, no reference, no date, 1910, C.C. N.C. 4/66.
9 Edward Carpenter to W.C. Goodwin, September 3, 1910.
10 'In Case of Strike, Mr. Edward Carpenter says the Miners Might Work the Mines', *Socialist Outlook*, October 8, 1911, C.C. N.C. 1/92.

11 Edward Carpenter, 'Beauty in Civic Life', Leeds Arts Club, *Yorkshire Daily Observer*, October 24, 1911, N.C. A.M. quoted in Steele, *Alfred Orage and the Leeds Arts Club*, p. 165.

12 *Leeds Weekly Citizen*, October 28, 1911, N.C. A.M. in Steele, *Alfred Orage and the Leeds Arts Club*, pp. 165–166.

13 Edward Carpenter, 'Long Live Syndicalism', *The Syndicalist*, Vol. 1, No. 4, May 1912, C.C. C.Per 129; Thomas Johnston, 'The Anarchists and Edward Carpenter', *Forward*, May 4, 1912, C.C. N.C. 4/84.

14 John Bruce Glasier, 'Review of Edward Carpenter, The Drama of Love and Death', *Socialist Review*, no date, C.C: N.C. 5/64.

15 P.M. Atkinson and Odon Por, 'Syndicalism', *Daily Herald*, June 20, 1912.

16 Edward Carpenter, Inaugural Meeting of the Beautiful Sheffield League, April 29, 1910, C.C. N.C. 4/99; Edward Carpenter, 'Beauty in Civic Life', Caxton Hall, November 22, 1911, Croydon Humanitarian League; *The Humanitarian*, Vol. IV, No. 119, January 1912, p. 2, C.C. C.Per 57/2; The Progressive League and the Bolton Housing and Town Planning League, October 21, no date, C.C. N.C. 4/86; Oxford University Fabian Society, Tuesday May 14, 1912, C.C: N.C. 4/86.

17 Edward Carpenter, 'Beauty in Civic Life: Report of Lecture Given at the Oxford University Fabian Society', *Oxford Chronicle*, May 24, 1912, C.C. N.C. 1/91.

18 'Co-operation and Syndicalism: Interview with Edward Carpenter', *Co-operative News*, June 29, 1912, C.C. C.Per 23.

19 Por, *Work's Coming-of-Age*, cutting, no reference, C.C. C.Per 62.

20 C.R. Ashbee, *The Building of Thelema* (London: J.M. Dent, 1910), pp. 36, 39–40, 57, 79; Fiona MacCarthy, *The Simple Life: C.R. Ashbee in the Cotswolds* (London: Lund Humphries, 1981), p. 140.

21 Fry in Fiona MacCarthy, 'Roger Fry and the Omega Idea', in Crafts Council Gallery, *The Omega Workshops 1913–19: Decorative Arts of Bloomsbury* (London: Crafts Council, 1983), p. 9.

22 To Prince Peter Kropotkin from his English friends, C.C. Mss. 93.

23 Peter Kropotkin, *The Conquest of Bread*, Preface to the 1913 edition (London: Allen Lane, 1972), pp. 38-39.

24 Reynolds to Carpenter, May 25, 1913, C.C. 386/215.

25 Stephen Reynolds and Bob and Tom Woolley, *Seems So! A Working-class View of Politics* (London: Macmillan, 1911), p. 278, quoted in Eileen Yeo, *The Contest for Social Science: Relations and Representations of Gender and Class* (London: Rivers Oram Press, 1996), pp. 242–245.

26 Reynolds to Carpenter, May 25, 1913, C.C. 386/215.

27 Edward Carpenter, 'A Christmas Greeting to Socialist Women', *Clarion*, December 27, 1907, C.C. N.C. 1/7. (This appears alongside a poem by Charlotte Perkins Gilman.)

28 Carpenter to Mattison, October 9, 1903, A.M; Hannam, *Isabella Ford*, p. 110.

29 Edward Carpenter, Notes on Women's Suffrage, no date, C.C. Mss. 165.

30 Carpenter to Sixsmith, October 22, 1908, C.F.S./W.W./E.C.

31 'The Suffragettes' Demonstrations', *Manchester Evening News*, October 26, 1908, C.C. N.C. 2/11.

32 Despard to Carpenter, February 17, 1908, C.C. 386/147.

33 Despard to Carpenter, March 17, 1908, C.C. 386/148.

34 Carpenter to Sixsmith, July 6, 1909, C.F.S./W.W./E.C.

35 Courtney to Carpenter, October 31, 1909, C.C. 271/110.

36 Men's League for Women's Suffrage, Great Demonstration (Three Platforms), no reference, no date, C.C. N.C. 4/64.

37 Men's League for Women's Suffrage, A Declaration of Representative Men in Favour of Women's Suffrage, 1909, Mss. in Box 5, Folder 33, M.E.G. papers.

38 Annie Kenney, *Memories of a Militant* (London: Edward Arnold, 1924), pp. 23, 114–115.

39 Mary Gawthorpe, *Up Hill to Holloway* (Penobscot, Maine: Traversity Press, 1962), p. 178.

40 Ibid., pp. 230–231.

41 Ellis to Gawthorpe, September 18, 1912; Carpenter to Gawthorpe, September 14, 1912; Carpenter to Gawthorpe, September 16, 1915, M.E.G. papers.

42 Lytton to Carpenter, January 17, 1909, C.C. 386/164.

43 Lytton to Carpenter, June 26, 1909, C.C. 386/168.

44 Ed. Ralph Darlington, *Molly Murphy: Suffragette and Socialist* (Salford: Institute for Social Research, University of Salford, 1998), p. 25.

45 Ibid., pp. 20–27, 70–71.

46 Angela V. John, *War, Journalism and the Shaping of the Twentieth Century: The Life and Times of Henry W. Nevinson* (London: I.B. Tauris, 2006), pp. 80, 83, 98–99. 101–104.

47 H.N.D., August 5, 1912; B.Mss.Eng.misc.e.617; H.N.D., August 10, 1912, B.Mss.Eng.misc.e.617.

48 H.N.D., August 22, 1914, B.Mss.Eng.misc.e.618.

49 Evelyn Sharp in ed. Beith, *Edward Carpenter*, pp. 208–209.

50 Evelyn Sharp, *Unfinished Adventure: Selected Reminiscences from an English Woman's Life* (London: John Lane, The Bodley Head, 1933), p. 128.

51 Edward Carpenter, 'A Vision of the Future: A Review', *The Reformer*, Vol. VII, No. 70, October 1904, pp. 617–619, N.C. C.F.S./W.W./E.C.

52 Jane Hume Clapperton, *A Vision of the Future: Based on the Application of Ethical Principles* (London: Swan Sonnenschein, 1904), pp. 145–159, C.F.S./W.W./E.C.

53 Edward Carpenter, 'The New Morality', Notes for article in *Albany Review*, September 1907, C.C. Mss. 143.

54 Constance Malleson (Colette O'Niel), *After Ten Years* (London: Jonathan Care, 1931), pp. 78–79.

55 John Worthen, *D.H. Lawrence: The Early Years: 1885–1912* (Cambridge: Cambridge University Press, 1992), pp. 360–366; Nehls, *D.H. Lawrence: A Composite Biography*, pp. 135–136.

56 Tierl Thompson, ed., *Dear Girl: The Diaries and Letters of Two Working Women 1897–1917* (London: The Women's Press, 1987), pp. 154, 211.

57 Ibid., p. 154.

58 Edward Carpenter, *New Freewoman*, July 1, 1913, p. 40.

59 Greenway, 'It's What You Do with It That Counts', in Bland and Doan, eds., *Sexology in Culture*, p. 37.

60 Harry J. Birnstingl, 'Uranians', *Freewoman*, January 4, 1912, p. 110.
61 Charles J. Whitby, 'Tertium Quid', *Freewoman*, January 18, 1912, pp. 167–168.
62 Harry J. Birnstingl, 'The Human Minority', *Freewoman*, February 8, 1912, p. 235; Albert Löwy, 'The Intellectual Limitations of the "Normal"', *Freewoman*, February 1, 1912, p. 212.
63 Edward Carpenter, 'The Status of Women in Early Greek Times', *New Freewoman*, August 1, 1913, p. 68.
64 Tasker to Carpenter, July 21, 1913, C.C. 386/218; Moore to Carpenter, September 26, 1914, C.C. 376/1.
65 Corke to Emile Delavenay, August 13, 1971, E.D. Letters.
66 Carpenter to Bartholomew, January 28, 1910, C.C. 391/1.
67 Oswald Dawson, ed., *The Bar Sinister and Illicit Love, The Biennial Proceedings of the Legitimation League* (London: W. Reeve, 1895), pp. 50–51; Carpenter to Vance, August 27, 1913.
68 Carpenter to Vance, June 12, 1914, John Baker Private Collection.
69 Ibid.
70 Oliver to Carpenter, October 25, 1915, C.C. 386/262. On Oliver see Bland, *Banishing the Beast*, pp. 281–282, 291–292.
71 Fry to Carpenter, January 14, 1911, C.C. 386/176.
72 Sassoon to Carpenter, August 2, 1911, C.C. 386/181.
73 Sassoon to Carpenter, July 27, 1911, C.C. 386/179.
74 Carpenter to Sassoon, March 13, 1912, in Jean Moorcroft Wilson, *Siegfried Sassoon: The Making of a War Poet* (London: Duckworth, 1998), p. 157.
75 Graves to Carpenter, May 30, 1914, C.C. 386/234.
76 See Miranda Seymour, *Robert Graves: Life on the Edge* (London: Doubleday, 1995), pp. 22–27.
77 Graves to Carpenter, May 30, 1914, C.C. 386/234.
78 E.M. Forster, Terminal Note, *Maurice* (London: Penguin Books, 1972), p. 217.
79 Ibid.
80 Ibid.
81 E.M. Forster, *Locked Diary*, Mss. photocopy (catalogued as the Locked Journal), December 31, 1913, E.M.F.
82 Lytton Strachey in P.N. Furlong, *E.M. Forster: A Life*, Volume II (London: Cardinal Sphere Books, 1988), p. 15.
83 Carpenter to Forster, August 23, 1914, E.M. Forster's *Letter Book*, E.M.F.
84 Seward to Carpenter, October 7, 1912, C.C. 370/7.
85 Seward to Carpenter, October 12, 1912, C.C. 370/8.
86 Ibid.
87 Ashbee, M. March 1913.
88 E. Bertram Lloyd to Carpenter, August 15, 1913, C.C. 368/1.
89 Ibid.
90 Bertram Lloyd to Carpenter, October 14, 1913, C.C. 368/2; November 12, 1913, C.C. 368/3.
91 Winsten, *Salt and his Circle*, p. 187.
92 Carpenter to Ellis, July 16, 1913, H.R.C.
93 Housman in Beith, ed., *Edward Carpenter*, pp. 110–111; Lesley Hall, '"Disinterested Enthusiasm for Sexual Misconduct": The British Society for the

Study of Sex Psychology, 1913–1917', *Journal of Contemporary History*, Vol. 30, No. 4, October 1995, p. 666.

94 Bertram Lloyd to Carpenter, March 19, 1914, C.C. 368/6.
95 Bertram Lloyd to Carpenter, November 12, 1913, C.C. 368/3
96 Bertram Lloyd to Carpenter, March 4, 1914, C.C. 368/5.
97 Hall, "'Disinterested Enthusiasm for Sexual Misconduct'", pp. 668–670.
98 Laurence Housman in the *British Society for the Study of Sex Psychology, Policy and Principles*, Publication No. 1 (London: B.S.S.S.P., 1914), p. 7.
99 Bertram Lloyd to Edward Carpenter, January 12, 1913, C.C. 386/4.
100 Edward Carpenter and E.S.P. Haynes, 'The Taboos of the British Museum Library', *The English Review*, December 1913, pp. 123–125, C.C. C.Per 28.
101 Carpenter to Moll, no date, C.C. 271/147; Moll to Carpenter, July 6, 1914, C.C. 271/148.
102 Carpenter to Moll, no date, C.C. 271/147.
103 Hirschfeld to Carpenter, July 26, 1914, C.C. 270/150.

19 Image and Impact

1 'The Sage of Holmesfield', *Sheffield Independent*, July 6, 1910, C.C. N.C. 2/84; J. William Lloyd, *The Free Comrade. An Utterance of the Free Spirit*, October 1902, C.F.S./W.W./E.C.
2 Ellis, *Three Modern Seers*, p. 200.
3 Harry Beswick, 'A Night with a Prophet', *Clarion*, November 13, 1906, C.C. N.C. 4/80.
4 J. William Lloyd, quoted in Will S. Monroe, Beith, ed., *Edward Carpenter*, p. 153.
5 Constantine Sarantchoft, 'Sparks from A Literary Anvil: A Day with Edward Carpenter', *The Teacher's World*, October 27, 1915, p. 92, C.C. N.C. 2/14; Salt in Beith, ed., *Edward Carpenter*, p. 185.
6 Edward Lewis, *Edward Carpenter: an exposition and an appreciation* (London: Methuen, 1915), p. 294.
7 Lloyd quoted in Monroe, Beith, ed., *Edward Carpenter*, p. 253.
8 Ferrando in ibid., pp. 68–69.
9 Cramp in ibid., pp. 20, 22–23.
10 Forster in ibid., p. 79.
11 Forster, Terminal Note, *Maurice*, p. 219.
12 Lytton Strachey to Pippa Strachey, February 9, 1904, in Michael Holroyd, *Lytton Strachey: A Biography* (London: Penguin, 1971), p. 218. Michael Holroyd says Edward Carpenter officiated, but it was the Unitarian clergyman from Manchester College, J. Estlin Carpenter. See Laura Trevelyan, *A Very British Family: The Trevelyans and their World* (London: I.B. Tauris, 2006), p. 162.
13 Frances Spalding, *Roger Fry: Art and Life* (Berkeley and Los Angeles: University of California Press, 1980), p. 46.
14 Rupert Brooke, 'Democracy and the Arts', 1909, in Christopher Hassall, *Rupert Brooke: A Biography* (London: Faber and Faber, 1964), p. 242.
15 Alfred E. Randall, 'Edward Carpenter's Play, The Promised Land', *New Age*, February 31, 1910, C.C.: C.Per 84. See John Carswell, *Lives and Letters 1906–1957* (London: Faber and Faber, 1978), pp. 64–65, 145.

16 Enid Nesbit, *New Treasure Seekers* (London: T. Fisher Unwin, 1904), p. 14.
17 'The Simple Life, Sweeping Indictment of Modern Society', *Tribune*, March 8, 1906, C.C. N.C. 1/62.
18 Cartoon, *Morning Leader*, March 13, 1906, reproduced in Carpenter, *My Days and Dreams*, opposite p. 257.
19 Ashbee M. March 1913; Janet Ashbee in M. June 1, 1906.
20 Janet Ashbee in M. June 1, 1906.
21 Holbrook Jackson, 'Edward Carpenter', *Yorkshire Weekly Post*, January 13, 1906, C.C. N.C. 2/4.
22 Conrad Noel, 'The Art of Living: A Chat with Edward Carpenter', *The Hindu*, July 13, 1905, C.C. N.C. 2/8. (Also *Daily News*, June 20, 1905, C.C. N.C. 2/27.)
23 Charles Sixsmith, Notes from lectures on Edward Carpenter, 1912–1913. C.F.S./W.W./E.C.
24 Carpenter to Sixsmith, February 25, 1913, C.F.S./W.W./E.C.
25 Lewis, *Edward Carpenter*, pp. 300–301.
26 Haynes, *The Lawyer*, p. 161.
27 Carpenter to Mattison, December 17, 1905, A.M.
28 Alvin Langdon Coburn in Helmut and Alison Gernschein, eds., *Alvin Langdon Coburn Photographer: An Autobiography* (New York: Dover, 1978), p. 34.
29 Carpenter to Sixsmith, March 9, 1913, C.F.S./W.W./E.C.
30 Sir Stanley Unwin, *The Truth About a Publisher: An Autobiographical Record* (London: George Allen and Unwin, 1960), p. 149.
31 Stockham to Carpenter, no date, C.C. 269/4.
32 Stockham to Carpenter, October 23, 1910, C.C. 269/96.
33 Stanley Unwin to Edward Carpenter, August 4, 1915, C.C. 267/138.
34 Carpenter, Diary, December 24, 1915, Mss. 259; Carpenter to Ellis, December 24, 1915, H.R.C.
35 Mitchell Pirie Briggs, *George D. Herron and the European Settlement*, 1932, in Stanford University Publications University Series, History, Economics and Political Science, Volume III, No. 2 (Stanford: Stanford University, no date), pp. 233–236.
36 George D. Herron to Carpenter, November 7, 1908, C.C. 386/158; November 13, 1908, C.C. 386/161; November 26, 1908, 386/162.
37 Burke, *Becoming Modern*, pp. 146–147; Ferrando in Beith, ed., *Edward Carpenter*, pp. 66–71.
38 Herron to Carpenter, June 29, 1909, C.C. 386/167.
39 Biagio di Paulo to Carpenter, no date, C.C. 379/15.
40 Carpenter, *My Days and Dreams*, pp. 269–272.
41 'A Renounced Birthright: Hungarian Count's Socialistic Tendencies', *Daily Telegraph*, March 11, 1913, N.C.; in *Letters Addressed to Alf Mattison*, inserted, p. 139, A.M.
42 Federn to Carpenter, May 13, 1901, C.C. 270/13.
43 Federn to Carpenter, June 6, 1904, C.C. 270/18.
44 Federn to Carpenter, February 17, 1912, C.C. 270/106.
45 Robert Wohl, *The Generation of 1914* (Cambridge, Mass.: Harvard University Press, 1979), pp. 47, 62.
46 Carpenter, *My Days and Dreams*, pp. 274–75.

47 Ibid. Mabel Dodge Luhan, *European Experiences*, Vol. 2 (New York: Harcourt Brace and Company, 1933), pp. 70–76, 223–224.

48 Carpenter, *My Days and Dreams*, p. 275; Marcelle Senard, *Edward Carpenter et Sa Philosophie* (Paris: Librarie de l'Art Indépendent, 1914).

49 Edward Carpenter, Introduction to Romain Rolland's, *Beethoven 1909–10*, Mss. and letters, C.C. 214, 215.

50 Bazalgette to Carpenter, August 7, 1908, C.C. 377/1.

51 Egbert, *Social Radicalism and the Arts in Western Europe*, pp. 609–616; Herbert, *The Artist and Social Reform*, pp. 198–202; Dalrymple Henderson, 'Mysticism as the "Tie That Binds"', p. 34.

52 Federn to Carpenter, June 6, 1904, C.C. 270/18.

53 Mesnil to Carpenter, January 9, 1914, C.C. 377/9.

54 Herron to Carpenter, November 7, 1908, C.C. 386/158.

55 Carpenter, *My Days and Dreams*, p. 280, Dosseff and Vaptzaroff to Carpenter, October 22, no date, C.C. 271/168.

56 Maude to Carpenter, October 21, 1905, C.C. 386/119.

57 Carpenter, *My Days and Dreams*, p. 280.

58 James Webb, *The Harmonious Circle, The Lives and Work of G. I. Gurdjieff, P.D. Ouspensky, and their Followers* (London: Thames and Hudson, 1980), pp. 115–123; Maria Carlson, '*No Religion Higher than Truth': A History of the Theosophical Movement in Russia 1875–1824* (Princeton: Princeton University Press, 1993), pp. 54–73.

59 Ouspensky to Carpenter, December 6, 1913, C.C. 382/10.

60 Edward Carpenter, Constantine, Mss. C.C. 382/16.

61 Sarantchoft to Edward Carpenter, February 17, 1910, C.C. 382/13.

62 Carpenter to Sarantchoft, May 23, 1914, C.S.

63 Sheffield City Libraries, *A Bibliography of Edward Carpenter*, p. 16, Chushichi Tsuzuki, '"My Dear Sanshiro": Edward Carpenter and his Japanese Disciple', *Hitotsubashi Journal of Social Studies*, Vol. 6, No. 1 (Whole Number 6), November 1972, pp. 1–3.

64 Ishikawa to Carpenter, December 14, 1909, C.C. 380/21.

65 Abé to Carpenter, May 26, 1910, C.C. 380/23.

66 Tsuzuki, '"My Dear Sanshiro"', p. 4.

67 Ishikawa to Carpenter, August 10, 1910, C.C. 380/22.

68 Tsuzuki, '"My Dear Sanshiro"', pp. 4–5; Otsu to Carpenter, October 8, 1912, C.C. 380/45.

69 Tsuzuki, '"My Dear Sanshiro"', pp. 5–6.

70 Bertram Lloyd to Carpenter, November 12, 1913, C.C. 368/3.

71 Reynolds to Carpenter, April 2, 1914, C.C. 386/225.

72 Carpenter to Sixsmith, March 16, 1914, C.F.S./W.W./E.C.

73 Ishikawa to Carpenter, March 2, 1914, C.C. 380/32.

74 Ishikawa to Carpenter, January 28, 1914, C.C. 380/31.

75 Baruch Hirson, *The Cape Town Intellectuals: Ruth Schechter and her Circle 1907–1934* (London: Merlin, 2001), pp. 41–45; Margaret Chatterjee, *Gandhi and his Jewish Friends* (London: Macmillan, 1992), pp. 51, 79.

76 Gandhi to Carpenter July 29, 1911, C.C. 376/9.

77 Bhagavan Das, inscription in Bhagavan Das, *The Science of Social Organisation or the Laws of Mana in the Light of Theosophy* (Adyar, Madres: The Theosophist

Office, 1910), C.C. C181.4S; Dixon, *Divine Feminine*, p. 107.

78 Allen to Carpenter, November 18, 1913, C.C. 267/71.

79 Chakraverti (Chakravarti) to Carpenter, June 14, 1911, C.C. 378/19.

80 Copley, *A Spiritual Bloomsbury*, p. 79.

81 Michael Maiwald, 'Race, Capitalism and the Third-Sex Ideal: Claude McKay's Home to Harlem and the Legacy of Edward Carpenter', *Modern Fiction Studies*, Vol. 48, No. 4, Winter 2002, pp. 829–834.

82 Leonard D. Abbott, 'The Poetry of Edward Carpenter', *The Comrade*, November 1901, C.C. C.Per 20.

83 Ashbee, M. November 1900.

84 Janet Ashbee to Ashbee, J. December, no date, 1900.

85 Ernest Crosby, *Edward Carpenter: Poet and Prophet* (Philadelphia: The Conservator, 1901).

86 Ernest Crosby, 'Edward Carpenter', *The Whim*, Vol. 6, No. 1, August 1903.

87 Leonard D. Abbott, 'The Poetry of Edward Carpenter', *The Comrade*, November, 1901, C.C. C.Per 20.

88 Leonard D. Abbott, 'The Renaissance of Paganism', *The International*, no date, C.C. N.C. 2/136.

89 Leonard D. Abbott, 'Homosexual Love', *The Free Comrade*, June 1911.

90 J. William Lloyd, *The Free Comrade*, October 1902, N.C. C.F.S./W.W./E.C.

91 Laurence Veysey, *Communal Experience: Anarchist and Mystical Counter-Cultures in America* (New York: Harper and Row, 1973), pp. 18–32.

92 J. William Lloyd and Leonard D. Abbott, *The Free Comrade: An Utterance of the Free Spirit*, Vol. I, No. 1, July 1910.

93 See Leonard D. Abbott, *Francisco Ferrer: His Life, Work and Martyrdom* (New York: Francisco Ferrer Association, 1910).

94 See 'Helena Bailie' in Paul Avrich, ed., *Anarchist Voices* (Princeton: Princeton University Press, 1995), pp. 14–15.

95 Dalrymple Henderson, 'Mysticism as the "Tie That Binds"', p. 34.

96 Henry Bryan Binns, 'Review of Edward Carpenter, My Days and Dreams', *The Friend*, July 21, 1916, C.C. N.C. 5/34.

97 Carpenter to Hukin, September 30, 1903, C.C. 361/46.

98 Dalrymple Henderson, 'Mysticism as "The Tie That Binds"', p. 32.

99 Floyd Dell, *Intellectual Vagabondage: An Apology for the Intelligentsia* (New York: George H. Doran, 1926), pp. 168–175.

100 Duncan to Carpenter, May 16, 1912, C.C. 386/196.

101 Carpenter, *My Days and Dreams*, p. 245.

102 Terence S. Kissack, *Anarchism and Homosexuality*, PhD, City University of New York, 2004, pp. 212–213.

103 Oscar Lovell Triggs, *Edward Carpenter* (Chicago: Charles H. Kerr, 1913), first edition, 1905, pp. 37, 93, 110.

104 Dalrymple Henderson, 'Mysticism as the "Tie That Binds"', fn. 70, p. 37.

105 John Spargo, 'Edward Carpenter, The Philosopher, His Gospel of Friendship and Simplicity', *The Craftsman*, Vol. XI, No. 1, October 1906, p. 52.

106 'Literary Notes', no date, enclosed in Abbott to Carpenter, January 21, 1905, C.C. 375/3.

107 Abbott to Carpenter, January 21, 1905, C.C. 375/3.

108 *Current Literature*, 1909, cited in Dalrymple Henderson, 'Mysticism as the "Tie that Binds"', pp. 31–32.

109 Bragdon to Carpenter, January 22, 1914, C.C. 271/143.

110 Carpenter to Bragdon, February 12, 1914, CO140. BRA-BRI C.F.B.

111 Ashbee, M., January 24, 1903.

112 Forster, Terminal Note, *Maurice*, p. 217.

113 Edward Carpenter, 'The Drawing Room Table Literature', *New Age*, March 17, 1910, C.C: C.Per 84.

20 Healer of Nations

1 Edward Carpenter to Charles Sixsmith, June 7, no date (1914), C.F.S./W.W./E.C.

2 Cousins, 'Edward Carpenter as I found him', *The Irish Citizen*, June 12, 1915, C.C. N.C. 2/50.

3 Foxwell to Sixsmith, July 30, 1914, C.F.S./W.W./E.C.

4 See 'The list of signatures to the 1914 Address to Edward Carpenter on the occasion of his seventieth birthday from the Carpenter Collection, Sheffield Archive', in Delavenay, *D.H. Lawrence and Edward Carpenter*, Illustrations, 3, between pages 146–147.

5 Mattison, Note-book B, no date, 1914, p. 43, A.M.

6 Carpenter to Sixsmith, August 28, 1914, C.F.S./W.W./E.C.

7 Furniss to Pearson, May 3, 1903, W.C.M.

8 Friedenson to Carpenter, August 27, 1914, 311/60.

9 Carpenter to Sixsmith, August 31, 1914, m C.F.S./W.W./E.C.

10 H.N.D. September 6, 1914; September 9, 1914, B.Mss.Eng.misc.e.618.

11 H.A.L. Fisher, *The War: Its Causes and Issues*, three addresses, August 31, September 1 and September 2 in Sheffield, 1914, C.C. CO42S; Edward Carpenter, *The Healing of Nations and the Hidden Sources of their Strife* (London: George Allen and Unwin, 1915), pp. 22–25, 56, 60–61, 78–80, 97–100.

12 Ibid., pp. 138–139.

13 Kathleen Bunting quoted in Hill, 'Edward Carpenter, Memories of a "True Socialist"', *Morning Telegraph*, February 28, 1973.

14 Edward Carpenter, Belgian Book, Mss. Notes, C.C. Mss. 287; 'The Belgian Book' was *King Albert's Book: A Tribute to the Belgian King and People from Representative Men and Women throughout the World* (London: Hodder and Stoughton [for the *Daily Telegraph*], 1914). Winston Churchill, Norman Angel and Romain Rolland were among the other contributors.

15 Edward Carpenter, 'Patriotism and Internationalism', *The Herald*, December 19, 1914, N.C. C.F.S./W.W./E.C. Reprinted in *The Healing of Nations*, p. 133.

16 Ibid., p. 136.

17 Ibid., p. 212.

18 Romain Rolland, *Above the Battlefield* (Cambridge, 1914) quoted in ibid., p. 247.

19 Skinner to Carpenter, March 27, 1915, C.C. 267/123.

20 Carpenter to Sixsmith, January 22, 1915, C.F.S./W.W./E.C.

21 Laurence Housman, *The Unexpected Years* (London: Jonathan Cape, 1937), pp. 298, 305–306.

22 Henry Nevinson in John, *War, Journalism and the Shaping of the Twentieth Century*, p. 139.

23 R.F. Muirhead in Beith, ed., *Edward Carpenter*, p. 157.

24 Brockway, *Towards Tomorrow*, p. 43; Keith Robbins, *The Abolition of War: The Peace Movement in Britain 1914–1919* (Cardiff: University of Wales Press, 1976), p. 27.

25 Bertram Lloyd to Carpenter, June 2, 1915, C.C. 368/13.

26 'Conference on Pacifist Philosophy of Life', Caxton Hall, July 8 and 9, no reference, no date, C.C. N.C. 1/92.

27 Carpenter to Sixsmith, August 24, 1915, C.F.S./W.W./E.C.

28 Edward Carpenter, 'Conscription and National Service: The Plan of Self Compulsion', Letter to the *Daily Chronicle*, August 12, 1915, C.C. N.C. 2/122.

29 *Morning Post*, August 14, 1915, C.C. N.C. 2/122. See also Professor J.F.C. Hearnshaw, *Morning Post*, August 20, 1915, C.C. N.C. 3/101.

30 Notices of Meetings in October and November 1915, C.C. N.C. 4/64, 4/75, 4/97.

31 Rolland to Carpenter, July 20, 1915, C.C. 377/23.

32 Edward Carpenter, 'Conscription and National Service: The Plan of Self Conscription', letter to the *Daily Chronicle*, August 12, 1915, C.C. N.C. 2/122.

33 Edward Carpenter, 'Against Conscription', no reference, November 24, 1915, C.C. N.C. 1/70.

34 'Thousands of Young Men Will Resist Conscription, Impressive Convention of the No-Conscription Fellowship in London', *Labour Leader*, December 2, 1915.

35 Stanley Unwin to Carpenter, December 8, 1915, C.C. 267/147.

36 Kinkead-Weekes, *D.H. Lawrence: Triumph to Exile*, pp. 279–282; D.H. Lawrence, *The Rainbow*, Chapter XII, 'Shame' (London: Penguin, 1966), pp. 334–352.

37 Carpenter to Stanley Unwin, December 9, 1915 (rough copy in pencil), C.C. 267/148.

38 Edward Carpenter, statement enclosed in ibid.

39 Carpenter to Stanley Unwin, December 10, 1915, C.C. 267/149.

40 Ibid.

41 Browne to Ellis, February 1, 1916, H.E.P.

42 Unwin, *The Truth About Publishing*, pp. 323–326.

43 Basil Thomson, *Queer People: My Experiences at Scotland Yard* (London: Hodder and Stoughton, 1922), p. 266.

44 Unwin, *The Truth about a Publisher*, p. 149.

45 Stanley Unwin to Carpenter, December 14, 1915, C.C. 267/150.

46 Browne to Ellis, February 1, 1916, H.E.P.

47 Bertram Lloyd to Carpenter, March 20, 1916, C.C. 386/16 and enclosed letters from Picton to Bertram Lloyd, March 13, 1916; March 17, 1916.

48 Carpenter to Sarantchoft, January 12, 1916, C.S.; Carpenter, Diary, March 18, 1916, C.C. Mss. 260; Carpenter to Mattison, March 19, 1916, A.M.

49 Carpenter, Diary, March 4, 1916; April 8, 1916, C.C. Mss. 260.

50 Ibid., April 20, 1916, C.C. Mss. 260.

51 Malleson to Carpenter May 10, 1916, C.C. 386/269. Fenner Brockway, *Inside the Left: Thirty Years of Platform, Press, Prison and Parliament* (London: New Leader Ltd, 1942), pp. 77–78.
52 Olivier to Carpenter, August 28, 1916, C.C. 386/261.
53 Samuel Hynes, *A War Imagined; The First World War and English Culture* (New York: Collier Books, 1990), pp. 145–152; Carpenter, Diary, April 23, Easter Day, 1916, C.C. Mss. 260.
54 Edward Carpenter, 'The Use of Blinkers', *War and Peace*, Vol. III, No. 33, June 1916, p. 142, C.C. CPer 142.
55 Carpenter to Clemas, June 11, 1916, C.C. 390/2.
56 Edward Carpenter, *Never Again: A Protest and a Warning Addressed to the Peoples of Europe* (London: George Allen and Unwin, 1916), pp. 5, 7, 19, 21.
57 Carpenter to Sarantchoft, January 12, 1916, C.S.
58 H.N.D July 14, 1916; B.Mss.Eng.misc.e.619.
59 Ibid. July 17, 1916; B.Mss.Eng.misc.e619. Carpenter, Diary, July 15, 1916, C.C. Mss. 260.
60 Bonham Carter to Carpenter, July 18, 1916, C.C. 386/274.
61 Correspondence and Papers of A. Conan Doyle and C.K. Shorter, Concerning Roger Casement, Petition to H. H. Asquith, p. 1, Conan Doyle/Shorter, British Library.
62 Carpenter to Shorter, July 21, 1916, in ibid.
63 John, *War, Journalism and the Shaping of the Twentieth Century*, pp. 168–172; Henry W. Nevinson, *Fire of Life* (London: James Nisbet, 1935), pp. 338–339.
64 Carpenter, Diary, November 7, 1915, C.C. Mss. 259.
65 Ibid. August 3, 1916, C.C. Mss. 260.
66 Sheffield City Libraries, *A Bibliography of Edward Carpenter*, p. 54.
67 Bazalgette to Carpenter, October 15, 1916, C.C. 377/3.
68 Mesnil to Carpenter, October 17, 1916, C.C. 377/15.
69 Edward Carpenter, 'Fighting to a Finish', Letter to the Editor of the *Daily Chronicle*, October 10, 1916, C.C. N.C. 1/70.
70 Edward Carpenter, 'The Trojan War and Constantinople', *The Nation*, February 17, 1917, p. 677, C.C. CPer 81; Tsuzuki, *Edward Carpenter*, p. 178.
71 Carpenter, Diary, January 7, 1917, C.C. Mss. 261.
72 'Alex Gordon', Notes on the Strike Movement Now Developing in the North and West of England, Part 1, 1916, pp. 62–3, M.P.
73 Unnamed Informer, ibid., p. 146.
74 Carpenter, Diary, March 12, 1917, C.C. Mss. 261.
75 Ibid. June 4, 1917, C.C. Mss. 262.
76 'This Statement is made by Second-Lieutenant Siegfried Lorraine Sassoon MC 3rd Batt. Royal Welch Fusiliers, July 1917', enclosed in Siegfried Sassoon to Edward Carpenter, July 7, 1917, C.C. 386/291; Moorcroft Wilson, *Siegfried Sassoon: The Making of a War Poet*, pp. 379.
77 Carpenter to Sassoon, July 10, 1917, in Rupert Hart-Davis, ed., *Siegfried Sassoon Diaries 1915–1918* (London: Faber and Faber, 1983), p. 180.
78 Sassoon to Carpenter, August 29, 1917, C.C. 386/296.
79 Ibid. October 9, 1917, C.C. 386/298.
80 Carpenter, Diary, September 11, 1917; September 15, 1917, C.C. Mss. 262; Sassoon to Carpenter, October 9, 1917, C.C. 386/298.

81 Carpenter, Diary, September 22, 1917; October 14, 1917; October 24, 1917.

82 Carpenter, Diary, December 28, 1917, C.C. Mss. 262.

83 Carpenter to George Clemas, December 30, 1917, C.C. 390/24.

84 Edward Carpenter, 'Russia and Non-Resistance', Herald, March 16, 1917, C.C. N.C. 1/20.

85 Clemas to Carpenter, April 28, 1918, C.C. 386/305.

86 Carpenter, Diary, April 12, 1918, C.C. Mss. 263.

87 Carpenter to Granville Bantock, May 7, 1918, G.B.L.

88 Carpenter, Diary, May 2, 1918, C.C. Mss. 263 and repeated at the end of the note-book after July entries.

89 Carpenter to Clemas, no date (1918), C.C. 386/29.

90 Carpenter, Diary, July 24, 1918, C.C. Mss. 263.

91 Sassoon to Carpenter, August 15, no date (1918), C.C. 386/295.

92 Siegfried Sassoon to Edward Carpenter, September 3, 1918, C.C. 386/313; Siegfried Sassoon to Edward Carpenter, October 8, 1918, 386/315.

93 Jean Moorcroft Wilson, Siegfried Sassoon: The Journey from the Trenches: A Biography 1918–1967 (London: Duckworth, 2003), p. 9.

94 See the letters mistakenly catalogued as from 'William Walton' to Edward Carpenter 1904–1905, C.C. 386/115–118 and 124–125.

95 Sergeant Walter (Wilfred) to Carpenter, March 7, 1916, C.C. 386/265.

96 Carpenter to Sarantchoft, October 31, 1915, C.S.

97 'Dennis' to Edward Carpenter, April 24, 1918, C.C. 384/22.

98 Hobson to Carpenter, November 4, 1917, C.C. 367/2.

99 Hobson to Carpenter, January 7, 1918, C.C. 367/5.

100 Nelly (Lady Hyett) to Edward Carpenter, October 10, 1916, J.C.

101 'Fighting Carpenters', Daily Sketch, April 30, 1916, C.C. N.C. 2/154; 'Captain Carpenter', Sheffield Daily Telegraph, May 2, 1918, C.C. N.C. 2/82.

102 Carpenter to Mattison, May 12, 1918, A.M.

103 Hyndman to Carpenter, December 9, 1917, C.C. 386/302; Chushichi Tsuzuki, Tom Mann, 1856–1941; The Challenge of Labour (Oxford: The Clarendon Press, 1991), p. 182; Reynolds to Carpenter, April 14, 1916, C.C. 386/266.

104 Tsuzuki, '"My Dear Sanshiro"', p. 7.

105 Di Paulo to Edward Carpenter, June 22, 1916, C.C. 379/43; Biagio di Paulo, August 22, 1916, C.C. 379/44.

106 Briggs, George D. Herron and the European Settlement, pp. 237–258.

107 Rolland to Carpenter, July 20, 1915, C.C. 377/73; Mesnil to Carpenter, March 24, 1915, C.C. 377/12.

108 Marcelle Senard to Edward Carpenter, November 22, 1914, C.C. 377/42. Carpenter to Ishikawa, June 10, 1915, in Tzuzuki, '"My Dear Sanshiro"', p. 7.

109 Bishop to Carpenter, March 20, 1915, C.C. 365/40.

110 Woolf, Roger Fry: A Biography, p. 213.

111 P.N. Furbank, E. M. Forster, A Life, Vol. 2 (London: Cardinal Sphere Books, 1988), pp. 19–27.

112 Carpenter, Diary, October 25, 1916, C.C. Mss. 260.

113 Carpenter, Diary, March 26, 1916, C.C. Mss. 260.

114 Richard Hawkin, Conscience and Liberty, An Address delivered to the No-Conscription Fellowship, Sheffield, March 14th 1916 (Sheffield Rushlight Pamphlet I, 1916), p. 3, Sheffield Local History Library.

115 Carpenter, Diary, June 20, 1917, C.C. Mss. 262; June 28, 1917, C.C. Mss. 262.
116 Carpenter to Hawkin, August 23, 1917, J.R.L.
117 Carpenter to Uttley, August 30, 1917, J.R.L.
118 Edward Carpenter, 'The Society of Friends and Free Discussion', Mss. Letter, May 27, 1918 and Edward Carpenter, 'The Silence Rule in Gaol', *Manchester Guardian*, May 30, 1918, C.C.N.C. 1/70.
119 Picton in Beith, ed., *Edward Carpenter*, p. 171.
120 Carpenter to Clemas, no date (1918), C.C. 390/29.

21 Hope Against Hope

1 Housman, *The Unexpected Years*, p. 306.
2 Carpenter to Sixsmith, August 24, 1914, C.F.S./W.W./E.C.
3 Carpenter to Hopkin, March 28, 1916, in Delavenay, *D.H. Lawrence and Edward Carpenter*, p. 31.
4 Carpenter, Diary, June 20, 1915, C.C. Mss. 259.
5 Alf Mattison, Note-book C, September 14, 1918, pp. 99, A.M.
6 Carpenter, Diary, June 12, 1918, July 8, 1918, C.C. Mss. 263.
7 Carpenter, Diary, June 26, 1915, C.C. Mss. 259.
8 Carpenter, Diary, July 4, 1915, C.C. Mss. 259.
9 Frederic Brooks, 'A Visit to Edward Carpenter', *The Epoch*, Vol. 5, No. 11, November 1915, p. 330, C.C. CPer 29.
10 H.N.D. May 13, 1917; B. Mss. Eng.misc.e.620.
11 Kathleen Bunting, interviewed by Rony Robinson, early 1980s.
12 Carpenter, *My Days and Dreams*, pp. 297-298; Carpenter, Diary, September 12, 1918, C.C. Mss. 261; November 16, 1917; November 18, 1917, C.C. Mss. 262; Edward Carpenter, *Common Place Book*, no page numbers, C.C. Mss. 303.
13 H.N.D. May 12, 1917; B. Mss. Eng.misc. e.620; Carpenter, Diary, May 12, 1918, C.C. Mss. 263.
14 Ibid., July 12, 1917, C.C. Mss. 262
15 Ibid. October 22, 1917; November 2, 1917, C.C. Mss. 262.
16 Carpenter, Diary, July 31, 1916, C.C. Mss. 260. On George's death see ibid., January 1, 1917, C.C. Mss. 261, and Memoranda at end of Diary, January to May 1917, C.C. Mss. 261.
17 Ibid., July 30, 1916, C.C. Mss. 260.
18 Ibid. August 1, 1916, C.C. Mss. 260.
19 Ibid., January 10, January 14, 1918, C.C. Mss. 263.
20 Carpenter to Bantock, February 26, 1918, G.B.L.
21 Carpenter to Ellis, September 14, 1916, H.R.C.
22 Ellis to Carpenter, September 19, 1916, H.E.P.
23 Preface by Edward Carpenter, *The New Horizon Memoir of Edith Ellis*, Mss. H.E.P.
24 Edward Carpenter, *Love Unfulfilled*, from c. 1873, revised 1915 and newspaper cutting, C.C. Mss. 3/23.
25 Carpenter, Diary, March 13, 1917, C.C. Mss. 261; February 26, 1917, C.C. Mss 261.
26 Ibid., March 13, 1917, C.C. Mss. 261.

27 Ibid., March 17, 1917, C.C. Mss. 261; Fannie Hukin to Sixsmith, Monday Night, no date (March 1917), C.F.S./W.W./E.C.

28 Carpenter, Diary, March 20, 1917, C.C. Mss. 261.

29 Ibid., March 21, 1917, C.C. Mss. 261.

30 Carpenter to Sixsmith, Wednesday evening, no date (March 1917), with an enclosed note from Merrill to Sixsmith, C.F.S./W.W./E.C.

31 Carpenter, Diary, March 22, 1917, C.C. Mss. 261.

32 Carpenter to Sixsmith, March 22, 1917, C.F.S./W.W./E.C.

33 Carpenter, Diary, March 22, 1917, C.C. Mss. 261.

34 Kate Salt to Carpenter, no date, C.C. 355/57.

35 Carpenter, Diary, March 26, 1917, C.C. Mss. 261.

36 Edward Carpenter, G.E.H. (funeral), C.C. Mss. 361–56.

37 Carpenter, Diary, September 15, 1917, C.C. Mss. 262.

38 Ibid., January 28, 1918; February 2, 1918; February 3, 1918, C.C. Mss. 263.

39 Ibid., August 25, 1917, C.C. Mss. 262; Clemas to Carpenter, October 28, 1918, C.C. 386/317.

40 Carpenter to Clemas, July 18, 1917, C.C. 390/10; Fenner Brockway, *Socialism Over Sixty Years: The Life of Jowett of Bradford (1864–1944)* (London: National Labour Press and George Allan and Unwin, 1946), p. 70.

41 H.N.D. July 15, 1916; B.Mss.Eng.misc.e.619. Edward Carpenter to George Clemas, July 18, 1917, C.C. 390/10.

42 Carpenter to Clemas, December 23, 1917, C.C. 390/26.

43 Ibid., July 30, 1916, C.C. 390/3; Carpenter, Diary, August 6, 1916, C.C. Mss. 260.

44 Carpenter to Clemas, August 6, 1917, C.C. 390/14.

45 H.N.D. July 15, 1916; B.Mss.Eng.misc.e.619.

46 Carpenter to Clemas, May 15, 1917, C.C. 390/17.

47 Carpenter, Diary, February 5, February 7, 1917, C.C. Mss. 261; August 7, 1917, C.C. Mss. 262.

48 On Brice's Restaurant see H.N.D., September 9, 1914; B.Mss.Eng.misc.e.618. On St George's see Edward Carpenter to Havelock Ellis, November 1, no date, H.R.C. and Rupert Hart-Davis, ed., *The Autobiography of Arthur Ransome* (London: Jonathan Cape, 1985), p. 82.

49 Carpenter, Diary, January 24, 1918, C.C. Mss. 263; see also on the 1917 Club, Robert Skidelsky, *John Maynard Keynes: Hopes Betrayed 1883–1920* (London: Macmillan, 1983), p. 348. On the Bomb Shop see Henderson to Carpenter, July 12, 1918, C.C. 268/44.

50 Malleson, *After Ten Years*, pp. 89–90.

51 Carpenter, Diary, July 27, 1917, C.C. Mss. 262.

52 See Jeffrey Weeks, *Sex, Politics and Society: The Regulation of Sexuality Since 1800* (London: Longman, 1981), pp. 114–115, 181–184; Hall, "'Disinterested Enthusiasm for Sexual Misconduct'", pp. 666–678; Timothy D'Arch Smith, *Love in Earnest: Some Notes on the Lives and Writings of the English Uranian Poets from 1889 to 1930* (London: Routledge and Kegan Paul, 1970), pp. 137–138; Sheila Rowbotham, *A New World for Women: Stella Browne, Socialist Feminist* (London: Pluto Press, 1977), pp. 16, 64, 69.

53 Carpenter, Diary, April 29, 1915, C.C. Mss. 259.

54 Carpenter, Diary, October 14, 1915, C.C. Mss. 259.

55 F.W. Stella Browne, 'The Sexual Variety and Variability Among Women', 1917, Reprinted in Rowbotham, *A New World for Women*, pp. 87–105.

56 Carpenter, Diary, July 19, 1916, C.C. Mss. 260; Carpenter to Haynes, July 4, 1916, J.C.

57 D'Arch Smith, *Love in Earnest*, pp. 138–139.

58 Bertram Lloyd to Carpenter, November 1, 1917, C.C. 368/28.

59 Edward Carpenter, Diary, October 15, 1918, C.C. Mss. 261. Eden Paul's paper was later published by the B.S.S.S.P., as a pamphlet. Eden Paul, *The Sexual Life of the Child* (London: British Society for the Study of Sex Psychology, pamphlet No. 10, 1921).

60 Eden Paul, *Literary Guide*, October, no date, 1915, C.C. N.C. 6/125.

61 Browne to Sanger, April 18, 1917, M.S.P.P.; British Society for the Study of Sex Psychology, *Third Annual Report, 1917–1918* (London: B.S.S.S.P., 1918), p. 4.

62 Bertram Lloyd to Edward Carpenter, March 25, 1915, C.C. 368/12.

63 Bertram Lloyd to Edward Carpenter, February 28, 1916, C.C. 368/15.

64 Carpenter to Stopes, May 26, 1916, M.S.

65 Carpenter, Diary, June 10, 1916, C.C. Mss. 260.

66 Bertram Lloyd to Edward Carpenter, June 24, 1916, C.C. 368/20.

67 Carpenter to Stopes, March 26, 1918, M.S.

68 Carpenter, Diary, February 2, 1917, C.C. Mss. 261; April 10, 1918, C.C. Mss. 263; September 23, 1918, C.C. Mss. 261.

69 Ellis to Carpenter, January 6, 1915, H.E.P.

70 Carpenter, Diary, January 30, 1915, C.C. Mss. 259; Sanger to Carpenter, April 13, 1918, C.C. 375/28.

71 Edward Carpenter to the President of the United States, September, no date, 1915, M.S.

72 Sanger to Carpenter, April 13, 1918, C.C. 375/28.

73 Carpenter, *The Healing of Nations*, p. 192.

74 Ibid.

75 Carpenter, *My Days and Dreams*, p. 208.

76 Ibid., p. 97.

77 Gerald Gould, 'Edward Carpenter's Message', *Herald*, September 16, 1916, N.C. C.F.S./W.W./E.C.

78 Carpenter to Fairbanks, August 21, 1918, J.C.

79 Lomer to Carpenter, June 9, 1916, C.C. 386/271; Lomer to Carpenter, May 3, 1917, C.C. 386/286.

80 Forster to Barger, March 23, 1918, E.M.F.

81 Carpenter to Clemas, November 18, 1917, C.C. 390/17.

82 Clemas to Carpenter, October 28, 1917, 386/317.

83 Picton in Beith, ed., *Edward Carpenter*, p. 168.

84 Cousins, 'Edward Carpenter as I found him', *The Irish Citizen*, June 12, 1915, C.C. N.C. 2/50.

85 Salt to Mattison, August 7, 1924, *Letters Addressed to Alf Mattison*, p. 394, A.M.

86 Salt to Mattison, March 1, 1930, ibid., p. 423, A.M.

87 Forster to Barger, January 31, 1918, E.M.F.

88 H.N.D. July 15, 1916; B.Mss.Eng.misc.e.619.

89 Carpenter, Diary, March 27, 1916, C.C. Mss. 260.

90 Clemas to Carpenter, January 22, 1916, C.C. 386/263; April 28, 1916, C.C. 386/267.

91 Carpenter to Clemas, June 11, 1916, C.C. 390/2.

92 Carpenter to Clemas, July 30, 1916, C.C. 390/3.

93 Clemas to Carpenter, April 28, 1916, C.C. 386/267; Carpenter, Diary, October 14, 1916, C.C. Mss. 260.

94 Clemas to Carpenter, May 15, 1916, C.C. 386/270.

95 Carpenter to Clemas, April 16, 1917, C.C. 390/7.

96 Carpenter, Diary, September 22, 1918, C.C. Mss. 261.

97 Carpenter to Clemas, November 18, 1917, C.C. 390/17.

98 Hobson to Carpenter, November 4, 1917, C.C. 367/2.

99 Carpenter, Diary, February 2, 1915, C.C. Mss. 259; August 5, 1917, C.C. Mss. 262.

100 Carpenter to Clemas, July 30, 1916, C.C. 390/3.

101 Carpenter, My Days and Dreams, p. 321.

102 Carpenter to Clemas, December 3, 1917, C.C. 390/27.

103 A.E.R. [and all], 'Views and Reviews', New Age, October 5, 1916, C.C. N.C. 6/64. On Randall see Carswell, Lives and Letters, pp. 65, 145.

104 Carpenter to Ellis, December 21, 1916, H.R.C.

105 Carpenter to Corke, October 9, 1916, quoted in Corke to Delaveney, October 9, 1968, E.D. Letters.

106 Carpenter to Hopkin, April 4, 1916, in Delaveney, D.H. Lawrence and Edward Carpenter, p. 31.

107 Lawrence, The Rainbow, Contents, p. 5; Carpenter, 'Widening Circles', Towards Democracy, p. 482.

108 Carpenter, Diary, December 27, 1917, C.C. Mss. 262.

109 D.H. Lawrence, 'Notes on Philosophy of Social Reconstruction', quoted in Ray Monk, Bertrand Russell: The Spirit of Solitude (London: Vintage 1997), p. 423.

110 Lawrence to Russell, September 25, 1915, in ibid., p. 426.

111 Lawrence to Hopkin, September 25, 1915, in George J. Zytaruk and James T. Boulton, ed., The Letters of D.H. Lawrence, June 1913–October 1916, Vol. II (Cambridge: Cambridge University Press, 1979), p. 401.

112 Lawrence to Hopkin, September 14, 1915, in ibid., p. 391; Lawrence to William and Sallie Hopkin, September 25, 1915, in ibid.

113 Ibid. (September 25, 1915.)

114 E.M. Forster, Locked Diary, photocopy, September 8, 1915, E.M.F.

115 Malleson, After Ten Years, pp. 106–107.

116 Ibid., pp. 104–105, 108.

117 Ibid., p. 109.

118 Bertrand Russell to Colette O'Niel, September 24, 1917, in Nicholas Griffin, ed., The Selected Letters of Bertrand Russell: The Public Years, 1914–1970 (London, Routledge, 2001), pp. 121–122.

119 Bertrand Russell to Colette O'Niel, January 4, 1918, in ibid., p. 131.

120 Edward Carpenter, The Liberation of Industry, Lecture Notes, June to November 1917, C.C. Mss. 216.

121 Por to Carpenter, May 7, 1915, C.C. 386/255.

122 Carpenter, Diary, July 22, 1917, C.C. Mss. 262.

123 Alf Mattison, Note-book B, Edward Carpenter's Lecture Engagements, 1917, p. 70. A.M.

124 Carpenter to Bantock, October 9, 1917, G.B.L.

125 Lloyd to Carpenter, October 14, 1917, C.C. 386/27.

126 Edward Carpenter, *Towards Industrial Freedom* (London: George Allen and Unwin, 1917), p. 31.

127 Ibid., p. 94.

128 Reynolds to Carpenter, November 9, 1918, C.C. 386/318.

129 Carpenter, *My Days and Dreams*, p. 209.

130 Carpenter, *The Healing of Nations*, 1915 (back cover); Nield, 'The Uses of Utopia', in Brown, *Edward Carpenter and Late Victorian Radicalism*, p. 20.

131 Lewis, *Edward Carpenter: An Exposition and an Appreciation*; A.H.M. Sime, *Edward Carpenter: His Ideas and Ideals* (London: Kegan Paul, 1916).

132 Carpenter, *My Days and Dreams*, pp. 323–324.

133 Goodway, *Anarchist Seeds Beneath the Snow*, p. 35.

134 Randall, 'Views and Reviews', *New Age*, October 5, 1916, C.C. N.C. 6/64.

135 On Carpenter's working-class readership, see Jonathan Rose, *The Intellectual Life of the British Working Classes* (New Haven: Yale University Press, 2001), pp. 190–194; Picton in Beith, ed., *Edward Carpenter*, p. 168.

136 Carpenter to Bantock, May 7, 1918, G.B.L.

137 Carpenter to Bantock, May 14, 1918, G.B.L.

138 Carpenter, Diary, June 16, 1918, C.C. Mss. 263.

139 David Stevenson, *Cataclysm: The First World War as Political Tragedy* (New York: Basic Books), pp. 448–449.

140 Carpenter, Diary, November 11, 1918, C.C. Mss. 261.

22 Reconstruction and Revolution?

1 Carpenter to Clemas, March 5, 1919, C.C. 390/30.

2 *Westminster Gazette*, June 18, 1919, C.C. N.C. 4/93.

3 Edward Carpenter Letter, 'The Appeal of the Russian Intellectuals', *The Nation*, May 15, 1920, C.C. N.C. 1/20; Edward Carpenter letter *Herald*, 'Russia' no date, c1920, C. N.C. 1/72.

4 Carpenter, Diary, April 19, 1919, C.C. Mss. 264.

5 Carpenter to Clemas, April 23, 1919, C.C. 390/36.

6 C.T. Cramp, Presidential Address to the A.G.M. of the N.U.R. reported in the *Railway Review*, June 20, 1919, quoted in Philip S. Bagwell, 'The Triple Industrial Alliance 1913–1922', in Asa Briggs and John Saville, eds., *Essays in Labour History 1886–1923* (London: Macmillan, 1971), p. 104.

7 Edward Carpenter, 'Object Lessons in Guild Socialism, I, The Miners', *Daily Herald*, September 22, 1919, C.C. N.C. 1/49; The 'Herald' League. Ticket for A Grand Re-Union at the Holborn, Concert Hall, Grays Inn Road, WC. Friday September 26, 1919. Dancing, Speaking etc. from 7.30, C.C. N.C. 4/89; Carpenter, Diary, September 26, 1919, C.C. Mss. 265.

8 H.N.D., September 26, 1919, B.Mss.Eng.misc.e.621.

9 Carpenter, Diary, October 1 and October 6, 1919, C.C. Mss. 265.

10 Edward Carpenter, 'Object Lessons in Guild Socialism II, The Police', *Daily Herald*, October 17, 1919, C.C. N.C. 1/49; Edward Carpenter, 'Object

Lessons in Guild Socialism III, The Soldiers', *Daily Herald*, November 27, 1919, C.C. N.C. 1/47.

11 Edward Carpenter, 'Art and Beauty in Actual Life', *The Building News*, January 30, 1920, C.C. N.C. 2/46.

12 Edward Carpenter, Back to the Land, Lecture Notes, C.C. Mss. 220.

13 Reeves to Carpenter, September 8, 1919, C.C. 271/173.

14 Carson Scott to Carpenter, October 17, 1919, C.C. 271/174.

15 Reeves to Carpenter, September 8, 1919, C.C. 271/173.

16 Yuko Kikuchi, *Japanese Modernisation and Mingei Theory: Cultural Nationalism and Oriental Orientalism* (London: Routledge Curzon, 2004), pp. 31–32.

17 Ishikawa to Sixsmith, September 2, 1920, C.F.S./W.W./E.C. Tsuzuki, "'My Dear Sanshiro'", pp. 8–9.

18 Arthur J. Penty, *A Guildsman's Interpretation of History* (New York: Sunrise, 1920), p. 299.

19 Edward Carpenter, Communism, 1919–1920, C.C. Mss. 224.

20 Bertram Lloyd to Carpenter, March 31, 1920, C.C. 368/34.

21 Bertram Lloyd to Carpenter, June 11, 1920, C.C. 368/36

22 Carpenter to Bragdon, June 26, 1920, CO140 BRA-BRI. C.F.B.

23 Carpenter, Diary, March 30, March 31, April 1, 1920, C.C. Mss. 266.

24 Carpenter to Dalton, July 5, 1920, D.P.

25 Carpenter, Diary, May 22, 1919, Mss. 264.

26 Carpenter, Diary, December 14, 1919, C.C. Mss. 265.

27 Carpenter to Clemas, January 26, 1920, C.C. 390/39.

28 Edward Carpenter, *The Teaching of the Upanishads: Being the Substance of Two Lectures to a Popular Audience: I Rest. II The Nature of the Self* (London: George Allen and Unwin, 1920), p. 3.

29 Edward Carpenter, Self-Consciousness, no date, p. 11, C.C. Mss. 275.

30 Carpenter, Diary, January 11, 1919, C.C. Mss. 264.

31 Carpenter to Clemas, May 30, 1919, C.C. 390/37.

32 Carpenter, Diary, October 3, 1919, C.C. Mss. 265.

33 Ford to Carpenter, November 22, 1921, C.C. 386/364.

34 Carpenter, Diary, January 16, 1919, C.C. Mss. 264.

35 Kate Salt to Carpenter, February 7, 1919, C.C. 355/67.

36 Carpenter to Florrie Mattison, February 19, 1919, A.M.

37 Salt to Carpenter, April 5, 1919, C.C. 356/40.

38 Ford to Carpenter, August 2, 1919, C.C. 380/330.

39 Carpenter, Diary, August 27, 28, and 29, 1919, C.C. Mss. 265.

40 Carpenter, 'Last Visits to Bruce Glasier', *Labour Leader*, Supplement, June 10, 1920, C.C. N.C. 1/40.

41 W.W. Young, *Robert Weare of Bristol, Liverpool and Wallasey, b. 1858, died 1920: An Appreciation and Four of his Essays for Private Circulation* (Manchester: C.W.S. Printing Works, no date), pamphlet, pp. 3–45, S.B.C.

42 Schreiner to Carpenter, August 4 (?), 1920, C.C. 359/102.

43 Ford to Carpenter, November 22, 1921, C.C. 386/364.

44 Carpenter to Clemas, March 10, 1919, C.C. 390/31.

45 Carpenter to Clemas, April 5, 1919, C.C. 390/34; Carpenter, Diary, June 28, 1919, C.C. Mss. 264.

46 Carpenter, Diary, March 15, 1920, C.C. Mss. 266.

47 Ibid., March 4, 1919, June 6, 1919, C.C. Mss. 264.
48 Ibid., December 24 and December 25, 1919, C.C. Mss. 265.
49 Ibid., December 29, 1919, C.C. Mss. 265.
50 Ibid., December 30, 1919, C.C. Mss. 265.
51 Ibid., January 2, 1920, C.C. Mss. 266.
52 Ibid., October 13, 1919, C.C. Mss. 265.
53 Ibid., February 15, 1920, C.C. Mss. 266.
54 Ibid., March 11, 1920; March 19, 1920, C.C. Mss. 266.
55 Ibid., March 20, 1920; March 25, 1920; March 27, 1920, C.C. Mss. 266.
56 'H' [Herbert Mills] to Carpenter, June 12, 1920, C.C. 386/336.
57 Carpenter, Diary, February 25, 1920, C.C. Mss. 266.
58 Ibid., March 18, 1920, C.C. Mss. 266.
59 'H' [Herbert Mills] to Carpenter, June 12, 1920, C.C. 386/336.
60 Carpenter, Diary, February 21, 1920 and February 22, 1920, C.C. Mss. 266.
61 Carpenter to Clemas, July 30, 1921, C.C. 390/46.
62 License, January 1, 1920, C.C. Mss. 323.
63 Chambers to Carpenter, August 19, 1921, C.C. 386/355.
64 Lomer to Carpenter, July 21, 1919, C.C. 386/329.
65 Forster, *Locked Diary*, photocopy, August 28, 1920, E.M.F.
66 See Maiwald, 'Race, Capitalism and the Third-Sex Ideal', p. 7.
67 Carpenter to Stopes, November 25, 1918, M.S.
68 Carpenter, Diary, June 15, 1919, C.C. Mss. 264.
69 Ibid., August 24, 1919, C.C. Mss. 265.
70 Ibid., August 25, 1919.
71 Carpenter to Stopes, March 2, 1921, M.S.; Keith Briant, *Marie Stopes: A Biography* (London: The Hogarth Press, 1962), pp. 134−136.
72 F.W. Stella Browne, 'Liberty and Democracy', *The Birth Control Review*, Vol. 5, No. 2, February 1921, pp. 6−7.
73 D.H. Lawrence, Foreword to *Women in Love*, in Warren Roberts and Harry T. Moore, eds. *Phoenix II. Uncollected, Unpublished and Other Prose Works by D.H. Lawrence* (London: Heinemann, 1968), pp. 275−276.
74 Edward Carpenter, *Pagan and Christian Creeds* (London: George Allen and Unwin, 1920), pp. 218−219.
75 'Unconventional Anthropology', *The Athenaeum*, February 20, 1920, p. 240, N.C. 6/48.
76 Edward Carpenter, Preface to the Complete Edition (1920), *Civilisation: Its Cause and Cure and Other Essays* (London: George Allen and Unwin, 1921), pp. 9−10.
77 Ibid., p. 267.
78 Ibid., p. 247.
79 Ibid., pp. 255, 263.
80 Carpenter to MacDonald, April 17, 1921, Carpenter (Edward) P.R.O. J.R.M.
81 Edward Carpenter, 'The Miners' Instinct', *Daily News*, May 3, 1921, C.C. N.C. 1/47.
82 Edward Carpenter, 'Sunshine and Coal', *Daily News*, May 28, 1921, C.C. N.C. 1/10.
83 Edward Carpenter, 'Coal and Wet Weather: An Object Lesson from Sheffield', *Daily News*, June 21, 1921, C.C. N.C. 1/10.

84 Edward Carpenter, 'Free Bread for All', *Daily News*, August 17, 1921, C.C. N.C. 1/1. Muirhead to Carpenter, August 28, 1921, C.C. 386/358.
85 Muirhead to Carpenter, August 28, 1921, C.C. 386/358.
86 Carpenter, 'Free Bread for All', C.C. N.C.1/1.
87 Carpenter to Clemas, July 25, 1921, C.C. 390/45.
88 Arthur Reade to Edward Carpenter, September 14, 1921, C.C. 386/359. Edward Carpenter, 'Back to the Wild', *Free Oxford*, Vol. 1, No. 2, October 22, 1921, C.C. Mss. 250/2.
89 Carpenter, 'Back to the Wild', C.C. Mss. 250/2.
90 Editor's Note, 'Edward Carpenter, Back to the Wild', *Free Oxford*, Vol. 1, No. 2, October 22, 1921, C.C. Mss. 250/2.
91 'Naked and Unashamed', *Plain English*, December 3, 1921, C.C. N.C. 2/113.
92 Basil Blackwell, quoted in M.P. Ashley and C.T. Sanders, *Red Oxford: A History of the Growth of Socialism in the University of Oxford* (Oxford: Oxford University Labour Club, 1930), p. 35.
93 Salt to Carpenter, December 27, 1921, C.C. 356/49.
94 Salt to Mattison, June 14, 1922, *Letters Addressed to Alf Mattison*, p. 192, A.M.

23 Guildford

1 Coxeter to Carpenter, March 8, 1922, C.C. 386/374.
2 'Scholar Recluse, 80 To-day', *Evening Standard*, no date (August 29, 1924), C.C. N.C. 2/68.
3 Sixsmith in Beith, ed. *Edward Carpenter*, p. 229.
4 Carpenter to Mattison, July 15, 1922, A.M.
5 Carpenter to Ellis, February 27, 1922, H.R.C.
6 Fannie Hukin to Mattison, May 23, 1922, *Letters Addressed to Alf Mattison*, p. 191, A.M.
7 A Correspondent, 'A Memory of Carpenter', no reference, no date (1929), N.C. C.F.S./W.W./E.C.; Forster, *Locked Diary*, photocopy, May 11, 1922, E.M.F.
8 Carpenter to Mattison, July 27, 1922, A.M.
9 Ford to Mattison, July 23, 1922, *Letters Addressed to Alf Mattison*, p. 195, A.M.
10 Fannie Hukin to Mattison, May 23, 1922, ibid., p. 191, A.M.
11 Forster, *Locked Diary*, May 11, 1922, E.M.F.
12 Sixsmith to Mattison, November 13, 1922, *Letters Addressed to Alf Mattison*, p. 201, A.M.
13 Deeds of Carpenter House, July 7, 1922. I am grateful to Jo McGhee for allowing me to look through the deeds.
14 Carpenter to Mattison, July 15, 1922, A.M.
15 Helen Chapman to Carpenter, September 3, 1922, C.C. 386/375.
16 Carpenter to Helen Chapman, September 4, 1922, C.C. 386/376.
17 Coxeter to Carpenter, October 17, 1923, C.C. 386/384.
18 Deeds of Carpenter House, June 4, 1924. See also, 'Scholar Recluse 80 To-day', *Evening Standard*, C.C. N.C. 2/68.
19 Carpenter to Sixsmith, October 2, 1922, C.F.S./W.W./E.C.
20 Helen Chapman to Carpenter, October 16, 1922, C.C. 386/378.
21 Edward Carpenter, *Some Friends of Walt Whitman: A Study in Sex Psychology*

(London: The British Society for the Study of Sex Psychology, Publication No. 13, 1924), p. 14, C.C. Mss. 333/334, pp. 12, 14.
22 Ibid., p. 15.
23 Carpenter to Shaw, July 1, 1921, S.P.
24 Cutting, 'A Third Sex? Scientist's Fresh Theory', *Daily News*, January 19, 1922, enclosed in C.T. Bamforth to Edward Carpenter, January 20, 1922, C.C. 386/387.
25 Edward Carpenter, *Love's Coming of Age* (London: George Allen and Unwin, 1923), pp. 204–205.
26 H.N.D. April 11 and 18, 1923; B.Mss.Eng.misc.e.622.
27 Illit Gröndahl in ed. Beith, *Edward Carpenter*, p. 104.
28 H.N.D. May 27, 1923; B.Mss.Eng.misc.e.622.
29 Dalton to Carpenter, June 12 and 22, 1923, C.C. 386/381 and C.C. 386/381; Pimlott, *Hugh Dalton*, pp. 64–65, 77; Hugh Dalton, D.D. Mss. Vol. 4, 25/6/23–29/6/23, p. 116, L.S.E.
30 Gavin (Chester) Arthur, *The Circle of Sex* (New York: University Books, 1966), p. 131.
31 Arthur to Carpenter, September 8, 1923, C.C. 271/187.
32 Michael Davidson, *The World, The Flesh and Myself* (London: A. Mayflower-Dell Paperback, 1962), p. 120.
33 H.N.D. October 28, 1923; B.Mss.Eng.misc.623
34 Senard to Carpenter, April 7, 1923, C.C. 377/61.
35 Senard to Carpenter, February 25, 1924, C.C. 377/62.
36 David James Fisher, 'The Rolland-Barbusse Debate', *Survey: A Journal of East and West Studies*, Vol. 20, No. 2/3 (91/92), Double Issue Spring–Summer 1974, pp. 121–175.
37 Carpenter to Sharp, November 26 (1923), E.S.P.; B.Mss.Eng.lett.c.277.
38 Ashbee, M. December 20, 1923.
39 W.J. Godfrey in Beith, ed., *Edward Carpenter,* pp. 92–94.
40 Carpenter to Sixsmith, June 5, 1917, C.F.S./W.W./E.C.; Carpenter to Clemas, February 4, 1924, C.C. 390/50.
41 Carpenter to Clemas, February 18, 1924, C.C. 390/51.
42 Laing to Carpenter, February 16, 1924, C.C. 386/392.
43 Carpenter to Ashelford, March 4, 1924, J.C.
44 H.N.D. April 27, 1924; B.Mss.Eng.misc.e.623.
45 Edward Carpenter, 'At the Very Edge of Death', *The English Review*, May 1924, p. 655, N.C. C.F.S./W.W./E.C. On Carpenter's preoccupation with the graveyard, see 'Carpenter's Old School', *Manchester Guardian*, July 2, 1929, N.C. C.F.S./W.W./E.C.
46 West to Edward Carpenter, May 9, 1924, C.C. 386/395; see Jean Overton Fuller, *The Magical Dilemma of Victor Neuburg* (London: W.H. Allen, 1965).
47 Arthur to Carpenter, May 14, 1924, C.C. 386/397.
48 Ibid.
49 Arthur, *The Circle of Sex*; 'Allen Ginsberg', in Winston Leyland, ed., *Gay Sunshine Interviews*, Vol. I (San Francisco: Gay Sunshine Press, 1978) and 'Gavin Arthur, The Gay Succession', in Winston Leyland, ed., *Gay Roots: Twenty Years of Gay Sunshine* (San Francisco: Gay Sunshine Press, 1991).
50 Arthur, *The Circle of Sex*, pp. 130, 138.

51 'Allen Ginsberg', in Leyland, ed., *Gay Sunshine Interviews*, p. 126; 'Gavin Arthur, The Gay Succession', in Leyland, ed., *Gay Roots*, p. 323.

52 Ted Inigan quoted in Arthur, *The Circle of Sex*, p. 132.

53 I am grateful to Marilyn Wilkes' research on the electoral register which records 'Edward Inigan' in Autumn 1924 and to Joey Cain for information on Arthur's May 13, 1924, letter to his mother.

54 Arthur, *The Circle of Sex*, p. 135.

55 'Gavin Arthur, The Gay Succession', in Leyland, ed., *Gay Roots*, p. 325.

56 Ibid.

57 Arthur, *The Circle of Sex*, pp. 135–136.

58 Ibid., pp. 136–137.

59 Alan Watts, Introduction, Arthur, *The Circle of* Sex, p. 8; Allen Ginsberg, Introduction to 'Gavin Arthur, The Gay Succession', in ed. Leyland, *Gay Roots*, p. 323.

60 Goldy to Carpenter, May 26, 1924, C.C. 375/4.

61 Carpenter, Constantine, p. 2, C.C. Mss. 382/16.

62 Carpenter to Sarantchoft, no date, C.C. Mss. 299.

63 'Guildford Railway Tragedy: Russian Official's Suicide', Newspaper Cutting, no reference, no date, enclosed in Carpenter to Clemas, June 6, 1924, C.C. 390/54.

64 Carpenter, Constantine, p. 2, C.C. Mss. 382/16.

65 Hannam, *Isabella Ford*, pp. 200–201.

66 'Yorkshire Pioneer of Woman Suffrage', *Yorkshire Evening Post*, July 15, 1924, N.C., in *Letters Addressed to Alf Mattison*, p. 249, A.M.

67 Olivier to Carpenter, July 24, 1924, C.C. 386/403.

68 MacDonald to Carpenter, July 26, 1924, C.C. 386/404.

69 Weinbren, 'Against *All* Cruelty: The Humanitarian League, 1891–1919', *History Workshop Journal* Issue 38, no. 86, 1994, p. 92.

70 Carpenter to Robert Trevelyan, June 26, 1924, R.C.T.; Carpenter to Colenso, August 2, 1924, J.C.

71 Carpenter to Besant, June 10, 1924, C.C. 396/1.

72 Carpenter to Forster, August 14, 1924; *E.M. Forster's Letter Book*, E.M.F.

73 H.N.D. August 10, 1924; B.Mss.Eng.misc.e.623.

24 Last Years

1 Roughton to Sixsmith, September 7, 1924, C.F.S./W.W./E.C.

2 Merrill to Annie and Tom Nicholson, Monday, no date, C.C. 271/14.

3 'Scholar Recluse 80 Today', *Evening Standard*, no date (August 1924), C.C. N.C. 2/68.

4 F.R. Swan, 'England Arise: A Notable Anniversary', *Daily Herald*, August 29, 1924, C.C. N.C. 2/71; Tom Swan, 'Wreathe the Living Brow', *Clarion*, August 29, 1924, C.C. N.C. 2/69; Anon, 'An Eminent Victorian', *New Statesman*, August 30, 1924, C.C. N.C. 2/69; Anon, 'Happy Returns', *Justice*, August 28, 1924, C.C. N.C. 2/145; Anon, 'Edward Carpenter 80', *Observer*, no date (August 1924), C.C. N.C. 2/66; 'Scholar Recluse 80 Today', *Evening Standard*, no date (August 1924), C.C. N.C. 2/68.

5 C.E.M. Joad, 'Edward Carpenter', The Book Mark, *New Leader*, October 3, 1924, C.C. N.C. 2/154.

6 Edward Carpenter, 'Mad Hatters, Edward Carpenter's views on Business', *Daily News*, September 4, 1924, C.C. N.C. 1/46.
7 Merrill to Annie and Tom Nicholson, Monday, no date, C.C. 271/14.
8 Godfrey in Beith, ed., *Edward Carpenter*, p. 92.
9 I.L.P. Sheffield, C.C. 313/20; I.L.P. Typed Congratulatory Message, C.C. 313/20–24, *Clarion*, C.C. 313/29; Neighbours and Friends of Millthorpe, C.C. 313/25–28.
10 Morel to Carpenter, September, no date, 1924, C.C. 313/41.
11 Roughton to Sixsmith, September 7, 1924, C.F.S./W.W./E.C.
12 Forster, *Locked Diary*, photocopy, September 20, 1924, E.M.F.
13 Carpenter to Clemas, October 6, 1924, C.C. 390/55.
14 Carpenter to Barnard, August 9, 1924, C.C. 271/88.
15 Stanley Unwin to Carpenter, August 14, 1924, C.C. 267/446.
16 Unwin, *The Truth About a Publisher*, p. 149.
17 Edward Carpenter and George Barnefield: *The Psychology of the Poet Shelley* (London: Allen and Unwin, 1925), pp. 30, 32.
18 H.N.D. January 31, 1925, B.Mss.Eng.misc.e.623.
19 Carpenter and Barnefield, *The Psychology of the Poet Shelley*, p. 7.
20 Rodgers to Carpenter, May 1, 1925, C.C. 386/410.
21 Forster to Barger, October 2, 1924, E.M.F.P.
22 Goldman to Berkman, May 28, 1925, E.G.P./A.B.A.
23 Ibid.
24 Goldman to Carpenter, December 1, 1924, E.G.P./E.G.
25 Goldman to Carpenter, February 20, 1825 [sic] (1925), E.G.P./ E.G.; see Terence Kissack, *Free Comrades: Anarchism and the Politics of Homosexuality, 1895–1917* (Oakland: AK Press 2008), pp. 122–125.
26 Goldman to Berkman, May 28, 1925, E.G.P./A.B.A.
27 H.N.D. February 27, 1925; B.Mss.Eng.misc.623.
28 Carpenter to Ellis, June 17, 1925, H.R.C.
29 Merrill to Sixsmith, no date, (autumn 1925), in Notes by Charles Sixsmith, C.F.S./W.W./E.C.
30 Carpenter to Ellis, March 5, 1925, H.R.C.
31 Leaflet, Guildford Trades and Labour Council, The Great Rally in the Borough Halls, North Street, Guildford, on Friday January 16, 1925 (copy in my possession).
32 Lansbury's Labour Weekly, *Sixteen Songs for Sixpence* (London: Lansbury's Labour Weekly, no date).
33 Carpenter to Nevinson, October 25, 1925, H.N.P.; B.Mss.Eng.lett.c.278.
34 Carpenter to Sharp, September 4, 1926, E.S.P.; B.Mss.Eng.lett.c.277.
35 Carpenter to Ellis, October 12, 1926.
36 Carpenter to Colenso, April 28, 1924, J.C.
37 Carpenter to Clemas, November 10, 1925, C.C. 390/59.
38 Carpenter to Clemas, August 6, 1926, C.C. 390/61.
39 Carpenter to Sixsmith, August 2, 1926, C.F.S./W.W./E.C.
40 Carpenter to Sixsmith, August 17, 1926; October 26, 1926, C.F.S./W.W./E.C.
41 Carpenter to Sharp, September 4, 1926, E.S.P.; B.Mss.Eng.lett.c.277.
42 'Keep up your pecker, we are not dead yet', message to the Daily News, *Daily News*, no date (August 1926), N.C. C.F.S./W.W./E.C.

43 Edward Carpenter, 'The Miners As I Have Known Them', *Manchester Guardian*, October 8, 1926, C.C. N.C.1/46.

44 Carpenter to Dalton, October 11, 1926, D.P.

45 Carpenter to Dalton, October 19, 1926, D.P.

46 Forster to Barger, December 26, 1926; Carpenter to Clemas, January 3, 1927, C.C. 390/65.

47 Carpenter to Clemas, April 20, 1927, C.C. 390/67; April 25, 1927, C.C. 390/68.

48 H.N.D. April 9, 1927; B.Mss.Eng.misc.e.624.

49 Carpenter to Sharp, April 22, 1927, E.S.P.; B.Mss.Eng.lett.277.

50 Gröndahl in Beith, ed., *Edward Carpenter*, p. 105.

51 Edward Inigan ('Ted') in ed. Beith, *Edward Carpenter*, p. 119.

52 Henry S. Salt, 'Edward Carpenter and Brighton', no reference, no date, N.C. C.F.S./W.W./E.C.

53 Carpenter to Pearson, August 11, 1927, C.C. Mss. 333.

54 Carpenter to Clemas, April 25, 1926, C.C. 390/60.

55 Carpenter to Clemas, April 25, 1927, C.C. 390/68.

56 Carpenter to Clemas, August 30, 1927, C.C. 390/70.

57 Carpenter to Clemas, August 31, 1927, C.C. 390/71.

58 Cramp in Beith, ed., *Edward Carpenter*, pp. 24-25.

59 Arunachalam to Carpenter, August 29, 1917, in Carpenter, ed., *Light from the East*, pp. 77-80.

60 Svarnam Arunachalam to Edward Carpenter, October 8, 1925, C.C. 378/7; Edward Carpenter to Lady Arunachalam, March 12, 1926, C.C. 378/9; Svarnam Arunachalam to Edward Carpenter, June 29, 1926, C.C. 378/10; January 28, 1927, C.C. 378/11.

61 Edward Carpenter, 'Introduction' in Carpenter, ed., *Light from the East*, p. 13.

62 Ibid., p. 97, Tariq Rahman, 'The Literary Treatment of Indian Themes in the Works of Edward Carpenter', *Durham University Journal*, Vol. 80 (1), December 1987, p. 81.

63 Carpenter, *Light from the East*, p. 97, note 1, see Copley, *A Spiritual Bloomsbury*, pp. 58-59.

64 Parminder Kaur Bakshi, 'Homosexuality and Orientalism: Edward Carpenter's Journey to the East', in Brown, ed., *Edward Carpenter and Late Victorian Radicalism*, p. 175; Mitter, *Much Maligned Monsters*, pp. 75, 84; Tariq Rahman, 'The Alienated Prophet: The Relationship between Edward Carpenter's Psyche and the Development of his Metaphysic', *Forum for Modern Languages*, Vol. xxiii, No. 3, July 1987, pp. 205-206.

65 Carpenter, *Light from the East*, p. 24.

66 Ibid., pp. 103-104.

67 Ibid., pp. 133, 139.

68 Salt to Mattison, February 14, 1928, *Letters Addressed to Alf Mattison*, p. 388, A.M.

69 H.N.D. September 24, 1927; B.Mss.Eng.misc.e.624.

70 Ed. Proctor, *The Autobiography of G. Lowes Dickinson*, p. 157.

71 Arthur, *The Circle of Sex*, p. 132.

72 R.H. Minshall in Beith, ed., *Edward Carpenter*, p. 141.

73 Fannie Hukin to Mattison, January 18, 1928, *Letters Addressed to Alf Mattison*, p. 350, A.M.

74 Alf Mattison, 'A Visit to Edward Carpenter', *The Journal of Alf Mattison of Leeds*, Mss. February 4, 1928, p. 108. Leeds Reference Library.

75 Inigan in ed. Beith, *Edward Carpenter*, p. 120.

76 Vera G. Pragnell, *The Story of the Sanctuary* (London and Steyning: The Vine Press, 1928), p. v.

77 Muirhead to Mattison, June 2, 1928, *Letters Addressed to Alf Mattison*, p. 364, A.M.

78 Frank F. Smith, 'Notes and Comments', *The Surrey Advertiser*, February 9, 1944, C.C. Mss. 387/31.

79 H.N.D. July 8, 1928, B.Eng.misc.e.624.

80 'Edward Carpenter at Eighty-Four', no reference, August, no date, 1928, N.C. C.F.S./W.W./E.C.

81 'Hearty Congratulations to Edward Carpenter, 84th Birthday', no reference, August, no date, 1928, C.C. N.C. 2/67.

82 Inigan in Beith, ed., *Edward Carpenter*, p. 120.

83 Mattison, *The Journal of Alf Mattison*, Mss. Whit Sunday 1928, p. 161. Leeds Reference Library.

84 Inigan in Beith, ed., *Edward Carpenter*, p. 120.

85 Gröndahl in ibid., p. 106.

86 E.M. Forster, 'Book Talk, The Life and Work of Edward Carpenter', Radio Broadcast, September 1944, Typed Mss. C.F.S./W.W./E.C.

87 H.N.D. June 9, 1929; B.Eng.misc.e.624.

88 Beith to Luckhurst Scott, June 19, 1929 enclosed in Luckhurst Scott to MacDonald, June 22, 1929, R.M.P.

89 Barker to Sixsmith, June 28, 1929, C.F.S./W.W./E.C.

90 H.N.D. June 30, 1929, and July 1, 1929; B.Eng.misc.e.624.

91 Ted (Inigan) to Sixsmith, Telegram, July 1, 1929, C.F.S./W.W./E.C.

92 Mattison, *The Journal of Alf Mattison*, Mss. July 3, 1929, p. 25. Leeds Reference Library; H.N.D. July 1, 1929; B.Eng.misc.e.624.

93 'Into the Sun', no reference, no date, N.C. C.F.S./W.W./E.C.

94 H.N.D. July 1, 1929; B.Eng.misc.e.624.

95 Henry Nevinson, 'Funeral of Edward Carpenter. The Simple Ceremony at Guildford', *Manchester Guardian*, July 2, 1929, C.F.S./W.W./E.C.

96 Hyett to Mattison, July 12, 1929; July 15, 1929, *Letters Addressed to Alf Mattison*, p. 390, A.M.; Hyett to Dalton, July 12, 1929, D.P.; Green to Dalton, July 24, 1929, D.P.

97 Recent Wills, no reference, no date, N.C. C.F.S./W.W./E.C.; Tsuzuki, *Edward Carpenter*, p. 193; Mattison, *The Journal of Alf Mattison*, Mss. Bank Holiday, August 3, 1929, p. 31, Leeds Reference Library.

98 'Mr Edward Carpenter, Democratic Author and Poet', *The Times*, June 29, 1929, N.C. C.F.S./W.W./E.C.; 'Edward Carpenter', *Manchester Guardian*, June 29, 1929, N.C. C.F.S./W.W./E.C.; Right Hon. T.P. O'Connor M.P., 'Socialist Mystic and Poet', *Daily Telegraph*, June 30, 1929, N.C. C.F.S./W.W./E.C.; H.S.S. (Henry Salt), 'Edward Carpenter', *Cruel Sports: The Official Journal of the League for the Prohibition of Cruel Sports*, no date, p. 98, N.C. C.F.S./W.W./E.C.; 'The Passing of Edward Carpenter', *Daily Herald*,

no date, N.C. C.F.S./W.W./E.C.; Fenner Brockway, 'A Memory of Edward Carpenter', *New Leader*, July 5, 1929; 'Poet and Socialist', *Forward*, July 6, 1929, N.C. C.F.S./W.W./E.C.; 'Edward Carpenter', *Clarion*, July, no date, 1929, N.C. C.F.S./W.W./E.C.; Robert Sharland, 'Edward Carpenter', *The Social Democrat*, August 1929, N.C.S.B.; T. Ashcroft, 'Edward Carpenter', *Plebs*, no date, N.C. C.F.S./W.W./E.C. 'Edward Carpenter', *The Singer and Sower*, no date, N.C. C.F.S./W.W./E.C.

99   H.J. Dion Byngham, 'The Passing of Edward Carpenter', *The Healthy Life: The Independent Health Magazine*, no date, pp. 300-301, N.C. C.F.S./ W.W./E.C.

100 Mattison, *The Journal of Alf Mattison*, Mss. Bank Holiday, August 3, 1929, p. 30, Leeds Reference Library.

101 H.N.D. September 3, 1929, B.Eng.misc.e.624.

102 Clemas to Sixsmith, January 30, 1930, C.F.S./W.W./E.C.; Salt to Mattison, January 2, 1930, *Letters Addressed to Alf Mattison*, p. 417.

103 Mattison, *The Journal of Alf Mattison*, Mss. April 13 to April 20, 1931, p. 232, Leeds Reference Library; Salt to Mattison, January 15, 1930, *Letters Addressed to Alf Mattison*, p. 420. A.M.

104 Salt to Clemas, September 25, 1930, C.C. 390/76.

105 Forster to Clemas, December 16, 1929, C.C. 390/77; Forster to Sharp, December 27, 1929, E.M.F.

106 Inigan in Beith, ed., *Edward Carpenter*, p. 121.

25 Bearing the Memory

1   E.M. Forster, December 1929, *Commonplace Book* (London: Scolar Press, 1978), p. 62.

2   MacDonald in Beith, ed., *Edward Carpenter*, p. 132; Lowes Dickinson in ibid., p. 34; Housman in ibid., p. 107; Lloyd quoted in Monroe in ibid., p. 153.

3   Forster in ibid., pp. 77-78.

4   George Orwell, *The Road to Wigan Pier* (London: Gollancz, 1937), p. 206.

5   George Orwell to Jack Common, April 16 (?), 1936, in Sonia Orwell and Ian Angus, eds., *The Collected Essays, Journalism and Letters of George Orwell, Volume 1, An Age Like This 1920-1940* (London: Penguin, 1970), p. 245.

6   Rayner Heppenstall, 'Edward Carpenter and the Idea of Democracy', *The Adelphi*, Vol. 7, No. 5 (new series), February 1934, p. 360.

7   Karl Federn, *The Materialist Conception of History: A Critical Analysis* (London: Macmillan, 1939), pp. 13-14, 16.

8   Carpenter, Preface to Complete Edition (1920), *Civilisation: Its Cause and Cure*, pp. 7-11; Picton in Beith, ed., *Edward Carpenter*, p. 178.

9   Claude Bragdon, *More Lives Than One* (New York: Alfred A. Knopf, 1938), pp. 176-179; Sheldon Cheney, *Expressionism in Art* (New York: Liveright Publishing Corporation, 1958), first edition 1934, pp. 34, 329-332, 386. Dalrymple Henderson, 'Mysticism as the "Tie that Binds"', note, p. 37. David Goodway, *Herbert Read Reassessed* (Liverpool: Liverpool University Press, 1998), pp. 178-189, 203, 216-218, 279; Donald L. Miller, *Lewis Mumford: A Life* (Pittsburgh: University of Pittsburgh Press, 1989), pp. 162-166.

10 Laurence Veysey, *The Communal Experience: Anarchist and Mystical Counter-*

Cultures in America (New York: Harper and Row, 1973), pp. 103, 208–334; *The Happy Valley Foundation History*, http://www.happyvalleyfdn.org/history.html

11 Patrick Wright, *The Village that Died for England* (London: Faber and Faber, 2002), first edition 1995, pp. 180–193.

12 Emma Hopley, *Campaigning Against Cruelty: The Hundred Year History of the British Union for the Abolition of Vivisection* (London: The British Union of Abolition, 1998), pp. 30–51; Brown, *A Consideration of Some Parallels in the Personal and Social Ideals of E.M. Forster and Edward Carpenter*, PhD, University of Wales, 1982, p. 535; 'Liberty [National Council for Civil Liberties]', in John Button, ed., *The Radicalism Handbook: A Complete Guide to the Radical Movement in the Twentieth Century* (London: Cassell, 1995), pp. 395–396; Furbank, *E.M. Forster: A Life*, pp. 186–188.

13 Kumari Jayawardena, *Doreen Wickremasinghe: A Western Radical in Sri Lanka* (Colombo: Women's Education and Research Centre, 1991), pp. 11–29.

14 Hendrick, *Henry Salt*, pp. 166–168; Henry Salt, 'Concerning Rules and Principles', *The Vegetarian News*, Vol. II, No. 128, August 1931, pp. 221–225, N.C. C.F.S./W.W./E.C.

15 Brown, *A Consideration of Some Parallels*, p. 535, fn. 7. Copley, *A Spiritual Bloomsbury*, pp. 242–258; Parminder Kaur Bakshi, *Distant Desire: The Theme of Friendship in E.M. Forster's Fiction*, PhD, University of Warwick, 1992.

16 Virginia Nicholson, *Among the Bohemians: Experiments in Living 1900–1939* (London: Viking, 2002), pp. 7–10, 87–91, 124–127, 139–143.

17 Desmond MacCarthy, 'Edward Carpenter: Minor Prophet', *The Listener*, September 7, 1944, N.C. C.F.S./W.W./E.C.

18 Forster, 'Book-Talk, The Life and Work of Edward Carpenter', B.B.C. Talk, September, 1944, Typed Mss. C.F.S./W.W./E.C.

19 Diana Souhami, *The Trials of Radclyffe Hall* (London: Weidenfeld and Nicolson, 1998), pp. 176–222; Laura Doan, *Fashioning Sapphism: The Origins of a Modern English Lesbian Culture* (New York: Columbia University Press, 2001), pp. xi–xxiii, 117–125, 126–163; Laura Doan, 'The Outcast of One Age is the Hero of Another', Radclyffe Hall, Edward Carpenter and the Intermediate Sex', in Laura Doan and Jay Prosser, eds., *Palatable Poisons: Critical Perspectives on the Well of Loneliness* (New York: Columbia University Press, 2001), pp. 162–178.

20 Ross McKibbin, *Classes and Cultures: England 1918–1951* (Oxford: Oxford University Press 1998), pp. 325–326.

21 Jean Overton Fuller, *The Magical Dilemma of Victor Neuburg* (London: W.H. Allen, 1965), pp. 234, 237–241, 260–263.

22 Kevin Porter and Jeffrey Weeks, *Between the Acts: Lives of Homosexual Men 1885–1967* (London: Routledge, 1991), pp. 35–37, 61–62, 69.

23 Simon Karlinsky, 'Russia's Gay Literature and Culture: The Impact of the October Revolution', in eds. Martin Bauml Duberman, Martha Vicinus and George Chauncey Jr., *Hidden from History: Reclaiming the Gay and Lesbian Past* (London: Penguin 1991), pp. 356–362; Kevin Morgan, Gidon Cohen and Andrew Flinn, *Communists and British Society 1920–1991* (London: Rivers Oram Press and Pandora Press, 2006), pp. 126–127.

24 See Stuart Timmons, *The Trouble with Harry Hay: Founder of the Modern Gay*

Movement (Boston: Alyson Publications, 1990), and ed. Will Roscoe, *Harry Hay, Radically Gay: Gay Liberation in the Words of its Founder* (Boston: Beacon Press, 1996).

25 Winston Leyland, *Allen Ginsberg: Gay Sunshine Interviews*, Vol. 1, p. 106.

26 Aldous Huxley, *Science, Liberty and Peace* (London: Chatto and Windus, 1947), pp. 30–31, quoted in Goodway, *Anarchist Seeds Beneath the Snow*, p. 57.

27 Sheffield Clarion Central Committee, Report from S. Harpham, 1930, pp. 1–2, cutting in C.F.S./W.W./E.C.; Sheffield's Lost Opportunity, Edward Carpenter Memorial Service, Great Demonstration, Sheffield Co-operator, no date, C.C. N.C. 2/109.

28 Harpham to Mattison, July 5, 1930, *Letters Addressed to Alf Mattison*, p. 428, A.M.

29 Minute Book of the Edward Carpenter International Memorial Trust, 1931–1934, C.C. Mss. 388; Edward Carpenter, Programme of Service 1844–1929, The Second Annual Memorial Service to be held at Millthorpe (Holmesfield), at the rear of his late Residence, or if wet in Mr. Kay's Barn, Sunday 5, July, 1931 at 2.30 o'clock, C.F.S./W.W./E./C.

30 Kathleen Bunting quoted in Hill, 'Edward Carpenter: Memories of a "True Socialist"', *Morning Telegraph*, February 28, 1973, N.C. Private Collection of Jo McGhee, Carpenter House.

31 Meeting held T.U. Club, London, Friday 7, August 1931, C.C. Mss. 388; Edward Carpenter International Memorial Appeal, The 'Edward Carpenter' International Memorial Trust, Hon. Secretary S. Harpham, no date (1931–1932), C.F.S./W.W./E.C.

32 Edward Carpenter Memorial Service 1953, A Brief History of the Edward Carpenter Fellowship, Miscellaneous Papers, Edward Carpenter Centenary, 1944; Correspondence and cuttings, C.C. Mss. 387; Deeds of Carpenter House, December 12, 1933. I am grateful to Jo McGhee for allowing me access to the deeds.

33 Carpenter Service Fellowship, May 11, 1935, C.C. Mss. 388; Carpenter Service Fellowship, Minutes July 3, 1935, C.C. Mss. 388; Notes and Extracts. Correspondence between Leonard Green and the Town Clerk of Sheffield, E.B. Gibson, over Carpenter's books presented by Tom Nicholson to Sheffield Library 1933–1934, C.F.S./W.W./E.C.

34 Florence Mattison, My Memories of Carpenter, Edward Carpenter Memorial Service, Sunday July 4, 1937, C.F.S./W.W./E.C.

35 Stanley Unwin to Mattison, February 8, 1944, C.F.S./W.W./E.C.

36 Green to Beith, November 29, 1943, C.C. 387/6.

37 Forster to Beith, March 14, 1944, C.C. 387/1.

38 Sixsmith to Beith, June 5, 1944, C.C. 387/24.

39 S.K. Ratcliffe, 'Edward Carpenter', *Manchester Guardian*, August 29, 1944, C.C. N.C. Mss. 387/29; Charles Morgan, 'Poet of Democracy; Edward Carpenter's Dream, Aeons of Peace and Progress', *Times Literary Supplement*, September 2, 1944, p. 426, N.C. C.F.S./W.W./E.C.; Desmond MacCarthy, 'Edward Carpenter: Minor Prophet', *The Listener*, September 7, 1944, pp. 270–271, C.C. N.C. Mss. 387/3; 'Hardly Known Now', *Evening Standard*, no date, C.C. W.C. Mss. 387/35; C.F. Sixsmith, 'Centenary of a Prophet: Edward Carpenter's Bolton Following', *Bolton Journal*, August 29, 1944,

N.C. C.F.S./W.W./E.C.; 'Edward Carpenter and Leeds', *Yorkshire Post and Leeds Mercury*, August 29, 1944, N.C. C.F.S./W.W./E.C.; *Southport Announcer*, July 23, 1944, C.C. N.C. Mss. 387/39; Reference to *Sheffield Telegraph* in Leonard Green to Gilbert Beith, September 5, 1944, C.C.387/17; E.M. Forster, 'Edward Carpenter, A Centenary Note', Book Section, *Tribune*, No. 404, September 22, 1944, pp. 12–13, N.C. C.F.S./W.W./E.C.; John Stewart Collis, 'Edward Carpenter', *Health and Life*, Issue 125, October 1944, p. 137, N.C. C.F.S./W.W./E.C.; Gabriel Seal, 'Centenary of a Forgotten Countryman', *The Countryman*, Vol. xxx, No. 1, Autumn, 1944, p. 40, N.C. C.F.S./W.W./E.C.; Ussher to Sixsmith, October 3, 1944 (on E.M. Forster's B.B.C. Talk), C.F.S./W.W./E.C.

40 *Surrey Advertiser*, no date, hand-written notes, C.C. Mss. 387/30; Our London Correspondent, 'In a Surrey Garden', *Manchester Guardian*, August 29, 1944, N.C. C.F.S./W.W./E.C.; Philip Unwin to Beith, August 19, 1944.

41 Edward Carpenter Memorial Service, July 7, 1946, C.F.S./W.W./E.C.

42 Edward Carpenter Memorial Service, July 6, 1947, C.F.S./W.W./E.C. On Adams, see Barua, *Edward Carpenter 1844–1929*, p. 240.

43 G.H.B. Ward quoted in 'Society Want Reformer's Home', *Sheffield Telegraph*, September 6, 1955, C.C. N.C. Mss. 387.

44 'Socialist Pioneer Honoured', no reference, June 29, 1955, C.C. N.C. Mss. 387; Gordon to Mattison, October 12, 1925, *Letters Addressed to Alf Mattison*, p. 282, A.M.

45 Lamb to Mattison, November 8, 1929, *Letters Addressed to Alf Mattison*, p. 410, A.M.

46 Notes and Extracts, Correspondence between Leonard Green and the Town Clerk of Sheffield, E.B. Gibson, 1933–1934, C.F.S./W.W./E.C.

47 Sheffield City Libraries, *A Bibliography of Edward Carpenter* (Sheffield: Sheffield City Libraries, 1949). Additions to list in C.S. Sixsmith's Carpenter Collection, September 26, 1949, C.F.S./W.W./E.C.

48 Lamb to Sixsmith, March 11, 1950, C.F.S./W.W./E.C.

49 *Bolton Evening News*, October 24, 1950, N.C. C.F.S./W.W./E.C. Correspondence between Charles Sixsmith and Harold Hamer, October, November 1950, January 1951, September 1953, C.F.S./W.W./E.C.

50 Keith Nield, 'Edward Carpenter', in Joyce Bellamy and John Saville, eds., *Dictionary of Labour Biography*, Vol. II (London: Macmillan, 1974), p. 92.

51 The judgements of labour historians during the 1950s were inclined to be dismissive. Henry Pelling, *The Origins of the Labour Party 1880–1900* (Oxford: Clarendon Press, 1965; first edition 1954), pp. 142–143, says Carpenter 'suited the new intelligentsia of socialism' but 'proved of no permanent value to the working class' G.D.H. Cole, *A History of Socialist Thought, Vol. III, Part I, The Second International, 1889–1914* (London: Macmillan, 1956), p. 143, describes him as a 'crank' but a 'considerable minor prophet', adding that he took little part in the socialist movement except through his writings; Thompson, *William Morris*, pp. 289–290, presents Carpenter as an individualistic, if sincere rebel, claiming that his market gardening backed by a private income was not 'especially arduous'. On their response see Nield, 'Edward Carpenter: The Uses of Utopia', Brown, ed., *Edward Carpenter and Late Victorian Radicalism*, pp. 19, 31.

52 Barua, *The Life and Work of Edward Carpenter*; see also Terence Francis Eagleton, *Nature and Spirit: A Study of Edward Carpenter in his Intellectual Context*, PhD, Cambridge University, 1968; Stephen Clair Immer, *The Philosophy of Edward Carpenter: British Poetic Radicalism*, M.A. Department of History and the Graduate School of the University of Oregon, 1968.

53 C.M. Kelly, 'The Sage of Cordwell', *Derbyshire Life and Countryside*, Vol. 34, No. 8, August 1969, p. 43, N.C. Jo McGhee.

54 Kathleen Bunting quoted in Hill, 'Memories of a "True Socialist"', N.C. Jo McGhee.

55 Bruce to Sheila Rowbotham, June 16, 1977, Private Collection, Sheila Rowbotham.

56 Brown, *A Consideration of Some Parallels*, fn. 2, p. 532.

57 Getting Started: Edward Carpenter Trust and Gamut Magazine, http://www.diggersanddreamers.org.uk/Articles/199004.html. I am grateful to John Spencer for this reference and to John Baker for information on the Edward Carpenter community. The Edward Carpenter forum was founded in 2007; it has its own web page. ·

58 Edward Carpenter Celebration Programme, Guildford, Saturday May 3, 1986. Private Collection, Jonathan Cutbill. The event is recorded in the Channel 4 documentary *Utopias*, Lusia Films, Director Marc Karlin.

59 I am grateful to Judith Williamson for this information.

60 Erlend Clouston, 'Best Feet Forward: Barefoot campaigner makes strides towards a healthier way of life', *Guardian*, Society, March 24, 2004.

61 Thomas Patrick Barclay, *Memoirs and Medleys, The Autobiography of a Bottle Washer (1852–1933)* (Leicester: Edgar Backus, 1934), p. 68.

62 Angus Gellatly and Oscar Zarate, *Introducing Mind and Brain* (Thriplow, Royston: Icon Books, 2005), pp. 160–170; Ian Sample, 'A Fine Romance: how humans and chimps just couldn't let go', *Guardian*, May 18, 2006, p. 17; Paul Broks, *Into the Silent Land* (London: Atlantic Books, 2003), pp. 132–143; Carolin Crawford, 'Braneworlds, Review of Brian Greene, The Fabric of the Cosmos: Space, Time and the Texture of Reality', *London Review of Books*, May 19, 2005, pp. 33–34; Brian Greene, 'The Universe on a String', *The New York Times*, op.ed., October 20, 2006, p. 3; Frank Close, 'Me and My Breakfast Cereal, Review of Robert Laughlin, A Different Universe: Reinventing Physics from the Bottom Down', *London Review of Books*, February 9, 2006, pp. 28–29.

63 Frank Close, *Particle Physics: A Very Short Introduction* (Oxford: Oxford University Press, 2004), p. 129.

64 Carpenter to Clemas, January 3, 1927, C.C. 390/65.

65 Edward Carpenter, 'In a Manufacturing Town', *Towards Democracy*, p. 145.

66 Edward Carpenter, 'The Dream Goes By', *Towards Democracy*, p. 387.

67 Nevinson in Beith, ed., *Edward Carpenter*, p. 165.

68 Carpenter, *My Days and Dreams*, p. 304.

Acknowledgements

Writing, and particularly writing at length, is necessarily lonely, but I have received such generous help and support that I have felt myself at times to be working in co-operative association. From the start, the conviction of my colleague at Manchester University, Laura Doan, that I should embark on the biography was a vital inspiration, while discussions with Angela John, the biographer of Carpenter's friends Henry W. Nevinson and Evelyn Sharp, provided enlightenment and insights. I am greatly indebted to the indefatigable John Baker whose enthusiasm for the biography sustained me with references to material, critical comments and ideas. Joey Cain generously shared his research on Whitman and Carpenter and on Chester (Gavin) Arthur with me and his contribution has really enriched the book. Jonathan Cutbill, Carpenter's literary executor, offered me the secular equivalent to a blessing and access to his private collection of letters. Rosemary Fitch, Carpenter's great, great niece allowed me to look at papers and kindly read the manuscript.

I am deeply grateful to my agent Faith Evans who read several drafts as I struggled to bring the vast amount of material on Edward Carpenter together. She brought to bear a skilled literary eye, combining enthusiasm with honest criticism. Thanks too to the staff at Verso for their stalwart support, and especially to my editor Tom Penn, who displayed great fortitude and gave me much needed reassurance. Tim Clark performed the Herculean task of cutting with sensitivity and precise understanding, to the great benefit of the manuscript. Several friends read drafts and provided critical expertise at moments of doubt and confusion: Ros Baxandall, Nigel Fountain, Paul Kelemen, Jenny Taylor, Hilary Wainwright. My partner, Derek Clarke, steadfastly endured Edward Carpenter, accompanied by an ever widening circle of friends and acquaintances, moving in with us for several years amidst mounting piles of paper. A crucial figure in the emergence of this manuscript is Anne Morrow who heroically typed the bulk of it, noted inconsistencies and gave me her thoughts on the characters and their doings. At various points of crisis when my repetitive stress injury flared up and I could not write, I was rescued by John Spencer and Bunny Martin's practical skills, physiological intelligence and humour. Mark Wilding copied material for me at the Sheffield Archive.

When I read through the pages I recall a mosaic of people and memories. D.A. Sachs copied letters and manuscripts from his J. William Lloyd collection. Felicity Ashbee, Michael Barrett Brown and Dennis Goodwin kindly gave me their time in talking about their fathers' friendship with Carpenter, and Annie McEwen allowed me to see a letter from Dolly Radford to Carpenter in her possession. Loretta and Jason Capper's detective work in New Zealand put me in touch with A.J. Furniss, who sent family memories and letters relating to John Furniss, one of the early Sheffield socialists who emigrated. Keith Gull dug out information on Carpenter's great love George Hukin's first marriage. Sally Goldsmith located where Carpenter had lived in Bradway, which led us to a descendant of Charles Fox, the farmer and adult student who had owned the farm in the early 1880s, still living in exactly the same spot. Jo McGhee, the present owner of 'Carpenter House', shared her memories of local farming families in Holmesfield and Millthorpe, while Marilyn Wilkes' research located Carpenter's first house in Guildford and revealed the second had been knocked down. Rony Robinson told me about Totley, his grand-mother, and the Bunting sisters from Holmesfield who knew Carpenter, and Judith Williamson about the commemorative council flats 'Carpenter House' on Brecknock Road, London. My cousin, Mary Gamble, found a distant relative who had delivered eggs to Carpenter.

Carol Ewing attempted to explain to me the basics of contemporary medical views on the relation between nerves and brain, and John Pickstone patiently listened to my agitated efforts to embark on the history of science and checked my progress. Judith Okely checked through material on the history of anthropology. Paul Atkinson sent me material on the history of psychoanalysis and maths. Derek Sederman guided me through the history of Abbotsholme School. Françoise Barret-Ducrocq produced infor-mation on Carpenter's French contacts. John Stokes' comments on the cultural history of the 1890s and Temma Kaplan's on Spanish anarchism were extremely helpful. Thanks to Partha Mitter for sharing his knowledge of Western perceptions of India, to Kumari Jayawardena for introducing me to the history of the labour and women's movement in Sri Lanka and her interest in Robert Weare and Bristol socialism. Thanks are also due to Logie Barrow, David Beetham, Lucy Bland, John Blishen, Catherine Burke, Jay Critchley, Vincent Geoghegan, David Goodway, Lesley Hall,

Karen Hunt, Martin Kenner, Terence Kissack, Jill Liddington, Ellen Malos, Tara Martin, Simon Miller, Jean Moorcroft Wilson, Kevin Morgan, Theresa Moriarty, Robin Murray, Julian Putkowski, John Quail, Liz Stanley, Dorothy Thompson, Laura Trevelyan, Joyce Wainwright, and Barbara Winslow for references as well as to Michaela Mazzei for translating letters in Italian and to Paul Kelemen, Rachel Ramsay, and Barbara Dubrowski for translating material in German.

Sally Alexander, Tariq Ali, Howard Booth, Shravika Damunupola, Gary Daniels, Joy Dixon, Catherine Hall, Brian Heaphy, Jonathan Ned Katz, Chris Leach, Swasti Mitter, Nikos Papastergiadis, Lynne Segal, Gareth Steadman Jones, Chushichi Tsuzuki, Jeffrey Weeks, Janet Wolff and Patrick Wright all expressed their faith that it was worthwhile at points along what seemed sometimes like a journey without end. Members of the Edward Carpenter Community of Gay Men and the Edward Carpenter Forum encouraged me by their interest and by inviting me to speak at their weekend school. I have also enthused on aspects of Carpenter's life and ideas at the Bolton Socialist Club; for the National Assembly of Women at Wortley Hall; at the Working Class Movement Library in Salford; at Hull University Social Anthropology Department; at the 'Writing in Opposition' Conference and to members of my own department, Sociology, at Manchester University. I am grateful for comments from these meetings.

One of the most delightful aspects of writing the biography has been retracing Carpenter's steps on convivial outings to Sheffield, Totley, Bradway, Millthorpe, Guildford, Bolton and Lyme Regis with members of the Edward Carpenter Community of Gay Men and the Edward Carpenter Forum, along with Derek Clarke, Barbara Davy, Nigel Fountain, Sally Goldsmith, Gabrielle Mander, Rony Robinson and Mark Wilding. On my alternative Carpenterian heritage trails I met with warm hospitality from Jo McGhee at Carpenter House, Millthorpe (now a bed and breakfast), from Karen Lamb at Moorhay farm, from Pam and Peter Levell in Carpenter's former home in Guildford and from Martin Daunton who showed me Trinity Hall's paintings of Edward Anthony Beck and Robert Farren's 'Senate-House Hill: Degree Morning'.

Thanks to the many dedicated archivists and librarians who assisted my searches, particularly Ruth Harman, Cheryl Bailey and their colleagues in the Sheffield Archives along with Fran Baker and Dorothy Clayton and the staff of the John Rylands Library, both of which became rather like second homes, as well as to Candace Falk, Barry Pateman and Jessica Moran of the Emma Goldman Papers, University of California, Berkeley, for help in locating anarchist material on my two visits and sending on sources after I had left.

For permission to quote I am grateful to the following: Felicity Ashbee and Francis Ames-Lewis (C.R. Ashbee); Nicholas Deakin (Havelock Ellis); Michael Aryton Estate (Henry W. Nevinson and Evelyn Sharp); Barbara Levy Literary Agency (Siegfried Sassoon); Pollinger Limited and the Estate of Frieda Lawrence Ravagli, for correspondence from and relating to D.H. Lawrence; A.P. Watt Ltd for Robert Graves' letter to Edward Carpenter; Jon Wynne-Tyson (the Salts); the Provost and Fellows of Worcester College (John Dalton Papers); New College, Oxford (Milner Papers); Charlotte Perkins Gilman Papers, Schlesinger Library, Radcliffe Institute, Harvard University; the Society of Authors, on behalf of the Bernard Shaw Estate, and the Society of Authors as the Literary Representative of the Estate of Holbrook Jackson; Annabel Cole (Roger Fry); the Society of Authors and the Provost and Scholars of King's College Cambridge (E.M. Forster published and unpublished material); thanks also to King's College, Cambridge, Archive Centre for permission to quote from the journal of C.R. Ashbee and the papers of Roger Fry (REF/3/28), and to the National Art Library, Victoria and Albert Museum for permission to reprint material from Ashbee's *Memoirs*. Material from the collections of C.F. Sixsmith, Walt Whitman and the Edward Carpenter Collection, Richard Hawkin, Alison Uttley and Raymond Unwin are reproduced by courtesy of the University Librarian and Director, the John Rylands University Library, University of Manchester. I am similarly grateful to Colin Harris at the Bodleian Library, Oxford (Henry W. Nevinson, Evelyn Sharp, Carpenter's letters to Bertram Dobell and Edith Nesbit, Milner Papers); the Brotherton Library, University of Leeds (Alf Mattison); Bolton Archives and Local Studies Service (the Bolton Whitmanites); Norfolk Record Office (Carpenter's letter to Fred Henderson); the University of Nottingham Library (Carpenter's letters to Constantine Sarantchoft and Helen Corke's letters to Emile Delavenay); Birmingham University Library (Carpenter's letters to Granville Bantock); the Sidney Jones Library, Liverpool University (Glasier Papers); London School of Economics Archives (Percival Chubb and Fabian Papers); the British Library (Carpenter's letters to Marie Stopes, Bernard Shaw, Rutland Boughton, the Ellis Papers, A. Conan-Doyle and C.K. Shorter Papers Concerning Roger Casement); the Women's Library (Carpenter's letter to Edith How-Martyn); Betty Ballantine and the International Institute for Social History (Emma Goldman); the Tamiment Library New York University (Helena Born Papers); Hilda M. Wick at Beeghly Library, Ohio Wesleyan University (Carpenter's letter to 'Benjamin'); the Harry Ransom Center, University of Texas at Austin (Carpenter's letters to Ellis); Syracuse University Library, Special Collections Research Centre (Carpenter's letters to Whitman); the

Manuscripts Division, Department of Rare Books and Special Collections, Princeton University Library (Carpenter's letters to Bragdon). For permission to reproduce images thanks are due to: Sheffield Archives; Bolton Central Library and Archives; the John Rylands Library, Manchester; the Master and Fellows of Trinity Hall, Cambridge; the Chicago Historical Society; the National Portrait Gallery, London; the British Library; Colindale James Nisbet and Co. The archive references for the images from the Sheffield Archives are: 1 (Carp/8/103), 4 (Carp/8/74), 5 (Carp/8/6), 9 (Carp 8/57), 10 (Carp/10/198), 12 (Carp/8/48), 16 (Carp/8/54), 18 (Carp/8/31) and 24 (Carp/8/95). Images 8, 17, 26, 27 and 28 are from the John Rylands Library. Image 2 is from Trinity Hall, Cambridge, and image 13 is from the Bolton Central Library and Archives. Image 11, 'Edward Carpenter by Roger Fry', is the copyright of the National Portrait Gallery, London. Image 22, by Alvin Langdon Coburn, copyright reserved, is from the collection of the National Portrait Gallery, London. Image 25 is the copyright of the Chicago Historical Society. Every effort has been made to secure all necessary permissions. The author and publisher will be glad to recognise any holders of copyright who have not been acknowledged above.

Archives Consulted

(With abbreviations used in the Notes)

A. Conan-Doyle and C.K. Shorter Papers Concerning Roger Casement; British Library.

Alexander Berkman Archive; The International Institute of Social History, Amsterdam. (A.B.A.)

Alf Mattison Collection; Brotherton Library, University of Leeds. (A.M.)

Alfred Orage Papers; Brotherton Library, University of Leeds.

Alison Uttley Collection; John Rylands Library, Deansgate, Manchester.

Andre Raffalovich Collection; John Rylands Library, Deansgate, Manchester.

Angela Tuckett Manuscript on Enid Stacy; Working Class Movement Library, Salford. (A.T.Mss)

Bayley–Whitman Collection; Ohio Wesleyan University.

Bernard Shaw Papers; British Library.

Bolton Whitman Fellowship Collection; Bolton Library. (B.W.F.C.)

Carpenter Collection; Sheffield Archives. (C.C.)

Carpenter to Edith How-Martyn Correspondence; Women's Library, London Metropolitan University.

Carpenter to Florence Farr; Goldsmiths Library, Senate House, University of London Library.

Carpenter to George Lansbury; London School of Economics.

Carpenter to Lady Carnarvon; Hampshire Record Office.

Carpenter to Rev. Henry S. McClelland; Glasgow City Council, Archives and Special Collections, Mitchell Library.

Carpenter to Rutland Boughton; British Library.

Cecil Roberts Papers; Churchill College Cambridge.

Cecil Sharp Papers; Cecil Sharp House, London.

Charles Frederick Sixsmith, Walt Whitman and Edward Carpenter

Collection; John Rylands Library, Deansgate, Manchester. (C.F.S./W.W./E.C.)

Charles Robert Ashbee Papers; Journal (GBR/0272/CRA), King's College, Cambridge, Archive Centre. (J.)

Charlotte Perkins Gilman Papers, Schlesinger Library, Radcliffe Institute, Harvard University. (C.P.G.)

Chubb Papers; London School of Economics.

Claude. F. Bragdon Collection; Princeton University. (C.F.B.)

Constantine Sarantchoft, Harold Bing Collection; University of Nottingham. (C.S.)

C.R. Ashbee Memoirs; National Art Library, Victoria and Albert Museum. (M.)

Dalton Diaries, Hugh; London School of Economics Archives. (D.D.)

Dalton Papers, John. Worcester College, Oxford. (D.P.)

Edward Morgan Forster, King's College, Cambridge. (E.M.F.)

E.J. Dent Papers; King's College, Cambridge.

Emma Goldman; The International Institute of Social History, Amsterdam. (E.G.)

Emma Goldman Papers; University of California, Berkeley. (E.G.P.)

Emmeline Pethick-Lawrence Letters; Trinity College, Cambridge.

Emile Delavenay Papers; University of Nottingham. (E.D.)

Evelyn Sharp Papers; Bodleian Library, Oxford. (E.S.P.)

Fabian Papers; London School of Economics. (F.P.)

Ford family papers; Brotherton Library, University of Leeds.

Ford Scrapbook, Leeds Archives.

Foxwell Papers; St John's College, Cambridge.

Fred Henderson Papers; Norfolk Record Office, Norwich. (H.E.N.)

Glasier Papers; Sidney Jones Library, University of Liverpool. (G.P.)

Granville Bantock Letters relating to Edward Carpenter; Worcestershire Record Office. (G.B.W.)

Granville Bantock Letters; University of Birmingham. (G.B.L.)

Havelock Ellis Papers; British Library. (H.E.P.)

Helena Born Papers; Tamiment Library and Robert F. Wagner Labor Archives, New York. (H.B.)

Henry W. Nevinson Diary; Bodleian Library, Oxford. (H.N.D.)

Henry W. Nevinson Papers; Bodleian Library, Oxford. (H.N.P.)

H.J. Wilson Papers; Sheffield Archives.

Independent Labour Party Papers; London School of Economics.

Joey Cain Private Collection.

John Baker Private Collection.

Jonathan Cutbill Private Collection. (J.C.)

Joseph Estlin Carpenter Papers; Harris Manchester College, Oxford. (J.E.C.)

Karl Pearson Collection; University College, London.

Margaret Ashton Papers; Manchester Central Reference Library.

Margaret Sanger Papers Project; Department of History, New York University. (M.S.P.P.)

Marie Stopes Papers; British Library. (M.S.)

Mary E. Gawthorpe Papers; Tamiment Library and Robert F. Wagner Labor Archives. (M.E.G.)

Milner Papers; Bodleian Library, Oxford. (M.P.)

Oglander Collection; Isle of Wight Record Office.

Patrick Geddes Collection; University of Strathclyde, Glasgow.

Percy Withers Collection; Somerville College, Oxford.

Ramsay MacDonald Papers; The National Archive, London. (R.M.P.)

Raymond Unwin Papers; Kantorowich Library, John Rylands, University of Manchester. (R.U.P.)

Richard Hawkin's Papers; John Rylands Library, Deansgate, Manchester.

Riley Papers; Beinecke Library, Yale University. (R.P.)

Robert C. Trevelyan Papers; Trinity College, Cambridge. (R.C.T.)

Roger Fry Papers; King's College, Cambridge, Archive Centre. (R.E.F)

Rupert Chawner Brooke Papers; King's College, Cambridge.

Samuel Bale Collection; Bristol Public Library. (S.B.C.)

Sprott Papers; King's College, Cambridge, Archive Centre. (W.J.H.S.)

Sydney Olivier Papers; Rhodes House, Oxford.

Walt Whitman Collection; Manuscript Division, Library of Congress, Washington D.C. (W.W.L.O.C.)

Abbreviations used for sites of manuscript collections

(B.)	Bodleian Library, Oxford.
(B.L.)	British Library, London.
(H.R.C.)	Harry Ransom Center, University of Texas at Austin.
(King's)	King's College, Cambridge, Archive Centre.
(J.R.L.)	John Rylands Library, Manchester University, Deansgate.
(L.S.E.)	London School of Economics Archive.
(S.C.R.C.)	Walt Whitman; Special Collections Research Center, Syracuse University.
(U.C.L.)	University College Library, London.
(W.C.M.)	Waikato Coalfields Museum, Huntly, New Zealand.

Selected Bibliography

Works by Edward Carpenter
(With the date of the first edition and the date of the edition cited in the Notes)

Narcissus and Other Poems (London: Henry S. King, 1873)

Towards Democracy (Manchester and London: The Labour Press, 1883. Reprint of complete edition, George Allen and Unwin, 1921)

England's Ideal (London: Swan Sonnenschein, 1887. Reprint 1895)

(ed.) *Chants of Labour: A Song Book of the People* (London: Swan Sonnenschein, 1888. Reprint sixth edition, George Allen and Unwin, 1922)

Civilisation: Its Cause and Cure (London: Swan Sonnenschein, 1889. Reprint 1893)

From Adam's Peak to Elephanta: Sketches in Ceylon and India (London: Swan Sonnenschein, 1892. Reprint, George Allen and Unwin, 1921)

(ed. with Alf Mattison) *Tom Maguire: A Remembrance* (Manchester: Manchester Labour Press, 1895)

Love's Coming of Age: A Series of Papers on the Relations Between the Sexes (Manchester: The Labour Press, 1896)

(ed.) *Forecasts of the Coming Century* (Manchester: The Labour Press, 1897)

Angel's Wings: A Series of Essays on Art and its Relation to Life (London: Swan Sonnenschein, 1898. Reprint, George Allen and Unwin, 1920)

(ed.) *Ioläus: An Anthology of Friendship* (London: Swan Sonnenschein, 1902. Second edition, enlarged, 1902)

The Art of Creation: Essays on the Self and its Powers (London: George Allen, 1904. Enlarged edition, 1907)

Prisons, Police and Punishment: An Enquiry into the Causes and Treatment of Crime and Criminals (London: Arthur C. Fifield, 1905)

Days With Walt Whitman: With Some Notes on his Life and Work (London: George Allen, 1906)

Sketches from Life in Town and Country (London: George Allen, 1908)

The Intermediate Sex: A Study of Some Transitional Types of Men and Women
(London: Swan Sonnenschein, 1908. Reprint, George Allen and Unwin,
1918)

The Drama of Love and Death: A Study of Human Evolution and Transfiguration
(London: George Allen, 1912)

Intermediate Types Among Primitive Folk (London: George Allen, 1914)

The Healing of Nations and the hidden sources of their strife (London: George
Allen and Unwin, 1915)

My Days and Dreams: being autobiographical notes (London: George Allen
and Unwin, 1916. Third edition 1918)

Never Again! a protest and a warning addressed to the peoples of Europe (London:
George Allen and Unwin, 1916)

Towards Industrial Freedom (London: George Allen and Unwin, 1917.
Second edition 1918)

Pagan and Christian Creeds: Their Origin and Meaning (London: George
Allen and Unwin, 1920)

With G.C. Barnard (pseudonym George Barnefield), *The Psychology of the
Poet Shelley* (London: George Allen and Unwin, 1925)

(ed.) *Light from the East: being letters on gnanam, the divine knowledge, by P.
Arunachalam* (London: George Allen and Unwin, 1927)

For Carpenter's complete works see *A Bibliography of Edward Carpenter*,
prepared by Sheffield City Libraries (Sheffield 1949), pp. 1–59.

Other Works

(Further references are in the longer manuscript version of Sheila
Rowbotham, *Edward Carpenter: A Life of Liberty and Love*, deposited in
the Sheffield Archives)

Abbott, Leonard D. *Francisco Ferrer: His Life, Work and Martyrdom* (New
York: Francisco Ferrer Association, 1910)

Aldrich, Robert. *The Seduction of the Mediterranean: Writing, Art and Homosexual Fantasy* (London: Routledge, 1992)

Armytage, W.H.G. *Heavens Below: Utopian Experiments in England 1560–
1960* (London: Routledge and Kegan Paul, 1961)

Arthur, Gavin. *The Circle of Sex* (New York: University Books, 1966)

Ashbee, C.R. *A Few Chapters in Workshop Reconstruction and Citizenship*
(London: The Guild and School of Handicraft, Essex House, 1894)

Ashbee, C.R. *The Building of Thelema* (London: J.M. Dent, 1910)

Ashbee, Felicity. *Janet Ashbee: Love, Marriage and the Arts and Crafts Movement*
(New York: Syracuse University Press, 2002)

Ashley, M.P., and Sanders C.T. *Red Oxford: A History of the Growth of*

Socialism in the University of Oxford (Oxford: Oxford University Labour Club, 1930)

Avrich, Paul. *Anarchist Voices* (Princeton: Princeton University Press, 1995)

Barker, A.T. *The Letters of H.P. Blavatsky to A.P. Sinnett and other Miscellaneous Letters* (Pasadena, California: Theosophical University Press, 1973)

Barrow, Logie and Bullock, Ian. *Democratic Ideas and the British Labour Movement 1880–1914* (Cambridge: Cambridge University Press, 1996)

Barua, Dilip Kumar. *Edward Carpenter 1844–1929, An Apostle of Freedom* (Burdwan: University of Burdwan, 1991)

Beith, Gilbert (ed.) *Edward Carpenter: In Appreciation* (London: George Allen and Unwin, 1931)

Bergson, Henri. *L'Évolution Créatrice* (Paris: Félix Alcan et Guillaumin Réunis, 1911)

Bergson, Henri. *Creative Evolution* (London: Macmillan, 1964)

Bland, Lucy. *Banishing the Beast: English Feminism and Sexual Morality 1885–1914* (London: Penguin, 1995)

Bland, Lucy and Doan, Laura. *Sexology in Culture: Labelling Bodies and Desires* (Oxford: Polity Press, 1998)

Blodgett, Harold. *Walt Whitman in England* (Ithaca, New York: Cornell University Press, 1934)

Blum, Deborah. *Ghost Hunters: William James and the Search for Scientific Proof of Life After Death* (London: Century, 2007)

Bowler, Peter J. *The Eclipse of Darwinism: Anti-Darwinian Evolution Theories in the Decades Around 1900* (Baltimore: Johns Hopkins University Press, 1983)

Briggs, Julia. *A Woman of Passion: The Life of E. Nesbit 1858–1924* (London: Penguin, 1987)

Briggs, Mitchell Pirie. *George D. Herron and the European Settlement.* Stanford University Publications University Series, History, Economics and Political Science, Vol. 3, No. 2 (Stanford: Stanford University, no date, c. 1932)

Brockway, Fenner. *Inside the Left: Thirty Years of Platform, Press, Prison and Parliament* (London: New Leader Ltd, 1942)

Brockway, Fenner. *Towards Tomorrow: The Autobiography of Fenner Brockway* (London: Hart-Davis, 1977)

Brown, Tony, 'Figuring in History: The Reputation of Edward Carpenter 1883–1987 Annotated Secondary Bibliography', *English Literature in Transition*, Vol. 32, Nos. 1/2 (1989)

Brown, Tony (ed.) *Edward Carpenter and Late Victorian Radicalism* (London: Frank Cass, 1990)

Bryher, Samson. *An Account of the Labour and Socialist Movement in Bristol* (Bristol: Labour Weekly, 1929–1931)

Bucke, Richard Maurice. *Cosmic Consciousness: A Study in the Evolution of the Human Mind* (London: The Olympia Press, 1972)

Burke, Carolyn. *Becoming Modern: The Life and Times of Myrna Loy* (New York: Farrar, Strauss and Giroux, 1985)

Calder-Marshall. Arthur. *Havelock Ellis: A Biography* (London: Rupert Hart-Davis, 1959)

Carlson, Maria. *'No Religion Higher than Truth': A History of the Theosophical Movement in Russia 1875–1924* (Princeton, New Jersey: Princeton University Press, 1993)

Carswell, John. *Lives and Letters 1906–1957* (London: Faber and Faber, 1978)

Challinor, Raymond. *The Origins of British Bolshevism* (London: Croom Helm, 1977)

Chatterjee, Margaret. *Gandhi and his Jewish Friends* (London: Macmillan, 1992)

Clapp, B.W. *An Environmental History of Britain since the Industrial Revolution* (London: Longman, 1994)

Clapperton, Jane Hume. *A Vision of the Future: Based on the Application of Ethical Principles* (London: Swan Sonnenschein, 1904)

Clarke, Edwin and Jacyna, L.S. *Nineteenth-Century Origins of Neuroscientific Concepts* (Berkeley and Los Angeles: University of California Press, 1987)

Clarke, J. J. *Oriental Enlightenment: The Encounter Between Asian and Western Thought* (London: Routledge, 1997)

Close, Frank. *Particle Physics: A Very Short Introduction* (Oxford: Oxford University Press, 2004)

Coates, Chris (ed.) *Utopia Britannica: British Utopian Experiments 1325–1945* (London: Diggers and Dreamers Publications, 2001)

Coburn, Alvin Langdon. *Men of Mark* (London: Duckworth, 1913)

Cocks, H.G. *Nameless Offences: Homosexual Desire in the 19th Century* (London: I.B. Tauris, 2003)

Collins, Marcus. *Modern Love: An Intimate History of Men and Women in Twentieth Century Britain* (London: Atlantic Books, 2003)

Cook, Matt. *London and the Culture of Homosexuality 1885–1914* (Cambridge: Cambridge University Press, 2003)

Copley, Antony. *A Spiritual Bloomsbury: Hinduism and Homosexuality in the Lives and Writing of Edward Carpenter, E.M. Forster and Christopher Isherwood* (Lanham, Rowman and Littlefield, 2006)

Crawford, Alan. *C.R. Ashbee: Architect, Designer and Romantic Socialist* (New Haven: Yale University Press, 1985)

Crawford, Elizabeth. *The Women's Suffrage Movement: A Reference Guide, 1866–1928* (London: UCL Press, 1999)

Crawley, Charles. *Trinity Hall: The History of a Cambridge College* (Cambridge: Printed for the College, 1976)

Cronwright-Schreiner, S.C. *The Letters of Olive Schreiner 1876–1920* (London: T. Fisher Unwin, 1924)

Daniels, Gary. 'Reflections on New Unionism', *Historical Studies in Industrial Relations*, No. 21 (Spring 2006)

D'Arch Smith, Timothy. *Love in Earnest: Some Notes on the Lives and Writings of the English Uranian Poets from 1889 to 1930* (London: Routledge and Kegan Paul, 1970)

Darlington, Ralph. *Molly Murphy: Suffragette and Socialist* (Salford: Institute for Social Research, University of Salford, 1998)

Dawson, Oswald. *The Bar Sinister and Illicit Love: The Biennial proceedings of the Legitimation League* (London: W. Reeve, 1895)

Delany, Paul. *The Neo-Pagans: Rupert Brooke and the Ordeal of Youth* (New York: The Free Press, 1987)

Delavenay, Emile. *D.H. Lawrence: The Man and His Work* (London: Forum House, 1969)

Delavenay, Emile. *D.H. Lawrence and Edward Carpenter: A Study in Edwardian Transition* (London: Heinemann, 1971)

Dixon, Joy. *Divine Feminine: Theosophy and Feminism in England* (Baltimore: The Johns Hopkins University Press, 2001)

Doan, Laura and Prosser, Jay (eds.) *Palatable Poisons: Critical Perspectives on the Well of Loneliness* (New York: Columbia University Press, 2001)

Egbert, Donald Drew. *Social Radicalism and the Arts: Western Europe. A Cultural History from the French Revolution to 1968* (London: Gerald Duckworth and Co., 1970)

Ellenberger, Henri F. *The Discovery of the Unconscious: The History and Evolution of Dynamic Psychiatry* (London: Pimlico, 2005)

Ellis, Edith. *Three Modern Seers* (London: Stanley Paul and Co., no date, c. 1910)

Ellis, Havelock. *Studies in the Psychology of Sex, Vol. 2, Sexual Inversion* (Philadelphia: F.A. Davis, 1923, third edition)

Ellis, Havelock. *Views and Reviews: A Selection of Uncollected Articles 1884–1932* (London : Desmond Harmsworth, 1932)

Ellis, Havelock. *My Life* (London, Heinemann, 1940)

Ellman, Richard, *Oscar Wilde* (London: Penguin, 1988)

Ewen and Ewen, *Typecasting: On the Arts and Science of Human Inequality* (New York: Seven Stories Press, 2006)

Fawcett, Millicent Garrett. *What I Remember* (London: T. Fisher Unwin, 1924)

Finger, Stanley. *Origins of Neuroscience: A History of Exploration into Brain Function* (New York: Oxford University Press, 1994)

First, Ruth and Scott, Ann. *Olive Schreiner: A Biography* (London: Andre Deutsch, 1980)

Fishman, William J., *East End Jewish Radicals 1875–1914* (London: Croom Helm, 1983)

Forster, E.M. *Goldsworthy Lowes Dickinson* (London: Edward Arnold and Co., 1934)

Forster, E.M. *The Longest Journey* (London: Penguin, 1964)

Forster, E.M. *Maurice* (London: Penguin, 1972)

Fremantle, Anne. *This Little Band of Prophets: The Story of the Gentle Fabians* (London: George Allen and Unwin, 1960)

Furbank, P.N. *E.M. Forster: A Life* (London: Cardinal Sphere Books, 1988)

Gawthorpe, Mary. *Up Hill to Holloway* (Penobscot, Maine: Traversity Press, 1962)

Geoghegan, Vincent. 'Edward Carpenter's England Revisited', *History of Political Thought*, Vol. xxiv, No. 3 (August 2003)

Gernschein, Helmut and Gernschein, Alison (eds.) *Alvin Langdon Coburn: Photographer, An Autobiography* (New York: Dover, 1978)

Giesbers, J.H.G.I. *Cecil Reddie and Abbotsholme* (Druk Centrale Drukkerij N.V.: Nijamegan, 1970)

Goodway, David. *Anarchist Seeds Beneath the Snow: Left Libertarian Thought and British Writers from William Morris to Colin Ward* (Liverpool: Liverpool University Press, 2006)

Gould, Peter C. *Early Green Politics: Back to Nature, Back to the Land and Socialism in Britain 1880–1900* (Brighton: Harvester Press, 1988)

Greig, Noel. *Edward Carpenter: Selected Writings, Vol. 1, Sex* (London: GMP Publishers, 1984)

Grosskurth, Phyllis. *Havelock Ellis: A Biography* (New York: New York University Press, 1980)

Grosskurth, Phyllis (ed.) *The Memoirs of J.A. Symonds* (New York: Random House, 1984)

Hall, Lesley. 'Disinterested Enthusiasm for Sexual Misconduct', *Journal of Contemporary History*, Vol. 30, No. 4 (October 1995)

Hannam, June. *Isabella Ford* (Oxford: Basil Blackwell, 1989)

Hannam, June and Hunt, Karen. *Socialist Women: Britain 1880s–1920s* (London: Routledge, 2002)

Hardy, Dennis. *Alternative Communities in Nineteenth-Century England* (London: Longman, 1979)

Hassell, Christopher. *Rupert Brooke: A Biography* (London: Faber and Faber, 1964)

Haynes, E.S.P. *The Lawyer, A Conversation: Pieces Selected from the Lawyer's Notebooks and Other Writings by Renee Haynes* (London: Eyre and Spotiswood, 1951)

Henderson, Linda Dalrymple. *The Fourth Dimension and Non-Euclidean Geometry in Modern Art* (Princeton: Princeton University Press, 1983)

Henderson, Linda Dalrymple. 'Mysticism as the "Tie that Binds"', *Art Journal*, Vol. 46, No. 1 (Spring 1987)

Hendrick, George. *Henry Salt: Humanitarian Reformer and Man of Letters* (Urbana: University of Illinois Press, 1977)

Herbert, Eugenia W. *The Artist and Social Reform: France and Belgium 1885–1898* (New Haven: Yale University Press, 1961)

Hill, Mary A. *Charlotte Perkins Gilman: The Making of a Radical Feminist* (Philadelphia: Temple University Press, 1980)

Hilton, Tim. *John Ruskin* (New Haven: Yale University Press, 2002)

Hirson, Baruch. *The Cape Town Intellectuals: Ruth Schecter and her Circle 1907–1934* (London: Merlin, 2001)

Holroyd, Michael. *Lytton Strachey: A Biography* (London: Penguin, 1971)

Holt, Ann. *G.H.B. Ward 1876–1957: His Lifelong Campaign for Access to the Countryside* (London: The Ramblers Association, 1985)

Hopley, Emma. *Campaigning Against Cruelty: The Hundred Year History of the British Union for the Abolition of Vivisection* (London: The British Union of Abolition, 1998)

Howell, David. *British Workers and the Independent Labour Party 1888–1906* (Manchester: Manchester University Press, 1983)

Hughes, Jeff. 'Occultism and the Atom: The curious story of isotopes', *Physics World* (September 2003)

Hunt, Barry and Preston, Adrian (eds.) *War Aims and Strategic Policy in the Great War 1914–1918* (London: Croom Helm, 1977)

Hyndman, H.M. *England for All: The Text Book of Democracy* (Brighton: The Harvester Press, 1973)

Hynes, Samuel. *A War Imagined: The First World War and English Culture* (New York: Collier Books, 1990)

Janaway, Christopher. *The Cambridge Companion to Schopenhauer* (Cambridge: Cambridge University Press, 1999)

Janaway, Christopher. *Schopenhauer: A Very Short Introduction* (Oxford: Oxford University Press, 1994, 2004)

Javadi, Hasan. *Persian Literary Influence on English Literature* (Calcutta: Iran Society, 1983)

Jayawardena, Visakha Kumari. *The Rise of the Labor Movement in Ceylon* (Colombo, Sri Lanka: Sanjiva Prakashana, 1972)

Jayawardena, Kumari. *Doreen Wickremasinghe: A Western Radical in Sri Lanka* (Colombo: Women's Education and Research Centre, 1991)

Jayawardena, Kumari. *Nobodies to Somebodies: The Rise of the Colonial Bourgeoisie in Sri Lanka* (London: Zed Books, 2002)

John, Angela V., *War, Journalism and the Shaping of the Twentieth Century: The Life and Times of Henry W. Nevinson* (London: I.B. Tauris, 2006)

Jones, Nigel. *Rupert Brooke: Life, Death and Myth* (London: Richard Cohen Books, 1999)

Karlinsky, Simon. 'Russia's Gay Literature and Culture: the Impact of the October Revolution' in Duberman, Martin, Vicinus, Martha and Chauncey, George Jr. (eds.) *Hidden from History: Reclaiming the Gay and Lesbian Past* (London: Penguin, 1991)

Katz, David S. *The Occult Tradition: From the Renaissance to the Present Day* (London: Pimlico, 2007)

Katz, Jonathan Ned. *Love Stories: Sex Between Men Before Homosexuality* (Chicago: University of Chicago Press, 2001)

Kenney, Annie. *Memories of a Militant* (London: Edward Arnold, 1924)

Kern, Stephen. *The Culture of Time and Space 1880–1918* (Cambridge, Mass.: Harvard University Press, 1983)

Kikuchi, Yuko. *Japanese Modernisation and Mingei Theory: Cultural Nationalism and Oriental Orientalism* (London: Routledge Curzon, 2004)

Kinkead-Weekes, Mark. *D.H. Lawrence: Triumph to Exile 1912–1922* (Cambridge: Cambridge University Press, 1996)

Kissack, Terence. *Free Comrades: Anarchism and Homosexuality in the United States, 1895–1917* (Oakland: AK Press, 2008)

Kropotkin, Peter. *Memoirs of a Revolutionist* (New York: Grove Press, 1899, 1968)

Kuper, Adam. *The Invention of Primitive Society* (London: Routledge, 1988)

Laurence, Dan H. *Bernard Shaw: Collected Letters 1874–1897* (London: Max Reinhardt, 1965)

Laurence, Dan H. *Bernard Shaw: Collected Letters 1898–1910* (London: Max Reinhardt, 1972)

Lauritsen, John and Thorstad, David. *The Early Homosexual Rights Movement (1864–1935)* (New York: Times Change Press, 1974)

Lawrence, D.H. 'Prologue to *Women in Love*' in Roberts, Warren and Moore, Harry T. (eds.) *Phoenix II: Uncollected, Unpublished and Other Prose Works by D.H. Lawrence* (London: Heinemann, 1968)

Lawrence, D.H. *The Rainbow* (London: Penguin, 1966)

Lelyveld, David. *Aligarh's First Generation: Muslim Solidarity in British India* (Princeton, New Jersey: Princeton University Press, 1978)

Lewis, Edward. *Edward Carpenter: An Exposition and an Appreciation* (London: Methuen, 1915)

Leyland, Winston. *Gay Sunshine Interviews, Vol. 1* (San Francisco: Gay Sunshine Press, 1991)

Liddington, Jill. *Rebel Girls: Their Fight for the Vote* (London: Virago, 2006)

Luft, David S. *Eros and Inwardness in Vienna* (Chicago: University of Chicago Press, 2003)

MacCarthy, Fiona. *The Simple Life: C.R. Ashbee in the Cotswolds* (London: Lund Humphries, 1981)

MacCarthy, Fiona. 'Roger Fry and the Omega Ideal' in Crafts Council Gallery, *The Omega Workshops 1913–19* (London: Crafts Council and the Author, 1983)

MacCarthy, Fiona. *William Morris: A Life for Our Time* (London: Faber and Faber, 1994)

MacKenzie, Norman (ed.) *The Letters of Sidney and Beatrice Webb, Vol. 2, Partnership 1892–1912* (Cambridge and London: Cambridge University Press and L.S.E., 1978)

MacKenzie, Norman (ed.) *The Letters of Sidney and Beatrice Webb, Vol. 3, Pilgrimage 1912–1947* (Cambridge and London: Cambridge University Press and L.S.E., 1978)

MacKenzie, Norman and Jeanne (eds.) *The Diaries of Beatrice Webb* (London: Virago, 2000)

Magee, Bryan. *The Philosophy of Schopenhauer* (Oxford: Clarendon Press, 1983)

Martin, David E., and Rubinstein, David. *Ideology and the Labour Movement: Essays Presented to John Saville* (London: Macmillan, 1979)

Miller, Edward Haviland (ed.) *Walt Whitman: The Correspondence, Vol. 3, 1876–1885* (New York: New York University Press, 1964)

Mitter, Partha. *Much Maligned Monsters: History of European Reactions to Indian Art* (Oxford: Clarendon Press, 1977)

Mix, Katherine Lyon. *A Study in Yellow: The Yellow Book and its Contributors* (Lawrence: University of Kansas Press, 1960)

Monk, Ray. *Bertrand Russell: The Spirit of Solitude* (London: Vintage, 1997)

Myers, Frederic W. *Human Personality and its Survival of Bodily Death* (London: Longmans, Green and Co., 1903)

Nehls, Edward. *D.H. Lawrence: A Composite Biography, Vol. 1, 1885–1919* (Wisconsin: University of Wisconsin Press, 1957)

Nesbit, Enid. *New Treasure Seekers* (London: T. Fisher Unwin, 1904)

Nevinson, Henry W. *Changes and Chances* (London: Nisbet and Co., 1923)

Nicoll, D. J. *Stanley's Exploits, or, Civilising Africa* (London: Kate Sharpley Library, B.M. Hurricane, 2001)

Nield, Keith. 'Edward Carpenter 1844–1929. Socialist and Author' in Bellamy, Joyce and Saville, John, *Dictionary of Labour Biography, Vol. 2* (London: Macmillan, 1974).

Oliver, Hermia. *The International Anarchist Movement in Late Victorian London* (London: Croom Helm, 1983)

Olivier, Margaret. *Sydney Olivier: Letters and Selected Writings* (London: George Allen and Unwin, 1948)

O'Toole, Alan. *With the Poor People of the Earth: A Biography of Doctor John Creaghe of Sheffield and Buenos Aires* (London: Kate Sharpley Library, B.M. Hurricane, 2005)

Pemble, John (ed.) *John Addington Symonds and the Demon Desire* (London: Macmillan, 2000)

Penty, A.J. *The Restoration of the Gild System* (London: Swan Sonnenschein, 1906)

Penty, A.J. *A Guildsman's Interpretation of History* (New York: Sunrise, 1920)

Pierson, Stanley. 'Edward Carpenter, Prophet of a Socialist Millennium', *Victorian Studies* Vol. XIII, No. 3 (March 1970)

Pimlott, Ben. *Hugh Dalton* (London: Macmillan, 1985)

Plato. *Phaedrus*, translation and commentary by C.J. Rowe (Warminster, Wiltshire: Aris and Phillips, 1986)

Porter, Kevin and Weeks, Jeffrey. *Between the Acts: Lives of Homosexual Men 1885–1967* (London: Routledge, 1991)

Price, A.W. *Love and Friendship in Plato and Aristotle* (Oxford: Clarendon Press, 1989)

Proctor, Dennis (ed.) *The Autobiography of G. Lowes Dickinson and other Published Writings* (London: Duckworth, 1973)

Putnam, Ruth Anna (ed.) *The Cambridge Companion to William James* (New York: Cambridge University Press, 1997)

Pye, Denis. *Fellowship is Life: The National Clarion Cycling Club 1895–1995* (Bolton: Clarion Publishing, 1995)

Quail, John. *The Slow Burning Fuse: The Lost History of the British Anarchists* (London: Paladin, 1978)

Rahman, Tariq. 'Edward Carpenter and E.M. Forster', *Durham University Journal* Vol. LXXIX, No.1 (December 1986)

Rahman, Tariq. 'The Literary Treatment of Indian Themes in the Works of Edward Carpenter', *Durham University Review* 80 (1987)

Rahman, Tariq. 'The Alienated Prophet', *Forum for Modern Languages* Vol. XXIII, No. 3 (July 1987)

Reclus, Élie. *Primitive Folk: Studies in Comparative Ethnology* (London: Walter Scott, 1890)

Reynolds, David. *Walt Whitman's America: A Cultural Biography* (New York: Alfred A. Knopf, 1995)

Richards, Huw. *The Daily Herald and the Left* (London: Pluto Press, 1997)

Robb, Graham, *Homosexual Love in the Nineteenth Century* (Basingstoke and Oxford: Picador, 2003)

Robertson, Michael. *Worshipping Walt: The Whitman Disciples* (Princeton: Princeton University Press, 2008)

Roscoe, Will (ed.) *Harry Hay, Radically Gay: Gay Liberation in the Words of its Founder* (Boston: Beacon Press, 1996)

Rose, Jonathan. *The Edwardian Temperament 1895–1919* (Athens, Ohio: Ohio University Press, 1986)

Rothblatt, Sheldon. *The Revolution of the Dons: Cambridge and Society in Victorian England* (London: Faber and Faber, 1968)

Roud, Steve, Upton, Eddie, and Taylor, Malcolm. *Still Growing: English Traditional Songs and Singers from the Cecil Sharp Collection* (London: The English Folk Dance and Song Society, 2003)

Rowbotham, Sheila. 'The Call to University Teaching 1873–1900', *Birmingham Historical Journal* (Autumn 1969)

Rowbotham, Sheila and Weeks, Jeffrey. *Socialism and the New Life: The Personal and Sexual Politics of Edward Carpenter and Havelock Ellis* (London: Pluto Press, 1977)

Rowbotham, Sheila. *A New World for Women: Stella Browne, Socialist Feminist* (London: Pluto Press, 1977)

Rowbotham, Sheila. 'In Search of Carpenter', *History Workshop Journal* 3 (Spring 1977)

Rowbotham, Sheila. 'Commanding the Heart: Edward Carpenter and Friends', *History Today* 37 (September 1987)

Rowbotham, Sheila. 'Our Party is the People', in Rule, John and Malcolmson, Robert (eds.) *Protest and Survival, the Historical Experience: Essays for E.P. Thompson* (London: Merlin Press, 1993)

Rowbotham, Sheila. 'The Sheffield Anarchists in the 1890s' (Sheffield 1979). Reprinted in Rowbotham, Sheila, *Threads Through Time* (London: Penguin, 1999)

Rowbotham, Sheila. 'Travellers in a Strange Country: Responses of University Extension Students to the University Extension Movement', in Rowbotham, Sheila, *Threads Through Time* (London: Penguin, 1999)

Ruskin, John. *Fors Clavigera*, in Cook, E.T. and Wedderburn, Alexander (eds.) *The Works of John Ruskin* (London: George Allen, 1907)

Salt, Henry S. *Seventy Years Among Savages* (London: George Allen and Unwin, 1921)

Salt, Henry. *Company I Have Kept* (London: George Allen and Unwin, 1930)

Salveson, Paul. 'Loving Comrades: Lancashire's Links to Walt Whitman', *Walt Whitman Quarterly Review* Vol. 14, Nos 2/3 (Fall 1996/Winter 1997)

Salveson, Paul. *With Walt Whitman in Bolton: Spirituality, Sex and Socialism in a Northern Mill Town* (Huddersfield: Little Northern Books, 2008)

Sarracino, Caroline. 'Redrawing Whitman's Circle', *Walt Whitman Quarterly Review* Vol. 14, Nos 2/3 (Fall 1996/Winter 1997)

Schueller, Herbert M. and Peters, Robert L. *The Letters of John Addington Symonds, Vol. 3, 1885–1893* (Detroit: Wayne State University Press, 1969)

Searle, G.R. *A New England? Peace and War 1886–1918* (Oxford: Clarendon Press, 2004)

Sederman, Derek. *A History of Abbotsholme School 1889–1989* (Rocester, Staffordshire: Abbotsholme School, 1989)

Sedlar, Jean W. *India and the Greek World: A Study of the Transmission of Culture* (Totowa, New Jersey: Rowman and Littlefield, 1980)

Senard, Marcelle. *Edward Carpenter et sa Philosophie* (Paris: Librarie de l'Art Indépendént, 1914)

Sénéchal, Christian. *Les Grands Courants de la Littérature Française Contemporaine* (Paris: S.F.E.L.T. Editions Edgar Malfère, 1941)

Sharp, Evelyn. *Unfinished Adventure: Selected Reminiscences from an English Woman's Life* (London: John Lane, The Bodley Head, 1933)

Sharpe, Eric J. *The Universal Gita: Western Images of the Bhagavadgita: A Bicentenary Study* (London: Duckworth, 1985)

Shepherd, John. *George Lansbury: At the Heart of Old Labour* (Oxford: Oxford University Press, 2002)

Shi, David E. *The Simple Life: Plain Living and High Thinking in American Culture* (New York: Oxford University Press, 1985)

Sime, A.H.M. *Edward Carpenter: His Ideas and Ideals* (London: Kegan Paul, 1916)

Sinfield, Alan. *The Wilde Century: Effeminacy, Oscar Wilde and the Queer Moment* (New York: Columbia University Press, 1994)

Skidelsky, Robert. *John Maynard Keynes, Hopes Betrayed, 1883–1920* (London: Macmillan, 1983)

Skidelsky, Robert. *John Maynard Keynes, Economist, Philosopher, Statesman, 1883–1946* (London: Macmillan, 2003)

Smith, Roger. *The Fontana History of the Human Sciences* (London: Fontana, 1997)

Stamp, Sir Dudley. *Nature Conservation in Britain* (London: Collins, 1969)

Stanley, Liz. *Imperialism, Labour and the New Woman: Olive Schreiner's Social Theory* (Durham: Sociology Press, 2002)

Stansky, Peter. *William Morris, C.R. Ashbee and the Arts and Crafts Movement* (London: Nine Elms Press, 1984)

Steele, Tom. *Alfred Orage and the Leeds Arts Club 1893–1923* (Aldershot, Hants: Scolar Press, 1990)

Stevenson, David. *Cataclysm: The First World War as Political Tragedy* (New York: Basic Books, 2004)

Stokes, John. *In the Nineties* (New York: Harvester Wheatsheaf, 1989)

Stokes, John. *Oscar Wilde: Myths, Miracles and Limitations* (Cambridge: Cambridge University Press, 1996)

Stokes, John (ed.) *Eleanor Marx (1855–1898): Life, Work, Contacts* (Aldershot: Ashgate, 2000)

Sutton, Denys (ed.) *Letters of Roger Fry* (London: Chatto and Windus, 1972)

Swenarton, Mark. *Artisans and Architects: The Ruskinian Tradition in Architectural Thought* (London: Macmillan, 1989)

Taddeo, Julie Anne. *Lytton Strachey and the Search for Modern Sexual Identity: The Last Eminent Victorian* (New York: Harrington Park Press, 2002)

Thomas, M. Wynn. *Transatlantic Connections: Whitman U.S., Whitman U.K.* (Iowa City: University of Iowa Press, 2005)

Thompson, Dorothy. *Queen Victoria: Gender and Power* (London: Virago, 1990)

Thompson, E.P. *William Morris: Romantic to Revolutionary* (London: Merlin Press, 1955, 1977)

Thompson, E.P. 'Homage to Tom Maguire', in Briggs, Asa and Saville, John (eds.) *Essays in Labour History* (London: Macmillan, 1960)

Thompson, Laurence. *The Enthusiasts: A Biography of John and Katharine Bruce Glasier* (London: Victor Gollancz, 1971)

Thompson, Tierl. *Dear Girl: The Diaries and Letters of Two Working Women 1897–1917* (London: The Women's Press, 1987)

Thomson, Basil. *Queer People: My Experiences at Scotland Yard* (London: Hodder and Stoughton, 1922)

Thomson, Mathew. *Psychological Subjects: Identity, Culture and Health in Twentieth Century Britain* (Oxford: Oxford University Press, 2006)

Timmons, Stuart. *The Trouble with Harry Hay: Founder of the Modern Gay Movement* (Boston: Alyson Publications, 1990)

Traubel, Horace. *With Walt Whitman in Camden, Vols. 1, 3* (New York: Rowman and Littlefield, 1961); *Vol. 4* (Philadelphia: University of Pennsylvania Press, 1953); *Vol. 5* (Carbondale, Illinois: Southern Illinois University Press, 1964)

Trevelyan, Laura. *A Very British Family: The Trevelyans and Their World* (London: I.B. Tauris, 2006)

Tsuzuki, Chushichi. *H.M. Hyndman and British Socialism* (Oxford: Oxford University Press, 1961)

Tsuzuki, Chushichi. 'My Dear Sanshiro', *Hitotsubashi Journal of Social Studies* Vol. 6, No. 1 (Whole No. 6) (November 1972)

Tsuzuki, Chushichi. *Edward Carpenter: Prophet of Human Fellowship 1844–1929* (Cambridge: Cambridge University Press, 1980)

Tsuzuki, Chushichi. *Tom Mann 1856–1941: The Challenge of Labour* (Oxford: Clarendon Press, 1991)

Tufts, Helen (ed.) *Helena Born: Whitman's Ideal Democracy* (Boston, Mass.: Everitt Press, 1902)

Unwin, Stanley. *The Truth About Publishing* (London: Allen and Unwin, 1926)

Unwin, Sir Stanley. *The Truth About a Publisher: An Autobiographical Record* (London: George Allen and Unwin, 1960)

Van der Linden, Marcel and Thorpe, Wayne (eds.) *Revolutionary Syndicalism: An International Perspective* (Aldershot, Hants: Scolar Press, 1990)

Veysey, Laurence. *Communal Experience: Anarchist and Mystical Counter-Cultures in America* (New York: Harper and Row, 1973)

Ward, Colin (ed.) *Kropotkin's Fields, Factories and Workshops* (Oakland: AK Press, 1974)

Waters, Chris. *British Socialists and the Politics of Popular Culture 1884–1914* (Manchester: Manchester University Press, 1990)

Webb, James. *The Harmonious Circle: The Lives and Work of G.I. Gurdjieff, P.D. Ouspensky and their Followers* (London: Thames and Hudson, 1980)

Weeks, Jeffrey. *Coming Out: Homosexual Politics in Britain from the Nineteenth Century to the Present* (London: Quartet Books, 1977)

Weeks, Jeffrey. *Sex, Politics and Society: The Regulation of Sexuality Since 1800* (London: Longman, 1981)

Weintraub, Stanley. *Bernard Shaw: The Diaries 1885–1897* (University Park: Pennsylvania State University Press, 1986)

Wilson, A. Jeyaratnam. *Sri Lankan Tamil Nationalism: Its Origins and Development in the 19th and 20th Centuries* (London: Hurst and Company, 2000)

Wilson, Jean Moorcroft. *Siegfried Sassoon: The Making of a War Poet* (London: Duckworth, 1998)

Wilson, Jean Moorcroft. *Siegfried Sassoon: The Journey from the Trenches: A Biography 1918–1967* (London: Duckworth, 2003)

Winsten, Stephen. *Salt and his Circle* (London: Hutchinson and Co., 1951)

Woolf, Virginia. *Roger Fry: A Biography* (London: The Hogarth Press, 1940)

Worthen, John. *D.H. Lawrence: The Early Years 1885–1912* (Cambridge: Cambridge University Press, 1992)

Wright, Patrick. *The Village that Died for England* (London: Faber and Faber, 2002)

Wrigley, Chris. *David Lloyd George and the British Labour Movement: Peace and War* (Hassocks, Brighton: The Harvester Press, 1976)

Yeo, Eileen. *The Contest for Social Science* (London: Rivers Oram Press, 1996)

Zytaruk, George and Boulton, James T. (eds.) *The Letters of D.H. Lawrence, June 1913–October 1916, Vol. 2* (Cambridge: Cambridge University Press, 1979)

Theses

Bakshi, Parminder Kaur. *Distant Desire: The Theme of Friendship in E.M. Forster's Fiction.* University of Warwick PhD (1992)

Barua, Dilip Kumar. *The Life and Work of Edward Carpenter in the Light of Religious, Political and Literary Movements of the later half of the Nineteenth Century.* University of Sheffield PhD (1966)

Brown, Anthony David. *A Consideration of Some Parallels in the Personal and Social Ideals of E.M. Forster and Edward Carpenter.* University of Warwick PhD (1982)

Eagleton, Terence. *Nature and Spirit: A Study of Edward Carpenter in his Intellectual Context.* University of Cambridge PhD (1968)

Hall, Duncan. *A Pleasant Change from Politics: The Musical Culture of the British Labour Movement.* University of Warwick PhD (2000)

Kissack, Terence S. *Anarchism and the Politics of Homosexuality.* City University of New York PhD (2004)

Newspapers and Periodicals Consulted

Albany Review
Amalgamated Engineers' Monthly Journal
The Athenaeum
British Medical Journal
Christian Commonwealth
The Citizen
Clarion
Commonweal
The Comrade (US)
The Conservator (US)

Cooperative News
The Craftsman (US)
Cruel Sports
Daily Chronicle
Daily Herald
Daily News
Daily Telegraph
The Ethical World
Evening Standard
Forward
The Free Comrade (US)
Freedom
Freewoman
The Healthy Life
Herald of the Star (India)
Humane Review
The Humanitarian
I.L.P. News
Independent Review
The International (US)
International Socialist Review (US)
Irish Citizen
Justice
Labour Leader
Labour Prophet
Leeds Weekly Citizen
Light: A Journal of Psychical, Occult and Mystical Research
Liverpool Daily Courier
Lucifer
Manchester Evening News
Manchester Guardian
Medical Times
Morning Leader
Morning Post
The Nation
New Age
New Freewoman
New International Review
New Statesman
Pioneer (India)
Progress

The Schoolmaster
Sheffield and Rotherham Weekly Independent
Sheffield Daily Telegraph
Sheffield Guardian
Sheffield Weekly Echo
The Social Democrat
Socialist Outlook
The Syndicalist
Teacher's World
The Times of India (India)
To-day
T.P.s Weekly
Tribune
War Commentary
Western Daily Press
The Whim
Yorkshire Daily Observer
Yorkshire Free Press
Yorkshire Weekly Post

Index